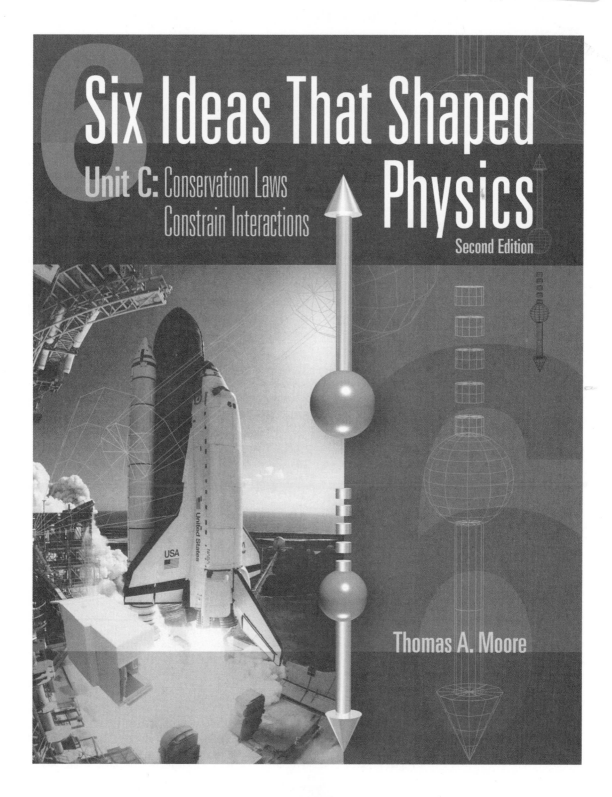

Six Ideas That Shaped Physics

Unit C: Conservation Laws Constrain Interactions

Physics

Second Edition

Thomas A. Moore

McGraw Hill

Boston   Burr Ridge, IL   Dubuque, IA   Madison, WI   New York   San Francisco   St. Louis
Bangkok   Bogotá   Caracas   Kuala Lumpur   Lisbon   London   Madrid   Mexico City
Milan   Montreal   New Delhi   Santiago   Seoul   Singapore   Sydney   Taipei   Toronto

McGraw-Hill Higher Education

A Division of The **McGraw-Hill** *Companies*

SIX IDEAS THAT SHAPED PHYSICS, UNIT C: CONSERVATION LAWS
CONSTRAIN INTERACTIONS, SECOND EDITION

 This book is printed on recycled, acid-free paper containing 10% postconsumer waste.

6 7 8 9 0 QPD/QPD 0 9

ISBN 978-0-07-229152-0
MHID 0-07-229152-4

Publisher: *Kent A. Peterson*
Sponsoring editor: *Daryl Bruflodt*
Developmental editor: *Spencer J. Cotkin, Ph.D.*
Marketing manager: *Debra B. Hash*
Senior project manager: *Susan J. Brusch*
Senior production supervisor: *Sandy Ludovissy*
Coordinator of freelance design: *David W. Hash*
Cover/interior designer: *Rokusek Design*
Cover image: *© Corbis Images*
Senior photo research coordinator: *Lori Hancock*
Photo research: *Chris Hammond/PhotoFind LLC*
Media project manager: *Sandra M. Schnee*
Supplement producer: *Brenda A. Ernzen*
Media technology associate producer: *Judi David*
Compositor: *Interactive Composition Corporation*
Typeface: *10/12 Palatino*
Printer: *Quebecor World Dubuque, IA*

Credit List: **Chapter 2** C2.2a: © Michael P. Gadomski/Photo Researchers; C2.2b: © Richard Pasley/Stock Boston. **Chapter 3** C3.7: © Joel Gordon; Pg. 59: © Corbis/Vol.#75; Pg. 60: © Lee Snider/Image Works. **Chapter 4** C4.1(top left): © P. Hawtin, University of South Hampton/SPL/Photo Researchers; C4.1(top right): NASA; C4.1(bottom left): © PhotoDisc/Vol. #39; C4.1(bottom right): NASA/S. Gallagher (Penn State University/STScl-PRC01-22; C4.4: © Richard Megna/Fundamental Photographs; C4.5: NASA; Pg. 77: © Stephen Dunn/Allsport. **Chapter 5** C5.4: Photo courtesy of Cessna Aircraft Company; C5.6a: JPL/NASA; C5.6b: Courtesy of NASA/JPL/Caltech; Pg. 96: © Todd Warshaw /Allsport; Pg. 97: NASA. **Chapter 6** Pg. 114(left): © Bettmann/CORBIS; Pg. 114(right): Jet Propulsion Laboratory/NASA. **Chapter 8** Pg. 147: © Mark Burnett/Photo Researchers; Pg. 151: © The Kobal Collection/ Alta Vista/Village Roadshow/Boland, Jasin. **Chapter 9** Pg. 170: NASA; Pg. 172: © R. Sidney/Image Works. **Chapter 10** C10.1b: © Science Museum/Science & Society Picture Library; Pg. 189(left): NASA; Pg. 189(right): © PhotoDisc Website; Pg. 190: © John V. A. F. Neal/Photo Researchers. **Chapter 11** C11.4a: © Alex Bartel/Science Photo Library/Photo Researchers; C11.4b: © PhotoDisc/ Vol. 6; Pg. 207: © John Nordell/Image Works; Pg. 208(top): © M. Antman/Image Works; Pg. 208(bottom): © Eastcott/Momatiuk/Image Works. **Chapter 12** C12.4: NASA; Pg. 228: © PhotoDisk/Vol. 89. **Chapter 14** Pg. 24: © Anglo-Australian Observatory, Photograph by David Malin.

Library of Congress Cataloging-in-Publication Data
Moore, Thomas A. (Thomas Andrew)
    Six ideas that shaped physics. Unit C, Conservation laws constrain interactions / Thomas A. Moore. — 2nd ed.
      p. cm.
    Includes index.
    ISBN 0-07-229152-4 (acid-free paper)
    1. Conservation laws (Physics). I. Title: Conservation laws constrain interactions. II. Title

QC793.3.C58 M66   2003   2002020009
                                                  CIP

www.mhhe.com

6 Six Ideas That Shaped Physics

Unit C: Conservation Laws Constrain Interactions

Property of

Brad Clarke,

winter, 2009

Dedication

For All My Family, Near and Far
(and in Memory of Anne Moore),
whose love has conserved what is best.

Table of Contents for
Six Ideas That Shaped Physics

Unit C
Conservation Laws Constrain Interactions

C1   Introduction to Interactions
C2   Vectors
C3   Interactions Transfer Momentum
C4   Particles and Systems
C5   Applying Momentum Conservation
C6   Introduction to Energy
C7   Some Potential Energy Functions
C8   Force and Energy
C9   Rotational Energy
C10 Thermal Energy
C11 Energy in Bonds
C12 Power, Collisions, and Impacts
C13 Angular Momentum
C14 Conservation of Angular Momentum

Unit N
The Laws of Physics Are Universal

N1   Newton's Laws
N2   Vector Calculus
N3   Forces from Motion
N4   Motion from Forces
N5   Statics
N6   Linearly Constrained Motion
N7   Coupled Objects
N8   Circularly Constrained Motion
N9   Noninertial Reference Frames
N10 Projectile Motion
N11 Oscillatory Motion
N12 Introduction to Orbits
N13 Planetary Motion

Unit R
The Laws of Physics Are Frame-Independent

R1   The Principle of Relativity
R2   Synchronizing Clocks
R3   The Nature of Time
R4   The Metric Equation
R5   Proper Time
R6   Coordinate Transformations
R7   Lorentz Contraction
R8   The Cosmic Speed Limit
R9   Four-Momentum
R10 Conservation of Four-Momentum

Unit E
Electric and Magnetic Fields Are Unified

E1   Electrostatics
E2   Electric Fields
E3   Electric Potential
E4   Conductors
E5   Driving Currents
E6   Analyzing Circuits
E7   Magnetic Fields
E8   Currents and Magnets
E9   Symmetry and Flux
E10 Gauss' Law
E11 Ampere's Law
E12 The Electromagnetic Field
E13 Maxwell's Equations
E14 Induction
E15 Introduction to Waves
E16 Electromagnetic Waves

Unit Q
Particles Behave Like Waves

Q1   Standing Waves
Q2   The Wave Nature of Light
Q3   The Particle Nature of Light
Q4   The Wave Nature of Matter
Q5   The Quantum Facts of Life
Q6   The Wavefunction
Q7   Bound Systems
Q8   Spectra
Q9   Understanding Atoms
Q10   The Schrödinger Equation
Q11   Energy Eigenfunctions
Q12   Introduction to Nuclei
Q13   Stable and Unstable Nuclei
Q14   Radioactivity
Q15   Nuclear Technology

Unit T
Some Processes Are Irreversible

T1   Temperature
T2   Ideal Gases
T3   Gas Processes
T4   Macrostates and Microstates
T5   The Second Law
T6   Temperature and Entropy
T7   Some Mysteries Resolved
T8   Calculating Entropy Changes
T9   Heat Engines

Contents: Unit C
Conservation Laws Constrain Interactions

About the Author   xi

Preface   xii

Introduction for Students   xvi

Chapter C1

Introduction to Interactions   02

	Chapter Overview	02
C1.1:	The Nature of Science	04
C1.2:	The Development and Structure of Physics	05
C1.3:	An Overview of This Unit	08
C1.4:	Introduction to Mechanics	08
C1.5:	Fundamental Interactions	10
C1.6:	Macroscopic Interactions	12
C1.7:	Describing "Motion"	14
C1.8:	Physics Skills: Technical Terms	16
C1.9:	Physics Skills: Units	17
	Aristotelian Thinking Diagnostic Test	19
	Two-Minute Problems	21
	Homework Problems	21
	Answers to Exercises	23
	Answers to the Aristotelian Diagnostic	23

Chapter C2

Vectors   24

	Chapter Overview	24
C2.1:	Vectors and Scalars	26
C2.2:	Basic Vector Operations	27
C2.3:	Components	29
C2.4:	The Magnitude of a Vector	31
C2.5:	Vectors in One and Two Dimensions	31
C2.6:	Vector Operations in Terms of Components	34
C2.7:	Vectors Have Units	37
C2.8:	Reference Frames	37
	Two-Minute Problems	39
	Homework Problems	40
	Answers to Exercises	42

Chapter C3

Interactions Transfer Momentum   44

	Chapter Overview	44
C3.1:	Velocity	46
C3.2:	Interactions Transfer Momentum	48
C3.3:	Impulse and Force	50
C3.4:	Mass and Weight	53
C3.5:	Momentum Flow and Motion	55
C3.6:	Physics Skills: Illegal Vector Equations	57
	Two-Minute Problems	58
	Homework Problems	59
	Answers to Exercises	61

Chapter C4

Particles and Systems   62

	Chapter Overview	62
C4.1:	Systems of Particles	64
C4.2:	Conservation of Momentum	64
C4.3:	A System's Center of Mass	66
C4.4:	How the Center of Mass Moves	69
C4.5:	Inertial Reference Frames	72
C4.6:	Interactions with the Earth	74
	Two-Minute Problems	76
	Homework Problems	76
	Answers to Exercises	79

Chapter C5

Applying Momentum Conservation   80

	Chapter Overview	80
C5.1:	Momentum Conservation Without Isolation	82
C5.2:	Degrees of Isolation	83
C5.3:	A Problem-Solving Framework	84
C5.4:	Constructing Model Diagrams	86
C5.5:	Solving Conservation of Momentum Problems	88

C5.6: Airplanes and Rockets 92
Two-Minute Problems 94
Homework Problems 95
Answers to Exercises 97

Chapter C6

Introduction to Energy 98

Chapter Overview 98
C6.1: Interactions and Energy 100
C6.2: Kinetic Energy 101
C6.3: Measuring Potential Energy 103
C6.4: Negative Energy? 107
C6.5: A Look Ahead 108
C6.6: Adapting the Framework to
Energy Problems 109
Two-Minute Problems 112
Homework Problems 113
Answers to Exercises 114

Chapter C7

Some Potential Energy Functions 116

Chapter Overview 116
C7.1: The Electromagnetic Interaction 118
C7.2: The Gravitational Interaction 120
C7.3: Gravitation near the Earth 121
C7.4: The Potential Energy of a Spring 123
C7.5: Some Examples 126
C7.6: Physics Skills: Significant Digits 130
Two-Minute Problems 131
Homework Problems 132
Answers to Exercises 134

Chapter C8

Force and Energy 136

Chapter Overview 136
C8.1: Momentum and Kinetic Energy 138
C8.2: The Dot Product 139
C8.3: An Interaction's Contribution to dK 140
C8.4: The Meaning of k-Work 142
C8.5: The Earth's Kinetic Energy 143
C8.6: Force Laws 144
C8.7: Contact Interactions 146

Two-Minute Problems 149
Homework Problems 150
Answers to Exercises 152

Chapter C9

Rotational Energy 154

Chapter Overview 154
C9.1: Introduction to Rotational Energy 156
C9.2: Measuring Angles 156
C9.3: Angular Velocity 158
C9.4: The Moment of Inertia 160
C9.5: Calculating Moments of Inertia 161
C9.6: Translation and Rotation 164
C9.7: Rolling Without Slipping 165
Two-Minute Problems 168
Homework Problems 169
Answers to Exercises 173

Chapter C10

Thermal Energy 174

Chapter Overview 174
C10.1: The Case of the Disappearing Energy 176
C10.2: Caloric Is Energy 176
C10.3: Thermal Energy 178
C10.4: Friction and Thermal Energy 179
C10.5: Heat and Work 180
C10.6: Specific "Heat" 182
C10.7: Problems Involving Thermal Energies 184
Two-Minute Problems 188
Homework Problems 189
Answers to Exercises 191

Chapter C11

Energy in Bonds 192

Chapter Overview 192
C11.1: Potential Energy Diagrams 194
C11.2: Bonds 197
C11.3: Latent "Heat" 198
C11.4: Chemical and Nuclear Energy 201
C11.5: Other Forms of Hidden Energy 205
Two-Minute Problems 205
Homework Problems 206
Answers to Exercises 209

Chapter C12

Power, Collisions, and Impacts 210

	Chapter Overview	210
C12.1:	Power	212
C12.2:	Types of Collisions	215
C12.3:	Elastic Collisions	216
C12.4:	The Slingshot Effect	221
C12.5:	Inelastic Collisions	222
C12.6:	Asteroid Impacts	224
	Two-Minute Problems	227
	Homework Problems	228
	Answers to Exercises	230

Chapter C13

Angular Momentum 232

	Chapter Overview	232
C13.1:	The Case of the Rotating Person	234
C13.2:	The Cross Product	235
C13.3:	The Angular Momentum of a Particle	238
C13.4:	The Angular Momentum of a Rigid Object	239
C13.5:	The Angular Momentum of a Moving Object	241
C13.6:	Twirl and Torque	242
	Two-Minute Problems	245
	Homework Problems	247
	Answers to Exercises	248

Chapter C14

Conservation of Angular Momentum 250

	Chapter Overview	250
C14.1:	Precession of a Top	252
C14.2:	Applications	254
C14.3:	Conservation of Angular Momentum	255
C14.4:	Some Worked Examples	257
C14.5:	Application: Neutron Stars	263
	Two-Minute Problems	265
	Homework Problems	266
	Answers to Exercises	269

| Glossary | 271 |
| Index | 281 |

About the Author

Thomas A. Moore graduated from Carleton College (magna cum laude with Distinction in Physics) in 1976. He won a Danforth Fellowship that year that supported his graduate education at Yale University, where he earned a Ph.D. in 1981. He taught at Carleton College and Luther College before taking his current position at Pomona College in 1987, where he won a Wig Award for Distinguished Teaching in 1991. He served as an active member of the steering committee for the national Introductory University Physics Project (IUPP) from 1987 through 1995. This textbook grew out of a model curriculum that he developed for that project in 1989, which was one of only four selected for further development and testing by IUPP.

He has published a number of articles about astrophysical sources of gravitational waves, detection of gravitational waves, and new approaches to teaching physics, as well as a book on special relativity entitled *A Traveler's Guide to Spacetime* (McGraw-Hill, 1995). He has also served as a reviewer and an associate editor for American Journal of Physics. He currently lives in Claremont, California, with his wife Joyce and two college-aged daughters. When he is not teaching, doing research in relativistic astrophysics, or writing, he enjoys reading, hiking, scuba diving, teaching adult church-school classes on the Hebrew Bible, calling contradances, and playing traditional Irish fiddle music.

Preface

Introduction

Opening comments about Six Ideas That Shaped Physics

This volume is one of six that together comprise the text materials for *Six Ideas That Shaped Physics*, a fundamentally new approach to the two- or three-semester calculus-based introductory physics course. *Six Ideas That Shaped Physics* was created in response to a call for innovative curricula offered by the Introductory University Physics Project (IUPP), which subsequently supported its early development. In its present form, the course represents the culmination of more than a decade of development, testing, and evaluation at a number of colleges and universities nationwide.

This course is based on the premise that innovative approaches to the presentation of topics and to classroom activities can help students learn more effectively. I have completely rethought from the ground up the presentation of every topic, taking advantage of research into physics education wherever possible, and I have done nothing just because "that is the way it has always been done." Recognizing that physics education research has consistently underlined the importance of active learning, I have also provided tools supporting multiple opportunities for active learning both inside and outside the classroom. This text also strongly emphasizes the process of building and critiquing physical models and using them in realistic settings. Finally, I have sought to emphasize contemporary physics and view even classical topics from a thoroughly contemporary perspective.

I have not sought to "dumb down" the course to make it more accessible. Rather, my goal has been to help students become *smarter*. I intentionally set higher-than-usual standards for sophistication in physical thinking, and I then used a range of innovative approaches and classroom structures to help even average students reach this standard. I don't believe that the mathematical level required by these books is significantly different from that of a standard university physics text, but I do ask students to step beyond rote thinking patterns to develop flexible, powerful conceptual reasoning and model-building skills. My experience and that of other users are that normal students in a wide range of institutional settings can, with appropriate support and practice, meet these standards.

The six volumes of the Six Ideas text

The six volumes that comprise the complete *Six Ideas* course are:

Unit C (**C**onservation Laws):	Conservation Laws Constrain Interactions
Unit N (**N**ewtonian Mechanics):	The Laws of Physics are Universal
Unit R (**R**elativity):	The Laws of Physics are Frame-Independent
Unit E (**E**lectricity and Magnetism):	Electricity and Magnetism are Unified
Unit Q (**Q**uantum Physics):	Matter Behaves Like Waves
Unit T (**T**hermal Physics):	Some Processes are Irreversible

I have listed these units in the order that I recommend that they be taught, though other orderings are possible. At Pomona, we teach the first three units during the first semester and the last three during the second semester of a year-long course, but one can easily teach the six units in three quarters or even over three semesters if one wants a lower pace. The chapters of all these texts have been designed to correspond to what one might realistically discuss in a single 50-minute class session at the *highest possible pace*. A reasonable course syllabus will therefore set an average pace of not more than one chapter per 50 minutes of class time.

The *Six Ideas* website

For more information than I can include in this short preface about the goals of the *Six Ideas* course, its organizational structure (and the rationale behind that structure), and the evidence for its success, as well as many other resources for both teachers and students, please visit the *Six Ideas* website (see the next section).

Important Resources

Instructions about how to use this text

I have summarized important information about how to read and use this text in an *Introduction for Students* immediately preceding chapter C1. Please look this over, particularly if you have not seen other volumes of this text.

The *Six Ideas* web site contains a wealth of up-to-date information about the course that I think both instructors and students will find very useful. The URL is

www.physics.pomona.edu/sixideas/

Essential computer programs

One of the most important resources available at this site are a number of computer applets that illustrate important concepts and aid in difficult calculations. Past experience indicates that students learn the ideas much more effectively when these programs are used in both the classroom and the homework. These applets are freeware and are available for both the Mac (Classic) and Windows operating systems.

Some Notes Specifically About Unit C

This unit is the foundation on which the rest of the *Six Ideas* course is built. The current course structure assumes that unit C will be taught first and will be immediately followed by unit N.

Why study conservation laws first?

Why study conservation laws *before* newtonian mechanics? The most important reasons are as follows: (1) Conservation laws are easy to understand and use, which helps build student confidence at the beginning of the course; (2) using conservation laws does not really require calculus, thus delaying the introduction of calculus for several weeks; (3) studying conservation of momentum and angular momentum *does* require vectors, allowing vector concepts to be developed for several weeks in simple contexts before getting into vector calculus; and (4) conservation laws really are more fundamental than even newtonian mechanics, so it is good to start the course with physical concepts that are crucially important and will be useful throughout the course.

We did not intuit these benefits at first: the earliest versions of *Six Ideas* presented mechanics in the standard order. Rather, this inversion emerged naturally as a consequence of observations of student learning and some reflection about the logic of the course. (Interestingly, a number of people interested in reforming the course have independently come to the same conclusion.)

This approach can be good even for well-prepared students

Inverting the order *can* be a challenge (in both the positive and negative sense) for the student who has already had some mechanics. Studying mechanics "backward" in this way can actually be very good for such a student, because it makes her or him really *think* about the subject again, and the new perspective gives greater flexibility. The instructor can play a key role in helping such students appreciate this by emphasizing the power and breadth of the conservation law approach and its importance in contemporary physics, as well as celebrating with them the strength that one gains by being able to look at a situation from multiple perspectives.

The importance of the momentum-transfer model

The momentum-transfer model of interactions (which is introduced in chapter C3) is really what makes it possible to talk about conservation laws without starting with Newton's laws. This model will be a new and challenging idea to almost everyone. Instructors should work carefully with students, giving them enough practice with the model to *ensure* that they understand it and can talk about it correctly. The payoff is that when students really grasp this model, it by its very nature helps them avoid many of the standard misconceptions that tend to plague students in introductory courses. It takes a little work to get used to the new language, but I think that you will find it worth the effort.

Some unusual terminology

Instructors should note that I have coined a couple of new terms. A number of physicists have recently pointed out the contradictory ways in which we define and use the concept of *work*. I have therefore defined the term **k-work** $[dK]$ strictly to mean what might be called "center-of-mass work": this is the form of work that appears in the standard work-energy theorem and which is easiest to apply to both particles and extended objects. Students who are going on in physics need to understand that this idea is traditionally called *work*, but that I am renaming and more sharply defining it to avoid confusion with thermodynamic work (where I do use the traditional term) and the idea of "a force acting through a distance," both of which are very different concepts. The second invented term is **twirl** $[d\vec{L}]$, which is to angular momentum what impulse is to momentum and k-work is to energy. Having such a term makes the similarity of these concepts more apparent. One should also note that I have sharpened the meaning of impulse, k-work, and twirl to mean specifically what a *particular interaction* contributes to an object's momentum, kinetic energy, and angular momentum, respectively. Again, getting used to these new terms and definitions takes a bit of effort, but I believe that the payoff is a much clearer understanding of these important and difficult concepts. Instructors can greatly contribute to the pedagogical effectiveness of these ideas by learning these terms and by using them consistently and carefully.

Taking advantage of "puzzles"

Several chapters of this unit begin with a "puzzle" about the behavior of interacting objects. The pedagogical effectiveness of these puzzles can be greatly enhanced if they are demonstrated and discussed in class *before* students do the assigned reading. This helps students connect the puzzle with the real world and gives them a chance to "discover" the issue actively before they passively read about it. The website offers suggestions about how one can do these demonstrations in a way that actively engages the students.

What can be cut?

Almost every chapter in this unit is essential preparation or background for other parts of the course (indeed, most chapters have been deliberately pared down so that only what is essential remains). If one is desperate for something to cut, one *might* omit chapter C12 (which looks at some interesting and contemporary applications of conservation of energy as well as studying elastic and inelastic collisions). The rest of the unit is pretty much an indivisible whole.

Appreciation

A project of this magnitude cannot be accomplished alone. I would first like to thank the others who served on the IUPP development team for this project: Edwin Taylor, Dan Schroeder, Randy Knight, John Mallinckrodt, Alma Zook, Bob Hilborn, and Don Holcomb. I'd like to thank John Rigden and other members of the IUPP steering committee for their support of the project in its early stages, which came ultimately from an NSF grant and the special efforts of Duncan McBride. Users of the texts—especially Bill Titus, Richard Noer, Woods Halley, Paul Ellis, Doreen Weinberger, Nalini Easwar, Brian Watson, Jon Eggert, Catherine Mader, Paul De Young, Alma Zook, Daniel Schroeder, Alfred Kwok, David Tanenbaum, and Dave Dobson—have offered invaluable feedback and encouragement. I'd also like to thank Alan Macdonald, Roseanne Di Stefano, Ruth Chabay, Bruce Sherwood, and Tony French for ideas, support, and useful suggestions. Thanks also to Robs Muir for helping with several of the indexes. My editors Jim Smith, Denise Schanck, Jack Shira, Karen Allanson, Lloyd Black, J. P. Lenney, and Daryl Bruflodt as well as Spencer Cotkin, Donata Dettbarn, David Dietz, Larry Goldberg, Sheila Frank, Jonathan Alpert, Zanae Roderigo, Mary Haas, Janice Hancock, Lisa Gottschalk, Debra Hash, David Hash, Patricia Scott, Chris Hammond, Brittney Corrigan-McElroy, Rick Hecker, and Susan Brusch, have all worked very hard to make this text happen, and I deeply appreciate their efforts. I'd like to thank reviewers Doreen Weinberger (Smith College), Carmen Shephard (Southwestern Illinois College), Shane Burns (Colorado College), Catherine Mader (Hope College), Edwin Carlson, David Dobson, Irene Nunes, Miles Dressler, O. Romulo Ochoa, Qichang Su, Brian Watson, and Laurent Hodges for taking the time to do a careful reading of various units and offering valuable suggestions. Thanks to Connie Wilson, Hilda Dinolfo, Connie Inman, and special student assistants Michael Wanke, Paul Feng, Mara Harrell, Jennifer Lauer, Tony Galuhn, and Eric Pan, and all the Physics 51 mentors for supporting (in various ways) the development and teaching of this course at Pomona College. Thanks also to my Physics 51 students, and especially Win Yin, Peter Leth, Eddie Abarca, Boyer Naito, Arvin Tseng, Rebecca Washenfelder, Mary Donovan, Austin Ferris, Laura Siegfried, and Miriam Krause, who have offered many suggestions and have together found many hundreds of typos and other errors. Eric Daub was indispensable in helping me put this edition together. Finally, very special thanks to my wife, Joyce, and to my daughters, Brittany and Allison, who contributed with their support and patience during this long and demanding project. Heartfelt thanks to all!

Thanks!

Thomas A. Moore
Claremont, California

Introduction for Students
How to Read and Use This Text Effectively

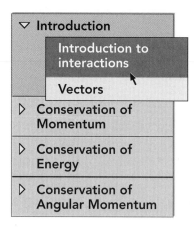

Introduction

Welcome to *Six Ideas That Shaped Physics!* This text has been designed using insights from recent research into physics learning to help you learn physics as effectively as possible. It thus has many features that may be different from science texts you have probably encountered. This section discusses these features and how to use them effectively.

Why Is This Text Different?

Research consistently shows that people learn physics most effectively if they participate in *activities* that help them *practice* applying physical reasoning in realistic situations. This is so because physics is not a collection of facts to absorb but rather a set of *thinking skills* requiring practice to master. You cannot learn such skills by going to factual lectures any more than you can learn to play the piano by going to concerts!

This text is designed, therefore, to support *active learning* both inside and outside the classroom by providing (1) resources for various kinds of learning activities, (2) features that encourage active reading, and (3) features that make it easier for the text (as opposed to lectures) to serve as the primary source of information, so that more class time is available for active learning.

The Text as Primary Source

Features that help the text serve as the primary source of information

To serve the last goal, I have adopted a conversational style that I hope will be easy to read, and I tried to be concise without being so terse that you need a lecture to fill in the gaps. There are also many text features designed to help you keep track of the big picture. The unit's **central idea** is summarized on the front cover where you can see it daily. Each chapter is designed to correspond to one 50-minute class session, so that each session is a logically complete unit. The two-page **chapter overview** at the beginning of each chapter provides a compact overview of that chapter's contents to consider before being submerged by the details (it also provides a useful summary when you review for exams). An accompanying **chapter-location diagram** uses a computer-menu metaphor to display how the current chapter fits into the unit (see the example at the upper left). Major unit subdivisions appear as gray boxes, with the current subdivision highlighted in color. Chapters in the current subdivision appear in a submenu with the current chapter highlighted in black and indicated by an arrow.

All technical terms are highlighted using a bold type like **this** when they first appear, and a **glossary** at the end of the text summarizes their definitions. Please also note the tables of useful information, including definitions of common symbols, that appear inside the front cover.

A physics *formula* is both a mathematical equation and a *context* that gives the equation meaning. Every important formula in this text appears in a **formula box.** Each contains the equation, a **Purpose** (describing the formula's meaning and utility), a definition of the **Symbols** used in the equation, a description of any **Limitations** on the formula's applicability, and possibly some other useful **Notes.** Treat everything in such a box as an *indivisible unit* to be remembered and used together.

Active Reading

Like passively listening to a lecture, passively scanning a text does not really help you learn. *Active* reading is a crucial study skill for effectively learning from this text (and other types of technical literature as well). An active reader stops frequently to pose internal questions such as these: *Does this make sense? Is this consistent with my experience? Am I following the logic here? Do I see how I might use this idea in realistic situations?* This text provides two important tools to make this easier.

What it means to be an *active reader*

Use the **wide margins** to (1) record *questions* that occur to you as you read (so that you can remember to get them answered), (2) record *answers* when you receive them, (3) flag important passages, (4) fill in missing math steps, and (5) record insights. Doing these things helps keep you actively engaged as you read, and your marginal comments are also generally helpful as you review. Note that I have provided some marginal notes in the form of *sidebars* that summarize the points of crucial paragraphs and help you find things quickly.

Tools to help you become an active reader

The **in-text exercises** help you develop the habits of (1) filling in missing math steps and (2) posing questions that help you *practice* using the chapter's ideas. Also, although this text has many worked examples of problems similar to homework or exam problems, *some* of these appear in the form of in-text exercises (as you are more likely to *learn* from an example if you work on it some yourself instead of just scanning someone else's solution). Answers to *all* exercises appear at the very end of each chapter, so you can get immediate feedback on how you are doing. Doing at least some of the exercises as you read is probably the *single most important thing you can do* to become an active reader.

The single most important thing you can do

Active reading does take effort. *Scanning* the 5200 words of a typical chapter might take 45 minutes, but active reading could take twice as long. I personally tend to "blow a fuse" in my head after about 20 minutes of active reading, so I take short breaks to do something else to keep alert. Pausing to fill in missing math also helps me keep focused longer.

Class Activities and Homework

The problems appearing at the end of each chapter are organized into categories that reflect somewhat different active-learning purposes. **Two-minute problems** are short, concept-oriented, multiple-choice problems that are primarily meant to be used *in* class as a way of practicing the ideas and/or exposing conceptual problems for further discussion. (The letters on the back cover make it possible to display responses to your instructor.) The other types of problems are primarily meant for use as homework *outside* of class. **Basic** problems are simple drill-type problems that help you practice in straightforward applications of a single formula or technique. **Synthetic** problems are more challenging and realistic questions that require that you

End-of-chapter problems support active learning

bring together multiple formulas and/or techniques (maybe from different chapters) and think carefully about physical principles. These problems define the level of sophistication that you should strive to achieve. **Rich-context** problems are yet more challenging problems that are often written in a narrative format and ask you to answer a practical, real-life question rather than explicitly asking for a numerical result. Like situations you will encounter in real life, many provide too little information and/or too much information, requiring you to make estimates and/or discard irrelevant data (this is true of some *synthetic* problems as well). Rich-context problems are generally too difficult for most students to solve alone; they are designed for *group* problem-solving sessions. **Advanced** problems are very sophisticated problems that provide supplemental discussion of subtle or advanced issues related to the material discussed in the chapter. These problems are for instructors and truly exceptional students.

Class time works best if you are prepared

Read the Text *Before* Class! You will be able to participate in the kinds of activities that promote real learning *only* if you come to each class having already read and thought about the assigned chapter. This is likely to be *much* more important in a class using this text than in science courses you may have taken before! Class time can also (*if* you are prepared) provide a great opportunity to get your *particular* questions about the material answered.

Introduction
to Interactions

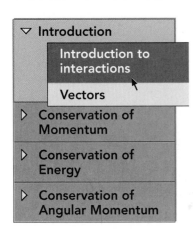

▽ **Introduction**

Introduction to interactions

Vectors

▷ **Conservation of Momentum**

▷ **Conservation of Energy**

▷ **Conservation of Angular Momentum**

Chapter Overview

Introduction

Welcome to *Six Ideas That Shaped Physics!* This introductory chapter presents an overview of physics as a discipline, a description of this course unit, and an introduction to the crucial concept of *interactions*.

Section C1.1:   The Nature of Science

One of the main goals of science is the development of imaginative **conceptual models** of physical reality. A good simplified model can capture the essence of a complex phenomenon and help organize our thinking about it. *This text's main purpose is to teach you the art of scientific model building*, by helping you not only to understand and appreciate the grand models we call **theories** but also to practice building the small-scale models needed to apply a theory in any given situation.

Science is an unusually effective *process* for generating powerful models of reality that happens when four crucial elements come together:

1. A sufficiently large community of scholars.
2. A commitment to logical consistency as an essential feature of models.
3. An agreement to use **reproducible experiments** to test models.
4. An overarching theory that provides a context for research.

In the case of physics, the Greek philosophical tradition created a community that recognized the power of logical reasoning. Early Renaissance thinkers championed the value of reproducible experiments as being crucial for testing models. But physics was not really launched until 1687, when Newton provided an overarching theory broad enough to provide a solid context for research.

Section C1.2:   The Development and Structure of Physics

Since the days of Newton, physicists have sought to create models able to embrace originally distinct areas of study. A map of this quest for "unification" appears in figure C1.1. The current conceptual structure of physics, illustrated in figure C1.2, rests on two fundamental theories: **general relativity** (GR) and the **standard model** (SM) of particle physics. In practice, physicists use five simpler theories (which are approximations valid in various limited contexts): **newtonian mechanics, special relativity, electromagnetic field theory, quantum mechanics,** and **statistical mechanics.** Units N, R, E, Q, and T of this text explore these theories in that order.

Physicists have recently learned to appreciate the role that **symmetries** play in physics. Both GR and the SM acknowledge (as almost any imaginable future theory must) certain basic symmetries (such as the time and position independence of physical laws) that give rise to **conservation laws** (such as the laws of conservation of energy and of momentum). These conservation laws thus have a validity beyond the particular theories currently in vogue.

Section C1.3: An Overview of This Unit

This unit focuses on conservation laws. It has four major subdivisions, one providing some basic background and one for each of the three great conservation laws common to all physical theories: **conservation of (linear) momentum, conservation of energy,** and **conservation of angular momentum.**

Section C1.4: Introduction to Mechanics

A theory of *mechanics* is a model of how an object moves in the absence of interactions and how its motion is affected by interactions with other things. The Aristotelian model (widely accepted until the early 1600s) stated that in the absence of interactions an object is at *rest*; it moves only when an active agent applies a push or pull. This model makes intuitive sense, but fails in a number of situations.

The breakthrough came when Newton, building on work by Galileo and others, created a new mechanics based on the following ideas:

Newton's first law: Any object not interacting with something else moves with a constant speed in a fixed direction.

An **interaction** is a physical relationship *between two objects* that, in the absence of other interactions, *changes* the motion of each.

This model successfully explains a *much* broader range of phenomena, partly because it categorizes friction as an *interaction* instead of an intrinsic aspect of motion.

Section C1.5: Fundamental Interactions

The SM states that all matter consists of **elementary particles** known as **quarks** and **leptons,** which we can model as mathematical point particles. (The electron is a lepton, while the proton and the neutron are quark triplets.) It also asserts that these particles participate in just four possible interactions: the **strong nuclear interaction,** the **weak nuclear interaction,** the **electromagnetic interaction,** and the **gravitational interaction.** As the first two have effective ranges smaller than an atomic nucleus, only the last two can act between larger objects.

Section C1.6: Macroscopic Interactions

We can more usefully categorize interactions between two **macroscopic** objects (consisting of more than a handful of atoms) as being either **long-range interactions,** which operate between physically separated objects, or **contact interactions,** which arise only from direct physical contact. Contact interactions include **friction** interactions that oppose the relative motion of the objects, **compression** interactions that oppose their merging, and **tension** interactions that oppose their separation. Long-range interactions include *all* gravitational interactions and long-range **electrostatic** and/or **magnetic** interactions. (According to the SM, all contact interactions are *really* electromagnetic interactions between atoms on the objects' interacting surfaces.)

Section C1.7: Describing "Motion"

What do we mean by "motion" in the idea that "interactions change motion"? Simple experiments show that when an object interacts with something else, its **speed** *may* change. But it may *not* change (1) if the object is involved in *multiple* interactions that cancel or (2) if the interaction changes the object's *direction* of motion instead. The last suggests that an object's **velocity vector,** which describes both the rate *and* the direction of its motion, might be a better description of motion. We will study the mathematics of vectors in chapter C2.

Section C1.8: Physics Skills: Technical Terms

This section discusses technical terms and how to learn them successfully.

Section C1.9: Physics Skills: Units

This section describes **SI units,** the internationally accepted system of scientific units, and the unit operator method for changing units. The fact that units must be consistent on both sides of an equation provides a useful tool for checking results; indeed, keeping track of units is one of the easiest ways to increase your problem-solving power!

C1.1   The Nature of Science

To explain is human

It is part of human nature that we strive to discern order in the cosmos and love to tell each other stories that *explain* what we discern, using ideas common to our experience. Science stands firmly in this ancient tradition: stories about how the gods guide the planets around the sky and modern stories about how the curvature of space-time does the same have much in common! What distinguishes science from the rest of the worldwide storytelling tradition is (1) the *types* of stories that scientists tell and (2) the *process* that science uses for creating and evaluating these stories.

Scientists express their stories in the form of **conceptual models,** which bear roughly the same relation to the real world as a model airplane does to a real airplane. A good physical model captures a phenomenon's *essence* while remaining small and simple enough to grasp. Model building is an essential aspect of science because reality is much too complicated to understand fully; models compress complex phenomena into bite-sized chunks that can be digested by finite minds. Inventing a model is less an act of discovery than an act of *imagination:* a good model is a vivid *story* about reality that creatively ignores complexity.

This text is about models and model building

Model making in science happens at all levels. **Theories**—grand models able to embrace a huge range of phenomena—are for science what great novels are for literature: extraordinary works of imagination that we strive to understand and cherish. But to apply such a grand model to a real-life situation, we must also construct a smaller model of the situation itself, simplifying it and making approximations so that we can connect it to the right grand model. Scientists do this second kind of model building daily, and one of the main goals of this course is to help you practice this art.

Models are limited

It is crucial to note that because models are necessarily simpler than reality, all models have their limits: the full "truth" about any phenomenon remains forever beyond our grasp. Even so, one *can* distinguish *better* models from *poorer* models. Good models are more logically self-consistent, more powerfully predictive in a broader range of cases, and more elegant in construction than their competitors.

Science is a *process* for producing powerful models

Science is, more than anything, a uniquely powerful *process* for generating and evaluating models, one that (since its development in the 1600s) has proved to be an astonishingly prolific producer of rich and powerful models.

A discipline becomes a science when the following four elements come together:

1. A sufficiently large *community* of scholars.
2. A commitment to *logical consistency* as an essential feature of all models.
3. An agreement to use **reproducible experiments** to test models.
4. An *overarching theory* rich enough to provide a solid context for research.

In the case of physics, the Greek philosophical tradition created a community of scholars who appreciated the power of logical reasoning. In fact, this community found its power so liberating that for a long time it imagined that pure logic should be *sufficient* to understand the world. The idea of using experiments to *test* one's logic was not even fully expressed until the 13th century and did not gain full acceptance as being *necessary* until the 17th century. Eventually, however, people recognized that the human desire to order experience is so strong that one of the most difficult tasks facing any thinker is to distinguish the order that is really out there from that which only *seems* to exist. Reproducible experiments make what would otherwise be individual experience available to the wider community, anchoring models more firmly to reality. Galileo Galilei (1564–1642) was a great champion of this approach. His use of the newly invented telescope to display features of heavenly bodies unimagined by any models of the time underlined to his sharpest contemporaries the inadequacy of pure reason and the importance of observation.

If only the first three elements are present, the prescientific community, even if it agrees on certain data, is generally fragmented into schools, each exploring its own model. Some progress is made, but at a much slower rate than when the whole community can work together. This was the situation in physics between the times of Galileo and Isaac Newton. In 1687, Newton published the first model of physics broad enough to embrace both terrestrial and celestial phenomena. This brilliant model captured the imagination of the whole physics community, and as this happened, physics became a science. The physics community shifted from arguing about smaller partial models to working *together* to refine, test, and extend Newton's extraordinarily rich model, confident that it would be shown to be completely true and valid.

The irony is that the community that strove to extend Newton's model to cover everything eventually amassed the evidence needed to prove it *false!* Only a community that is *devoted* to exploring a powerful model can collect the kind of detailed and careful evidence necessary to prove it false and thus move on to better models. This paradox is the engine that drives science forward.

The paradox at the heart of science

C1.2   The Development and Structure of Physics

The history of physics since Newton (which is summarized in figure C1.1) has involved both broadening the reach of physics and the *unification* of models. While Newton's model provided the general backdrop for physics until 1905, topics such as thermal physics, electricity, magnetism, and optics initially required their own separate theories. However, starting in the early 1800s, physicists began constructing models that unified these areas of physics, showing, for example, that electricity, magnetism, and light are different manifestations of something called an *electromagnetic field*; that thermal physics could be explained by Newton's model; and so on. This program was going so well in the late 1800s that some physicists wrote that there was probably little left to learn about physics!

In the early decades of the 1900s, though, physicists began to see that the basic newtonian backdrop was incompatible with an increasing number of experimental results. After a period of turmoil, physicists found two new theories—the theory of **general relativity** (1915) and the theory of **quantum mechanics** (1926)—that essentially covered the same territory as Newton's theory and yet were completely consistent with modern experiments. After this bifurcation, the process of unification began again. Old ways of unifying various areas of physics with Newton's model were updated to be consistent with the new backdrop theories, and quantum mechanics was unified with the electromagnetic field theory and **special relativity** (the nongravitational part of general relativity) to yield the theory called *quantum electrodynamics*. This in turn was generalized to include fields other than the electromagnetic field and became *relativistic quantum field theory*, and this in turn was unified with various models describing subatomic particles to create the **standard model** of particle physics.

The history of physics since Newton

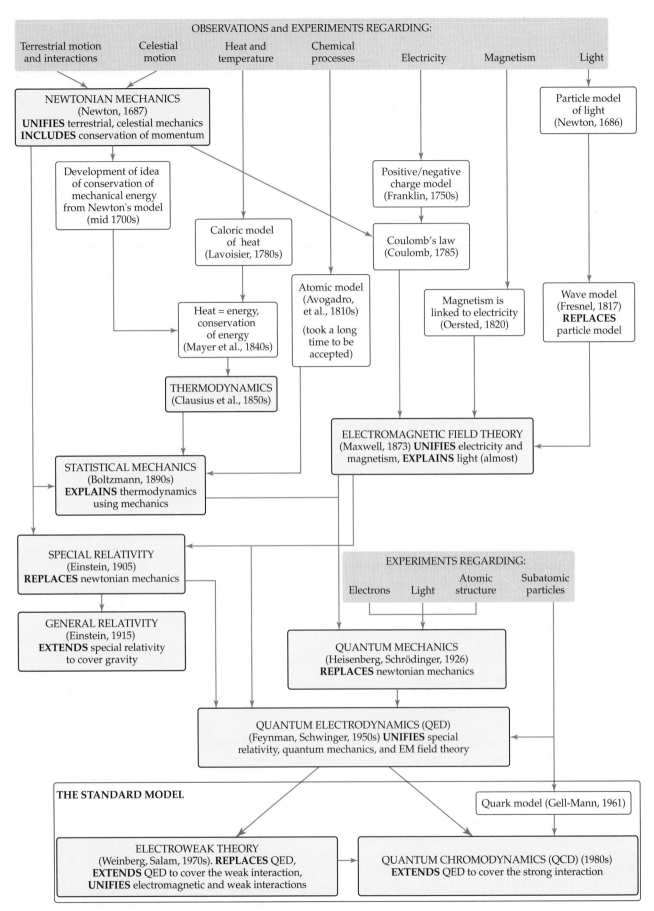

Figure C1.1
A schematic history of physics.

Currently, **general relativity,** which covers gravity and other phenomena at distance scales larger than atoms, and the **standard model,** which theoretically works for all distance scales but does not cover gravity, stand as the two fundamental models of physics. Although physicists are dissatisfied with both (for different reasons) and are *especially* dissatisfied to have *two* theories instead of one, no known experimental result contradicts these theories.

In practice, physicists rarely use these fundamental theories to explain phenomena except in exotic cases. Instead they use one of five simpler theories: **newtonian mechanics, special relativity, electromagnetic field theory, quantum mechanics,** or **statistical mechanics.** Each of these theories has its own more limited range of validity than the two fundamental theories but is typically *much* easier to use within that range. These theories, their limitations, and their relationships to the fundamental theories are illustrated in figure C1.2.

Since about the 1960s, physicists have come to appreciate the importance of **symmetry principles** in physics (see the top line of figure C1.2). Early in the 1900s, the mathematician Emmy Noether showed that, given some reasonable assumptions about what kinds of physical theories are possible, a symmetry principle stating that "the laws of physics are unaffected if you do such and such" automatically implies a **conservation law.** For example, the time independence of the laws of physics implies that a quantity (which we call *energy*) exists whose value in an isolated system is *conserved* (it does not change with time).

Conservation laws, therefore, stand in a certain sense *above* the particular models of physics: conservation of energy is a feature of newtonian mechanics, electromagnetic field theory, general relativity, and so on because *all* these theories (1) have the form assumed by Noether's theorem and (2) assume that the laws of physics are time-independent. Moreover, our current fundamental theories are based on symmetry principles in the sense that they propose (and work out the consequences of) *new,* nonobvious symmetry principles.

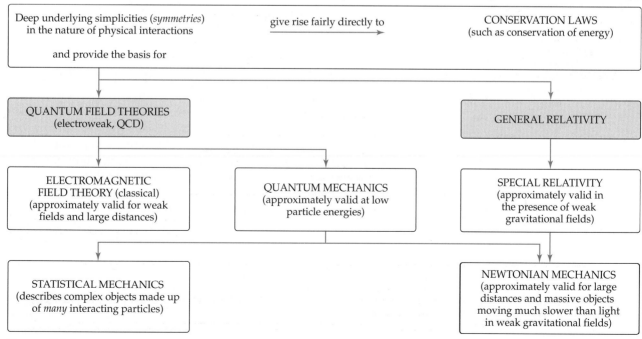

Figure C1.2
The current conceptual structure of physics.

C1.3   An Overview of This Unit

Why we have to learn the five simpler theories first

It might seem logical in a course like this one to start with the two fundamental theories and work downward to the five approximate theories at the bottom of figure C1.2. However, this is impractical because (1) the fundamental theories (in spite of their awesome breadth and beauty) are very sophisticated, hard to learn, and unnecessarily complicated to use and (2) they are expressed using the language and concepts of the five simpler theories. One must therefore begin by learning the five simpler theories. Each of the *other* five units of this six-unit text introduces you to one of these theories (units N, R, E, Q, and T look at Newtonian mechanics, special Relativity, Electromagnetic field theory, Quantum mechanics, and Thermal physics/statistical mechanics, respectively).

This unit will focus on conservation laws

In this first unit, though, we will focus on the conservation laws that lie at the foundation of *all* current physical theories. When an isolated set of objects interacts with one another, we find that (no matter how the objects interact) certain quantities (which we call the set's total **energy, momentum, and angular momentum**) are *conserved* (i.e., have values that do not change with time). These laws provide powerful tools for analyzing the behavior of a set of objects *without* having to delve into exactly *how* they interact.

The symmetries behind these conservation laws

Noether's theorem states that conservation of energy, of momentum, and of angular momentum follows from three basic symmetry principles: that the laws of physics are independent of (1) *time,* (2) *place,* and (3) *orientation,* respectively (meaning, for example, that an experiment done on an isolated set will yield the same result whether we do it today or tomorrow, here or on the moon, or facing west or east). These principles (and the other assumptions Noether makes) are so basic that these conservation laws will also almost certainly be a part of future theories. Since a proof of Noether's theorem is (alas!) beyond us here, in this course we will just assume that the conservation laws are true and go from there.

Even though these conservation laws appear in all current theories of physics, we will see that the *definitions* of energy, momentum, and angular momentum are somewhat different in different theories. We will start with the definitions used in newtonian mechanics and develop modifications as needed.

An overview of the unit

This unit is divided into four subdivisions, as shown in figure C1.3. The first provides crucial background for the others, which explore conservation of momentum, energy, and angular momentum, respectively. The colored boxes in the figure correspond to these four subdivisions, and the chapters in each subdivision are listed below and to the right of each subdivision heading.

The remainder of this chapter discusses the currently accepted model of matter and interactions. We will see that an accurate description of motion also requires working with *vectors,* so the other chapter in this introductory subdivision reviews the mathematics of vectors. Discussion of these issues provides an essential foundation for the rest of the unit.

C1.4   Introduction to Mechanics

An introduction to *mechanics*

Mechanics is the area of physics that deals with how the physical interactions between objects affect their motion. A person cannot survive long without constructing mental models about how objects move and interact. However, the commonsense models that people unconsciously develop tend to be numerous, each working well only in a narrow range of situations. This is acceptable in most everyday circumstances, but more than casual reflection often exposes such models to be mutually (or even self-) contradictory, and relying on them can lead to incorrect predictions in unusual situations.

Einstein once said that physics is simply "refined common sense." Your mission in this unit will be to *refine* your common sense by thoughtfully displacing the unconscious models you personally have developed during your life with the much more powerful and comprehensive models that physicists have developed during the past 300 years. This is not easy! By definition, your unconscious models make *sense* to you, and the models preferred by physicists will seem abstract and counterintuitive in comparison, at least at first.

More than anything, success in this mission requires thinking carefully and self-critically about ideas that at first seem self-evident. Let us start by thinking carefully about the definition of mechanics given before. To understand how physical interactions between objects affect their motions, we first should ask, How does an object move in the *absence* of interactions?

The intuitively *obvious* answer is that it *remains at rest*. To get something moving, one might say, some active agent has to push it or pull on it, and when the agent stops doing this, the object comes to rest. The Greek philosopher Aristotle may have been the first to state this model clearly (probably in the 330s B.C.), but it is still a typical feature of people's unconscious models today.

Sensible as this answer might seem, a bit of commonsense reflection shows that it gets into serious trouble in a number of cases. Aristotle himself recognized that continued forward motion of an arrow after it left a bow was hard to explain with this model. He proposed an explanation that even his followers quickly recognized was inadequate. His followers instead proposed that the arrow continued to be pushed forward by what amounted to a "memory" of the initial push that got it moving, a memory that the arrow eventually "forgets." However, this answer had its own problems. (For example, if you push a child in a wagon, why does the "memory of the push" that keeps the wagon rolling after you let go, *feel* to the child very different from the original push?) In spite of these problems, the respect that Aristotle earned for the quality of the bulk of his work (and the lack of a good alternative) kept this flawed model of motion alive for 2000 years.

The breakthrough required to move forward finally came in 1687 when Isaac Newton published a simple but quite different answer to the question:

Newton's first law: Any object that does not interact with something else moves with a *constant speed* in a *fixed direction.*

Therefore, the continuing motion of an arrow or wagon requires no explanation in this model: it is *expected.* However, this raises a different question: What causes an object to *stop*? According to Newton, the answer is *interactions:*

An **interaction** is a physical relationship *between two objects* that, in the absence of other interactions, *changes* the motion of each.

For example, when Aristotle's flying arrow comes into physical contact with its target, the target interacts with the arrow—*this* is what brings the arrow to rest.

One of the crucial aspects of Newton's model (as outlined by the two ideas above) is that it helps us to think clearly about *friction*. In Aristotle's

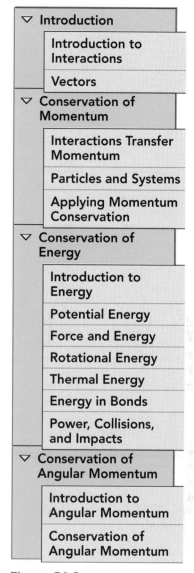

▽ **Introduction**

| **Introduction to Interactions** |

| **Vectors** |

▽ **Conservation of Momentum**

| **Interactions Transfer Momentum** |

| **Particles and Systems** |

| **Applying Momentum Conservation** |

▽ **Conservation of Energy**

| **Introduction to Energy** |

| **Potential Energy** |

| **Force and Energy** |

| **Rotational Energy** |

| **Thermal Energy** |

| **Energy in Bonds** |

| **Power, Collisions, and Impacts** |

▽ **Conservation of Angular Momentum**

| **Introduction to Angular Momentum** |

| **Conservation of Angular Momentum** |

Figure C1.3
A schematic map describing the structure of unit C.

The most basic principles of Newton's mechanics

model, "coming to rest" is an intrinsic feature of motion, so friction is built into the model in a way that hides it from view. Newton's model, on the other hand, sees friction as being an *interaction* between a moving object and something else which actively *slows down the object.* This enables us to imagine motion in the *absence* of friction (something that is nearly a contradiction in terms in Aristotle's model!) and thus think clearly about cases such as planetary motion that Aristotle's model cannot address.

Newton's model also emphasizes that *inanimate* things can affect motion. Aristotle thought that creating what he called "violent" motion (as opposed to the "natural" motions of a massive object toward the earth or fire toward the sky) requires an animate agent. Newton's model removes these artificial distinctions, making it possible to offer inanimate explanations of motion.

Newton's model can in fact handle any situation that Aristotle's model can and many more that it cannot. This is more than sufficient reason to abandon Aristotle's approach! However, since our daily experience rarely exposes us to objects moving without friction, seeing the world with newtonian (instead of Aristotelian) eyes initially requires a *conscious* act of imagination. Fully embracing Newton's model also means being vigilant against the Aristotelian ideas periodically served up by our subconscious. But the desired goal is not to *discard* your intuition (which is a powerful and useful tool!) but rather, with some careful reflection, to *refine* your intuition to become more newtonian. This takes effort; but when you succeed, your retrained intuition will have much greater reach and power than before.

(If you are interested to know where you currently stand in this process, you can find an Aristotelian Thinking Diagnostic Test at the end of the chapter. Do not expect to do well: It may take all term to reshape your intuition thoroughly!)

C1.5   Fundamental Interactions

The fundamental structure of matter

How can two objects interact? To understand the currently accepted answer to this question, we need to discuss briefly the deep structure of matter according to the standard model of particle physics. You probably already know that matter is constructed of molecules, which are in turn constructed of interacting atoms, and that each atom consists of a cloud of electrons orbiting a nucleus constructed of protons and neutrons (see figure C1.4). According to the standard model, an electron is an example of a more general class of six elementary particles called **leptons,** while protons and neutrons

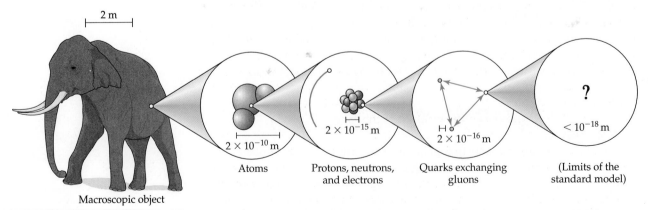

Figure C1.4

An overview of the structure of matter as viewed by the standard model.

Table C1.1   **Table of lepton and quark properties.** Masses and charges are expressed in terms of the proton mass and charge, respectively. (The fact that leptons and quarks both appear in three pairs is suggestive of some deeper order that is not yet understood.)

Leptons				Quarks			
Name	**Symbol**	**Mass**	**Charge**	**Name**	**Symbol**	**Mass***	**Charge**
Electron	e^-	1/1836	−1	Down	d	0.33	$-\frac{1}{3}$
Electron-neutrino	ν_e	≈ 0	0	Up	u	0.33	$+\frac{2}{3}$
Muon	μ^-	0.1126	−1	Strange	s	0.57	$-\frac{1}{3}$
Muon-neutrino	ν_μ	≈ 0	0	Charmed	c	1.6	$+\frac{2}{3}$
Tau	τ^-	1.894	−1	Bottom	b	5.0	$-\frac{1}{3}$
Tau-neutrino	ν_τ	≈ 0?	0	Top	t	184	$+\frac{2}{3}$

*Because quarks cannot exist as isolated particles, their masses cannot easily be determined (we will see why in unit Q). The masses listed here follow one scheme for defining quark masses, but should be used only for comparisons and not taken too literally.

are constructed of elementary particles called **quarks,** of which there are also (perhaps not coincidentally) six types. See table C1.1 for a list of the names and properties of these fundamental particles. Each of these particles also has a corresponding **antiparticle,** which has the same mass and most other properties except for opposite electrical charge. All known types of matter (including exotic forms currently only found in particle accelerator experiments and energetic astrophysical objects) are constructed of these particles.

The standard model offers a fascinating account of why the quark triplets that we call the proton and neutron are the *only* quark configurations that can survive for more than a millionth of a second, and why the electron is the only stable lepton other than the neutrinos, which are extremely hard to detect. The only thing we need to know at present, though, is that our best available theory of particle physics states that *all* matter is comprised of interacting **elementary particles** that have no known deeper structure and thus can be modeled as mathematical points. This idea will prove very useful to us in chapter C4.

Now we can talk about the contemporary view of fundamental interactions. The standard model asserts that elementary particles can participate in four fundamentally different kinds of interactions. The **strong nuclear interaction** acts only between quarks. It is what binds quarks together to form protons and neutrons and binds protons and neutrons into nuclei. The next-strongest interaction is the **electromagnetic interaction,** which acts only between electrically *charged* particles. The **weak nuclear interaction** acts between all quarks and leptons. As we will see in unit Q, it plays an important role in determining nuclear structure. The **gravitational interaction** acts between *all* particles, but is *by far* the weakest of the four.

The four fundamental interactions

Each interaction has one or more associated **mediators** that represent the interaction in quantum-mechanical calculations. These calculations imagine a pair of particles interacting by exchanging mediators in a way that usually makes the mediators undetectable even in principle. Under the right circumstances, though, certain particle interactions emit these mediators as independent and detectable particles. The best-known mediator is the **photon,** the mediator of the electromagnetic interaction: Light consists of independent

Table C1.2   **Table of fundamental interactions.** Relative strengths are expressed as approximate fractions of the strong nuclear interaction strength. The rightmost three columns describe the mediating particles, whose masses and charges are given in terms of the proton mass. (We will see what zero mass means in unit R.) Mediators have no antiparticles.

Name	Acts between	Strength	Effective Range	Mediator(s)	Name	Mass	Charge
Strong (nuclear)	Quarks and/or gluons	$\equiv 1$	$\approx 10^{-15}$ m	Gluons (eight types)		0	0
Electromagnetic	All charged particles	$\approx 10^{-2}$	∞	Photon		0	0
Weak (nuclear)	Quarks and/or leptons	$\approx 10^{-13}$	$\approx 10^{-18}$ m	Vector bosons	W^+	85.7	+1
					Z^0	97.19	0
					W^-	85.7	−1
Gravitational	*All* particles	$\approx 10^{-38}$	∞	Graviton (? not seen)		0	0

Only electromagnetic and gravitational interactions have a range larger than an atomic nucleus

photons. The properties of the four interactions and their mediators are shown in table C1.2.

Note that the strong and weak nuclear interactions have an effective range smaller than the typical size of an atomic nucleus! This means that while these interactions help determine nuclear structure (as we will see in unit Q), *only the electromagnetic and gravitational interactions are able to act between particles separated by more than the width of a nucleus.*

Exercise C1X.1

The proton is constructed of two *u* quarks and a *d* quark. The neutron is constructed of two *d* quarks and a *u* quark. The Δ^{++} "particle" is an unstable quark triplet similar in mass to the proton but with double the charge. What quarks must it contain?

Exercise C1X.2

In what ways can a proton interact with a muon? In what ways can a neutrino interact with a free photon?

C1.6   Macroscopic Interactions

Useful categories for interactions between macroscopic objects

While it is good to know something about the nature of interactions at the fundamental level, it proves more helpful to use different categories for the interactions between **macroscopic** objects (objects consisting of more than a handful of atoms). We can divide interactions between macroscopic objects into two general categories: **long-range interactions** that allow the objects to influence one another even when they are separated by a significant distance and **contact interactions** that arise *only* when the objects come into direct physical contact.

The only possible long-range interactions are **electrostatic** interactions that involve at least one electrically charged object, **magnetic** interactions that involve at least one magnet, and **gravitational** interactions. Since the fundamental gravitational interaction is so weak, unless at least one of the interacting objects has a mass larger than that of a large mountain, this interaction will only immeasurably affect the objects' motions. The electrostatic and

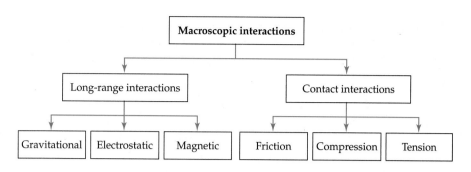

Figure C1.5
A diagram illustrating the hierarchical relationship of the most useful model for categorizing interactions at the macroscopic level.

magnetic interactions are at the fundamental level simply different manifestations of the electromagnetic interaction, but superficially they seem pretty different. (We will see how these two interactions fit together in unit E.)

We can further subdivide contact interactions into **friction** interactions, which oppose the *relative* motion of the objects in contact; **compression** interactions, which seek to keep them from merging; and **tension** interactions, which oppose their separation.

Figure C1.5 illustrates the hierarchical relationship of the categories presented here. *You should be able to place any physically real interaction that affects the motion of macroscopic objects into one of these categories.*

Exercise C1X.3

Think of realistic examples from your experience, at least one for each type of long-range interaction, where one object affects another's motion even when they are separated by a significant distance.

Please understand that *all* contact interactions are, at the fundamental level, just complicated *electromagnetic* interactions between the atoms on the interacting objects' touching surfaces. When these atoms approach one another closely, some of the electrically charged particles in the atoms are pushed more closely together than other particles, leading to either repulsive or attractive electromagnetic interactions. Remember that even atoms are actually mostly empty space, so what looks like surfaces in contact at the macroscopic level looks at the atomic level like point particles interacting over a distance.

However, understanding that contact interactions are *really* electromagnetic interactions does not really help us much at the macroscopic level. In terms of the way we handle them at the macroscopic level (for reasons that will become clearer as we move through the unit), gravitational interactions and long-range electrostatic and magnetic interactions have more in common with each other than the latter have with the microscopic electromagnetic interactions involved in contact. The distinction between long-range and contact interactions thus not only is intuitive but also helps us find the right methods to bring to bear in realistic circumstances.

It is worth remembering that the real physical world is always unimaginably complex: we can never know fully what is going on. We are *always* seeking simplified mental models that are *useful* for helping our limited minds think clearly about the world and make good predictions. If categorizing interactions in this way is helpful in a wide range of contexts, then that is great! At the same time, we need to recognize the acceptable range of this model: this model is *not* helpful at the level of elementary particle physics,

All contact interactions are *really* electromagnetic

. . . but the macroscopic categories are helpful

while the standard model is not all that useful at the macroscopic level. Part of being a good physicist is learning to use *appropriate* models for a given context while at the same time recognizing the limits of those models.

Exercise C1X.4

A car skids to a stop with its wheels locked. What interactions affect the car's motion? (Use the categories of this section.) Qualitatively, *how* do the interactions affect its motion? (It may help you to think about what would change if each interaction were switched off somehow.)

C1.7   Describing "Motion"

The definition of *interaction* in section C1.4 states that an interaction (when acting alone) "changes the motion" of the participating objects. Now that we have discussed interactions in some detail, it is time to think more carefully about "motion." What is the best way to describe motion in this context?

One way might be to talk about an object's **speed.** I will carefully and quantitatively define this term in chapter C3, but for now let us rely on our intuitive understanding of speed as a numerical quantity that increases as an object moves faster and decreases as it slows down. How do interactions affect an object's speed? Imagine a shopping cart full of groceries with very well-greased wheels on a level surface. If the cart is already moving at a good clip and you leave it alone, you know from experience that it will continue to move at roughly the same speed for quite a while. On the other hand, if you push forward on it from behind, its speed will increase, and a strong push will cause its speed to increase faster. If you pull backward on the cart, it will slow down, and a strong pull will slow it down faster. So we see that in the absence of interactions, the cart's speed remains (roughly) the same, but a contact interaction between you and the cart can change the cart's speed at a rate that tells us something about the interaction's strength.

However, speed is not the best quantity for describing motion, because it is also possible for an object to participate in interactions and yet *not* experience a change in speed. This may happen in at least two ways.

Imagine first sitting at rest on a trampoline. Your speed in this case is constant (zero). Can we conclude that you participate in no interactions? No! You can *feel* both the downward pull of gravity and the upward push exerted by the contact interaction between the trampoline and your seat. If the trampoline were to suddenly vanish, you know what would happen: the gravitational interaction between you and the earth (now acting alone) would cause you to fall toward the ground. Similarly, if you can imagine suddenly switching off gravity, you know that the contact interaction between you and the stretched trampoline surface (now acting alone) would launch you toward the sky. What is happening here is that the two interactions exert opposite effects on your motion in such a way that they cancel each other out.

The definition of *interaction* given in section C1.5 actually already handles this particular problem: I was careful to say there that an interaction necessarily causes changes in motion only when it acts *alone.* However, it is important to be *aware* that multiple interactions can oppose one another in such a way as to cancel their effects on an object's motion.

There is, however, a more serious problem with identifying "motion" in the definition of interaction with "speed." If you lightly tap a rolling soccer

Interactions *can* change an object's speed

But "speed" is not the best description of motion

ball sideways with your foot, you can change the ball's direction without changing its speed. The contact interaction between your foot and the ball pretty clearly does something to change the ball's "motion," but the effect in this case is *not* a change in the ball's speed. We see from this that *direction* is an important aspect of "motion" as we are using the term in the definition of interaction.

Example C1.1

Problem   Imagine a puck floating above an air table. (Such a table uses flowing air to support the puck a small distance above the table so that the puck can move almost frictionlessly around the table.) Imagine that the puck is connected by a string to a peg on the table. If we hold the puck so the string is taut and then launch the puck in a direction perpendicular to the string, the puck will follow a circular path around the peg at a constant speed (as you can verify!), as shown in figure C1.6a. How does the puck interact with its surroundings? How do these interactions affect the puck's motion?

Solution   The puck participates in three interactions: (1) a long-range gravitational interaction with the earth, (2) a compression contact interaction with the flowing air, and (3) a tension contact interaction with the string. The puck touches nothing but the supporting air and the string, so the puck cannot be involved in any other contact interactions. If we assume that the puck is uncharged and nonmagnetic, it cannot participate in any other long-range interactions either.

The gravitational interaction would, in the absence of the other interactions, cause the puck to fall toward the floor. The contact interaction with the flowing air would, in the absence of other interactions, puff it toward the ceiling. In this situation, these two interactions cancel each other. The interaction with the string causes a constant change in the puck's *direction* of motion without changing its speed (if the string were cut, the puck would move in a straight line at a constant velocity, as shown in figure C1.6b). This is therefore another example of an interaction that changes an object's *direction* but not its *speed*.

But, you might argue, must there not be a fourth interaction that pulls *outward* on the puck? Is the fact that the string is taut not evidence for such an interaction? According to Newton's model of motion, no and no! First, with what else could the puck possibly be interacting? As noted before, because the puck does not touch anything but the string and air and because it could well be uncharged and not magnetic, we have excluded all other possibilities available in our model! The string in this case is taut because it has to pull on the puck to cause it to deviate from the straight path that it would naturally take if the string were not there, and a string can only pull on something if it is taut!

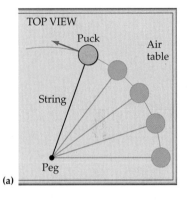

(a)

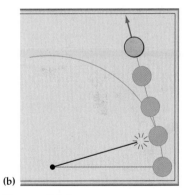

(b)

Figure C1.6

(a) A puck floating on an air table will follow a circular path at a constant speed if it is tethered to a peg by a string. (b) If the string breaks, the puck will travel in a straight line instead (by Newton's first law).

Let us imagine a quantity, which we will call **velocity** $\vec{v}$ to distinguish it from speed, that expresses both the rate *and* the direction of an object's motion. We can visualize this quantity as being an arrow which points in the object's direction of motion and whose length is proportional to its speed. Such an arrow would be "changed" by the interactions in the wagon example (where the arrow's *length* changes) as well as in the soccer ball example (where the arrow's *direction* changes). Moreover, in the trampoline case we can more easily see

An intuitive definition of *velocity*

how equal upward and downward changes in a velocity arrow during a given time interval might yield no net change. Velocity thus better describes the "motion" that gets changed by an interaction than speed does.

An arrowlike quantity that has both a magnitude and a direction is a **vector.** To progress with our quantitative description of motion, we need to study the mathematics of vectors. This will be our task in chapter C2.

Exercise C1X.5

A satellite in a circular orbit around the earth moves at a constant speed. How does this satellite interact with its surroundings? How does this interaction or do these interactions affect its motion?

C1.8   Physics Skills: Technical Terms

To clearly and concisely communicate ideas to one another, physicists, like people in any close-knit community, have developed a community language involving **technical terms** with special meanings. We have seen a number of such terms introduced in this chapter.

In physics, these technical terms are usually English words or phrases. This means that English-speakers may *think* that they understand what they hear or read in a discussion of physics, but if they are not familiar with the *special* meanings that certain words have to physicists, they can become quickly lost.

Mechanics, law, velocity, force, inertia, mass, weight, energy, momentum, impulse, and *work* are words that are important in this unit and that mean quite different things in physics than they do in common English. In physics, *mechanics* refers to a theory about motion rather than to people who fix cars. In physics, a *law* describes how physical objects *naturally* behave; in colloquial English, a law *prescribes* behavior precisely because humans do *not* naturally follow the law. As we will see, we will have similar problems with the other terms on the list. Such terms can easily confuse a reader who is unaware of their technical meanings!

Correct use of technical terms is also more than just a matter of good style. The precise definitions of these terms make it easier both to express physical ideas clearly and to *think* about them correctly. In my experience, careless use of technical terms (usually arising from mixing in meanings from common English) is a leading cause of confusion among introductory-level students.

Part of your task in this course is to learn the language of practicing physicists. Doing this successfully means realizing that you *are* learning a new language: treat technical terms as you would vocabulary in any foreign language! Specifically, you have to (1) learn to *recognize* technical terms and (2) *memorize* their definitions (using flash cards or other aids). When you later use the term, pause to *think* about whether you are using it correctly; be particularly aware of connotations from everyday English that may creep in.

It will help you to identify and study these terms if you remember that I highlight each technical term in **boldface** type when it is first introduced, define the term clearly nearby, and then *restate* the definition in the glossary at the end of the book. If you make *sure* that you know the technical meaning of each term in the glossary, you will greatly reduce opportunities for confusion.

C1.9   Physics Skills: Units

Units attach physical meaning to bare numbers. If you catch a fish and brag to your friends that it was "3" long, they will not know how to react until you specify the units—3 meters, 3 feet, or 3 cm. To clearly and precisely communicate the magnitude of a measured quantity to someone, we must state it in terms of a previously agreed-upon standard unit for that quantity. The purpose of a **system of units** is to define such standards.

Standard SI Units and Prefixes   An international committee has been working since 1960 to provide clear and reproducible definitions of standard units to help scientists communicate results more precisely. The system of units adopted by the committee as the standard for all scientific communication is an adaptation of what used to be called the *metric* system, but the units are now called **SI units** (from the French term *Système Internationale*). This system defines seven fundamental units, each with a standard abbreviation: the **meter** (abbreviation: m) for distance, the **second** (s) for time, the **kilogram** (kg) for mass, the **kelvin** (K) for temperature, the **mole** (mol) for counting molecules, the **ampere** (A) for electric current, and the **candela** (cd) for luminous intensity, which we will not use in this course. The committee has carefully defined most of these basic units so that scientists can easily recreate the unit in their own laboratories. For example, the second is currently defined to be 9,192,631,770 oscillations of the radio waves emitted by a cesium-133 atom under certain well-defined conditions. A scientist anywhere in the world can therefore, in principle, create a cesium-based atomic clock that measures time in standard seconds.

In addition to these basic units, the SI committee has defined a set of **derived units** that are combinations of these basic units. The most important of these are the **joule** ($1 \text{ J} \equiv 1 \text{ kg·m}^2/\text{s}^2$) for energy, the **watt** ($1 \text{ W} \equiv 1 \text{ J/s}$) for power, the **newton** ($1 \text{ N} \equiv 1 \text{ kg·m/s}^2$) for force, the **pascal** ($1 \text{ Pa} \equiv 1 \text{ N/m}^2$) for pressure, the **coulomb** ($1 \text{ C} = 1 \text{ A·s}$) for electric charge, the **volt** ($1 \text{ V} = 1 \text{ J/C}$) for electric energy per unit charge, and the **ohm** ($1 \text{ W} = 1 \text{ V/A}$) for electrical resistance. Future chapters will explore the reasons behind the definitions of these and other derived units.

The SI committee has also defined a set of standard prefixes and prefix abbreviations (see figure C1.7) that one attaches to a unit to multiply it by various powers of 10. Thus 1 *millimeter* (abbreviation: mm) is equal to 10^{-3} m, 1 *gigajoule* (GJ, which is pronounced with a hard g as in *get*) is 10^9 J, 1 *nanosecond* (ns) is 10^{-9} s, and so on.

Units for angles (the *radian* and the *degree*) are standard, but for historical reasons are not treated as formal SI units. We will also occasionally refer to English units such as the *mile*, the *foot*, and the *pound* (which is a unit of force).

STANDARD PREFIXES

Power	Prefix	Symbol
10^{18}	exa	E
10^{15}	peta	P
10^{12}	tera	T
10^{9}	giga	G
10^{6}	mega	M
10^{3}	kilo	k
10^{-2}	centi	c
10^{-3}	milli	m
10^{-6}	micro	μ
10^{-9}	nano	n
10^{-12}	pico	p
10^{-15}	femto	f
10^{-18}	atto	a

Figure C1.7

Standard SI prefixes for powers of 10.

Developing an Intuitive Feel for the Units   How big is a megameter? How much energy is a microjoule? You probably do not have an intuitive feeling for such quantities. There are two things that you can do to feel more at home with SI units: (1) *memorize the prefixes* and (2) *learn some benchmarks*.

The SI prefixes are used frequently in physics literature and increasingly in everyday speech (as in "a 10-gigabyte disk drive"). It will slow you down considerably if you do not at *least* memorize the prefixes between 10^{-12} and 10^{+12}. The prefix *milli* is particularly difficult for speakers of U.S. English (it means one-*thousandth*, *not* one-millionth).

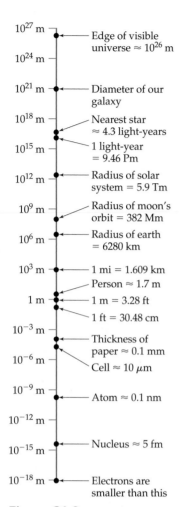

Figure C1.8a
Benchmarks for distances in meters.

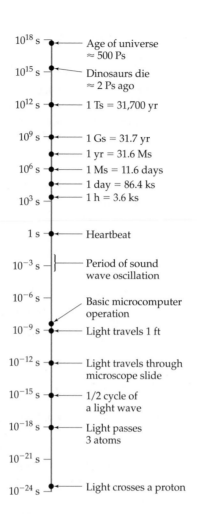

Figure C1.8b
Benchmarks for times in seconds.

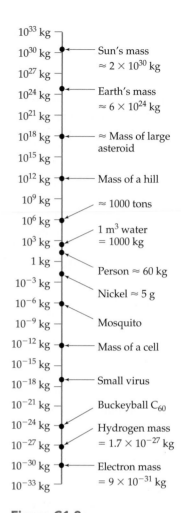

Figure C1.8c
Benchmarks for masses in kilograms.

The best way to get a feeling for multiples of the basic SI units is to study the benchmark charts shown in figure C1.8. Knowing these charts can help you to recognize absurd answers when you solve problems. (For example, if you compute how high you can throw a ball and you get a result larger than the size of the solar system, you've made a mistake somewhere.)

Conversion of Units   Often in this course you will need to convert a quantity expressed in one unit to the equivalent quantity expressed in another unit. For example, imagine that we are told that the distance to a nearby town is 23 miles (mi), and we want to convert this to a distance in meters. We would start by writing down the equation that defines the relationship between the units:

$$1 \text{ mi} = 1609 \text{ m} \tag{C1.1a}$$

Since 1 mi is *equivalent* to 1609 m, the *ratio* of these quantities is 1:

$$\frac{1609 \text{ m}}{1 \text{ mi}} = 1 \tag{C1.1b}$$

Such a ratio of equivalent units is called a **unit operator.** Since we can always multiply a quantity by 1 without changing its value, we can multiply our original distance of 23 mi by 1 in the form of the unit operator to get

$$(23 \text{ mi})(1) = (23 \text{ mi})\left(\frac{1609 \text{ m}}{1 \text{ mi}}\right) \qquad \text{(C1.1c)}$$

Note that we cancel the unit "mi" that appears in the numerator and denominator exactly as if it were an algebraic symbol. In general, when writing equations involving units, you treat the units as if they were algebraic symbols, carrying any uncanceled units through to the right side.

This method amounts to being a useful mnemonic device that helps you do unit conversions correctly. When you multiply a quantity by one or more unit operators and cancel any units that appear in both the numerator and denominator, then if the units that remain are the final units that you wanted, you can be assured that your quantity has been correctly converted.

Let us consider another example that illustrates how to treat powers of units. Consider a rock whose density of 3000 kilograms per cubic meter (kg/m^3) and volume is 10 cubic centimeters (cm^3). What is its mass? Since density $\rho \equiv m/V$ (where m is the object's mass and V is its volume), $m = \rho V$. When we multiply ρ and V, we have to include *three* powers of the unit operator converting meters to centimeters in order to get the units to come out to be simply kilograms:

$$\left(3000 \, \frac{kg}{m^3}\right)(10 \, cm^3)\left(\frac{1 \text{ m}}{100 \text{ cm}}\right)\left(\frac{1 \text{ m}}{100 \text{ cm}}\right)\left(\frac{1 \text{ m}}{100 \text{ cm}}\right) = 0.03 \text{ kg} \quad \text{(C1.2)}$$

Unit Consistency Any equation relating physical quantities *must* have the same units on both sides. For example, in the equation $v = D/T$, if D is a distance in meters and T is a time interval in seconds, then the speed v *must* have units of meters per second (m/s). Note also that it is possible to multiply or divide quantities having different units; but two quantities being added or subtracted must have the *same* units (e.g., adding 10 m to 2.3 s is nonsense!).

Unit consistency provides a very useful way to check algebraic work or other calculations: algebraic errors almost always yield inconsistent units. *This is probably the simplest and yet most underutilized method for checking one's work.* Developing the habit of *constantly* thinking about unit consistency is a giant step toward being able to solve problems both quickly *and* correctly.

ARISTOTELIAN THINKING DIAGNOSTIC TEST

Note: The questions on this page and the next constitute a test for diagnosing signs of Aristotelian thinking. Some of these questions can be answered correctly (i.e., from a newtonian perspective) using ideas from this chapter, but others explore topics to be covered in the future. I have not formally defined *force* yet in this course; use your own intuitive sense of what the word means. The newtonian answers are found at the end of the chapter, after the exercise answers. (You should *not* expect to score well on this test, even if you have taken physics in high school. Aristotelian-like intuitive models are very difficult to displace, and it may take you much of the course to make progress.)

AD1 A bicyclist coasts without pedaling on a level road. Why does the cyclist eventually come to rest?
A. All moving objects naturally come to rest.

B. Friction steadily slows down the bike.
C. Friction eventually overpowers the force keeping the bicycle moving.
D. The force of the bike's initial motion wears out.
E. B and D.
F. C and D.

AD2 A child throws a baseball into the air. *After* the ball leaves the child's hand, the ball moves vertically upward for a while, reaches a certain maximum height, and then falls back toward the ground. Ignoring air resistance, the force(s) acting on the ball during this time is (are)
A. The constant downward force of gravity alone.
B. The constant force of gravity and a steadily decreasing upward force.

(more)

C. The constant force of gravity and a steadily decreasing upward force that acts only until the ball reaches its maximum height.

D. A decreasing upward force before the ball reaches its maximum height and an increasing downward force of gravity afterward.

E. Nonexistent. No forces act on the ball; it returns to the ground because that is its natural place of rest.

AD3   A hockey puck sliding due north on a frictionless plane of ice is given a very brief eastward "tap" by a hockey player. What path in the drawing will the hockey puck follow after the tap is over (circle one)?

TOP VIEW

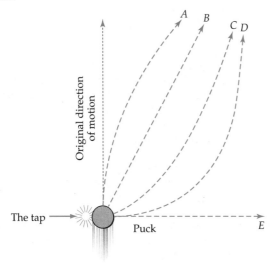

AD4   Imagine that a small car rear-ends a large truck that is initially at rest. During the collision, the force that the *truck* exerts on the car is
A. Zero (the truck is just sitting there).
B. Smaller than the force that the *car* exerts on the truck.
C. Equal to the force that the *car* exerts on the truck.
D. Greater than the force that the *car* exerts on the truck.

AD5   A child on a playground merry-go-round is holding on for dear life as the merry-go-round turns rapidly.

TOP VIEW

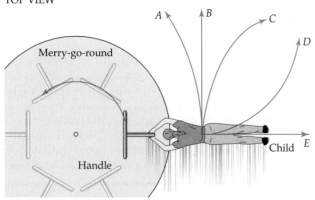

If the child's grip fails, what path will the child follow before hitting the ground? Choose the letter corresponding to the path on the diagram that you think best describes the child's path relative to the ground after letting go.

AD6   Imagine that you throw a rock off a 30-m (100-ft) cliff facing a still lake when the sun is directly overhead. The initial velocity of the ball is 10 m/s horizontally due west. Assume that the effect of the air on the rock is negligible. Just before the rock hits the water, the westward component of its velocity (which will be the same as the speed of its shadow on the water) will be
A. Roughly zero (the rock drops straight into the water).
B. Significantly less than 10 m/s.
C. Very close to 10 m/s.
D. Significantly larger than 10 m/s.

AD7   Imagine that you jump from a tree to the ground. Why do you come to rest when you reach the ground?
A. The ground pushes up on your feet.
B. Gravity stops acting on you when you reach the ground.
C. Anything that is falling naturally comes to rest when it finally reaches the ground.
D. Friction.
E. Your feet push against the ground; that push stops you.

AD8   Imagine that you are standing by the side of a road facing the road. Just as a pickup truck passes you (moving toward your right), a person in the passenger side of the cab happens to drop a stone out the window. If the person drops the stone at the instant the truck passes closest to you, the stone hits the ground
A. Somewhat to the right of your position.
B. Somewhat to the left of your position.
C. In front of you, straight below where it was dropped.

AD9   Imagine a wagon with truly frictionless wheels sitting at rest on level ground. To get this wagon moving, you would have to exert a push
A. Larger than the wagon's weight.
B. Larger than the wagon's inertia.
C. Of any magnitude.

AD10   A person is moving a crate along the floor at a steady speed by pulling on a rope tied to the crate. The rope suddenly breaks. At the instant the rope breaks, the crate
A. Immediately stops.
B. Immediately starts slowing down.
C. Continues moving until the force of the pull wears out.
D. Continues moving until inertia overcomes the force of its forward motion.

TWO-MINUTE PROBLEMS

C1T.1 According to the definition of *science* given in this chapter, *astrology* is not a science. What does it lack?
A. A community of scholars devoted to its study.
B. Agreement that models must be logically consistent.
C. Reliance on reproducible experiments to test models.
D. A fundamental theory embracing the discipline.

C1T.2 According to the definition of *science* given in this chapter, which of the following do you think are sciences? Show the letter of the first discipline on the list that you think is *not* a science. Be prepared to defend your answer! (The answers are open to debate!)
A. Geology
B. Psychology
C. Anthropology
D. Economics
E. Political science
F. Philosophy

C1T.3 A baseball player slides into third base. Why, according to the newtonian model of motion, does the player eventually come to rest?
A. All moving objects naturally come to rest.
B. Friction overpowers the force of the player's motion.
C. The force of the player's motion eventually wears out.
D. A friction interaction changes the player's motion.
E. B and C.
F. C and D.
T. Other (specify).

C1T.4 An object moving at a constant speed must have something acting on it to maintain its motion, true (T) or false (F)?

C1T.5 *Mesons* are subatomic "particles" that actually consist of a quark bound to an antiquark. The lowest-mass mesons are the *pions* ($\pi^+ = u\bar{d}$, $\pi^- = \bar{u}d$, $\pi^0 = u\bar{u}$ or $d\bar{d}$, where the overbar indicates an antiparticle). The kaons (K^+, K^0, K^-) are mesons with masses substantially larger than the pions but smaller than other mesons. The quark composition of the K^- must be
A. $u\bar{s}$
B. $\bar{u}s$
C. $d\bar{s}$
D. $\bar{d}s$
E. $c\bar{s}$
F. $\bar{c}s$

C1T.6 The quark triplet called the Σ^0 is the lowest-mass uncharged triplet except for the neutron, which is substantially less massive. The quark composition of the Σ^0 must be
A. udd
B. uds
C. $\bar{u}dd$
D. sdd
E. cdd
F. cds

C1T.7 Imagine that I throw a ball toward the floor. It hits the floor and rebounds upward. What type of fundamental interaction between the atoms of the floor and the ball causes the ball to rebound upward?
A. Strong nuclear
B. Electromagnetic
C. Weak nuclear
D. Gravitational
E. Some combination of the above
F. Some other kind of interaction

C1T.8 An empty floating boat interacts gravitationally with the earth. A different interaction with something else keeps the boat from responding to the gravitational interaction by sinking. What is the other object that interacts with the boat? What is the *type* of macroscopic interaction involved? (Choose one from each column.)
A. The surrounding water.   A. A tension interaction.
B. The atmosphere.   B. A electrostatic interaction.
C. The earth.   C. A friction interaction.
D. The lake floor.   D. A compression interaction.

C1T.9 A bicyclist rounds a curve at a constant speed. The bicyclist's velocity is also constant, T or F?

C1T.10 A car moves 10 m backward in 2 s at a steady rate. The car's speed is therefore −5 m/s, T or F?

HOMEWORK PROBLEMS

Basic Skills

C1B.1 Consider a kite being flown on a windy day. What kinds of interactions does this kite participate in, and what other object is it interacting with in each case? (Use the macroscopic interaction categories.)

C1B.2 Consider a hockey puck sliding on rough ice. What kinds of interactions does the puck participate in, and what other object is it interacting with in each case? (Use the macroscopic interaction categories.)

Solve problems C1B.3 through C1B.7 using the unit operator technique shown in section C1.9.

C1B.3 If you say to a friend on the phone, "I'll be over in half a kilosec," how many minutes will your friend wait?

C1B.4 Show that $1.00 \text{ m/s} = 2.24$ miles per hour (mi/h).

C1B.5 What is the speed of light in furlongs per fortnight? (You can find the speed of light in meters per second on the inside front cover of the text. 1 furlong = $\frac{1}{8}$ mi = length of a typical furrow in a medieval farm, and 1 fortnight = 14 days.)

C1B.6 A light-year (abbreviation: ly) is the distance that light travels in 1 year. Find this distance in both miles and meters. (The speed of light is $c = 3.00 \times 10^8 \text{ m/s}$.)

C1B.7 The density of water is very nearly 1000 kg/m^3. Use unit conversion to show that a cube of water 10 cm on a side has a mass of 1 kg, and that a cube of water 1 cm on a side has a mass of 1 gram (g). (This was originally the international *definition* of the kilogram, enabling one to create a standard kilogram without having to go to France to look at the platinum-iridium cylinder that now defines the kilogram. The standard was redefined when it became clear that the difficulty of measuring volumes of water precisely makes defining the unit of mass in terms of an actual object more reproducible.)

Synthetic

C1S.1 Can the question "What is justice?" ever be investigated scientifically? If you think not, does this mean that justice does not exist or that it is not worth thinking about? If you think it can, can your belief be verified scientifically? Support your case with reasoned arguments.

C1S.2 *Baryons* are subatomic "particles" constructed of quark triplets (the proton is a baryon). Make a table of all baryons with masses smaller than about 1.8 times the proton mass, and predict the mass and charge of each of these combinations. (The actual baryon masses will be different from these predictions because of issues we will discuss in unit Q, but will be close.)

C1S.3 Neutrinos very rarely interact with *anything* and thus are very hard to detect. About 10^{14} neutrinos from the sun pass through your body every second, even at midnight (the neutrinos easily go through the earth), but this is of no concern since (very roughly) one a *day* interacts with any quark or lepton in your body. In fact, a neutrino would have to pass through several thousand light-years of solid lead before it would have a 50–50 chance of being absorbed. Given the information in section C1.5, see if you can explain why neutrinos so rarely interact with normal matter.

C1S.4 The radius of a proton is roughly 10^{-15} m, while the radius of a hydrogen atom is about 0.5×10^{-10} m. If we were to enlarge both proportionally until the proton was as large as a marble, about how large would the atom be?

C1S.5 How big on a side would a cube of rock have to be to be more massive than you are? Solve this problem by using the unit operator technique discussed in section C1.9. (*Hint:* Rock has a density of roughly 3 times that of water. See problem C1B.7.)

Rich-Context

C1R.1 Estimate the total mass of the water in the earth's oceans. [*Hints:* About what fraction of the earth's surface is ocean? The greatest depths in the ocean are about 11 kilometers (km). What might one estimate the average depth to be?]

C1R.2 Working in groups, make a list of some questions of practical importance in people's lives that cannot be answered scientifically at present. Discuss among yourselves whether it might be possible in the future to address such questions scientifically, or whether at least some of your questions cannot even *in principle* be addressed scientifically according to the definition of *science* presented in this chapter. If you believe there are questions that cannot be addressed scientifically even in principle, is it worth studying or thinking about such questions at all? If you believe such questions do *not* exist, then discuss how you would prove *that* belief scientifically.

C1R.3 Pick biology, chemistry, or geology (whichever your group knows most about) and see whether you can come to consensus about when and how your selected discipline became a science according to the definitions given in this chapter. Focus on the last of the four required elements to fall into place for your selected discipline, and be prepared to make a case for your consensus. Is the answer clear, or is it open to debate in your particular case? Pinpoint any uncertainties or weaknesses in your argument.

C1R.4 Each part of this problem describes an object in a specific physical context in which it interacts with other objects. In each case, use the macroscopic interaction categories to list the ways that the object interacts with its surroundings; and for each listed interaction, state the *other* object involved. Remember that an interaction, if unopposed, will act to change the object's velocity, but two opposed interactions may cancel each other's effect on the velocity. Do the best you can; some of these are *hard!*
   a. A person sits on a chair.
   b. A leaf falls from a tree. (Consider the leaf after it has left the tree but before it hits the ground.)
   c. A magnet sticks to the side of a refrigerator.

d. A tiny bit of paper jumps from a tabletop toward an electrically charged comb. (Consider the bit after it has left the tabletop but before it reaches the comb.)

e. *Difficult:* A child hangs on to a playground merry-go-round that is rotating so rapidly that the child is suspended above the ground. (See the diagram associated with problem AD5 on page 20. If we ignore air friction, there are only *two* interactions involved here.)

f. *Difficult:* A car accelerates down a road. We will see later in this unit that processes internal to an object can *never* change the motion of the object as a whole: only an interaction with something *external* can do this. If this is so, what interaction increases the car's speed? Would the acceleration be possible if the road were very slippery?

Advanced

C1A.1 A neutrino must pass within about 10^{-18} m of a quark to have any chance of interacting with it. Thus, the maximum target area that a quark presents to a neutrino is about 10^{-36} m^2. However, a neutrino moves so quickly and the weak interaction is so weak that experimentally only about 1 in 10^{12} typical neutrinos passing a quark within this radius actually interacts significantly with it. Use this information, the fact that Avogadro's number of protons and/or neutrons has a mass of about 1 g, and the fact that the density of lead is about 11 g/cm^3 to estimate (in light-years) how far a given typical neutrino would have to travel through lead to have a 50–50 chance of significantly interacting.

ANSWERS TO EXERCISES

C1X.1 The quark composition of the Δ^{++} must be *uuu*: Only this triplet has a charge of +2 times the proton charge and yet has a mass even close to the proton's mass.

C1X.2 The muon and the proton can participate in weak nuclear interactions, electromagnetic interactions (since both are charged), and gravitational interactions. The neutrino and photon can only participate in gravitational interactions, as both are uncharged and the neutrino cannot participate in strong nuclear interactions and the photon cannot participate in strong or weak nuclear interactions.

C1X.3 Here are some simple examples. The earth affects a dropped ball gravitationally even though the ball does not touch the earth. A charged balloon electrostatically repels another charged balloon even when they do not touch. Two magnets attract or repel each other magnetically, depending on their orientation.

C1X.4 The car participates in a gravitational interaction with the earth, a contact friction interaction with the air, a contact friction interaction with the road, and a contact compression interaction with the road. The gravitational interaction, acting alone, would cause the car to fall toward the earth's center. The compression interaction with the road pushes upward on the car, preventing it from falling (if gravity were suddenly turned off, this interaction would launch the car toward the sky!). The friction interactions with the road and air cause the car to slow down.

C1X.5 The satellite (assuming that it orbits above the earth's atmosphere) participates in only one significant interaction: a gravitational interaction with the earth. This interaction causes the satellite to deviate from the straight-line path it would follow if the earth were not there. As in the case of the puck in example C1.1, this interaction causes a change in the satellite's velocity but not its speed.

ANSWERS TO THE ARISTOTELIAN DIAGNOSTIC

A score of 80% or above is great!

1. B   2. A   3. B   4. C   5. B   6. C   7. A   8. A   9. C   10. B

C2

Vectors

Chapter Overview

Introduction

As chapter C1 hinted, we need to understand the mathematics of *vectors* to describe "motion" in newtonian mechanics. This will help with more than just describing motion; we will find that *many* physical quantities are described by vectors.

▽ **Introduction**

Introduction to interactions

Vectors

▷ **Conservation of Momentum**

▷ **Conservation of Energy**

▷ **Conservation of Angular Momentum**

Section C2.1: Vectors and Scalars

A **vector** has both a numerical **magnitude** and an associated **direction,** while a **scalar** has only a magnitude. An italic symbol represents a vector if it has an arrow over it (for example, $\vec{v}$) but a scalar if it does not. One can visualize a vector as an arrow whose direction indicates the vector's direction and whose length is proportional to its magnitude.

Section C2.2: Basic Vector Operations

A **displacement** is a vector that describes a *shift in position* by specifying the direction and distance traveled. If we arrange two vectors $\vec{u}_1$ and $\vec{u}_2$ so that one's tip coincides with the other's tail, we define their **vector sum** $\vec{u}_1 + \vec{u}_2$ as going from the first's tail to the second's tip (see figure C2.1a). A vector $\vec{u}$'s **vector inverse,** denoted by $-\vec{u}$, has the same magnitude but opposite direction (see figure C2.1b). We can think of the **vector difference** $\vec{u}_2 - \vec{u}_1$ as being either the sum of $\vec{u}_2$ and $-\vec{u}_1$ or the vector that when added to $\vec{u}_1$ yields $\vec{u}_2$ (see figure C2.1c).

Section C2.3: Components

If we set up an imaginary cubical grid in space and define three mutually perpendicular directions parallel to the grid lines to be the $+x$, $+y$, and $+z$ **directions,** we can write any vector $\vec{u}$ as a sum of three **component vectors:**

$$\vec{u} = \vec{u}_x + \vec{u}_y + \vec{u}_z = u_x\hat{x} + u_y\hat{y} + u_z\hat{z} \qquad \text{(C2.4)}$$

Purpose: This equation describes how we can reconstruct a vector $\vec{u}$ given its (scalar) **components** u_x, u_y, and u_z (and it implicitly defines those signed component numbers).

Symbols: $\vec{u}_x$, $\vec{u}_y$, and $\vec{u}_z$ are *component vectors* parallel to the x, y, and z **coordinate directions,** respectively, and $\hat{x}$, $\hat{y}$, and $\hat{z}$ are **directionals,** or shorthand expressions for the $+x$ direction, the $+y$ direction, and the $+z$ direction, respectively.

Limitations: This equation assumes we have already established a cubical grid in space and defined the $+x$, $+y$, and $+z$ directions.

Note that each component's absolute value specifies the magnitude of the corresponding component vector, and its sign specifies whether the component vector points in the positive or negative coordinate direction. Note also that, given a grid, merely listing a vector's component scalars (say, in the form of a **column vector**) completely describes the vector.

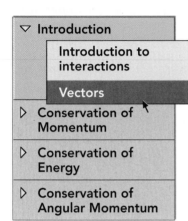

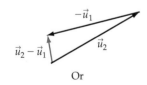

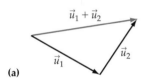

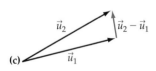

Figure C2.1
(a) How to construct the sum of two vectors. (b) How to construct a vector's inverse. (c) Two ways to construct the difference between two vectors.

Section C2.4: The Magnitude of a Vector

In analogy to a displacement's length, we can use an arbitrary vector $\vec{u}$'s components to calculate its magnitude as follows:

$$u = \text{mag}(\vec{u}) = \sqrt{u_x^2 + u_y^2 + u_z^2} \qquad \text{(C2.7)}$$

Purpose: This equation describes how to calculate a vector $\vec{u}$'s magnitude $u = \text{mag}(\vec{u})$ from its components u_x, u_y, and u_z.

Limitations: There are none (in the context of this course).

Notes: This definition implies that $u \geq 0$ *always*: a negative vector magnitude is a contradiction in terms! Note that a component vector's magnitude is $\text{mag}(\vec{u}_x) = |u_x|$, not u_x.

Section C2.5: Vectors in One and Two Dimensions

In situations where all the vectors of interest lie on a plane, we can describe a vector's direction by specifying its angle relative to some given direction. We can use trigonometry to convert from vector components to the vector's magnitude and direction angle, or vice versa. (*Please read this very important section for the details, which are important but too complicated to summarize here.*)

Section C2.6: Vector Operations in Terms of Components

We can use components to calculate the vector sum $\vec{u} + \vec{w}$, the vector inverse $-\vec{u}$, and the difference $\vec{u} - \vec{w}$ of two vectors. In component vector notation, the equations are

$$\begin{bmatrix} u_x \\ u_y \\ u_z \end{bmatrix} + \begin{bmatrix} w_x \\ w_y \\ w_z \end{bmatrix} = \begin{bmatrix} u_x + w_x \\ u_y + w_y \\ u_z + w_z \end{bmatrix} \qquad - \begin{bmatrix} u_x \\ u_y \\ u_z \end{bmatrix} = \begin{bmatrix} -u_x \\ -u_y \\ -u_z \end{bmatrix} \qquad \text{and}$$

$$\begin{bmatrix} u_x \\ u_y \\ u_z \end{bmatrix} - \begin{bmatrix} w_x \\ w_y \\ w_z \end{bmatrix} = \begin{bmatrix} u_x - w_x \\ u_y - w_y \\ u_z - w_z \end{bmatrix}$$

respectively (see equations C2.16, C2.17, and C2.18, respectively). The components of the **scalar multiple** $b\vec{u}$ of a scalar b and a vector $\vec{u}$ are simply $[bu_x, bu_y, bu_z]$: this operation stretches $\vec{u}$ by the factor $|b|$ but either does not change its direction (if $b > 0$) or exactly reverses it (if $b < 0$). *Dividing* a vector by a scalar b is the same as multiplying it by $1/b$.

Section C2.7: Vectors Have Units

Since a vector has a numerical magnitude, it also generally has units. The units of a vector as a whole and of each of its components are the same as the units of its magnitude.

Section C2.8: Reference Frames

We call the process of establishing a cubical grid setting up a **reference frame.** To define a frame, we *must* (but may freely) choose

1. The object to which the frame is attached.
2. The orientation of the frame's *x*, *y*, and *z* **axes** in space.
3. The location of the frame's **origin** (which defines the zero point for all axes).
4. Which side of each axis represents the "positive" direction.

It is *conventional* to choose axis directions to be **right-handed** (meaning that one's right index finger, second finger, and thumb indicate the positive sides of the *x*, *y*, and *z* axes, respectively). In a frame in **standard orientation** on the earth's surface, these axes point east, north, and upward, respectively. Once we have established a reference frame, three **coordinates** [*x, y, z*] specify the components of any point's **position** $\vec{r}$, which is defined to be the displacement from the origin to that point. We can calculate a displacement from *A* to *B* as a *change in position* $\Delta\vec{r} = \vec{r}_B - \vec{r}_A$. Realistic reference frames are not usually literal cubical grids, but must be functionally equivalent.

C2.1   Vectors and Scalars

The distinction between *vectors* and *scalars*

At the end of chapter C1, we found that an object's *velocity* (which specifies both its rate and its direction of motion) provides a more useful description of its motion in the context of the newtonian model than its *speed* (which specifies only its rate of motion). A **scalar** quantity is any quantity (such as speed) that we can completely describe using a single numerical value. In contrast, a **vector** is a quantity (such as velocity) that has a **direction** in addition to a numerical **magnitude.** Intrinsically *scalar* quantities in physics include *energy, mass, time, electric charge,* and *temperature;* intrinsically vector quantities include *displacement, force, momentum, angular momentum,* and *torque.* Figure C2.2 illustrates the distinction. Note that when describing a vector, one should *always* specify its magnitude *and* direction; *both* are essential aspects of a vector. Thus we might describe a car's velocity $\vec{v}$ as being 65 mi/h west, while we would describe its *speed* as being simply 65 mi/h.

Notation for vectors and scalars

The distinction between a vector and a scalar is so important that physicists have developed notation that clearly distinguishes the symbols used for vectors and scalars. In this text, an italic letter with an arrow over it *always* represents a vector, while an italic letter without such an arrow is *always* a scalar. For example, the symbol for *velocity* is $\vec{v}$, while the symbol for *speed* is v. Blurring the distinction between vectors and scalars is a sure path to confusion, so please strive to use this notation correctly.

(I should say here that it is still common in *printed* texts to use nonitalicized boldface letters as vector symbols, for example, **v** for velocity instead of $\vec{v}$. However, this notation is not easy to reproduce by hand, and evidence suggests that many beginners do not readily recognize the boldface letters as being different from ordinary symbols. Many new introductory textbooks are therefore using the arrow-over notation.)

One can visualize a vector quantity as an *arrow* whose direction specifies the vector's direction and whose length is proportional to the vector's magnitude. When I draw arrows to represent vector quantities, I always label the arrow with the *vector's* symbol (rather than with the scalar symbol representing its magnitude, as is done in some texts).

Figure C2.2

(a) Temperature is a *scalar* quantity: it is completely specified by a single numerical value. (b) The push these people exert acts in a certain direction and has a certain strength; this force is thus a *vector* quantity.

(a)

(b)

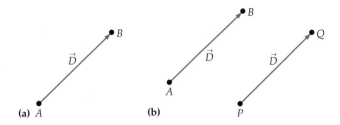

Figure C2.3
(a) An arrow representing a displacement. (b) These two displacements are equivalent.

Exercise C2X.1

Is the *drag* an object experiences when moving through air a scalar or a vector? What about an object's *volume?* Defend your response in both cases.

C2.2   Basic Vector Operations

The most fundamental kind of vector is a *displacement:* indeed, we define the properties of all other vectors in analogy to those of displacements. A **displacement** describes a *shift in position* from one point in space to another. Since we can completely describe such a shift by specifying a magnitude (the distance between the points) and a direction (the direction we go to get from the first point to the second), a displacement qualifies as a vector quantity. (The Latin word *vector* in fact means "carrier," expressing the way a displacement *carries* us from one point to the other.) Figure C2.3a illustrates how we can visually represent a displacement by using an arrow.

Definition of a *displacement*

Note that a displacement represents *only* the magnitude and direction of a *shift* in position; it does *not* specify where the shift begins or ends. For example, if point B lies 2.0 m northeast of point A and point Q lies 2.0 m northeast of point P, the *same* displacement vector $\vec{D}$ (whose magnitude is 2.0 m and whose direction is northeast) carries us from A to B and from P to Q (see figure C2.3b). By analogy, we consider *any* two vectors (not just displacements) that have the same magnitude and direction to be equivalent, even if they were originally defined at different places and/or times. Therefore, we can freely transport vectors from place to place and/or from time to time, because as long as we have not changed its magnitude or direction, the transported vector is equivalent to the original.

Vectors are movable

We can now define operations of vector addition and vector subtraction analogous to the addition and subtraction of scalars. Imagine that we travel from point A to point B (displacement $\vec{D}_1$ in figure C2.4a), then from point B to point C (displacement $\vec{D}_2$). Our "total" displacement in this trip is from A to C (displacement $\vec{D}_3$). It makes sense to define the **vector sum** of $\vec{D}_1$ and $\vec{D}_2$ to be this total displacement $\vec{D}_3$. We define the sum of *any* two vectors $\vec{u}_1$ and $\vec{u}_2$

Definition of *vector addition*

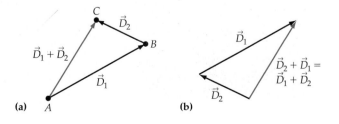

Figure C2.4
(a) How to construct the sum of two displacements. (b) Adding the vectors in the reverse order does not change the result.

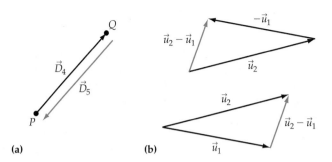

Figure C2.5
(a) Two displacements that are vector inverses of each other.
(b) Two methods for constructing a vector difference.

(a)   **(b)**

Definition of the vector inverse

analogously: if we align the vectors so that the tail end of $\vec{u}_2$ coincides with the tip of $\vec{u}_1$, then the sum $\vec{u}_1 + \vec{u}_2$ is the vector stretching from the tail end of $\vec{u}_1$ to the tip of $\vec{u}_2$. Figure C2.4b shows that vector addition is **commutative:** if we line up the vectors in the reverse order, the sum is still the same.

Now consider traveling from point P to point Q (displacement $\vec{D}_4$ in figure C2.5a) and then back to point P (displacement $\vec{D}_5$). These two displacements add up to the **zero vector** (*no* displacement). Since two *scalars a and b* that add to zero are negatives of each other ($a + b = 0$ implies $a = -b$ and $b = -a$), we analogously define two vectors that add to nothing to be negatives (technically, **vector inverses**) of each other:

$$\text{If} \qquad \vec{D}_4 + \vec{D}_5 = 0 \qquad \text{then} \qquad \vec{D}_4 \equiv -\vec{D}_5 \qquad \text{and} \qquad \vec{D}_5 \equiv -\vec{D}_4$$

$$(C2.1)$$

Note that vector inverses will only add to zero if they have the same magnitude (arrow length) but opposite directions. A minus sign in front of a vector therefore indicates *a reversal of the vector's direction.* (Note also that because a vector with zero magnitude has no well-defined direction, it is not really different from the zero scalar; so we conventionally write it as simply 0 without the arrow.)

Definition of the vector difference

We can define the **vector difference** $\vec{u}_2 - \vec{u}_1$ of two vectors $\vec{u}_1$ and $\vec{u}_2$ to be the sum of $\vec{u}_2$ and the vector inverse of $\vec{u}_1$:

$$\vec{u}_2 - \vec{u}_1 \equiv \vec{u}_2 + (-\vec{u}_1) \qquad (C2.2a)$$

Alternatively, we can define $\vec{u}_2 - \vec{u}_1$ to be the vector that when added to $\vec{u}_1$ yields $\vec{u}_2$:

$$\vec{u}_2 = (\vec{u}_2 - \vec{u}_1) + \vec{u}_1 \qquad (C2.2b)$$

Figure C2.5b shows that these two approaches yield equivalent vectors. The second definition implies that if we align $\vec{u}_1$ and $\vec{u}_2$ so that their tail ends coincide, then the vector difference $\vec{u}_2 - \vec{u}_1$ is a vector going from the tip of $\vec{u}_1$ to the tip of $\vec{u}_2$. We will find this second approach to calculating the vector difference most useful in the chapters that follow.

Exercise C2X.2

In the spaces provided, construct the vector sum $\vec{u}_1 + \vec{u}_2$, the vector inverses $-\vec{u}_1$ and $-\vec{u}_2$, and the vector difference $\vec{u}_2 - \vec{u}_1$ of the vectors $\vec{u}_1$ and $\vec{u}_2$ shown.

C2.3   Components

So far, I have described these vector operations only qualitatively. To do *quantitative* calculations with vectors, we need to know how to express not only a vector's magnitude but also its direction in terms of purely scalar quantities. We can do this most naturally by resolving a vector into *components*.

Suppose that we permeate the space in a region of interest with an imaginary cubical grid consisting of three mutually perpendicular sets of straight, evenly spaced, and parallel lines. By arbitrarily picking a "positive" direction for each of these sets of lines, we define three mutually perpendicular **coordinate directions** in space, which we conventionally call the *x* **direction,** the *y* **direction,** and the *z* **direction.** It might help you visualize this if we align this grid so that these coordinate directions correspond to "east," "north," and "up," respectively.

Once we have defined such a grid, we can write any vector (such as the displacement $\vec{D}$ at a certain time between me and a bat circling around the classroom) as a sum of three mutually perpendicular displacement **component vectors** $\vec{D}_x$, $\vec{D}_y$, $\vec{D}_z$ parallel to the *x*, *y*, and *z* grid lines, respectively (see figure C2.6). For example, if to get from me to the bat at a given instant you have to go 4.0 m along the grid's *x* direction, 2.0 m opposite to the grid's *y* direction, and 2.5 m along the grid's *z* direction, then we could write the displacement as

Definition of a vector's component vectors

$$\vec{D} = \vec{D}_x + \vec{D}_y + \vec{D}_z \qquad\qquad (C2.3a)$$

where

$$\vec{D}_x = 4.0 \text{ m in } +x \text{ direction} \equiv (4.0 \text{ m})\hat{x} \qquad (C2.3b)$$

$$\vec{D}_y = 2.0 \text{ m in } -y \text{ direction} \equiv -(2.0 \text{ m})\hat{y} \qquad (C2.3c)$$

$$\vec{D}_z = 2.5 \text{ m in } +z \text{ direction} \equiv (2.5 \text{ m})\hat{z} \qquad (C2.3d)$$

where you can think of the **directionals** $\hat{x}$, $\hat{y}$, and $\hat{z}$ as standing for the phrases "in the $+x$ direction," "in the $+y$ direction," and in the "$+z$ direction," respectively. Thus $(2.0 \text{ m})\hat{y}$ describes a displacement of 2.0 m in the $+y$ direction, and (according to the definition of vector inverse in section C2.2) $-(2.0 \text{ m})\hat{y}$ describes a 2.0-m displacement in the *opposite* direction, that is, the $-y$ direction.

(The directionals $\hat{x}$, $\hat{y}$, and $\hat{z}$ are also often written **i**, **j**, and **k**, respectively, and called *unit vectors*, but the notation and terminology I am using here

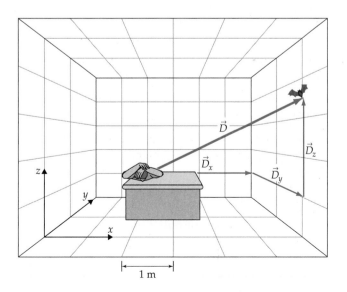

Figure C2.6

Once we have defined a cubical grid, we can write any vector as a sum of component vectors.

seem to me to be less arbitrary and more to the point. For example, calling $\hat{x}$ a unit vector obscures the most important issue at this level, which is that $\hat{x}$ simply *indicates a direction*, in this case, the $+x$ direction.)

Definition of a vector's (scalar) components

Note that in equation C2.3, we have *completely described* the displacement vector $\vec{D}$ in terms of the three signed scalar values $+4.0$ m, -2.0 m, and $+2.5$ m! By analogy, we can describe *any* vector $\vec{u}$ in terms of three *scalar components* u_x, u_y, and u_z such that

$$\vec{u} = u_x\hat{x} + u_y\hat{y} + u_z\hat{z} \qquad\qquad \text{(C2.4)}$$

Purpose: This equation describes how we can reconstruct a vector $\vec{u}$ from its components u_x, u_y, and u_z (and implicitly defines those components).

Symbols: $\hat{x}$, $\hat{y}$, and $\hat{z}$ are *directionals*, short for the "$+x$ direction," the "$+y$ direction," and the "$+z$ direction," respectively.

Limitations: This equation assumes that we have already established a cubical grid in space defining the $+x$, $+y$, and $+z$ directions.

We call u_x, u_y, and u_z the **x component,** the **y component,** and the **z component** of the vector $\vec{u}$, respectively. Please carefully note the difference between a *component* and a *component vector:* the component u_x is simply a scalar (with no intrinsic direction), while the component vector $\vec{u}_x \equiv u_x\hat{x}$ is a full-fledged vector pointing in the $\pm x$ direction.

Formally, we describe a given vector's x component (say) as being "the x component of (the vector's name)." To save writing, I will also use the phrase "x-(vector name)" to refer to the same component. For example, we could call v_x either "the x component of the object's velocity" (its formal name) or "the object's x-velocity" (for short). We can describe the other components analogously. (Please note, however, that I will use this terminology to refer *only* to the vector's *scalar* components, not its component vectors.)

Column vector notation for listing components

Since we can reconstruct *any* vector $\vec{u}$ from its scalar components u_x, u_y, and u_z by using equation C2.4, simply *listing* these components in order is equivalent to specifying the vector. In what follows, I will usually describe a vector by listing its components in the form of a **column vector,** like this:

$$\vec{u} = \begin{bmatrix} u_x \\ u_y \\ u_z \end{bmatrix} \qquad\qquad \text{(C2.5)}$$

Column vector notation makes doing calculations with vectors very efficient and clear, so I will use this notation often in all units of this text. (Note that if I need to list the components without taking up so much vertical space, I will write $\vec{u} = [u_x, u_y, u_z]$ instead.)

Exercise C2X.3

Imagine that we find (using a cubical grid whose x, y, and z directions correspond to east, north, and up, respectively) that one can get from my desk lamp to the nearest wall outlet by traveling 1.5 m south, 0.5 m down, and 1.0 m east. What are the components of the displacement vector $\vec{D}$ from the lamp to the outlet?

C2.4   The Magnitude of a Vector

Note that if the displacement $\vec{D}$ that carries us from a point A to another point B has components D_x, D_y, and D_z, the distance between points A and B (which is the magnitude of $\vec{D}$ by definition) is, according to the three-dimensional pythagorean theorem,

$$D = \sqrt{D_x^2 + D_y^2 + D_z^2} \tag{C2.6}$$

By analogy, we define the **magnitude** of an arbitrary vector $\vec{u}$ to be

$$u = \text{mag}(\vec{u}) = \sqrt{u_x^2 + u_y^2 + u_z^2} \tag{C2.7}$$

Definition of the *magnitude* of a vector

Purpose: This equation describes how to calculate the magnitude $u = \text{mag}(\vec{u})$ of a vector $\vec{u}$ from the vector's components u_x, u_y, and u_z.
Limitations: There are none in the context of this course.
Notes: This definition implies that $u \geq 0$ *always*: a negative vector magnitude is a contradiction in terms!

Equation C2.7 displays both notations that we will use for a vector's magnitude in this text. The *conventional* notation for the magnitude of a vector $\vec{u}$ is simply u—the same symbol without the arrow. This notation can be problematic because it is easy to blur the important distinction between u (which is a scalar) and $\vec{u}$ (which is a vector). To make the distinction clearer, I will use the $\text{mag}(\vec{u})$ notation often in unit C, and I urge you to do the same. This will help you habitually think clearly about both the connection and the distinction between vectors and their magnitudes.

Notation for vector magnitudes

Note that in the case of component vectors, $\text{mag}(\vec{u}_x)$ (for example) $= |u_x|$, not u_x. This is so because we have already reserved the symbol u_x to represent a *signed* component, and the rule that a vector's magnitude is always positive trumps the rule that the symbol for a vector's magnitude is the same symbol without the arrow. This is the *only* exception to the latter rule, though.

Exercise CX2.4

What is the magnitude of the displacement described in exercise C2X.3?

C2.5   Vectors in One and Two Dimensions

Sometimes all the vectors of interest in a given situation are parallel to a given direction in space. When this is true, we can align our grid so that this corresponds to one of the coordinate directions, which for the present we will assume is the x direction. Any vector of interest then is completely equivalent to a single component vector ($\vec{u} = u_x\hat{x}$) and is therefore completely described by a single signed number u_x [note that $u \equiv \text{mag}(\vec{u}) = |u_x|$].

Vectors in one dimension

Figure C2.7 illustrates that two vectors $\vec{u}$ and $\vec{w}$ that point one way or the other along a given coordinate direction add just as their components u_x and w_x in that direction do:

$$\vec{u} + \vec{w} = u_x\hat{x} + w_x\hat{x} = (u_x + w_x)\hat{x} \tag{C2.8}$$

We will find this result useful in section C2.6.

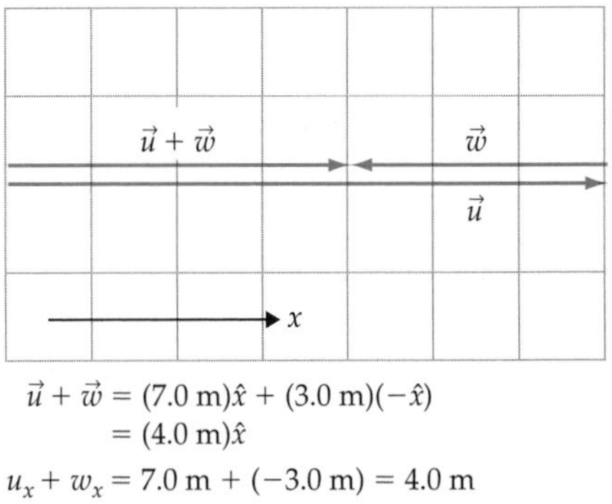

Figure C2.7

Vectors whose directions are parallel to a given direction add just as their components in that direction do.

$\vec{u} + \vec{w} = (7.0 \text{ m})\hat{x} + (3.0 \text{ m})(-\hat{x})$
$\qquad\quad = (4.0 \text{ m})\hat{x}$

$u_x + w_x = 7.0 \text{ m} + (-3.0 \text{ m}) = 4.0 \text{ m}$

When analyzing objects moving in one dimension, some texts drop the subscript and say things like "the car's velocity is $v = -32$ m/s" which means really that "$v_x = -32$ m/s." This is very confusing, because the symbol v normally (and sometimes even in the same book!) refers to the object's speed, which cannot be negative. Even in one-dimensional cases, it is important to keep clear the conceptual distinctions between a vector $\vec{u}$, its component u_x, and its magnitude u. Many physics educators now consider this to be poor usage. (It is like writing a headline that reads "Milk drinkers turn to powder" when the slightly longer sentence "People are drinking more powdered milk" would avoid the ambiguity and leave the reader with a better impression of the writer's intelligence.)

When all vectors of interest are confined to a certain plane, we can generally orient our grid so that one coordinate direction is *perpendicular* to the plane. All vectors of interest then have zero components in this direction and are thus completely described by their *two* components in the plane. In such cases, it is often useful to describe a vector's direction in terms of an angle measured in the plane from some reference direction. If we need to, we can use simple trigonometry to translate back and forth between a vector's components and its magnitude and this "direction angle." Let us see how this works.

Computing a two-dimensional vector's components from its magnitude and direction

For the sake of argument, assume that we have oriented the grid so that all vectors of interest lie in the xy plane. Consider an arbitrary vector $\vec{u}$ in this plane. As illustrated in figure C2.8a, $\vec{u}$ and its component vectors $\vec{u}_x$ and $\vec{u}_y$ form a right triangle whose hypotenuse has length $\text{mag}(\vec{u}) = u$ and whose legs have lengths $\text{mag}(\vec{u}_x) = |u_x|$ and $\text{mag}(\vec{u}_y) = |u_y|$. The definitions of sine and cosine then imply that

$$\sin\theta \equiv \frac{\text{opp}}{\text{hyp}} = \frac{|u_y|}{\text{mag}(\vec{u})} \quad \text{and} \quad \cos\theta \equiv \frac{\text{adj}}{\text{hyp}} = \frac{|u_x|}{\text{mag}(\vec{u})} \qquad (C2.9a)$$

$$\sin\phi \equiv \frac{\text{opp}}{\text{hyp}} = \frac{|u_x|}{\text{mag}(\vec{u})} \quad \text{and} \quad \cos\phi \equiv \frac{\text{adj}}{\text{hyp}} = \frac{|u_y|}{\text{mag}(\vec{u})} \qquad (C2.9b)$$

where "opp," "adj," and "hyp" stand for the lengths of the triangle's leg opposite to the angle, its leg adjacent to the angle, and its hypotenuse, respectively. So if we know $\vec{u}$'s magnitude $u = \text{mag}(\vec{u})$ and either angle θ or angle ϕ, we can calculate the absolute values of its components as follows:

$$|u_x| = u\cos\theta \qquad \text{or} \qquad |u_x| = u\sin\phi \qquad (C2.10a)$$

$$|u_y| = u\sin\theta \qquad \text{or} \qquad |u_y| = u\cos\phi \qquad (C2.10b)$$

To determine each component's *sign*, we check to see whether the corresponding component *vector* points in the positive or negative component

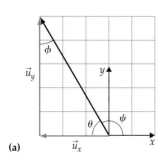
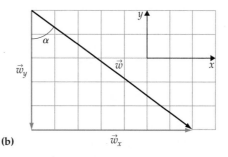

(a)   **(b)**

Figure C2.8
(a) The triangle formed by $\vec{u}$ and its component vectors. (b) The triangle formed by $\vec{w}$ and its component vectors.

direction. In the case at hand, $\vec{u}_x$ points in the $-x$ direction while $\vec{u}_y$ points in the $+y$ direction, so

$$u_x = -|u_x| = -u \cos\theta = -u \sin\phi \qquad (C2.11a)$$

$$u_y = +|u_y| = +u \sin\theta = +u \cos\phi \qquad (C2.11b)$$

Exercise C2X.5

Find analogous expressions for the absolute values $|w_x|$ and $|w_y|$ of the components of vector $\vec{w}$ shown in figure C2.8b in terms of the angle α and $w = \text{mag}(\vec{w})$, and then determine w_x and w_y in terms of these absolute values.

On the other hand, if we know $\vec{u}$'s components u_x and u_y, we can calculate its magnitude and either of the direction angles θ or ϕ as follows:

$$u = \text{mag}(\vec{u}) = \sqrt{u_x^2 + u_y^2} \qquad (C2.12a)$$

$$\tan\theta = \frac{\text{opp}}{\text{adj}} = \left|\frac{u_y}{u_x}\right| \quad\Rightarrow\quad \theta = \tan^{-1}\left|\frac{u_y}{u_x}\right| \qquad (C2.12b)$$

$$\tan\phi = \frac{\text{opp}}{\text{adj}} = \left|\frac{u_x}{u_y}\right| \quad\Rightarrow\quad \phi = \tan^{-1}\left|\frac{u_x}{u_y}\right| \qquad (C2.12c)$$

where $\tan^{-1}(\ )$ is the *inverse tangent* (or *arctangent*) function.

Computing a two-dimensional vector's magnitude and direction from its components

Exercise C2X.6

Given the values of w_x and w_y, how could you calculate the angle α?

Note that I defined both θ and ϕ to be *interior* angles of the triangle formed by the vector $\vec{u}$ and its vector components $\vec{u}_x$ and $\vec{u}_y$. What if we wanted to find the angle ψ between $\vec{u}$ and the $+x$ direction in figure C2.8? The sine, cosine, and tangent functions are defined for all angles from $0°$ to $360°$, so in principle, if we carefully keep track of the signs of these functions, we *could* rewrite equations C2.10 or C2.12 in terms of $\sin\psi$, $\cos\psi$, and/or $\tan\psi$. However, I personally find it *much* easier to deal with a triangle's *interior* angles, because they are all less than $90°$, so I *know* that their sines, cosines, and tangents are always positive, reducing the probability of sign errors. So if I know $\text{mag}(\vec{u})$ and ψ and want to compute u_x and u_y, I first calculate the triangle's interior angle $\theta = 180° - \psi$ and then calculate u_x and u_y from $\cos\theta$ and $\sin\theta$. Similarly, if I am given u_x and u_y and asked to calculate ψ, I first calculate the interior angle θ, using equation C2.12b, and then calculate $\psi = 180° - \theta$.

How to handle angles greater than $90°$

Exercise C2X.7

A displacement $\vec{D}$ has a magnitude of 5.0 m and a direction 127° counter-clockwise from the $+y$ direction. What are its components D_x and D_y?

Exercise C2X.8

A car's velocity is $\vec{v} = [v_x, v_y, v_z] = [-20 \text{ m/s}, +15 \text{ m/s}, \ 0 \text{ m/s}]$ at a certain time in a grid whose x, y, and z directions correspond to east, north, and up, respectively. What are this velocity's magnitude v and direction, expressed as an angle measured counterclockwise from east?

C2.6   Vector Operations in Terms of Components

Writing vectors in terms of *components* allows us to calculate vector sums, in-verses, and differences precisely and quantitatively *without* drawing pictures (as the methods of section C2.2 would seem to require). For example, imag-ine we want to compute the *sum* of two arbitrary vectors $\vec{u}$ and $\vec{w}$. Using equation C2.4, we can write this as a sum of six component vectors:

$$\vec{s} = \vec{u} + \vec{w} = u_x\hat{x} + u_y\hat{y} + u_z\hat{z} + w_x\hat{x} + w_y\hat{y} + w_z\hat{z} \qquad \text{(C2.13)}$$

Since we can sum these vectors in any order we like (because vector addition is *commutative*, as discovered in section C2.2), we can group the terms as follows:

$$\vec{s} = \vec{u} + \vec{w} = u_x\hat{x} + w_x\hat{x} + u_y\hat{y} + w_y\hat{y} + u_z\hat{z} + w_z\hat{z} \qquad \text{(C2.14)}$$

In section C2.5, we saw that component vectors that lie one way or the other along a coordinate direction add as ordinary numbers do; so we can write equation C2.14 as

$$\vec{s} = \vec{u} + \vec{w} = (u_x + w_x)\hat{x} + (u_y + w_y)\hat{y} + (u_z + w_z)\hat{z} \qquad \text{(C2.15)}$$

as shown in figure C2.9 for a pair of vectors in two dimensions (see also equa-tion C2.8). So the components of $\vec{u} + \vec{w}$ are simply the ordinary numerical sums of the corresponding components of $\vec{u}$ and $\vec{w}$! In column vector format,

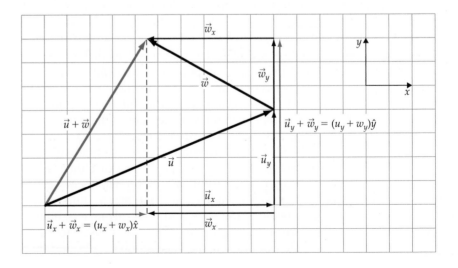

Figure C2.9

The component vectors of a sum are the sums of the two vectors' component vectors.

we write

$$\begin{bmatrix} s_x \\ s_y \\ s_z \end{bmatrix} = \begin{bmatrix} u_x \\ u_y \\ u_z \end{bmatrix} + \begin{bmatrix} w_x \\ w_y \\ w_z \end{bmatrix} = \begin{bmatrix} u_x + w_x \\ u_y + w_y \\ u_z + w_z \end{bmatrix} \qquad \text{(C2.16)}$$

How to calculate a vector sum using components

Imagine now that $\vec{u} + \vec{r} = 0$: this means that vector $\vec{r}$ is the same as $\vec{u}$'s vector inverse $-\vec{u}$. Equation C2.16 therefore implies that the components of this vector inverse $\vec{r} = -\vec{u}$ are simply the components of $\vec{u}$ multiplied by -1

$$\begin{bmatrix} 0 \\ 0 \\ 0 \end{bmatrix} = \begin{bmatrix} u_x + r_x \\ u_y + r_y \\ u_z + r_z \end{bmatrix} \quad \Rightarrow \quad -\vec{u} \equiv \begin{bmatrix} r_x \\ r_y \\ r_z \end{bmatrix} = \begin{bmatrix} -u_x \\ -u_y \\ -u_z \end{bmatrix} \qquad \text{(C2.17)}$$

How to calculate a vector inverse using components

since u_x and r_x add to zero if and only if $r_x = -u_x$ (and analogously for the other components).

This in turn means that the components of the vector *difference* $\vec{q} = \vec{u} - \vec{w} = \vec{u} + (-\vec{w})$ are simply the differences of the corresponding components of $\vec{u}$ and $\vec{w}$:

$$\begin{bmatrix} q_x \\ q_y \\ q_z \end{bmatrix} = \begin{bmatrix} u_x \\ u_y \\ u_z \end{bmatrix} - \begin{bmatrix} w_x \\ w_y \\ w_z \end{bmatrix} = \begin{bmatrix} u_x \\ u_y \\ u_z \end{bmatrix} + \begin{bmatrix} -w_x \\ -w_y \\ -w_z \end{bmatrix} = \begin{bmatrix} u_x - w_x \\ u_y - w_y \\ u_z - w_z \end{bmatrix} \qquad \text{(C2.18)}$$

How to calculate a vector difference using components

We can easily use components to define the **scalar multiple** of a vector. The product $b\vec{u}$ of an arbitrary scalar b and an arbitrary vector $\vec{u}$ is defined to be the vector whose components are the product of b with the corresponding components of $\vec{u}$:

The definition of a scalar multiple of a vector

$$b\vec{u} \equiv \begin{bmatrix} bu_x \\ bu_y \\ bu_z \end{bmatrix} \qquad \text{(C2.19)}$$

What does this mean geometrically? The magnitude of $b\vec{u}$ is

$$\mathrm{mag}(b\vec{u}) = \sqrt{(bu_x)^2 + (bu_y)^2 + (bu_z)^2} = \sqrt{b^2\left(u_x^2 + u_y^2 + u_z^2\right)}$$

$$= |b|\sqrt{u_x^2 + u_y^2 + u_z^2} = |b|\,\mathrm{mag}(\vec{u}) \qquad \text{(C2.20)}$$

meaning that multiplication by b stretches the vector $\vec{u}$ by a factor of $|b|$ (or shrinks it if $|b| < 1$). On the other hand, since all of $\vec{u}$'s component vectors are stretched by the same factor, the directions of $b\vec{u}$ and $\vec{u}$ are the same if b is positive (see figure C2.10a). If b is negative, all of $\vec{u}$'s component vectors are reversed in addition to being stretched by the same factor, so $b\vec{u}$ is exactly opposite to $\vec{u}$ (see figure C2.10b). Note that this means that -1 times $\vec{u}$ is simply $\vec{u}$ reversed in direction, which (by definition of the vector inverse) is $-\vec{u}$. This makes perfect sense!

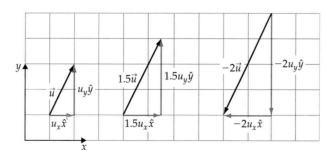

Figure C2.10
Multiplying by a positive scalar changes its length without changing its direction. Multiplying it by a negative scalar reverses its direction while changing its length.

We define *dividing* a vector $\vec{u}$ by a scalar b to be the same as multiplying it by $1/b$:

$$\frac{\vec{u}}{b} \equiv \left(\frac{1}{b}\right)\vec{u} \tag{C2.21}$$

Operations *not* defined

Note that we have *not* defined what it means to multiply a vector by a vector or divide either a scalar or a vector by another vector. Therefore, notations such as $\vec{u}\vec{w}$, $\vec{u}^2$, $\vec{u}/\vec{w}$, and $b/\vec{u}$ make no sense. (Later we will define two *different* kinds of vector multiplication, but division by a vector *cannot* be defined in any way that makes mathematical sense.)

Exercise C2X.9

What are the components of the vector sum of the displacements $\vec{D}_1 = [5\text{ m}, 4\text{ m}, 0\text{ m}]$ and $\vec{D}_2 = [-1\text{ m}, -3\text{ m}, 0\text{ m}]$?

Exercise C2X.10

Using the grid provided, sketch the vectors $\vec{D}_1$ and $\vec{D}_2$ described in exercise C2X.9, and convince yourself that the geometric definition of the vector sum yields the same result that you found in that exercise.

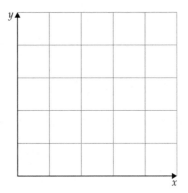

Exercise C2X.11

Subtract the displacement vector $\vec{D}_3 = [3\text{ m}, -5\text{ m}, 0\text{ m}]$ from the displacement $\vec{D}_4 = [2\text{ m}, -2\text{ m}, 0\text{ m}]$. Again, sketch the vectors in the space provided, and show that the tail-to-tail method of constructing the vector difference shown in figure C2.5b yields an arrow whose components are the same as the ones you calculated directly.

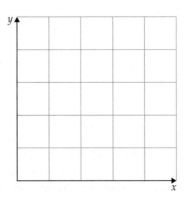

Exercise C2X.12

If we multiply the displacement vector $\vec{D}_5 = [3\text{ m}, -1\text{ m}, 0\text{ m}]$ by -4, what do its components become? How does the magnitude of $-4\vec{D}_5$ compare to that of $\vec{D}_5$? How do their directions compare?

C2.7   Vectors Have Units

Just as a scalar numerical quantity generally has associated units, a vector's magnitude also generally has associated units. For example, a displacement's magnitude has units of meters, a velocity's magnitude has units of meters per second, and so on.

The definition of the magnitude given by equation C2.7 makes it clear that each of a vector's components must have the same units as its magnitude (remember that we cannot add quantities that have different units!). So if a displacement's magnitude is measured in meters, *each* of the displacement's *components* must also have units of meters. We therefore say that the vector as a *whole* has the same units as its magnitude.

Just as we cannot add numbers with different units, so we cannot add vectors with different units. But just as we can multiply two numbers that have different units, so can we multiply a vector and a scalar having different units, and we treat the multiplied units exactly as if we had multiplied two ordinary numbers. For example, if we divide a displacement in meters by an interval of time in seconds, the resulting vector has units of meters per second.

Rules for working with vector units

When writing vectors in the form of a component list, one can write something like either $\vec{v} = [3\text{ m/s}, -5\text{ m/s}, 1\text{ m/s}]$ or $\vec{v} = [3, -5, 1]\text{ m/s}$. I will generally use the former notation, which I think is clearer, but the other method is acceptable. What is *not* acceptable is to not specify the units at all. (The only exception is that it is conventional *not* to attach units to the zero vector; the units simply do not matter in such a case.)

How to specify vector units in writing

C2.8   Reference Frames

Components make vector calculations easy and natural, but before we can even *think* about using components, first we must set up the "imaginary cubical grid" we have been talking about, a process we call "setting up a **reference frame**."

Setting up a reference frame first involves choosing the frame's **origin** as its fundamental point of reference. We can define this origin to be attached to any point on any object that we like. Then we need to define three mutually perpendicular lines going through the origin to serve as the frame's *x*, *y*, and *z* **axes,** and then which direction along each line will be the positive direction, thus defining the frame's +*x*, +*y*, and +*z* **directions.** Finally, we need to establish some mechanism for measuring an object's (vector) **position** $\vec{r}$ in the reference frame, which is defined to be *its displacement from the origin*.

How to set up a reference frame

A straightforward mechanism for measuring positions is to construct a *literal* cubical grid using straight, rigid measuring rods (see figure C2.11a). To determine the components of an object's position in such a frame, we merely count along the measuring rods how far we have to travel parallel to each coordinate direction to get from the origin to the object. We call the three components of an object's position $\vec{r}$ its **coordinates** in the given frame, and conventionally we write them not as $[r_x, r_y, r_z]$ but rather simply as

Using a literal cubical grid to measure positions and displacements

Figure C2.11
(a) The *position* of a point is its displacement from the origin.
(b) The displacement vector between two points is the vector difference $\Delta \vec{r}$ of their positions.

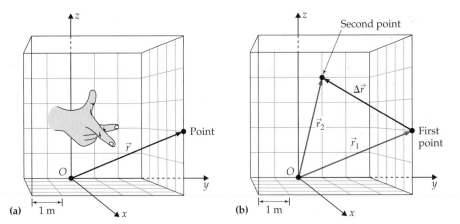

$[x, y, z]$ (which is shorter without being ambiguous). Since a displacement is defined to be a *change* in position, to determine the components of the displacement from point A at position $\vec{r}_A$ to point B at position $\vec{r}_B$, we need only calculate the vector difference $\Delta \vec{r} \equiv \vec{r}_B - \vec{r}_A$ between the two positions, as illustrated in figure C2.11b.

$$\Delta \vec{r} = \begin{bmatrix} x_B \\ y_B \\ z_B \end{bmatrix} - \begin{bmatrix} x_A \\ y_A \\ z_A \end{bmatrix} = \begin{bmatrix} x_B - x_A \\ y_B - y_A \\ z_B - z_A \end{bmatrix} \equiv \begin{bmatrix} \Delta x \\ \Delta y \\ \Delta z \end{bmatrix} \qquad (C2.22)$$

Note again that we conventionally write the components of $\Delta \vec{r}$ as $[\Delta x, \Delta y, \Delta z]$ instead of $[\Delta r_x, \Delta r_y, \Delta r_z]$. Physicists use Δ to denote a *change* in something, and because they generally think of a displacement as a change in position, they conventionally use $\Delta \vec{r}$ instead of $\vec{D}$ as the symbol for a displacement (a practice I will follow from now on).

The point I want to make is that if we can use a literal cubical grid to compute positions, we can also compute displacements and so work our way up to more complicated vectors. However, constructing a literal cubical grid in a region of space of interest is often awkward, and such grids get in the way of the motion of objects we might be interested in. Air traffic controllers use a more practical system to locate planes in the sky. Radar pulses sent from the control tower (which serves as the frame's origin) are reflected by planes in the vicinity and return to the control tower. The direction the returning pulse comes from indicates the plane's direction from the origin, and the time it takes the pulse to make the round trip determines the plane's distance from the origin. One can then use trigonometry to *calculate* the same position coordinates for the plane we would have gotten if we could have used a literal cubical grid. In a similar way, a **Global Positioning System (GPS)** receiver uses radio signal travel time to measure the receiver's distance from a number of orbiting satellites with known positions and then uses trigonometry to calculate its vector position relative to any origin point attached to the earth that you define. These methods provide a way to set up an intangible grid that is nonetheless *functionally* equivalent to a literal grid. Since any reference frame indeed *must* deliver the same results as a literal grid, though, a literal grid represents a useful way to *visualize* a reference frame and what it does.

We have considerable freedom in setting up reference frames. We can

1. Attach a frame to *any* object that we please.
2. Choose which is the positive side of each axis.
3. Orient the frame in any way that we like.
4. Specify whatever origin is convenient.

More practical reference frames

Freedoms and conventions in setting up reference frames

We have so much freedom because a reference frame is a *human* creation that we superimpose on the universe to help us measure things, not something that already exists in the world.

In practice, we apply certain *conventions* that limit our choices but make things easier. (1) We will discuss attaching reference frames to different kinds of objects (including moving objects) later, but for now (unless explicitly stated otherwise) we will assume our frames are attached to the earth's surface. (2) No matter how we orient a reference frame, it is conventional *always* to choose the axis directions so that if you point your right index finger in the $+x$ direction and right second finger in the $+y$ direction, your extended right thumb points in the $+z$ direction. We will call such a frame a **right-handed reference frame** (see figure C2.11a). (3) While other orientations are acceptable, we will say that a right-handed frame on the earth's surface is in **standard orientation** if its $+x$, $+y$, and $+z$ directions point east, north, and up, respectively.

Because you still have complete freedom to choose an origin (which is useful, because an appropriate choice can make a problem simpler), if you do not clearly *specify* your choice when writing a problem solution, you may confuse the reader. This goes *doubly* if you choose to violate any of the conventions discussed. For example, if you are working a problem where something is moving along a line due northwest, you may find it easier to orient your reference frame so that, say, the $+x$ direction points northwest. This is fine, but you should *describe* your nonstandard orientation in your solution.

It is important to *describe* the choices that you make

It is important to be clear about these things because the coordinates of a given object are *different* in frames having different origins and orientations. For example, an object might have position coordinates [3 m, 5 m, −2 m] in one frame, [3 m, 5 m, 3 m] in a frame with the same orientation but whose origin is lower by 5 m, and [5 m, −3 m, −2 m] in a frame with the same origin as the first but rotated 90° counterclockwise around the z axis. The coordinates of an object are thus *ambiguous* unless we clearly describe the frame's characteristics!

Exercise C2X.13

The x, y, and z axes of a reference frame on the surface of the earth point north, up, and west, respectively. Is the frame right-handed?

Exercise C2X.14

A point's position coordinates are [2 m, 2 m, −1 m] in a frame in standard orientation on the earth's surface. What are its coordinates in a frame whose origin is 2 m west of the first frame's origin and whose x, y, and z axes point south, up, and west, respectively? (*Hint:* Draw a picture!)

TWO-MINUTE PROBLEMS

C2T.1 The magnitude and direction of a vector can be described without using a reference frame, true (T) or false (F)?

C2T.2 The *components* of a given displacement vector depend on one's choice of reference frame origin, T or F?

C2T.3 The x, y, and z directions of a reference frame point up, west, and north, respectively. Such a coordinate system is right-handed, T or F?

C2T.4 A reference frame drawn on a sheet of paper has its y direction oriented toward the top of the sheet and its x direction toward its right edge. What direction must the *z* direction point if the frame is right-handed?

A. Outward, perpendicular to the plane of the paper.
B. Inward, perpendicular to the plane of the paper.
C. Diagonally to the lower left, in the plane of the paper.
D. Diagonally to the lower right, in the plane of the paper.
E. Vertically downward in the plane of the paper.
F. Other (specify).

C2T.5 If an object is located 3.0 m north and 1.0 m west of the origin of a frame in standard orientation on the earth's surface, its coordinates in that frame are

A. [3.0 m, 1.0 m, 0 m]
B. [−3.0 m, −1.0 m, 0 m]
C. [1.0 m, 3.0 m, 0 m]
D. [−1.0 m, 3.0 m, 0 m]
E. [−1.0 m, 0 m, −3.0 m]
F. Other (explain)

C2T.6 An object whose initial position coordinates are [1.5 m, 2.0 m, −4.2 m] in a frame in standard orientation is found a short time later at a position whose coordinates are [1.5 m, −3.0 m, −4.2 m]. What is the direction of this object's displacement during this time interval?

A. East.
B. West.
C. North.
D. South.
E. Down.
F. Other (specify).

C2T.7 The components u_x, u_y, and u_z of a certain vector $\vec{u}$ are *all* negative numbers. The vector's magnitude u is then certainly negative as well, T or F?

C2T.8 The *only* way that a vector can have zero magnitude is for *all* its components to be zero, T or F?

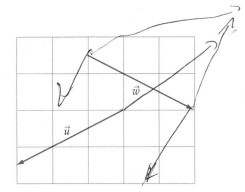

Figure C2.12
Vectors for problems C2T.9 through C2T.11.

C2T.9 Consider the two vectors shown in figure C2.12. The sum of these vectors points most nearly
A. Up   B. Down.   C. Right.   D. Left.

C2T.10 Consider the two vectors shown in figure C2.12. The vector $\vec{w} - \vec{u}$ points most nearly
A. Up.   B. Down   C. Right.   D. Left.

C2T.11 Consider the two vectors shown in figure C2.12. To change $\vec{u}$ into $\vec{w}$, one would have to
A. Multiply by −1.
B. Multiply by 120°.
C. Add the vector $\vec{u} + \vec{w}$.
D. Add the vector $\vec{w} - \vec{u}$.
E. Add the vector $\vec{u} - \vec{w}$.
F. Do none of the above.

C2T.12 For all possible orientations and lengths of $\vec{u}$ and $\vec{w}$, $\mathrm{mag}(\vec{u} + \vec{w}) = \mathrm{mag}(\vec{u}) + \mathrm{mag}(\vec{w})$, true or false?

C2T.13 For all possible orientations and lengths of $\vec{u}$ and $\vec{w}$, $\mathrm{mag}(\vec{u} - \vec{w}) \geq |\mathrm{mag}(\vec{u}) - \mathrm{mag}(\vec{w})|$, true or false?

HOMEWORK PROBLEMS

Basic Skills

C2B.1 A reference frame on the surface of the earth has an *x* axis that points upward and a *y* axis that points eastward. What direction should the *z* axis point to create a right-handed coordinate system? Explain, using a picture.

C2B.2 Imagine that you walk 200 m south, 300 m up, and 60 m west in a reference frame in standard orientation on the earth's surface. Write your displacement as a column vector, and compute its magnitude.

C2B.3 If you walk 85 m south and 25 m east from a certain starting position, what are the magnitude and the direction of your displacement? (Specify the direction by specifying an angle relative to an appropriately chosen direction.)

C2B.4 A sailboat sails 25 km south and then 14 km west of Malibu. What are the magnitude and direction of its total displacement? (Specify the direction by specifying an angle relative to an appropriately chosen direction.)

C2B.5 Imagine that you walk 500 m in a direction 30° south of east. What are the components of your displacement in a reference frame in standard orientation on the earth's surface?

C2B.6 Imagine that during a certain interval of time, a jetliner flies a distance of 38 km along a straight line 35° west of north at a constant altitude of 10 km. What are the components of its displacement during this interval?

C2B.7 Compute the components of the vector sum $\vec{u} + \vec{w}$ and the magnitude of that sum for the displacements $\vec{u}$ and $\vec{w}$ given by equation C2.23. (Please show your work.)

$$\vec{u} = \begin{bmatrix} 2\ \text{m} \\ -3\ \text{m} \\ 1\ \text{m} \end{bmatrix} \qquad \vec{w} = \begin{bmatrix} -4\ \text{m} \\ -1\ \text{m} \\ 3\ \text{m} \end{bmatrix}$$

C2B.8 Compute the components of the vector difference $\vec{w} - \vec{u}$ and the magnitude of that difference for the displacements given in equation C2.23. (Please show your work.)

C2B.9 Compute the components of the vector given by $\vec{u} - 3\vec{w}$ for $\vec{u}$ and $\vec{w}$ as given in equation C2.23.

C2B.10 Compute the components of the vector given by $\vec{u} + 2\vec{w}$ for $\vec{u}$ and $\vec{w}$ as given in equation C2.23.

Synthetic

C2S.1 An object is at position [2.0 m, 3.0 m, −1.0 m] in a reference frame in standard orientation on the earth's surface. This reference frame is lifted vertically 3.0 m and then is turned 90° around the x axis (so that the y axis now points vertically upward). (The object remains fixed relative to the earth in this process: only the frame's position and orientation are changed.) What are the object's coordinates now? Explain, using a picture.

C2S.2 If a vector $\vec{u}$ is added to a vector $\vec{w}$, under what circumstances will $\text{mag}(\vec{u} + \vec{w}) = \text{mag}(\vec{u}) + \text{mag}(\vec{w})$? Under what circumstances will $\text{mag}(\vec{u} + \vec{w}) = 0$? Can the value of $\text{mag}(\vec{u} + \vec{w})$ ever be *greater* than $\text{mag}(\vec{u}) + \text{mag}(\vec{w})$? Present a careful argument (preferably using diagrams) supporting each answer.

C2S.3 Can $\text{mag}(\vec{u} - \vec{w})$ ever equal $\text{mag}(\vec{u}) + \text{mag}(\vec{w})$? If so, specify the circumstances. If not, explain why not.

C2S.4 An object initially has a velocity of 3 m/s due west. After interacting with something else for a while, the object ends up with a velocity of 4 m/s due south. What are the magnitude and the direction of the object's *change* in velocity? Specify the direction as being roughly northwest, southeast, northeast, or whatever is appropriate. (*Hint:* You do not need to know anything about velocity to solve this problem except that

it is a vector with units of meters per second. Define the change in a vector in a way analogous to how we would define the change in a number.)

C2S.5 A jetliner takes off from Los Angeles International Airport. After 5 minutes (min), the jet has an altitude of 5 km above the level of the airport and is 25 km west and 10 km north of the airport. What are the magnitude and the direction of its displacement during this time interval? Specify the direction by stating *two* angles: the angle of the displacement's direction west of north and the angle of the displacement's direction above the horizontal.

C2S.6 A boat leaves San Pedro and travels 35 km 15° west of south before its engine dies. You left San Pedro earlier in the morning and have traveled 42 km 23° south of west by the time the first boat's distress call reaches you. How far from and in what direction is the first boat relative to you at that point?

Rich-Context

C2R.1 Is it possible to see the top of Mount Everest from a boat floating in the Bay of Bengal? Assume that the air is perfectly clear and that there are no other mountains, clouds, or buildings obstructing your line of sight. (*Hint:* What might possibly obstruct the view if there are no mountains, clouds, or buildings in the way? Use an atlas or map to estimate distances.)

C2R.2 Two teams of explorers leave a common point. The first team travels 5 km north across a plain, then follows a river 15° west of north for 7 km before making camp for the night. The second climbs a ridge, traveling basically due northeast for 6 km along a trail that climbs upward to an altitude of 2.5 km. This team then follows the ridge northward at approximately the same altitude for 4 km before setting up camp. Can the two teams communicate that night if their radios have a range of 5 km?

C2R.3 Imagine that you want to measure the height of an inaccessible mountain peak on an island in the South Pacific. First you line up your boat so that it is due west of the peak, and you find that the peak is an angle of $\phi = 12°$ up from the horizon. Then you move your boat a displacement of 25 km 37° south of east (according to your GPS receiver) and find that the mountain is now due north. You are about to take another measurement of the peak's angle from the horizon, but your first mate, walking by, spills hot coffee on your back, you drop your transit on the deck, and it breaks. You severely cuss out the first mate and take the transit to the chief engineer, who tells you that it will take at least 3 days to fix ("Ye canna expec' me to work miracles, Cap'n!" he says.) After calming down, though, you realize that you already have enough information to determine the mountain's height. Do so.

Advanced

C2A.1 (a) Prove mathematically that for any two vectors $\vec{u}$ and $\vec{w}$ lying in the xy plane of a given reference frame

$$\text{mag}^2(\vec{u} + \vec{w}) = \text{mag}^2(\vec{u}) + \text{mag}^2(\vec{w}) + 2\,\text{mag}(\vec{u})\,\text{mag}(\vec{w})\cos\theta \quad \text{(C2.24)}$$

where θ is the angle between the directions of $\vec{p}$ and $\vec{q}$.

(b) Use this result to argue that

$$|\text{mag}(\vec{u}) - \text{mag}(\vec{w})| \\ \leq \text{mag}(\vec{u} + \vec{w}) \\ \leq \text{mag}(\vec{u}) + \text{mag}(\vec{w}) \quad \text{(C2.25)}$$

ANSWERS TO EXERCISES

C2X.1 The drag that a moving object experiences is a *vector* quantity: It has not only a magnitude (expressing how strongly the air resists the object's motion) but also a clear associated direction (the direction that the air resistance pushes on the object). Drag is in fact a subcategory of *force*, which is a vector. An object's volume, on the other hand, has an obvious magnitude, but it does not make sense to assign it a direction: volume is a *scalar*.

C2X.2 The completed drawings should look like this:

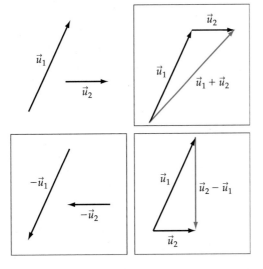

C2X.3 The displacement's components are $[D_x, D_y, D_z] = [+1.0\text{ m}, -1.5\text{ m}, -0.5\text{ m}]$.

C2X.4 According to equation C2.7, the displacement's magnitude is

$$D = \sqrt{D_x^2 + D_y^2 + D_z^2}$$
$$= \sqrt{(1.0\text{ m})^2 + (-1.5\text{ m})^2 + (-0.5\text{ m})^2} = 1.9\text{ m} \quad \text{(C2.26)}$$

C2X.5 In this case, $|w_x| = w\sin\alpha$ and $|w_y| = w\cos\alpha$, where $w \equiv \text{mag}(\vec{w})$. Since $\vec{w}_x$ points in the $+x$ direction but $\vec{w}_y$ points in the $-y$ direction, the components are

$$w_x = +|w_x| = w\sin\alpha \quad \text{(C2.27a)}$$

$$w_y = -|w_y| = -w\cos\alpha \quad \text{(C2.27b)}$$

C2X.6 In this case, the lengths of the triangles' sides opposite and adjacent to the angle α are $|w_x|$ and $|w_y|$, respectively, so $\alpha = \tan^{-1}|w_x/w_y|$.

C2X.7 Here is a drawing of the vector $\vec{D}$.

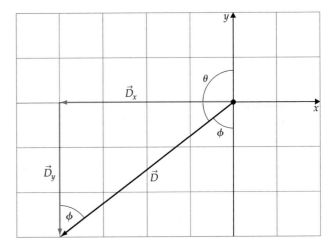

Note that the interior angle ϕ has a value of $180° - 127° = 53°$. From the triangle and the directions of the component vectors $\vec{D}_x$ and $\vec{D}_y$ relative to the coordinate directions, we then see that

$$D_x = -|D_x| = -\text{mag}(\vec{D})\sin\phi$$
$$= -(5.0\text{ m})(\sin 53°) = -4.0\text{ m} \quad \text{(C2.28a)}$$

$$D_y = -|D_y| = -\text{mag}(\vec{D})\cos\phi$$
$$= -(5.0\text{ m})(\cos 53°) = -3.0\text{ m} \quad \text{(C2.28b)}$$

C2X.8 Here is a drawing of this vector and its vector components $\vec{v}_x$ and $\vec{v}_y$.

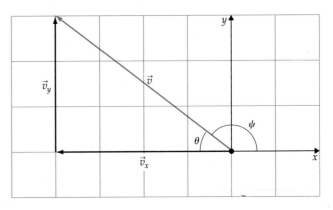

According to equation C2.4, the magnitude of the car's velocity (i.e., its speed) is

$$v \equiv \mathrm{mag}(\vec{v})$$
$$= \sqrt{(-20 \text{ m/s})^2 + (15 \text{ m/s})^2 + (0 \text{ m/s})^2}$$
$$= 25 \text{ m/s} \qquad \qquad (C2.29a)$$

The interior angle θ drawn on the diagram is given by

$$\tan \theta = \frac{\mathrm{opp}}{\mathrm{adj}} = \left| \frac{v_y}{v_x} \right|$$

$$\Rightarrow \quad \theta = \tan^{-1} \left| \frac{v_y}{v_x} \right| = \tan^{-1} \left| \frac{15 \text{ m/s}}{20 \text{ m/s}} \right| = 37°$$

$$(C2.29b)$$

The angle measured from the eastward ($+x$ direction) is therefore $\psi = 180° - 37° = 143°$.

C2X.9 The sum is [4 m, 1 m, 0 m].

C2X.10 See figure C2.13a.

C2X.11 $\vec{D}_4 - \vec{D}_3 = [-1 \text{ m}, 3 \text{ m}, 0 \text{ m}]$. See figure C2.13b.

C2X.12 $-4\vec{D}_5 = [-12 \text{ m}, +4 \text{ m}, 0 \text{ m}]$. The magnitude is 4 times that of the original vector, and the direction is *opposite* to that of the original vector.

C2X.13 No.

C2X.14 [−2 m, −1 m, −4 m]

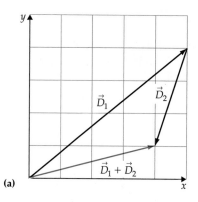

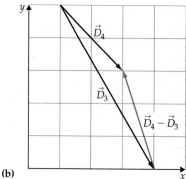

Figure C2.13

(a) The answer to exercise C2X.10.
(b) The answer to exercise C2X.11.

C3

Interactions Transfer Momentum

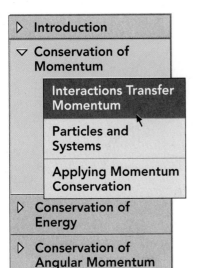

▷ **Introduction**

▽ **Conservation of Momentum**

    Interactions Transfer Momentum

    Particles and Systems

    Applying Momentum Conservation

▷ **Conservation of Energy**

▷ **Conservation of Angular Momentum**

Chapter Overview

Introduction

This chapter opens the subdivision on *conservation of momentum*. In this chapter, we will apply what we learned in chapter C2 about vectors to explore fundamental principles and concepts at the very heart of mechanics.

Section C3.1:   Velocity

A **particle** is a hypothetical object whose position is a mathematical point. In what follows, I will describe concepts in terms of *particles*, but will apply them to macroscopic objects as well. (We will see why we can do this in chapter C4.)

We define a particle's **velocity** $\vec{v}$ at a given instant of time in this way:

$$\vec{v} \equiv \frac{d\vec{r}}{dt} \quad \text{or} \quad \begin{bmatrix} v_x \\ v_y \\ v_z \end{bmatrix} = \frac{1}{dt}\begin{bmatrix} dx \\ dy \\ dz \end{bmatrix} = \begin{bmatrix} dx/dt \\ dy/dt \\ dz/dt \end{bmatrix} \qquad \text{(C3.2)}$$

Purpose: This equation defines a particle's velocity vector $\vec{v}$.
Symbols: $d\vec{r}$ is the particle's displacement during the time interval dt.
Limitations: The interval dt must be so short that $\vec{v} \approx$ constant during dt.
Notes: Speed $v \equiv \text{mag}(\vec{v})$.

Section C3.2:   Interactions Transfer Momentum

All known interactions obey the following principle:

> **The momentum-transfer principle:** Any interaction between two objects affects their motion by *transferring momentum* from one to the other.

Experimentally, we find that this works if we define a particle's **momentum** to be

$$\vec{p} \equiv m\vec{v} \qquad \text{(C3.4)}$$

Purpose: This equation defines a particle's momentum vector $\vec{p}$.
Symbols: m is the particle's mass, $\vec{v}$ is its velocity.
Limitations: This equation applies to particles only (but see chapter C4).

Gaining an amount of momentum in one direction is the same as *losing* the same amount of momentum in the opposite direction, so we can consider *either* particle to be the source of the momentum transfer (to switch donors, switch signs).

Section C3.3:   Impulse and Force

We call the amount of momentum $[d\vec{p}]_A$ that a *specific* interaction A contributes to a given particle's total momentum during a short time interval dt the **impulse** delivered by that interaction during dt. Experiments show that

$$d\vec{p} = [d\vec{p}]_A + [d\vec{p}]_B + \cdots \qquad \text{(C3.5)}$$

Purpose: This equation describes how multiple interactions affect a particle's motion.

Symbols: $[d\vec{p}]_A$, $[d\vec{p}]_B$, ... are the impulses contributed to the particle by interactions A, B, etc. during a given short time interval dt, and $d\vec{p}$ is the resulting change in the particle's actual momentum $\vec{p}$ during dt.

Limitations: This equation applies to particles only (but see chapter C4).

Note: The brackets in the notation $[d\vec{p}]_A$ distinguish the small amount of momentum that a specific interaction A *contributes* to a particle during dt from the *net change* $d\vec{p}$ in the particle's *actual* momentum during that interval.

We define the **force** that an interaction between objects exerts on either object to be the *rate* at which the interaction delivers impulse to the object:

$$\vec{F}_A \equiv \frac{[d\vec{p}]_A}{dt} \qquad \text{(C3.6)}$$

Purpose: This defines the force $\vec{F}_A$ that interaction A exerts on a particle.

Symbols: $[d\vec{p}]_A$ is the impulse delivered by the interaction to the particle during the small time interval dt.

Limitations: The interval dt should be small enough that $\vec{F}_A \approx$ constant during dt. (If it is not, $\vec{F}_A$ becomes the **average force** during the interval.)

Notes: The SI unit of force is the **newton,** where $1\,\text{N} \equiv 1\ \text{kg·m/s}^2$. (The English unit is the **pound,** where $1\ \text{lb} = 4.45\ \text{N}$.) Force $\vec{F}_A$ has the same direction as the impulse $[d\vec{p}]_A$ being delivered.

Since the momentum that an interaction between two particles contributes to one must come from the other, the forces that a given interaction exerts on two particles must be equal in magnitude but opposite in direction (this is **Newton's third law**).

Section C3.4: Mass and Weight

In physics, *mass* and *weight* are completely distinct concepts. A particle's **mass** expresses how much impulse is required to produce a certain change in the particle's velocity. An object's **weight** $\vec{F}_g$ is the total *force* that gravitational interactions exerts on the object at a given point. *Weight* is a vector measured in newtons, while *mass* is a scalar measured in kilograms. Experimentally, though,

$$\vec{F}_g = m\vec{g} \qquad \text{(C3.8)}$$

Purpose: This equation describes how weight is related to mass.

Symbols: $\vec{F}_g$ is the weight acting on an object; m is the object's mass; $\vec{g}$ is the **gravitational field vector** at a certain point in space.

Limitations: There are none (until we study general relativity, at least).

Notes: Near the earth's surface, $\vec{g}$ points toward the earth's center, and the **gravitational field strength** $g \equiv \text{mag}(\vec{g}) = 9.8\ \text{N/kg}$.

Section C3.5: Momentum Flow and Motion

One can use momentum-transfer ideas to make qualitative predictions about a particle's motion. See the section for details.

Section C3.6: Physics Skills: Illegal Vector Equations

This section discusses errors that beginners often make in dealing with vectors.

C3.1   Velocity

What we mean by the term *particle*

A **particle** is a hypothetical object having zero volume, and thus its position is a mathematical point in space. We saw in chapter C1 that this idealization is an excellent model for an elementary particle. However, we will see in chapter C4 that it also proves to be a useful model for macroscopic objects.

In the remainder of this chapter, I am going to talk about various quantities and principles as if they applied only to particles, because particles are so well defined mathematically. However, I will freely *apply* these quantities and principles to macroscopic objects in examples and arguments. We will see why we can get away with this in chapter C4.

Position and displacement

In chapter C2, we defined the position $\vec{r}$ of a point in space to be its displacement from the reference frame origin to the point in question (see figure C3.1a). We also saw that we can consider the displacement $\Delta\vec{r}$ between two arbitrary points to be the difference of their positions:

$$\Delta\vec{r} \equiv \vec{r}_2 - \vec{r}_1 \quad \text{or} \quad \begin{bmatrix} \Delta x \\ \Delta y \\ \Delta z \end{bmatrix} \equiv \begin{bmatrix} x_2 \\ y_2 \\ z_2 \end{bmatrix} - \begin{bmatrix} x_1 \\ y_1 \\ z_1 \end{bmatrix} = \begin{bmatrix} x_2 - x_1 \\ y_2 - y_1 \\ z_2 - z_1 \end{bmatrix} \quad \text{(C3.1)}$$

(see figure C3.1b). Since at every instant of time a particle occupies a mathematical point in space, we can describe its motion as a sequence of displacements at various instants of time.

The definition of a particle's *velocity*

In chapter C1, we *qualitatively* defined a particle's **velocity** $\vec{v}$ at a given instant of time t to be a vector whose magnitude is the particle's speed v and whose direction is the particle's direction of motion at that instant of time. We are now in a position to define $\vec{v}$ more *quantitatively*. Let dt be the duration of a time interval containing the instant t at which we want to know $\vec{v}$, and let $d\vec{r}$ be the particle's tiny displacement during that tiny time interval. If dt is sufficiently short that neither the particle's speed nor its direction of motion changes appreciably during that time interval, then the particle's velocity is $\vec{v} \equiv d\vec{r}/dt$ (that is, the displacement vector $d\vec{r}$ multiplied by the scalar $1/dt$):

A quantitative definition of a particle's velocity

$$\vec{v} \equiv \frac{d\vec{r}}{dt} \quad \text{or} \quad \begin{bmatrix} v_x \\ v_y \\ v_z \end{bmatrix} = \frac{1}{dt} \begin{bmatrix} dx \\ dy \\ dz \end{bmatrix} = \begin{bmatrix} dx/dt \\ dy/dt \\ dz/dt \end{bmatrix} \quad \text{(C3.2)}$$

Purpose: This equation defines a particle's vector velocity $\vec{v}$.
Symbols: $d\vec{r}$ is the particle's displacement during the time interval dt.
Limitations: The interval dt must be short enough that $\vec{v} \approx$ constant during dt.
Notes: The *direction* of $\vec{v}$ is the direction of motion; $\mathrm{mag}(\vec{v}) =$ speed v.

Does this definition coincide with the our earlier qualitative definition? Consider the direction aspect first. Since $1/dt$ is a positive scalar, the vector $\vec{v}$ ends up having the same direction as the short displacement $d\vec{r}$, which in turn accurately reflects the direction that the object is moving *if and only if dt is sufficiently short*, as shown in figure C3.2 (this is why this limitation is important). As for the magnitude, you probably learned in junior high school that an object's speed is the distance traveled in a time interval divided by

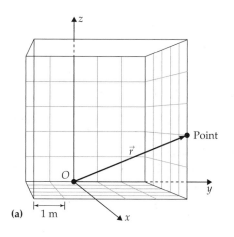

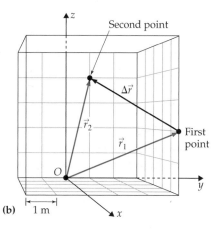

Figure C3.1
(a) The *position* vector of a point is its displacement from the origin. (b) The displacement vector between two points is the difference between their position vectors.

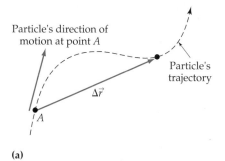

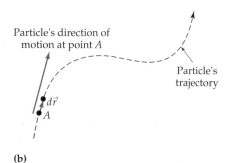

Figure C3.2
(a) A particle's displacement during a long time interval Δt beginning when it passes point A may only poorly reflect its direction of motion at point A. (b) The direction of the particle's displacement during a sufficiently short interval dt *does* accurately reflect the object's direction of motion at point A.

that time interval. According to equation C3.2, the particle's speed is

$$v \equiv \mathrm{mag}(\vec{v}) \equiv \sqrt{v_x^2 + v_y^2 + v_z^2}$$

$$= \sqrt{\left(\frac{dx}{dt}\right)^2 + \left(\frac{dy}{dt}\right)^2 + \left(\frac{dz}{dt}\right)^2}$$

$$= \frac{\sqrt{dx^2 + dy^2 + dz^2}}{dt} = \frac{|dr|}{dt} \qquad (C3.3)$$

where $|dr| = \mathrm{mag}(d\vec{r})$ is the distance the particle travels during the time interval dt. So equation C3.3 is consistent with the familiar definition of speed.

Exercise C3X.1

A particle moves with a constant speed around a circle. Is its velocity constant?

Exercise C3X.2

During a "sufficiently short" time interval of 0.25 s, a hypothetical particle moves a displacement of 4.0 m east, 1.0 m south, and 0.1 m downward relative to the earth's surface. What are the components of this particle's velocity at this time in a reference frame in standard orientation on the earth's surface? What is the particle's speed?

C3.2   Interactions Transfer Momentum

We are now ready to address the fundamental question of mechanics

In chapter C1 we defined an *interaction* between two objects to be a physical relationship between them that allows each to affect the other's motion. We are finally in a position to construct a model that describes more precisely what happens during an interaction.

Consider the experiment shown in figure C3.3, where a cart moving with a certain initial speed v_0 collides with an identical cart at rest. If you actually do the experiment (assuming that the effects of friction are small and the carts' bumpers are sufficiently "springy"), you will find that the collision interaction affects the carts' motion by bringing the first to rest and sending the second cart away with the same speed the first had initially. Qualitatively it looks as if the contact interaction between the carts during the collision causes the first cart's motion to be entirely transferred to the second cart! Is this what *always* happens in a collision?

We can check this by doing the experiment shown in figure C3.4, which is just like the collision shown in figure C3.3 except that the initially moving cart is now twice as massive as before. If you do this experiment (assuming low friction and springy bumpers), you will find that the initially moving cart is *not* brought to rest by the collision interaction, but rather continues to move forward with about one-third of its original speed v_0, while the lighter cart moves away from the collision with a speed of about $\frac{4}{3}v_0$.

This experiment scuttles the idea that one cart's motion is entirely transferred to the other cart. Indeed, in this case we seem to have more "motion" after the collision than we did before, since the total of the carts' speeds before the collision was v_0 and but $\frac{5}{3}v_0$ afterward. On the other hand, the front cart still gains motion, and the other loses it in the collision. Let us see if we can save the basic concept that *some* quantity related to motion is being transferred from the initially moving cart to the one initially at rest.

Since the only change we made was in the mass of the moving cart, perhaps the "quantity related to motion" has something to do with mass. Indeed, you may know from painful experience that the effects you suffer when an object moving at a given speed hits you worsen as its mass increases (would you rather be hit by a tennis ball moving at 20 mi/h or a truck moving at the same speed?). On the other hand, your suffering increases with the object's speed, too! So perhaps the "quantity of motion" we are interested in here is the *product* of the object's mass and speed. Let us see where this hypothesis gets us.

Figure C3.3

An example collision between identical carts. (The final speeds are the actual experimental results in this situation.)

Figure C3.4

An example collision where one cart is twice as massive as the other. (The final speeds are the actual experimental results in this situation.)

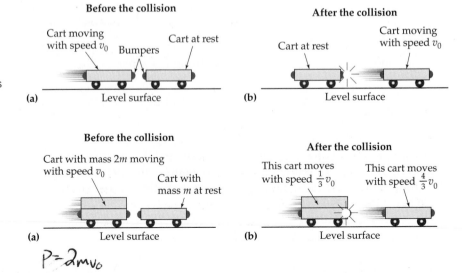

$P = 2mv_0$

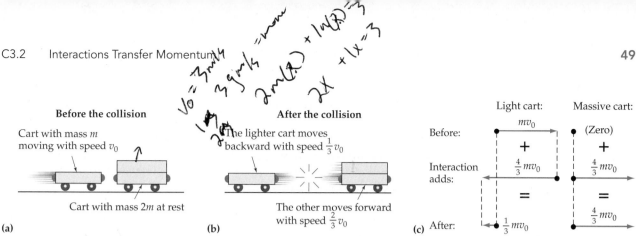

Before the collision

Cart with mass m
moving with speed v_0

Cart with mass $2m$ at rest

(a)

After the collision

The lighter cart moves
backward with speed $\frac{1}{3}v_0$

The other moves forward
with speed $\frac{2}{3}v_0$

(b)

Light cart: Massive cart:

Before: mv_0 (Zero)

+   +

Interaction $\frac{4}{3}mv_0$ $\frac{4}{3}mv_0$
adds:

=   =

After: $\frac{1}{3}mv_0$ $\frac{4}{3}mv_0$

(c)

Figure C3.5
(a), and (b) A collision between two carts where the right cart is twice as massive as the left cart. (c) Note that the collision interaction transfers a "quantity of motion" (assumed here to be a *vector*) equal to $\frac{4}{3}mv_0$ rightward from the left cart to the right cart.

Let us take the mass of the lighter cart to be m; the mass of the initially moving cart is then $2m$. Our hypothetical "quantity of motion" for the initially moving cart is thus $2mv_0$. The collision gives the right cart a "quantity of motion" of $m(\frac{5}{3}v_0) = \frac{5}{3}mv_0$. If we subtract this from $2mv_0$, we get $\frac{2}{3}mv_0$, which is indeed the mass of the left cart $(2m)$ times its observed speed of $\frac{1}{3}v_0$! So this collision interaction does indeed seem to transfer a "quantity of motion" equal to $\frac{5}{3}mv_0$ from the back cart to the right cart, with some remaining in the left cart. The explanation works for the initial experiment as well, where the first cart transferred to the second cart a "quantity of motion" equal to mv_0 (although it is curious that the magnitude of the "quantity of motion" transferred is different in the two experiments).

Flush from this success, let us now try an experiment where we reverse the masses of the carts. The results of such an experiment (as you can verify) are shown in figure C3.5. After the collision, the massive right cart moves ahead with a speed of $\frac{2}{3}v_0$, and the lighter left cart rebounds *backward* with a speed of $\frac{1}{3}v_0$! These results are catastrophic for our model. Our "quantity of motion" for the initially moving cart is mv_0; but its value for the right cart after the collision is $2m(\frac{2}{3}v_0) = \frac{4}{3}mv_0$ and that for the left cart is $\frac{1}{3}mv_0$. Again, we seem to end up with more "quantity of motion" than we had before.

But wait! What if *direction* matters? What if our "quantity of motion" in fact should be a *vector* with a direction parallel to the direction of motion? Then the initial quantity of motion is an *arrow* pointing forward with a length proportional to mv_0. The interaction gives the right cart a quantity of motion equivalent to a rightward arrow of length $\frac{4}{3}mv_0$. To find out what this gift does to the first cart, we have to *subtract* this arrow from the first cart's initial arrow, which is the same as *adding* a *leftward* arrow of length $\frac{4}{3}mv_0$. The result (as shown in figure C3.5c) is that the final quantity of motion for the left cart is $\frac{1}{3}mv_0$ in the leftward direction, consistent with what is observed.

Physicists now call the vector quantity that we have discovered **momentum** (although "quantity of motion" is in fact the English translation of the Latin term that Newton used). We formally define a particle's momentum to be

A vector model of momentum

$$\vec{p} \equiv m\vec{v} \qquad (C3.4)$$

Purpose: This equation defines a particle's momentum vector $\vec{p}$.
Symbols: m is the particle's mass; $\vec{v}$ is its velocity.
Limitations: This equation applies to particles only (but see chapter C4), and only in the context of newtonian mechanics.
Notes: The SI units for $\vec{p}$ are kilogram-meters per second (kg·m/s).

The definition of the
momentum of a particle

You can easily verify that the *vector* model of momentum transfer we developed for the experiment shown in figure C3.5 also works for the experiments shown in figures C3.4 and C3.3, as well as for collisions where the carts have arbitrary relative masses, where bumpers that are *not* springy or involve interactions that are *not* contact interactions (e.g., magnetic repulsion), or even where both carts move initially. Our model does not predict the *amount* of momentum transferred in the collision (that depends somewhat on the type of interaction—see chapter C12), but still tells us something very important about interactions.

Exercise C3X.3

Imagine that a cart with mass m moving with speed v_0 collides with an identical cart at rest. After the collision, the carts stick together and move together at a speed of $\frac{1}{2}v_0$ in the same direction as the originally moving cart. Show (by drawing a picture analogous to figure C3.5c) that we can also think of *this* collision as transferring momentum from the left cart to the right cart. Compute the magnitude and direction of that momentum transfer.

We are encouraged by this evidence to generalize boldly:

The momentum-transfer principle: Any interaction between two objects affects their motion by *transferring momentum* from one to the other.

The model of motion that this principle expresses has proved over the centuries to be an extremely powerful and far-reaching model for understanding interactions, and (with some refinements) it applies even in our most modern theories. In fact, you may recall from chapter C1 that in quantum field theory, we model an interaction between two particles by imagining that they exchange the interaction's mediator particles: these mediators quite literally carry momentum between the interacting particles! This model is the very heart of modern mechanics, and many of the ideas in this unit (and essentially *everything* in unit N) follow as logical consequences of this model. The rest of this chapter and chapter C4 are devoted to giving you just an overview of these consequences.

The core idea of this section

We can consider either interacting object as donating the momentum

By the way, it does not matter in this model which of the two interacting objects we consider to be the donor and which the recipient of the momentum transferred by the interaction. In the collision shown in figure C3.5, either we can think of the left cart as giving the right cart $\frac{4}{3}mv_0$ of rightward momentum and *losing* $\frac{4}{3}mv_0$ of rightward momentum as a result, or we can think of the right cart as giving $\frac{4}{3}mv_0$ of *leftward* momentum to the left cart and losing $\frac{4}{3}mv_0$ of leftward momentum as a result. The definition of the vector inverse ensures that the results are the same either way. This is good, because it would be strange if the fundamental model of the interactions between two objects treated the two objects asymmetrically.

C3.3   Impulse and Force

The definition of impulse

Physicists call the amount of momentum that a *particular* interaction A between two particles transfers to either particle during a short interval of time the **impulse** $[d\vec{p}]_A$ that the interaction delivers to that particle during that interval. For example, the impulse delivered to the right cart by the collision interaction C shown in figure C3.4 is $[d\vec{p}]_C = \frac{4}{3}mv_0$ right.

A financial analogy may help us understand some subtle distinctions in meaning between the terms *a particle's momentum* $\vec{p} = m\vec{v}$, *impulse*, and *momentum* in general. Think of the *particle's momentum* ($\vec{p} = m\vec{v}$) as being like a person's net financial worth. An *interaction* is like a financial transaction that increases one person's net worth at the expense of the other's. An *impulse* is like a check that a person writes or receives in the transaction. The term *momentum* is, like *money*, a general term for both what each particle (person) has and what is being transferred. (The only flaw in this analogy is that momentum is a *vector* quantity, while money is a *scalar*.)

A financial analogy

If a particle participates in only a *single* interaction (call it interaction A) with one other particle, then the total change in its momentum due to the interaction during a short interval of time will be equal to the impulse that it receives from the interaction during that time: $d\vec{p} = [d\vec{p}]_A$. But what happens if a particle participates in multiple interactions with multiple partners? The financial analogy suggests the answer. During a given month, a person may write and/or receive checks involving many other people. The change in the person's net worth during that month is just the *arithmetic sum* of the check amounts (treating incoming checks as positive numbers and outgoing checks as negative numbers). By analogy, the change $d\vec{p}$ in the momentum of a particle that participates in multiple interactions during a given interval is the *vector sum* of the impulses it receives during that interval:

What happens when a particle participates in many interactions

$$d\vec{p} = [d\vec{p}]_A + [d\vec{p}]_B + \cdots \qquad (C3.5)$$

Purpose: This equation describes how multiple interactions affect a particle's motion.

Symbols: $[d\vec{p}]_A, [d\vec{p}]_B, \ldots$ are the impulses (momentum contributions) delivered to the particle by interactions A, B, etc. during a given short time interval dt, and $d\vec{p}$ is the resulting change in the particle's actual momentum $\vec{p}$ during that time interval.

Limitations: This equation applies to particles only (but see chapter C4).

In spite of the analogy, it is not *obvious* that impulses should really add this way, but 300 years of experiments support this simple model.

Please note in the preceding paragraphs that I am using brackets to distinguish the amount of momentum $[d\vec{p}]_A$ (i.e., impulse) that a given interaction A *contributes* to a particle from the actual change $d\vec{p}$ in the value of that particle's momentum $\vec{p} = m\vec{v}$. As equation C3.5 makes clear, these quantities are *not* equal in general: the net change $d\vec{p}$ in the particle's momentum during a given time interval dt is determined by the vector sum of *all* of the impulses that various interactions contribute during that interval. I believe that recognizing this distinction is very important if one is to develop a clear understanding of the momentum-transfer model, so I will use this notation carefully and deliberately in what follows, and I recommend that you do likewise. Read $[d\vec{p}]_A$ as meaning "the *contribution* that interaction A makes to $d\vec{p}$."

The term *impulse* fairly intuitively expresses what a collision interaction does to a particle's motion, but you can even think of a continuing interaction as delivering a continuous series of very tiny impulses to a particle, which you can think of as little "taps" in a certain direction. For example, you perhaps know that the speed of a dropped object increases as the object falls. We can see why this is so if we imagine the gravitational interaction between the object and the earth as delivering a continuous series of tiny downward taps

Imagining a continuing interaction as a series of tiny impulses to the object, each one increasing the object's downward momentum by a tiny amount. As a result, the falling object accumulates downward momentum (and thus downward speed) as time passes.

In the limit as the taps become extremely tiny and the time between them becomes infinitesimal, the momentum flow into the particle becomes continuous, almost like a fluid accumulating in the particle. This "momentum flow" image is very useful for interactions that, unlike collisions, last a significant amount of time.

The definition of force

We define the **force** $\vec{F}$ that an interaction exerts on a given object to be the *rate* at which momentum flows into the object because of that interaction:

$$\vec{F}_A \equiv \frac{[d\vec{p}]_A}{dt} \qquad\qquad \text{(C3.6)}$$

Purpose: This equation defines the force $\vec{F}_A$ that interaction A exerts on a particle.
Symbols: $[d\vec{p}]_A$ is the small impulse the interaction delivers to the particle during the small time interval dt.
Limitations: The interval dt must be small enough that $\vec{F}_A \approx$ constant during dt.
Notes: The SI unit of force is the **newton**, where $1\,\text{N} \equiv 1\,\text{kg·m/s}^2$. Force $\vec{F}_A$ has the same direction as the impulse $[d\vec{p}]_A$ being delivered.

The units of force

The first note in the box acknowledges that force is such a useful concept in newtonian mechanics that it has its own special SI unit. Since $[d\vec{p}]_A$ must have the same units as momentum (kilogram-meters per second, the units of mass times velocity), consistency requires that the units of force be those of momentum/time, or kilogram-meters per second, per second $[(\text{kg·m/s})/\text{s}] =$ kilogram-meters per second squared (kg·m/s^2). We define one *newton* to be the force experienced by a particle receiving an impulse of one kilogram-meter per second every second $(1\,\text{N} \equiv 1\,\text{kg·m/s}^2)$. A newton is very roughly the magnitude of the upward push required to hold a music CD (in its case) at rest in the earth's gravitational field.

Force as a push or pull

How well does this definition of force coincide with the colloquial idea of force as a push or pull? Consider an object floating at rest that is not interacting with anything. If you push on this object in a certain direction for a certain time interval dt, the contact interaction between your hand and the object will give it an impulse $[d\vec{p}]_C = \vec{F}_C\, dt$ in the same direction, and if it was initially at rest, it will end up moving in that direction. A small $\vec{F}_C$ delivers a small impulse during dt, so the object's change in velocity will be small, as we would expect from a weak push. On the other hand, a large $\vec{F}_C$ gives it a proportionally larger impulse, prompting it to respond more vigorously, just as we would expect from a stronger push. Thus our technical definition does seem to reproduce what we would expect from the "force = push" concept, while also providing a quantitative definition of a force's strength and its exact effect on a particle's motion.

Exercise C3X.4

Consider the collision between carts shown in figure C3.5. Imagine that $m = 1.0$ kg, $v_0 = 1.0$ m/s, and the contact interaction lasts for 0.05 s. Assume that the force that the contact interaction exerts on the front cart is *constant* (this is not *really* likely, but let us pretend). What is the magnitude of this force?

(*Note:* When we compute the force by *pretending* it is constant over a certain interval when it really probably is not, we signal this by saying that we are computing the **average force** over the time interval.)

We can visualize an interaction between two particles as a being like a hose that carries a flow of momentum from one to the other. Since any momentum that flows *out* of one must flow *into* the other, the *magnitude* of the rate of momentum flow must be the same for both particles. This statement and the definition of force directly imply that

An interaction as a momentum-carrying hose

> A given interaction between particles A and B must exert a force on B that is equal in magnitude and opposite in direction to the force that it exerts on A: $\vec{F}_{\text{on }B} = -\vec{F}_{\text{on }A}$.

(The minus sign is there because any momentum that flows into B has flowed out of A.) For example, figure C3.5c in section C3.2 shows that in the collision shown, the impulses delivered to the two carts (and thus the forces) are indeed equal in magnitude and opposite in direction. Physicists call this statement **Newton's third law;** we will study it in greater detail in unit N.

C3.4   Mass and Weight

Equation C3.4 defines *momentum* in terms of *mass* and *velocity*. While I carefully defined *velocity* in equation C3.2 in terms of more basic ideas, I really have not yet defined what I mean by *mass*, trusting instead that you intuitively knew what I meant. I would like to deal with this issue more carefully now.

Mass is defined in terms of *momentum*, not vice versa

The *principle of momentum transfer* is the most fundamental physical idea in this chapter. We in fact *discovered* the definition $\vec{p} = m\vec{v}$ by trying to make this principle work experimentally. The point is that we can define momentum *independently* of mass as being whatever "quantity of motion" an interaction transfers.

Viewed from this perspective, a particle's **mass** simply expresses the relationship between its momentum and its velocity, each of which we can define separately. *Qualitatively*, a particle's mass expresses how much impulse we need in order to change its velocity by a given amount. Conversely, the greater a particle's mass, the *smaller* its velocity change will be for a given impulse: a particle's mass expresses the degree to which it *resists* changes in its motion.

Mass expresses an object's resistance to changes in its motion

An **operational definition** defines a physical quantity by describing a procedure for measuring that quantity. (Operational definitions are useful in physics because they firmly anchor quantities in empirical reality, avoiding the potential vagueness of verbal definitions.) An operational definition of mass based on the principle of momentum transfer goes as follows. Imagine we have particle of known mass m_1 and a particle whose mass m_2 we would like to measure. We set things up so that the two particles participate in a repulsive interaction with each other (perhaps by placing a compressed spring between them) but do not interact significantly with anything else. We hold them initially at rest, and then we release them so that the repulsive interaction, acting alone, drives them apart (see figure C3.6). We then measure the particles' speeds v_1 and v_2 after some given interval of time. (Note that each speed is equal to the magnitude of that particle's change in velocity, since the initial velocity of each was zero.)

An operational definition of *mass*

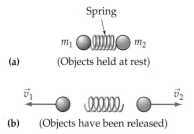

(a)   (Objects held at rest)

(b)   (Objects have been released)

Figure C3.6
(a) The initial situation in an experiment to measure the mass m_2.
(b) The final situation after the objects have been released. We measure $\vec{v}_1$ and $\vec{v}_2$ at the same instant.

The principle of momentum transfer means that each particle must get the same magnitude of impulse. Therefore, if we want mass to express the particle's resistance to changes in its velocity for a given impulse, then the simplest way to do this is to define a particle's mass to be proportional to $1/\mathrm{mag}(\Delta\vec{v})$ for a given impulse. This means that

$$\frac{m_2}{m_1} \equiv \frac{\mathrm{mag}(\Delta\vec{v}_1)}{\mathrm{mag}(\Delta\vec{v}_2)} = \frac{v_1}{v_2} \qquad \Rightarrow \qquad m_2 \equiv m_1\frac{v_1}{v_2} \quad \text{in this experiment}$$

(C3.7)

This definition of mass is consistent with the definition $\vec{p} = m\vec{v}$.

The SI unit of mass

This definition allows us to determine the mass of any object, given an object of known mass. However, even to begin using this definition, we must have *one* object whose mass we know. By international convention, the defining object is a particular metal cylinder stored under controlled conditions near Paris, France. This object has a mass of one **kilogram** (the SI unit of mass) by definition. Given this object, we can determine the mass of anything else in kilograms.

Mass and weight are completely distinct concepts!

It is crucial to note that in physics, *mass* and *weight* are *completely distinct concepts*. An object's mass expresses its resistance to changes in its velocity. An object's **weight** $\vec{F}_g$, however, expresses the force that a gravitational interaction exerts on the object at a certain point in space. *Mass* is a *scalar* measured in kilograms; *weight* is a *vector* measured in newtons.

On the basis of their definitions, we might not expect there to be any connection between an object's mass and the weight force it experiences in a gravitational interaction. Experiments show, however, that at a given point in space, an object's weight is in fact directly proportional to its mass:

The relationship between mass and weight

$$\vec{F}_g = m\vec{g} \qquad\qquad (C3.8)$$

Purpose: This equation describes the relationship between weight and mass.

Symbols: $\vec{F}_g$ is the weight acting on an object, m is the object's mass; $\vec{g}$ is the **gravitational field vector** at a certain point in space.

Limitations: There are none (until we study general relativity, at least).

Notes: Near the earth's surface, $\vec{g}$ points toward the earth's center, and the **gravitational field strength** $g \equiv \mathrm{mag}(\vec{g}) = 9.8\ \mathrm{N/kg}$.

Surprisingly, the gravitational field vector $\vec{g}$ in equation C3.8, while it does depend on one's exact position relative to a strongly gravitating object such as the earth, is *completely independent* of the nature of the object involved, meaning that $\mathrm{mag}(\vec{F}_g)$ is strictly proportional to m for *all* objects at a given point in space (a fact that has no explanation in Newton's mechanics, but is explained by general relativity). Within any region of space where $\mathrm{mag}(\vec{g}) \approx$ constant (such as points relatively near the surface of the earth), we consider the magnitude of the weight force acting on an object to be proportional to its mass for all practical purposes.

Note that the **pound** is an English system unit of *force* (1 lb = 4.45 N), not mass! A 1-kg object experiences a weight force of about 2.2 lb near the earth's surface.

Exercise C3X.5

In an experiment of the type shown in figure C3.6, an object whose mass is known to be 0.50 kg has a final speed of 3.0 m/s, while the other object has a final speed of 2.0 m/s. What is its mass?

Exercise C3X.6

What is your weight in newtons?

C3.5   Momentum Flow and Motion

One can fairly easily use either impulse or momentum flow ideas to make qualitative predictions about an object's motion. Consider, for example, throwing a ball so that its initial velocity has both an upward and a forward component, and imagine that after it is launched, the ball interacts only gravitationally with the earth (friction interactions are negligible). Figure C3.7 shows how we can predict the trajectory by treating the gravitational force on the ball as a series of small downward taps separated by a given time interval dt. The ball's displacement between taps will be parallel to its momentum $\vec{p}$ after the last tap (and proportional in length to $\vec{p}$, because the ball's displacement is proportional to its velocity between the taps, which in turn is proportional to $\vec{p}$). Each tap, however, changes the ball's momentum so that its new momentum (black arrow) is the vector sum of its old momentum (gray arrow) and the downward impulse (colored arrow) delivered by the tap (since $d\vec{p} \equiv \vec{p}_{\text{final}} - \vec{p}_{\text{initial}} = [d\vec{p}]_{\text{tap}}$ according to equation C3.5, implying that $\vec{p}_{\text{final}} = \vec{p}_{\text{initial}} + [d\vec{p}]_{\text{tap}}$). The ball subsequently moves in the direction indicated by the new momentum until the next tap. Figure C3.7 shows the resulting trajectory. Perhaps you can imagine that in the limit that the taps become very small and the time between taps becomes small, the trajectory will become a smooth parabola.

The multitap model for predicting trajectories

Another whole approach (which I actually find easier to visualize) is to imagine each component of the ball's momentum to be like a graduated cylinder reservoir containing a certain amount of fluid. If the fluid level in the reservoir corresponding to, say, the momentum x component is *above* the zero mark, the ball's x-momentum is positive; if below, the x-momentum is negative. Pouring fluid into this reservoir thus increases the component of the ball's momentum in the $+x$ direction, while draining momentum from it decreases that component.

The graduated reservoir model for predicting trajectories

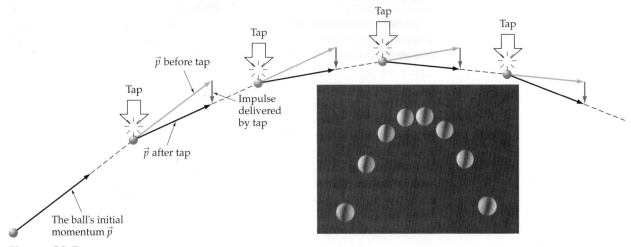

Figure C3.7

How to predict the trajectory of a thrown ball by modeling the effect of the gravitational interaction as a series of small taps. The gray arrows represent the ball's momentum before each tap, the colored arrows the impulse delivered by that tap, and the black arrows the ball's momentum after each tap. The inset multiflash picture shows that the actual trajectory of a thrown ball is consistent with this prediction.

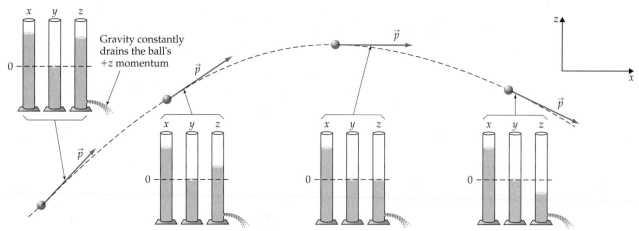

Figure C3.8

How to predict a ball's trajectory using a fluid flow model of momentum. In this model, we represent each of the object's momentum components by a fluid-filled graduated reservoir whose level specifies the component's value. Interactions either fill or drain reservoirs. Here I am assuming that the ball's y momentum is zero initially.

In the particular case of the thrown ball, the force exerted by the ball's gravitational interaction with the earth adds downward momentum to the ball at a constant rate. This is equivalent to draining the reservoir corresponding to the $+z$ component of the ball's momentum at a constant rate. So the fluid level in this z reservoir steadily drops, eventually passing the zero and continuing into negative territory. On the other hand, since the impulse delivered by the gravitational interaction is purely downward, it has no component in either the x or y direction, so the corresponding x and y reservoirs get neither drained nor filled. By imagining what happens to the levels in these reservoirs as time passes, one can sketch the ball's momentum vectors at successive instants of time. This allows one to sketch the ball's trajectory qualitatively, as shown in figure C3.8.

These models for understanding motion have their own strengths and weaknesses. The **multitap model** can yield a fairly *precise* prediction of the trajectory, but is somewhat abstract and does not work well for continuously acting forces if you use too few taps. The **three-reservoir model** is more concrete, but is good for only qualitative predictions. Note also that the model is not completely realistic: one can add to or drain an object's momentum indefinitely without either overflowing or emptying the "reservoirs"! Use whichever model you understand better and/or better fits the context.

Consider now a cart rolling forward in the $+x$ direction along a level track with nonnegligible friction. This case is more complicated than the case of the ball because the cart participates in multiple interactions. We can usefully think of the cart as participating in *three* interactions: a gravitational interaction with the earth, a compression contact interaction with the track that prevents it from sinking into the track, and a friction contact interaction with the track that seeks to oppose its motion relative to the track.

In this case, I find the reservoir model most natural. Note that the cart's vertical momentum is always zero; so since gravity drains the cart's z reservoir at a constant rate, the compression contact interaction must fill it at the same rate. The impulses delivered by these interactions are entirely vertical, so they leave the x and y reservoirs alone. The friction contact interaction, though, opposes the cart's motion relative to the track, so transfers momentum in the $-x$ direction to the cart, which is equivalent to draining the cart's x reservoir. Thus the cart's x-momentum (and thus forward velocity)

Strengths and weaknesses of the two models

The case of a cart rolling with friction

decreases steadily until the cart stops. At that point, there is no more relative motion for the friction interaction to resist, so it stops draining the x reservoir, and the cart subsequently remains at rest. Figure C3.9 illustrates the situation as the cart is slowing down.

For our purposes in this unit, a *qualitative* understanding of the effects of interaction motion at the level of these examples is sufficient. We will discuss the effects of interactions on motion in detail in unit N.

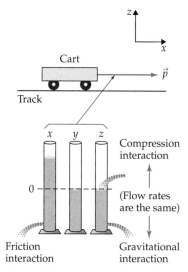

Exercise C3X.7

Imagine a pool ball that is initially rolling due north on a pool table. Your opponent, in a blatantly illegal attempt to foil your great shot, blows constantly directly eastward on the ball. Model the ball as a particle that is moving initially northward but experiences a constant eastward force. Sketch momentum arrows for the ball at successive times during your friend's blowing, using both the multitap and graduated-reservoir models.

Figure C3.9
The three-reservoir model applied to the moving cart problem at one instant of time. The level in the z reservoir never changes from zero, but friction slowly drains the x reservoir to zero.

C3.6   Physics Skills: Illegal Vector Equations

Since so many important physical quantities are described by vectors, we will be doing a *lot* of mathematics with vectors from this chapter onward. Doing algebra with vector quantities is a lot like doing algebra with ordinary scalars *except* in a few important cases. Here is a list of things to keep in mind when doing vector algebra that will help you avoid making common mistakes.

1. **Do not set a vector equal to a scalar.** A vector quantity has both a magnitude *and an associated direction,* while a scalar quantity has only a numerical value. Therefore, a vector is *never* equivalent to a scalar (even if their magnitudes are the same). So avoid writing equations like $\vec{v} = 20$ m/s when what you *really* mean is $\text{mag}(\vec{v}) = 20$ m/s or perhaps $\vec{v} = 20$ m/s south or $\vec{v} = (20 \text{ m/s})\hat{x}$. (The *only* exception is that an equation like $\vec{v} = 0$ is acceptable: We conventionally take this to mean that all the *components* of $\vec{v}$ are zero.)

2. **Vector magnitudes are *always* positive** (by definition!). For example, saying that $v = -32$ m/s is absurd: a particle's speed is the *magnitude* of its velocity vector and so *must* be positive. (If you are tempted to write this, you probably mean something like $v_x = -32$ m/s: a vector *component* can be negative.)

3. **Division by a vector is *not defined.*** If you are given an equation like $\vec{v} = d\vec{r}/dt$ and are asked to find dt, you might be tempted to rearrange it in the usual way to get $dt = d\vec{r}/\vec{v}$. But the latter equation is meaningless, since division by a vector is not defined: *you cannot divide both sides of an equation by a vector.* [The *right* way to solve the vector equation $\vec{v} = d\vec{r}/dt$ for dt is to take the magnitude of both sides, to get $\text{mag}(\vec{v}) = \text{mag}(d\vec{r})/dt$, and then to rearrange these *scalar* values in the usual way to get $dt = \text{mag}(d\vec{r})/\text{mag}(\vec{v})$.]

4. **Remember that $\text{mag}(\vec{u}_1 + \vec{u}_2) \neq \text{mag}(\vec{u}_1) + \text{mag}(\vec{u}_2)$.** See figure C3.10 for an example. To take an even more extreme example, note that if $\vec{u}_1$ and $\vec{u}_2$ have equal magnitudes but opposite directions, $\text{mag}(\vec{u}_2) + \text{mag}(\vec{u}_2) \neq 0$, but $\text{mag}(\vec{u}_1 + \vec{u}_2) = 0$! Similarly, $\text{mag}(\vec{u}_1 - \vec{u}_2) \neq \text{mag}(\vec{u}_1) - \text{mag}(\vec{u}_2)$. Therefore, whenever you take the magnitude of both sides of a vector equation, check carefully that you do not break up the magnitude of a vector sum (or difference) into the sum (or difference) of magnitudes.

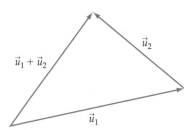

Figure C3.10
Note that the length of the arrow representing $\vec{u}_1 + \vec{u}_2$ is *not* the same as the sum of the lengths of the arrows representing $\vec{u}_1$ and $\vec{u}_2$ (in fact it is somewhat smaller).

(It may help you to remember that we have to treat the *square root* of a sum or difference in the same way, since $\sqrt{a \pm b} \neq \sqrt{a} \pm \sqrt{b}$, so treat vector magnitudes as you would treat square roots.)

5.   **Components are *not* vectors.** A vector $\vec{u}$'s components u_x, u_y, and u_z are *scalars* (simple signed numbers), not vectors. The quantities $\vec{u}_x$, $\vec{u}_y$, and $\vec{u}_z$, on the other hand, are component *vectors,* which have magnitude and direction. Keep these distinctions clear!

Observing the following general rule (which I call the **column vector rule**) will help you avoid making many of the specific errors listed above: *If any symbol in an equation has an arrow or hat over it, you should be able to replace that symbol with a three-component column vector without changing the equation's meaning.* For example, the equation $\vec{v} = 20$ m/s is wrong according to this rule because a column vector is obviously not the same as a single number. The equation $dt = d\vec{r}/\vec{v}$ is absurd according to this rule because division by a column vector makes no sense. The converse to this rule is also useful: *A symbol without an arrow over it can never be replaced by a column vector.* If you are careful to observe both of these general rules when writing equations, you will sidestep the vast majority of common beginner's errors.

Exercise C3X.8

Find the mistakes (if any) in each of these statements:

a.   A 2.0-kg particle moving in the $-x$ direction at 10 m/s has momentum components $\vec{p}_x = -20$ kg·m/s and $\vec{p}_y = \vec{p}_z = 0$, so the magnitude of its momentum is $p = -20$ kg·m/s.

b.   A system consists of two particles, one moving northward with a momentum of $p_1 = 20$ kg·m/s and the other westward with a momentum of $p_2 = 10$ kg·m/s. The system's total momentum is thus $p_{tot} = 30$ kg·m/s.

c.   If a particle moves with a velocity of $\vec{v} = 10$ m/s and has a momentum of $\vec{p} = 5$ kg·m/s, then its mass must be $m = \vec{p}/\vec{v} = 0.5$ kg.

TWO-MINUTE PROBLEMS

C3T.1 "The car rounded the corner at a constant velocity." Would this statement make sense to a physicist?
A. No, the word *velocity* is being used incorrectly.
B. No, a car has to slow down to turn a corner.
C. It could make sense or not, depending on the corner.
D. Yes, this statement is acceptable.

C3T.2 Imagine that a 1.0-kg cart traveling rightward at 1.0 m/s hits a 3.0-kg cart at rest. Afterward, the smaller cart is observed to move leftward with a speed of 0.75 m/s. What impulse did the collision give the smaller cart at the expense of the larger?
A. None; the larger cart was at rest and so had no momentum to give.
B. None; the lighter cart gave an impulse to the more massive cart, not the other way round.
C. 0.75 kg·m/s leftward.
D. 1.00 kg·m/s leftward.
E. 1.75 kg·m/s leftward.

F. Other (specify).
T. Both A and B are correct.

C3T.3 Imagine that a moving cart (cart *A*) hits an identical cart (cart *B*) at rest. Cart *B* remains at rest, and cart *A* rebounds with a speed equal to its original speed. Cart *B* must have participated in some other interaction during the collision process, true (T) or false (F)?

C3T.4 Imagine that two identical carts traveling toward each other at the same speed collide and come to rest. According to the momentum-transfer principle, if one of the carts is observed to be at rest after the collision, the other
A. Must be at rest also.
B. Must rebound backward with its original speed.
C. Must rebound backward with twice its original speed.

$P_{L} = 1.0kg \cdot 1m/s = 1 kg \cdot m/s$

$P_{LA} = 1.0kg \cdot .75m/s = -.75m/s$

D. Must continue forward with twice its original speed.

E. Does none of the above. This process violates the momentum-transfer principle!

F. Other (specify).

C3T.5 An 8.0-kg bowling ball hits a 1.2-kg bowling pin. The force that the contact interaction exerts on the pin has the same magnitude that it exerts on the ball, T or F?

C3T.6 It is possible for a human being to have a weight of 150 kg, T or F?

C3T.7 A cup sitting on a table constantly receives upward momentum from the table, T or F?

C3T.8 A particle is launched horizontally with an initial speed of 5 m/s and subsequently interacts *only* gravitationally with the earth. According to the three-reservoir model, the horizontal component of the particle's velocity after a few seconds has passed is
A. Somewhat greater than 5 m/s.
B. Essentially equal to 5 m/s.
C. Somewhat less than 5 m/s.
D. 0.
E. Other (specify).

C3T.9 Which of the following statements involving vectors are correct? Answer T if it is correct and F if it is not (be prepared to identify the error if you answer F).
a. $\vec{p}_{tot} = \vec{p}_1 + \vec{p}_2$ implies that $p_{tot} = p_1 + p_2$. F, need vectors
b. $\vec{p} = m\vec{v}$ implies that $m = \vec{p}/\vec{v}$. T
c. If $\vec{v} = [0, -5.0 \text{ m/s}, 0]$, then $\vec{v}_y = -5.0 \text{ m/s}$. T
d. If $\vec{v} = [0, -5.0 \text{ m/s}, 0]$, then $v = +5.0 \text{ m/s}$. F, -5.0m/s
e. If $\vec{v} = 5.0 \text{ m/s}$ and $m = 2.0 \text{ kg}$, then $\vec{p} = 10 \text{ kg·m/s}$. T

HOMEWORK PROBLEMS

Basic Skills

C3B.1 An object is observed in a certain reference frame to move from the position [2.2 m, −3.5 m, 1.6 m] to the position [−1.8 m, 1.3 m, −0.1 m] during a time interval of 0.65 s. What are the components of the object's velocity during this interval (assuming that the interval is sufficiently short that the velocity is essentially constant)? -1.8 -2.2, 1.3 + +3.5, -.01-1.6

$\left(\dfrac{-4}{.65}, \dfrac{2.8}{.65}, \dfrac{-1.61}{.65}\right)$ m/s

C3B.2 During a certain interval of time, an object whose velocity components in a certain frame are essentially constant [1.5 m/s, −2.0 m/s, 0 m/s] moves a distance of 5.0 m. How long was the interval of time?

C3B.3 A 2.0-kg object's momentum at a certain time is 10 kg·m/s 37° vertically upward from due west. What are the components and magnitude of its velocity vector at this time (in a frame in standard orientation)? ((cos37)·10, sin37·10)

C3B.4 A 1.0-kg cart traveling at 1.0 m/s rightward hits a 4.0-kg cart at rest. After the collision, the lighter cart is observed to move to the left at 0.5 m/s. What impulse did the interaction deliver to the massive cart (magnitude and direction)? What is that cart's velocity after the collision (magnitude and direction)? Construct an arrow diagram something like the one shown in figure C3.5c.

P 1 kg·m/s
-.5 kg·m/s = -1.5 kg·m/s

C3B.5 Imagine that a 1.0-kg cart traveling at 1.0 m/s rightward collides with a cart at rest. If the collision interaction gives an impulse of 1.5 kg·m/s of rightward momentum to the cart originally at rest, what is the velocity of the originally moving cart *after* the collision?

C3B.6 The value of $g \equiv \text{mag}(\vec{g})$ near the surface of the moon is about one-sixth of its magnitude near the surface of the earth. What would your mass be on the moon? What would your weight be on the moon?

C3B.7 A rocket at time $t = 0$ is moving at a constant velocity in deep space in the $+x$ direction. The rocket turns 90° so that it points in the $+y$ direction, and at $t = 3$ s it fires its rocket engine for 3 s. It then turns 180° to facee the $-y$ direction and at $t = 9$ s fires its engine again at the same thrust for 6 s.
(a) Use either the multitap or the three-reservoir model to draw a qualitatively accurate trajectory for the rocket out to at least $t = 18$ s.
(b) Is its final direction of motion same as its initial direction?
(c) Is the rocket pointing at the end in its final direction of motion? (Explain your results for all parts.)

C3B.8 Each of the equations or statements listed below is incorrect in some way. Describe the error in each case.
(a) Object A has a momentum of $\vec{p} = 2 \text{ kg·m/s}$.
(b) At the time in question, the object's x velocity was $\vec{v}_x = -10 \text{ m/s}$.

(more)

(c) At the time, the object's velocity was 25 m/s.

(d) The displacement between points A and B is [3, 5, −1].

(e) Particle A's momentum is $\vec{p}_A = 2.0$ kg·m/s west while particle B's is $\vec{p}_B = 2.0$ kg·m/s eastward. The magnitude of the sum of these momenta is 4.0 kg·m/s.

Synthetic

C3S.1 At a certain time, a car is 150 m due west of your house. If it is traveling with a constant velocity of 30 m/s 30° south of east, what are the magnitude and the direction of its position relative to your house 5 s later?

C3S.2 A cart with a mass m moving to the right with an initial speed v_0 hits a cart with mass M at rest. After the collision, the first cart rebounds to the left with a speed of $v_A = \frac{3}{5}v_0$, and the other cart moves to the right with a speed of $v_B = \frac{2}{5}v_0$. Construct a momentum-arrow diagram analogous to figure C3.5c, and use this to infer the value of the unknown mass M (express it as some multiple of m).

C3S.3 A cart with mass m moving to the right at an initial speed of v_0 hits a cart with mass $2m$ that is moving at a speed of $\frac{3}{4}v_0$ to the left. Imagine that the carts stick together after the collision. Construct a momentum-arrow diagram analogous to figure C3.5c, and use this to infer the carts' common final velocity $\vec{v}_f$ (magnitude and direction).

C3S.4 A book sitting at rest on a table receives a downward impulse of 18.6 kg·m/s every second from its gravitational interaction with the earth.

(a) What is the magnitude of the gravitational *force* acting on the book (i.e., the book's weight)?

(b) What is the book's mass (assuming that it is near the earth's surface)?

(c) What impulse (magnitude and direction) does the book's contact interaction with the table exert on the book every second?

C3S.5 Answer the questions posed in the Aristotelian Thinking Diagnostic Test at the end of chapter C2, carefully explaining your answers by using some kind of momentum flow model. (In principle, you can use such a model to correctly answer all of them, although some are still tricky.)

C3S.6 A tugboat of mass $m = 20{,}000$ kg pushes a barge with a mass of 80,000 kg so that starting from rest, they reach a speed of 2.0 m/s after 10 s. Assume that the effects of gravity on the tug and barge are canceled by the effects of their supporting contact interactions with the water; and assume that friction interactions are negligible and that all forces are constant during the 10-s interval. The front bumper on the tug might buckle if a force of more than 150,000 N acts on it, and its propeller might fracture if it is asked to provide more than 250,000 N of force. Is this tug operating within these limits? Answer as follows:

(a) Start with the barge. How much impulse did the contact interaction with the tug give the barge during the time interval in question? Argue that your answer implies that the barge's contact interaction with the tug must have exerted a force of magnitude 160,000 N on the barge, and explain carefully why this means that the force exerted on the tug's bumper also has a magnitude of 160,000 N, violating the limit.

(b) Argue that the tug must therefore get a backward impulse of 1,600,000 kg·m/s from the barge during this interval. Yet you can calculate the tug's actual net change in momentum during the interval from the information given. Using an arrow diagram, find the magnitude of the impulse that it must receive from the propeller, and show that this implies a propeller force of 200,000 N, which is within the operating limits of the propeller.

(c) This result assumes no friction. Carefully explain, using a momentum-transfer model, how including friction would qualitatively affect these results. (That is, will the forces involved get larger or smaller? How do you know?)

Rich-Context

C3R.1 You are the pilot of a jet plane traveling due north at 250 m/s. At a certain time, you see another plane at the same altitude at the 4 o'clock position relative to you and about 5 km away. Thirty seconds later, this plane is at the 3 o'clock position relative to you and 3 km away. Are you in danger of colliding with this plane?

C3R.2 Perhaps you have felt a garden hose exert a backward force on your hand when you are using a nozzle that creates a high-speed spray of water. Roughly estimate how long it would take the water coming out of a typical garden-hose nozzle to fill up a 2-quart jar [$\approx$ 2 liters $\approx$ 2000 cm³]; also make a guess about the water's speed in meters per second. Use your esti`mates and the fact that 1 cm³ of water has a mass of 1 g to estimate the magnitude of force that the contact interaction between the water and nozzle must exert on the outgoing water. Explain carefully why this is also the force that your hand must exert on the nozzle if you hold it at rest. Does your answer seem reasonable, in your experience?

Advanced

C3A.1 The duration of a "sufficiently short" time interval depends on the accuracy you require. Imagine that an object travels at a constant speed once around a circle in time Δt. How big can dt be (as a fraction of Δt) if the magnitude of $\vec{v}$ in equation C3.2 is to be correct within 0.1%?

ANSWERS TO EXERCISES

C3X.1 No, because the particle's direction of motion is changing with time.

C3X.2 $\vec{v} = [16 \text{ m/s}, -4.0 \text{ m/s}, -0.4 \text{ m/s}]$, $v = 16.5 \text{ m/s}$

C3X.3 The originally moving cart gains $\frac{1}{2}mv_0$ of backward momentum, and the other cart gains the same amount of forward momentum. The picture looks like this:

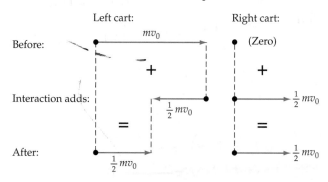

C3X.4 According to the diagram, the impulse the collision interaction contributes to the front cart is $[d\vec{p}]_C = \frac{4}{3}mv_0$ forward = 1.33 kg·m/s forward. If this is constant during the collision, then $\vec{F}_C = [d\vec{p}]_C/dt$, so $\text{mag}(\vec{F}_C) = \text{mag}([d\vec{p}]_C/dt) = \text{mag}([d\vec{p}]_C)/dt = (1.33 \text{ kg·m/s})/(0.05 \text{ s}) = 27 \text{ kg·m/s}^2 = 27 \text{ N}$.

C3X.5 The unknown mass is

$$m_2 = m_1 \frac{v_1}{v_2} = (0.5 \text{ kg})\left(\frac{3.0 \text{ m/s}}{2.0 \text{ m/s}}\right) = 0.75 \text{ kg} \quad \text{(C3.9)}$$

C3X.6 My weight is

$$155 \text{ lb}\left(\frac{4.45 \text{ N}}{1 \text{ lb}}\right) = 690 \text{ N} \quad \text{(C3.10)}$$

The weight of an adult human being generally lies between 400 and 1400 N.

C3X.7 A multitap picture will look something like that shown to the right. Each tap transfers a bit of eastward momentum (colored arrow) to the ball which when added to its original momentum (gray arrow), produces the ball's new momentum after each tap. We see that the ball's path bends eastward at a steadily increasing angle. In the three-reservoir model, the ball's x reservoir is steadily filled by its contact interaction with the

blowing air. The ball's z reservoir is simultaneously emptied and filled at the same rate by the ball's gravitational interaction with the earth and its contact interaction with the table; as a result, its level remains fixed at zero. The y (north) reservoir is unaffected: its level remains fixed and positive throughout.

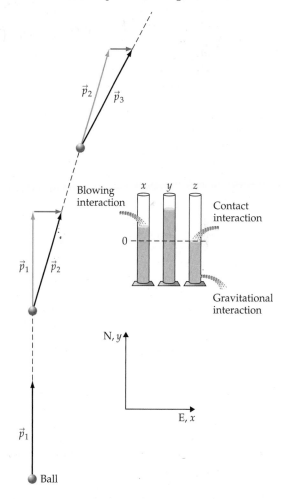

C3X.8 (a) The momentum components are written incorrectly with arrows, and the magnitude of the momentum vector is quoted as being negative. (b) The magnitude of a sum of momentum vectors is not equal to the sum of the magnitudes. (c) Vectors are set equal to scalar values, and the final equality involves division by a vector.

C4

Particles and Systems

▷ **Introduction**

▽ **Conservation of Momentum**

   Interactions Transfer Momentum

   Particles and Systems

   Applying Momentum Conservation

▷ **Conservation of Energy**

▷ **Conservation of Angular Momentum**

Chapter Overview

Introduction

Every object in our daily experience is a vast system of interacting elementary particles. The goal of this chapter is to show that *we can in fact treat interactions between macroscopic objects* (even *nonrigid* objects!) *as if they were interactions between particles.* This simplification makes a simple physics of macroscopic objects possible.

Section C4.1: Systems of Particles

A **system** of interacting particles is any set of particles having a well-defined boundary. An **extended object** is a system of elementary particles having a well-defined surface in space that serves as the system boundary. The macroscopic objects of our daily experience are extended objects according to this definition.

Any interaction that involves particles in a system can be placed into one of two categories. If *both* particles involved in the interaction are inside the system, we call it an **internal interaction;** if one particle involved in the interaction is inside the system and the other is outside, then we call it an **external interaction.**

Section C4.2: Conservation of Momentum

A system's **total momentum** is the vector sum of the momenta of all its particles:

$$\vec{p}_{\text{tot}} \equiv \vec{p}_1 + \vec{p}_2 + \cdots + \vec{p}_N \tag{C4.1}$$

Purpose: This equation defines a system's total momentum vector $\vec{p}_{\text{tot}}$.
Symbols: $\vec{p}_1, \vec{p}_2, \ldots, \vec{p}_N$ are the momenta of the system's N particles.
Notes: This equation applies to systems of N extended objects too (see section C4.4).

The distinction between internal and external interactions is important because *only external interactions can transfer momentum into or out of a system* and thus change a system's total momentum: internal interactions merely transfer momentum around *within* the system and thus cannot affect $\vec{p}_{\text{tot}}$. So, if we define an **isolated system** to be a system that participates in no external interactions, then

> **The law of conservation of momentum:** The total momentum $\vec{p}_{\text{tot}}$ of an *isolated* system does not change with time.

This is an important direct consequence of the principle of momentum transfer.

Section C4.3: A System's Center of Mass

A system's **center of mass** (CM) is a mathematical point in space whose vector position is the *weighted average* of the positions of the system's particles:

$$\vec{r}_{CM} \equiv \frac{1}{M}(m_1\vec{r}_1 + m_2\vec{r}_2 + \cdots + m_N\vec{r}_N) \qquad \text{(C4.2)}$$

Purpose: This equation defines the position $\vec{r}_{CM}$ of a system's CM.
Symbols: $\vec{r}_1, \vec{r}_2, \ldots, \vec{r}_N$ are the positions of the system's N particles; $m_1, m_2, \ldots, m_N$ are their masses; and $M \equiv m_1 + \cdots + m_N$ is the system's mass.
Limitations: There are none (this is a fundamental definition).

If a system consists of a set of *macroscopic* objects, we can find the system's center of mass simply by treating each macroscopic object as if it were a point particle located at its center of mass. We will not spend much time calculating CM positions. It will generally be enough in what follows to know that every system has a well-defined CM and that the CM of a symmetric object is typically at its geometric center.

Section C4.4: How the Center of Mass Moves

The definition of the center of mass directly implies that

$$\vec{p}_{tot} = M\vec{v}_{CM} \qquad \text{(C4.14)}$$

Purpose: This equation describes how a system's total momentum $\vec{p}_{tot}$ is related to the velocity $\vec{v}_{CM}$ of its center of mass.
Symbols: M is the system's total mass.
Limitations: Relativity requires adjusting the definition of $\vec{v}_{CM}$.

The center of mass of an *isolated* system thus moves at a constant velocity. If a system is *not* isolated, the total change in its momentum is due only to external interactions: $d\vec{p}_{tot} = [d\vec{p}]_{ext, A} + [d\vec{p}]_{ext, B} + \cdots$. Comparing this and $\vec{p}_{tot} = M\vec{v}_{CM}$ with $d\vec{p} = [d\vec{p}]_A + [d\vec{p}]_B + \cdots$ and $\vec{p} = m\vec{v}$ in chapter C3, we see the following:

The particle model: A system's center of mass responds to *external* interactions exactly as a point particle would respond to those interactions.

This *extremely* important simplifying principle makes a physics of macroscopic objects possible. Among other things, it implies that *all* the equations and ideas in chapter C3 describing the behavior of *particles* also apply to *systems* if we substitute "the system's center-of-mass position" for "the particle's position" and "*external* interactions" for "interactions."

Section C4.5: Inertial Reference Frames

One can find reference frames where Newton's first law fails. We will learn how to handle such **noninertial reference frames** in chapter N9, but for now we will attempt to do physics calculations only in **inertial reference frames** where Newton's first law holds. An ideal inertial frame would be a nonrotating frame floating in space far from any gravitating objects. In practice, we can treat a frame attached to the center of mass of a system as being inertial if (1) the frame is not rotating, (2) the system's *only* external interactions are *gravitational* interactions with objects far away compared to the size of both the system and the frame, and (3) we *ignore* those gravitational interactions. We say that such a frame **floats in space.** An example is a frame fixed to the earth's surface (although the earth's slow rotation makes such a frame slightly noninertial).

Section C4.6: Interactions with the Earth

Small objects interacting with the earth seem to gain or lose momentum without apparently affecting the earth's momentum. However, the momentum of the earth *does* change in such interactions (when viewed in an appropriate *inertial* frame); but because of the earth's huge mass, changes in the earth's velocity are negligible.

C4.1   Systems of Particles

Definition of a *system*

A **system** in physics is a set of interacting particles having a well-defined "boundary" that allows us to determine whether a given particle is inside or outside the system. We can define the boundary in any way we like as long as it does this job. (Note that a system boundary is a completely imaginary artifact that we superimpose on the universe to help us think more clearly about it.)

Definition of an *extended object*

An **extended object** is a material object with a well-defined *surface* in space that defines its boundary and encloses a nonzero volume. As we discussed in chapter C1, we can think of *any* material object as being a system of interacting elementary particles. An extended object is thus a special case of a system with a certain kind of boundary. The macroscopic objects of our daily experience are virtually all extended objects according to this definition. Figure C4.1 shows some examples of extended objects.

Definition of *internal* and *external* interactions

Any interaction involving at least one particle in a system can be placed into one of two categories. If *both* particles involved in the interaction are inside the system, we call it an **internal interaction;** if one of the two particles involved in the interaction is inside the system and the other is outside, then we call it an **external interaction.** For example, if our system is a baseball, the interactions that hold the baseball's particles together are *internal* interactions; the gravitational interactions between its particles and the earth's particles are *external* interactions.

Exercise C4X.1

Consider a system consisting of two billiard balls on a pool table. If the balls collide, is the contact interaction between the balls an internal or external interaction? How about the balls' contact interaction with the table?

C4.2   Conservation of Momentum

We define a system's **total momentum** $\vec{p}_{\text{tot}}$ to be the vector sum of the momenta of its constituent particles:

Definition of a system's total momentum

$$\vec{p}_{\text{tot}} \equiv \vec{p}_1 + \vec{p}_2 + \cdots + \vec{p}_N \qquad \text{(C4.1)}$$

Purpose: This equation defines a system's total momentum vector $\vec{p}_{\text{tot}}$.

Symbols: $\vec{p}_1, \vec{p}_2, \ldots, \vec{p}_N$ are the momenta of the system's N particles.

Note: This equation applies to systems of N extended objects, too (see section C4.4).

This definition is very clear and precise, but literally applying the definition to the task of calculating a system's total momentum would be hard in practice, because we would have to know the momenta of all its quarks, leptons, and field mediators. Fortunately, we will discover a more practical way to calculate this quantity in the next few sections.

Figure C4.1
Examples of extended objects.

Only *external* interactions can change a system's momentum

The momentum-transfer principle means that a system's internal interactions only transfer momentum back and forth *within* the system and therefore cannot affect a system's total momentum. *Only external interactions can transfer momentum into or out of a system* and thus change its total momentum.

If a system participates in *no* external interactions, we call it an **isolated system.** Since no momentum can flow either into or out of such a system, the following holds:

The law of conservation of momentum

The law of conservation of momentum: The total momentum $\vec{p}_{tot}$ of an *isolated* system is *conserved*; that is, it does not change with time.

This is a *central* consequence of the momentum-transfer principle, and it will be our sole focus of study in chapter C5. In fact, this law and the momentum-transfer principle are essentially two sides of the same coin: Although I have derived this law as a consequence of the momentum-transfer principle, I could have just as easily taken conservation of momentum to be more basic and derived the law of momentum transfer from it. Both are just different ways of expressing the consequences of the deep symmetry principle that the laws of physics are independent of where you are in the universe, as discussed in chapter C1.

C4.3   A System's Center of Mass

Now, in the newtonian model of mechanics, a particle's position is sharply defined and unambiguous, and so its velocity and momentum are also sharply defined, as discussed in sections C3.1 and C3.2. When we attempt to describe the motion of extended objects, we would like to be able to define the object's position in a similarly precise way. Newton found that the concept of the *center of mass* of a system of particles solves this problem.

Definition of a system's center of mass (CM)

The **center of mass** of *any* system of particles is a mathematical point whose position we define as follows:

$$\vec{r}_{CM} \equiv \frac{1}{M}(m_1\vec{r}_1 + m_2\vec{r}_2 + \cdots + m_N\vec{r}_N) \qquad (C4.2)$$

Purpose: This equation defines the position $\vec{r}_{CM}$ of a system's center of mass.

Symbols: $\vec{r}_1, \vec{r}_2, \ldots, \vec{r}_N$ are the positions of the system's N particles; $m_1, m_2, \ldots, m_N$ are their masses; and $M \equiv m_1 + \cdots + m_N$ is the system's mass.

Limitations: There are none (this is a fundamental definition).

Note that the position of a system's center of mass is essentially a *weighted average* that weights each particle's position in proportion to its mass.

In column vector notation, equation C4.2 becomes

$$\begin{bmatrix} x_{CM} \\ y_{CM} \\ z_{CM} \end{bmatrix} = \frac{1}{M}\left(m_1 \begin{bmatrix} x_1 \\ y_1 \\ z_1 \end{bmatrix} + m_2 \begin{bmatrix} x_2 \\ y_2 \\ z_2 \end{bmatrix} + \cdots + m_N \begin{bmatrix} x_N \\ y_N \\ z_N \end{bmatrix} \right) \qquad (C4.3)$$

which is equivalent to three separate component equations:

$$x_{CM} = \frac{1}{M}(m_1x_1 + m_2x_2 + \cdots + m_Nx_N) \qquad (C4.4a)$$

$$y_{CM} = \frac{1}{M}(m_1 y_1 + m_2 y_2 + \cdots + m_N y_N) \qquad (C4.4b)$$

$$z_{CM} = \frac{1}{M}(m_1 z_1 + m_2 z_2 + \cdots + m_N z_N) \qquad (C4.4c)$$

Does this definition make sense? Imagine a system consisting of only *two* particles separated by some distance D. For the sake of simplicity, let us choose a reference frame in which both particles lie on the x axis (so that both have zero y and z coordinates) and where the first particle is located at the origin, meaning that $x_1 = 0$ and $x_2 = D$ (see figure C4.2). Equation C4.3 then reduces to

Checking the definition in a
simple two-particle case

$$\begin{bmatrix} x_{CM} \\ y_{CM} \\ z_{CM} \end{bmatrix} = \frac{1}{M}\left(m_1 \begin{bmatrix} 0 \\ 0 \\ 0 \end{bmatrix} + m_2 \begin{bmatrix} D \\ 0 \\ 0 \end{bmatrix} \right) = \frac{1}{M} \begin{bmatrix} m_2 D \\ 0 \\ 0 \end{bmatrix} \qquad (C4.5)$$

meaning that in this particular case

$$x_{CM} = \frac{m_2}{M} D = \left(\frac{m_2}{m_1 + m_2} \right) D \qquad y_{CM} = z_{CM} = 0 \qquad (C4.6)$$

We see from equation C4.6 that the center of mass of a two-particle system

1. *Lies along the line connecting the two particles* (the x axis in this particular case).
2. Has an x-position that lies *between* the two particles, as $m_2/(m_1 + m_2) < 1$.
3. Is exactly halfway between the two particles (at $x = \frac{1}{2}D$) when $m_1 = m_2$.
4. Is closer to the more massive particle if $m_1 \neq m_2$. For example, if $m_2 < m_1$, then $m_2/(m_1 + m_2) < \frac{1}{2}$, so the CM is closer to m_1.

These features probably coincide with whatever intuitive sense you might have about where the center of mass of a two-particle system ought to be.

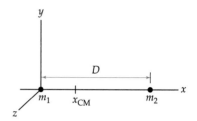

Figure C4.2
The center of mass of a system consisting of two point particles. The center of mass shown here would be accurate if $m_1 \approx 2m_2$.

Exercise C4X.2

Imagine that particle A has a mass of 22 kg and particle B has a mass of 2.0 kg. These particles are separated by a distance of 1.2 m. Where is the center of mass of this system relative to the position of particle A? (*Hint:* Choose your reference frame so that this system looks like that in figure C4.2.)

We can, in principle, find the center of mass of any multiparticle system at a given time in a similar way by averaging the weighted vector positions of each of its elementary particles at that time. However, this is impossible in practice because of the outrageously huge number of elementary particles involved. A more practical (but approximate) method would be to break the object up into a moderate number of macroscopic chunks that are still small enough that we can consider the particles in each to have essentially the same position. For example, when computing a galaxy's center of mass, we can, to an excellent degree of approximation, treat its stars as if they were point particles, rather than go all the way back to the galaxy's quarks and leptons (in a galaxy-sized reference frame, all the particles in a given star *will* have the same position, unless we are keeping track of positions to better than 1 part in 10^{12}!).

Finding the center of mass
by breaking the system into
small chunks

Example C4.1

Problem   A water molecule consists of one oxygen atom (O) and two hydrogen atoms (H) in roughly the configuration shown in figure C4.3a (actually, the angle between the arms is more like 105°, but taking it to be 90° makes the calculation simpler). The mass of the oxygen atom is very nearly 16 times that of the hydrogen atom, and the distance D between the hydrogen and oxygen nuclei is measured to be 0.096 nanometer (nm) (1 nm = 10^{-9} m). Note that virtually all the mass of any atom is concentrated in its nucleus, which is typically about 10^5 times smaller than the atom. Where is the center of mass of this system?

Figure C4.3
(a) A schematic diagram of a water molecule (the sizes of the atomic nuclei have been greatly exaggerated and the electrons have been ignored). (b) One possible reference frame for analyzing this system.

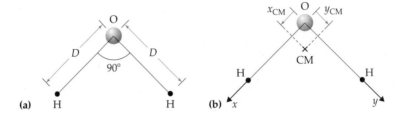

Solution   Since virtually all the mass of each atom is in its nucleus, and since these nuclei are so small that particles in the nucleus essentially all have the same position compared to the scale molecule as a whole, we will model the molecule as a system of *three* particles (corresponding to the three nuclei), rather than go back to the molecule's constituent quarks and electrons.

It is always helpful to choose a reference frame where as many quantities are zero as possible. Note that in the frame shown in figure C4.3b, the z-positions of all the nuclei are zero. In addition, the y-position of the hydrogen atom on the left is zero, the x-position of the hydrogen atom on the right is zero, and both the x and y-positions of the oxygen nucleus are zero. Let us define m to be the unknown mass of the hydrogen atom. Equation C4.3 then implies that

$$\begin{bmatrix} x_{CM} \\ y_{CM} \\ z_{CM} \end{bmatrix} = \frac{1}{18m}\left(16m\begin{bmatrix} 0 \\ 0 \\ 0 \end{bmatrix} + m\begin{bmatrix} D \\ 0 \\ 0 \end{bmatrix} + m\begin{bmatrix} 0 \\ D \\ 0 \end{bmatrix} \right) = \begin{bmatrix} D/18 \\ D/18 \\ 0 \end{bmatrix} \quad \text{(C4.7)}$$

This means that $x_{CM} = y_{CM} = D/18 = 0.0053$ nm $= 5.3$ picometers (pm) in this reference frame, which means that the center of mass is a distance of roughly

$$\text{mag}(\vec{r}_{CM}) = \sqrt{x_{CM}^2 + y_{CM}^2 + z_{CM}^2} = \sqrt{\left(\frac{D}{18}\right)^2 + \left(\frac{D}{18}\right)^2 + 0^2}$$

$$= \frac{D}{18}\sqrt{2} = 7.5 \text{ pm} \quad \text{(C4.8)}$$

from the origin (i.e., the oxygen nucleus). Since the position of the center of mass has equal x and y components, it is located directly *downward* from the oxygen nucleus in figure C4.3b.

Important things to know
about the center of mass

We will *not* spend time actually computing the centers of mass for extended objects in this text. It will be enough for our purposes to know that (1) every extended object or system *has* a well-defined center of mass and (2) the center of mass of a *symmetric* object, such as a sphere, cube, or cylinder, is located at that object's geometric center (as one might expect).

One can also prove the following useful theorem:

We can calculate the position of the center of mass of any *set* of extended objects by treating each object as if it were a point particle with all its mass concentrated at its *individual* center of mass.

A useful theorem for computing the center of mass of a system of extended objects

In outline, the proof goes like this: The definition of the center of mass says that $M\vec{r}_{CM} = m_1\vec{r}_1 + m_2\vec{r}_2 + \cdots + m_N\vec{r}_N$. Group the terms in the sum on the right into sets that each pertain to the particles in a single object. By the same equation applied to each object, the terms for object A add up to $m_A\vec{r}_{CM,A}$, the terms for object B add up to $m_B\vec{r}_{CM,B}$, and so on. Therefore,

$$M\vec{r}_{CM} = m_A\vec{r}_{CM,A} + m_B\vec{r}_{CM,B} + \cdots$$

$$\Rightarrow \quad \vec{r}_{CM} = \frac{1}{M}(m_A\vec{r}_{CM,A} + m_B\vec{r}_{CM,B} + \cdots) \qquad (C4.9)$$

just as if the objects were particles located at their centers of mass.

This theorem makes it easy to find the center of mass of a system of objects when we know where their centers of mass are. So, for example, the center of mass of two *spheres* with masses m_1 and m_2 whose centers are separated by a distance D is the same as that of two *point particles* with masses m_1 and m_2 separated by a distance D, no matter how large the spheres might be.

Exercise C4X.3

In a binary star system (where two stars orbit each other), one star has 3 times the mass of the other. If the stars are 100 million km apart, how far is this system's center of mass from the center of the larger star?

C4.4   How the Center of Mass Moves

Why do we define the center of mass as we do? It turns out that because of the principle that interactions mediate momentum transfers, a system's center of mass (as we have defined it) moves in an especially simple and predictable way in response to external interactions involving its particles.

Why we define the center of mass as we do

Imagine that we look at the system at the beginning and end of a very short time interval dt. Let the positions of its particles at the beginning and at the end of the interval be $\vec{r}_{1i}, \vec{r}_{2i}, \ldots, \vec{r}_{Ni}$ and $\vec{r}_{1f}, \vec{r}_{2f}, \ldots, \vec{r}_{Nf}$, respectively. The position of the system's center of mass at the beginning of the interval is therefore

$$\vec{r}_{CM,i} \equiv \frac{1}{M}(m_1\vec{r}_{1i} + m_2\vec{r}_{2i} + \cdots + m_N\vec{r}_{Ni}) \qquad (C4.10)$$

and an analogous formula gives $\vec{r}_{CM,f}$. The change in the CM's position during this interval is therefore

$$dr_{CM} \equiv \vec{r}_{CM,f} - \vec{r}_{CM,i}$$

$$= \frac{1}{M}(m_1\vec{r}_{1f} + m_2\vec{r}_{2f} + \cdots + m_N\vec{r}_{Nf}) - \frac{1}{M}(m_1\vec{r}_{1i} + m_2\vec{r}_{2i} + \cdots + m_N\vec{r}_{Ni})$$

$$= \frac{1}{M}(m_1[\vec{r}_{1f} - \vec{r}_{1i}] + m_2[\vec{r}_{2f} - \vec{r}_{2i}] + \cdots + m_N[\vec{r}_{Nf} - \vec{r}_{Ni}])$$

$$= \frac{1}{M}(m_1\,d\vec{r}_1 + m_2\,d\vec{r}_2 + \cdots + m_N\,d\vec{r}_N) \qquad (C4.11)$$

where $d\vec{r}_1, d\vec{r}_2, \ldots, d\vec{r}_N$ are the particles' tiny displacements during this interval. If we now multiply both sides by M and divide by dt, we get

$$M\frac{d\vec{r}_{CM}}{dt} = m_1\frac{d\vec{r}_1}{dt} + m_2\frac{d\vec{r}_2}{dt} + \cdots + m_N\frac{d\vec{r}_N}{dt} \tag{C4.12}$$

But the definitions of velocity and momentum therefore imply that

$$M\vec{v}_{CM} = m_1\vec{v}_1 + m_2\vec{v}_2 + \cdots + m_N\vec{v}_N = \vec{p}_1 + \vec{p}_2 + \cdots + \vec{p}_N \tag{C4.13}$$

By the definition of a system's total momentum, then,

How a system's momentum is linked to the motion of its center of mass

$$\vec{p}_{tot} = M\vec{v}_{CM} \tag{C4.14}$$

Purpose: This equation describes how a system's total momentum $\vec{p}_{tot}$ is related to the velocity $\vec{v}_{CM}$ of its center of mass.
Symbols: M is the system's total mass.
Limitations: Relativity requires adjusting the definition of $\vec{v}_{CM}$.

So, to find a system's total momentum, all that we need to do is to multiply its total mass M by the velocity of its center of mass $\vec{v}_{CM}$, *exactly as if the system were a single particle located at its center of mass!* This follows directly from the definitions of velocity, momentum, and the center of mass.

Exercise C4X.4

Consider a system of extended objects A, B, ... Use equation C4.14 and an argument like that for the system-of-objects theorem to show that we can calculate the total momentum of such a system as follows:

$$\vec{p}_{tot} = \vec{p}_{tot,A} + \vec{p}_{tot,B} + \cdots = m_A\vec{v}_{CM,A} + m_B\vec{v}_{CM,B} + \cdots \tag{C4.15}$$

This shows that equation C4.1 applies to systems of objects as well as particles.

Newton's first law for extended objects

Equation C4.14, in conjunction with the law of conservation of momentum, implies that an *isolated* system's $\vec{v}_{CM}$ is a constant. Since an extended object is a system, if an isolated object's center of mass is at rest, it will remain at rest; and if it is moving, it will continue to move in the same direction at a constant speed. This is simply *Newton's first law*, except we now see that it applies to arbitrary systems, not just to particles! (See problem C4S.8 for a discussion of how we can apply this result to the problem of finding planets orbiting distant stars.)

Exercise C4X.5

Imagine a 60-kg person holding a 6-kg stone at rest at the origin of a reference frame in deep space. The person throws the stone in the $+x$ direction. If after 5 s the stone has traveled 30 m from the origin in that frame, how many meters has the person moved in the $-x$ direction? (*Hint:* A system in "deep space" is isolated, by sheer distance, from significant external interactions.)

What if the system is not isolated? Because *internal* interactions do *not* change a system's momentum, the change in a system's total momentum must be due to impulses delivered from external interactions: $d\vec{p}_{tot} = [d\vec{p}]_{ext,A} + [d\vec{p}]_{ext,B} + \cdots$. If we compare this equation and $\vec{p}_{tot} = M\vec{v}_{CM}$ to

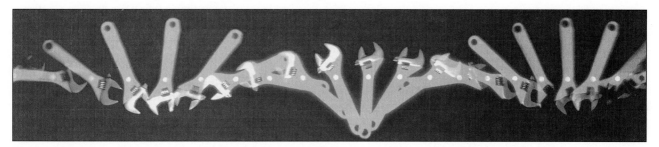

Figure C4.4
A multiflash top view of a wrench that rotates as it slides toward the right on a horizontal surface. Note that the wrench's center of mass follows a straight line (although it slows down due to external friction interactions with the surface).

the analogous equations for particles $d\vec{p} = [d\vec{p}]_A + [d\vec{p}]_B + \cdots$ and $\vec{p} = m\vec{v}$ (equations C3.5 and C3.4), we see the following:

> **The particle model:** A system's center of mass responds to its *external* interactions *exactly* as a point particle would respond to those interactions.

We can treat a system's CM as if it were a particle!

Since extended objects qualify as "systems," this statement applies to all extended objects.

This means that every idea or equation that we have formulated up to now for interacting *particles* also applies to any *system* of particles, as long as we substitute the system quantities $\vec{r}_{CM}$, $\vec{v}_{CM}$, and $\vec{p}_{tot}$ for the particle quantities $\vec{r}$, $\vec{v}$, and $\vec{p}$, respectively, and put the qualifier *external* in front of any references to *interactions*. If we are interested only in the motion of a system's CM in response to external interactions, we can accurately model any system as if it were a structureless particle located at its center of mass (see figure C4.4).

This is a *very* important result! Imagine how difficult it would be to do physics (or even stay alive!) if the motion of an extended object depended on the detailed character of its *internal* interactions (which are so complicated we could never hope to understand them in detail). It would be hard even to play catch in your backyard, for example, if the motion of a thrown ball depended on the details of how the atoms *inside* the ball happen to be interacting with one another.

Indeed, this idea is the only thing that makes a physics of extended objects practical. It is also so basic that we typically take it for granted. We have just seen, though, that this idea is a nonobvious consequence of the idea that *interactions transfer momentum*. Because *that* principle in turn is valid in all accepted physical theories, the idea that we can model a system's response to external interactions by ignoring internal interactions and treating the system as if it were a particle is also valid in all current theories of physics (although *particle* is defined somewhat differently in quantum mechanics). This is one of the most important and useful principles in all of physics!

From now on, I will use this model implicitly whenever we deal with extended objects. Whenever I refer to an extended object's *position, velocity, or momentum*, please understand that I am really talking about the position, velocity, or momentum of that object's *center of mass*. Whenever I talk about the interactions that an object participates in, please understand that I am really talking about the *external* interactions involving the object's particles.

Conventions for the future

We define a **rigid** object to be an object whose dimensions and shape do not change significantly, even in response to interactions. Many everyday objects are at least approximately rigid. Note that if an object is rigid and is not

Rigid objects

rotating, any given point in the object has a fixed position relative to its center of mass. This means that as the object moves, its center of mass and the given point will undergo the same displacement in a given interval of time, which in turn means the two points have the same *velocity*. Thus if we want to determine the velocity of a cart's center of mass, for example, we can instead measure the velocity of *any* given point on the cart, say, its front edge. You have probably done this intuitively in the past; now you know *why* this is a reasonable thing to do.

C4.5   Inertial Reference Frames

In chapter C2, I stated that in principle we could attach a reference frame to any object that we choose. However, it turns out that some choices are better than others. Before we can dig into realistic applications of the ideas in this chapter, we need to discuss this issue in greater detail.

Newton's first law is the starting point of our model of mechanics. If an isolated object does *not* move with a constant velocity, then the momentum of an object can change without receiving any transfers from interactions, the total momentum of a system is not conserved, and our whole model falls apart.

Now, it is technically impossible in any reference frame near the surface of the earth to find a *truly* isolated object, because *any* object near the earth interacts gravitationally with it, and we cannot shield an object from gravity. But let us imagine a small ball with a tiny jet engine that exerts an upward thrust on the ball that exactly cancels the ball's weight, so that the net momentum flow from these interactions is always zero. If there are no *other* interactions acting on the ball, it should then behave just as an isolated object does.

So according to Newton's first law, if we place such a ball at rest in midair, it should remain floating there exactly at rest indefinitely. Perhaps you can imagine that if we did this in a reference frame attached to the earth, the ball *would* in fact remain floating at rest. However, we can also easily imagine reference frames where we know intuitively that the ball would *not*.

For example, imagine that we set up a reference frame in the enclosed empty space in the back of a large truck. Our jet ball should float nicely at rest if the truck is not moving. You may even be able to believe that the ball will float at rest relative to the truck if we release it when the truck is moving smoothly at a constant velocity relative to the ground. But what would happen to the ball if the driver were to slam on the brakes? You *know* intuitively that the ball would fly toward the front of the truck (partly because you have seen loose objects in your car behave in this way under similar circumstances!). If the truck pulls away from a stop sign, you also know that the ball will zoom toward the back of the truck. You know that if the truck rounds a curve, the ball will drift to the side of the truck farthest from the curve's center. If the truck were placed on a rotating turntable, you know the ball would drift away from the axis of rotation.

We cannot explain this by assuming that somehow the ball starts interacting with something. It does not participate in any significant contact interactions, and assuming the ball is uncharged and unmagnetic, it cannot participate in any long-range interactions except gravitational interactions, and it is not plausible that pressing the brakes on a truck magically creates a planet-sized mass in front of the truck! We are forced to admit that under these circumstances an isolated object is *not* observed in the truck's reference frame to obey Newton's first law.

Inertial reference frames are reference frames in which we find Newton's first law to be obeyed; **noninertial reference frames** are frames (such as the

Testing frames with Newton's first law

Example frames which Newton's first law fails

The definition of *inertial* and *noninertial* frames

truck frame in question) in which we find it to be violated. The models of motion we have been developing work in inertial reference frames but fail in noninertial reference frames. There *are* actually ways of making sense of noninertial reference frames (which we will explore in chapter N9); but until then, we will only make progress by taking the following pledge (hold up your right hand, please!): *I solemnly swear never to analyze a physical process, either qualitatively or quantitatively, using a (significantly) noninertial reference frame.* The consequences of violating this pledge at this point in the course will be nonsensical or paradoxical results.

How do we distinguish an inertial frame from a noninertial frame? Ultimately the only way is to *test Newton's first law.* Indeed, most contemporary physicists will tell you that the real importance of Newton's first law is not so much that it clearly states the distinction between Newton's and Aristotle's models of motion (although that is why *Newton* thought it was important) but that it *defines* the crucial distinction between inertial and noninertial reference frames.

Distinguishing inertial from noninertial frames

However, jet-powered floating balls are hard to come by, so let me suggest general guidelines for choosing frames. A truly inertial reference frame would be a nonrotating reference frame located in deep space far from gravitating objects. Such frames are, however, accessible only in our imaginations.

However, one of the fundamental predictions of the theory of general relativity is that a frame attached to the center of mass of a system is (for all practical purposes) physically indistinguishable from a frame in deep space *if* (1) the frame is not rotating, (2) the system's *only* external interactions are *gravitational* interactions with objects whose centers are far away compared to the size of both the system and the frame, and (3) we *ignore* those external gravitational interactions (!). Physicists conventionally call such frames *freely falling frames* (because, like a freely falling object near the earth, their only external interactions are gravitational); but I find it more helpful to think of such frames as **floating in space,** so that I do not focus on the external gravitational interactions that general relativity instructs us to ignore.

Freely floating reference frames

An example is a frame attached to the center of mass of an orbiting Space Shuttle. The *external* interactions for the system consisting of the orbiting Space Shuttle and all its contents are purely gravitational interactions with the earth and more distant astronomical objects. The earth's center is very far from the Space Shuttle compared to the Space Shuttle's size (and other astronomical objects are even more distant). So according to my assertion, a reference frame attached to this system's center of mass should behave as if it were an inertial frame, if we ignore all external gravitational interactions. And this is true! Perhaps you have seen video images from the Space Shuttle where objects released at rest float at rest and objects that are launched continue to move with a constant velocity. It therefore *appears* that Newton's first law is satisfied in the Space Shuttle's reference frame (see figure C4.5).

An example: the Space Shuttle

Are these objects really isolated? Not *really,* according to the newtonian model we have been developing—the Space Shuttle and all its contents *do* interact gravitationally with their surroundings. The earth's gravitational field is actually quite strong where the Space Shuttle orbits (an orbiting Space Shuttle is only a few percent farther from the earth's center than you are right now!). However, in spite of this, objects in the Space Shuttle frame behave *as if* they were in an inertial frame where *all* external gravitational interactions have been shut off!

Another frame of this type would be a nonrotating frame attached to the center of mass of a system consisting of the earth and its contents. This system participates in external gravitational interactions with the moon, sun, and other astronomical objects, which are all pretty distant compared to the

Figure C4.5
Floating objects initially at rest in the Space Shuttle's reference frame remain at rest.

Another example: a nonrotating reference frame attached to the earth's center

Frames attached to the earth's surface are *almost* inertial

size of the earth (although the moon is only about 60 earth radii away). So we can *pretend* that a reference frame attached to the earth's center of mass is an inertial frame if we ignore all gravitational interactions with other astronomical objects.

Of course, we daily work with reference frames attached to the earth's *surface*. These are *almost* as good as a nonrotating reference frame attached to the earth's center except that such frames do rotate once a day with respect to the rest of the universe along with the earth. Since the earth's rotation is pretty slow, these frames are only very *slightly* noninertial, and you actually have to look pretty hard to see any violations of Newton's first law. (But such violations do exist, offering hard evidence that the earth does indeed rotate.)

Nice features of such *effectively inertial* frames

Newtonian mechanics also offers an explanation as to *why* freely floating reference frames are effectively inertial when we ignore all external gravitational interactions, an explanation that we will discuss in detail in chapter N9. But for now, let us accept this gift from nature with gratitude. It actually makes doing physics much simpler because (1) we do not have practical access to any *real* (deep space) inertial frames and (2) it is nice that we do not have to even *think* about gravitational interactions with distant astronomical objects, which would increase the complexity of our calculations.

Exercise C4X.6

Should we expect a reference frame attached to any of the following objects to be an effectively inertial frame? Why or why not? (a) A merry-go-round. (b) An airplane accelerating for takeoff. (c) An elevator that falls frictionlessly in its shaft after its cable has been cut.

C4.6   Interactions with the Earth

A puzzle: Does the earth's momentum change when interacting with you?

Here is a puzzle. Imagine that you jump vertically up from the floor. As you start your leap, your contact interaction with the floor gives you a significant upward momentum. Your partner in this interaction is the earth itself. So as you push against the ground, the model developed in chapter C3 predicts that the earth must get an downward impulse from the contact interaction that is equal in magnitude to the downward impulse you get. If it does not, the total momentum of the system consisting of you and the earth will not be conserved.

But this seems absurd! The earth is *obviously* unmoved by your jump and therefore has zero momentum always. But your momentum definitely changes, so the total momentum of this system is *not* conserved, and the law of conservation of momentum is therefore false!

Choosing the right reference frame

This is an example of the paradoxes we can generate by violating the pledge we took in section C4.5. If we use a reference frame attached to the earth (as we often do), then the earth is always at rest in that frame by definition, and momentum is indeed *not* conserved. An earth-based frame is *not* a good one to use in this particular case, though. If we want to study how the earth responds to interactions, clearly we need to use a frame in which the earth is free to move!

According to section C4.5, the *right* reference frame to use in a case like this is a reference frame fixed to the center of mass of the *system* containing both you and the earth. The external interactions involving this *system* are purely gravitational with distant astronomical objects, so a frame attached to its center of mass satisfies the qualifications for a "freely floating frame" and is therefore effectively inertial. By contrast, a frame attached to the earth does *not* qualify, because in *this* case the system to which the frame is attached (the earth) has a *non*gravitational external interaction with *you*. If we use such a noninertial frame, we can *expect* absurd results. So to verify that the earth recoils from your jump, we would have to set up a frame tied to the system's center of mass and measure the earth's velocity relative to that frame.

The earth does move in a valid reference frame, but not very much!

Let us try to estimate how difficult this would be. Let us estimate that a person's mass is roughly 50 kg, and that a person jumping off the floor can achieve a vertical speed of about 3 m/s (6.6 mi/h) very roughly. The impulse that the contact interaction between you and the earth delivers to you is very roughly 150 kg·m/s upward. The earth should therefore get an impulse of 150 kg·m/s downward. How fast will it move in response in an inertial frame?

The earth has a mass of about 6×10^{24} kg. If the earth is originally at rest and then gains 150 kg·m/s of momentum, it (or more correctly, its center of mass) will be moving (just after you leave the ground) at a speed of very roughly

$$v_f \equiv \text{mag}(\vec{v}_f) = \frac{\text{mag}(\vec{p}_{\text{earth}})}{m_{\text{earth}}} = \frac{150 \text{ kg·m/s}}{6 \times 10^{24} \text{ kg}} \approx 25 \times 10^{-24} \text{ m/s} \quad \text{(C4.16)}$$

If the earth continued moving undisturbed at this rate for 10^{15} years or so (about 100,000 times the age of the universe), it would only move about a meter. If the contact interaction lasted approximately 0.4 s, the earth would move about 10^{-23} m, which is about 100 million times smaller than an atomic nucleus.

In other words, the earth's motion in this circumstance is not just *hard* to detect, it is so impossibly small that we can hardly imagine *ever* being able to detect it. Therefore our model is not at all inconsistent with the observation that the earth seems to remain at rest: Even though our model predicts that the earth's center of mass does *not* remain at rest in a valid reference frame, it also predicts that the motion will be so small as to be completely unobservable.

Here is an analogy. Imagine that you take a bucket of water from the ocean. Did you notice that the ocean's level falls a bit? No? Why not? You probably believe that the ocean's level really *does* fall a little bit: You intuitively know that if you take some water from the ocean, it does indeed have less water than it had before. But because the ocean is so immense, taking a bucket of water from it does not *measurably* affect its level. Similarly, the earth (because of its enormous mass) can provide (or absorb) impulses without measurable effect.

An analogy

The same kind of argument applies to situations where an object collides with a wall or barrier and either bounces off or is brought to rest. The object's horizontal momentum clearly changes, so the earth must get a momentum transfer in the opposite direction, but the earth's motion will not measurably change.

The bottom line is that to resolve the paradox *intellectually*, we have to imagine using a reference frame attached not to the earth's center but to the center of mass of the system that contains you and the earth. However, we have just seen that even when we use such a frame, the change in the earth's motion due to normal, human-scale interactions is immeasurably small (because the earth's mass is so immense). Therefore, for all purposes *other* than calculating the earth's own response to an interaction, a frame fixed to the earth's center of mass is indistinguishable from a frame fixed to the *system*'s center of mass: the distinction between these frames is completely immeasurable. We will, therefore, continue to use earth-based frames without worrying about this issue too much. We simply keep in mind that the earth can absorb or supply impulses without discernible effect.

For virtually all purposes, a frame attached to the earth is just fine

Exercise C4X.7

A friend proposes the following doomsday scenario: What if China's leaders arrange for its entire population ($\approx 10^9$ people) to jump simultaneously from ladders to the ground. Would this not wreak global havoc as the earth shifted in response? Using a system-based reference frame in which the earth is initially at rest, estimate the speed of the earth's center of mass just before the entire population of China hits the ground. Do you think that the motion of the earth's center of mass in this case is something to worry about? (*Hint:* Estimate the gravitational impulse one gets in the process of falling a few meters.)

TWO-MINUTE PROBLEMS

C4T.1 Which of the following things qualifies as being an "extended object"? For each object, answer T if it qualifies, F if it does not, and D if it is debatable.
   a. An electron. F
   b. An atom. T
   c. A rock. F
   d. A human being. F
   e. A swarm of bees. T
   f. The earth's atmosphere. T
   g. The water in an ocean current. F
   h. A cluster of galaxies. T

C4T.2 The following diagrams show hypothetical results for collisions between two identical balls floating in space. The white ball was initially moving to the right along the dotted line before it hit the gray ball, which was initially at rest. (The collision is not necessarily head-on.) The arrows depict the balls' final velocities. Which outcomes are physically possible? For each case, answer T if it is, F if not.

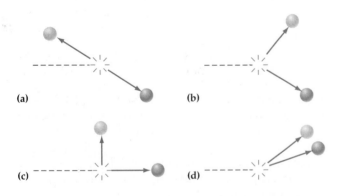

C4T.3 Consider a system consisting of two particles, one with 3 times the mass of the other. If the distance between the particles is 1.0 m, the system's center of mass is what distance from the lighter object?
   A. ≈ 1.0 m
   B. 0.75 m
   C. 0.66 m
   D. 0.33 m
   E. 0.25 m
   F. Other (specify)

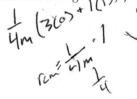

C4T.4 In example C4.1, if we had modeled the atoms as solid spheres instead of point nuclei, we would have gotten the same result for the center of mass, true (T) or false (F)?

C4T.5 In a reference frame fixed on the sun, which do you think follows the straighter path?
   A. The earth.
   B. The moon.
   C. The center of mass of the earth-moon system.

C4T.6 Which of the following would be an appropriate inertial reference frame for analyzing the effects on the earth of the gravitational interaction between the earth and the moon? Answer T if this frame would be okay, F if not.
   a. A frame attached to the earth's surface.
   b. A nonrotating frame attached to the earth's CM.
   c. A nonrotating frame attached to the CM of the earth-moon system.
   d. A nonrotating frame attached to the sun's CM.
   e. A nonrotating frame attached to the solar system's CM.

HOMEWORK PROBLEMS

Basic Skills

C4B.1 The nuclei of the hydrogen and chlorine atoms in an HCl molecule are 0.13 nanometer (nm) apart. How far from the nucleus of the chlorine atom is the molecule's center of mass? (The mass of the chlorine nucleus is roughly 35 times that of the hydrogen nucleus. Electron masses are negligible.)

C4B.2 Consider a system consisting of two point particles A and B. The particles are 25 cm apart, and the distance between particle A and the system's center of mass is *[handwritten at top: $r_1 = (0,0)$ $r_{cm} = 5 cm$ $r_2 = (25,0)$ $r_{cm} = \frac{1}{m}(m_1 r_1 + m_2 r_2)$ $5 = \frac{1}{A+B}(A(0) + 25(B))$ $5 = \frac{25B}{A+B}$ $A = 5$ $A+B = 5$ $B = 1$ $A = 4$]*

5 cm. What is the mass of particle B compared to the mass of A?

C4B.3 Two particles with a mass of 1.0 kg lie on along the x axis at $x = \pm50$ cm, respectively. Two particles also lie on the y axis. One, with mass 1.0 kg, is at $y = +40$ cm; and the other, with mass 2.0 kg, is at $y = -40$ cm. Where is the center of mass of this system?

C4B.4 In a certain reference frame, a 0.20-kg point particle lies 22 cm due north of the origin, another 0.15-kg particle lies 38 cm due west of the origin, while a 0.40-kg particle lies at the origin. Locate the center of mass of this system in this reference frame.

C4B.5 How far from the earth's geometric center is the center of mass of the earth-moon system? Is this inside the earth? The earth has a mass of 6.0×10^{24} kg and a radius of 6380 km. The moon has a mass of 7.4×10^{22} kg, and its center orbits about 384,000 km from the earth's center. (Note that the earth and moon are *not* particles!)

[handwritten: 384,000 $\frac{1}{7.4 \times 10^{22} + 6 \times 10^{24}}(0 + \text{...})$ r_{cm}]

C4B.6 You want to predict how the sun reacts to its gravitational interaction with Jupiter. Which would be the best place to attach the center of a nonrotating reference frame for the purposes of this analysis, the center of mass of the sun, that of Jupiter, or that of the solar system as a whole? Justify your choice or choices, and explain why the other choices would not be appropriate.

Synthetic

C4S.1 Prove that in a two-particle system, the distance between the system's center of mass and each particle is inversely proportional to that particle's mass. That is, if d_A and d_B are the distances between the system's center of mass and particles A and B, respectively, show that $d_A/d_B = m_B/m_A$ (note the order reversal!).

C4S.2 In a certain piece of modern sculpture, four iron spheres are connected in a line by lightweight rods. The separation between each sphere's geometric center and the next along the line is 42 cm. The spheres decrease in size along the line; their masses are 44 kg, 22 kg, 11 kg and 5.5 kg respectively; and their diameters are 22 cm, 17 cm, 14 cm, and 11 cm respectively. The artist wants to suspend this system of spheres by a single wire so that it rotates ponderously in the breeze above the viewers' heads. We will see in unit N that the appropriate place to attach the wire is at the system's center of mass. Where is this point (relative to the center of the most massive sphere)?

C4S.3 Estimate how far you would have to raise your personal center of mass to clear a bar 1.8 m high when performing a high jump. (*Hints:* What experiment might you perform to find the vertical position of your personal center of mass? Experienced high jumpers arrange their bodies nearly horizontally; why? How far above the bar do you think your center

of mass would need to go? Make some thoughtful estimates and explain your choices.)

C4S.4 Two space walkers, one with a mass of 120 kg and the other with a mass of 85 kg, hold on to the ends of a lightweight cable 12 m long. The astronauts are originally at rest in deep space. How will this system's center of mass move? If the astronauts then start pulling themselves toward each other along the cable until they meet, roughly how far will the less massive astronaut move? Does your answer depend on which astronaut is more active in the pulling process?

C4S.5 An asteroid is spotted moving directly toward the center of Starbase Alpha. The frightened residents fire a missile at the asteroid, which breaks it into two chunks, one with 2.4 times the mass of the other. The chunks both pass the starbase at the same time. If the lighter chunk passes 1800 m from one edge of the 2.2-km-wide starbase, will the other chunk hit or miss the starbase?

C4S.6 In a test of a new missile defense system, a missile is fired on a trajectory that would directly strike a certain bunker. A laser flash from the bunker ignites the missile's fuel, causing it to explode into two fragments, one with 1.8 times the mass of the other. If the fragments land at the same time 45 m apart, by how much does the larger fragment miss hitting the bunker? Ignore the effects of air resistance. (*Hint:* The external gravitational interaction between the missile and the earth would have caused the missile's center of mass to reach the ground at the location of the bunker if the missile had not exploded.)

C4S.7 The sun has a mass of 2×10^{30} kg, while Jupiter has a mass of about 1.9×10^{27} kg. If Jupiter is about 7.8×10^8 km from the sun, what is the approximate radius of the sun's motion about the solar system's center of mass due to its interaction with Jupiter? (Ignore the rest of the planets.) Compare this to the radius of the sun, which is about 700,000 km.

C4S.8 Even with the best telescopes currently available, planets orbiting even the stars closest to the earth are too dim compared to their parent stars to be imaged directly. However, one might indirectly detect a planet's presence by observing its gravitational effect on the star. Assuming that the star-planet system is very far from other stars, it will be essentially isolated, so its center of mass should move in a straight line. If the planet's mass is large enough, the system's center of mass will be displaced significantly from the star's center of mass. When the planet orbits the star, therefore, the planet and the star really both orbit the system's center of mass (like a pair of waltzing ballroom dancers), as shown in figure C4.6. We might therefore hope to detect a planet by observing how much a star's position "wobbles" around its general line of motion.

How difficult would this be? Assume that the star in question is a red dwarf that has a mass of about 0.30 times that of the sun (whose mass is 2.0×10^{30} kg) and that the planet has 1.5 times the mass of Jupiter (whose mass is 1.9×10^{27} kg) orbiting at a distance of about 1.5×10^{12} m (about 10 times the distance from the earth to the sun).

(a) About how far is the star's center of mass from the system's center of mass?

(b) If the star is 8.1 ly from us, what will be the star's maximum angular distance from the system's center of mass as seen by an earth-based telescope? Express your result in milliarcseconds, where 1 milliarcsecond = 1 mas = $(1/3,600,000)°$.

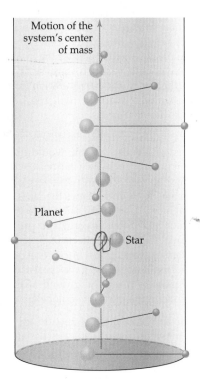

Figure C4.6
The motion of a star and planet through the sky. The large ball represents the star and the small ball the planet. The solid colored line represents the path of the system's center of mass. One can see how the star "wobbles" around the system's center of mass as it interacts with the planet. (This wobble has been *greatly* exaggerated.)

(c) Considering that atmospheric disturbances blur a star's apparent size to a blob about 250 mas across, would detection of such a planet using this method be straightforward?

Note: I did not choose the parameters of this problem randomly. In 1996, George Gatewood at the University of Pittsburgh announced tentative discovery of a planet of this mass and distance orbiting Lalande 21185, a red dwarf star 8.1 ly from earth, after carefully analyzing more than a half-century's worth of measurements of the star's position relative to distant stars. (More data need to be collected over a period of many years to confirm or disprove this discovery.) More extrasolar planets have been discovered using careful measurements of the Doppler shift of the star's light due to its wobbling motion (this turns out to be marginally easier than making direct position measurements).

Rich-Context

C4R.1 A 56-kg canoeist sits at rest at the back end of a 23-kg canoe. The canoe is at rest in the still water of a lake with its front end about 0.50 m from the dock. The canoeist realizes that she has left the paddle on the dock, so she carefully works her way to the front of the 3.8-m canoe. Is she likely to be able to reach the dock from the front of the boat? (*Hint:* We can treat the system of the canoe and canoeist as if it were isolated, for reasons we will discuss in chapter C5. How does this help?)

C4R.2 You are the captain of a spaceship exploring a star system consisting of two visible stars, one a blue giant with a mass of $11M$ (where M is the mass of the sun) and the other a red dwarf with a mass of about $0.5M$. Earlier missions also reported that the system contained a black hole of mass $2M$, but the black hole is not visible and you are unsure exactly where it is. You set up a reference frame fixed to your ship, with yourself at the origin and the x axis pointing toward the blue star and the xy plane containing both stars. The blue giant is 700 gigameters (Gm) (700 million km) away from you along your x axis, while the red dwarf is 825 Gm from you, 14° below your x axis (i.e., in the $-y$ direction).

(a) Draw a picture of the situation, and argue that the coordinates of the blue giant are $x_g = 700$ Gm, $y_g = 0$ Gm while those for the red dwarf are $x_d = 800$ Gm, $y_d = -200$ Gm.

(b) One of the things that you learned at Starfleet Academy is that stellar systems tend to form in such a way that the members' orbits (1) are approximately circular about the system's center of mass, (2) all lie in the same plane, and (3) all orbit in the same direction (all clockwise or all counterclockwise). Your measurements indicate that the giant is moving in the $+y$ direction, while the dwarf moves in a direction 45° clockwise of that direction. *Assuming* that you are at rest with respect to the system's center of mass (the previous mission's charts suggest that you are) and that the visible stars really *are* in circular orbits, locate the system's center of mass.

(c) Given these assumptions, locate the black hole and make a guess about its current direction of motion. Are you safe in your present location?

Advanced

C4A.1 Argue that if frame S is effectively inertial, frame S' moves relative to S at a constant velocity, and both are able to make measurements in the same volume of space, then S' must also be inertial. (*Hint:* Consider an isolated object floating at rest with respect to frame S.)

ANSWERS TO EXERCISES

C4X.1 The contact interaction between the balls is *not* an external interaction because the particles in both balls are members of the system. The contact interaction with the table *is* an external interaction, because the particles in the table are not part of the system as we have defined it.

C4X.2 If we set up our reference frame so that the massive particle (particle A) is at the origin and particle B is a distance $D = 1.2$ m in the $+x$ direction from the origin, then equation C4.6 tells us that the center of mass is 0.10 m = 10 cm from the origin (which is the position of particle A).

C4X.3 Let us choose our reference frame so that the more massive star (whose mass is $3m$) is at $x = 0$ and the lesser star (whose mass is m) is at $x = 100$ million km. Then the x position of the system's center of mass is given by $x_{CM} = (0 + mx)/4m = x/4 = 25$ million km.

C4X.4 The definition of any system's total momentum is

$$\vec{p}_{tot} = \vec{p}_1 + \vec{p}_2 + \cdots \qquad (C4.17)$$

where $\vec{p}_1, \vec{p}_2, \ldots$ are the momenta of its constituent particles. If the system consists of extended objects, then we can group the terms of this sum into sets, each of which pertains to the particles in each object. The set corresponding to the momenta of the particles in object A, for example, will add up to $\vec{p}_{tot,A} = m_A \vec{v}_{CM,A}$ by equation C4.14, and similarly for all the other objects. So, assuming that there are no particles left over, the sum in equation C4.17 after grouping boils down to

$$\begin{aligned} \vec{p}_{tot} &= \vec{p}_{tot,A} + \vec{p}_{tot,B} + \cdots \\ &= m_A \vec{v}_{CM,A} + m_B \vec{v}_{CM,B} + \cdots \end{aligned} \qquad (C4.18)$$

C4X.5 If the system consisting of the person and the rock is really isolated (by virtue of being in "deep space") and its center of mass is initially at rest in our chosen reference frame, then it will *remain* at rest no matter what the person does to the stone (since any interactions between the person and the stone are *internal* to the system). Let the person's mass be $m_p = 60$ kg and the stone's mass be $m_s = 6.0$ kg. If we interpret $d = 30$ m to be the distance between the origin and the stone's *center of mass* after 5 s, then the distance D

between the *person's* center of mass and the origin at this time can be found from the equation

$$\vec{r}_{CM} \equiv \begin{bmatrix} 0 \\ 0 \\ 0 \end{bmatrix} = \frac{1}{M} \left(m_s \begin{bmatrix} d \\ 0 \\ 0 \end{bmatrix} + m_p \begin{bmatrix} -D \\ 0 \\ 0 \end{bmatrix} \right) \qquad (C4.19)$$

The x component of this equation then tells us that

$$0 = \frac{1}{M}(m_s d - m_p D) \quad \Rightarrow \quad m_s d = m_p D \qquad (C4.20)$$

Solving this equation for D and plugging in the numbers, we find that the person has moved a distance $D = 3.0$ m in the $-x$ direction from the origin.

C4X.6 Only the last has a real chance of being effectively inertial. The merry-go-round frame is rotating, and so it does not qualify. We can guess that a jet ball placed initially at rest in the plane would zoom backward when the plane started accelerating forward, so this frame is not going to be inertial. The elevator, if it is really falling frictionlessly, only interacts gravitationally with the earth and other astronomical bodies, whose centers are far away compared to the elevator's size. So the elevator can qualify as an effectively inertial frame if we ignore all those gravitational interactions (including those with the earth!) when analyzing things in that frame.

C4X.7 Let us estimate that the average mass of a person in China is 50 kg, and that the people get on sufficiently tall ladders that everybody hits the ground traveling at about 10 m/s (roughly 22 mi/h). So the total momentum transferred to the earth by 10^9 people doing this is $\approx 5 \times 10^{11}$ kg·m/s, which will cause the earth's center of mass to move at a final speed (just before they all hit the ground) of about

$$\text{mag}(\vec{v}) = \frac{\text{mag}(\vec{p}_{earth})}{m_{earth}} = \frac{5 \times 10^{11} \text{ kg·m/s}}{6 \times 10^{24} \text{ kg}}$$
$$\approx 10^{-13} \text{ m/s} \qquad (C4.21)$$

At this speed, the earth's center of mass would take about 20 min to cover the diameter of an atom. While the seismic waves radiated by this event might be measurable, the motion of the earth's center of mass is insignificant.

C5

Applying Momentum Conservation

Chapter Overview

Introduction

This chapter closes the subsection on momentum by considering practical applications of the law of conservation of momentum, a topic that we will revisit in chapter C12. This chapter also introduces a general problem-solving framework and other useful techniques for solving challenging physics problems, tools which we will use throughout the course.

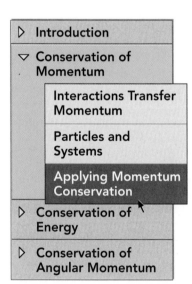

▷ Introduction

▽ Conservation of Momentum

    Interactions Transfer Momentum

    Particles and Systems

    Applying Momentum Conservation

▷ Conservation of Energy

▷ Conservation of Angular Momentum

Section C5.1: Momentum Conservation Without Isolation

In chapter C4, we saw that an *isolated* system's total momentum is conserved, but real physical systems are never completely isolated. However, if momentum flows coming into a system from its external interactions happen to cancel each other out, then the system's total momentum is conserved in *spite* of the external interactions. In particular, if the system consists of objects moving on a level surface, external interactions will cancel as long as there is no significant friction.

Section C5.2: Degrees of Isolation

More generally, we can treat a system *as if* it were isolated under the following circumstances:

1. The system and the reference frame we use to describe it both **float in space** subject to only gravitational interactions with relatively distant objects. Since we can ignore distant gravitational interactions in such a frame and these are the system's only external interactions, it behaves as if it were isolated.

2. The net flow of momentum into the system from external interactions is zero, making the system **functionally isolated** even if those interactions are strong. This is the situation considered in section C5.1.

3. The system's objects participate in a very brief but strong internal interaction (a **collision**). If we look at the system's total momentum *just before* and *just after* this process, external interactions will have too little time to transfer much momentum (the system is **momentarily isolated**).

Section C5.3: A Problem-Solving Framework

Research suggests that almost all expert physics problem solvers solve serious physics problems using the same general framework, which involves four main tasks: (1) **translating** the problem into mathematical symbols, almost always with the help of a *picture;* (2) building a **conceptual model** of the situation that coherently and logically links together enough physics equations to solve the problem; (3) working out an algebraic **solution** for the quantities to be determined; and (4) **evaluating** (checking) the results to see that they make sense. The section discusses each of these tasks in greater detail.

Section C5.4: Constructing Model Diagrams

The conceptual model step of this framework is challenging because it involves thinking skills that novices find unnatural. This section describes a set of rules for constructing a **conceptual model diagram.** The rules are as follows:

1. Start with an appropriate *helping diagram* to organize your thinking about the conceptual aspects of the problem.
2. Use this diagram to construct a *master equation* that expresses the fundamental physical principle you will use to solve the problem.
3. Briefly note what principle the equation expresses and why it applies in a cartoon balloon attached to the equals sign.
4. Identify symbols whose values are known and/or cancel out symbols that appear on both sides of the equation.
5. Circle or highlight the unknown symbols and compare to the number of equations. You are done if there are at least as many equations as unknowns.
6. If you need more equations, select an equation that applies in the situation and contains one or more of the unknown symbols. Connect any symbols to the same symbol in previous equations with a line.
7. Repeat from step 3 until you are done.

Following these rules essentially walks you through a expertlike thinking process, and writing the cartoon balloons ensures that you have both thought and written about the physical principles involved. For simple problems, one can also write out the same thought process in prose.

Section C5.5: Solving Conservation of Momentum Problems

In conservation of momentum problems, the conceptual model will begin with a column vector version of the basic conservation of momentum equation $\vec{p}_{1i} + \vec{p}_{2i} + \vec{p}_{3i} + \cdots = \vec{p}_{1f} + \vec{p}_{2f} + \vec{p}_{3f} + \cdots$. Your translation step should include the items in this checklist:

1. *Two* pictures showing the initial and final states of the system.
2. Reference frame axes to define coordinate directions.
3. Labels defining symbols for *masses, velocities,* and other useful quantities.
4. A list of symbols with known values.

This section includes several examples illustrating the use of the problem-solving framework.

Section C5.6: Airplanes and Rockets

An airplane wing works by deflecting downward air that passes around it. Since the interaction between the wing and air gives the air downward momentum, it must also give the wing upward momentum so that momentum is conserved by the interaction. This upward momentum flow keeps the plane aloft.

Rocket engines work by ejecting propellant at high velocity. Since the interaction between the engine and the propellant gives the latter rearward momentum, the engine must get forward momentum if the interaction is to conserve momentum. This pushes the rocket forward.

A rocket engine's performance turns out to depend essentially entirely on the propellant's ejection speed relative to the engine. Chemical rockets can eject propellant at up to 4 km/s and ion engines at up to 32 km/s. An ideal rocket engine would eject propellant at the speed of light.

C5.1   Momentum Conservation Without Isolation

We saw in chapter C4 that the total momentum of a system of particles and/or objects that is *isolated* from external interactions is conserved (since internal interactions only transfer momentum around *within* the system). In reality, *no* system is ever completely isolated from its surroundings. Even so, we find that in a number of practical situations, a system's momentum is conserved anyway. How does this work?

Let us consider the specific example of the cart collision shown in figure C5.1. We saw in chapter C3 that such a collision transfers momentum from one cart to the other, implying that the total momentum of the two carts is conserved. The two-cart system, however, is clearly *not* isolated, as each participates in a gravitational interaction with the earth and a contact interaction with the surface on which it rolls. So *why* is its momentum conserved?

Consider for the moment a *single* cart rolling along a level surface. The gravitational interaction between the earth and the cart constantly pours downward momentum into the cart. When the cart is rolling on the level surface, though, the vertical component of its momentum has a constant value of zero. This means that the cart's contact interaction with the surface must pour upward momentum into the cart at the same rate as gravity pours in downward momentum. The wheels' suspension in fact *ensures* that the net flow of vertical momentum into the cart is zero on average. For example, imagine that the cart, for some reason, begins to move upward. This causes its wheels' suspension to relax, making the interaction between the wheels and the surface less intense, which decreases the rate at which upward momentum from that interaction flows into the cart. This in turn causes the cart to accumulate uncanceled downward momentum from gravity, which eventually causes the cart to move back toward the surface, which makes the momentum flows more balanced again.

A puzzle: How can a collision between carts conserve momentum when the carts are not isolated?

Exercise C5X.1

By analogy, explain how the cart will self-correct if it is jostled downward.

Remember from chapter C3 that the *force* an interaction exerts on an object expresses the flow rate and direction of the momentum that the interaction delivers to the object. We can consider the total force that the contact interaction exerts on the cart to be a sum of two component vectors, a vertical one perpendicular to the surface and a horizontal one parallel to the surface (see figure C5.2). We define the parts of the contact interaction exerting the vertical and horizontal force component vectors to be the *compression* and *friction* parts of the interaction, respectively. The point of the previous paragraph is that the cart's suspension ensures that, on average, the momentum flow from the contact interaction's compression part exactly cancels the

Figure C5.1

An example collision between carts that does conserve momentum. (This is an example that we have examined in both chapters C3 and C4.)

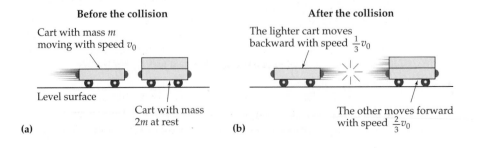

Before the collision

Cart with mass m moving with speed v_0

Level surface

Cart with mass $2m$ at rest

(a)

After the collision

The lighter cart moves backward with speed $\frac{1}{3}v_0$

The other moves forward with speed $\frac{2}{3}v_0$

(b)

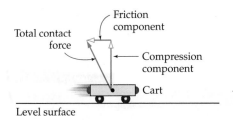

Total contact force

Friction component

Compression component

Cart

Level surface

Figure C5.2

The two components of the contact interaction between a cart and a surface.

momentum flow from the gravitational interaction. Therefore only the frictional part of the interaction provides any *net* flow of external momentum into or out of the cart.

In the limit that friction is negligible, though, the net flow of external momentum into the cart is essentially zero. This means that the net flow of external momentum into a system consisting of two such carts is *also* essentially zero. Since internal interactions between the carts only transfer momentum between the carts, and since the system gets no net momentum from the outside, its total momentum is conserved, *exactly as if it were isolated.*

Exercise C5X.2

A friend claims that a passive thing like a level surface *obviously* cannot deliver an active flow of upward momentum to a cart, so the surface must somehow shield the cart from the effects of gravity. Flesh out an argument *against* this model by considering the following thought experiment. Imagine lifting the cart a small distance above the table and releasing it from rest. What happens to the cart? Why is this a problem for the shielding model?

C5.2 Degrees of Isolation

We can see from section C5.1 that a system does not have to be strictly isolated for its total momentum to be conserved. In general, a system's momentum is conserved in any process where its external interactions do not change its total momentum *significantly* during that process. There are three distinct types of situations in which this is true.

Consider first a system that interacts only gravitationally with objects whose centers of mass are distant compared to the system's size. As discussed in chapter C4, we can treat a reference frame freely floating in the same vicinity as an inertial frame if we ignore external gravitational interactions. Since these are the system's *only* external interactions by hypothesis, the system as viewed in this frame will behave as if it were isolated. We say that such a system is isolated because it **floats in space.** (Remember, though, that this works only if *both* the system and the frame float freely in space and respond gravitationally to the *same* distant bodies.)

First case: systems that *float in space*

Consider now a system that participates in strong nongravitational external interactions whose momentum flows nonetheless essentially cancel, so that its total momentum remains constant in *spite* of those interactions. This is exactly the kind of situation we explored at length in section C5.1. We say that such a system is **functionally isolated,** since it *functions* as if it *were* isolated even though it is not.

Second case: *functionally isolated* systems (whose external interactions cancel)

The way to *test* for functional isolation is to verify that *each* of the system's objects (when not interacting with other objects in the system) moves with constant momentum in spite of its external interactions. If there is significant friction (or the surface on which the objects move is not level), at least one object will fail this test, and the system is not functionally isolated.

In the third case, the system participates in strong external interactions that do *not* cancel, but we only look at the system's momentum *just before* and *just after* a very strong and brief interaction. In physics, a **collision** is *any* process in which the internal interaction between two system objects (1) lasts only for a short time but (2) delivers to the objects a much larger impulse than any other interaction during that time. (Note that this definition does *not* require that the objects actually *touch* during a collision!) If the collision process is sufficiently brief, external interactions simply do not have *time* to transfer significant momentum to the system. So, as long as we look at the system just before and just after such a "collision," its total momentum is approximately conserved. We will describe such a system as being **momentarily isolated.**

Exercise C5X.3

Two billiard balls collide on a billiard table. According to the definitions presented above, is the system consisting of the two balls *functionally* isolated, *momentarily* isolated, or isolated because it *floats in space?*

Exercise C5X.4

Two cars skidding on a road hit each other. Can we apply conservation of momentum to this situation? If so, what justifies treating the cars as an isolated system?

C5.3   A Problem-Solving Framework

Part of the aim of this course is to raise your problem-solving skills from the level of predigested "plug-and-chug" problems of the type common in high school physics courses (even advanced-placement courses) to an entirely new level suited to addressing more realistic problems (exemplified by the synthetic and rich-context problems in this text). In this section, I will give you a leg up by describing the general problem-solving "framework" that essentially all experts (but few novices) use to solve serious physics problems, an approach that both research and long experience show to be efficient and effective in generating correct solutions.

This framework involves completing four main tasks: (1) **translating** the problem into mathematical symbols, almost always with the help of a *picture;* (2) building a **conceptual model** of the situation that coherently and logically links together enough physics equations to solve the problem; (3) working out an algebraic **solution** for the quantities to be determined; and (4) **evaluating** (checking) results to see that they make sense. Let us look at each of these tasks in greater detail.

In the *translation* step, you take the verbal statement of the problem, identify physical quantities of interest, translate those quantities into mathematical symbols so that you can link them to equations, and list the quantities whose values you know. Doing this well prepares you to think more clearly about the conceptual model in the next step and helps you avoid certain beginner errors (such as using the same symbol for different quantities). One *can* do this verbally (e.g., "Let v_i be the ball's initial speed" and so on), but experts know that it is almost always better to define symbols by drawing a schematic *picture* of the situation and labeling the picture's features with those symbols. Pictures are better because (1) human minds are better at processing visual relationships than verbal information, so drawing a picture helps organize one's thinking about a problem; (2) for the same reason, defining symbols visually makes it much easier for both you and your grader to find and remember those definitions; (3) defining reference frame axes (an essential step in any problem involving vectors) is much more easily done on a picture than in words; and (4) defining symbols on a picture *saves time,* since lengthy verbal explanations are not needed.

In the *conceptual model* step, you wrestle with essential questions such as the following: What theories and/or principles apply here? What simplifications and/or approximations do I have to make to construct a usable model of the situation? What do I need to know to solve the problem, and how can I determine quantities I am not given directly? The goal is to select the equations you need and develop a coherent and physically reasonable plan for using them to solve the problem.

The *conceptual model* step

This part is, in my opinion, *by far* the most important part of a problem solution, as it involves about 90% of the thinking you do about the physics of the situation. Yet this is the most important problem-solving skill that typical plug-and-chug problems do not really require and thus do not help you practice. This step is so important at this stage of your education that I will devote the entire next section of this chapter to describing a scheme that makes it easier.

Your job in the *algebraic solution* step is take the plan you developed in the previous step and execute it by solving your selected equations *symbolically* for the quantity or quantities of interest. If the problem requests a numerical result, you will *then* plug known values into the symbolic equation and calculate the result, *keeping careful track of units throughout the process.*

The *algebraic solution* step

It is important to solve your equations symbolically *before* inserting any numbers (other than zeros or simple unitless integers or fractions). Some problems may ask for purely symbolic results, which are often more useful than numerical results because they clearly display how quantities relate to one another. But even if a problem asks for a numerical result, solving equations symbolically is *still* worthwhile because (1) you are *much* less likely to make errors when doing symbolic algebra, (2) using symbols exclusively makes it *much* easier for you or your grader to review your work to find errors, and (3) it *saves time*, because writing a multidigit number with its required units usually takes about 5 to 10 times as much effort of writing a symbol (compare, e.g., writing 2.28×10^6 m/s to writing v_0). Do not make extra work for yourself!

I am *not* saying that you cannot calculate intermediate numerical results in the process of solving a problem: calculating intermediate results can be very helpful when solving complicated problems. What I *am* saying is this: *Never do* algebra *with numbers* (unless they are very simple *unitless* numbers). Observing this simple rule will save you endless grief when solving complicated problems.

The *evaluation* part of the framework is where you thoughtfully assess whether an equation or numerical result *makes sense.* Experts do this kind of assessment *continually* as they work through a problem, but it is essential to do it at the end at least.

The *evaluation* step

The most important way to check a result is to look for *unit consistency:* conceptual and algebraic errors very often lead to unit inconsistencies. For example, if my final expression for a speed is $v = D/\tau^2$ (where D is a distance and τ is a time) or its numerical value has units of meters per second, then I know I have made an error. Long experience has taught me the value of being *constantly* aware of units, yet this powerful tool is consistently underutilized by beginners. I strongly urge you to (1) attach (appropriate) units to *every* numerical quantity you write, (2) keep careful track of units when you calculate, and (3) learn to quickly assess the units implied by symbolic equations.

It is also important to check the *signs* and *magnitudes* of numerical results. For example, if a speed comes out negative or a car ends up with a mass greater than that of a galaxy, there is an error somewhere. Correct numerical results also *tend* to be of the same order of magnitude as known values of the same kind of quantity appearing in the problem. We will discuss methods of assessing the validity of *symbolic* results as we go on in the course.

Experts do *some* of these steps in their heads, which is fine when you are an expert. But just as I learned valuable skills as a beginner when my violin teacher made me think through and write out bowing patterns, you will learn empowering thinking habits if you consciously practice this expert problem-solving framework by consciously writing out each step on paper. The worked examples in the rest of this text will illustrate how to use the framework.

The importance of practicing these steps on paper

C5.4   Constructing Model Diagrams

The conceptual modeling step of this framework is challenging because doing it well involves a number of thinking processes that research suggests beginners find unnatural. For example, experts typically construct a model from the top down (starting with fundamental physical principles and working toward equations) while novices usually work from the bottom up (starting from equations having the variables mentioned in the problem and trying to stitch them together into a coherent whole). Experts are conscious of the physical meaning and limitations of the equations they use; novices tend not to be (and thus end up using inappropriate equations). Experts learn to remember which *symbols* represent known quantities, while novices seek to make this clear by plugging in numbers too early (so that only unknown symbols are left).

This section describes a set of rules for constructing a **conceptual model diagram.** Following these simple rules will automatically walk you through an expertlike thinking process, which in turn will help you solve complicated problems quickly and accurately. The diagram's very structure addresses all the novice difficulties mentioned above.

The rules for constructing a conceptual model diagram

The rules (which assume that you have completed the translation step) are as follows:

1. You will almost always begin a conceptual model diagram by drawing what I call a *helping diagram*. A helping diagram is an abstract representation of the object or system of interest that helps you visualize and think clearly about conceptual aspects of the system (e.g., internal or external interactions) that are not easy to represent in the more realistic diagram you drew for the translation step. Different kinds of problems call for different kinds of helping diagrams: we will discuss the appropriate kind of helping diagram for each type of problem as we go along.

2. Use the helping diagram to construct a *master equation* that expresses the most fundamental physical principle that applies to the problem. If this is a vector equation, write it in *column vector* form, and feel free to use simple definitions (such as $\vec{p} \equiv m\vec{v}$) to express this equation in terms of symbols you have defined in the translation step. (For example, *this* chapter is about applying conservation of momentum, so the master

equation for any problem in this chapter will be a column vector equation expressing conservation of momentum.)

3.   Above the equation's equals sign write a brief note explaining what physical principle the equation expresses and *why* it applies in this case. Surround it with a cartoon balloon as if it were spoken by the equals sign. (The explanation can be pretty brief. It might read, "CoM: functionally isolated," short for "this equation describes the principle of conservation of momentum, which applies here because the system is functionally isolated." We will define standard abbreviations such as CoM for important principles as we go along.)

4.   Look at every symbol in the equation. (a) If you know that its value is zero or a simple unitless number like 2 or $\frac{1}{2}$, draw an arrow through the symbol and write the value at the arrow's tip. (b) Draw a slash mark through any symbols that cancel on both sides of an equation. (c) Check to see whether the symbol appears on your list of symbols with known values.

5.   Circle any symbols whose values remain unknown after step 4. If such a symbol appears more than once in your equations, circle only one instance of the symbol and use lines to link that circle to all other instances of the symbol. Count the circled symbols, and compare to the number of equations. (Count each meaningful row of a vector equation as a *separate* equation. A row that says $0 + 0 = 0$ is *not* meaningful.) If you have at least as many independent equations as unknowns, you should be able to solve the problem, and your model is complete.

6.   Otherwise, consider a different equation containing one or more of your unknowns, carefully assessing whether it applies in this situation (or whether making a reasonable approximation or assumption would *allow* it to apply). If it does, write the equation below the master equation and draw a line connecting any symbol appearing in the new equation with the same symbol in previous equations.

7.   Repeat, starting at step 3, until you have enough equations to solve. In step 3, the equivalence sign $\equiv$ is sufficient explanation for definitions, but you should attach an explanatory cartoon balloon to the equals sign of any other equations.

Occasionally (most often in rich-context problems), you may need to make an estimate to determine a symbol's value. If so, treat the equation linking the symbol to its estimated value as just another equation in step 6, and write "estimated" (along with any appropriate explanation if the estimation is not trivial) in the equation's cartoon balloon. You may also encounter known or unknown quantities that ultimately prove to be irrelevant. Keep focused on solving for the unknowns that the problem asks you to solve.

You may also need to be flexible in adapting the above rules to specific problems. If you do something outside the rules, simply explain what you are doing.

I also find it very helpful to express vector components (whenever possible) in terms of symbols representing intrinsically *positive* numbers (such as vector magnitudes or distances). This means that any minus signs associated with the components get displayed explicitly in the equation instead of being "buried" inside the symbol. I find that this markedly reduces the number of sign errors I make.

If you complete such a diagram well, (1) you will always know which symbols are known and unknown, (2) you will know without doing any algebra that your model is complete, (3) your "equals sign" notes will have provided sufficient physical reasoning to support your model, and (4) your diagram will essentially tell you how to solve the problem mathematically. Most importantly, though, you will have followed an expertlike reasoning process that focuses first on important principles and depends on *physical* reasoning to fill in the details.

You *can* write your conceptual model step in *prose* instead of constructing a diagram; this is sometimes easier for simple problems. But if you do write a prose model, make sure that you follow a thinking process like that you would use to build the diagram, and use complete sentences to describe the equations you will use and why they apply in this situation (or what approximation you are making that allows them to apply). Examples in this text will typically provide model steps in both diagram and prose form. Follow your instructor's advice about which approach to use for your homework solutions. (I personally recommend that you use conceptual model diagrams for any homework problem whose number is marked with an asterisk.)

C5.5   Solving Conservation of Momentum Problems

The helping diagram for conservation of momentum problems

The conceptual model diagram for any problem in *this* chapter will begin with a helping diagram that we will call an **interaction diagram.** You can construct an interaction diagram as follows. Draw a large circle to represent the system, and draw one rectangular box inside that circle for each object inside the system, labeling the box with the object's name. If the objects inside the system interact with objects outside the system, draw a box outside the circle for each relevant object outside the system, and label these boxes as well. Then draw lines connecting the boxes to represent the internal and external interactions between these objects, and label these lines to indicate the type of interaction involved. (If the system floats in space, simply write "floats in space" along the margin of the circle and do not include any external gravitational interactions.)

An interaction diagram helps you clearly visualize the system and sharply distinguish between external and internal interactions. In conservation of momentum problems we are especially interested in understanding the *external* interactions, so that we know what approximations we have to make to say that the system is isolated.

The master equation for conservation of momentum problems

The master equation for any problem in this chapter will express the law of conservation of momentum (CoM), which states that a suitably isolated system's total momentum before some process of interest is equal to its total momentum after that process:

$$\vec{p}_{1i} + \vec{p}_{2i} + \vec{p}_{3i} + \cdots = \vec{p}_{1f} + \vec{p}_{2f} + \vec{p}_{3f} + \cdots \qquad (C5.1)$$

where the subscripts 1, 2, 3, . . . refer to the objects in the system and subscripts i and f mean initial and final, respectively. Adapt this equation for the number of objects in the system in question, use the definition $\vec{p} \equiv m\vec{v}$ to rewrite the momenta in terms of masses and velocities, and write it out in column vector form. Your explanation for the equals sign in this equation should include this principle's abbreviation **CoM** followed by some statement of how this system is isolated (using the categories discussed in section C5.2).

The translation step for conservation of momentum problems

The *translation* step for any conservation of momentum problem should include all items on the following checklist:

1. *Two* pictures that show the system in its initial and final states, respectively.

2. Reference frame axes to define coordinate directions.
3. Labels defining symbols for *masses* and *velocities* of all system objects (as well as any other useful quantities).
4. A list of all symbols having known values.

Including all the items on this list will leave you well prepared for the conceptual model step.

On the next two pages, you will find example solutions to conservation of momentum problems that illustrate the use of the problem-solving framework. These solutions provide both a diagram version *and* a prose version of the conceptual model step, so that you can see what is involved in each.

Example C5.1

Problem   ("Captain, we've got a problem in engineering . . .") A 10,000-kg spaceship in deep space travels at 40 km/s toward the Andromeda galaxy. Its engines suddenly explode, blowing the ship apart into two hunks. The front (8000-kg) hunk continues moving toward Andromeda at 60 km/s. What is the velocity (magnitude and direction) of the back hunk?

Translation

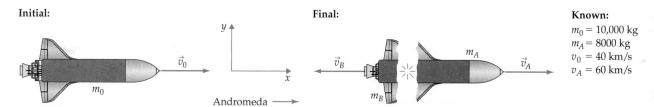

Known:
$m_0 = 10{,}000$ kg
$m_A = 8000$ kg
$v_0 = 40$ km/s
$v_A = 60$ km/s

Conceptual Model Diagram

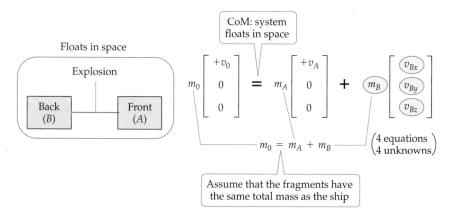

Prose Model   The problem statement implies that our reference frame floats in space at rest relative to the Andromeda galaxy; let us assume this. If so, then both our system and the frame are floating in space subject to the same external gravitational interactions; so according to observers in this frame, the system's total momentum is conserved. In this case, expressed in terms of the symbols defined above, this law states that

$$m_0 \begin{bmatrix} v_{0x} \\ v_{0y} \\ v_{0z} \end{bmatrix} = m_A \begin{bmatrix} v_{Ax} \\ v_{Ay} \\ v_{Az} \end{bmatrix} + m_B \begin{bmatrix} v_{Bx} \\ v_{By} \\ v_{Bz} \end{bmatrix} \qquad \text{(C5.2)}$$

We are given that $m_0 = 10{,}000$ kg and $m_A = 8000$ kg, and the way we have set up our axes implies that $v_{0x} = +\mathrm{mag}(\vec{v}_0) = +40$ km/s, $v_{Ax} = +\mathrm{mag}(\vec{v}_A) = +60$ km/s and $v_{0y} = v_{0z} = v_{Ay} = v_{Az} = 0$. The components of $\vec{v}_B$ and m_B are unknown; but if we assume that the total mass of the two fragments is the same as that of the original ship, then we also have $m_0 = m_A + m_B$, giving us four equations (three vector rows and this last equation) for our four unknowns.

Solution The last two rows of equation C5.2 imply that $v_{By} = v_{Bz} = 0$. Solving $m_0 = m_A + m_B$ for m_B and plugging it into the first row of equation C5.2, we get

$$m_0 v_{0x} = m_A v_{Ax} + (m_0 - m_A)v_{Bx} \quad \Rightarrow \quad v_{Bx} = \frac{m_0 v_{0x} - m_A v_{Ax}}{m_0 - m_A}$$

$$v_{Bx} = \frac{(10{,}000 \text{ kg})(+40 \text{ km/s}) - (8000 \text{ kg})(+60 \text{ km/s})}{10{,}000 \text{ kg} - 2000 \text{ kg}}$$

$$= -40 \text{ km/s} \tag{C5.3}$$

Evaluation The answer has the right units, and its magnitude seems reasonable (comparable to other speeds in the problem). The sign seems okay, too, showing that the diagram's complete guess that the back hunk might move *away* from Andromeda (in the $-x$ direction) was correct.

Example C5.2

Problem (Stoplight? What stoplight?) A 1000-kg car traveling west at 20 m/s collides with an 800-kg car traveling north at 16 m/s. The collision locks the cars together. What is the velocity of the two-car unit just after the collision? (Describe in terms of a magnitude and direction angle.)

Translation

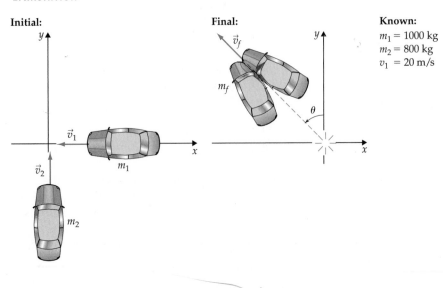

Initial:

Final:

Known:
$m_1 = 1000$ kg
$m_2 = 800$ kg
$v_1 = 20$ m/s

Conceptual Model Diagram

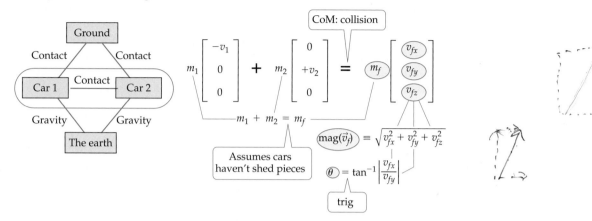

Prose Model Friction between the cars' tires and the road will likely be significant here, so the system is not isolated. However, we are only interested in the velocity right after a violent collision, so we can treat the system as being momentarily isolated. Conservation of momentum in this case implies that

$$m_1 \begin{bmatrix} v_{1x} \\ v_{1y} \\ v_{1z} \end{bmatrix} + m_2 \begin{bmatrix} v_{2x} \\ v_{2y} \\ v_{2z} \end{bmatrix} = m_f \begin{bmatrix} v_{fx} \\ v_{fy} \\ v_{fz} \end{bmatrix} \tag{C5.4}$$

We know that $m_1 = 1000$ kg and $m_2 = 800$ kg, and the way we have set up our frame axes implies that $v_{1x} = -\text{mag}(\vec{v}_1) = -20$ m/s and $v_{2y} = +\text{mag}(\vec{v}_2) = +16$ m/s, and $v_{1y} = v_{1z} = v_{2x} = v_{2z} = 0$. We do not know m_f or the components of $\vec{v}_f$; moreover, we want to find $\text{mag}(\vec{v}_f)$ and θ, so we have *six* unknowns. But if the cars do not shed significant pieces in the collision, then $m_f = m_1 + m_2$, and $\text{mag}(\vec{v}_f) \equiv [v_{fx}^2 + v_{fy}^2 + v_{fz}^2]^{1/2}$ by definition and $\theta = \tan^{-1}|v_{fx}/v_{fy}|$ by trigonometry. This gives us enough equations to solve.

Solution The last row of equation C5.4 tells us that $v_{fz} = 0$, so the cars do not move vertically (as we might have guessed). After we plug in $m_1 + m_2$ for m_f, the top two rows of this equation yield $m_1 v_{1x} = (m_1 + m_2)v_{fx}$ and $m_2 v_{2y} = (m_1 + m_2)v_{fy}$, respectively. Solving these equations for v_{fx} and v_{fy}, we get

$$v_{fx} = \frac{m_1 v_{1x}}{m_1 + m_2} = \frac{(1000 \text{ kg})(-20 \text{ m/s})}{1800 \text{ kg}} = -11 \text{ m/s} \tag{C5.5a}$$

$$v_{fy} = \frac{m_2 v_{2y}}{m_1 + m_2} = \frac{(800 \text{ kg})(+16 \text{ m/s})}{1800 \text{ kg}} = +7.1 \text{ m/s} \tag{C5.5b}$$

(Note that these units are correct for velocity components.) Since v_{fx} is negative but v_{fy} is positive, $\vec{v}_f$ points northwest, as I guessed in the diagram. Specifically,

$$\theta = \tan^{-1}\left|\frac{v_{fx}}{v_{fy}}\right| = \tan^{-1}\left|\frac{-11 \text{ m/s}}{+7.1 \text{ m/s}}\right| = \tan^{-1}(1.55) = 57° \text{ (west of north)} \tag{C5.6a}$$

and $\text{mag}(\vec{v}_f) = \sqrt{v_{fx}^2 + v_{fy}^2 + 0} = \sqrt{(11 \text{ m/s})^2 + (7.1 \text{ m/s})^2} = 13 \text{ m/s}$

$$\tag{C5.6b}$$

Evaluation Note that $\text{mag}(\vec{v}_f)$ is positive and comparable in magnitude to $\vec{v}_1$ and $\vec{v}_2$.

These examples are pretty straightforward

Using the full power of the expert framework and the conceptual model diagram to solve these relatively simple problems is a bit like using a supersonic fighter jet to go to the grocery store: there is excessive fire and noise, and when all the setting up and mopping up are complete, you have not really gotten there all that much faster than you would have if you had walked. But practicing some simple takeoffs and landings will help prepare you to fly cross-country when you need to (if you understand my metaphor).

C5.6   Airplanes and Rockets

What keeps an airplane from falling? Textbooks often appeal to *Bernoulli's principle*, which describes how the pressure of a fluid, such as air, varies with flow speed. But we can answer this question more directly and generally using conservation of momentum.

Perhaps you can see that the *shape* of a typical airplane wing redirects the airflow above the wing somewhat *downward* in the end, since as the air moves over the wing, the air must follow the curve of the wing's rear upper surface, as shown in figure C5.3a. (Otherwise, there would be a vacuum above the downward-sloping part of the wing's upper surface.) If the interaction between the wing and air gives the air some downward momentum, the interaction must give the wing upward momentum to conserve momentum. *This* is what provides the required lift. (During level flight, the flow of upward momentum that the plane gets from its interaction with the air exactly cancels the flow of downward momentum it gets from gravity.)

This effect is greatly enhanced if the wing is tipped somewhat upward (this is called increasing the wing's *angle of attack*; see figure C5.3b), partly because then even some of the air flowing *under* the wing is redirected downward. The wing flaps that pilots of commercial jets extend during takeoff and landing also are designed to do this. While both of these options more firmly direct air downward, they also increase the friction between the air and the wing and so are only used during takeoff and landing (when having greater lift at low airspeeds is more important than fuel economy). Figure C5.4 vividly illustrates that wings *do* push air downward.

Conservation of momentum keeps a plane in the air

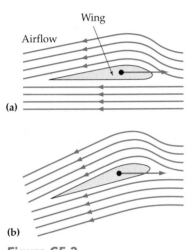

Figure C5.3
(a) A diagram of the airflow around a cross section of a typical airplane wing, as viewed by someone at the end of the wing. Note how the air flowing over the top of the wing is deflected downward. (b) The same wing at a higher *angle of attack*.

Figure C5.4
The deep trough this Cessna Citation jet leaves in the clouds below it shows that its wings do push air downward.

This explanation depends on the principle that *interactions transfer momentum*. It may comfort you to know that your airplane is being supported by one of the universe's most fundamental physical principles!

Conservation of momentum also explains how a rocket can increase its momentum even in space (where it seems that there is nothing to "push" against). All rocket engines in fact operate by pushing propellant backward at as high a velocity as possible. To do this, the rocket engine has to transfer backward momentum to the propellant. The forward momentum of the remainder of the rocket must then increase by the same amount to conserve momentum (see figure C5.5).

In a standard liquid-fuel rocket, the body of the rocket consists of tanks holding two substances that react energetically when combined (e.g., liquid hydrogen and liquid oxygen). These substances are brought into contact in the rocket engine nozzle and ignited. The resulting chemical reaction increases the temperature of the exhaust gases dramatically, which makes these gases expand rapidly. Since they have no place to go except backward out of the nozzle, they are propelled rearward with a large speed (commonly $\approx$ 2 to 3 km/s).

A natural quantity for describing rocket performance is the *impulse* (i.e., momentum transferred) *per unit mass* of propellant. The greater this quantity is, the less propellant the rocket has to carry to achieve the same change in momentum, and the less propellant the rocket has to carry, the smaller its mass and thus the smaller the momentum change it needs to achieve a given final velocity. So increasing the momentum transferred per mass of a rocket's propellant *doubly* contributes to its performance.

How might we improve this quantity? Consider a liquid-fuel rocket engine that ejects propellant with an exhaust speed of 2000 m/s. To do this, the engine must transfer 2000 kg·m/s of backward momentum to each kilogram of fuel, so this is also the magnitude of the forward impulse the rocket gets from that kilogram of fuel. The momentum transfer per unit mass is therefore (2000 kg·m/s)/kg = 2000 m/s, which is simply the exhaust speed! Thus the crucial thing determining a rocket's performance is its *exhaust speed*.

How can we increase the exhaust speed? In a chemical rocket, one can do this by increasing the fuel combustion temperature. But these temperatures cannot be made too high, or else the engine nozzle will melt. The exhaust speed of the best available chemical rockets is about 4.5 km/s.

Ion engines are sometimes used in deep space probes where keeping propellant mass small is especially important. These engines use electrical fields to accelerate charged atoms to *very* high velocities. For example, the ion engine used by NASA's Deep Space 1 probe (see figure C5.6), which visited the asteroid Braille in 1999 and comet Borrelly in September 2001, ejects xenon propellant at a speed of 31.5 km/s. The *rate* (in kilograms per second) at which it ejects that propellant is very small, so it exerts a small thrust (0.02 lb), but it exerts that thrust *very* efficiently.

The best possible rocket engine would use matter and antimatter, which when combined, annihilate each other to create pure energy in the form of gamma rays, which can (at least in principle) be directed rearward. As we will see in unit R, the gamma rays produced by the annihilation of equal amounts of matter and antimatter of total mass m would carry away momentum equal in magnitude to mc, where c is the speed of light. This means that the momentum transferred per unit mass would also be c = 300,000 km/s. Since the speed of light is the highest exhaust velocity possible, such an engine would deliver the highest possible performance. (Matter/antimatter engines are still hypothetical at present.)

See problem C5S.1 for more information about rocket engine performance.

Rockets also employ conservation of momentum

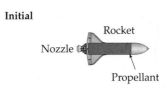

Initial

Final

Figure C5.5
A rocket works by pushing propellant backward as rapidly as possible. Since momentum has to be conserved, the rocket's forward momentum increases as it transfers backward momentum to the propellant.

A rocket engine's performance depends on the propellant's exhaust speed

Figure C5.6a

NASA technicians ready the Deep Space 1 probe for launch. The flat black objects on either side are the probe's folded solar panels. The ion rocket engine is at the bottom: its nozzle is roughly 30 cm across.

Figure C5.6b

Deep Space 1's engine in action during a test.

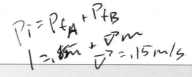

TWO-MINUTE PROBLEMS

C5T.1 A 0.5-kg cart moving at a speed of 1.0 m/s in the $+x$ direction along a level track runs into a 1.0-kg cart initially at rest. Someone claims to have determined that after the collision, the massive cart moves in the $+x$ direction at 0.6 m/s and the other moves in the $-x$ direction at 0.2 m/s. This claim is consistent with the law of conservation of momentum, true (T) or false (F)? Be prepared to explain your response. (Assume that the carts have nearly frictionless wheels.)

C5T.2 A 1.0-kg cart moving at a speed of 1.0 m/s in the $+x$ direction along a level track runs into a 0.5-kg cart initially at rest. After the collision, the lighter cart moves in the $+x$ direction at 1.5 m/s and the massive cart with a speed 0.25 m/s. Assume that the carts have nearly frictionless wheels. In what direction does the massive cart move?
  A. The $+x$ direction.
  B. The $-x$ direction.
  C. Neither direction makes the supplied information consistent with the conservation of momentum.
  D. This system is not isolated, so it is impossible to say.

C5T.3 Hockey puck A slides due north on a level plane of essentially frictionless ice. It then collides with puck B, which was initially at rest. Just after the collision, puck A is observed to move due west. If this is so, in what (approximate) direction must puck B move just after the collision?
  A. Northeast.

  B. Northwest.
  C. Southeast.
  D. Southwest.
  E. This system is not isolated, so it is impossible to say.
  F. Some other direction (specify).
  T. The answer depends on the pucks' masses.

C5T.4 Two football players run into each other at midfield. We can (or cannot) realistically apply conservation of momentum to calculate the players' velocities just after the impact because
  A. The system of interest floats in space.
  B. The players are functionally isolated.
  C. We can treat the interaction as a collision.
  D. Conservation of momentum does *not* apply here.

C5T.5 Two magnetic hockey pucks sliding on a flat plane of frictionless ice attract each other, changing each other's direction of motion as they pass. We can (or cannot) realistically apply conservation of momentum to this situation because
  A. The system of interest floats in space.
  B. The pucks are a functionally isolated system.
  C. We can treat the interaction as a collision.
  D. Conservation of momentum does not apply here.

C5T.6 Two stars in deep space pass near to each other, gravitationally changing each other's direction of motion as they pass. We can (or cannot) realistically apply conservation of momentum to this situation because

A. The system of interest floats in space.
B. The stars are a functionally isolated system.
C. We can treat the interaction as a collision.
D. Conservation of momentum does not apply here.

The remaining two-minute problems all imagine a situation where two hockey pucks are sliding on a flat, horizontal plane of frictionless ice. One puck has twice the mass of the other. They approach each other as described in each problem, collide, and then *stick together*.

C5T.7 Initially, the light puck is moving east at 3 m/s while the heavy puck is moving west at 2 m/s. The final velocity of the joined pucks is
A. Eastward.
B. Westward.
C. Zero.

D. Impossible to determine.
E. Some other direction (explain).

C5T.8 Initially, the light puck is moving west at 4 m/s while the heavy puck is moving south at 2 m/s. The final velocity of the joined pucks is
A. Northeast.
B. Northwest.
C. Southeast.
D. Southwest.
E. Zero.
F. Some other direction (explain).

C5T.9 Originally the light puck was moving south, and the final speed of the joined pucks is zero. The original velocity of the heavy puck *must* have been northward, T or F?

HOMEWORK PROBLEMS

Basic Skills

C5B.1 A 0.3-kg cart rolling on essentially frictionless wheels at an initial speed of 1.0 m/s in the +x direction collides with a 0.6-kg cart initially at rest. After the collision, the more massive cart is observed to move in the +x direction with a speed of 0.55 m/s. What is the velocity (magnitude and direction) of the lighter cart?

C5B.2 A cart rolling on essentially frictionless wheels at an initial speed of 1.0 m/s in the +x direction collides with an identical cart initially at rest. After the collision, the front cart is observed to move in the +x direction with a speed of 0.85 m/s. What is the velocity (magnitude and direction) of the other cart?

C5B.3 A person firing a rifle feels it recoil against his or her shoulder. Explain why.

C5B.4 Imagine a cannon that is free to roll on wheels. Initially, both the cannon and cannonball are at rest. When the cannonball is fired, though, the momentum transferred to the cannonball comes at the expense of the cannon, so the cannonball and cannon end up with momenta having equal magnitudes but opposite directions. If this is so, why does the cannonball fly away at a large speed while the cannon recoils only very modestly? Explain your response.

C5B.5 Two identical hockey pucks slide on a flat, frictionless plane of ice. Originally, one is sliding westward at a speed of 3 m/s, while the other is sliding eastward at a speed of 1 m/s. The pucks collide and stick together. What is their joint velocity (magnitude and direction) after the collision?

C5B.6 Two hockey pucks, one with mass m and the other with mass $3m$, slide on a flat, frictionless plane of ice. Originally, the lighter puck is sliding westward at a speed of 2 m/s, while the other is sliding eastward at a speed of 1 m/s. The pucks collide and stick together. What is their joint velocity (magnitude and direction) after the collision?

C5B.7 Two hockey pucks, one with mass m and the other with mass $3m$, slide on a flat, frictionless plane of ice. Originally, the lighter puck is sliding eastward at a speed of 2 m/s, while the other is sliding northward at a speed of 2 m/s. The pucks collide and stick together. What is their joint velocity (magnitude and direction) after the collision? [*Hint:* Draw a picture.]

C5B.8 Two hockey pucks, one with mass m and the other with mass $3m$, slide on a flat, frictionless plane of ice. Originally, the lighter puck is sliding westward at a speed of 6 m/s, while the more massive puck is sliding southward at a speed of 2 m/s. The pucks collide and stick together. What is their joint velocity (magnitude and direction) after the collision? [*Hint:* Draw a picture.]

Synthetic

The starred problems are especially well suited for practicing the use of the problem-solving framework and conceptual model diagrams.

C5S.1 For historical reasons, a rocket engine's performance is often stated in terms of its **specific impulse,** which is the momentum transferred per unit *weight* of propellant instead of mass (where the propellant's weight is measured at the earth's surface).
(a) Argue that the units of specific impulse are simply seconds.
(b) Argue that the specific impulse of a rocket engine is proportional to the propellant's exhaust velocity, and find the constant of proportionality.
(c) A chemical rocket engine gives its propellant an exhaust speed of 4.5 km/s. What is the specific impulse of this engine?

C5S.2 A 110-kg football player running at 3 m/s collides head-on with a 55-kg referee by accident. This collision gives an impulse to the referee at the expense of the player. Irrespective of how *large* the impulse is, how will the magnitude of the change in the referee's velocity during the collision compare with that of the player? Explain carefully.

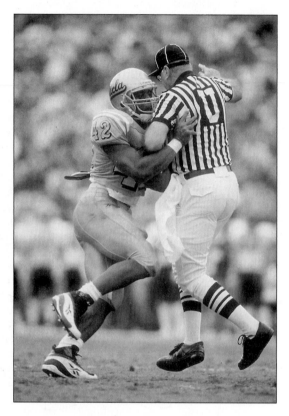

C5S.3 Imagine that someone places you at rest on a flat, utterly frictionless surface. You cannot walk to the edge of the surface, because your shoes will not grip it. Is there another way to use those shoes and the law of conservation of momentum to get off the surface? Explain your solution.

C5S.4 Imagine that a rocket is launched from an asteroid in deep space and fires its engines until the speed of the rocket relative to the asteroid is equal to the speed of the rocket's exhaust. The exhaust ejected by the engine is now at *rest* with respect to the asteroid. If the engines continue to fire, will the rocket's speed with respect to the asteroid still increase? (If it does, note that the exhaust will now move in the same direction as the rocket relative to the asteroid.) Explain whether the rocket can still go faster from the point of view of an observer on the asteroid.

*C5S.5 Two hockey pucks, one with mass m and the other with mass $2m$, slide on a flat, frictionless plane of ice. Originally, the lighter puck is sliding in a direction 30° west of south at a speed of 3 m/s while the more massive puck is sliding in a direction 60° north of east

at 1.5 m/s. The pucks collide and stick together. What is their joint velocity (magnitude and direction) after the collision?

*C5S.6 Two identical hockey pucks slide on a flat, frictionless plane of ice. Originally, one is sliding in a direction 60° south of west at a speed of 2 m/s, while the other is sliding in a direction 30° west of north at a speed of 2 m/s. The pucks collide and stick together. What is their joint velocity (magnitude and direction) after the collision?

*C5S.7 Two people slide on a frictionless, flat, horizontal plane of ice. Person A, whose mass is 54 kg, is sliding due east at a speed of 2.5 m/s. Person B, whose mass is 68 kg, is sliding due south at a speed of 1.8 m/s. These people collide and hold on to each other. What are the magnitude and direction of their joint velocity after the collision?

*C5S.8 In the All-Alaska Ice Floe Softball finals, the right fielder for the Nome IceSox (who is floating on a small chunk of ice in still water) makes an outstanding catch of a line drive. If the combined mass of the fielder and the ice is 540 kg, and it was traveling due north at 0.15 m/s (due to the fielder's frenzied paddling) before the catch, and the ball has a mass of 0.25 kg and is traveling at 32 m/s due east when caught, what is the final heading of the fielder just after the ball is caught?

*C5S.9 A pontoon boat (weight 1200 lb) sits at rest on a still lake near a dock. Your friend Dana, whose weight is 160 lb, runs off the end of the dock at a speed of 15 mi/h and jumps onto the deck of the boat. Dana does not know anything about physics and so is surprised that the boat ends up moving away from the dock. How fast is it moving after Dana lands?

*C5S.10 During the filming of a certain movie scene, the director wants a small car (mass 750 kg) traveling due east at 35 m/s to collide with a small truck (mass 3200 kg) traveling due north. The director also wants the collision to be arranged so that just afterward the interlocked vehicles travel straight toward the camera (which is placed at a safe distance, of course). If the line between the camera and the collision makes an angle of 29° with respect to north, at what speed should the trucker drive?

Rich-Context

*C5R.1 A small asteroid of mass 2.6×10^9 kg is discovered traveling at a speed of 18 km/s on a direct heading for Starbase Alpha, which is in deep space well outside the solar system. Lacking weapons of sufficient power to destroy the asteroid, the frightened starbase inhabitants decide to deflect it by hitting it with a remote-controlled spaceship. The spaceship has an empty mass of 25,000 kg and a top speed of 85 km/s when its fuel is exhausted. The asteroid has to be deflected so that by the time it reaches the starbase, its center is 1800 m away from its original path. What is the minimum time before the asteroid's projected impact that the spaceship must reach the asteroid? Explain carefully (lives are at stake here!).

*C5R.2 An astronaut repairing a communications satellite in deep space floats at rest with respect to the astronaut's spaceship but at a distance of 22 m away from

its open airlock door. The astronaut is not tethered to the ship, but instead uses a jet pack to maneuver around the satellite. The jet pack suddenly fails. The astronaut needs to get back to the ship, but does not want to push on the communications satellite, for fear of changing its position. The astronaut has in hand a power tool, which has a mass of about 0.45 kg. How can the astronaut use it to get back to the ship? Estimate the time (within about a factor of 2 or so) that it will take to get back to the shuttle if the astronaut uses this method.

Advanced

C5A.1 Consider a rocket in deep space whose empty mass is 5200 kg that can carry 52,000 kg of propellant. If the rocket engine can eject 1300 kg/s of propellant from its nozzle at a speed of 3300 m/s relative to the rocket, and if the rocket starts at rest, what is its final speed? This problem is difficult because the ship's mass changes constantly as the propellant is ejected. Either solve the problem *mathematically* using calculus, taking the constantly decreasing mass of the rocket into account, or *numerically* using a calculator or a computer program. If you do the former, note that conservation of momentum implies that the rate of change of the *total* momentum of the rocket and the exhaust must be zero. If you do the latter, pretend that each 1 s the rocket ejects a 1300-kg "chunk" of propellant, and use conservation of momentum to compute the final speed of the rocket (including the remaining propellant). You will have to repeat this calculation for each second that the engines fire.

ANSWERS TO EXERCISES

C5X.1 If the cart begins to move downward, the wheels' suspension is compressed, so the wheels interact more strongly with the surface, causing an excess of upward momentum to flow into the cart until it moves away from the surface enough to restore the balanced momentum flow.

C5X.2 If your friend's model is correct, the surface should shield the cart from gravity just as effectively (or at least almost as effectively) if it is a small distance above the surface instead of being right on the surface. But if you release the cart, it will fall back to the surface just as vigorously as it would do in midair. Indeed, the only situation where the surface seems to "shield" the cart effectively occurs when the cart is in physical contact with the surface, something that is easy for our model to explain but hard for your friend's model.

C5X.3 Depending on the level of approximation you are willing to tolerate, the balls can be either *functionally*

isolated or *not isolated*. The downward momentum transfer each ball gets from gravity during any given time interval would be exactly canceled by an upward momentum transfer from the ball's contact interaction with the table if the balls roll frictionlessly; but with billiard balls there is some friction that leads to imperfect cancellation of these momentum transfers. The cancellation is fairly good, though, because the momentum of a ball usually does not change much as it rolls.

C5X.4 In this case, the frictional part of the interaction between the cars' tires and the road is pretty significant, so the system is not isolated. Even so, we *can* usefully apply conservation of momentum to the collision if we focus on the cars' momenta *just before* and *just after* the collision: the duration of the collision is so short that the net momentum transferred to the system due to the imperfect cancellation of external momentum transfers will be small.

C6

Introduction to Energy

▷ **Introduction**

▷ **Conservation of Momentum**

▽ **Conservation of Energy**

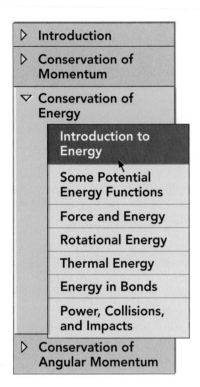

    Introduction to Energy

    Some Potential Energy Functions

    Force and Energy

    Rotational Energy

    Thermal Energy

    Energy in Bonds

    Power, Collisions, and Impacts

▷ **Conservation of Angular Momentum**

Chapter Overview

Introduction

The law of conservation of energy is one of the richest and most productive ideas in all of physics. This chapter launches a long subsection that explores various aspects of this law and lays important foundations for all the remaining units in the course.

Section C6.1: Interactions and Energy

Every fundamental interaction between two particles contains **potential energy** V, a scalar that depends on the particles' separation. A particle has **kinetic energy** K, a scalar that depends only on the particle's mass and speed. A multiparticle system's **total energy** E is

$$E = K_1 + K_2 + K_3 + \cdots + V(r_{12}) + V(r_{13}) + V(r_{23}) + \cdots \qquad \text{(C6.2)}$$

Purpose: This equation defines the total energy E of a multiparticle system.
Symbols: $K_1, K_2, K_3, \ldots$ are the kinetic energies of particles $1, 2, 3, \ldots$; $V(r_{12})$ is the potential energy of the interaction between particles 1 and 2 when they are separated by a distance r_{12}, and so on.
Limitations: This simple form of the equation applies whenever the newtonian model applies (the equation can become more complex in extreme situations).
Note: If a given pair of particles participates in more than one type of interaction, we should include a separate potential energy term for each interaction.

Since any fundamental interaction between a pair of particles simply transfers some of the interaction's potential energy to the particles' kinetic energies (or vice versa), the total energy of an isolated system will be conserved.

Section C6.2: Kinetic Energy

In the context of the newtonian model, this model works empirically if we define

$$K \equiv \tfrac{1}{2}mv^2 \qquad \text{(C6.3)}$$

Purpose: This equation defines the kinetic energy K of a particle of mass m moving at speed v.
Limitations: This turns out to be an approximation that is accurate when the particle's speed is much smaller than that of light.
Notes: Equivalently, $K \equiv p^2/2m$ (equation C6.5). The SI unit of kinetic energy (and thus of energy in general) is the **joule**, where $1\,\text{J} \equiv \text{kg·m}^2/\text{s}^2 = 1\,\text{N·m}$.

One implication of this definition is that whenever the earth interacts with a much lighter object, the earth's kinetic energy is negligible compared to the object's.

Section C6.3: Measuring Potential Energy

If we give the particles of an isolated two-particle system an initial separation r_i and then allow a single interaction to take them to a final separation r_f, conservation of energy implies that we can use their initial and final kinetic energies to calculate the change in the interaction's potential energy:

$$V(r_f) - V(r_i) = K_{1i} - K_{1f} + K_{2i} - K_{2f} \qquad (C6.9)$$

We can explore how V varies with separation by changing r_i or r_f. However, this only gives us the *difference* in V for two different separations, not V at any specific separation. This scheme thus only determines V up to a constant, because if $V(r)$ satisfies equation C6.9, so does $V(r) + C$. This ambiguity in the value of V allows us to *choose* V to be zero at a convenient **reference separation** (the potential energy at any *other* separation is then fixed by equation C6.9).

Experimentally, we find that for the gravitational interaction,

$$V(z) = mgz \qquad (C6.12)$$

Purpose: This equation describes (a possible choice for) the potential energy function for the gravitational interaction between the earth and an object of mass m.

Symbols: $V(z)$ is the interaction's potential energy when the object has a vertical coordinate z in some reference frame and $g = 9.8$ N/kg.

Limitations: This equation assumes that we have chosen our reference separation to be the object's separation from the earth's center when its vertical coordinate is $z = 0$. It applies only when the object is close to the earth's surface.

Section C6.4: Negative Energy?

Our freedom to choose a reference separation means we can *choose* a system's potential energy (and thus its total energy) to be as positive or negative as we like. A negative total energy *only* means the system has less total energy than it would if its particles were at rest at the reference separation. (*Kinetic* energies, though, cannot be negative.)

Section C6.5: A Look Ahead

As we will see, contact interactions between macroscopic objects can convert energy to "hidden" forms that don't behave like either kinetic or potential energy (we will use ΔU to represent a change in a hidden energy). Conservation of energy implies that an isolated system's total energy does not change, so

$$0 = \Delta K_1 + \Delta K_2 + \cdots + \Delta V + \cdots + \Delta U + \cdots \qquad (C6.16)$$

This equation will have one kinetic energy term for each system object and at least one interaction term (usually a potential or hidden energy) for each internal interaction between any pair of objects. In each chapter we will learn how to add appropriate terms for new types of interactions.

Section C6.6: Adapting the Framework to Energy Problems

The translation section of a conservation of energy problem should include

1. Pictures showing initial and final system states.
2. Frame axes on each picture (*if needed*).
3. Labels defining symbols for masses, initial and final velocities, and separations.

The conceptual model diagram will begin with an interaction diagram followed by a master equation in the form of equation C6.16, with a balloon for the equals sign. If you can, write out each term as an explicit difference using the symbols you defined in the translation step. See the section for more details and an example.

C6.1   Interactions and Energy

The law of conservation of energy is one of the richest and most productive ideas in all of physics. It is also in a certain sense more subtle than conservation of momentum: while Newton himself understood that interactions conserve momentum, it was not until the middle decades of the 1800s that the physics community realized fully that energy was also universally conserved.

My goal in this section is to introduce the concept of energy as it applies to fundamental particles and interactions, where the idea appears in its simplest form. Later, we will see that as we attempt to apply the model to *macroscopic* interactions between *macroscopic* objects, the model becomes more complicated: indeed, it will take us a number of chapters to work out all the details. (This is why it took the community so long to develop the idea in the first place!) Our quest to understand the full meaning of this powerful idea will take us on a journey into new realms of physics and greatly broaden our understanding of the physics of everyday phenomena.

The basic energy model

As we saw in chapter C1, the fundamental elements of physical reality are *particles* and the four fundamental *interactions*. We have seen that we can consider any of these interactions to be like a hose that carries momentum from one particle to another. However, it also turns out that we can consider an interaction between two particles as being something that contains a certain amount of **potential energy** V, a *scalar* quantity that depends only on the characteristics of the interaction, the participating particles, and the physical *separation* of those particles. Each particle also contains a certain amount of **kinetic energy** K, a scalar quantity that increases as the particle's mass and speed increase. Any change in the separation of two interacting particles leads to a *transfer* of energy from the interaction's potential energy to the particles' kinetic energies or vice versa: the **total energy** E involved in the interaction, which is defined to be

The total energy involved in an interaction between two particles

$$E = K_1 + K_2 + V(r) \tag{C6.1}$$

(where K_1 and K_2 are the kinetic energies of the two particles and r is their separation), is *conserved*. All four fundamental interactions behave in this way.

Figure C6.1 illustrates this idea in the context of two particles floating in space that attract each other gravitationally. The potential energy V of a gravitational interaction happens to decrease as the particles get closer, but the interaction also causes the particle's speeds to increase at just the right rate so that the increase in their kinetic energies balances the decrease in the interaction's potential energy.

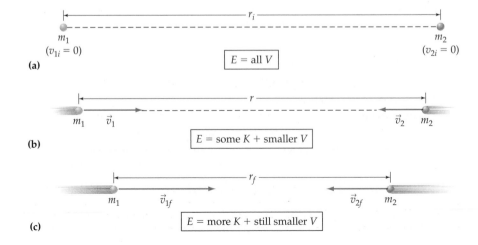

Figure C6.1

The gravitational interaction between two particles transforms gravitational potential energy to the particles' kinetic energies without changing the system's total energy.

What happens if we have a system that involves more than two interacting particles? As one might guess, the total energy of the system is the simple sum of *all* the particles' kinetic energies and the potential energies of *all* internal interactions involving those particles:

The total energy of a multiparticle system

$$E = K_1 + K_2 + K_3 + \cdots + V(r_{12}) + V(r_{13}) + V(r_{23}) + \cdots \quad \text{(C6.2)}$$

Purpose: This equation defines the total energy E of a multiparticle system.

Symbols: K_1, K_2, K_3, ... are the kinetic energies of particles 1, 2, 3, ...; $V(r_{12})$ is the potential energy of the interaction between particles 1 and 2 when they are separated by a distance r_{12}, and so on.

Limitations: This simple form of the equation applies whenever the newtonian model applies (the equation can become more complex in extreme situations).

Note: If a given pair of particles participates in more than one type of interaction, we should include a separate potential energy term for each interaction.

Since internal interactions only involve transfers between the kinetic and potential energies that appear in this sum, a system's total energy is not affected by such internal interactions. But the definition of a system's total energy E excludes potential energies involved in any *external* interactions, which can transfer energy into or out of the kinetic energies of particles in the system and therefore change a system's total energy. Therefore, a system's total energy E will be conserved if the system is *isolated*.

Why energy is conserved

Let me emphasize that K, V, and E are *scalar* quantities that ignore everything about the directions of any motions or separations involved. This is an advantage over momentum, which is intrinsically a vector quantity. However it is a bit more complicated that we have *two* fundamental forms of energy (potential and kinetic) compared to just one form of momentum.[†]

I hope that you can see that the basic *idea* of conservation of energy is pretty simple. The only thing that remains is to define K and V more concretely. We will address this issue in the next two sections.

C6.2   Kinetic Energy

Physicists in the 18th and 19th centuries found that the scheme outlined in the previous section works experimentally as long as we define a particle's kinetic energy to be

$$K \equiv \tfrac{1}{2}mv^2 \quad \text{(C6.3)}$$

The definition of kinetic energy

Purpose: This equation defines the kinetic energy K of a particle of mass m moving at speed v.

Limitations: This turns out to be an approximation that is accurate when the particle's speed is much smaller than that of light.

[†]Actually, momentum and energy are more symmetric than they appear in this regard. Interactions *can* store "potential momentum" just as they store potential energy. But for reasons beyond our scope here, this is important only in unusual, highly dynamic circumstances, whereas potential energy is important and useful in much more common situations.

We will see more clearly *why* kinetic energy should be defined in this way in unit R. For now, you should take this simply as a definition that makes the whole scheme work empirically.

The SI unit of energy

This equation implies that the SI units of kinetic energy must be $kg \cdot (m/s)^2 = kg \cdot m^2/s^2$. Unit consistency in equation C6.1 implies that V and E must have the same units. Since energy is such an important concept in physics, it has its own SI unit, called the **joule,** defined such that

$$1\,J \equiv 1\,\text{joule} \equiv 1\,kg \cdot m^2/s^2 \qquad (C6.4)$$

This is the kinetic energy of a 2-kg object (roughly the mass of a half-gallon carton of milk) moving at 1 m/s (strolling speed). The unit is named for James Joule, one of the physicists who helped develop the modern concept of conservation of energy.

Exercise C6X.1

Show that $1\,J = 1\,N \cdot m$, where N is abbreviation for newton, the SI unit of force.

Exercise C6X.2

Estimate the kinetic energies of a 50-kg person running at 3 m/s and a 1000-kg car moving at 30 m/s.

Note also that if we multiply the right side of equation C6.3 by $1 = m/m$, and use the definition $p \equiv mag(\vec{p}) = mv$, we find that

$$K \equiv \frac{(mv)^2}{2m} = \frac{p^2}{2m} \qquad (C6.5)$$

This is an alternative expression for the kinetic energy that we will find very useful.

Why we can often ignore the earth's kinetic energy

Consider now an isolated system of two particles with masses m_1 and m_2 initially at rest in some inertial reference frame (see figure C6.2). Imagine that the particles interact for a certain amount of time. Since the total momentum of the system is initially zero, if the first particle ends up with momentum $\vec{p}_1$ at the end of this period of time, the other must end up with a momentum of $\vec{p}_2 = -\vec{p}_1$, implying that the magnitudes of their final momenta are equal: $p_1 \equiv mag(\vec{p}_1) = mag(\vec{p}_2) \equiv p_2$. The particles also both have zero initial kinetic energy. How do their final kinetic energies compare? According to the definition of kinetic energy in equation C6.5,

$$\frac{K_2}{K_1} = \frac{p_2^2/2m_2}{p_1^2/2m_1} = \frac{m_1}{m_2} \qquad (C6.6)$$

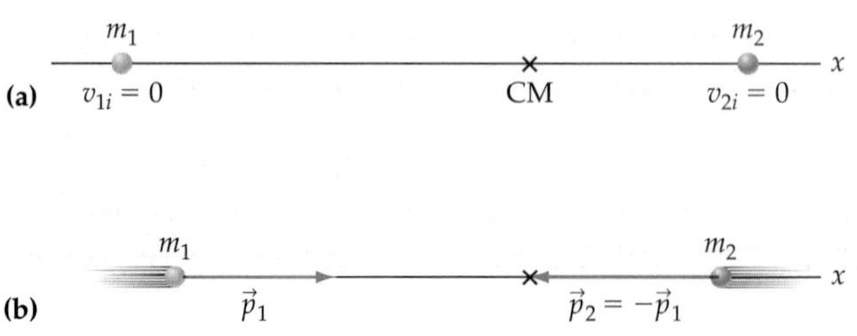

Figure C6.2

(a) Two particles initially at rest in a given frame. (b) After the particles participate in an attractive interaction for a short time, each ends up with a momentum that is the vector inverse of the other's.

We see that while this interaction always gives the particles *equal* magnitudes of momentum (assuming the particles start from rest), it gives each particle a kinetic energy *inversely proportional to its mass*.

This has the very important implication that *when something of normal mass interacts with the earth, the earth's kinetic energy can be completely ignored,* since if $m_2 \gg m_1$, equation C6.6 implies that $K_2 \ll K_1$. We will find this useful when we consider gravitational potential energy in section C6.3.

Exercise C6X.3

Imagine that a 6000-kg truck initially at rest with respect to the earth interacts with the earth and ends up with 100,000 J of energy. What is kinetic energy that the entire earth gains as a result of this interaction?

C6.3   Measuring Potential Energy

Consider now a single interaction acting between two otherwise isolated particles. Let the particles' kinetic energies be K_{1i} and K_{2i} and their separation be r_i at a certain initial instant of time and K_{1f}, K_{2f}, and r_f at some later instant. Equation C6.1 implies that

A scheme for measuring potential energy

$$E_i = K_{1i} + K_{2i} + V(r_i) \qquad (C6.7a)$$

$$E_f = K_{1f} + K_{2f} + V(r_f) \qquad (C6.7b)$$

Conservation of energy implies that $E_i = E_f$. Therefore, if we subtract equation C6.7a from C6.7b, we get

$$0 = [K_{1f} - K_{1i}] + [K_{2f} - K_{2i}] + [V(r_f) - V(r_i)] \qquad (C6.8)$$

If we measure the particles' kinetic energies when they have a certain separation r_i, allow the system to evolve until the particles reach a new separation r_f, and measure their kinetic energies again, then equation C6.8 implies that we can calculate the change in the interaction's potential energy in the process as follows:

$$V(r_f) - V(r_i) = K_{1i} - K_{1f} + K_{2i} - K_{2f} \qquad (C6.9)$$

By repeating this measurement scheme for different values of r_f and/or r_i we can graph how the interaction's potential energy V depends on the particles' separation r. The energy model predicts that we should find the potential energy difference $V(r_f) - V(r_i)$ to depend *only* on the characteristics of the particles, the type of interaction, and the *values* of the separations r_i and r_f, but *not* on the particles' initial kinetic energies or the path the particles follow in getting from separation r_i to separation r_f.

Let's apply this scheme to measuring the potential energy of the gravitational interaction between a freely falling object of mass m (say, a ball) and the earth. Since gravity is one of the four fundamental interactions, it *should* have a well-defined potential energy $V(r)$.

Application to a simple falling object

We have seen in previous chapters that interactions between macroscopic objects can be treated as interactions between point particles, so we will model both the ball and the earth as point particles located at their respective centers of mass. The system of the earth and the ball floats in space, so if we also use a frame that floats in space, we can ignore the system's external gravitational interactions with the rest of the universe and treat the system as isolated.

For the sake of simplicity, assume that we do a series of experimental runs where the final position of the ball's center of mass is fixed, so that the final separation between the ball and the earth has a fixed value r_f. Let us simplify things further by dropping the ball from rest. This means that the ball's initial kinetic energy is zero. Moreover, we saw in section C6.2 that under such circumstances, the earth's kinetic energy is always negligible, so $\Delta K_{earth} \approx 0$. Therefore, equation C6.9 in this case simplifies to

$$V(r_i) - V(r_f) = +K_f = \tfrac{1}{2}mv_f^2 \qquad (C6.10)$$

where K is the ball's final kinetic energy, m is its mass, and v_f is its final speed at the separation r_f from the earth. An experimental setup we might use to do the job is shown in figure C6.3a. Note that if we set up a reference frame whose z axis is vertical, the *change $r_i - r_f$* in the object's separation from the earth's center is the same as the change $z_i - z_f$ in its vertical coordinate.

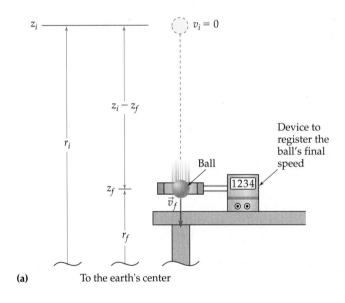

(a)   To the earth's center

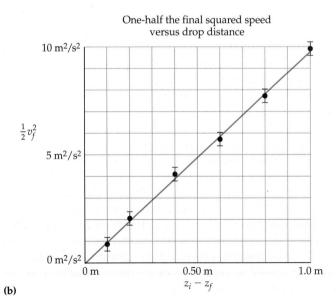

Figure C6.3

(a) An experiment to measure how the potential energy of an object's gravitational interaction with the earth varies with separation. (b) A graph of the experimental results.

(b)

Figure C6.3b shows a graph of experimental results for $\frac{1}{2}v_f^2 = K_f/m$ plotted as a function of drop distance $z_i - z_f$. No matter what the ball's mass is, it turns out (for values of h small compared to the radius of the earth anyway) that the graph is a straight line with slope 9.8 $(\text{m}^2/\text{s}^2)/\text{m} = 9.8$ m/s^2. Since $1\,\text{N} = 1\,\text{kg}\cdot\text{m/s}^2$, we could also express this value as 9.8 N/kg, which is precisely the magnitude of the gravitational field vector $\vec{g}$ near the surface of the earth (see equation C3.8). Therefore, we see experimentally that

An empirical formula for gravitational potential energy

$$\frac{1}{2}v_f^2 = g(z_i - z_f) \qquad \text{but} \qquad \frac{1}{2}v_f^2 = \frac{K_f}{m} = \frac{V(r_i) - V(r_f)}{m}$$

$$\Rightarrow \qquad V(r_i) - V(r_f) = mg(z_i - z_f) = mg(r_i - r_f) \qquad \text{(C6.11)}$$

We will learn more about *why* $V(r)$ should be related to g in chapter C8, but it is certainly plausible that the potential energy might depend on the strength of the earth's gravitational field, which is what g expresses.

We see that (assuming $z_i > z_f$) the gravitational interaction's potential energy is *larger* when the ball is at its initial position than at its final position. This makes perfect sense: as the ball falls, the potential energy of its gravitational interaction with the earth *decreases*, but its kinetic energy *increases*, conserving its total energy.

Exercise C6X.4

In circumstances where an object interacts with the earth, it is tempting to think of the potential energy as belonging to the *object* instead of the interaction, since the potential energy varies as the *object* changes position (the earth seems fixed). Many textbooks in fact would say that "the object's potential energy is converted to kinetic energy" as it falls. Why is this kind of language *not* helpful when the interacting objects have comparable mass?

One might be tempted to conclude from equation C6.11 that the potential energy function $V(r)$ for the gravitational interaction (at least at points near the earth) is $V(r) = mgr$. Such a function certainly would be consistent with equation C6.11, but so would the function $V(r) = mgr + C$, where C is any constant value (note that the C's will simply cancel out in equation C6.11). This problem arises because our experiment only allows us to measure the *difference* $V(r_i) - V(r_f)$. Indeed, *any* experiment based on the scheme outlined in equation C6.9 only allows us to measure the potential energy difference $V(r_i) - V(r_f)$, never $V(r_i)$ or $V(r_f)$ separately. In fact, there are no known laws of physics that allow us to determine anything *but* the difference $V(r_i) - V(r_f)$ unambiguously. Therefore, we can only determine an interaction's potential energy up to a constant.

Potential energy is defined only up to a constant

You may find this disturbing. After all, in section C6.1, I told you that an interaction between two objects separated by a given distance r "has" a potential energy $V(r)$; but now I am telling you that we can never know for certain what the value of that potential energy is! What good is this? Well, the flip side of ambiguity in this case is *freedom*. The laws of physics never involve anything but the *difference* $V(r_f) - V(r_i)$ in the interaction's potential energy at two separations. This means that while we cannot unambiguously define the value of $V(r)$ at a given separation, it also means that the laws of physics don't ever *care* what value we assign to the potential energy, so we can choose that value to be anything that is *convenient!*

Our freedom to define a *reference separation*

In other words, we are completely free to *determine* the value of V at a given separation by arbitrarily choosing a **reference separation** r_0 and *defining* the interaction's potential energy to be zero at that separation: $V(r_0) \equiv 0$ (this essentially chooses the value for the overall constant that we are free to choose). Then, if we use that reference separation as either r_i or r_f in equation C6.9, we can measure $V(r)$ at any other position.

For example, imagine that we set up a coordinate system in standard orientation on the earth's surface. We can use our freedom to define a reference separation to set $V = 0$ when an object interacting gravitationally with the earth is at vertical position $z = 0$ in our frame. This is convenient because (1) we don't have to even think about the *actual* separation between the object and the earth's center of mass (which will be in excess of 6300 km, an inconveniently large number) and (2) the potential energy function for the interaction becomes simply

A potential energy formula for the gravitational interaction

$$V(z) = mgz \qquad \text{(C6.12)}$$

Purpose: This equation describes (one possible choice for) the potential energy function for the gravitational interaction between the earth and an object of mass m.

Symbols: $V(z)$ is the interaction's potential energy when the object has vertical coordinate z in some given reference frame, and g is the gravitational field strength $= \text{mag}(\vec{g}) = 9.8$ N/kg near the earth's surface.

Limitations: This equation assumes that we have chosen our reference separation to be the object's separation from the earth's center when its vertical coordinate is $z = 0$. It applies only when the object is close to the earth's surface.

We could have just as easily chosen V to be zero at $z = +22$ m or $z = -47$ m. It also doesn't matter whether our origin is at the top of a mountain or the bottom of the sea (even though $z = 0$ corresponds to very different separations between the object and the earth's center in such cases). Since the predictions that the law of conservation of energy makes in each case depend only on the *difference* between $V(r_i)$ and $V(r_f)$, all choices of reference separation are physically equivalent.

Example C6.1

Problem Imagine that we define the reference separation for the potential energy of a 5-kg object's gravitational interaction with the earth to be when that object is at a vertical position of $z = -10$ m in our given reference frame. What is the interaction's potential energy when the object is at $z = 0$? When it is at $z = -15$ m? What constant would we be adding to equation C6.12 in this case?

Translation Let $z_0 = -10$ m, $z_1 = 0$, and $z_2 = -15$ m; and let $V(z)$ be the gravitational interaction's potential energy when the object is at some arbitrary vertical position z.

Model   Equation C6.11 implies that

$$V(z) - V(z_0) = mg(z - z_0) \qquad\qquad \text{(C6.13a)}$$

Solution   If we choose the reference separation to be when $z = z_0$, then we are *defining* $V(z_0) \equiv 0$, so the expression above becomes simply

$$V(z) = mg(z - z_0) = mgz - mgz_0 \qquad\qquad \text{(C6.13b)}$$

Note that this is the same as expression C6.12 except that we have added a constant term with the value $-mgz_0 = -(5\text{ kg})(9.8\text{ N/kg})(-10\text{ m}) = +490\,\text{N·m} = 490\,\text{J}$ (according to the result of exercise C6X.1). Therefore

$$V(z_1) = mgz_1 - mgz_0 = 0 + 490\text{ J} = +490\text{ J} \qquad\qquad \text{(C6.14a)}$$

$$V(z_2) = mgz_2 - mgz_0 = (5\,\cancel{\text{kg}})(9.8\,\cancel{\text{N/kg}})(-15\,\cancel{\text{m}})\left(\frac{1\text{ J}}{1\,\cancel{\text{N·m}}}\right) + 490\text{ J}$$

$$= -735\text{ J} + 490\text{ J} = -245\text{ J} \qquad\qquad \text{(C6.14b)}$$

Evaluation   Note that the units are all consistent. The sign of the last result may seem surprising, but see section C6.4.

Exercise C6X.5

Imagine that we define the reference separation for the potential energy of a 3-kg object's gravitational interaction with the earth to be when that object is at $z = z_0 = +10$ m. (a) What constant would we be adding to equation C6.12 in this case? (b) What is the interaction's potential energy when the object is at $z = z_1 = 0$? When it is at $z = z_2 = +20$ m? (c) If we defined the reference position to be $z = 0$, what would the interaction's potential energies be when the object was at these two positions? (d) Demonstrate explicitly that the potential energy *difference* $V(z_2) - V(z_1)$ is the same whether we define the reference position to be $z = +10$ m or $z = 0$.

C6.4   Negative Energy?

Our freedom to choose the reference separation where $V = 0$ means that we can choose an interaction's potential energy to be *negative*. For example, if we set up a standard coordinate system on the surface of the earth and choose the reference separation for an object interacting gravitationally with the earth to be when the object is at $z = 0$ (on the surface of the earth), then if the object is anywhere *below* the surface of the earth (say, in a pit or well) its gravitational potential energy will be *negative* [since $V(z) = mgz$ and $z < 0$]. To be specific, if a 3-kg object is placed 5.0 m below the ground, the interaction's potential energy is $mgz = (3.0\text{ kg})(9.8\text{ m/s}^2)(-5.0\text{ m}) = -147\text{ kg·m}^2/\text{s}^2 = -147\text{ J}$.

What does it mean for a system to have a negative potential energy? The minus sign here has nothing to do with *direction* (as it does when we are considering vectors): energy is a *scalar* and thus has no direction. If an interaction's potential energy is negative at a given separation, this simply means its value at that separation is *smaller* than it would be at the reference separation, that's all! So when we say that the interaction potential energy is -147 J when

How to interpret negative potential energies

our 3-kg object is 5 m below the ground, we are really saying only that this energy is in this case 147 J smaller than it would be when the object was at ground level.

Perhaps you can see that our freedom to choose the reference separation means that we can *choose* to make the system's potential energy at any given separation either positive or negative. *Neither the sign nor the value of a potential energy has any direct physical meaning:* only the *difference* between potential energy values at different separations has any physical meaning.

How to interpret negative total energies

By choosing the reference separation in a certain way, we might even make our system's *total* energy negative. For example, if we have a 3-kg object gravitationally interacting with the earth at rest at $z = -5$ m and our reference separation is when the object is at $z = 0$, the *total* energy E of the system involving the earth and the object is $E = K_1 + K_2 + V = 0 - 0 - 147\,\text{J} = -147\,\text{J}$. This negative total energy should be interpreted as meaning simply that the system's total energy in this situation is 147 J smaller than it would be if the earth and object were at rest at the reference separation. Negative potential or total energies should *not* be a source of alarm (although a negative kinetic energy *is* impossible).

We can *never* determine the absolute total energy in a system!

This emphasizes, though, that because there is no known way to determine the absolute amount of *potential* energy involved in an interaction, there is no way to determine the absolute amount of total *energy* in a system. The total energy in a system is conserved, but its actual *value* depends on choices we make.

C6.5   A Look Ahead

In this chapter, we have learned how to write the potential energy $V(r)$ of the gravitational interaction between the earth and an object near the earth's surface. In chapter C7 we will learn how to write potential energy functions for electrostatic interactions as well as gravitational interactions in more general situations. Since these interactions are fundamental interactions (even when they operate between macroscopic objects), they fit nicely into the simple energy model discussed in this chapter.

Handling contact interactions

Contact interactions between macroscopic objects, however, are another story. At the deepest level, contact interactions are simply electromagnetic interactions, so energy *is* conserved by such interactions. But, as we will discuss in chapter C9, contact interactions such as friction can seem to remove energy from a system. What such interactions really do is channel energy into "hidden" forms of energy (e.g., the kinetic and potential energy of individual vibrating atoms) that at the macroscopic level often do not seem much like either potential or kinetic energy. We will describe changes in "hidden" energies by using the symbol ΔU.

Example expressions of the law of conservation of energy

For the case of an isolated system consisting of just two objects participating in a single fundamental interaction, we can write the law of conservation of energy in the form

$$0 = \Delta K_1 + \Delta K_2 + \Delta V \qquad\qquad (C6.15a)$$

where $\Delta K_1 \equiv K_{1f} - K_{1i}$ is the change in the first object's kinetic energy, ΔK_2 is the same for the second object, and ΔV is the change in the interaction's potential energy during some process of interest. This version of the law essentially states that the *change* in an isolated system's total energy during the process must be zero. For each *additional* fundamental interaction between the two objects, we would add another potential energy term to this equation.

For example, if the objects participate in both a gravitational and an electrostatic interaction, we might write

$$0 = \Delta K_1 + \Delta K_2 + \Delta V_g + \Delta V_e \qquad \text{(C6.15b)}$$

For each different type of *contact* interaction acting between the objects we will also add at least one term, usually a hidden energy term (but sometimes a kinetic or potential energy term). For example, a tennis ball converts some of its kinetic energy to hidden energy when it bounces (this is why it does not rebound quite as high). In a conservation of energy problem involving a bouncing tennis ball, therefore, we might write

$$0 = \Delta K_1 + \Delta K_2 + \Delta V_g + \Delta U \qquad \text{(C6.15c)}$$

In chapters C7 through C12, we will look at various kinds of interactions. Each time we consider a possible new interaction between objects, we will learn exactly what kind of energy term or terms we have to add to equation C6.15 to represent that interaction and how to calculate that change in energy in terms of macroscopically measurable variables. At present we really know how to handle only *one* kind of interaction: a gravitational interaction between the earth and an object close to the earth. We represent this interaction in equation C6.15 by including a potential energy term of the form $V(z) = mgz$ (see equation C6.12 for details and restrictions).

We will only rarely consider systems involving more than two distinguishable objects, but in such a case, as discussed in section C6.1, we have to include a kinetic energy term for each moving object and a potential energy or some other interaction energy term for each interaction between each *pair* of objects.

In *principle*, we could write the law of conservation of energy in the form $E_i = E_f$, where E_i is the system's total energy before the process of interest and E_f is its total energy after that process. However, as we have seen, only potential energy *differences* are physically meaningful. The same is true of *internal* energies: indeed, we will see that it is even *more* awkward to define a unique value for an object's internal energy at a given time than it is to define a unique value for an interaction's potential energy at a given separation! Moreover, as we will see in section C6.6, we can directly link the terms in equation C6.15 to items in an interaction diagram, and this makes interaction diagrams more effective as helping diagrams for solving conservation of energy problems. For all of these reasons, I will consistently express the law of conservation of energy in *difference* form in this volume.

C6.6   Adapting the Framework to Energy Problems

We can adapt the problem-solving framework discussed in chapter C5 to conservation of energy problems by making a few minor changes of emphasis. Since kinetic, potential, and total energies are all scalars, reference frame *directions* are typically less important than they are for problems involving vectors, and may not be necessary at all (although it is often useful to define a vertical z axis in problems that involve something interacting gravitationally with the earth). Your *translation* section should, however, include the items on this checklist (in addition to the usual list of symbols with known values):

What you should do in a *translation* step

1. *Two* pictures that show the system in its initial and final states, respectively.
2. Reference frame axes on each picture to define coordinate directions (*if needed*).

The helping diagram for conservation of energy problems

3. Labels defining symbols for masses and initial and final velocities and separations of all system objects (as well as any other useful quantities).

Your *conceptual model diagram* for a conservation of energy problem solution, just as for a conservation of momentum problem solution, should begin with an *interaction diagram*. However, in addition to drawing and labeling boxes for objects and lines for interactions, write a symbol (such as ΔK_1 or ΔK_2) in each box that corresponds to an object *inside* the system to represent the change in that object's kinetic energy during the process of interest, and write a symbol (such as ΔV) near the line that corresponds to each significant *internal* interaction to represent the change in that interaction's potential energy during the same process. If you are treating an internal interaction (such as friction) as negligible, write "(small)" or "(negl.)" near the line instead. We will discuss in subsequent chapters what to write for macroscopic interactions that involve significant internal energy changes.

The master equation for conservation of energy problems

The master equation for your model will express the law of conservation of energy (abbreviation CoE) for your system. First write a version of this equation, using the symbols you defined in your interaction diagram, in the following form:

$$0 = \Delta K_1 + \Delta K_2 + \cdots + \Delta V + \cdots \qquad (C6.16)$$

(Include only *significant* interactions in this equation). Then immediately rewrite the equation in the same order, expressing each term using the more basic quantities you defined in your *translation* step. For example, you might rewrite the term ΔK_1 as $\frac{1}{2}m_1 v_{1f}^2 - \frac{1}{2}m_1 v_{1i}^2$ if m_1 is the mass of object 1 and v_{1f} and v_{1i} are its final and initial speeds, respectively. Use cartoon balloons to explain anything that is not obvious or any approximations that you make.

Now you can proceed to finish the conceptual model diagram in the usual way. In many problems involving gravity, the object's mass often cancels out. Watch for this.

Example C6.2 illustrates the process (again, note that I have provided both a prose and a diagram version of the model). Carefully note how I have noted the fact that $V(z) = mgz$ only applies near the earth's surface and how I have handled the fact that the earth's kinetic energy is approximately zero (because the earth is so much more massive than the penny): the same issues arise in many problems. The latter case illustrates that it is sometimes useful to draw a cartoon balloon when one assigns a *value* to a symbol when that value represents an approximation or involves an assumption.

Note also that in a prose version of the model, it is often easier to start with an abstract version of the conservation of energy equation and then explain each term. (Doing the same thing on the diagram, though, would make it needlessly complex.)

Example C6.2

Problem (A Penny from Heaven) Imagine that you accidentally drop a penny from the observation deck of the Empire State Building (height $\approx$ 1200 ft = 370 m). Ignoring air friction, what will be the penny's approximate speed when it hits the ground? Why would you guess that throwing things off the observation deck is forbidden?

Translation

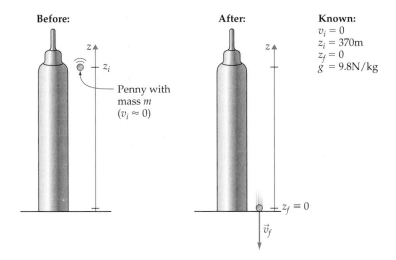

Before:

z_i

Penny with
mass m
($v_i \approx 0$)

After:

$z_f \equiv 0$

$\vec{v}_f$

Known:
$v_i = 0$
$z_i = 370\text{m}$
$z_f = 0$
$g = 9.8\text{N/kg}$

Conceptual Model Diagram

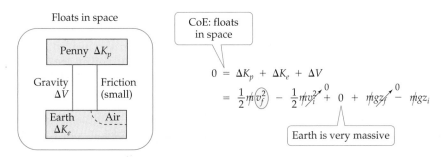

Floats in space

Penny ΔK_p

Gravity
ΔV

Friction
(small)

Earth
ΔK_e

Air

CoE: floats
in space

$$0 = \Delta K_p + \Delta K_e + \Delta V$$
$$= \tfrac{1}{2}m v_f^2 - \tfrac{1}{2}m\cancelto{0}{v_i^2} + 0 + \cancelto{0}{mgz_f} - mgz_i$$

Earth is very massive

Prose Model   Conservation of energy in this case implies that $0 = \Delta K_p + \Delta K_e + \Delta V + \Delta U$, where the four terms refer to the change in the penny's kinetic energy, the change in the earth's kinetic energy and the change in the potential energy of the gravitational interaction between the earth and penny, and the possible change in hidden energy due to the friction interaction between the penny and the air. Here $\Delta K_e \approx 0$ because the earth is so much more massive than the penny. We will also assume that air friction is negligible, so $\Delta U \approx 0$. The penny's initial kinetic energy is zero, so $\Delta K_p = \tfrac{1}{2}m v_f^2$. Since the penny is near the earth's surface at all times, we can write the gravitational potential energy change as $\Delta V = mgz_f - mgz_i = -mgz_i$, since $z_f = 0$. Note that the penny's mass m factors out of each of these surviving terms, so it should cancel out of the problem. The only unknown is v_f, so we should be able to solve.

Solution   Plugging $\Delta K_p = \tfrac{1}{2}m v_f^2$ and $\Delta V = -mgz_i$ into the master equation and solving for v_f, we get

$$0 = \tfrac{1}{2}m v_f^2 - mgz_i \quad \Rightarrow \quad \tfrac{1}{2}v_f^2 = gz_i \quad \Rightarrow \quad v_f = \sqrt{2gz_i} \quad \text{(C6.17)}$$

$$\Rightarrow \quad v_f = \sqrt{2gz_i} = \sqrt{2\left(9.8\frac{\text{N}}{\text{kg}}\right)(370\,\text{m})\left(\frac{1\,\text{kg·m/s}^2}{1\,\text{N}}\right)}$$

$$= 85\,\text{m/s}\left(\frac{2.2\,\text{mi/h}}{1\,\text{m/s}}\right) = 187\,\text{mi/h} \quad \text{(C6.18)}$$

Evaluation This answer does have the right units and is positive (as a speed should be). The final speed is pretty large, but doesn't seem unbelievable. It is pretty clear, though, that throwing things off the observation deck is forbidden because even something as small as a penny traveling this fast could have potentially fatal consequences if anyone were hit by it.

Again, arraying the full power of the conceptual model diagram against such a simple problem is overkill. But don't fret; we will hit challenging problems soon enough, and by practicing simple problems first, you will be a lean, mean, problem-solving machine by then.

TWO-MINUTE PROBLEMS

C6T.1 Which has the larger kinetic energy, a 50-kg person running at a speed of 2 m/s or a 5-g nickel falling at a speed of 200 m/s?
A. The running person.
B. The falling nickel.
C. Both have the same kinetic energy.

C6T.2 How does the kinetic energy K_{fast} of a car traveling at 50 mi/h compare with the kinetic energy K_{slow} of an identical car traveling at 25 mi/h? (The consequences of a collision are in rough proportion to the energy involved!)
A. Both cars are identical, so $K_{fast} = K_{slow}$.
B. $K_{fast} \approx 1.5 K_{slow}$.
C. $K_{fast} \approx 2 K_{slow}$.
D. $K_{fast} \approx 4 K_{slow}$.
E. Other (explain).

C6T.3 A person throws three identical rocks off a cliff of height h with exactly the same speed v_0 each time (see the drawing). Rock A is thrown almost vertically upward, rock B is thrown horizontally, and rock C is thrown almost vertically downward. Which rock hits the ground with the greatest *speed*? (Ignore air friction.)

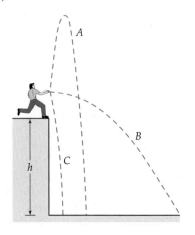

A. Rock A.
B. Rock B.
C. Rock C.
D. All rocks hit with the same speed.
E. Other (specify).

C6T.4 Imagine that we know from experiments that when the object moves from point A to point B, the potential energy of its gravitational interaction with the earth *increases* by 24 J, and that when the object moves from point B to point C, the potential energy of its system *decreases* by 18 J. If we define the system's reference separation to be when the object is at point C, what is the value of the system's potential energy when the object is at point A?
A. +6 J
B. −6 J
C. −52 J
D. +52 J
E. 0
F. Other (specify)

C6T.5 In a coordinate system where the z axis is vertical, we choose the gravitational potential energy of a 4-kg rock interacting with the earth to be zero when $z = -5$ m. The formula for the potential energy as a function of z is thus $V(z) = mgz + C$. What is the (approximate) value of C?
A. −50 J
B. +50 J
C. −200 J
D. +200 J
E. 0
F. Other (specify)

C6T.6 There is no way to *experimentally* determine the actual value of a system's total energy, true (T) or false (F)?

C6T.7 Consider a rock interacting gravitationally with the earth. Imagine that we define the interaction's potential energy to be zero if the rock is at ground level. A person standing at the bottom of a well throws the rock vertically upward from 20 m below ground level. The rock makes it all the way up to 1 m below ground level before falling back into the well. The total energy of the rock-earth system is

A. Negative.
B. Zero.
C. Positive (in this particular case).
D. Positive because energy is *always* positive.
E. The answer depends on the rock's mass.
F. The answer depends on the rock's initial speed.
T. The answer depends on something else (specify).

HOMEWORK PROBLEMS

Basic Skills

C6B.1 A car is traveling north at 30 mi/h. A truck having 4 times the mass of the car is traveling at 60 mi/h west. How many times greater is the truck's kinetic energy than the car's? Explain your reasoning.

C6B.2 A typical arrow might have a mass of 100 g and move at a speed of about 100 m/s. How does its kinetic energy compare to that of person weighing 110 lb running at a speed of 8.8 mi/h?

C6B.3 Consider an object interacting gravitationally with the earth. If we move the object from vertical position A to vertical position B, we find that the system's gravitational potential energy *increases* by 10 J. If we move it from vertical position B to vertical position C, the system's potential energy *decreases* by 5 J. If we take the system's reference separation to be when the object is at position B, what is the system's potential energy when the object is at each of the three points?

C6B.4 Consider a 5-kg object interacting gravitationally with the earth. Imagine that we set up a standard reference frame with the z axis pointing vertically upward. If the interaction's potential energy when the object is at $z = 5$ m is -50 J, what is the approximate z-position of the object when it is at its reference separation from the earth?

C6B.5 Consider a 0.25-kg ball interacting gravitationally with the earth. Imagine that we set up a reference frame in standard orientation on the earth's surface and define ground level to be the reference separation and set $z = 0$ there. Imagine that a person throws the ball upward into the air and that as the ball leaves the person's grasp 2.0 m above the ground, it has a speed of 12 m/s. What is the *system* involved here, and what is its total energy at this time?

C6B.6 Consider a 0.20-kg ball interacting gravitationally with the earth. Imagine that we set up a reference frame in standard orientation on the earth's surface and define ground level to be the reference separation and set $z = 0$ there. Imagine that a person at the bottom of a well throws the ball upward and that when the ball leaves the person's grasp 8.0 m below the ground, it has a speed of 6 m/s. What is the system's total energy at this time?

Synthetic

The starred problems are especially well suited for practicing the use of the problem-solving framework and conceptual model diagrams.

C6S.1 A 1000-kg car travels down a road at 25 m/s (55 mi/h). What is its kinetic energy? Now imagine that the car's speed increases to 35 m/s (77 mi/h), which is 40% faster. Is the kinetic energy 40% larger or not? (Note that the severity of a crash is roughly proportional to the kinetic energy that participants bring to it.)

C6S.2 Imagine that if you drop an object from a certain height, its final speed is 20 m/s when it reaches the ground. If you throw the object vertically downward from the same height with an initial speed of 20 m/s, will its final speed be 40 m/s? Carefully explain why or why not.

*C6S.3 A 2.0-kg coconut (initially at rest) falls from the top of a coconut tree 15 m high. What is the coconut's kinetic energy when it hits the ground? What is its speed?

*C6S.4 If a person wanting to dive from a seaside cliff does not feel safe hitting the water faster than 20 m/s (44 mi/h), what is the maximum height from which he or she should dive?

*C6S.5 Imagine that you are standing at the top of a cliff 45 m high overlooking the ocean and you throw a rock straight downward at a speed of 15 m/s. What is the rock's speed when it hits the water?

*C6S.6 Imagine that you are throwing a tennis ball at a Frisbee lodged in a tree 15 m above the ground. If you want the ball's speed to be at least 5 m/s when it hits the Frisbee, what should its speed be as it leaves your hand? Does your answer depend on the angle that the ball's velocity makes with the horizontal when it leaves your hand?

Rich-Context

*C6R.1 You are designing a safety net for use by firefighters that can safely catch a person jumping from the top of a 30-story building. What will be the person's approximate speed when hitting the net? How much kinetic energy will the net have to convert safely to other forms? (Make appropriate estimates.)

C6R.2 In July 1994, about 20 fragments of comet Shoemaker-Levy struck the planet Jupiter, each traveling at a final speed of roughly 60 km/s. These impacts were closely studied because they promised to be the most cataclysmic impacts ever witnessed. No one knew

exactly *how* cataclysmic, though, because the fragments' sizes (and thus masses) were too small to measure. One estimate of the total energy released by fragment G's impact was 4×10^{22} J (equivalent to the detonation of roughly 100 million typical atomic bombs). Use *this* to estimate fragment G's size, first assuming first that it was solid rock and then that it was solid ice, which have densities of about 3000 kg/m^3 and 920 kg/m^3, respectively. Don't worry about being excessively precise. (This illustrates how even a little knowledge about kinetic energy can help answer questions about objects that can barely be *seen* by the best telescopes!)

An infrared image of the fireball created when fragment G hit Jupiter. The energy released by the impact can be estimated from images like this.

ANSWERS TO EXERCISES

C6X.1 According to chapter C3, $1 \text{ N} \equiv 1 \text{ kg·m/s}^2$, so

$$1 \text{ J} = 1 \text{ J} \left(\frac{1 \text{ kg·m}^2/\text{s}^2}{1 \text{ J}} \right) \left(\frac{1 \text{ N}}{1 \text{ kg·m/s}^2} \right) = 1 \text{ N·m}$$

(C6.19)

C6X.2 The person's kinetic energy is $\frac{1}{2}(50 \text{ kg})(3 \text{ m/s})^2 = 225 \text{ kg·m}^2/\text{s}^2 = 225 \text{ J}$, while the car's kinetic energy is $\frac{1}{2}(1000 \text{ kg})(30 \text{ m/s})^2 = 450,000 \text{ kg·m}^2/\text{s}^2 = 450,000 \text{ J}$.

C6X.3 According to the inside front cover, the earth's mass is about 6×10^{24} kg. Therefore equation C6.6 implies

that

$$\frac{K_{\text{earth}}}{K_{\text{truck}}} = \frac{m_{\text{truck}}}{m_{\text{earth}}} = \frac{6 \times 10^3 \text{ kg}}{6 \times 10^{26} \text{ kg}} = 10^{-23}$$

(C6.20)

Therefore, the earth's kinetic energy is about $10^{-23}(10^5 \text{ J}) = 10^{-18}$ J, which is immeasurably small compared to the truck's energy.

C6X.4 When the two objects have comparable mass (e.g., like repelling magnetic carts on a track), the positions of *both* carts change appreciably during the interaction and both carts' kinetic energies change in response to changes in the interaction's potential energy. Which cart in such a situation would you want to say "has" the potential energy? Talking about the *interaction's potential energy* also emphasizes the fact that there would *be* no potential energy without the interaction. We will also see in unit E that the model is more literally true than we might think: we can actually calculate how much energy an electromagnetic field stores per unit volume in the space surrounding charged objects!

C6X.5 (a) As in example C6.1, $V(z) = mgz - mgz_0$, where $mgz_0 = (3\,\text{kg})(9.8\,\text{N/kg})(10\,\text{m}) = 294\,\text{N·m} = 294\,\text{J}$.

(b) Therefore, $V(z_1) = 0 - 294\,\text{J} = -294\,\text{J}$ and $V(z_2) = (3\,\text{kg})(9.8\,\text{N/kg})(20\,\text{m}) - 294\,\text{J} = +294\,\text{J}$.

(c) When the reference separation is defined to be when the object is at $z = 0$, we can use equation C6.12 without modification to compute the potential energies: $V(z_1) = 0\,\text{J}$ and $V(z_2) = +588\,\text{J}$.

(d) Note that $V(z_2) - V(z_1) = 294\,\text{J} - (-294\,\text{J}) = +588\,\text{J}$ if the reference point is at $z = +10\,\text{m}$, and $V(z_2) - V(z_1) = +588\,\text{J} - 0\,\text{J} = +588\,\text{J}$ if it is at $z = 0$.

C7

Some Potential Energy Functions

Chapter Overview

Introduction

In chapter C6, we saw that we could write the law of conservation of energy in the form $0 = \Delta K_1 + \Delta K_2 + \cdots + \Delta V + \cdots + \Delta U + \cdots$, where the ΔK, ΔV, and ΔU terms refer to changes in kinetic, potential, and hidden energies, respectively. Our main task from here through chapter C11 is to learn what terms we have to add to this equation to describe various common types of interactions. We begin the process in this chapter by discussing potential energy functions for several important interactions.

Section C7.1: The Electromagnetic Interaction

The potential energy function for the interaction between two **charged** particles is

$$V(r) = +k\frac{q_1 q_2}{r} \qquad \begin{array}{l}\text{reference separation:} \\ V(r) \equiv 0 \text{ when } r = \infty\end{array} \qquad \text{(C7.1)}$$

Purpose: This equation describes the **electrostatic** potential energy function $V(r)$ for an electromagnetic interaction between two charged particles.

Symbols: q_1 and q_2 are the two particles' charges, r is their separation, and k is the **Coulomb constant** $= 8.99 \times 10^9$ J·m/C^2.

Limitations: This equation strictly applies only to particles, and assumes neither particle's speed is close to that of light. The formula assumes the choice of reference separation noted.

Notes: The SI unit of charge is the **coulomb;** a proton has a charge of $+e$, where $e \equiv 1.602 \times 10^{-19}$ C, while an electron's charge is $-e$. This formula also applies to spherical charge distributions if we model each as a point charge located at the sphere's center.

If the charges have like signs $(q_1 q_2 > 0)$, the potential energy function decreases with increasing separation, implying that the kinetic energies of a pair of isolated like charges will increase as they move apart, the hallmark of a repulsive interaction. Similarly, the kinetic energies of an isolated pair with opposite charges will decrease with increasing separation, signaling an attractive interaction.

Section C7.2: The Gravitational Interaction

The potential energy function for a gravitational interaction between two particles is

$$V(r) = -G\frac{m_1 m_2}{r} \qquad \begin{array}{l}\text{reference separation:} \\ V(r) \equiv 0 \text{ when } r = \infty\end{array} \qquad \text{(C7.3)}$$

Purpose: This equation describes the potential energy function $V(r)$ for a gravitational interaction between two particles separated by a distance r.

Symbols: m_1 and m_2 are the particles' masses, and G is the **universal gravitational constant** (empirically, $G = 6.67 \times 10^{-11}$ J·m/kg^2).

▷ Introduction

▷ Conservation of Momentum

▽ Conservation of Energy

　Introduction to Energy

　Some Potential Energy Functions

　Force and Energy

　Rotational Energy

　Thermal Energy

　Energy in Bonds

　Power, Collisions, and Impacts

▷ Conservation of Angular Momentum

Limitations: This equation strictly applies only to particles, and assumes neither particle is moving at a speed close to that of light. It only applies when we choose the reference separation noted.

    Note: This formula also applies to spherical objects if we model each as a point particle located at the sphere's center.

Note the similarities to the electrostatic formula: the main difference is that the gravitational interaction is *always* attractive because the masses are always positive.

Section C7.3: Gravitation near the Earth

It may seem puzzling that the general gravitational potential energy formula $V(r) = -Gm_1m_2/r$ in no way resembles the formula $V(z) = mgz$ discussed in chapter C6. But if we readjust the reference separation of the general formula to be consistent with the choice made for the other, we can see that $V(z) = mgz$ does in fact represent a useful approximation for the general formula in the limit that $z \ll r_e$, where r_e is the earth's radius. See figure C7.3 for a picture showing how this works.

Section C7.4: The Potential Energy of a Spring

We can treat two objects connected by a spring as if they were participating in a long-range interaction whose potential energy is very nearly

$$V(r) = \tfrac{1}{2}k_s(r - r_0)^2 \qquad \begin{array}{l}\text{reference separation:} \\ V(r) \equiv 0 \text{ when } r = r_0\end{array} \qquad \text{(C7.9)}$$

    Purpose: This equation describes the potential energy function $V(r)$ for a spring connecting two objects as a function of the separation r between the objects' centers.

    Symbols: r_0 is the separation of the objects' centers when the spring is relaxed, and k_s is a **spring constant** characterizing the spring's stiffness.

    Limitations: This **ideal spring** approximation accurately models real springs when $r - r_0$ is not large compared to r_0 and the spring's mass is very small compared to the masses of the objects it connects. It also applies only when we choose the reference separation as noted.

    This function is also a very useful approximation for the potential energy $V(r)$ of almost *any* interaction if $V(r)$ has a minimum when at an object separation of r_0, as long as the objects' separation remains sufficiently close to r_0.

    When an object interacts with a very massive object (such as the earth), we can consider it to be immobile. If the light object also moves in only one dimension (which we take to be the x axis) and if we define $x = 0$ to be its position when the spring is relaxed, then we can write

$$V(x) = \tfrac{1}{2}k_s x^2 \qquad V \equiv 0 \text{ at } x = 0 \qquad \text{(C7.10)}$$

Section C7.5: Some Examples

This section discusses three examples that illustrate the use of these potential energy formulas. Note especially example C7.2, which shows that an object traveling near the earth with a speed larger than a certain speed (called the earth's **escape speed**) will be able to coast out to essentially infinite distances in spite of the earth's attraction.

Section C7.6: Physics Skills: Significant Digits

This section discusses how to determine and specify an appropriate number of significant digits for a numerical quantity. A calculated quantity should not have more significant digits than the most uncertain quantity used in the calculation.

C7.1   The Electromagnetic Interaction

The electromagnetic interaction acts between *charged* particles

We begin our study of the potential energies associated with interactions by looking at the two long-range fundamental interactions, the *electromagnetic* and *gravitational* interactions. Of these two, the electromagnetic interaction is by far the one that is more crucial for objects that are much smaller than planets.

The electromagnetic interaction acts between any two particles that have electrical **charge.** You probably know from previous experience that there are exactly *two* kinds of electric charge, which are called *positive* and *negative*. The historical definition of positive and negative charge ends up implying that protons have positive charge and electrons have negative charge.

The SI unit of charge is the **coulomb,** where (for historical reasons) 1 C is equivalent to the charge of about 6.242×10^{18} protons. Positive and negative charges are represented by positive and negative numbers, respectively.

As long as two particles with charges q_1 and q_2 are not moving at relativistic speeds, the potential energy of their electromagnetic interaction depends on their separation r approximately as follows:

The formula for electrostatic potential energy

$$V(r) = +k\frac{q_1 q_2}{r} \qquad \begin{array}{l}\text{reference separation:} \\ V(r) \equiv 0 \text{ when } r = \infty\end{array} \qquad \text{(C7.1)}$$

Purpose: This equation describes the **electrostatic** potential energy function $V(r)$ for an electromagnetic interaction between two charged particles separated by a distance r.

Symbols: q_1 and q_2 are the two particles' charges, and k is the **Coulomb constant** $= 8.99 \times 10^9$ J·m/C².

Limitations: This equation strictly applies only to particles, and assumes neither particle's speed is close to that of light. The formula assumes the choice of reference separation noted.

Note: The SI unit of charge is the **coulomb;** a proton has a charge of $+e$, where $e \equiv 1.602 \times 10^{-19}$ C, while an electron's charge is $-e$.

This formula is an excellent approximation when the particles' speeds are much less than the speed of light, but is only *exact* when the particles are at rest; this is why the formula is called the *electrostatic* potential energy function. Note that to determine uniquely the value of $V(r)$ at a given r, we *must* choose a reference separation: the conventional choice for interacting point particles is to take $V(r)$ to be zero at infinite separation, which leads to the formula above.

The Coulomb constant

The *Coulomb constant k* expresses how strongly the interaction's potential energy depends on the magnitude of the charges involved (at a given separation): it thus characterizes the interaction's strength. The *value* of k (which is sometimes written $1/4\pi\varepsilon_0$ for historical reasons) depends on the unit of charge one uses: when charge is expressed in coulombs, k is

$$k = 8.99 \times 10^9 \frac{\text{J·m}}{\text{C}^2} \qquad \text{(C7.2)}$$

If $V(r)$ *increases* as r increases, the interaction is repulsive

Figure C7.1a and b shows graphs of equation C7.1 when $q_1 q_2 > 0$ (the particles' charges have *like* signs) and when $q_1 q_2 < 0$ (the particles' charges have *opposite* signs), respectively. Note that if the particles' charges have *like*

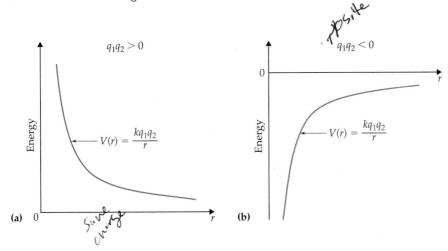

Figure C7.1
(a) A graph of the electrostatic potential energy function $V(r)$ as a function of separation r for a pair of particles whose charges have *like* signs. (b) A graph of $V(r)$ as a function of r for a pair of particles whose charges have *opposite* signs.

signs, their interaction potential energy *decreases* as their separation gets larger. If the particles are isolated, their total energy should remain constant, so their kinetic energy should increase as their separation increases, implying that the particles will speed up as they move away from each other. This is characteristic of a *repulsive* interaction; therefore, we say that *like charges repel*.

On the other hand, if the particles' charges are opposite, their potential energy (though it is always negative) *increases* as the particles' separation increases. This means that the kinetic energy of an isolated pair of such particles increases as they *approach* each other. This is characteristic of an attractive interaction: therefore, *opposite charges attract*.

These arguments show that we can understand much about the qualitative nature of an interaction by looking at a graph of $V(r)$. We will discuss this further in chapter C11.

If $V(r)$ *decreases* as r increases, the interaction is attractive

---

Exercise C7X.1

If two protons are separated by 10^{-12} m, what is the potential energy of their electrostatic interaction?

The reason we describe charges as being "positive" and "negative" is because the *physical* behavior of combined charges is analogous to the *mathematical* behavior of positive and negative numbers when added. For example, a hydrogen atom is a combination of a proton (whose charge is $+e$) and an electron (whose charge is $-e$). When viewed from a distance, the hydrogen atom behaves as if it were uncharged: the combination of the proton charge and the electron charge in close proximity is physically equivalent to *zero* charge. Analogously, if we add the numbers ($+e$ and $-e$) representing the proton and electron charges, we get the number 0.

An atom behaves as if it were neutrally charged only if its interaction partner is so far away that the atom seems like a point particle. A charged particle placed *close* to a hydrogen atom *can* interact with it electromagnetically since the particle (depending on its placement at a given time) may be significantly closer to either the proton or the electron, and as a result, the effects of a particle's interaction with the proton may *not* exactly cancel the effects of its interaction with the electron.

Indeed, when two hydrogen atoms are brought close together, such unbalanced interactions have the effect of changing the shape of the electron orbitals in the atoms so that there is a net electrostatic attraction that binds the atoms together: this is a chemical bond. Chemistry is fundamentally a

Why are charges "positive" and "negative"?

Neutral atoms *can* interact electromagnetically

detailed exploration of how atoms interact as a result of the imperfect cancellation of the electromagnetic interactions between atoms brought into close proximity. Such unbalanced interactions also give rise to contact interactions, as discussed in chapter C1.

When the two interacting charged particles also move with respect to each other, they interact *magnetically* as well as electrostatically. It turns out that the magnetic part of an interaction between two charged particles does not affect their kinetic energies, so we can ignore it in the electromagnetic potential energy. When other interactions are involved, magnetic effects can (indirectly) have energy implications. It turns out, for example, that the north and south magnetic poles of two interacting bar magnets behave *qualitatively* as positive and negative charges do, and we can treat such interactions between poles of such magnets *as if* they had potential energies with same inverse-*r* dependence as for point charges. But we will not worry about magnetism much until we explore it in depth in unit E.

C7.2   The Gravitational Interaction

Gravitation is observable because there is no such thing as negative mass!

It is ironic that the gravitational interaction, which is *by far* the weakest of the four fundamental interactions, is nonetheless the most obvious of the four in daily life, and more than any other shapes objects larger than asteroids. This is because the gravitational interaction acts between any pair of objects having mass, and *there is no such thing as negative mass*. Therefore, the gravitational effects of particles in an object tend to add instead of cancel out (as electromagnetic effects tend to do). Even an extraordinarily weak interaction between two elementary particles can become dominant when a huge number of particles pull together.

The potential energy formula for the gravitational interaction between two point particles is

The formula for gravitational potential energy

$$V(r) = -G\frac{m_1 m_2}{r} \qquad \begin{array}{l}\text{reference separation:} \\ V(r) \equiv 0 \text{ when } r = \infty\end{array} \qquad \text{(C7.3)}$$

Purpose: This equation describes the potential energy function $V(r)$ for a gravitational interaction between two particles separated by a distance r.
Symbols: m_1 and m_2 are the particles' masses, and G is the **universal gravitational constant** (empirically, $G = 6.67 \times 10^{-11}$ J·m/kg^2).
Limitations: This equation strictly applies only to particles, and assumes neither particle is moving at a speed close to that of light. It only applies when we choose the reference separation noted.

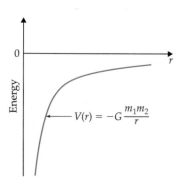

Figure C7.2

A graph of the gravitational potential energy $V(r)$ between a pair of particles with nonzero mass.

Note that, as in the case of the electrostatic potential energy function, we conventionally choose the reference separation to be $r = \infty$, as shown. Indeed, note that this function has *the same form* as the electromagnetic potential energy function given by equation C7.1, except that masses m_1 and m_2 here play the role that charges q_1 and q_2 did there, the constant G here replaces k there, and the sign of the gravitational potential energy is *always* negative. The minus sign is necessary so that the gravitational potential energy *increases* with increasing separation, which is a necessary characteristic of an *attractive* interaction, as we've seen. A graph of this potential energy function is shown in figure C7.2.

The universal gravitational constant G expresses how strongly the potential energy of a gravitational interaction depends on the magnitude of the masses involved (at a given separation): it thus characterizes the strength of the interaction. In SI units, this constant has the measured value

$$G = 6.67 \times 10^{-11} \ \frac{\text{J} \cdot \text{m}}{\text{kg}^2} \qquad\qquad \text{(C7.4)}$$

Equation C7.3 (like the electrostatic potential energy formula) strictly applies only to an interaction between *particles*. To find the total potential energy between two extended objects A and B (for either kind of interaction), we treat the extended objects as collections of microscopic particles (which is what they are), find the interaction potential energy for each possible *pair* of particles (such that one particle is in A and the other is in B), and then simply *add* these interparticle potential energies.

While the principle is simple, actually *doing* such a sum for a given pair of extended objects would be very tedious. In the case of gravitating objects, this is rarely necessary. An important characteristic of *both* the gravitational and electrostatic interactions is that when a *spherical* object (or charge distribution) interacts with another object, *the potential energy of the interaction turns out to be the same as what you would calculate for a particle with the same mass (or charge) located at the sphere's center* (assuming the other object is *outside* the sphere). You can prove this theorem fairly easily if you are handy with integrals (see problem C7A.1): otherwise, you can accept this on faith for now.

Since most objects in the universe that have a significant mass are very nearly spherical, this theorem means we can apply equation C7.3 directly to such objects, treating them as point particles. Any *non*spherical extended object (like a person) interacting with a planetary body will likely be so tiny compared to the planetary body that it can also be approximated as a point mass.

Spherical objects can be treated as point particles

Exercise C7X.2

What is the gravitational potential energy of a system of two 10-kg lead balls, separated (center to center) by 2 m?

C7.3   Gravitation near the Earth

It is puzzling, though, that the potential energy formula $V(r) = -Gm_1m_2/r$ looks *nothing* like the potential energy formula $V(z) = mgz$ that in chapter C6 we found empirically described gravitational interactions between the earth and objects near its surface. The first equation tells us that the gravitational potential energy is *negative*, and that it *decreases* in magnitude with $1/r$ as the separation between the objects increases. The other says that the gravitational potential energy is *positive* (for $z > 0$) and *increases* linearly as the separation z between the earth and the object increases. Yet equation C7.3 *should* apply to an object interacting with the earth! How can it when it seems to be so different?

Reconciling the two gravitational $V(r)$ formulas

Part of the difference between these equations has to do with different choices of *reference separation*. In the equation $V(r) = -Gm_1m_2/r$, the reference separation is $r = \infty$, whereas in the empirical formula $V(z) = mgz$, the reference separation is the separation between the object and the earth's center when the object has vertical coordinate $z = 0$ in whatever coordinate

First step: choose a common reference separation

system we are using. If the coordinate system is placed on the surface of the earth, then the actual separation between an object at $z = 0$ and the earth's center is the radius of the earth r_e. We can redefine equation C7.3 so that its reference separation is *also* at the earth's surface by adding an appropriate constant term to the potential energy:

$$V(r) = -G\frac{m_1 m_2}{r} + G\frac{m_1 m_2}{r_e} \qquad \text{now } V(r) \equiv 0 \text{ when } r = r_e \quad \text{(C7.5)}$$

$V(r) = mgz$ is an approximation valid near the earth

I will now show that equation C7.5 reduces to $V(z) = mgz$ for an object near the earth. Define M and m to be the masses of the earth and the object, respectively. Note that when an object is at position z, its distance from the earth's center is $r = z + r_e$. If you plug these things into equation C7.5 and massage things a bit, you can express $V(r) = -GMm/r$ as the following function of z:

$$V(z) = m\frac{GM}{r_e}\left[1 - \frac{1}{1 + (z/r_e)}\right] \qquad \text{(C7.6)}$$

Exercise C7X.3

Verify equation C7.6.

By putting the two terms in the square brackets over a common denominator and doing a bit more algebra, you can show that

$$V(z) = m\left[\frac{GM}{r_e^2} \frac{1}{1 + (z/r_e)}\right]z \qquad \text{(C7.7)}$$

Exercise C7X.4

Verify equation C7.7.

Now, notice that if the object is close to the earth's surface, then $z \ll r_e$ and the quantity in brackets in equation C7.7 will be *almost* equal to GM/r_e^2. The numerical value of GM/r_e^2 is 9.80 m/s^2, which is the empirical value of g. So

$$V(z) \approx m\left[\frac{GM}{r_e^2}\right]z = mgz \qquad \text{as long as } z \ll r_e \quad \text{(C7.8)}$$

Exercise C7X.5

Show by direct calculation that GM/r_e^2 has the same value and units as g. (See the inside front cover for the earth's mass and radius.)

So the empirical formula $V(z) = mgz$ represents an *approximation* to the true potential energy of an object's gravitational interaction with the earth, an approximation that is excellent as long as the object is always close to the earth's surface. Figure C7.3 illustrates what this approximation means. Figure C7.3a shows the actual potential energy for the interaction between an object and the earth as a function of the separation between that object and the earth's center. (Note that I have reset the reference point so that $V = 0$ at

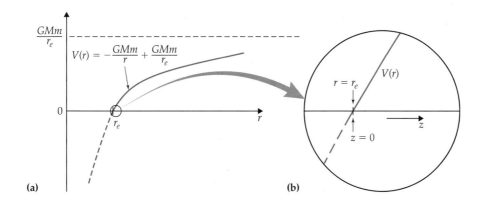

Figure C7.3
Any sufficiently tiny part of the gravitational potential energy function $V(r)$ will look like a straight line.

the earth's surface, as in equation C7.5.) But a sufficiently short segment of any curve will look like a straight line, as illustrated in figure C7.3b. This means that for sufficiently small displacements from the earth's surface, $V(r)$ increases almost linearly with z: mg is simply the constant of proportionality for this linear increase.

Whenever you do a problem involving an object interacting gravitationally with the earth, first look at whether the separation r between the earth and the object is ever likely to be significantly different from the earth's radius r_e. If so, you should use the general gravitational potential energy formula given by equation C7.3. If not, feel free to use the approximation $V(z) = mgz$.

Exercise C7X.6

Imagine that an object with mass $m = 3.0$ kg falls to the ground from an airplane flying at an altitude of $h = 20.0$ km. According to the formula $V(z) = mgz$, the change in the gravitational interaction's potential energy as the object falls is $\Delta V = mg\,\Delta z = (3.0 \text{ kg})(9.80 \text{ m/s}^2)(-20{,}000 \text{ m}) = -588{,}000$ J. What is ΔV according to the exact formula given by equation C7.3? (*Hint:* $GM = 3.99 \times 10^{14}$ J·m/kg for the earth. Keep track of at least four or five digits in your calculations.)

C7.4   The Potential Energy of a Spring

Consider now two objects connected by a lightweight spring. The interaction between the objects mediated by the spring is attractive if the spring is stretched beyond its natural length and repulsive if the spring is compressed to be shorter than its natural length.

This interaction would have to be classified as a *contact* interaction according to the scheme described in chapter C1: it arises because each object is in contact with the spring. As the string is stretched or compressed, the separations between its atoms change microscopically, which leads to energy being transferred to or from the microscopic potential energies of the interactions between atoms. In spite of the complexity of these interactions, it happens that the potential energy of these interactions can be almost exactly described by a simple function of the separation between the objects, *as if* the objects were participating in a long-range interaction like the gravitational or electrostatic interaction! An excellent approximation for the potential energy function for an interaction mediated by a spring is

Formula for potential energy of an ideal spring

$$V(r) = \tfrac{1}{2}k_s(r - r_0)^2 \qquad \begin{array}{l}\text{reference separation:}\\ V(r) \equiv 0 \text{ when } r = r_0\end{array} \qquad \text{(C7.9)}$$

Purpose: This equation describes the potential energy function $V(r)$ for a spring connecting two objects as a function of the separation r between the objects' centers.

Symbols: r_0 is the separation of the objects' centers when the spring is completely relaxed, and k_s is a **spring constant** characterizing the spring's stiffness.

Limitations: This **ideal spring** approximation accurately models real springs when $r - r_0$ is not large compared to r_0 and the spring's mass is very small compared to the masses of the objects it connects. It also applies only when we choose the reference separation as noted.

Note that the larger k_s is, the more energy has to be transferred to potential energy to stretch or compress the spring a given amount; so a spring with a large k_s will be difficult to compress or stretch. The conventional factor of $\tfrac{1}{2}$ makes certain other equations simpler.

This potential energy function, while idealized, generally describes the potential energy stored in a realistic spring quite well, particularly if the spring is not stretched or compressed very far from its natural length. If the spring also has a very small mass compared to the masses of the objects it connects, then we can ignore the small kinetic energy of the moving parts of the spring compared to the kinetic energies of the connected objects, and the system behaves very nearly *as if* the two objects were participating in a long-range interaction with this potential energy function.

A simplified version of the spring formula

In many realistic situations, a low-mass object is connected by a spring to a very massive object (such as the earth or something connected to the earth). In such a case, we can consider the massive object to be at rest and have essentially zero kinetic energy. If the low-mass object moves along a straight line parallel to the spring, we can define our reference frame so that one axis (say, the x axis) lies along this line, and the frame's origin so that the low-mass object is at $x = 0$ when the spring is relaxed (i.e., when the separation between the two objects is $r = r_0$). Then, when the position of the low-mass object is some $x \neq 0$, the separation of the two objects will be $r = r_0 + x$, implying that $x = r - r_0$ (see figure C7.4a). Plugging this into equation C7.9, we get

$$V(x) = \tfrac{1}{2}k_s x^2 \qquad \begin{array}{l}\text{reference separation:}\\ V(x) \equiv 0 \text{ at } x = 0\end{array} \qquad \text{(C7.10)}$$

This is the form of the spring potential energy function that we will most commonly use. Note that a graph of this $V(x)$ is a *parabola* (see figure C7.4b). Because the interaction's potential energy *increases* if the low-mass object moves away from $x = 0$, the object's kinetic energy must *decrease* as it does this (since the system's total energy is fixed). If the low-mass object slows down as it moves away from $x = 0$, the spring interaction is *attracting* it toward $x = 0$.

The spring interaction is a useful *model*

Understanding the spring interaction is important in physics not because objects connected by springs are all that common, but because this situation serves as a useful *model* for more complicated situations. For example, imagine that the complicated electromagnetic interaction between two atoms

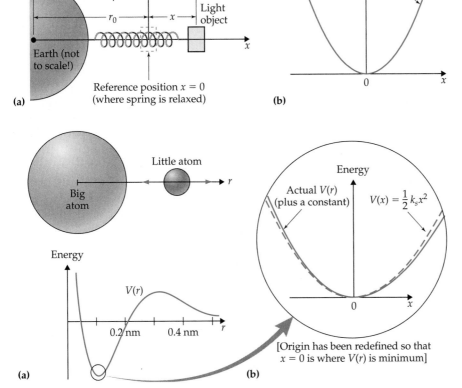

Figure C7.4
(a) A lightweight object is connected to the earth by a spring. We can define the origin of our reference frame so that the object is at $x = 0$ when the spring is relaxed. (b) The potential energy function for the spring in this situation is a parabola.

Figure C7.5
(a) A hypothetical potential energy function for the complicated electromagnetic interaction between two atoms. (b) If we add an appropriate constant to the potential energy, and redefine $x = 0$ to coincide with the bottom of the local minimum circled, then for values of x close to the new $x = 0$, $V(x) = \frac{1}{2}k_s x^2$.

has the potential energy function shown in figure C7.5a, which has a local minimum when the atoms are separated by $r = r_0$. If we redefine the origin of our reference frame so that $x = 0$ corresponds to $r = r_0$, and the reference separation where $V \equiv 0$ to be $x = 0$ (figure C7.5b), then the potential energy curve for values of x near zero looks a *lot* like a parabola and can be approximated by $V(x) = \frac{1}{2}k_s x^2$ with an appropriately chosen value of k_s. Thus when $x \approx 0$ ($r \approx r_0$), these two atoms will behave as if they were connected by a massless spring. Similarly, $V(r) = \frac{1}{2}k_s x^2$ is a good model for almost *any* situation where the interaction between two objects tends to push them toward a specific separation (and deviations from this separation r_0 are relatively small). Other examples include the interactions between the earth and a ball rolling in a bowl, and that between the earth and a pendulum bob. (Indeed, the fact that the microscopic interactions between atoms in spring steel are accurately described by this kind of potential energy function is why a spring itself behaves this way!)

Exercise C7X.7

Explain why k_s must have SI units of joules per meter squared.

Exercise C7X.8

A typical spring might have a k_s whose value is roughly 100 J/m². If such a spring has a relaxed length of 5.0 cm and is stretched to a length of 8.0 cm, what is the potential energy stored in the spring?

C7.5   Some Examples

The remainder of this chapter is devoted to some examples that illustrate applications of these potential energy formulas and further illustrate the use of the problem-solving framework in conservation of energy problems.

Note especially example C7.2, which introduces the idea of an **escape speed.** One of the most interesting implications of the gravitational potential energy formula is that if a rocket has a sufficiently high speed near a planet, the rocket can coast away from that planet *indefinitely* without using its engines (even though the planet is always pulling it back!). Example C7.2 shows how one can use conservation of energy to compute rather easily what this speed needs to be.

Example C7.1

Nuclear Fusion

Problem   The nucleus of a deuterium atom consists of a single positively charged proton bound to a single uncharged neutron of about the same mass. If one can get two such nuclei close enough together so that they essentially touch (i.e., so their separation is less than about 1.5 fm $= 1.5 \times 10^{-15}$ m), the strong interaction takes over and the nuclei fuse, releasing energy. However, since the nuclei have the same charge, they electrostatically repel each other. Imagine that we fire two deuterium nuclei directly toward each other with equal initial speeds. How large would this initial speed have to be for the nuclei to fuse? Express your answer as a fraction of the speed of light c.

Translation

Initial:

Final:

Known:
$m = 1.67 \times 10^{-27}$ kg
      $+ 1.68 \times 10^{-27}$ kg
$q_1 = q_2 = 1.60 \times 10^{-19}$ C
$k = 8.99 \times 10^9$ J·m/C^2
$r_f = 1.5 \times 10^{-15}$ m

Nucleus, charge q_1 ... $\vec{v}_{1i}$ ... m ... $r_i \approx \infty$ ... $\vec{v}_{2i}$ ... Nucleus, charge q_2 ... m

$\text{mag}(\vec{v}_{1i}) = \text{mag}(\vec{v}_{2i}) \equiv v_i$

r_f

$\vec{v}_{1f} = 0 \quad \vec{v}_{2f} = 0$

Conceptual Model Diagram

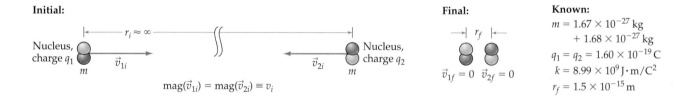

CoE: collision

$$0 = \Delta K_1 + \Delta K_2 + \Delta V$$

$$= \tfrac{1}{2}mv_{1f}^2{}^{\,0} - \tfrac{1}{2}m(v_i^2) + \tfrac{1}{2}mv_{2f}^2{}^{\,0} - \tfrac{1}{2}mv_i^2 + \frac{kq_1q_2}{r_f} - \frac{kq_1q_2}{r_i}{}^{\,0}$$

r_i is very large compared to r_f

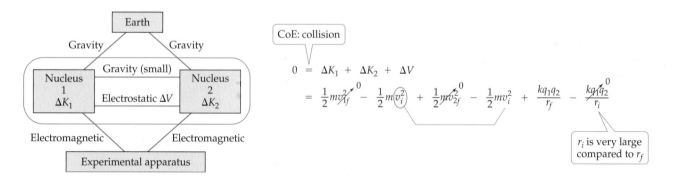

Prose Model   This interaction will probably happen so quickly that any external electromagnetic or gravitational interactions will not have time to transfer much energy, so we will treat this as a collision. There is also a gravitational interaction between the nuclei, but this will be completely negligible compared to the electrostatic interaction between the nuclei. So conservation of energy implies that $0 = \Delta K_1 + \Delta K_2 + \Delta V_e$, where the three terms refer to the kinetic energies of the two nuclei and the electrostatic potential energy, respectively. The separation between the nuclei will be smallest when as much of their initial kinetic energy as possible has been converted to electrostatic potential energy. Since the nuclei have the same mass and speed but opposite velocities, the system's total momentum is zero. This means the kinetic energies of both nuclei can go all the way to *zero* without violating conservation of momentum, as shown in the translation-step diagram. So $\vec{v}_{1f} = \vec{v}_{2f} = 0$, which implies that $\Delta K_1 = \Delta K_2 = 0 - \frac{1}{2}mv_i^2$. If we treat the nuclei as point particles, the electrostatic potential energy function is $V(r) = kq_1q_2/r$ (assuming the standard reference separation). We will *assume* that the initial separation of the nuclei is so large compared to their final separation that we can approximate it by infinity.

Solution   Conservation of energy then tells us that

$$0 = \left[0 - \frac{1}{2}mv_i^2\right] + \left[0 - \frac{1}{2}mv_i^2\right] + \left[\frac{ke^2}{r_f} - 0\right] = \frac{ke^2}{r_f} - mv_i^2 \quad \text{(C7.11)}$$

since $q_1 = q_2 = +e$. Solving for v_i, we get $v_i^2 = ke^2/mr_f$, so

$$\frac{v_i}{c} = \frac{e}{c}\sqrt{\frac{k}{mr_f}} = \frac{1.60 \times 10^{-19}\,\cancel{C}}{3.0 \times 10^8\,\text{m/s}}\sqrt{\frac{8.99 \times 10^9\,\text{J·m}/\cancel{C^2}}{2(1.67 \times 10^{-27}\,\text{kg})(1.5 \times 10^{-15}\,\cancel{m})}}$$

$$= \frac{0.023}{\cancel{m/s}}\sqrt{\frac{\cancel{J}}{\text{kg}}\left(\frac{1\,\text{kg·m}^2/\text{s}^2}{1\,\cancel{J}}\right)} = 0.023 \quad \text{(C7.12)}$$

Evaluation   This ratio is unitless and positive (as the ratio of speeds should be!) and less than 1, meaning that $v_i < c$ ($v_i > c$ would be suspicious).

Example C7.2

Escaping the Earth

Problem   Imagine that we launch a rocket away from the surface of the earth. Assuming that its engines fire only very briefly at the beginning of its flight, what is the *minimum* initial speed v_i that the rocket must have when its engines shut down if it is able to coast away from the earth forever? (We call this speed the earth's **escape speed.**)

Translation

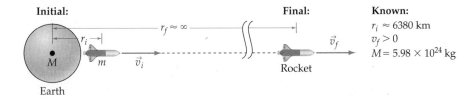

Conceptual Model Diagram

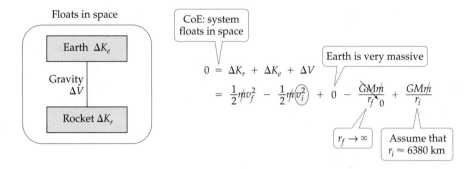

Prose Model   The system of the earth and rocket is isolated because it floats in space. If we assume the rocket is outside the earth's atmosphere, then the gravitational interaction is the only internal interaction in this system. Conservation of energy then implies that $0 = \Delta K_r + \Delta K_e + \Delta V$, where the terms refer to the kinetic energies of the rocket and earth and the potential energy of the gravitational interaction. Since the earth is so massive compared to the rocket, we will ignore its kinetic energy and consider the earth to be basically at rest in our frame throughout. Since the rocket's separation from the earth will eventually get large compared to r_e, we will use the exact gravitational potential energy formula $V(r) = -GMm/r$. Note that "coasting away forever" implies that $v_f > 0$ even as r_f approaches infinity, where $V(r_f) \approx 0$.

Solution   With these assumptions and approximations the conservation of energy equation reads

$$0 = \left[\frac{1}{2}mv_f^2 - \frac{1}{2}mv_i^2\right] + 0 + \left[-0 + \frac{GMm}{r_i}\right]$$

$$\Rightarrow \quad \frac{1}{2}mv_i^2 = \frac{1}{2}mv_f^2 + \frac{GMm}{r_i} \tag{C7.13}$$

Since v_f^2 must be greater than zero and r_i must be greater than r_e (implying that $GMm/r_i < GMm/r_e$), the rocket will definitely coast away forever as long as

$$\frac{1}{2}mv_i^2 > \frac{GMm}{r_e} \quad \Rightarrow \quad v_i^2 > \frac{2GM}{r_e} \quad \Rightarrow \quad v_i > \sqrt{\frac{2GM}{r_e}}$$

$$\Rightarrow \quad v_i > \sqrt{\frac{2(6.67 \times 10^{-11}\, N\cdot m/kg^2)(5.98 \times 10^{24}\, kg)}{6{,}380{,}000\, m} \left(\frac{1\, kg\cdot m^2/s^2}{1\, J}\right)}$$

$$\Rightarrow \quad v_i > 11{,}200\, m/s = 11.2\, km/s \tag{C7.14}$$

Evaluation   So the *minimum* speed that a rocket relatively close to the earth must attain to escape the earth completely is about 11.2 km/s: this is the earth's escape speed. This result's sign and units are appropriate for a speed. The magnitude does not seem outrageous; I seem to remember something about deep space probe speeds being tens of kilometers per second. (Note that the unknown rocket mass cancels out: this was nice!)

Example C7.3

A Friend Who Suddenly Pops Up

Problem   A friend of yours sits on a coiled spring that has been compressed to a length 55 cm shorter than its normal length and then held at that length. What is this spring's spring constant k_s if, when the spring is suddenly released, your friend flies into the air 2.0 m above his or her initial position?

Translation

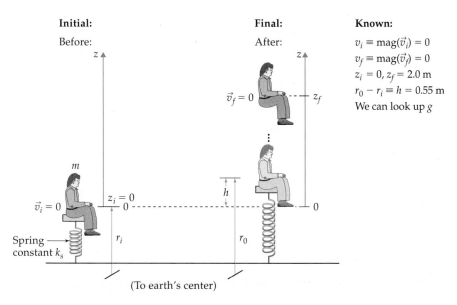

Initial:

Before:

m

$\vec{v}_i = 0$ $z_i = 0$

Spring constant k_s r_i

(To earth's center)

Final:

After:

$\vec{v}_f = 0$ ---- z_f

h

r_0

Known:

$v_i \equiv \text{mag}(\vec{v}_i) = 0$
$v_f \equiv \text{mag}(\vec{v}_f) = 0$
$z_i = 0, z_f = 2.0 \text{ m}$
$r_0 - r_i \equiv h = 0.55 \text{ m}$
We can look up g

Conceptual Model Diagram

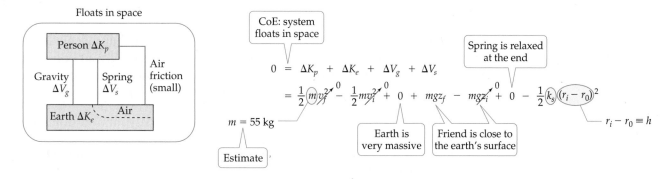

Floats in space

| Person ΔK_p |
| Gravity ΔV_g | Spring ΔV_s | Air friction (small) |
| Earth ΔK_e | Air |

CoE: system floats in space

$$0 = \Delta K_p + \Delta K_e + \Delta V_g + \Delta V_s$$
$$= \tfrac{1}{2} m v_f^2 \overset{0}{} - \tfrac{1}{2} m v_i^2 \overset{0}{} + 0 + mgz_f - mgz_i \overset{0}{} + 0 - \tfrac{1}{2} k_s (r_i - r_0)^2$$

$m = 55$ kg

Estimate

Earth is very massive

Friend is close to the earth's surface

Spring is relaxed at the end

$r_i - r_0 \equiv h$

Prose Model   The system in this case is your friend and the earth, which floats in space. We will ignore air friction. Two interactions act between the earth and your friend, a *gravitational interaction* and (initially at least) a *spring interaction*. Therefore conservation of energy for this system implies that $0 = \Delta K_p + \Delta K_e + \Delta V_g + \Delta V_s$, where the terms refer to the kinetic energies of the person and the earth and the potential energies of the gravitational and spring interactions, respectively. Since your friend always remains relatively near the earth, we will use the near-earth approximation $V_g(z) = mgz$ for the gravitational potential energy. If we assume the spring is ideal, we can use $V_s(r) = \tfrac{1}{2} k_s (r - r_0)^2$ for the spring potential energy. Note that after your friend leaves the seat, the spring is relaxed, and so $V_s(r_f) = 0$ and (as shown on the diagram) $r_i - r_0$ is equal to the distance h that the spring is initially compressed, which we are told is 0.55 m. We will assume that both the spring and the seat have very small masses compared to the person (and thus ignore these unknown masses). Note also that your friend is at rest both initially and finally, so the friend's net change in kinetic energy is zero. Your friend's mass does *not* cancel out in this case, so let's assume it is 55 kg (a fairly average human mass).

Solution   Conservation of energy implies that

$$0 = 0 + 0 + [mgz_f - 0] + \left[0 - \tfrac{1}{2}k_s(r_i - r_0)^2\right]$$

$$\Rightarrow \quad \tfrac{1}{2}k_s(r_i - r_0)^2 = mgz_f \quad \Rightarrow \quad k_s = \frac{2mgz_f}{(r_i - r_0)^2} \qquad \text{(C7.15)}$$

Plugging in the numbers, we get

$$k_s = \frac{2(55 \text{ kg})(9.8 \text{ m/s}^2)(2.0 \text{ m})}{(0.55 \text{ m})^2}\left(\frac{1 \text{ J}}{1 \text{ kg·m}^2/\text{s}^2}\right) = 7100 \text{ J/m}^2 \qquad \text{(C7.16)}$$

Evaluation   The units are right, and a plus sign is appropriate. Normal lab springs have $k_s \approx 100 \text{ J/m}^2$, but it makes sense that a spring that can throw a person 2.0 m in the air will have to be pretty strong!

C7.6   Physics Skills: Significant Digits

Unlike purely mathematical problems, physics problems involve quantities such as times, masses, distances, and speeds, that would have to be *measured* in real life, and thus would be somewhat uncertain (as all measured quantities are). This means the *answers* to such physics problems are uncertain as well. For example, if an object covers 100 m (± 1 m) in 30 s (± 1 s), then its speed could be anywhere from a maximum value of $(101 \text{ m})/(29 \text{ s}) = 3.5 \text{ m/s}$ to a minimum value of $(99 \text{ m})/(31 \text{ s}) = 3.2 \text{ m/s}$. In such a context it would be *absurd* to say that its speed is 3.333333333 m/s (which is what your calculator says): such an answer would suggest that you knew the speed to nine decimal places when in fact even the digit in the *first* decimal place is uncertain in this situation.

Conventions for dealing with significant figures

When doing an experiment or writing a formal journal article, you want to keep track of all uncertainties very carefully, but spending such effort on a homework problem solution is overkill. Even so, it is still important to recognize and communicate that quantities (and results) often have *some* uncertainty.

Let's deal with this problem by agreeing to abide by the following conventions. First, unless otherwise stated, let's *assume* in this course that the rightmost stated digit for any measurable quantity is uncertain (except in the case of integers greater than 100, where we will consider the last *nonzero* digit to be uncertain). Thus we will consider a stated value of 2.000 to be uncertain in the thousandths place, a value of 80 to be uncertain in the ones place, a value of 0.20 to be uncertain in the hundredths place, 23,000 to be uncertain in the thousands place, and so on. The digits from the leftmost nonzero digit to the uncertain digit (inclusive) are called the quantity's **significant digits**. Thus, 2.000 has four significant digits, 0.20 has two significant digits, and so on.

Second, we will assume that any *calculated* quantity has the same number of significant digits as whatever factor going into the calculation has the *least* number of significant digits. In *most* cases, this simple rule reasonably approximates the results of a more careful uncertainty analysis.

In problems in this text, I will *generally* state quantities to two significant digits. Therefore, you should generally state *results* to two significant digits unless you have specific reasons (which you should state) to do otherwise. If you want to keep track of *intermediate* results to three or maybe four significant digits, this is fine. But *whatever* you do, don't slavishly copy a long calculator result without considering the uncertainties involved: doing this shows all the world that you are not *thinking* about what you write.

A rule for determining the number of significant digits in a calculated result

TWO-MINUTE PROBLEMS

C7T.1 The electrostatic potential energy between the proton and electron in a normal hydrogen atom (with the conventional choice of reference separation) is
A. negative
B. zero
C. positive
D. any of the above

C7T.2 Water molecules weakly attract one another (this is why water molecules coalesce into a liquid and then a solid at decreasing temperatures). What do you think is the interaction responsible for this attraction?
A. Incompletely canceled strong interactions between the molecule's quarks.
B. Incompletely canceled electromagnetic interactions between the molecule's charged parts.
C. The weak interaction.
D. The gravitational interaction.

C7T.3 The general gravitational potential energy formula $V(r) = -Gm_1m_2/r$ is always negative for $r > 0$, but the empirical formula $V(r) = mgz$ is always positive for $z > 0$. Why are the signs in these expressions different?
A. The empirical formula is wrong.
B. The equations refer to different kinds of interactions.
C. The first equation does not apply to objects that are not point particles.
D. The equations assume different reference separations.
E. Other (specify).

C7T.4 The following graph shows the potential energy function of a certain interaction. This interaction is
A. always attractive.
B. always repulsive.
C. attractive for small r, repulsive for large r.
D. repulsive for small r, attractive for large r.
E. there is not enough information for a meaningful answer.

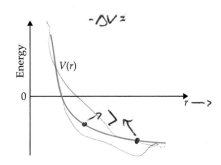

C7T.5 Assuming that $z = 0$ at the earth's surface, at roughly what value of z is the potential energy equation $V(r) = mgz$ (with $g = 9.80$ m/s) wrong by about 1%?
A. $z = 1$ km
B. $z = 15$ km
C. $z = 60$ km
D. $z = 250$ km
E. The equation is never in error: it is exact.

C7T.6 On a planet with twice the mass and twice the diameter of the earth, the value of g at its surface would be what factor times g at the surface of the earth?
A. 2 times larger
B. 4 times larger
C. 8 times larger
D. 2 times smaller
E. 4 times smaller
F. 8 times smaller
T. Other (specify)

C7T.7 When an atom in a crystal is moved 0.02 nm to the right or left, its potential energy of interaction with the crystal increases by 4×10^{-18} J. If the spring potential energy function is a good model for the potential energy of this interaction, what is the effective value of k_s?
A. 10^{-14} J/m^2
B. 2×10^{-14} J/m^2
C. 10,000 J/m^2

(more)

D. 20,000 J/m^2
E. Other (specify)

C7T.8 The potential energy function for a spring is shown in the graph to the right. What is the approximate spring constant for this spring?
A. 0.05 J/m^2
B. 5 J/m^2
C. 50 J/m^2
D. 100 J/m^2
E. 200 J/m^2
F. Other (specify)

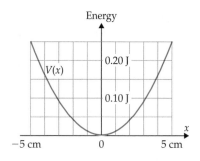

HOMEWORK PROBLEMS

Basic Skills

C7B.1 The two protons in a helium nucleus are separated by about 1.2 fm. What is the *approximate* potential energy of their electromagnetic interaction, assuming that $V = 0$ at infinite separation? (Assume that we can treat the protons as point particles, even though their size is comparable to their separation here.)

C7B.2 Imagine that two small objects are given equal charges of about $+1.0 \times 10^{-5}$ C and then are placed 25 cm apart. What is the potential energy involved in their electrostatic interaction, assuming that $V = 0$ at infinite separation?

C7B.3 Two spheres with a radius of 0.10 m and a mass of 25 kg are floating in deep space. Their gravitational attraction keeps them in contact. If we go in and manually separate these spheres to a large distance, by how much will the potential energy involved in their interaction increase?

C7B.4 Imagine that an object of mass $m = 0.10$ kg falls to the ground from a jet flying at an altitude of 35 km. What is its change in gravitational potential energy according to the formula $V(z) = mgz$? What is its change in potential energy according to the formula $V(r) = -GMm/r$?

C7B.5 A spring with a spring constant $k_s = 60$ J/m^2 has a relaxed length of 6.0 cm. If the spring is compressed to one-half its length, what is the change in its potential energy?

C7B.6 If it takes 50 J of energy to compress a spring so that it is 2.0 cm shorter than its equilibrium length, what is the spring's spring constant k_s?

C7B.7 The gravitational and contact interactions acting on a boat floating in a lake make it behave *as if* its vertical position were maintained by a spring connected to the lake bottom. If you have to put 100 J of energy into these interactions to push the boat 3 cm deeper into the water, what is the effective spring constant of this imaginary spring?

C7B.8 A mass hanging vertically from the end of a long string behaves when it is moved from side to side as if it were connected to its equilibrium position (directly below the point of suspension) by a weak spring with zero relaxed length. If the object has a mass of 0.10 kg and it takes 0.010 J of energy to move it 10 cm away from the central position, what is the effective spring constant k_s of the imaginary spring connecting it to the center point?

Synthetic

Starred problems are particularly well suited to practicing the use of the problem-solving framework and conceptual model diagrams.

*C7S.1 Jump vertically as high as you can from the ground. Use conservation of energy to estimate your speed just as you leave the ground.

*C7S.2 Imagine that two identical steel spheres, each having a mass of 1.0 kg, are placed a certain distance apart. They are given an equal charge q such that when the separation between the objects changes, the change in the gravitational potential energy between the objects is exactly balanced by an opposite change in the electrostatic potential energy between the objects. What is q?

*C7S.3 If aliens were to drop an asteroid of mass 10^{14} kg from about the radius of the moon's orbit (384,000 km), how much kinetic energy would it have (to convert to other forms of energy) when it hit the earth? Compare with the energy released by a very large nuclear bomb ($\approx 10^{16}$ J).

*C7S.4 A rocket is fired vertically from the surface of the earth. Its engines fire only briefly, and then the rocket continues to coast upward. What must the rocket's initial speed be if its speed is to be not less than 5.0 km/s when it is very far from the earth?

*C7S.5 You are trying to design a "rail gun" to launch canisters with masses ranging from 200 kg to 1200 kg from the surface of the moon so that they'd still have a speed of at least 500 m/s very far from the moon. What initial speed do you want the rail gun to give to each canister as it leaves the moon's surface? (The moon's radius is 1740 km, and its mass is 7.36×10^{22} kg.)

*C7S.6 (a) Imagine that a bullet is shot vertically into the air with an initial speed of 9800 m/s. If we ignore air friction, how high will it go?
        (b) Can we use the empirical gravitational potential energy formula here? Justify your response.

*C7S.7 Imagine that you fire a proton at the nucleus of a gold atom (which contains 79 protons and 118 neutrons). What does the proton's initial speed have to be if it is to penetrate the gold nucleus (whose radius is about 6 fm)? Express your answer as a fraction of the speed of light. (One way to measure nuclear radii is to find the speed that such a proton must have to be absorbed.)

*C7S.8 A 550-g glider sliding on a frictionless air track with a speed of 0.80 m/s hits a spring bumper at the end of the air track. It compresses the spring bumper a maximum distance of 1.0 cm before rebounding. What is the spring constant of the spring?

*C7S.9 You are trying to design a spring gun that is able to launch a 7.0-g marble to a vertical height of 22 m (measured from the starting position of the marble). The specifications for the gun state that when it is loaded, the spring will be compressed 8.0 cm from its relaxed length. (When the gun is fired, the ball is released when the spring reaches its relaxed length.) What should the spring's k_s be?

*C7S.10 A 2.0-kg block is dropped from a height of 48 cm above a plate supported by a spring. If the spring has a spring constant of $k_s = 1600$ J/m^2, what is the maximum distance that the spring will be compressed? (*Hints:* There is no potential energy associated with the spring interaction until the block hits the plate. Remember that the system's gravitational potential energy continues to decrease as the spring is compressed!)

Rich-Context

*C7R.1 A pogo stick is constructed of a long metal cylinder with two footrests at the bottom and a handle at the top. A spring-loaded pipe with a rubber "foot" fits into the bottom of the main cylinder, so that the spring resists the pipe being pushed into the cylinder.

A child can use the pogo stick to bounce around by grabbing the handle and placing both feet on the footrests and then bouncing up and down on the spring-loaded foot. Imagine that you are asked to design a pogo stick that will allow a typical 10-year-old to bounce high enough that the fully extended "foot" is about 50 cm above the ground, but no higher. What might be a reasonable range of possible values for the spring constant k of the spring you should use in the pogo stick? What constraints limit the value of k_s at either end?

*C7R.2 Imagine that you are prospecting for rare metals on a spherical asteroid composed mostly of iron (density ≈ 7800 kg/m^3) and whose radius is 4.5 km. You've left your spaceship in a circular orbit 400 m above the asteroid's surface and gone down to the surface using a jet pack. However, one of your exploratory explosions knocks you back against a rock, ruining your jet pack. (This is why you have a backup jet pack, which is, unfortunately, "back up" in the spaceship.) Is it possible for you to simply jump high enough in this situation to get back to the spaceship? (See problem C7S.1.)

Advanced

C7A.1 The gravitational potential energy of a sphere interacting with a point object is exactly as if the mass of the sphere's mass were concentrated at the sphere's center. We can prove this very useful theorem as follows. First, consider a very thin spherical *shell* of mass M and radius a. Let R be the distance between the shell's center and the external point object (mass m). To find the total potential energy of the shell's interaction with the point object, we have to sum the potential energies of each particle in the shell interacting with the point object. Consider the thin strip of shell shown in figure C7.6. If $d\theta$ is small, all particles in this strip are essentially the same distance r from the external point mass. The length of the strip is $2\pi a \sin \theta$ and its width is $a\, d\theta$, so its area is $2\pi a^2 \sin \theta \, d\theta$. Since the total mass M of the shell is spread evenly over the whole area $4\pi a^2$ of the shell, the total mass m_s in this strip is to M as its area is to

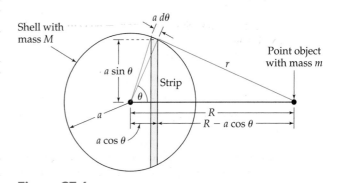

Figure C7.6

Computing the gravitational potential energy of a thin shell interacting with a point.

the shell's total area, implying that the mass of particles in the strip is

$$m_s = \frac{2\pi a^2 \sin\theta\, d\theta}{4\pi a^2} M = \frac{M}{2} \sin\theta\, d\theta \qquad (C7.17)$$

The bit of the gravitational potential energy associated with this strip interacting with the point particle is thus

$$dV = \frac{-Gm_s m}{r} = \frac{-GMm \sin\theta\, d\theta}{2r} \qquad (C7.18)$$

To find the total potential energy of all particles in the shell interacting with the point particle, we simply have to sum equation C7.18 for all such strips, which amounts to integrating this expression over all θ. Now, we can use the pythagorean theorem to express r in terms of θ:

$$r^2 = a^2 \sin^2\theta + (R - a\cos\theta)^2$$
$$= a^2 - 2Ra\cos\theta + R^2 \qquad (C7.19)$$

Verify this last expression, plug it into equation C7.18, and integrate from $\theta = 0$ to $\theta = \pi$. (I suggest a change of variables: define $u = \cos\theta$.) You should find that the total value of V for the interaction between the point and the shell is $V = -GMm/R$, which is what it would be if the shell's mass M were concentrated at its center. (Since a sphere can be constructed from a nested series of such shells, this proves the result for a sphere as well.)

C7A.2 If you know about Taylor series expansions, you can easily see *why* the spring potential energy function is a good approximation to almost any potential energy function $V(r)$ near a local minimum. Consider an *arbitrary* potential energy function $V(r)$ that has a local minimum at separation r_0. Write out a Taylor series expansion of $V(r)$ around the point r_0. Define $x \equiv r - r_0$, and let us assume that x is small (so that we are *close* to the minimum). Argue that we can make the first term in the expansion go away by using our freedom to choose a reference separation to make r_0 the reference separation. Argue that at a local minimum, the second term is automatically zero. Argue that the fourth and succeeding terms will be small compared to the third term if x is small, and so can be ignored. Under these conditions, then, the entire function $V(r)$ is well approximated by the third term in the Taylor series expansion. Then argue that the third term essentially has the form $V(x) = \frac{1}{2}k_s x^2$, and explain how k_s is linked to the second derivative of $V(r)$ with respect to r, evaluated at r_0. Since this works as long as the second derivative of $V(r)$ is defined and not zero, perhaps you can see just how general a model $V(x) = \frac{1}{2}k_s x^2$ might be!

ANSWERS TO EXERCISES

C7X.1 Defining $r = 10^{-12}$ m, noting that each proton's charge is $+e = 1.60 \times 10^{-19}$ C; and assuming that $V = 0$ at infinite separation, the interaction potential energy is

$$V(r) = +\frac{ke^2}{r}$$
$$= \frac{(8.99 \times 10^8 \text{ J·m/C}^2)(1.6 \times 10^{-19} \text{ C})^2}{10^{-12} \text{ m}}$$
$$= 2.3 \times 10^{-16} \text{ J} \qquad (C7.20)$$

C7X.2 Defining $r = 2$ m and $m_1 = m_2 = 10$ kg, and assuming that $V = 0$ at infinite separation, the interaction potential energy is

$$V(r) = -\frac{Gm_1 m_2}{r}$$
$$= -\frac{(6.67 \times 10^{-11} \text{ J·m/kg}^2)(10 \text{ kg})^2}{2 \text{ m}}$$
$$= -3.3 \times 10^{-9} \text{ J} \qquad (C7.21)$$

Remember that the negative result means only that the potential energy of the spheres' gravitational interaction when the spheres are separated by 2 m is 3.3 nJ *smaller* than it would be if their separation were essentially infinite.

C7X.3 Here are some of the missing steps:

$$V(r) = -G\frac{Mm}{r} + G\frac{Mm}{r_e} = \frac{GMm}{r_e}\left[-\frac{r_e}{r} + 1\right]$$
$$= \frac{GMm}{r_e}\left[-\frac{r_e}{r_e + z} + 1\right]$$
$$= \frac{GMm}{r_e}\left[-\frac{1}{1 + z/r_e} + 1\right] \qquad (C7.22)$$

C7X.4 Here are some of the missing steps:

$$V(z) = m\frac{GM}{r_e}\left[\frac{1 + (z/r_e)}{1 + (z/r_e)} - \frac{1}{1 + (z/r_e)}\right]$$
$$= m\frac{GM}{r_e}\left[\frac{1 + (z/r_e) - 1}{1 + (z/r_e)}\right]$$
$$= m\frac{GM}{r_e}\left[\frac{z/r_e}{1 + (z/r_e)}\right] \qquad (C7.23)$$

C7X.5 The earth's radius is 6380 km = 6,380,000 m, so

$$\frac{GM}{r_e^2} = \frac{(6.67 \times 10^{-11} \text{ J·m/kg}^2)(5.98 \times 10^{24} \text{ kg})}{(6,380,000 \text{ m})^2}\left(\frac{1 \text{ N·m}}{1 \text{ J}}\right)$$
$$= 9.8 \text{ N/kg} \qquad (C7.24)$$

C7X.6 Using the exact formula, we have

$$\Delta V = -\frac{GMm}{r_f} + \frac{GMm}{r_i} = -GMm\left(\frac{1}{r_e} - \frac{1}{r_e+h}\right)$$

$$= -(3.99 \times 10^{14}\ \text{J·m/kg})(3.0\ \text{kg})$$

$$\times \left(\frac{1}{6{,}380{,}000\ \text{m}} - \frac{1}{6{,}400{,}000\ \text{m}}\right)$$

$$= -586{,}000\ \text{J} \qquad\qquad (C7.25)$$

This is not much different from what we found using $V(z) = mgz$.

C7X.7 $V(x) = \frac{1}{2}k_s x^2$, so $2V(x)/x^2 = k_s$. Since V has units of joules and x has units of meters, k_s must have units of joules per square meter.

C7X.8 As the spring is stretched, the separation between the centers of objects connected to the spring's ends will grow from some value r_0 to some value r that is 3.0 cm larger (since the spring's length increases by 3 cm). Therefore, $r - r_0 = 3\ \text{cm} = 0.03\ \text{m}$, and

$$V(r) = \frac{1}{2}k_s(r - r_0)^2 = \frac{1}{2}(100\ \text{J/m}^2)(0.03\ \text{m})^2 = 0.045\ \text{J} \qquad (C7.26)$$

assuming that $V = 0$ when the spring is relaxed.

C8

Force and Energy

▷ Introduction

▷ Conservation of Momentum

▽ Conservation of Energy

    Introduction to Energy

    Some Potential Energy Functions

    Force and Energy

    Rotational Energy

    Thermal Energy

    Energy in Bonds

    Power, Collisions, and Impacts

▷ Conservation of Angular Momentum

Chapter Overview

Introduction

In this chapter, we develop a concept called *k-work* that describes how the force that an interaction exerts is related to the energy transfer that the interaction mediates. This concept will be useful throughout the course, but in this chapter it will help us understand how to handle several kinds of frictionless contact interactions in conservation of energy problems.

Section C8.1:   Momentum and Kinetic Energy

In this section, we show that if a particle's momentum changes by a tiny amount $d\vec{p}$ such that $dp \equiv \text{mag}(d\vec{p}) \ll \text{mag}(\vec{p})$, the resulting tiny change dK in its kinetic energy is given by $dK = v\,dp\cos\theta$, where v is the particle's speed and θ is the angle between the directions of $d\vec{p}$ and the particle's velocity $\vec{v}$.

Section C8.2:   The Dot Product

We define the **dot product** $\vec{u} \cdot \vec{w}$ of two arbitrary vectors $\vec{u}$ and $\vec{w}$ to be the following *scalar* quantity:

$$\vec{u} \cdot \vec{w} \equiv uw\cos\theta \tag{C8.5}$$
$$= u_x w_x + u_y w_y + u_z w_z \tag{C8.7}$$

where $u \equiv \text{mag}(\vec{u})$, $w \equiv \text{mag}(\vec{w})$, and θ is the angle between the directions of $\vec{u}$ and $\vec{w}$. The dot product has the following mathematical properties:

$$\vec{u} \cdot \vec{w} = \vec{w} \cdot \vec{u} \qquad \text{dot product is } \textit{commutative} \tag{C8.6a}$$
$$\vec{u} \cdot (\vec{w} + \vec{q}) = \vec{u} \cdot \vec{w} + \vec{u} \cdot \vec{q} \qquad \text{dot product is } \textit{distributive} \tag{C8.6b}$$
$$\vec{u} \cdot (b\vec{w}) = b(\vec{u} \cdot \vec{w}) \qquad \text{dot product is } \textit{linear} \tag{C8.6c}$$
$$\vec{u} \cdot \vec{u} = u^2 \tag{C8.6d}$$
$$\vec{u} \cdot \vec{w} = 0 \quad \Leftrightarrow \quad \vec{u} \perp \vec{w} \qquad \text{assuming } \vec{u} \neq 0 \text{ and } \vec{w} \neq 0 \tag{C8.6e}$$

We can therefore express the change in a particle's kinetic energy as being $dK = \vec{v} \cdot d\vec{p}$.

Section C8.3:   An Interaction's Contribution to dK

This means that if, during a brief time interval dt, multiple interactions $A, B, \ldots$ act on a particle and cause its momentum to change by $d\vec{p} = [d\vec{p}]_A + [d\vec{p}]_B + \cdots$, then the change in the particle's kinetic energy is $dK = \vec{v} \cdot [d\vec{p}]_A + \vec{v} \cdot [d\vec{p}]_B + \cdots$, where $\vec{v}$ is the particle's velocity and $[d\vec{p}]_A$, $[d\vec{p}]_B$, $\ldots$ are the impulses delivered by those interactions. Using the definitions of force and velocity, one can also show that $\vec{v} \cdot [d\vec{p}]_A = \vec{F}_A \cdot d\vec{r}$, where $d\vec{r}$ is the particle's displacement during dt. Therefore

$$[dK] \equiv \vec{F} \cdot d\vec{r} \tag{C8.15a}$$
$$dK = [dK]_A + [dK]_B + \cdots \tag{C8.15b}$$

Purpose: This equation describes how to compute the tiny change dK in a particle's kinetic energy from the tiny amount of **k-work** $[dK]$ that each interaction contributes during a tiny time interval dt.

Section C8.4:   The Meaning of k-Work

The k-work $[dK] \equiv \vec{F} \cdot d\vec{r}$ that an interaction contributes is analogous to the impulse $[d\vec{p}] = \vec{F}\,dt$ delivered by an interaction. Just as impulse is an interaction's withdrawal from or deposit into the particle's momentum bank account, k-work is a withdrawal from or deposit into the particle's kinetic energy bank account. The only difference is that an impulse deposit into one particle's momentum account comes out of the other particle's account, whereas (at the fundamental level) a k-work deposit into a particle's kinetic energy account comes out of the interaction's potential energy, not the other particle's kinetic energy. At the macroscopic level, this can be obscured, but it is still true that only rarely does an interaction even *seem* to transfer kinetic energy from one particle to another.

Section C8.5:   The Earth's Kinetic Energy

The expression $[dK] = \vec{F} \cdot d\vec{r} = \vec{v} \cdot [d\vec{p}]$ implies that even though an interaction between the earth and a much less massive object delivers impulses having the same magnitude to each, the k-work that interaction contributes to the earth is negligible, because the earth's velocity is negligible. Therefore, even though we cannot in practice measure the earth's motion, we can legitimately apply the law of conservation of energy to a system consisting of the earth and a smaller object because we can treat the change in the earth's kinetic energy as being negligible.

Section C8.6:   Force Laws

One can use an interaction's potential energy formula and the expression $[dK] = \vec{F} \cdot d\vec{r}$ to calculate the force that the interaction exerts on a particle. As illustrated by examples in this section, one can show that the near-earth gravitational potential energy formula implies that $\vec{F} = m\vec{g}$, the general gravitational potential energy formula implies **Newton's law of universal gravitation** $\vec{F}_g = (-Gm_A m_B/r^2)\hat{r}$ (where $\hat{r}$ is a directional = "away from the other particle"), and the spring potential energy formula implies that $\vec{F}_{sp} = -k_s(r - r_0)\hat{r}$. We will find these **force laws** useful in unit N.

Section C8.7:   Contact Interactions

The expression $[dK] = \vec{F} \cdot d\vec{r}$ also means that an interaction does not mediate *any* energy transactions if the force it exerts on an object is always perpendicular to that object's motion. Such interactions include the **normal** (perpendicular) part (as opposed to the *friction* part) of a contact interaction between a surface and an object that slides or rolls on wheels on that surface, the **lift** part (as opposed to the **drag** part) of the interaction between air and a wing, and the tension interaction between an inextensible string and an object swinging at the end of the string. We can therefore handle such a contact interaction in a conservation of energy problem by writing "$\perp$" next to its line in the solution's interaction diagram but *ignoring* it in the master equation.

C8.1   Momentum and Kinetic Energy

The most fundamental characteristic of an interaction between two particles is that it affects their motion by transferring momentum between them. In chapter C6, we saw that an interaction between two objects can also transfer energy from the interaction's potential energy to the kinetic energies of objects (or vice versa). In this section, we will explore how these ideas are connected.

We saw in chapter C6 that

$$K = \frac{p^2}{2m} \qquad \text{where } p \equiv \text{mag}(\vec{p}) \tag{C8.1}$$

This shows that if an interaction changes a particle's momentum, it will generally also change its kinetic energy. The interesting thing about this is that although a single interaction (or set of unbalanced interactions) will cause a particle's momentum to change by $d\vec{p}$, such an interaction or interactions do *not* necessarily cause a change in the particle's kinetic energy! Figure C8.1*a* shows that if $d\vec{p}$ is such that adding it to the particle's initial momentum $\vec{p}$ changes the *direction* of $\vec{p}$ but not its magnitude, then the object's kinetic energy does not change. Thus, the degree to which an interaction or set of interactions changes a particle's kinetic energy generally depends on the relative directions of $\vec{p}$ and $d\vec{p}$.

The change in a particle's kinetic energy resulting from a tiny change in its momentum

We can quantify this relationship as follows. Figure C8.1*b* shows what happens when we add an arbitrary momentum change $d\vec{p}$ to a particle's initial momentum $\vec{p}$. The **law of cosines** in this case tells us that the magnitude of the particle's new momentum $\vec{p}_{\text{new}}$ is given by

$$p^2_{\text{new}} \equiv [\text{mag}(\vec{p} + d\vec{p})]^2 = p^2 + 2p\,dp\cos\theta + dp^2 \tag{C8.2}$$

where $p \equiv \text{mag}(\vec{p})$, $dp \equiv \text{mag}(d\vec{p})$, and θ is the angle between the directions of $d\vec{p}$ and $\vec{p}$. You can easily prove that this is right: note on figure C8.1*b* that p_{new} is the hypotenuse of a right triangle whose legs have lengths $p + dp\cos\theta$ and $dp\sin\theta$. Equation C8.2 then follows directly from the pythagorean theorem and the trigonometric identity $\cos^2\theta + \sin^2\theta = 1$.

Exercise C8X.1

Verify equation C8.2.

The change dK that this $d\vec{p}$ produces in the particle's kinetic energy is

$$dK = K_{\text{new}} - K = \frac{p^2_{\text{new}}}{2m} - \frac{p^2}{2m} = \frac{2p\,dp\cos\theta + dp^2}{2m} \tag{C8.3}$$

If the time interval dt is sufficiently short that dp is very small compared to p,

Figure C8.1

(a) An interaction *can* transfer momentum to a particle without changing the magnitude of its momentum and thus its kinetic energy. (b) This happens when we add an arbitrary bit of momentum $d\vec{p}$ to a particle's momentum.

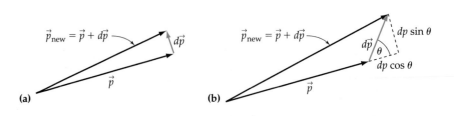

then dp^2 will be negligible compared to $2p\,dp\cos\theta$, meaning that

$$dK \approx \frac{p}{m}dp\cos\theta = v\,dp\cos\theta \qquad \text{when } dp \ll p \qquad (C8.4)$$

where v is the particle's speed when the momentum change occurs and θ is the angle between the directions of $d\vec{p}$ and $\vec{v}$. Note that figure C8.1b shows that if $\theta < 90°$, adding $d\vec{p}$ will increase the momentum arrow's length $p \equiv \text{mag}(\vec{p})$ and thus increase $K = p^2/2m$. This is consistent with equation C8.4, since if $\theta < 90°$, $\cos\theta$ is positive, making dK is positive. Similarly, if $\theta > 90°$, adding $d\vec{p}$ would decrease $p \equiv \text{mag}(\vec{p})$ and thus K, and (consistent with this prediction) equation C8.4 yields a negative value of dK.

Exercise C8X.2

Check that the units of equation C8.4 are correct.

C8.2   The Dot Product

We can express the relationship described in equation C8.4 more compactly in terms of the *dot product* between $\vec{v}$ and $d\vec{p}$. The **dot product** $\vec{u} \cdot \vec{w}$ of any two vectors $\vec{u}$ and $\vec{w}$ is defined to be the *scalar* quantity

$$\vec{u} \cdot \vec{w} \equiv uw\cos\theta \qquad (C8.5)$$

Definition of the dot product of two vectors

where $u \equiv \text{mag}(\vec{u})$, $w \equiv \text{mag}(\vec{w})$, and θ is the angle between the directions of $\vec{u}$ and $\vec{w}$. Figure C8.2 shows that we can interpret this product as being either u times the *projection* of $\vec{w}$ on $\vec{u}$ or w times the projection of $\vec{u}$ on $\vec{w}$.

From this definition, one can prove that the dot product has the following mathematical properties:

Mathematical properties of the dot product

$$\begin{aligned}
\vec{u} \cdot \vec{w} &= \vec{w} \cdot \vec{u} & \text{dot product is } \textit{commutative} & \quad (C8.6a)\\
\vec{u} \cdot (\vec{w} + \vec{q}) &= \vec{u} \cdot \vec{w} + \vec{u} \cdot \vec{q} & \text{dot product is } \textit{distributive} & \quad (C8.6b)\\
\vec{u} \cdot (b\vec{w}) &= b(\vec{u} \cdot \vec{w}) & \text{dot product is } \textit{linear} & \quad (C8.6c)\\
\vec{u} \cdot \vec{u} &= u^2 & & \quad (C8.6d)\\
\vec{u} \cdot \vec{w} = 0 \quad &\Leftrightarrow \quad \vec{u} \perp \vec{w} & \text{assuming } \vec{u} \neq 0 \text{ and } \vec{w} \neq 0 & \quad (C8.6e)
\end{aligned}$$

All these properties are easy to prove from the definition of the dot product except for the distributive property, whose proof is discussed in problem C8S.1. The basic point of these properties is that the dot product of two vectors behaves algebraically pretty much as the ordinary product of two numbers.

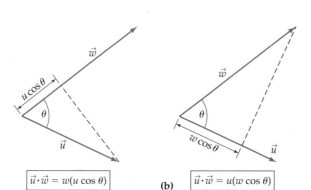

(a) $\boxed{\vec{u}\cdot\vec{w} = w(u\cos\theta)}$

(b) $\boxed{\vec{u}\cdot\vec{w} = u(w\cos\theta)}$

Figure C8.2

Alternative interpretations of the dot product. The *projection* of one vector on another is found by placing the tails of the two vectors together, dropping a perpendicular from the first vector's head to the second vector to form a right triangle, and then measuring the length of the leg along the second vector. The projection is considered to be negative if $\theta > 90°$. In this case, simple trigonometry implies that (a) the projection of $\vec{u}$ on $\vec{w}$ is $u\cos\theta$ and (b) the projection of $\vec{w}$ on $\vec{u}$ is $w\cos\theta$.

Exercise C8X.3

Prove the property in equation C8.6*d* follows from equation C8.5.

Exercise C8X.4

Prove the property in equation C8.6*e* follows from equation C8.5 (be sure to prove this for both directions of the double arrow!).

The dot product in terms of components

One important consequence of these properties is that we can calculate the dot product of two vectors from their components as follows:

$$\vec{u} \cdot \vec{w} = u_x w_x + u_y w_y + u_z w_z \tag{C8.7}$$

One can prove this pretty easily by writing $\vec{u}$ and $\vec{w}$ in terms of component vectors, using the distributive property to write out $\vec{u} \cdot \vec{w}$ in terms of dot products of these component vectors, and then applying the definition of the dot product. The details are left as an exercise (problem C8S.3).

The dot product seems made to order for equation C8.4, which can be rewritten very compactly in terms of a dot product between $\vec{v}$ and $d\vec{p}$:

The change in a particle's kinetic energy resulting from a tiny change in its momentum

$$dK = \vec{v} \cdot d\vec{p} \qquad \text{if } dp \ll p \tag{C8.8}$$

Exercise C8X.5

Imagine that during a certain tiny time interval dt, a particle whose velocity is $\vec{v} = [-4.0 \text{ m/s}, +2.0 \text{ m/s}, 0 \text{ m/s}]$ is involved in an interaction that changes its momentum by $d\vec{p} = [0.020 \text{ kg·m/s}, -0.010 \text{ kg·m/s}, 0 \text{ kg·m/s}]$. Using equation C8.8, compute the change dK in the particle's energy, and verify that it has the right units for an energy change.

Exercise C8X.6

Argue that the two vectors in exercise C8X.5 point in *opposite* directions. Then use equation C8.4 to compute dK and show that you get the same result as in exercise C8X.5.

C8.3   An Interaction's Contribution to dK

How a particle's kinetic energy is affected by multiple interactions

Now we are in a position to connect equation C8.8 to the interactions that cause the momentum change in the first place. If a particle participates in interactions $A, B, \ldots$, the total change $d\vec{p}$ in its momentum during a tiny time interval dt will be the vector sum of the tiny impulses that the interactions contribute during that time interval:

$$d\vec{p} = [d\vec{p}]_A + [d\vec{p}]_B + \cdots \tag{C8.9}$$

where $[d\vec{p}]_A, [d\vec{p}]_B, \ldots$ are the tiny impulses delivered by interactions $A, B, \ldots$, respectively. Plugging this into equation C8.4 and using the distributive property of the dot product, we get

$$dK = v \, dp \cos\theta = \vec{v} \cdot d\vec{p} = \vec{v} \cdot ([d\vec{p}]_A + [d\vec{p}]_B + \cdots)$$
$$= \vec{v} \cdot [d\vec{p}]_A + \vec{v} \cdot [d\vec{p}]_B + \cdots \tag{C8.10}$$

Now, we saw in chapter C3 that the *force* $\vec{F}$ that an interaction exerts on a particle is the rate at which it delivers impulse to that particle:

$$\vec{F} \equiv \frac{[d\vec{p}]}{dt} \quad \Rightarrow \quad \vec{F}\,dt = [d\vec{p}] \tag{C8.11}$$

as long as dt is small enough that $\vec{F}$ doesn't vary much during that interval. If dt is also small enough that the object's velocity $\vec{v}$ doesn't change much, then we also know that

$$\vec{v} = \frac{d\vec{r}}{dt} \tag{C8.12}$$

This means that

$$\vec{v} \cdot [d\vec{p}] = \left(\frac{d\vec{r}}{dt}\right) \cdot (\vec{F}\,dt) = \vec{F} \cdot d\vec{r} \tag{C8.13}$$

Plugging this into equation C8.10, we get

$$dK = \vec{F}_A \cdot d\vec{r} + \vec{F}_B \cdot d\vec{r} + \cdots \tag{C8.14}$$

where $d\vec{r}$ is the tiny displacement that the particle moves during a short time dt and $\vec{F}_A, \vec{F}_B, \ldots$ are the forces exerted on the particle by interactions A, $B, \ldots$, respectively, during that time.

Note that this equation applies as long as $d\vec{r}$ is small enough that neither $\vec{F}$ nor $\vec{v}$ changes significantly during that displacement. These were the conditions placed on equations C8.11 and C8.12. The condition that $\vec{v}$ not change much also ensures that $dp \ll p$, which was a required condition for equation C8.4 (and thus equations C8.10 and C8.14 as well).

Exercise C8X.7

If a particle participates in only a single interaction, then this is the *entire* contribution to dK. Argue that in this case, equation C8.14 means that an object's kinetic energy *increases* if the applied force $\vec{F}$ points in the direction the object is moving, and *decreases* if their directions are opposite. Does this make sense?

In this text, I will call each interaction's contribution to dK the tiny amount of **k-work** $[dK] \equiv \vec{F} \cdot d\vec{r}$ the interaction contributes to the particle during the time that it takes that particle to move a tiny displacement $d\vec{r}$. While I have discussed k-work in the context of interactions with a *particle*, in the usual way we can apply the same concept to an *extended object* by treating the object as a particle located at its center of mass: $\vec{F}_A, \vec{F}_B, \ldots$ in equation C8.14 become the total *external* forces interactions A, B, $\ldots$ exert on the object, $d\vec{r}$ becomes the displacement $d\vec{r}_{CM}$ of the object's center of mass, and dK becomes the change in the kinetic energy $K = \frac{1}{2}mv_{CM}^2$ of the object's center of mass. So in general,

$$[dK] \equiv \vec{F} \cdot d\vec{r} \tag{C8.15a}$$

$$dK = [dK]_A + [dK]_B + \cdots \tag{C8.15b}$$

Definition of k-work

Purpose: It describes how to compute the tiny change dK in a particle's kinetic energy from the tiny amount of *k-work* $[dK]$ each interaction contributes during a tiny time interval dt.

Symbols: $\vec{F}$ is the force that a specific interaction exerts on the particle; $[d\vec{p}]$ is the impulse the interaction delivers during dt; $\vec{v}$ is the particle's velocity; $d\vec{r}$ is the tiny displacement the particle moves during dt; and $[dK]_A$, $[dK]_B$, ... are the k-work contributed by interactions A, B, ..., respectively.

Limitations: The displacement $d\vec{r}$ must be small enough that each interaction's force $\vec{F}$ and the particle's velocity $\vec{v}$ are essentially constant during dt.

Notes: This applies to an extended object if we take $\vec{F}$ to be the total force that an *external* interaction exerts on an object, and $d\vec{r}$ and K to refer to the displacement and kinetic energy of the object's *center of mass*, respectively.

Explanation of the term *k-work*

Many texts call k-work (or something like it) simply *work*. However, only two chapters from now we will discuss an entirely different quantity, also traditionally called *work*. Moreover, physics educators have recently noted that one of the reasons beginners have difficulty with this concept is that physicists often unintentionally use the same word to refer to a *number* of subtly different quantities, particularly when applying the idea to extended objects. A.J. Mallinckrodt and H.S. Leff, in their article "All about Work" [*American Journal of Physics*, **60**(4), April 1992], discuss no less than *seven* distinct physical quantities all commonly called *work!*

I have deliberately chosen a technical term for this quantity that is similar but not identical to the traditional term (1) to distinguish this quantity from the quantity I will call *work* in chapter C10 and (2) to emphasize that in this text, this quantity has the *specific and well-defined meaning* stated in the box above, which may or may not coincide with what another text might call *work*. The "k" in both the name and the symbol is meant to remind you that this quantity is an interaction's contribution to the object's kinetic energy K.

Please note that the k-work that an interaction contributes can be either positive (if the smallest angle between the directions of $\vec{F}$ and $d\vec{r}$ is less than 90°) or negative (if that angle is greater than 90°). Positive k-work seeks to make an object's kinetic energy larger, while negative k-work seeks to make it smaller.

C8.4 The Meaning of k-Work

Similarities between impulse and k-work

The concept of k-work $[dK] \equiv \vec{F} \cdot d\vec{r}$ is to energy what the concept of impulse $[d\vec{p}] = \vec{F}\,dt$ is to momentum (indeed, note the similarity of the equations!). Just as the brackets in the symbol for impulse are meant to remind us that an impulse $[d\vec{p}]$ is only a specific interaction's *contribution* to the object's total change in momentum $d\vec{p}$ during a given time interval dt, so the brackets in the symbol for k-work are meant to remind us that an amount of k-work $[dK]$ is only a specific interaction's *contribution* to the object's total change in kinetic energy dK during the interval dt. Just as we call $[d\vec{p}]$ *impulse* to distinguish it from an *object's momentum* $\vec{p} \equiv m\vec{v}$ (even though they both have units of momentum), so we call $[dK]$ *k-work* to distinguish it from the *object's kinetic energy* $K \equiv \frac{1}{2}mv^2$ (even though they both have units of energy).

The financial analogy revisited

To revisit the financial analogy first described in chapter C3, both $[d\vec{p}]$ and $[dK]$ are analogous to a *cash transaction*, while $\vec{p}$ and K are analogous to *bank accounts*. Transactions imply some kind of money-transfer *process*, while a person's bank account holds money even in the absence of processes. At the end of the month, the change in a bank account's balance is the sum of all deposit and withdrawal transactions that have occurred that month, just as the change in an object's momentum $d\vec{p}$ during a time dt is the sum of all impulses $[d\vec{p}]$ it receives during dt and the change in an object's kinetic energy dK is the sum of all bits of k-work $[dK]$ it receives during dt. We can therefore think of $[d\vec{p}]$ as representing a deposit into or withdrawal from a particle's momentum account $\vec{p}$ and $[dK]$ as representing a deposit into or withdrawal from a particle's kinetic energy account K.

There is, however, one important difference between $[d\vec{p}]$ and $[dK]$. The impulse $[d\vec{p}]$ that an interaction between two particles delivers to one particle's momentum account comes directly out of the other particle's momentum account. At the most fundamental level, though, you should think of the $[dK]$ as representing a transaction between a particle's kinetic energy and the *interaction's potential energy* account, *not* the other kinetic energy account of the other particle involved in the interaction. The attractive gravitational interaction between two particles floating in space and released from rest, for example, increases the kinetic energy of *both* particles at the expense of the interaction's potential energy.

At the macroscopic level, things are more complicated, because transactions between kinetic and potential energies can occur at the microscopic level where they are out of sight. For example, it *looks* as if the contact interaction during a collision between two elastic balls transfers kinetic energy directly from one to the other. If you look at the collision more closely, you will see that as the balls first touch, their contact interaction deforms both balls, transferring kinetic energy from one or both balls to the potential energy of stretched rubber molecules before redistributing that energy to the balls' kinetic energies in different proportions. It is probably better not to worry about such details, though: just understand that a nonzero k-work $[dK]$ at the macroscopic level always signals an energy transaction between an object's kinetic energy and *some* other form of energy, which is only rarely the other object's kinetic energy.

An amount of k-work is a transaction between an object's K and the interaction's V

C8.5   The Earth's Kinetic Energy

In the remaining sections in this chapter, we will explore just a few of the many important applications of the k-work concept. In this section, we will use the idea to show quite generally why we can ignore the change ΔK_e in the earth's kinetic energy when it interacts with something much less massive.

Why we can neglect the change in the earth's kinetic energy

According to equations C8.10 and C8.13, we can also write the k-work contributed by any interaction that delivers an impulse $[d\vec{p}]$ to a particle moving with velocity $\vec{v}$ in the form

$$[dK] = \vec{v} \cdot [d\vec{p}] \tag{C8.16}$$

Now, *any* interaction between an object and the earth must, during a given tiny time interval dt, deliver impulses that are equal in magnitude but opposite in direction for the interaction to conserve momentum: $[d\vec{p}_e] = -[d\vec{p}_o]$ (where the subscripts e and o refers to the earth and the object, respectively). Therefore, the k-work that the interaction does on each object must be

$$[dK_o] = \vec{v}_o \cdot [d\vec{p}_o] \qquad [dK_e] = \vec{v}_e \cdot [d\vec{p}_e] = -\vec{v}_e \cdot [d\vec{p}_o] \tag{C8.17}$$

But we have already seen that in a reference frame floating in space where the earth is initially at rest, $\mathrm{mag}(\vec{v}_e) \ll \mathrm{mag}(\vec{v}_o)$, by something like a factor of 10^{23} or so for typical objects. Since the dot products in equation C8.17 are proportional to the magnitudes of the velocities appearing in them, $[dK_e] \ll [dK_o]$ by a comparable factor. So, quite generally, the change in the earth's kinetic energy in any interaction with something much less massive will be essentially zero when measured in a floating frame where the earth is initially at rest (or essentially at rest).

There is, therefore, a real difference between how we apply conservation of momentum and conservation of energy when an object interacts with the earth. In such an interaction the earth automatically gets the *same* magnitude of impulse the object gets, but we cannot really *apply* momentum conservation in such a case because the earth's response to that impulse cannot be measured in practice: we just shrug and write off what looks like a momentum transfer coming to the object from nowhere. On the other hand, we *can* apply conservation of energy to interactions between an object and the earth: since the earth essentially gets *no* kinetic energy in the interaction, we don't have to measure anything about the earth to know that its kinetic energy doesn't matter!

Applying conservation of energy and momentum to an interaction involving the earth

C8.6   Force Laws

Calculating the force of gravity near the earth's surface

The definition of k-work $[dK] = \vec{F} \cdot d\vec{r}$ provides a link between force and energy that we can use to determine the force that an interaction exerts on a particle from the formula for the interaction's potential energy. Consider first an object of mass m interacting gravitationally with the earth. If the object moves a tiny displacement $d\vec{r}$ in any direction near the earth's surface, the gravitational potential energy of its interaction with the earth changes by

$$dV = mg\,dz \qquad (C8.18)$$

(assuming the z axis points upward) since only the z component of the displacement $d\vec{r}$ has any effect on the object's separation from the earth's center. The k-work that the interaction contributes in this process is

$$[dK] = \vec{F}_g \cdot d\vec{r} = F_{gx}\,dx + F_{gy}\,dy + F_{gz}\,dz \qquad (C8.19)$$

where the last step follows from component definition of the dot product (equation C8.7) and the fact that the components of $d\vec{r}$ are usually written $[dx, dy, dz]$. This k-work comes at the *expense* of gravitational potential energy, so $[dK] = -dV$, implying that

$$F_{gx}\,dx + F_{gy}\,dy + F_{gz}\,dz = [dK] = -dV = -mg\,dz \qquad (C8.20)$$

Now, this equation has to be true no matter *what* the horizontal displacement components dx and dy might be, since displacements in these directions do not affect the object's separation from the earth. The only way that the left side of this equation can be automatically independent of dx and dy is if F_{gx} and F_{gy} are both identically *zero*, implying that the gravitational force is entirely vertical (something that does not come as a great shock to you, I expect). So the equation boils down to $F_{gz}\,dz = -mg\,dz$, implying that

$$F_{gz} = -mg \qquad (C8.21)$$

meaning that the gravitational force is vertically *downward* (since its z component is negative) and its magnitude has the constant value mg. This is completely consistent with equation C3.8. In this context, this result gives us confidence that our definitions of gravitational potential energy, kinetic energy, and k-work all make sense.

Calculating the force of gravity on the astronomical scale

We can do the same thing for the general gravitational potential energy formula. Consider a gravitational interaction between two arbitrary objects, which we will label A and B, and let's calculate the gravitational force on object B (to pick one object arbitrarily) when they are separated by a distance r. For the sake of simplicity, let's orient our reference frame so that the x axis connects the centers of A and B and so that the $+x$ direction points

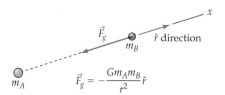

Figure C8.3
The gravitational force exerted on object B due to its interaction with object A.

away from object A at object B (see figure C8.3). Now let's imagine moving object B an arbitrary tiny displacement $d\vec{r}$ while holding the position of object A fixed. We will assume that the displacement is so small that $\text{mag}(d\vec{r}) \ll r$. For such a small displacement, only the displacement's component in the x direction significantly affects the separation between the two objects, so the gravitational potential energy will change by

$$dV = V(r + dx) - V(r) = -\frac{Gm_A m_B}{r + dx} + \frac{Gm_A m_B}{r}$$

$$= Gm_A m_B \frac{-r + (r + dx)}{r(r + dx)}$$

$$= Gm_A m_B \frac{dx}{r^2 + r\,dx} \approx \frac{Gm_A m_B}{r^2} dx \qquad (C8.22)$$

where in the last step I have used the fact that $|dx| < \text{mag}(d\vec{r}) \ll r$, so $r\,dx$ is negligible compared to r^2. Plugging this (instead of $dV = mg\,dz$) into equation C8.20 yields

$$F_{gx}\,dx + F_{gy}\,dy + F_{gz}\,dz = [dK] = -dV = -\frac{Gm_A m_B}{r^2}\,dx \qquad (C8.23)$$

Again, since this must be true no matter what dy and dz might be (as long as they are small), we see that $F_{gy} = F_{gz} = 0$ and $F_{gx} = -Gm_A m_B / r^2$. We can express this more abstractly by defining the directional $\hat{r}$ to represent the phrase "in the direction away from the other particle" (which is the same as the $+x$ direction if we are talking about object B). Then

$$\vec{F}_g = -\frac{Gm_A m_B}{r^2}\hat{r} \qquad (C8.24)$$

Newton's law of universal gravitation

(see figure C8.3). One advantage of this expression is that it applies equally well to particle A. (Note that the vector force acting on either particle points *toward* the other particle, which is appropriate for an attractive force.) Physicists call equation C8.24 **Newton's law of universal gravitation.**

Exercise C8X.8

Verify that the units are consistent in equation C8.24.

In a similar manner, you can show that the force exerted by an ideal spring interaction is

The force exerted by a spring

$$\vec{F}_{sp} = -k_s(r - r_0)\hat{r} \qquad (C8.25)$$

This has been left as a homework problem (see problem C8S.8).

Equations C8.21, C8.24, and C8.25 are **force laws:** they tell us how to calculate the force that an interaction exerts on a participating object. We will not use these formulas in this unit, although we will use them extensively in unit N. The point to understand now is that given a potential energy formula for an interaction, one can use the concept of k-work to find the corresponding force law.

C8.7   Contact Interactions

The *normal* part of a contact interaction contributes no k-work

Consider now the contact interaction between an object and a surface. In section C5.1, we talked about how we could describe the total force that this interaction exerts on that object as the sum of a component vector parallel to the surface (the *friction* part of the interaction) and a component vector perpendicular to the surface, traditionally called the **normal** part of the contact interaction (see figure C8.4). (*Normal* is being used here in its ancient sense of "perpendicular," not in its modern sense as "conventional" or "customary.") If the object slides or rolls parallel to the surface, then the force $\vec{F}_N$ that the normal part of the interaction exerts on an object is perpendicular to the object's displacement $d\vec{r}$ during any time interval dt by definition, so the k-work that this interaction contributes is $[dK] = \vec{F}_N \cdot d\vec{r} = 0$ (since the dot product of two perpendicular vectors is zero). The kinetic energy of an object sliding *frictionlessly* down a wire or track or moving on frictionless wheels on even an undulating or tilted track is therefore *not affected* by the contact interaction with the wire or track, and such an interaction can be *ignored* when we do a conservation of energy calculation.

Of course, if the interaction does exert a nonzero friction force $\vec{F}_F$, then that part of the interaction contributes k-work $[dK] = \vec{F}_F \cdot d\vec{r}$, which (because $\vec{F}_F$ almost always points opposite to the direction the object is moving) is negative, implying that it acts to slow the object down (no surprise here). Therefore, this part of the contact interaction must convert the object's kinetic energy to other forms of energy (forms we will discuss in chapters C9 and C10).

The *lift* part of a contact interaction between air and a wing contributes no k-work

Consider now the contact interaction between the air and an airplane wing. We can similarly think of the total force this interaction exerts on the wing as being the sum of two component vectors, a component opposite to the plane's motion (which we call the **drag**) and a component perpendicular to its motion (which we call the wing's **lift**: see figure C8.5). Again, by definition, the *lift* part of the interaction cannot contribute any k-work to the plane and thus cannot affect the plane's kinetic energy, no matter how the plane swoops or dives. The drag part, like the friction part of the contact interaction considered above, does convert the plane's kinetic energy to other forms of energy.

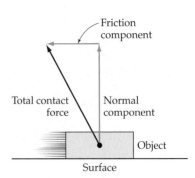

Figure C8.4

Normal and friction components of the total force exerted by the contact interaction between a surface and an object sliding on that surface.

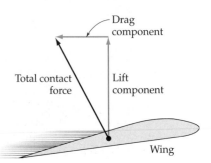

Figure C8.5

Lift and drag components of the total force exerted on a horizontally moving airplane wing by its contact interaction with the air. The lift part is perpendicular to the wing's *motion*, not necessarily the wing's surface.

Consider now an object swinging at the end of an inextensible string. Because the string is flexible, the contact interaction between the object and the string can only exert a force parallel to the string. But if the string is inextensible, the object can only move *perpendicular* to the string (because any displacement parallel to the string would change the string's length). Therefore, the k-work that this tension interaction contributes to the swinging object is also zero.

We see, therefore, that (in the absence of friction or drag) we can handle all these kinds of contact interactions in conservation of energy problems by recognizing that they contribute *zero* k-work to the objects in question and thus mediate no energy transactions at all. You can indicate that you recognize this in a conceptual model diagram by including the interaction in your interaction diagram and by labeling the interaction's line with a "⊥" symbol (instead of a potential energy symbol) as a shorthand way of saying that this interaction exerts a force that is always perpendicular to the object's motion and therefore has no energy implications. You can then ignore the interaction when you construct your master equation. (If a given contact interaction might also have a frictional component that you are going to ignore, treat the normal and frictional parts of the contact interaction as separate interactions on your interaction diagram.) Example C8.1 illustrates the process.

The contact force exerted on an object swinging on an inextensible string contributes no k-work

How to handle such interactions in a conservation of energy problem

Example C8.1

Problem   A roller-coaster car with effectively frictionless wheels rolls over a crest in the track at a speed of 3.0 m/s, then rolls down the track to a point that is 50 m east and 22 m lower than the crest. What is the car's speed at that point?

$$\vec{v}_r = 3 \, m/s$$

$$\vec{F} = -9.8 \, m/s^2$$

50m

? 22m

$$50^2 + 22^2 = c^2$$

$$c^2 =$$

$$c = 54.6$$

54.6 × 9.8

18.2 s.

30 m/s

Translation

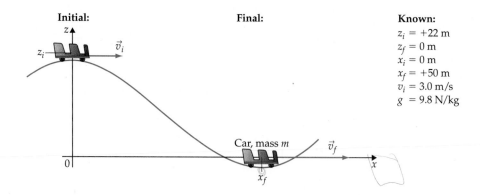

Conceptual Model Diagram

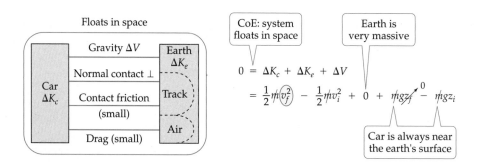

Prose Model   Our system here consists of the coaster car and the earth (we will consider the track to be part of the earth). This system is isolated because it floats in space. The car is involved in two interactions with the earth, a gravitational interaction and an essentially frictionless contact interaction with the track. The latter has no energy implications, so the law of conservation of energy in this case reads $0 = \Delta K_c + \Delta K_e + \Delta V_g$, where the symbols refer to the kinetic energies of the car and the earth and the potential energy of the gravitational interaction, respectively. Since the car is much less massive than the earth, $\Delta K_e \approx 0$. The car always remains near the earth's surface (or so we hope), so we can use $\Delta V_g = mgz_f - mgz_i$ (note that $z_f = 0$) and the car's change in kinetic energy is $\Delta K = \frac{1}{2}mv_f^2 - \frac{1}{2}mv_i^2$. We don't know the car's mass m, but it will cancel out. Therefore, we have enough information to solve for our unknown v_f. The eastward displacement is therefore irrelevant.

Solution   Our conservation of energy equation reduces to

$$0 = \left[\tfrac{1}{2}mv_f^2 - \tfrac{1}{2}mv_i^2\right] + 0 + [0 - mgz_i] + 0 \quad \Rightarrow \quad 0 = v_f^2 - v_i^2 - 2gz_i$$

$$\Rightarrow \quad v_f^2 = v_i^2 + 2gz_i \quad \Rightarrow \quad v_f = \sqrt{v_i^2 + 2gz_i} \tag{C8.26}$$

Plugging in the numbers, we get

$$v_f = \sqrt{(3.0 \text{ m/s})^2 + 2(9.8 \text{ N/kg})(22 \text{ m})\left(\frac{1 \text{ kg·m/s}^2}{1 \text{ N}}\right)} = 21 \text{ m/s} \tag{C8.27}$$

Evaluation   The plus sign and units are right for a speed (both terms under the radical end up have units of square meters divided by square seconds. The magnitude is about 45 mi/h, which is plausible.

TWO-MINUTE PROBLEMS

C8T.1 Two hockey pucks are initially at rest on a horizontal plane of frictionless ice. Puck *A* has twice the mass of puck *B*. Imagine that we apply the same constant force to each puck for the same interval of time *dt*. How do the pucks' kinetic energies compare at the end of this interval?
A. $K_A = 4K_B$
B. $K_A = 2K_B$
C. $K_A = K_B$
D. $K_B = 2K_A$
E. $K_B = 4K_A$
F. Other (specify)

C8T.2 Two hockey pucks are initially at rest on a horizontal plane of frictionless ice. Puck *A* has twice the mass of puck *B*. Imagine that we apply the same constant force to each puck until each puck crosses a finish line 1 m from its starting point. How do the pucks' kinetic energies compare when each crosses this finish line?
A. $K_A = 4K_B$
B. $K_A = 2K_B$
C. $K_A = K_B$
D. $K_B = 2K_A$
E. $K_B = 4K_A$
F. Other (specify)

C8T.3 A crate is being lifted vertically upward at a constant speed. Which interaction contributes *negative* k-work to the crate as it rises? (Ignore friction.)
A. The crate's contact interaction with the cable lifting it.
B. The crate's gravitational interaction with the earth.
C. Other (specify).
D. Neither A nor B; the crate's kinetic energy is constant!

C8T.4 Imagine that we suspend an object from the ceiling by a string and then set it swinging back and forth. Which of the following is/are responsible for significant changes in the object's kinetic energy as it swings?
A. The object's gravitational interaction with the earth.
B. The object's contact interaction with the string.
C. The centrifugal interaction pulling the object outward.

D. A and B only.
E. All the above.
F. None of the above.
T. Other (specify).

C8T.5 When an object slides down a frictionless incline, the contact interaction between the object and the incline does not contribute to the object's kinetic energy, true (T) or false (F)? This means that it also does not transfer any momentum to the object, T or F?

C8T.6 Imagine that a very heavy ball is suspended by a chain. Imagine that I pull the ball away from its equilibrium position, hold it against my nose (with the chain taut), and release the ball from rest. The ball swings away from me and then back toward me. I can be confident that it will not smash my nose (as long as I don't move), T or F?

C8T.7 A bead slides from rest down a frictionless wire in the earth's gravitational field. The diagram shows a set of possible shapes that the wire might have. At the bottom of which will the bead have the highest speed? (If the final speed is the same for all shapes, answer F.)

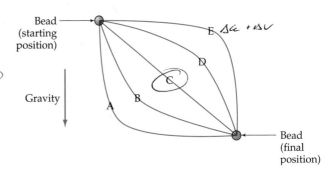

C8T.8 In the situation described in problem C8T.7, along the wire of which shape will the bead take the *shortest time* to get from the top to the bottom? (If the time is the same for all shapes, answer F.)

C8T.9 A skier starts from rest, slides down a frictionless slope, and slides off a ski jump angled upward at 45° with respect to the vertical. How does the skier's height h at the peak of the jump compare to his or her original height H?

A. $h < H$
B. $h \approx H$
C. $h > H$
D. There is not enough information provided to tell.

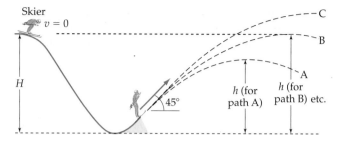

HOMEWORK PROBLEMS

Basic Skills

C8B.1 During a certain time interval, an object moving at 12 m/s receives an impulse of 200 kg·m/s opposite to its motion from a friction interaction. What k-work does this interaction contribute to the object? Does this increase or reduce the object's kinetic energy? Please explain.

C8B.2 An object is sliding at 2 m/s down an incline that makes an angle of 30° with respect to the horizontal. If the gravitational interaction contributes 10 kg·m/s of downward momentum to the object every second, what k-work does it contribute to the object every second?

C8B.3 Prove property C8.6c of the dot product.

C8B.4 What is the dot product of the two displacement vectors $\vec{u} = [2\text{ m}, -1\text{ m}, 3\text{ m}]$ and $\vec{w} = [5\text{ m}, 2\text{ m}, -2\text{ m}]$. What is the angle between these vectors?

C8B.5 Two displacement vectors $\vec{u} = [3\text{ m}, -5\text{ m}, 2\text{ m}]$ and $\vec{w} = [-4\text{ m}, -2\text{ m}, ?]$ are perpendicular. What is the value of w_z?

C8B.6 A car whose weight is 20,000 N (mass $\approx$ 2000 kg) is traveling at a constant speed of 25 m/s up an incline that makes an angle of 4° with respect to the horizontal. What k-work does the gravitational interaction contribute to the car every second? Does this particular interaction transform energy *to* or *from* the car's kinetic energy? Explain.

C8B.7 A car rolls 300 m down a straight incline that makes a constant angle of 8° with the horizontal. Equation C8.15a only applies if the time interval during which the displacement takes place is "tiny" in the sense described in the "Limitations" part of the box. Is the time that it takes the car to roll this distance "tiny" enough in this case for us to use equation C8.15a to compute the energy transformed by the gravitational interaction as the car rolls this distance?

Does it matter whether the car rolls at a constant speed? Please explain your answers carefully.

Synthetic

The starred problems are particularly well suited for practicing the use of the problem-solving framework and conceptual model diagrams.

C8S.1 We can prove that the dot product is distributive as follows. Let $\vec{a} \equiv \vec{w} + \vec{q}$. We can think of the dot product $\vec{u} \cdot \vec{a}$ as being $u \equiv \text{mag}(\vec{u})$ times the projection of $\vec{a}$ on $\vec{u}$. This projection, as well as the projections of $\vec{w}$ and $\vec{q}$ on $\vec{u}$, is shown in figure C8.6. Use this figure to prove that $\vec{u} \cdot (\vec{w} + \vec{q}) = \vec{u} \cdot \vec{w} + \vec{u} \cdot \vec{q}$. (The vectors $\vec{w}$ and $\vec{q}$ are shown lying in the same plane as $\vec{a}$ and $\vec{u}$, but the same basic argument applies even if they do not. Think about it!)

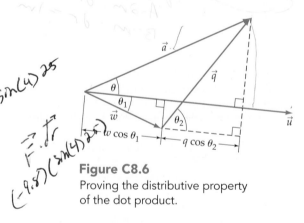

Figure C8.6
Proving the distributive property of the dot product.

C8S.2 Why not simply define the product of two vectors to be the product of their magnitudes: $\vec{u}\vec{w} \equiv uw$? Prove that this product does *not* satisfy the distributive property. (A product that does not satisfy the distributive property is much less useful than one that does.)

C8S.3 Prove that the component version of the dot product given by equation C8.7 is correct by writing $\vec{u}$ and $\vec{w}$ in terms of component vectors, using the distributive property to write out $\vec{u} \cdot \vec{w}$ in terms of dot products of these component vectors, and then applying the definition of the dot product given by equation C8.5. [*Hint:* Note that mag(u_x) = |u_x|, not u_x. Even so, you can show that $\vec{u}_x \cdot \vec{w}_x = u_x w_x$ by considering the possible cases for the signs of u_x and w_x.]

*C8S.4 Tarzan stands on a branch 3.0 m above the ground, holding onto a vine. He steps off the branch and swings downward on the vine. If his feet are about 1.0 m above the ground at the swing's lowest point, what is his speed there?

*C8S.5 You are investigating an accident where a 1500-kg car that was parked without its emergency brake on rolled down a hill with a slope of 8° a distance of 150 m (measured along the road) and hit a parked van. How fast was the car moving when it hit the van, assuming little friction?

*C8S.6 A bicyclist climbs a hill 32 m tall and then coasts down the other side without pedaling. If the cyclist's speed was 2.2 m/s at the top, what is it at the bottom (ignoring friction)?

C8S.7 A bicyclist coasts without pedaling down an incline that makes an angle of 3° with the horizontal at a steady speed of 13 m/s. If the mass of the cyclist and

the bike combined is 68 kg, use k-work (*not* Newton's second law) to estimate the force of friction that must be acting on the bicyclist. (*Hint:* Think about what happens during a time interval of 1 s.)

C8S.8 Using the technique shown in section C8.6, find the force law for an ideal spring interaction between two objects from the potential energy formula, and compare your result to equation C8.25.

C8S.9 Imagine that a certain interaction between two particles separated by a distance r has a potential energy $V(r) = br$, where b is a constant. (This potential energy function seems to at least approximately describe the interaction between two quarks.)
(a) Using the technique shown in section C8.6, find the force law for this interaction.
(b) Is this interaction attractive or repulsive? Explain.

Rich-Context

*C8R.1 A pilot makes a crash landing on the top of a mesa that stands 250 m above the surrounding plain (a mesa is a hill with very steep sides and a flat top). The pilot fixes the plane and wants to take off again, but the only reasonably smooth road that could be used for a runway is not long enough: the pilot estimates that the maximum speed the plane is likely to reach before going off the edge of the mesa is about 45 mi/h, but the plane needs an airspeed of about 120 mi/h before the wing's lift becomes significantly larger than the plane's weight. Noting that the side of the mesa is essentially a vertical cliff, the pilot thinks that by deliberately driving the plane off the edge at 45 mi/h and diving downward as well as forward, the pilot might cause the plane to pick up enough airspeed to pull out of the dive before hitting the ground. What would you advise the pilot to do: try it, or hope for rescue (and risk dying of exposure and dehydration)? Do not ignore either the lift or drag interactions between the plane and the air, but do remember that the plane also has a propeller.

*C8R.2 You are investigating a mishap on a mountain railroad. On the night of June 15, one railroad car was left parked at the top of a hill above another car of the same mass. In the morning, both cars are found coupled together in a lake, as shown in figure C8.7. (The

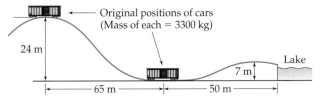

Figure C8.7
The situation for problem C8R.2.

tracks go right up to the lake to facilitate loading boats with ore.) The supervisor claims that the engineer must have not set the brake on the upper car; and during the night, it rolled down, hit, and coupled with the lower car; and its momentum carried both into the lake. The engineer disputes this, saying that someone must have released the brake and then *pushed* the upper car. Can you use physics to resolve this dispute? (*Hint:* Momentum is conserved in the collision. You will probably need to draw three conceptual model diagrams for this problem.)

Advanced

C8A.1 Use the component form of dot product of two arbitrary vectors $\vec{u}$ and $\vec{w}$ to prove the trigonometric identity

$$\cos(\theta - \phi) = \cos\theta\cos\phi + \sin\theta\sin\phi \qquad (C8.28)$$

C8A.2 Imagine that a person jumps vertically up from the ground after crouching at rest. The person clearly gains kinetic energy from the jumping process.

(a) Argue, using the principle of momentum transfer, that as the person exerts a downward force on the ground with his or her feet, the ground must exert an equal and opposite upward force on the person.

(b) Since the person gains kinetic energy, this upward force must contribute k-work to the person. But the point of contact between the person and the ground does not move, so the displacement $d\vec{r}$ of the point where the force is exerted is zero. Therefore, the k-work contributed by this upward force must be $[dK] = \vec{F} \cdot d\vec{r} = 0$! Resolve this paradox. (*Hint:* Think carefully about the definitions involved here.) *Comment:* One of the most common casual definitions of *work* appearing in the literature is that work is "a force acting through a distance." This illustrates one of the many paradoxes that can arise in people's minds if one uses this definition. The *correct* description of this situation using this definition is *much* more complex than a description that (correctly) uses k-work.

ANSWERS TO EXERCISES

C8X.1 According to the pythagorean theorem,

$$\begin{aligned} p_{new}^2 &= (p + dp\cos\theta)^2 + (dp\sin\theta)^2 \\ &= p^2 + 2p\,dp\cos\theta + dp^2\cos^2\theta + dp^2\sin^2\theta \\ &= p^2 + 2p\,dp\cos\theta + dp^2 \qquad (C8.29) \end{aligned}$$

since $\cos^2\theta + \sin^2\theta = 1$.

C8X.2 The SI units of v are m/s and the SI units of dp are kg(m/s), while $\cos\theta$ is unitless. Therefore, the units of dK are kg(m/s)^2 = kg·m^2/s^2 ≡ J, appropriate units for a change in energy.

C8X.3 The angle between a vector and itself is zero, so $\vec{u} \cdot \vec{u} = u^2\cos(0°) = u^2(1) = u^2$.

C8X.4 If $\vec{u} \cdot \vec{w} = 0$ but $u \neq 0$ and $w \neq 0$, then $\cos\theta$ must be zero, implying that θ must be $\pm90°$: thus the vectors are perpendicular. If the vectors are perpendicular, then the angle between the vectors is $\pm90°$, so $\cos\theta = 0$, implying that $\vec{u} \cdot \vec{w} = uw\cos(\pm90°) = uw(0) = 0$.

C8X.5 According to equation C8.6,

$$\begin{aligned} dK &= \vec{v} \cdot d\vec{p} = v_x\,dp_x + v_y\,dp_y + v_z\,dp_z \qquad (C8.30) \\ &= (-4.0 \text{ m/s})(0.020 \text{ kg·m/s}) \\ &\quad + (+2.0 \text{ m/s})(-0.010 \text{ kg·m/s}) + 0 \end{aligned}$$

$$\begin{aligned} &= -0.080 \text{ kg·m}^2/\text{s}^2 - 0.020 \text{ kg·m}^2/\text{s}^2 + 0 \\ &= -0.10 \text{ kg·m}^2/\text{s}^2 \qquad (C8.31) \end{aligned}$$

Since 1 kg·m^2/s^2 ≡ 1 J, these are the correct units for energy!

C8X.6 Note that $d\vec{p} = (-0.005 \text{ kg})\vec{v}$ in this particular case. Since multiplying a vector by a negative scalar flips its direction, this tells us that $d\vec{p}$ and $\vec{v}$ have opposite directions. So, the angle between them is 180°, and $\cos(180°) = -1$, so $dK = -v\,dp$. The pythagorean theorem implies that

$$\begin{aligned} v &\equiv \text{mag}(\vec{v}) \\ &= \sqrt{(-4.0 \text{ m/s})^2 + (2.0 \text{ m/s})^2 + 0} \\ &= \sqrt{20.0} \text{ m/s} \end{aligned}$$

$$\begin{aligned} dp &\equiv \text{mag}(d\vec{p}) \\ &= \sqrt{(0.020 \text{ m/s})^2 + (-0.010 \text{ m/s})^2 + 0} \\ &= \sqrt{5.0 \times 10^{-4}} \text{ m/s} \end{aligned}$$

$$\begin{aligned} dK &= -\left(\sqrt{20} \text{ m/s}\right)\left(\sqrt{5.0} \times 10^{-2} \text{ kg·m/s}\right) \\ &= -0.10 \text{ kg·m}^2/\text{s}^2 = -0.10 \text{ J} \qquad (C8.32) \end{aligned}$$

which is what we got before.

C8X.7 The displacement $d\vec{r}$ indicates the direction the object is moving during the time interval $d\vec{r}$. So if $\vec{F}$ and $d\vec{r}$ point in the same direction, then the angle θ between them is $0°$ and $\cos\theta = +1$, so dK is positive, meaning that the kinetic energy K is increasing. If $\vec{F}$ and $d\vec{r}$ point in opposite directions, then the angle θ between them is $180°$ and $\cos\theta = -1$, so dK is negative, meaning that K decreases. This makes sense: a push delivered in the direction of motion will cause the object to speed up (giving it a greater kinetic energy), while one in the reverse direction will slow it down.

C8X.8 Since G has SI units of $J \cdot m/kg^2$, the left side of equation C8.24 has units of

$$\frac{\cancel{J} \cdot \cancel{m} \, \cancel{kg^2}}{\cancel{kg^2} \, \cancel{m^2}} \left(\frac{1 \, N \cdot \cancel{m}}{1 \cancel{J}} \right) = N \tag{C8.33}$$

which are the appropriate units for force.

C9 Rotational Energy

▷ **Introduction**

▷ **Conservation of Momentum**

▽ **Conservation of Energy**

　　Introduction to Energy

　　Some Potential Energy Functions

　　Force and Energy

　　Rotational Energy

　　Thermal Energy

　　Energy in Bonds

　　Power, Collisions, and Impacts

▷ **Conservation of Angular Momentum**

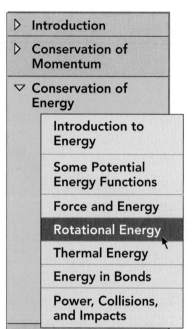

Chapter Overview

Introduction

In this chapter we look at rotational kinetic energy. In conservation of energy problems, including a rotational kinetic energy term allows us to handle friction interactions that cause an object to roll without slipping. This chapter also provides essential background for chapters C13 and C14 on angular momentum.

Section C9.1: Introduction to Rotational Energy

Empirically, an object that slides frictionlessly down an incline ends up moving faster than an object of the same mass that rolls down the same incline, even though the decrease in gravitational potential energy is the same for both. We could explain this if there is kinetic energy associated with the rolling object's rotation that soaks up some of the potential energy.

Section C9.2: Measuring Angles

For a number of reasons, it is easiest to quantify an object's rate of rotation if we define the absolute value of an angle θ to be

$$|\theta| \equiv \frac{s}{r} \tag{C9.1}$$

where s is the arclength **subtended** by the angle along the circumference of a circle of radius r. We say that an angle defined in this way has been expressed "in radians," even though the ratio is technically unitless. The **radian** is thus a peculiar "unitless unit" that we can choose to either display or not when specifying a quantity's units. We usually display it when we want to make it clear that the quantity involves measuring an angle or if we want to convert to or from other angular units, such as the **degree** or **revolution.**

Section C9.3: Angular Velocity

We define an object's **angular velocity** $\vec{\omega}$ to be

$$\vec{\omega} \equiv \left| \frac{d\theta}{dt} \right| \hat{\omega} \tag{C9.6}$$

Purpose: This equation defines a rotating rigid object's angular velocity $\vec{\omega}$.

Symbols: $d\theta$ is the tiny angle through which any particle in the object rotates during a tiny time interval dt, and $\hat{\omega}$ is a directional short for "in a direction parallel to the object's axis of rotation in the sense indicated by your right thumb when your fingers curl with its rotation."

Limitations: This equation only makes sense when applied to a rigid object rotating around a well-defined axis or to a particle moving in a plane around some origin.

The ordinary **rotational speed** v of any particle moving along a circular path of radius r (such as a particle in a rotating rigid object) is

$$v = \mathrm{mag}(\vec{v}) = r\omega \tag{C9.4}$$

Section C9.4: The Moment of Inertia

An object's **moment of inertia** I and its **rotational kinetic energy** K^{rot} for rotations around a given axis are given by

$$I \equiv m_1 r_1^2 + m_2 r_2^2 + \cdots + m_N r_N^2 \equiv \sum_{i=1}^{N} m_i r_i^2 \qquad \text{(C9.8)}$$

Purpose: This equation defines an extended object's moment of inertia I for a given axis of rotation.
Symbols: m_i is the mass of the ith particle in the object, and r_i is that particle's distance from the rotation axis.
Limitations: There are none; this is a definition.
Note: A given object's moment of inertia I will have different values for different axes of rotation (because the values of r_i will change).

$$K^{\text{rot}} = \tfrac{1}{2} I \omega^2 \qquad \text{(compare with } K = \tfrac{1}{2} m v^2 \text{)} \qquad \text{(C9.9)}$$

Purpose: This equation describes the kinetic energy K^{rot} associated with an object's rotation around its center of mass.
Symbols: I is the object's moment of inertia for the axis of its rotation, and ω is the angular speed of its rotation.
Limitations: The object must rotate as a rigid body does (otherwise ω is not well defined).

Note that I plays the same role for rotational motion that mass does for linear motion.

Section C9.5: Calculating Moments of Inertia

One can calculate an object's moment of inertia for a given axis of rotation by dividing it into small enough pieces that each particle in the piece is essentially the same distance from that axis. This section displays a number of examples of such calculations.

Section C9.6: Translation and Rotation

Although this is not obvious, the total kinetic energy of an object that is simultaneously moving and rotating turns out to be simply

$$K = K^{\text{cm}} + K^{\text{rot}} = \tfrac{1}{2} M v_{\text{CM}}^2 + \tfrac{1}{2} I \omega^2 \qquad \text{(C9.18)}$$

Where $K^{\text{cm}} \equiv \tfrac{1}{2} M v_{\text{CM}}^2$, the object's **translational kinetic energy,** would be its kinetic energy if it were not rotating, and $K^{\text{rot}} \equiv \tfrac{1}{2} I \omega^2$ would be its kinetic energy of rotation if it were not moving.

Section C9.7: Rolling Without Slipping

The angular speed ω of an object of radius R that rolls *without slipping* is linked to its center-of-mass speed v_{CM} by

$$\omega = \frac{v_{\text{CM}}}{R} \qquad \text{(C9.19)}$$

Rolling without slipping is caused by the friction part of a contact interaction between the object and a surface. Therefore, we can handle such an interaction in a conservation of energy problem by including a rotational kinetic energy term in our conservation of energy equation.

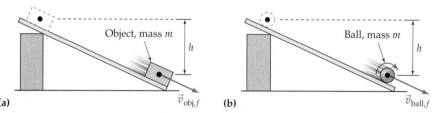

Figure C9.1

(a) An object of mass m slides from rest down a frictionless inclined track, going down a vertical distance h. (b) A ball with mass m rolls from rest without slipping along a similar incline, going the same vertical distance h as in part a. Its final speed is smaller than the sliding object's final speed.

C9.1   Introduction to Rotational Energy

A puzzle concerning the behavior of a rolling object

Here is a puzzle. Figure C9.1a shows an object sliding without friction down a straight inclined track. Figure C9.1b shows a ball with the same mass rolling without slipping down a straight track inclined at the same angle. Assume that both start from rest and move through the same vertical and horizontal distances. Since we can ignore the normal part of the contact interaction with the track in both cases, and since both objects have the same mass and move through the same vertical distance, they both have converted the same amount of gravitational potential energy to kinetic energy in this process. Therefore, they must have the same kinetic energy at the end, right? When we actually do this experiment, though, we find that the rolling ball is moving significantly more slowly than the sliding object when it reaches the end of the track! How can this be?

How taking account of rotational kinetic energy could solve the puzzle

There is a difference between these two situations, though: the ball is *rotating* around its center of mass when it reaches the end of the track, but the sliding object is not. This rotation causes the ball's constituent particles to move *around* its center of mass as well as along with it. If there is a kinetic energy associated with this rotational motion in addition to the kinetic energy of its forward motion, it could solve the puzzle. While the gravitational interaction must convert the same amount of potential energy to kinetic energy in each case, the energy released would go entirely to the kinetic energy of the sliding object's center-of-mass motion but only *partly* to the same for the ball, the rest going to the kinetic energy of the ball's rotational motion. This would explain why the ball's center of mass was not moving as rapidly as that of the sliding object at the end of the track.

To make sure that this qualitative proposal does indeed solve the puzzle, we need to know how to calculate the extra kinetic energy involved in the rotation, and then verify that including this energy accounts for the entire observed difference in speed. The purpose of this chapter is to explore how to calculate the kinetic energy associated with an extended object's rotational motion.

C9.2   Measuring Angles

How to quantify an angle

To quantify an object's rate of rotation, we need to quantify the *angle* through which the object rotates during a given interval of time. Two line segments that intersect at a point define an angle θ (see figure C9.2a). One way to quantify this angle is to superimpose on the line segments a circle whose center coincides with the point where they intersect. If we then divide the circle's circumference up into some number of equal-size parts, we can quantify the angle by counting the number of such parts bracketed (or **subtended**) by the segments (see figure C9.2b).

This is exactly what we do when we use a protractor to measure an angle: the protractor defines a circle whose center we align with the point where the lines intersect. We conventionally divide the circumference of a protractor's circle into 360 equal parts, called **degrees,** and reading the angle in degrees amounts to counting how many of these parts fit between the two line segments. But why 360 degrees and not 100, or 1000, or 47? This choice is simply conventional, but the numerical value of an angle measured in this way depends on that choice.

However, there is another way to quantify an angle that in a very real sense is much more natural. Consider figure C9.2c. Let r be the radius of the arbitrary circle that we superimpose on the angle, and let s be the arclength along that circle's circumference bracketed by the angle. We can *define* the magnitude of angle θ in this way:

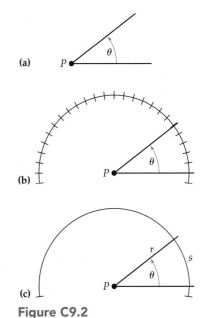

Figure C9.2
(a) Two line segments that intersect at some point P define an angle θ. (b) To quantify θ, we can superimpose a circle centered at P, divide its circumference into an arbitrary number of equally spaced units, and find out how many units the angle spans. (c) A more natural approach is to define θ to be the arclength s subtended, divided by the circle's radius r: $\theta \equiv s/r$.

$$|\theta| \equiv \frac{s}{r} \qquad\qquad (C9.1)$$

The ratio s/r is independent of the particular *circle* that we use because, just as the circle's total circumference is proportional to its radius r; so the arclength s subtended by the angle θ (which represents a fixed fraction of a circle) is proportional to r. Thus the ratio s/r remains fixed for a given angle as we vary r. The numerical value of this ratio is also independent of the *units* we use to express both s and r. Therefore, the angle defined in this way has a magnitude relatively free of "artificial ingredients."

Moreover, this definition proves to be very *convenient*, partly because it yields a *unitless* number (the ratio of two lengths is unitless). This is valuable because, technically, mathematical functions such as $\sin \theta$ and e^x are defined to convert a unitless number to another unitless number. Moreover, a number of mathematical relationships involving trigonometric functions obtain their simplest form when we define θ in this way.

According to equation C9.1, the angle corresponding to an entire circle has a value of $s/r = 2\pi r/r = 2\pi$. Since a right angle corresponds to a quarter of a circle, its numerical value is $2\pi/4 = \pi/2$. Similarly, the angle corresponding to $45°$ (one-eighth of a circle) is $\pi/4$, that corresponding to $30°$ is $\pi/6$, and so on.

It is conventional to say that when we define an angle in this way, we are expressing it "in radians," as if the radian were a unit of angle much as the meter is a unit of distance. However, θ as defined by equation C9.1 is strictly *unitless*. There is actually a continuing debate as to whether one should think of the **radian** (and by extension, the **degree,** the **revolution,** and other measures of angle) as being a unit like other units. In practice, I think that it is best to think of the radian as being a *special kind* of unit whose definition according to equation C9.1 is 1 rad = 1 m/m = 1. Since we can always multiply an equation by 1 without changing its meaning, we can (when calculating units) either supply or delete the radian unit at will. It is useful to *supply* this special unit in two cases:

Rules for handling angular "units" (which are rather peculiar)

1. When we want to make it clear that a given quantity is or involves an angle.
2. When we need to recalculate an angular quantity that has been given first in degrees or revolutions. In this case, we treat the radian, degree,

and/or revolution *as if* it were ordinary units. For example,

$$1 = 1 \text{ rad} = 1 \text{ rad} \left(\frac{1 \text{ rev}}{2\pi \text{ rad}} \right) = 0.159 \text{ rev} \left(\frac{360°}{1 \text{ rev}} \right) = 57.3° \qquad \text{(C9.2)}$$

In all *other* situations, we will avoid displaying the radian unit.

So from now on, let's *assume* that angles are defined as specified by equation C9.1. We will also *assume* that angles specified in units other than radians get converted to radians *before* they are used in calculations. Your calculator does this automatically when you calculate sin (15°), for example, but in other cases, you should do the conversion *explicitly*.

C9.3 Angular Velocity

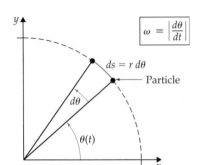

$$\omega \equiv \left| \frac{d\theta}{dt} \right|$$

$ds = r \, d\theta$

Particle

$d\theta$

$\theta(t)$

Figure C9.3
How to define the *angular speed* of a particle moving along a circular path.

A particle's *rotational speed* in a rotating object

Consider a point particle in circular motion around the origin of a reference frame in the *xy* plane of that frame (see figure C9.3). At every instant of time, the radius vector connecting the origin of the particle makes a certain angle $\theta(t)$ with the frame's *x* axis. We define the magnitude of this angle by using equation C9.1; we conventionally define the angle's *sign* to indicate whether we are measuring the angle to the radius vector counterclockwise (positive) or clockwise (negative) from the *x* axis.

We define the particle's **angular speed** ω at an instant to be the rate at which this angle changes at that instant

$$\omega \equiv \left| \frac{d\theta}{dt} \right| \qquad \text{(C9.3)}$$

where dt is an interval of time centered on the instant in question that is sufficiently short that the rotation speed does not change much during the interval, and $d\theta$ is the particle's change in angle during this interval. The absolute values ensure that we are talking about the *magnitude* of the change in the angle $d\theta$ whether the signed value of θ is increasing with time (so that $d\theta$ is positive) or decreasing with time (so that $d\theta$ is negative). This is a case where it is helpful to supply the unit of radians to make it clear that ω expresses the rate of change of an *angle*, so we often express ω in radians per second (rather than the equivalent but opaque units of 1/second).

According to equation C9.1, $|d\theta| \equiv s/r$, so if a particle's angle changes by $|d\theta|$ as it moves in a circular path of radius r, the arclength it covers is $ds = r|d\theta|$. Since the particle's *ordinary* speed v is the distance it covers in a tiny interval dt divided by dt, in this case v is

$$v = \text{mag}(\vec{v}) = \frac{ds}{dt} = \frac{r|d\theta|}{dt} = r\omega \qquad \text{(C9.4)}$$

Purpose: This equation describes how to calculate a particle's ordinary speed v due to its rotational motion in a circle of radius r at an angular speed ω.

Limitations: This equation only applies if the particle's trajectory is (at least momentarily) circular. It also assumes that ω is measured in radians per second.

Note that v is the ratio of the *distance* the particle covers (not the angle) to the time interval. When the particle is part of a rotating object, we call v the particle's **rotational speed** (to distinguish it from the particle's *angular speed ω*). We want the units of v to be meters per second to indicate that it is an ordinary speed; so we *drop* the radians in the units of ω, and the units of $r\omega$ become simply meters times 1/second (m·s^{-1}), which is equal to meters per second (m/s). Even so, it is *very* important to note that equation C9.4 *assumes* we are expressing ω in radians per second. If we initially express a rotation rate in some other units, we have to convert to radians per second before using equation C9.4. For example, if the object rotates at a rate of 10 turns per second, then we can calculate ω in radians per second as follows:

$$10 \, \frac{\text{rev}}{\text{s}} = 10 \, \frac{\text{rev}}{\text{s}} \left(\frac{2\pi \, \text{rad}}{1 \, \text{rev}} \right) = 62.8 \, \frac{\text{rad}}{\text{s}} = 62.8 \, \text{s}^{-1} = \omega \qquad \text{(C9.5)}$$

Now consider a rigid, extended object rotating around a certain axis (figure C9.4). We can treat *any* extended object as a set of particles. If the object is rigid, each of its particles follows a circular path in a plane perpendicular to the axis of rotation, and each rotates through the *same* angle in its plane during a given interval dt: thus all have the *same* angular speed ω. We define a rigid object's angular speed ω to be the common angular speed of its particles.

In linear motion, a particle's *speed* is the magnitude of its *velocity*: the particle's velocity vector specifies not only the rate at which the particle moves but also its direction of motion. Similarly, a rotating object's *angular speed* is the magnitude of its **angular velocity** $\vec{\omega}$, a vector that specifies not only the *rate* at which the object rotates but also its *direction* of rotation.

But how can we define a rotating object's "direction of rotation"? As the object rotates, the velocities of its various particles point in a variety of different directions. But a rotation *does* define an unambiguous line in space—the *axis* of the rotation! We therefore *define* the direction of $\vec{\omega}$ to be parallel to the axis of rotation.

This does not yet completely specify $\vec{\omega}$'s direction, since there are two possible directions parallel to the axis of rotation. The direction of $\vec{\omega}$ is defined *by convention* to be the direction along the axis indicated by your right thumb if you wrap your right fingers around the axis in the direction that the object's particles move as the object rotates (see figure C9.5). So to summarize:

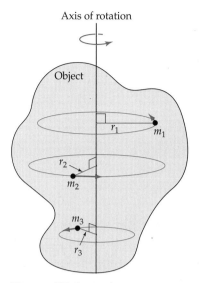

Figure C9.4
Particles (m_1, m_2, and m_3) in a rigid rotating object follow circular paths perpendicular to the axis of rotation.

$$\vec{\omega} \equiv \left| \frac{d\theta}{dt} \right| \hat{\omega} \qquad \text{(C9.6)}$$

Definition of angular velocity

Purpose: This equation defines a rotating rigid object's angular velocity $\vec{\omega}$.

Symbols: $d\theta$ is the tiny angle through which any particle in the object rotates during a tiny time interval dt, and $\hat{\omega}$ is a directional short for "in a direction parallel to the object's axis of rotation in the sense indicated by your right thumb when your fingers curl with its rotation."

Limitations: This equation only makes sense when applied to a rigid object rotating around a well-defined axis or to a particle moving in a plane around some origin.

Angular velocity $\vec{\omega}$ may seem less intuitive and more artificial than ordinary velocity $\vec{v}$. However, it is worth remembering that *both* are inventions of the human mind: neither refers to something that intrinsically exists in nature (although one might *almost* believe this about $\vec{v}$). Think of $\vec{\omega}$ as being not a name for something physically real, but rather a clever scheme for encoding into a compact mathematical package everything we need to know about an object's rotation: its rotational rate, axis of rotation, and direction of rotation around that axis. Knowing $\vec{\omega}$ therefore allows us to reconstruct completely the object's rotational behavior in our minds.

Exercise C9X.1

Does the earth's angular velocity vector point from the earth's center toward the earth's north pole or from the earth's center toward its south pole?

C9.4   The Moment of Inertia

Consider now a rigid object whose center of mass is at rest, but which is rotating with a certain angular velocity $\vec{\omega}$. Even though its center is at rest, most of its particles are actually moving, so they have kinetic energy. *An object's* **rotational kinetic energy** *is simply the total kinetic energy its particles have as a result of its rotation.*

How might we link this energy to $\vec{\omega}$? The speed at which any specific particle in the object moves as a result of this rotation is $v = r\omega$, where r is the distance between that particular particle and the axis of rotation. Let's number the particles in an object from 1 to N, and let the mass of the ith particle be m_i, its speed due to rotation be v_i, and its distance from the axis of rotation be r_i. The total kinetic energy of the particles in a rotating but otherwise motionless rigid object is thus

$$K^{\text{rot}} = \sum_{i=1}^{N} \tfrac{1}{2} m_i v_i^2 = \sum_{i=1}^{N} \tfrac{1}{2} m_i (r_i \omega)^2 = \tfrac{1}{2} \omega^2 \left(\sum_{i=1}^{N} m_i r_i^2 \right) \qquad \text{(C9.7a)}$$

where the angular speed ω can be pulled out of the sum because it is the same for all particles in the object. Note that the "rot" superscript on K^{rot} is not an exponent but simply means "rotational."

The $\sum$ notation I am using here, if you have not seen it before, is simply a compact way to write a lengthy sum of similar terms. Each $\sum$ in the equation above is essentially a shorthand that says "add up the following quantity evaluated for each particle from 1 to N." If I were to write out all the sums appearing in equation C9.7a in full, it would look like this:

$$\begin{aligned} K^{\text{rot}} &= \tfrac{1}{2} m_1 v_1^2 + \tfrac{1}{2} m_2 v_2^2 + \cdots + \tfrac{1}{2} m_N v_N^2 \\ &= \tfrac{1}{2} m_1 (r_1 \omega)^2 + \tfrac{1}{2} m_2 (r_2 \omega)^2 + \cdots + \tfrac{1}{2} m_N (r_N \omega)^2 \\ &= \tfrac{1}{2} \omega^2 \left(m_1 r_1^2 + m_2 r_2^2 + \cdots + m_N r_N^2 \right) \end{aligned} \qquad \text{(C9.7b)}$$

Note that since we can factor out in front of the sum any quantity that appears in all terms of the sum, we can pull the common factor of $\tfrac{1}{2} \omega^2$ out in front of the summation symbol in equation C9.7a. We will do this kind of thing quite commonly in what follows, so make sure you understand how this works. If you ever get confused about what is legal when working with $\sum$ notation, simply write the sums out explicitly as I did in equation C9.7b.

We call the final sum in parentheses in equation C9.7a the object's **moment of inertia** I for rotation around that axis:

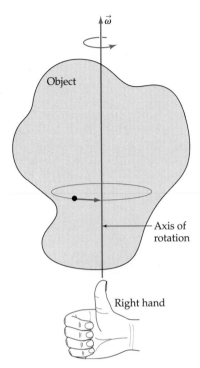

Figure C9.5
Right-hand rule for determining the direction of an object's angular velocity $\vec{\omega}$.

Comments about summation notation

$$I \equiv m_1 r_1^2 + m_2 r_2^2 + \cdots + m_N r_N^2 \equiv \sum_{i=1}^{N} m_i r_i^2 \qquad \text{(C9.8)}$$

Definition of an object's moment of inertia

Purpose: This equation defines an extended object's moment of inertia I for a given axis of rotation.
Symbols: m_i is the mass of the ith particle in the object, and r_i is that particle's distance from the rotation axis.
Limitations: There are none; this is a definition.
Note: A given object's moment of inertia I will have different values for different axes of rotation (because the values of r_i will change).

Note also that I depends on the object's *mass* and its *shape* (specifically, on the distances that particles in the object are from the axis of rotation).

The formula for an object's rotational kinetic energy looks quite a bit like the formula for the kinetic energy associated with the movement of its center of mass:

$$K^{\text{rot}} = \tfrac{1}{2} I \omega^2 \qquad (\text{compare with } K = \tfrac{1}{2} m v^2) \qquad \text{(C9.9)}$$

Formula for an object's rotational kinetic energy

Purpose: This equation describes the kinetic energy K^{rot} associated with an object's rotation around its center of mass.
Symbols: I is the object's moment of inertia for the axis of its rotation, and ω is the angular speed of its rotation.
Limitations: The object must rotate as a rigid body does (otherwise ω is not well defined).

In the rotational kinetic energy formula, the moment of inertia I and the angular speed ω play the same roles, respectively, as the mass m and speed v do in the usual formula. You can think of an object's moment of inertia I, therefore, as being its "effective rotational mass."

Exercise C9X.2

What are the SI units of an object's moment of inertia?

Exercise C9X.3

Imagine that a ball has a moment of inertia of 0.002 in SI units. If the ball spins at a rate of 10 rev/s, what is its rotational kinetic energy?

C9.5   Calculating Moments of Inertia

How can we calculate the value of I for a given object? The actual number of elementary particles in any extended object is so large that a *literal* application of equation C9.9 is impractical. But we *can* group the particles in an object into a reasonable number of pieces (each small enough that all its particles are *approximately* the same distance from the axis of rotation) and then sum over the pieces instead of the particles. The following examples illustrate this scheme.

Example C9.1

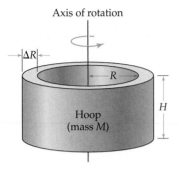

Axis of rotation

ΔR

R

Hoop
(mass M)

H

Figure C9.6
A thin hoop rotating around an axis through its center and parallel to its sides.

Calculating I for a Hoop

Problem   Imagine a thin cylindrical hoop of mass M, radius R, height H, and thickness $\Delta R \ll R$. What is its moment of inertia for rotations around an axis going through its center of mass and parallel to its sides (see figure C9.6)?

Model   The moment of inertia is fairly easy to calculate in this case. As long as the hoop's thickness ΔR is very small compared to its radius R, *all* particles in the hoop are approximately the same distance R from the axis of rotation.

Solution   This means that we can pull the factor R^2 out of the sum that defines the moment of inertia as follows:

$$I \equiv \sum_{i=1}^{N} m_i r_i^2 \approx \sum_{i=1}^{N} m_i R^2 = R^2 \sum_{i=1}^{N} m_i = MR^2 \qquad (C9.10)$$

since the sum of the masses m_i of all particles in the hoop is simply M.
   (In this case, we can accurately treat the entire hoop as a *single* "piece" because all particles in the hoop are equally distant from the axis.)

Example C9.2

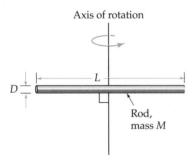

Axis of rotation

D L

Rod,
mass M

Figure C9.7
A thin rod rotating around an axis perpendicular to the rod.

A helpful trick

Calculating I for a Rod

Problem   Imagine a thin rod with mass M, length L, and diameter $D \ll L$. What is this rod's moment of inertia for rotations around an axis perpendicular to the rod and going through its center (see figure C9.7)?

Model and Translation   The trick here is to divide the rod into a countable number of pieces (each embracing a set of particles all approximately the same distance from the axis of rotation), as if the rod consisted of a countable number of fairly massive particles instead of a huge number of elementary particles. Let's divide the rod into n equal pieces, each with length $\Delta L = L/n$, and number the pieces using an index $j = 1$ to n. The mass of the particles in each piece compared to the total mass of the rod is

$$\frac{m_j}{M} = \frac{\Delta L}{L} \qquad \Rightarrow \qquad m_j = M\frac{\Delta L}{L} \qquad (C9.11)$$

(Computing m_j/M like this turns out to be very helpful in these kinds of problems.)

Solution   The rod's moment of inertia is thus approximately

$$I \approx \sum_{j=1}^{n} m_j r_j^2 = \sum_{j=1}^{n} \frac{M\,\Delta L}{L} r_j^2 = M\frac{\Delta L}{L} \sum_{j=1}^{n} r_j^2 \qquad (C9.12)$$

where r_j is the distance from the axis of rotation to the center of the jth piece. It turns out to be helpful to multiply the outside of the sum by L^2 and to divide each term on the inside by L^2 to compensate, as follows:

$$I \approx ML^2 \left[\frac{\Delta L}{L} \sum_{j=1}^{n} \left(\frac{r_j}{L} \right)^2 \right] \tag{C9.13}$$

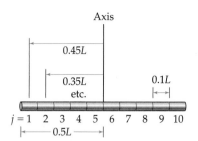

Figure C9.8
Dividing the rod into 10 equal pieces.

Note that the quantity inside the brackets is unitless, since it involves only ratios of lengths. So this sum will be a simple numerical factor that multiplies the ML^2 in the front.

Dividing the rod more finely (i.e., increasing the value of n) makes for more work computing the sum but also makes the result more accurate. Let's take $n = 10$. The values of r_j/L will then be (working from one end of the rod to the other) 0.45, 0.35, 0.25, 0.15, 0.05, 0.05, 0.15, 0.25, 0.35, and 0.45 for $j = 1$ to 10, respectively (see figure C9.8). The value of $\Delta L/L$ is 0.1. Our sum is thus

$$\frac{\Delta L}{L} \sum_{j=1}^{n} \left(\frac{r_j}{L} \right)^2 = (0.1)(0.45^2 + 0.35^2 + 0.25^2 + 0.15^2 + 0.05^2 + 0.05^2$$
$$+ 0.15^2 + 0.25^2 + 0.35^2 + 0.45^2)$$
$$= 0.0825 \tag{C9.14}$$

Exercise C9X.4

Verify the value of the sum, and that $0.0825 = 1/12.1$.

So $I = 0.0825\, ML^2 = (1/12.1)ML^2$. We would get a better approximation by choosing $n = 20$ or $n = 100$ or even larger. It turns out in this case that larger and larger values of n yield values for the sum that are closer and closer to $\frac{1}{12}$ (see problem C9B.4). Thus the theoretical value of the rod's moment of inertia is $I = \frac{1}{12}ML^2$. Even so, it is amazing how close we can get (within 1%) by dividing the rod into just 10 pieces!

Example C9.3

Calculating I for a Disk

Problem   Imagine a uniform solid disk with mass M, radius R, and height h. What is this disk's moment of inertia for rotations around an axis perpendicular to the disk and going through its center (see figure C9.9)?

Model and Translation   In this case, we imagine dividing the disk into n thin hoops with equal radial thickness $\Delta r \ll R$, one of which is shown shaded in figure C9.9. Note that all the particles in such a hoop are approximately the same distance r from the axis of rotation. Each hoop's volume is its circumference $2\pi r$ times its radial thickness Δr times its height h. The mass of the jth hoop is to the whole disk's mass what its volume is to the volume of the whole disk, so

$$\frac{m_j}{M} = \frac{(\text{volume})_j}{\text{total volume}} = \frac{2\pi r_j\, \Delta r\, h}{\pi R^2 h} = \frac{2r_j\, \Delta r}{R^2} \tag{C9.15}$$

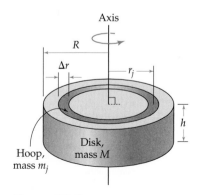

Figure C9.9
A disk rotating around an axis perpendicular to its face and going through its center.

Solution   The disk's moment of inertia is therefore

$$I \approx \sum_{j=1}^{n} m_j r_j^2 = \sum_{j=1}^{n} \left(\frac{M 2 r_j \, \Delta r}{R^2} \right) r_j^2 = MR^2 \left[\frac{2 \, \Delta r}{R} \sum_{j=1}^{n} \left(\frac{r_j}{R} \right)^3 \right] \quad \text{(C9.16)}$$

where in the last step I have pulled constant factors out of the sum and have again used the trick of multiplying the sum's outside by R^2 and dividing the terms inside the sum by R^2 to make it into sum of unitless numbers. If we divide the disk into 10 hoops with equal radial thickness Δr, then $\Delta r / R = 0.10$ and $r_j / R = 0.05, 0.15, \ldots, 0.95$, and the unitless quantity in the square brackets turns out to have a value of 0.4975. Therefore

$$I = 0.4975 MR^2 \approx \tfrac{1}{2} MR^2 \quad \text{(C9.17)}$$

As n becomes larger, the sum gets even closer to $\tfrac{1}{2}$ (see problem C9B.5).

lower I = greater v̄ (handwritten)

Exercise C9X.5

Verify that the quantity in square brackets in equation C9.16 is equal to 0.4975.

I am much more interested that you get out of these examples an *intuitive* understanding of the process of calculating I for an object than I am in your memorizing the particular results that we found. For easy future reference, I have listed moments of inertia for various simple objects in table C9.1.

If you are familiar with the methods of integral calculus, you can evaluate the sums involved exactly and more easily using integrals. This is not required at this point in the course, but if you are interested in the process, look at problem C9S.1.

Since any object's moment of inertia is simply a sum of $m_i r_i^2$ over all the particles in an object, it follows that if we can divide a complicated object into pieces with various moments of inertia $I_1, I_2, \ldots$, the object's total moment of inertia is $I = I_1 + I_2 + \cdots$ (as long as each moment of inertia is evaluated for rotations around the same axis), because the moment of inertia of each piece is simply a portion of the sum of $m_i r_i^2$ for that object. For example, we can evaluate the moment of inertia of a sphere by dividing it into *disks* of equal thickness and summing the moments of inertia of these disks (see problem C9A.1).

Table C9.1 Moments of inertia for various objects

Object and Axis		I
hoop	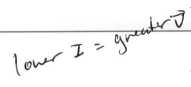	MR^2
cylinder or disk		$\tfrac{1}{2} MR^2$
thin rod		$\tfrac{1}{12} ML^2$
thin spherical shell		$\tfrac{2}{3} MR^2$
solid sphere		$\tfrac{2}{5} MR^2$

(All rotation axes here go through the object's center of mass.)

Exercise C9X.6

Consider an object consisting of two point particles each with mass m, connected by a rod of length L and mass m. What is the moment of inertia around an axis going through the center and perpendicular to the rod?

C9.6   Translation and Rotation

Now we are in a position to answer the question raised in section C9.1: what is the total kinetic energy of an object that is both moving *and* rotating (such as a rolling object)? It turns out that the object's total kinetic energy is just the simple sum of the **translational kinetic energy** of its center of mass (i.e., computed as if the object were a point particle located at its center of mass, ignoring the object's rotation) and its rotational kinetic energy (computed as if the object were not moving):

$$K = K^{cm} + K^{rot} = \tfrac{1}{2}Mv_{CM}^2 + \tfrac{1}{2}I\omega^2 \qquad (C9.18)$$

Purpose: This equation describes total kinetic energy K of a rigid object of mass M whose center of mass is moving with speed v_{CM} and whose angular speed of rotation is ω.
Symbols: $K^{cm} \equiv \tfrac{1}{2}Mv_{CM}^2$ would be the object's kinetic energy if it were not rotating, and $K^{rot} \equiv \tfrac{1}{2}I\omega^2$ would be its kinetic energy of rotation if it were not moving. The quantity I is the object's moment of inertia around the axis of its rotation.
Limitations: The object must rotate as a rigid body.

An object's total kinetic energy is the simple sum of its translational and rotational kinetic energies

This is a nice result, but it is by no means obvious. Consider an extended object that is both moving and rotating. The velocities of its particles point in all kinds of different directions and are constantly changing in very complicated ways. It is not at all clear that things should always work out as nicely as equation C9.18 claims. However, one can use properties of the dot product to prove fairly easily that C9.18 is correct under very general circumstances. Problem C9S.10 outlines the details if you are interested.

C9.7   Rolling Without Slipping

Now consider an object with circular cross section (such as a sphere, hoop, cylinder, or disk) that rolls without slipping along a surface. How can we compute its total kinetic energy (both rotational and translational)?

Assume the object has a mass M, its circular cross section has a radius R, and its center of mass moves with velocity $\vec{v}_{CM}$. Figure C9.10 shows such an object. Consider a point A on the object's bottom (where it touches the surface). If the object were sliding without rotating, this point would have a forward velocity equal to $\vec{v}_{CM}$. If it were rotating at an angular speed of ω

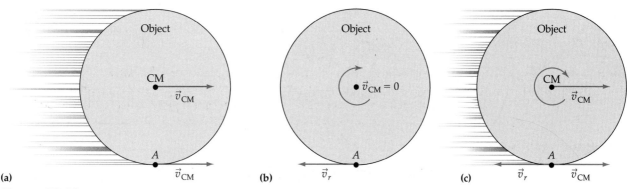

Figure C9.10
(a) If the object moves without rotating, the velocity of point A is the same as that of the center of mass. (b) If the object were to rotate without moving, the velocity of point A would be $\vec{v}_r$, where mag$(\vec{v}_r) = R\omega$. (c) If the object moves *and* rotates, the velocity of point A is $\vec{v}_r + \vec{v}_{CM}$.

without moving, it would have a *backward* velocity of magnitude $R\omega$. When the object is both moving and rotating, these velocities simply add, so the total speed of point A is $v_A = \text{mag}(\vec{v}_A) = |v_{CM} - R\omega|$.

But if the object is rolling *without slipping*, then the relative velocity between the particle at this point and the surface on which the object rolls should be *zero*. Assuming that the surface itself is not moving, this means that we must have $\vec{v}_A = 0$, implying that

The relationship between a rolling object's angular speed and its CM speed

$$|v_{CM} - R\omega| = 0 \quad \Rightarrow \quad v_{CM} = R\omega \quad \Rightarrow \quad \omega = \frac{v_{CM}}{R} \quad \text{(C9.19)}$$

Purpose: This equation links an object's angular speed ω to the speed v_{CM} of its center of mass for a rolling object.
Symbols: R is the object's radius.
Limitations: The object must roll without slipping.

Solving the puzzle from section C9.1

Let's apply this to the case of a ball of mass M and radius R rolling from rest a vertical distance $h \equiv z_i - z_f$ down an incline (refer to figure C9.1b). Conservation of energy in this situation implies that $0 = \Delta K^{\text{cm}} + \Delta K^{\text{rot}} + \Delta K_e + \Delta V_g$, where the first two terms refer to the ball's translational and rotational kinetic energies, respectively, ΔK_e refers to the kinetic energy of the earth, and ΔV_g refers to the potential energy associated with the gravitational interaction between the ball and the earth, respectively. The earth's kinetic energy $\Delta K_e \approx 0$ because the earth is very massive compared to the ball. Since the ball is always near the earth's surface, we can use $\Delta V_g = Mg(z_f - z_i) = -Mgh$. Where v_i and v_f are the initial and final speeds of its center of mass, $\Delta K^{\text{cm}} \equiv \frac{1}{2}Mv_f^2 - \frac{1}{2}Mv_i^2$. Where I is the ball's moment of inertia and ω_i and ω_f, respectively, are its initial and final angular speeds, $\Delta K^{\text{rot}} \equiv \frac{1}{2}I\omega_f^2 - \frac{1}{2}I\omega_i^2$. If we model the ball as a solid sphere, then $I = \frac{2}{5}MR^2$, and we can eliminate ω_i and ω_f in favor of v_i and v_f, using $\omega = v_{CM}/R$. If the ball is initially at rest, then $v_i = 0$; so if we are given M, R, g, and h, we can solve for v_f. Plugging this information into the conservation of energy equation yields

$$0 = \left[\tfrac{1}{2}Mv_f^2 - 0\right] + \left[\tfrac{1}{2}I\omega_f^2 - 0\right] + 0 - Mgh + 0$$

$$\Rightarrow \quad \tfrac{1}{2}Mv_f^2 + \tfrac{1}{2}I\omega_f^2 = Mgh$$

$$\Rightarrow \quad \frac{1}{2}Mv_f^2 + \frac{1}{2}\left(\frac{2}{5}MR^2\right)\left(\frac{v_f}{R}\right)^2 = Mgh$$

$$\Rightarrow \quad \frac{1}{2}Mv_f^2 + \frac{1}{5}Mv_f^2 = Mgh$$

$$\Rightarrow \quad \frac{7}{5}v_f^2 = 2gh \quad \Rightarrow \quad v_f = \sqrt{\frac{2gh}{7/5}} \quad \text{(C9.20)}$$

Note that if the rotational term weren't there (as in the case of an object sliding down a ramp), we would get the larger result $v_{fs} = \sqrt{2gh}$. So the rolling ball *does* move more slowly than the sliding object, and experiments indicate that the ratio v_f/v_{fs} is indeed $(\frac{5}{7})^{1/2}$ as predicted.

Note that it is the *frictional* part of the contact interaction between the ball and the incline that is involved in getting the object rolling, since the incline must exert a force on the ball parallel to the incline to get the ball rolling. (*Think:* Would the ball roll at all if it were on a *frictionless* incline?) Therefore, we now know how to handle the frictional part of a contact interaction between an object and a surface *if* its sole effect is to keep the object rolling without slipping: we simply include a rotational kinetic energy term in our conservation of energy equation. (You can indicate this on an interaction diagram by labeling the interaction's line with a ΔK^{rot} on the side nearest the rotating object.)

This is one situation in which we can handle the frictional part of a contact interaction

Example C9.4 illustrates a framework-based solution to a similar problem.

Example C9.4

Problem   A cylindrical hoop with a mass of 2.5 kg and a radius of 0.50 m rolls from rest down a hill 25 m tall. How fast is the hoop rotating (in revolutions per second) when it reaches the bottom? How fast is the hoop's center of mass moving at this point?

Translation

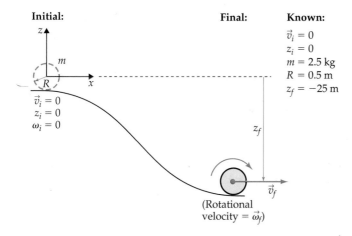

Initial: **Final:**   **Known:**
$\vec{v}_i = 0$
$z_i = 0$
$m = 2.5$ kg
$R = 0.5$ m
$z_f = -25$ m

$\vec{v}_i = 0$
$z_i = 0$
$\omega_i = 0$

z_f

$\vec{v}_f$

(Rotational
velocity $= \vec{\omega}_f$)

Conceptual Model Diagram

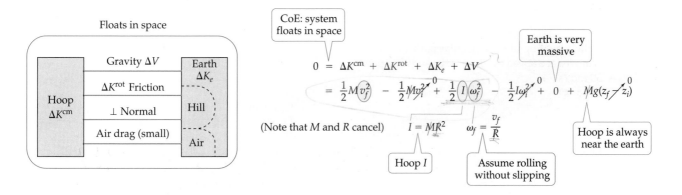

Floats in space

Hoop ΔK^{cm}	Gravity ΔV	Earth ΔK_e
	ΔK^{rot} Friction	
	$\perp$ Normal	Hill
	Air drag (small)	Air

CoE: system floats in space

Earth is very massive

$$0 = \Delta K^{\text{cm}} + \Delta K^{\text{rot}} + \Delta K_e + \Delta V$$
$$= \tfrac{1}{2}Mv_f^2 - \tfrac{1}{2}Mv_i^{2\,0} + \tfrac{1}{2}(I)\omega_f^2 - \tfrac{1}{2}I\omega_i^{2\,0} + 0 + Mg(z_f - z_i^{\,0})$$

(Note that M and R cancel) $I = MR^2$ $\omega_f = \dfrac{v_f}{R}$

Hoop I

Assume rolling without slipping

Hoop is always near the earth

Prose Model   The system of the hoop and the earth is isolated because it floats in space. The hoop participates in gravitational and contact interactions with the earth, and we can resolve the contact interaction into a normal part and a frictional part. If we assume that the hoop rolls without slipping, then we can handle the latter by keeping track of the hoop's rotational kinetic energy. The law of conservation of energy in this case reads $0 = \Delta K^{\text{cm}} + \Delta K^{\text{rot}} + \Delta K_e + \Delta V_g$, where the terms refer to the hoop's translational and rotational kinetic energies, the earth's kinetic energy, and the gravitational interaction's potential energy respectively. Because the earth is very massive compared to the hoop $\Delta K_e \approx 0$. Since the hoop remains close to the earth's surface, we can use $\Delta V = Mgz_f - Mgz_i$ for the gravitational potential energy change. Note that $z_i = 0$ in the frame defined in the translation step. Since $I = MR^2$ for a hoop of radius R, $\Delta K^{\text{cm}} \equiv \frac{1}{2}Mv_f^2 - \frac{1}{2}Mv_i^2$ and $\Delta K^{\text{rot}} \equiv \frac{1}{2}I\omega_f^2 - \frac{1}{2}I\omega_i^2$. We know everything in these terms except for ω_f and v_f; but if the hoop rolls without slipping, then $\omega_f = v_f/R$, so we have enough information to solve the problem.

Solution   Plugging this all into the conservation of energy equation, we get

$$0 = \left[\tfrac{1}{2}Mv_f^2 - 0\right] + \left[\tfrac{1}{2}I\omega_f^2 - 0\right] + 0 + \left[Mgz_f - 0\right] + 0$$

$$\Rightarrow \quad \tfrac{1}{2}Mv_f^2 + \tfrac{1}{2}I\omega_f^2 = -Mgz_f$$

$$\Rightarrow \quad \frac{1}{2}Mv_f^2 + \frac{1}{2}(MR^2)\left(\frac{v_f}{R}\right)^2 = -Mgz_f \quad \Rightarrow \quad Mv_f^2 = -Mgz_f$$

$$\Rightarrow \quad v_f = \sqrt{-gz_f} = \sqrt{-\left(9.8\,\frac{\text{N}}{\text{kg}}\right)(-25\text{ m})\left(\frac{1\,\text{kg·m/s}^2}{1\,\text{N}}\right)} = 15.7 \text{ m/s} \tag{C9.21}$$

The object's final angular speed of rotation ω_f is then

$$\omega_f = \frac{v_f}{R} = \frac{15.7\text{ m/s}}{0.5\text{ m}} = \frac{31.4\text{ rad}}{\text{s}}\left(\frac{1\text{ rev}}{2\pi\text{ rad}}\right) = 5.0 \text{ rev/s} \tag{C9.22}$$

Evaluation   Both results are positive (as appropriate for speeds) and have appropriate units. The magnitudes don't seem outrageous (15 m/s ≈ 33 mi/h). Note that the hoop's mass and radius turn out to be irrelevant.

TWO-MINUTE PROBLEMS

C9T.1   A particle moving along a circular path 10 cm in radius moves at a speed of 50 cm/s. Its angular speed is
A. 50 rad/s
B. 5 rad/s
C. 0.2 rad/s
D. 1.26 rad/s
E. 900° s^{-1}
F. Other (specify)

second) of a horse 5 m from the merry-go-round's center?
A. 0.80 m/s
B. 1.0 m/s
C. 1.26 m/s
D. 5.0 m/s
E. 31.4 m/s
F. Other (specify)

C9T.2   A merry-go-round makes a complete revolution once every 6.28 s. What is the speed (in meters per

C9T.3   A cylindrical barrel is rolling on the ground toward you. Its angular velocity points

A. To your right.
B. To your left.
C. Toward you.
D. Away from you.
E. Toward you at the top, away from you on the bottom.
F. Other (specify).

A. $\frac{1}{16}ML^2$
B. $\frac{1}{8}ML^2$
C. $\frac{1}{4}ML^2$
D. $\frac{1}{2}ML^2$
E. ML^2
F. Other (specify)

C9T.4 A bicyclist passes in front of you, moving perpendicular to your line of sight from your left to your right. The angular velocity of its wheels points roughly
A. To your right.
B. To your left.
C. Toward you.
D. Away from you.
E. To your right at the top, to your left on the bottom.
F. Other (specify).

C9T.7 Two wheels have the same total mass M and radius R. One wheel is a uniform disk. The other is like a bicycle wheel, with lightweight spokes connecting the rim to the hub. Which has the larger moment of inertia?
A. The solid disk.
B. The wheel with spokes.
C. There is insufficient information for a meaningful answer.

C9T.5 Four point particles, each with mass $\frac{1}{4}M$, are connected by massless rods so that they form a square whose sides have length L. What is the moment of inertia I of this object if it is spun around an axis going through the center of the square perpendicular to the plane of the square?
A. $\frac{1}{16}ML^2$
B. $\frac{1}{8}ML^2$
C. $\frac{1}{4}ML^2$
D. $\frac{1}{2}ML^2$
E. ML^2
F. Other (specify)

$I = w \cdot r$

$\frac{1}{\sqrt{2}}$

$2\,\frac{m}{4}\left(\frac{L}{\sqrt{2}}\right)^2$

$\frac{1}{2}m\,\frac{L^2}{2}\quad \frac{m}{4}L^2$

C9T.6 What would be the moment of inertia I of the square described in problem C9T.5 if it were spun around an axis going through one particle and its diagonal opposite?

C9T.8 A solid ball and a hollow ball are released from rest at the top of an incline and roll without slipping to the bottom. Which reaches the bottom first?
A. The solid ball.
B. The hollow ball.
C. Both balls arrive at the same time.
D. It depends on the masses of the balls.

C9T.9 A 10-kg sphere with a radius of 10 cm spinning at 10 rotations per second has a rotational kinetic energy of
A. 5 J
B. 10 J
C. 31 J
D. 63 J
E. 500 J
F. Other (specify)

HOMEWORK PROBLEMS

Basic Skills

$1.5\,h \times \dfrac{3600s}{1h} = 5400s$

C9B.1 A roughly spherical asteroid whose radius is 50 km rotates once every 1.5 h. What is its angular speed in radians per second?

$r = 50\,km$

$\frac{\pi}{45}\,rad/s$ $\quad 1.5\,h \times \frac{90s}{1h} = 90s$

C9B.2 An airplane flies clockwise around an airport control tower at a speed of 130 m/s. If that control tower is 8 km from the airplane at all times, what is the plane's angular velocity (magnitude and direction)?

$2\pi\,radian$

$.001164\,rad/s$

$k_{rot} = \frac{1}{2}I\omega^2$

C9B.3 A solid cylinder of iron with a radius of 20 cm, a height of 20 cm, and a mass of 200 kg rotates at a rate of 10 rev/s. What is its rotational kinetic energy?

$10\,rev \times \frac{2\pi\,rad}{}\quad \frac{1}{2}(200)\,(20\pi\,rad/s)$

C9B.4 Repeat the calculation shown in equation C9.14 for a rod divided into 20 equal pieces. Show that you get a value between 1/12.1 and 1/12. Repeat for 50 pieces

($r_j/L = 0.49, 0.47, 0.45$, etc.) and show that the result is even *closer* to $\frac{1}{12}$.

C9B.5 Evaluate the quantity in brackets in equation C9.16 for $n = 20$, and show that its value is even closer to $\frac{1}{2}$ than 0.4975.

C9B.6 In the calculation of the moment of inertia of a rod in section C9.5, it is important to assume that the rod is "thin." Explain why. How would the calculation be inaccurate if the rod were, say, as thick as it is long?

C9B.7 A 6-kg bowling ball whose radius is 12 cm rolls away from you without slipping at 4 m/s.
(a) What is its angular velocity (magnitude and direction)?
(b) What is its total kinetic energy (including rotational kinetic energy)?

C9B.8 A 20-kg piece of steel pipe that is 20 cm in diameter, 80 cm long, and 1 cm thick is rolling toward you at a speed of 3.0 m/s.
  (a) What is its angular velocity (magnitude and direction)?
  (b) What is its total kinetic energy (including rotational kinetic energy)?

C9B.9 (a) Estimate the rotational kinetic energy of the earth, treating it as a uniform sphere.
  (b) The earth is actually not a uniform sphere, but is denser at its center than at its surface. Does this make the estimate that you made in part (a) somewhat too large or somewhat too small? Explain.

What is its rotational kinetic energy?

Synthetic

The starred problems are especially well suited for practicing use of the problem-solving framework and conceptual model diagrams.

C9S.1 (Only for students already familiar with integral calculus.) We can use integral calculus to evaluate moments of inertia *exactly* and with less work than the method described in the chapter. To do this, we go through exactly the same process outlined in the examples up to the point of actually doing the sum. Then we define a new unitless variable $u \equiv r/L$ or $u \equiv r/R$ and convert the sum to an integral instead of calculating the sum by hand. For example, in the case of a rod of length L, we can rewrite the sum in equation C9.14 as follows:

$$\sum_{j=1}^{n} \left(\frac{r_j}{L}\right)^2 \frac{\Delta L}{L} = \sum_{j=1}^{n} u_j^2 \, \Delta u \qquad \text{(C9.23)}$$

where $\Delta u \equiv \Delta r/L = \Delta L/L = 1/n$ and $u_j = r_j/L$ for pieces on one side of the center and $u_j = -r_j/L$ for pieces on the other side (note that u_j will then range from $-\frac{1}{2}$ to $+\frac{1}{2}$). Note that as n goes to infinity, Δu will go to zero, so in this limit the sum becomes an integral

$$\lim_{n \to \infty} \sum_{j=1}^{n} u_j^2 \, \Delta u = \int_{-1/2}^{1/2} u^2 \, du \qquad \text{(C9.24)}$$

  (a) Show that the value of this integral is $\frac{1}{12}$.
  (b) Use the same technique to evaluate the moment of inertia of a disk.

C9S.2 Using a method similar to that used in example C9.2, find the moment of inertia of a thin rod of mass M and length L being rotated around an axis perpendicular to the rod but going through one end of the rod instead of through its center. Compare with the theoretical result $I = \frac{1}{3}ML^2$. (You may use calculus to evaluate any sum that you might need if you can; otherwise divide the rod into 10 pieces, calculate the value of each of the 10 terms in the sum for the moment of inertia, and then sum the terms.)

C9S.3 Using an approach similar to that used in example C9.3, find the moment of inertia of a disk just like the one shown in figure C9.9 except that it has a hole in the center of radius $\frac{1}{2}R$. Assume that the total mass of the modified disk is still M, and its outer radius is still R, and it still rotates around the same axis as before. Compare to the theoretical result $I = \frac{5}{8}MR^2$. (You may use calculus to evaluate any sum that you might need if you can; otherwise, divide the disk into 10 pieces and sum over the pieces.)

C9S.4 Calculate the moment of inertia of a wheel constructed as shown in figure C9.11 for rotations around an axis perpendicular to the drawing and going

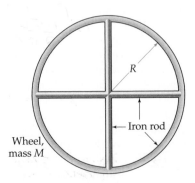

Figure C9.11

through the wheel's center. Assume that both the spokes and the circumference are constructed out of the same kind and thickness of iron rod. (*Hint:* Break the wheel down into three parts that all rotate around the same axis: two rods and one hoop. What fraction of the mass of the whole is the mass of the hoop? The mass of the two rods?)

C9S.5 A typical neutron star (what is left behind when a star goes supernova) has a mass of 1.4 solar masses and a radius of roughly 12 km. Just after formation, a neutron star can be spinning at a rate of 500 turns per second or so. Estimate the total rotational kinetic energy of the neutron star (describe any approximations or assumptions you make). If this energy were somehow converted to other forms of energy at the same rate as the sun radiates energy (which is roughly 3.9×10^{26} J/s), how long would it take to bring the neutron star to zero angular speed?

*C9S.6 A piece of concrete pipe being stored at a construction site is shaken loose in an earthquake and rolls down a hill. The pipe is a cylindrical shell 2.0 m in diameter, 3.2 m long, and 5 cm thick. Concrete has a density of roughly 2300 kg/m³. When the pipe reaches the street after descending a vertical distance of 45 m, how fast is it going?

*C9S.7 Imagine holding one end of the thread on a spool of thread and then releasing the spool from rest. What is the spool's vertical speed after it has fallen a distance h? You may assume that the thread is essentially massless compared to the spool; describe any other approximations that you make.

*C9S.8 A cylindrical section of a tree trunk 50 cm in diameter and 75 cm long is seen rolling down a road below a sawmill at a speed of 12 m/s. (Wood has a density of about 750 kg/m³.) Assuming that the road has an incline of 5% (meaning that if you travel 100 m along the slope of the road, you go up 5 m), at least how far

up the road is the sawmill? Describe any assumptions or approximations that you make.

*C9S.9 A length of thread is wrapped many times around a steel disk of mass M and radius R, which is free to rotate around a fixed, frictionless, horizontal axle. The end of the thread is connected to a small object of mass m. If this small mass is held at rest and then released, how fast is it moving after it has fallen through a vertical distance h? Express your answer in terms of M, R, m, g, and h (and be sure to check that your answer makes sense in the extreme limits $m \gg M$ or $M \gg m$ at least).

C9S.10 In this problem, we will prove that the total kinetic energy K of an object of mass M that is both moving with velocity $\vec{v}_{CM}$ and rotating with angular speed ω is the simple sum of the translational kinetic energy $K^{\text{rot}} = \frac{1}{2}Mv_{CM}^2$ it would have if it were not rotating and the rotational kinetic energy $K^{\text{rot}} = \frac{1}{2}I\omega^2$ it would have if it were not moving.

(a) Consider the ith particle in the object. If the object were not moving, the object's rotation during a short time interval dt would carry it from point a to b, a displacement of $d\vec{s}_i$, as shown in figure C9.12a. But if the object's center of mass moves a displacement $d\vec{r}_{CM}$ during that time, the object effectively moves from a to a' to b, as shown in figure C9.12b. Argue that this diagram implies that this ith particle's total velocity is

$$\vec{v}_i = \vec{v}_{CM} + \vec{u}_i \qquad (C9.25)$$

where $\vec{u}_i$ is the velocity it would have if the center of mass were at rest.

(b) Equation C8.6d implies that $v_i^2 = \vec{v}_i \cdot \vec{v}_i$. Use equation C9.25 and the distributive and commutative properties of the dot product to show that the ith particle's kinetic energy is

$$K_i = \tfrac{1}{2}m_i v_{CM}^2 + m\vec{v}_{CM} \cdot \vec{u}_i + \tfrac{1}{2}m_i u_i^2 \qquad (C9.26)$$

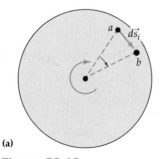 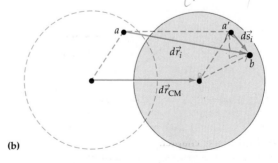

Figure C9.12

(a) If the object rotates at rest, the ith particle moves from some position a to a slightly different position b during the time dt. (b) If the object's center moves a displacement $d\vec{r}_{CM}$ during that time, the particle's displacement $d\vec{r}_i$ is the same as if the particle had moved from a to a' to b.

(c) Argue that if we now sum this over all particles, we get

$$K = K^{cm} + \vec{v}_{CM} \cdot \left(\sum_{i=1}^{N} m_i \vec{u}_i \right) + K^{rot} \quad \text{(C9.27)}$$

(d) Equation C9.27 would be the same as equation C9.18 if the middle term were not there. The most intuitive way to see that the term in parentheses must be zero is to recognize that this sum would give us the object's total momentum $\vec{p}_{TOT}$ if its center of mass were not moving. But since $\vec{p}_{TOT} = M\vec{v}_{CM}$ and $\vec{v}_{CM} = 0$ if the center of mass is not moving, the sum in parentheses must be zero. Prove that this result is correct (*without* the step of assuming the object is at rest) as follows. Use equation C9.25 to eliminate $\vec{u}_i$ in the sum enclosed in parentheses in favor of $\vec{v}_i$ and $\vec{v}_{CM}$, creating two independent sums. Then use $\vec{p}_{TOT} = M\vec{v}_{CM}$ to prove that the two sums cancel.

Rich-Context

*C9R.1 Imagine that you are replacing a tire on your car on a steep hill in San Francisco, and somehow your spare tire gets away and rolls down the hill. If the hill has an incline of 14°, about how fast is the tire moving when it reaches the intersection 85 m away (as measured down the slope)? Will this tire likely represent a hazard to pedestrians? Describe any approximations that you make.

*C9R.2 Two kids enter unpowered homemade carts in a soapbox derby race. The carts both have bodies with masses of 36 kg and four wheels that each has a mass of 3.0 kg. The racetrack is an incline 200 m long. The only significant difference between the carts is that one has solid, disklike wheels and the other has bicyclelike wheels where most of the mass is on the rim.

(a) Other things being equal, which cart will win, and why?

(b) If it takes the faster one 52 s to complete the race, roughly how long will the slower one take? (*Hint:* Show that at every point along the track, the carts' speeds are related by a fixed factor, if we ignore air friction.)

Advanced

C9A.1 Find the moment of inertia of a uniform sphere of radius R and mass M for rotations around any axis through its center by dividing the sphere into disks of equal thickness Δx, each perpendicular to the axis of rotation. Compare your result to the theoretical result $I = \frac{2}{5}MR^2$. (*Hints:* Draw a picture. Note that the squared radius of the jth disk is $r_j^2 = R^2 - x_j^2$, where x_j is the position of the center of that disk along the axis of rotation, assuming that $x = 0$ is the center of the sphere. Argue that $m_j/M = 3r_j^2\,\Delta x/R^3$. You may use calculus to evaluate any sum that you need if you can; otherwise, divide the sphere into 20 disks.)

C9A.2 Find the moment of inertia of a thin, uniform spherical shell of radius R, mass M, and thickness $\Delta R \ll R$, for rotations around any axis through its center, by dividing the shell into n thin hoops, each perpendicular to the axis of rotation and each having angular width $\Delta\theta = \pi/n$ (one such hoop is illustrated in figure C9.13). Compare your result to the theoretical result $I = \frac{2}{3}MR^2$. (*Hints:* Argue that the distance that the particles in the jth hoop are away from the axis is approximately $r_j = R\sin\theta_j$. Also argue that the mass of the jth hoop is given by the expression $m_j = M\frac{1}{2}r_j^2\,\Delta\theta/R^2$. You may use calculus to evaluate any sum that you need if you can; otherwise divide the sphere into 20 hoops with equal angular widths.)

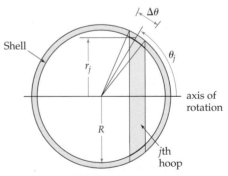

Figure C9.13
Evaluating the moment of inertia of a thin shell.

ANSWERS TO EXERCISES

C9X.1 The earth rotates toward the east, since the sun rises in the east. If we look down at the earth from above the north pole, the earth thus rotates counterclockwise. The right-hand rule then implies that the earth's angular velocity points toward us, and therefore away from the earth's center toward the *north* pole.

C9X.2 Since the moment of inertia I is the sum of terms involving the product of a mass and a squared distance, the units of I must be kilograms times meters squared.

C9X.3 Plugging the numbers into $K^{\mathrm{rot}} = \frac{1}{2} I \omega^2$, we get

$$K^{\mathrm{rot}} = \frac{1}{2}(0.002 \,\mathrm{kg \cdot m^2})(10 \,\mathrm{rev/s})^2 \left(\frac{2\pi \,\mathrm{rad}}{1 \,\mathrm{rev}}\right)^2 \left(\frac{1 \,\mathrm{J}}{1 \,\mathrm{kg \cdot m^2/s^2}}\right)$$
$$= 3.9 \,\mathrm{J} \qquad\qquad\qquad (C9.28)$$

C9X.4 (Alas, I can't show you how to type the numbers into your calculator.)

C9X.5 (Alas, I can't show you how to type the numbers into your calculator.)

C9X.6 Divide the object into three parts (two particles and the rod), and sum the moments of inertia for each part around the central axis (remembering that each particle is a distance of $L/2$ from the axis of rotation). The result is $I = \frac{1}{4}mL^2 + \frac{1}{4}mL^2 + \frac{1}{12}mL^2 = \frac{7}{12}mL^2 = \frac{7}{36}ML^2$, where $M = 3m$.

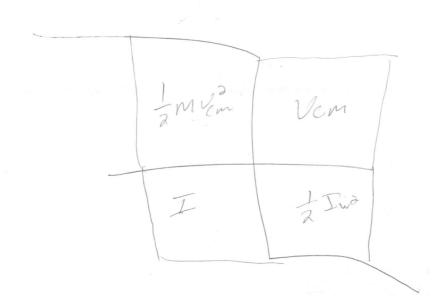

C10

Thermal Energy

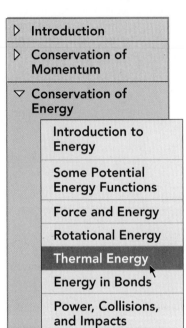

▷ Introduction

▷ Conservation of Momentum

▽ Conservation of Energy

    Introduction to Energy

    Some Potential Energy Functions

    Force and Energy

    Rotational Energy

    Thermal Energy

    Energy in Bonds

    Power, Collisions, and Impacts

▷ Conservation of Angular Momentum

Chapter Overview

Introduction

This chapter discusses *thermal energy*, the first form of "hidden" energy we will consider. Knowing about thermal energy will enable us to apply conservation of energy to a broader range of contact interactions, including friction, impact, and thermal contact interactions. The material in this chapter is essential background for chapters C11 and C12 and unit T, as well as providing deep background for the rest of the course.

Section C10.1: The Case of the Disappearing Energy

In many everyday processes (e.g., a book sliding on a tabletop) energy seems to disappear. This stumbling block prevented physicists from discovering the law of conservation of energy for more than 150 years after the advent of newtonian mechanics.

Section C10.2: Caloric Is Energy

The key to solving this puzzle lay in recognizing that an object's temperature is related to a hidden form of energy we now call *thermal energy*. In the 1700s and early 1800s, people working in the area of **thermal physics** thought that an object's temperature reflected how much of a hypothetical fluid called **caloric** it contained. The **calorie** was the amount of caloric needed to increase the temperature of 1 gram (1 g) of water by 1°C. Experiments done in the early 1800s established that caloric was actually a form of energy, with 1 calorie (cal) = 4.186 J. In the 1840s, the physics community came to understand that disappearing energy is really being *transformed* into thermal energy, conserving energy.

Section C10.3: Thermal Energy

We now know that thermal energy is simply the kinetic and potential energies associated with the random molecular motions and interactions. An object's **temperature** T expresses the intensity of these motions: indeed, under normal conditions T is linked to an object's average molecular translational *kinetic* energy by

$$K_{\text{avg}} \text{ (per molecule)} = \frac{3}{2} k_B T \qquad \text{(C10.3)}$$

where T is measured in the SI unit of **kelvins** from **absolute zero** (where all molecular motion ceases), and $k_B \equiv$ **Boltzmann's constant** $= 1.38 \times 10^{-23}$ J/K. The kelvin is defined so that temperature differences of 1 K and 1°C are equivalent (the only difference between the Kelvin and Celsius scales is the zero point: 0 K = −273.15°C).

Only the translational kinetic energy of an object's molecules is linked in a simple way to its temperature T. An object's *total* thermal energy is usually a complicated function of T.

Section C10.4: Friction and Thermal Energy

As an object slides on a surface, molecules on the contacting surfaces entangle, get pulled out of position, and then snap back to position as the surfaces move relative to each other. This leaves these molecules vibrating more violently, so the process has converted some of the object's energy of motion to molecular vibrational energy.

Similarly, collisions between objects can leave molecules in both vibrating more violently. This simplified model explains how such interactions transfer energy to thermal energy.

Section C10.5: Heat and Work

Internal energy U is the *total* energy that an object contains within the boundary defining its surface. We can keep track of *changes* in U by monitoring the energy flowing through that boundary. **Heat** Q is energy that flows across an object's boundary driven by a temperature difference between what is inside and what is outside. **Work** W is any *other* (macroscopic or hidden) energy that flows across the boundary (note that this can have little or nothing to do with k-work). Conservation of energy implies that in a given process, $\Delta U = Q + W$.

Formally, an object's **thermal energy** U^{th} is the part of its internal energy that increases with temperature. Note *heat* is an energy flow *across* an object boundary, whereas *thermal energy* is energy *enclosed* by that boundary. An object can *absorb* heat, but it never *contains* heat!

Section C10.6: Specific "Heat"

An object's thermal energy is generally a complicated function of temperature, but for relatively small temperature changes not too close to the temperatures where an object changes **phase** from solid to liquid or liquid to gas, we have

$$dU^{th} = Mc\, dT \qquad \text{(C10.7)}$$

Purpose: This equation connects a small change in an object's thermal energy dU^{th} with a small change in its temperature dT.

Symbols: M is the object's mass, and c is its **specific "heat."**

Limitations: The change in temperature dT must be small enough that $c \approx$ constant over the temperature range. Also, the process must involve no phase changes or changes in chemical or nuclear composition.

The quotation marks indicate that "heat" is a misnomer here: c really *should* be called *specific thermal energy*.

Section C10.7: Problems Involving Thermal Energies

Keeping track of thermal energies enables us to solve conservation of energy problems involving

1. Impact or friction interactions that do *work* on objects in the system   or
2. **Thermal contact interactions** that transfer heat between objects

To represent each such interaction, we add a ΔU^{th} term to our conservation of energy equation for *each* object involved.

We can use categories like those we used for conservation of momentum problems to characterize the degree to which a system is isolated. We can define a system to be *momentarily isolated* if there is not enough time for much external *energy* to flow into or out of the system. Systems that are *functionally isolated* with regard to external momentum flows are also isolated with regard to energy flows if the system's temperature is the same as that of its surroundings *or* it is surrounded by some kind of **thermal insulator** that prevents the flow of heat.

C10.1   The Case of the Disappearing Energy

Many natural processes seem
to destroy energy

Newton himself recognized that *momentum* was conserved when he proposed his theory of mechanics in 1686. However, it took another 150 years for the physics community to realize that *energy* was also conserved. Why? The main stumbling block was that many everyday physical processes involving macroscopic objects *seem* to destroy (or occasionally create) energy.

Consider, for example, a book sliding along a flat, horizontal tabletop. Typically, the contact interaction between the book and the table has a frictional component that exerts a force $\vec{F}_F$ opposite to its direction of motion. Since the angle between $\vec{F}_F$ and the book's displacement $d\vec{r}$ during a small time interval is $180°$, $[dK]_F = \vec{F}_F \cdot d\vec{r}$ is negative, so this part of the interaction drains the book's kinetic energy. Where does this energy go?

There is no potential energy
function for friction

Might it go to some form of potential energy? An interaction's potential energy, by definition, depends only on the characteristics of the interacting objects and their separation. In this case, the separation between the book and table does not change during the interaction, so whatever potential energy the interaction might have must remain constant in this process. Moreover, the amount of energy transformed by friction as the book slides a given distance depends on variables such as the book's speed: an interaction's potential energy should depend *only* on separation and the characteristics of the objects, not on quantities such as the speed. *We cannot, therefore, use a potential energy function to describe the frictional part of a contact interaction.* So if friction does not transform the book's kinetic energy to potential energy, where does that energy go?

There are other contact interactions that seem to make kinetic energy disappear without an increase in anything that might plausibly be considered potential energy. If we drop a book on the floor, gravitational potential energy is converted to kinetic energy as the book falls; but when the book hits the floor, that energy seems to vanish. Similarly, when you catch a baseball or hammer a nail or collide with a wall, kinetic energy seems to disappear.

C10.2   Caloric Is Energy

The insight physicists needed to move past this stumbling block came from work in an area of physics that initially seemed unrelated. Powerful as Newton's theory of mechanics was, it did not seem to have anything to say about physical processes involving heat and temperature change. Physicists studying such **thermal physics** problems in the 1700s and early 1800s therefore had to create their own models to explain the nature of heat and temperature.

The caloric model

Prior to the 1840s, the accepted model of thermal physics (proposed by Joseph Black in 1770) was that hot objects contained an abundance of a fluid called **caloric.** In this model, an object feels hot because of the caloric it holds, in much the same way as a sponge feels wet because of the water it holds. When we bring hot and cold objects into contact, caloric flows from the hot one to the cold one because caloric particles repel each other and thus naturally expand into the comparatively empty cold object.

The calorie

Caloric was measured in **calories,** where 1 cal was defined to be the amount of caloric required to increase the temperature of 1 g of water by 1°C. Just as squeezing two equally damp sponges yields twice as much water as squeezing either sponge separately, if the temperature of 2 g of water changes by 1°C, the water releases or absorbs 2 cal of caloric. Moreover, experiments showed that increasing the temperature of a substance by 2°C required almost exactly twice as much caloric as increasing it by 1°C. So the caloric absorbed or released by an amount of water with mass M undergoing a given (relatively small) temperature change ΔT is given by

$$\text{Caloric absorbed/released} = c\,M\,\Delta T \qquad \text{where } c = 1.00 \text{ cal} \cdot \text{g}^{-1} \cdot (\text{C}^\circ)^{-1}$$
(C10.1)

Physicists found that the same equation describes almost any substance undergoing a (relatively small) change in temperature as long as c is given a value appropriate to the substance.

The caloric model is intuitive and vivid, and it works well in most common circumstances. Starting in the late 1700s, though, physicists began to uncover significant weaknesses. The first steps toward a new theory were taken by Benjamin Thompson. Thompson, although born in colonial America, emigrated to Europe during the Revolutionary War, where he became director of the Bavarian Arsenal and was given the title Count Rumford. While supervising the boring of cannons, Thompson noticed that so much caloric seemed to be released by the drilling process that water used to cool the drill bit boiled away and had to be continuously replaced. The model of this process at the time was that grinding up the metal released caloric bound inside it. Thompson, however, determined that there seemed to be no limit to the caloric that could be released from a finite amount of iron. This seemed absurd, so he proposed that caloric was not really a substance at all but rather a form of motion created by the motion of the tool. Thompson later showed that the caloric generated by such a tool is approximately proportional to the mechanical energy supplied to the tool.

By the 1830s, a number of physicists were thinking about this general problem. In 1843, the British physicist James Prescott Joule provided a crucial piece of evidence by demonstrating experimentally that the effects of adding caloric to an object could be both qualitatively and quantitatively duplicated by transferring mechanical energy to the object (using friction as the agent of energy transfer). The apparatus Joule used is schematically illustrated in figure C10.1. In this experiment, water in a thermally insulated container is stirred by a paddlewheel driven by falling weights. Joule reasoned that the

The demise of the caloric model of thermal physics

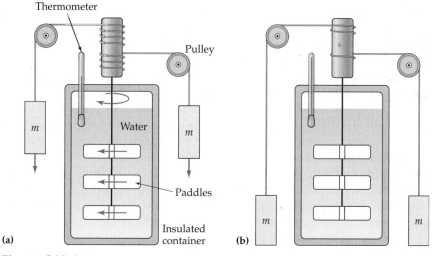

Figure C10.1a
A simplified diagram of the apparatus used by James Joule to demonstrate that adding mechanical energy to water was equivalent to adding caloric. Joule was able to use this apparatus to show that there was a fixed relationship between caloric and mechanical energy.

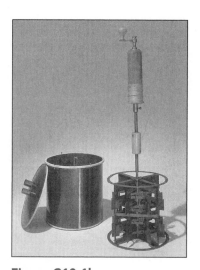

Figure C10.1b
Joule's actual paddlewheel apparatus.

gravitational potential energy released as the weights moved downward was absorbed by the water, and he showed that adding energy in this way caused the *same* kind of temperature increase that adding caloric would.

To appreciate the full significance of Joule's work, we need to remember that the calorie and the joule are *independently* defined. The calorie is an amount of caloric defined in terms of the temperature increase observed when the caloric is transferred to a known amount of water. The joule, on the other hand, is a unit of *energy* that is defined in terms of purely mechanical variables: $1\,J = 1\,kg \cdot m^2/s^2$. There is no obvious reason why there should be *any* connection between these two quantities. Yet Joule showed that

$$1\,cal = 4.186\,J \tag{C10.2}$$

consistently in a variety of circumstances: that is, putting a given amount of mechanical energy (4.186 J in modern units) into an object always had exactly the same effect as putting 1 cal of caloric into it. Joule also linked the calorie to units of chemical and electrical forms of energy.

Conservation of energy

By the end of the 1840s, the physics community understood that Joule's results (supplemented and supported by the work of other physicists) meant that the caloric model was incorrect: what had been called caloric was in fact a previously unknown form of *energy*, and the energy of an isolated system was *conserved*. It is hard to say who first thought of this idea in its full generality: various physicists at various times expressed versions of the idea in very different terms. Unlike some "discoveries" in physics, this extremely important and powerful idea (one of the greatest intellectual triumphs of the 19th century!) seems to have occurred gradually to a number of people at roughly the same time. In any case, by the end of the decade, the caloric model was dead, and the principle of conservation of energy had become firmly established.

Exercise C10X.1

Performing the experiment shown in figure C10.1 is not easy. Assume that the two weights have masses of 2.0 kg each and are able to drop a distance of 0.5 m. If there is 4 kg of water in the container (about 1 gal), what will be its approximate change in temperature?

C10.3   Thermal Energy

The contemporary model of internal energy storage

In the middle of the 19th century, it was still unclear *how* an object could absorb and hold energy and what this energy had to do with temperature. Since the early 1900s, though, physicists have understood that (1) all objects are constructed of a huge number of tiny molecules, (2) these molecules are in ceaseless random motion, and (3) an object's **temperature** is a measure of the intensity of this motion. We will discuss the definition of *temperature* more fully in unit T, but for gases and simple solids under everyday conditions, the temperature T (measured in the SI unit of **kelvins**) turns out to be directly proportional to the average *kinetic* energy per molecule of its molecules' random motions in the substance (treating the molecule as a point particle):

$$K_{avg}\text{ (per molecule)} = \frac{3}{2}k_B T \tag{C10.3}$$

where $k_B = 1.38 \times 10^{-23}$ J/K is called **Boltzmann's constant.**

The absolute temperature scale and absolute zero

This simple statement is possible only if we define temperature in such a way that an object whose molecules are all at rest has a temperature of *zero*. Since molecules cannot have negative kinetic energy, this is the lowest possible temperature an object can have: we therefore call this temperature **absolute zero.** The Kelvin temperature scale is defined so that 0 K corresponds to absolute zero and so that a *difference* in temperature of 1 K is the same as a difference in temperature of 1°C (= 0.01 times the temperature difference between freezing and boiling water). With these definitions, the temperature of freezing water (0°C) turns out to be 273.15 K, and other Celsius temperatures can be converted to kelvins by adding 273.15 K. (Note that while we read 0°C as "zero degrees Celsius," you should read 273.15 K as "273.15 kelvins." You should *not* say "degrees kelvin" or write K with a degree symbol. The SI unit of kelvins is treated exactly as any other SI unit.)

Equation C10.3 would *seem* to imply that the total **thermal energy** stored by an object containing N moving molecules would be

What counts as thermal energy

$$\text{Thermal energy} = \frac{3}{2} N k_B T \quad (?) \quad\quad \text{(C10.4)}$$

However, an object's thermal energy includes not only the kinetic energy associated with the random translational motion of its molecules but also any energy associated with the rotation or vibration of atoms within molecules, the potential energy of (ordinarily fairly weak) interactions between molecules, and so on. The fraction of a substance's total thermal energy that gets stored in the potential energies of intermolecular interactions and molecular rotations and vibrations can have a complicated relationship to its average translational molecular kinetic energy (and thus its temperature). Therefore, while equation C10.3 applies quite generally to many substances, equation C10.4 applies only to rarefied monatomic gases (such as helium), whose molecules are single atoms (which cannot vibrate or rotate) and are spaced so far apart that any interactions between them are negligible. In general, one can only say that the average thermal energy per molecule in a given substance is (virtually always) a monotonically increasing (but maybe quite complicated) function of its temperature T, and that its value is usually between $k_B T$ and $10\,k_B T$.

Exercise C10X.2

A cubic foot of helium gas at atmospheric pressure and room temperature (22°C = 295 K) contains roughly 7.5×10^{23} molecules. Estimate the total thermal energy in this gas. How fast would *you* have to be traveling to have this much *kinetic* energy?

C10.4   Friction and Thermal Energy

Now we are in a position to understand (at least qualitatively) how friction transforms kinetic energy to thermal energy. Consider again the book sliding on the table. When two surfaces are in contact and one moves past the other, their surface molecules often become entangled (see figure C10.2). As the book continues to push ahead, the entangled molecules are stretched away from their normal positions. Their interaction transforms a tiny bit of the book's kinetic energy to potential energy in the bonds between molecules (represented by springs here). At a certain point, the molecules suddenly become unstuck and snap back toward their initial positions, where they oscillate wildly. Interactions between molecules eventually transmit the energy of these oscillating surface molecules to the rest of the molecules in the book and the table.

How friction transforms kinetic to thermal energy

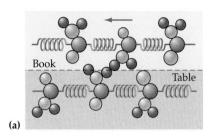
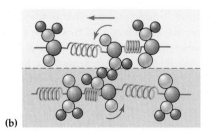
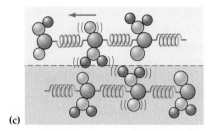

(a)   (b)   (c)

Figure C10.2

A schematic illustration of a book's molecules sliding past atoms on a table. In (a), two molecules become entangled. In (b), these molecules are pulled and twisted out of position by the motion of the book. In (c), the molecules snap back and oscillate wildly. (This scenario has been greatly simplified.)

Collisions also transform kinetic to thermal energy

This is a greatly simplified model, but it does explain how the macroscopic kinetic energy of the book can be converted to energy associated with molecular vibrations. From a microscopic point of view, this energy is simply ordinary kinetic and potential energy. But we cannot see these motions at the macroscopic level: the energy is "hidden." The only macroscopic indication that this process has occurred is that the temperatures of the interacting surfaces increase.

Similarly, when two objects collide, the complicated interaction between their surface molecules tends to set these molecules oscillating wildly at the expense of the objects' kinetic energies. This doesn't *always* happen; if a substance is especially *elastic*, then molecules pushed out of position by the collision simply return to their normal positions during the rebound without much random oscillation. Most collisions, however, transfer at least *some* of the objects' kinetic energy to thermal energy.

This model solves the mystery of the disappearing energy: the kinetic energy apparently lost in friction and collision interactions actually is transformed to *thermal energy*. Understanding this, as Joule and his contemporaries first saw, makes conservation of energy credible as a universal law of physics.

Exercise C10X.3

A 3.0-kg book experiences a constant 20-N rearward friction force as it slides along a tabletop. If it comes to rest after sliding 2 m, how much energy has the frictional part of the book's contact interaction converted to thermal energy in the book and tabletop? (*Hint:* Use k-work.)

C10.5   Heat and Work

Keeping track of thermal energy by watching the boundaries

In many practical situations, we have no way of knowing how much thermal energy an object contains at a given temperature. However, as is the case for potential energy, it is the *change* in thermal energy that is usually important. Since an object's thermal energy resides entirely *inside* the object, we can determine how that thermal energy changes by keeping careful track of the amount of energy that crosses the object's boundaries.

An analogy might help make this clear. You don't need to know how much oil is in your car's engine to keep it running. You can keep track of the oil level using the dipstick. If the oil is low, you put in enough to get you back to the correct level. If you see a greasy spot under the car, then you know there will be less oil in the engine. If no such spot appears but the oil level goes down anyway, then you can guess that your engine is burning oil. The point is that you can tell a lot about how the total amount of oil in your engine *changes* without actually knowing the total amount, and it is the *changes* that are important in practice.

Similarly, determining how an object's thermal energy changes involves keeping track of the amount of energy that crosses its boundaries. The crucial thermodynamic concepts of *heat* and *work* therefore are both defined to describe *energy transfer across a system boundary*.

When a hot object is placed in contact with a cold object, energy spontaneously flows across the boundary between them from the hot object to the cold object (we will see *why* in unit T) until both objects have the same temperature. In physics, **heat** is any energy that crosses the boundary between the two objects *because* of the temperature difference between them. Let me emphasize that to be *heat*, the energy in question *must*

Definition of *heat*

1. Be flowing across some kind of boundary between two objects, *and*
2. Do so as a direct result of a temperature difference across that boundary

We define **work** to be any *other* kind of energy flowing across an object's boundary. For example, if I stir a cup of water vigorously and it gets warm as a result, I have not "heated" the water, I have done *work* on it; the mechanical energy that flows across the water's boundary flows not because of a temperature difference but because of my stirring effort. (Note that *work* as defined here bears little conceptual resemblance to *k-work*.)

Definition of *work*

Note that both *heat* and *work* refer to energy in transit across a boundary. This sharply distinguishes both from **internal energy,** which refers to the energy *inside* an object's boundary. Both heat and work flows can contribute to changes in an object's internal energy. In fact, conservation of energy implies that

$$\Delta U = Q + W \qquad \text{(C10.5)}$$

where ΔU is the change in the object's internal energy in a given process, Q is the heat energy added in the process, and W is the work energy that has flowed into the system in the process. In words, this equation says that the change in an object's internal energy in a given process is equal to the sum of the heat and work energy that flows into it during the process. Note that Q and W are considered negative if energy flows *out* of the object: see figure C10.3. (Note that some texts define W to be *positive* when energy flows out of the object: in such texts, equation C10.5 becomes $\Delta U = Q - W$.)

Thermal energy U^{th} is *one form* of internal energy: it is the part of an object's internal energy that changes when its temperature changes (and is the only form we will consider in this chapter). The superscript "th" is *not* an exponent, but a label: it simply distinguishes thermal energy from internal energy U in general.

The definitions here make it clear that *heat is not the same as thermal energy* in physics. A hot object does *not* contain heat, it contains internal energy. Heat is always *energy in transit* across an object's boundary, never energy inside that boundary. An object can *absorb* heat, but it never *contains* any heat! Keeping these terms straight is essential to avoid confusion when studying thermal physics. Unfortunately, the word *heat* is used colloquially (and even in some science books) in ways incompatible with its technical meaning. Be careful to avoid using language (such as "friction converts energy to heat in the object") that confuses heat with internal energy.

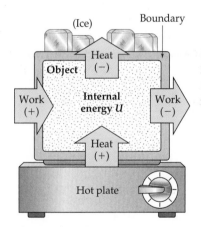

Figure C10.3
An illustration of the definitions of heat and work.

Heat is not the same as thermal energy

Exercise C10X.4

In each process described below, energy flows from object A to object B. Is the energy flow involved heat or work?

Heat or work?

(a) The water (B) in a pan sitting on an electric stove (A) gets hot.   _____

(b) The brake shoes (B) of your car (A) get hot when they are used.   _____

(c) Electricity flowing from a battery (A) makes a wire (B) warm.   _____

(d) A cup of water (B) in a microwave oven (A) gets hot.   _____

(e) Your ice cream (B) melts on a warm summer day (A).   _____

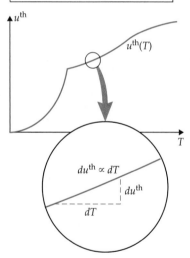

Thermal energy/molecule u as a function of temperature T

u^{th}

$u^{th}(T)$

T

$du^{th} \propto dT$

du^{th}

dT

Figure C10.4
When viewed on the large scale, the average thermal energy per molecule in a substance may be a complicated function of temperature; but over a sufficiently small range, it will look linear (except possibly near a temperature where the substance's phase changes).

The defining equation for *specific "heat"*

C10.6   Specific "Heat"

In section C10.3, we discussed how the average thermal energy per molecule in a given substance $u^{th} \equiv U^{th}/N$ (where N is the number of molecules) was generally some complicated function of temperature T. Figure C10.4 illustrates what a graph of $u^{th}(T)$ might look like for a hypothetical substance. This graph makes it clear that while temperature and thermal energy are clearly related, they are *not* equivalent. Temperature is to thermal energy roughly what the *depth* of water in a jar is to the *volume* of water in the jar. Just as the shape of a jar influences how the volume of water it holds is related to its depth, so the microscopic physics of a substance influences how the thermal energy in an object of that substance is related to its temperature. Also, just as two jars may have the same water depth and yet hold different amounts of water, so two objects may have the same temperature and yet contain different amounts of thermal energy. Temperature *indicates*, but is not *equivalent to*, thermal energy.

However, as figure C10.4 also illustrates, for sufficiently small ranges of temperature, u^{th} often increases fairly linearly with temperature, meaning that

$$du^{th} \propto dT \quad \Rightarrow \quad \frac{du^{th}}{dT} = \text{some constant} \qquad \text{(for small } dT\text{)} \quad \text{(C10.6)}$$

where the constant of proportionality between du^{th} and dT depends on the type of substance and on the approximate temperature. Thus, for a small temperature change dT, we can write the change in the thermal energy of a block of mass M of a substance made up of N molecules, each having mass m, as follows:

$$dU^{th} = N\,du^{th} = \left(\frac{M}{m}\right)du^{th} = M\left(\frac{1}{m}\frac{du^{th}}{dT}\right)dT = Mc\,dT \quad \text{(C10.7)}$$

Purpose: This equation connects a small change in an object's thermal energy dU^{th} with a small change in its temperature dT.

> **Symbols:** M is the object's mass, and c is its **specific "heat."**
> **Limitations:**   The temperature change dT must be small enough that $c \approx$ constant over the temperature range. Also, the process must involve no phase changes or changes in chemical or nuclear composition.

The value of $c \equiv (du^{th}/dT)/m = (dU^{th}/dT)/M$ depends sharply on the type of substance and even on the **phases** (i.e., solid, liquid, or gas) of the same substance. It may also depend weakly on its temperature and the surrounding pressure. For example, precise measurements indicate that the specific "heat" of liquid water at normal atmospheric pressure ranges from a high of about $4217\,\text{J}\cdot\text{kg}^{-1}\cdot\text{K}^{-1}$ near the freezing and boiling points to a low of $4178\,\text{J}\cdot\text{kg}^{-1}\cdot\text{K}^{-1}$ at about 34°C (a total variation of less than 1%). The value of c for liquid water usually quoted is $4186\,\text{J}\cdot\text{kg}^{-1}\cdot\text{K}^{-1}$ (its value at about 15°C and 65°C), and it is within about 0.2% of this value over the entire range from about 3°C to 97°C; so in this range, its temperature dependence is quite weak. The specific "heat" of *ice*, on the other hand, is about $2100\,\text{J}\cdot\text{kg}^{-1}\cdot\text{K}^{-1}$, less than one-half that of water that is only a few degrees warmer!

Equation C10.7 is therefore accurate as long as dT is sufficiently small that c is almost constant over the range in temperatures involved ("sufficiently small" in this context can be tens and even hundreds of degrees for some substances). Note also that since a kelvin is defined to be the same size as a degree on the Celsius scale, temperature *differences* in kelvins have the same numerical value as temperature differences in degrees Celsius. Table C10.1 lists specific "heats" for various substances near room temperature.

I put quotation marks around "heat" in the term *specific "heat"* to draw attention to a conceptual problem with this conventional term. *Specific* is fine: in physics and chemistry, the adjective usually describes a quantity defined so that it depends on the *type* but not the *amount* of substance. However, *heat* is misleading: c actually expresses the change in *thermal energy* per unit mass per unit temperature, not the "change in heat" (since an object does not contain "heat," it is unclear what that would even mean). You *could* cause an object's thermal energy to change by adding heat, but you could add energy in other ways as well. An object's specific "heat" therefore has essentially nothing to do with *heat*. Think of the quotation marks as saying, "we should be saying *thermal energy* instead of *heat*." (The term became conventional in the 19th century before heat and thermal energy had become firmly distinguished.)

Why the quotation marks?

Table C10.1   Specific "heats" of some common substances (evaluated at $\approx 20°\text{C}$)

Substance	Specific "Heat" ($\text{J}\cdot\text{kg}^{-1}\cdot\text{K}^{-1}$)	Substance	Specific "Heat" ($\text{J}\cdot\text{kg}^{-1}\cdot\text{K}^{-1}$)
Water	4186	Air	≈ 740
Alcohol	2400	Iron	450
Ice (−5°C)	2100	Copper	387
Wood	≈ 1700	Silver	234
Aluminum	900	Gold	129
Granite	790	Lead	128

Example C10.1

Problem How much thermal energy do we have to add to the water in a 10-gal aquarium to raise its temperature by 2°C? (10 gal ≈ 38 kg of water.)

Model A temperature difference of 2°C is the same as 2 K. The specific "heat" of water is going to be almost exactly constant (≈ 4186 J·kg^{-1}·K^{-1}) over this small a temperature range, so it should be fine to use equation C10.7.

Solution

$$dU^{\text{th}} = mc\, dT = (38\ \text{kg})(4186\ \text{J·kg}^{-1}\text{·K}^{-1})(2\ \text{K}) \approx 320{,}000\ \text{J} \quad (\text{C10.8})$$

Evaluation This is a lot of energy! To increase the tank's *kinetic* energy by this amount, we'd have to increase its speed from 0 to about 130 m/s (290 mi/h)!

Exercise C10X.5

How much thermal energy has to be removed from a glass of milk ($\approx$ water) to cool it from room temperature (≈ 20°C) to refrigerator temperature (≈ 5°C)? [*Hint:* 1 cup ≈ 0.25 liter (L) ≈ 250 cm^3 ≈ 250 g of water.]

C10.7   Problems Involving Thermal Energies

How to handle interactions involving heat and/or work

Our efforts in this chapter mean that we can now do conservation of energy problems involving contact interactions that mediate energy transfers to or from objects' thermal energies. These interactions generally fall into one of two categories:

Types of interactions that mediate thermal energy changes

1. Impact or friction interactions that do *work* on one or more of the involved objects.
2. **Thermal contact interactions** that directly transfer heat from one object to another.

When kinetic and/or potential energy seems to disappear in a process, an interaction of the first type is probably involved. The second type of interaction comes into play when objects having different temperatures are brought into physical contact.

How to handle contact interactions that cause thermal energy changes

When solving a conservation of energy problem that involves thermal energy changes, you should handle each *internal* contact interaction in your system that mediates thermal energy changes as follows. On your interaction diagram, draw a line (as usual) that represents the interaction between the boxes corresponding the two objects involved. Label this line according to the type of interaction involved, and then write an appropriately subscripted ΔU^{th} symbol just inside *each* object's box where the line meets the box. Make sure these internal energy terms also appear in the master equation that you construct using this interaction diagram.

Thinking about whether a system is isolated

We will now begin to encounter systems that *don't* involve something interacting with the earth, so we need to think more generally about when a system qualifies as being "isolated." It turns out that we can adapt the same categories we found useful for conservation of momentum problems to fit conservation of energy problems.

In chapter C5, we defined a *momentarily isolated* system to be one participating in a significant internal interaction so brief that there simply was not time for much external momentum to flow into or out of the system. In the context of conservation of energy, we define a system to be momentarily isolated if there is not enough time for much external *energy* to flow into or out of the system.

External interactions acting on a *functionally isolated* system, by definition, do not deliver any net impulse to any object in the system, ensuring conservation of momentum. Such interactions also contribute no net k-work to those objects (since $[dk] = \vec{v} \cdot [d\vec{p}]$), so they do not affect the system's total macroscopic energy either. However, a system sitting on a table might be functionally isolated with regard to nonhidden energy flows, and yet be in good *thermal* contact with the table or the surrounding air, allowing heat to flow into or out of the system. Therefore, a system will be fully functionally isolated from external energy flows only if (1) there are no significant temperature differences between objects inside and outside the system, or (2) the system is surrounded by a **thermal insulator** that does not allow much heat to flow even when there are large temperature differences. How good an insulator is needed depends on the time intervals and temperature differences involved. For processes lasting tens of seconds and involving temperature differences of tens of degrees, air is a pretty good insulator. For processes involving longer times and/or greater temperature differences, a better insulator such as Styrofoam may be required.

The following examples illustrate some problems involving thermal energy.

Example C10.2

Problem   Imagine that we drop a bag of lead shot (small lead spheres) from rest at the top of a 10-story building. When the bag of shot hits the ground, almost all its kinetic energy of motion will go to banging the lead spheres against each other inside the bag, and thus eventually to thermal energy in the lead (very little thermal energy gets deposited in the ground). If this model is accurate, about how much warmer should the lead shot be after it hits the ground?

Translation

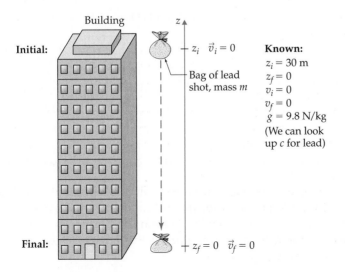

Initial: z_i $\vec{v}_i = 0$

Bag of lead shot, mass m

Final: $z_f = 0$ $\vec{v}_f = 0$

Known:
$z_i = 30$ m
$z_f = 0$
$v_i = 0$
$v_f = 0$
$g = 9.8$ N/kg
(We can look up c for lead)

Conceptual Model Diagram

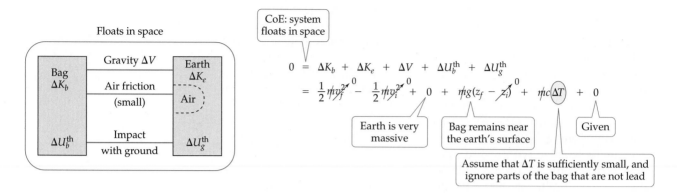

Prose Model   The system of the bag and the earth floats in space. The bag participates in a contact interaction with the ground and with the air (we will treat the latter as being negligible), as well as a gravitational interaction with the earth. So conservation of energy in this situation implies that $0 = \Delta K_b + \Delta K_e + \Delta V_g + \Delta U_b^{th} + \Delta U_g^{th}$, where the first two terms represent the changes in the kinetic energies of the bag and the earth, ΔV_g represents the gravitational interaction's change in potential energy, and ΔU_b^{th} and ΔU_g^{th} represent the thermal energy changes of the bag and the earth due to the contact interaction between them, respectively. We are told that the thermal energy of the ground doesn't change much, so we will take ΔU_g^{th} to be zero. Because the earth is very massive compared to the bag $\Delta K_e \approx 0$, and because the bag is at rest both initially and finally in the process in question $\Delta K_b = 0$. Since the bag remains near the earth, we can use $\Delta V_g = mgz_f - mgz_i$ to represent the change in gravitational potential energy. If we assume that the bag's change in temperature is small enough that its specific "heat" c is roughly constant, then $\Delta U_b^{th} = mc\,\Delta T$. The bag's mass m will cancel out, and we can look up c for lead in table C10.1, so we have enough information to solve for the remaining unknown ΔT.

Solution   So our conservation of energy equation reduces to

$$0 = 0 + 0 + [0 - mgz_i] + mc\,\Delta T + 0$$

$$\Rightarrow \quad \Delta T = \frac{mgz_i}{mc} = \frac{gz_i}{c}$$

$$= \frac{(9.8\ \text{N·kg}^{-1})(30\ \text{m})}{128\ \text{J·kg}^{-1}\text{·K}^{-1}}\left(\frac{1\ \text{J}}{1\ \text{N·m}}\right) = 2.3\ \text{K} \qquad (C10.9)$$

Evaluation   As we would expect, ΔT is positive (the lead gets warmer) and it has the right units. Its magnitude is also plausible.

Example C10.3

Problem   Imagine that we place a 50-g block of aluminum with an initial temperature of 100°C into an insulating covered Styrofoam cup containing 250 g of water at 22°C. Heat will flow from the aluminum to the water until both are at the same temperature. What is that temperature?

Translation

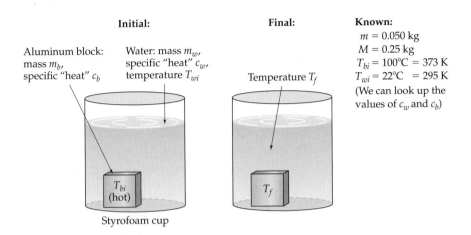

Initial:		Final:	Known:

Aluminum block: mass m_b, specific "heat" c_b

Water: mass m_w, specific "heat" c_w, temperature T_{wi}

Temperature T_f

Known:
$m = 0.050$ kg
$M = 0.25$ kg
$T_{bi} = 100°C = 373$ K
$T_{wi} = 22°C = 295$ K
(We can look up the values of c_w and c_b)

T_{bi} (hot)

T_f

Styrofoam cup

Conceptual Model Diagram

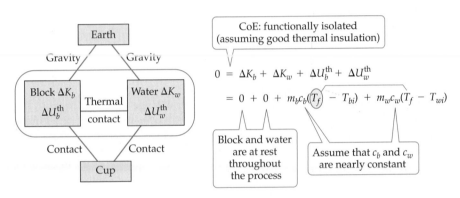

Earth

Gravity   Gravity

Block ΔK_b Thermal   Water ΔK_w
ΔU_b^{th} contact ΔU_w^{th}

Contact   Contact

Cup

CoE: functionally isolated
(assuming good thermal insulation)

$$0 = \Delta K_b + \Delta K_w + \Delta U_b^{th} + \Delta U_w^{th}$$

$$= 0 + 0 + m_b c_b (T_f - T_{bi}) + m_w c_w (T_f - T_{wi})$$

Block and water are at rest throughout the process

Assume that c_b and c_w are nearly constant

Prose Model   The system here is the block and the water. It is functionally isolated, because the contact interactions between each object and the Styrofoam container do not deliver any net k-work to either object, and because the Styrofoam thermally isolates the system from its surroundings. The only significant internal interaction here is the thermal contact interaction between the block and the water. Therefore, conservation of energy in this case implies that $0 = \Delta K_b + \Delta K_w + \Delta U_b^{th} + \Delta U_w^{th}$, where the first two terms refer to the kinetic energies of the block and water, respectively, and the last two terms (which represent the thermal contact interaction) refer to changes in the thermal energies of the same. Neither object moves at all, so the ΔK terms are both zero. We can write $\Delta U_b^{th} = m_b c_b (T_f - T_{bi})$ and $\Delta U_w^{th} = m_w c_w (T_f - T_{wi})$. We know the masses and initial temperatures, and can look up the specific "heats" in table C10.1, so we can solve for the unknown final temperature.

Solution   Therefore, the conservation of energy equation becomes

$$0 = 0 + 0 + m_b c_b (T_f - T_{bi}) + m_w c_w (T_f - T_{wi})$$

$$\Rightarrow \quad m_w c_w (T_f - T_{wi}) = m_b c_b (T_{bi} - T_f)$$

$$\Rightarrow \quad (m_w c_w + m_b c_b) T_f = m_b c_b T_{bi} + m_w c_w T_{wi}$$

$$\Rightarrow \quad T_f = \frac{m_b c_b T_{bi} + m_w c_w T_{wi}}{m_w c_w + m_b c_b} \qquad \text{(C10.10)}$$

In this case, we have $m_b c_b = (0.050 \text{ kg})(900 \text{ J} \cdot \text{kg}^{-1} \cdot \text{K}^{-1}) = 45 \text{ J/K}$ and $m_w c_w = (0.25 \text{ kg})(4186 \text{ J} \cdot \text{kg}^{-1} \cdot \text{K}^{-1}) = 1050 \text{ J/K}$, so

$$T_f = \frac{(45 \text{ J/K})(373 \text{ K}) + (1050 \text{ J/K})(295 \text{ K})}{45 \text{ J/K} + 1050 \text{ J/K}} = 298 \text{ K} (= 25°\text{C}) \quad \text{(C10.11)}$$

Evaluation   This final temperature is positive (necessary for an absolute temperature!) and has the right units. It is also between the initial temperatures of the block and water, which seems right.

TWO-MINUTE PROBLEMS

C10T.1   A railroad car collides with a similar car at rest. The cars lock togther. Does this process convert a significant amount of energy to thermal energy (compared to the first car's kinetic energy)?
A. No.
B. Yes.
C. We need more information to be sure.

C10T.2   The *root-mean-square* (rms) speed of a molecule's motion is the speed that the molecule would have if its actual kinetic energy were equal to its average kinetic energy K_{avg}. The rms speed of random motion of a nitrogen molecule in a container of air at room temperature is about 510 m/s. The mass of a hydrogen molecule is about 14 times smaller. What is *its* rms speed of random motion at the same temperature? Select the closest response.
A. 35 m/s
B. 140 m/s
C. 510 m/s
D. 1910 m/s
E. 7100 m/s

C10T.3   Say that the rms speed of random motion of helium gas molecules at room temperature (22°C) is v. If the temperature "doubles" (to 44°C), what is this speed now? Select the closest response. (*Hint:* Why the quotation marks?)
A. About the same
B. $\sqrt{2}v$
C. $2v$
D. $4v$

C10T.4   If you rub your hands together, they get warmer (try it!). Rubbing therefore heats your hands, true (T) or false (F)?

C10T.5   Is the change in the following objects' thermal energies due to a flow of heat (A) or work (B)?
a. A hot cup of tea on a table becomes cooler with time.

b. A meteorite entering the atmosphere glows white-hot.
c. Liquid nitrogen poured on a slab of ice boils furiously. (Liquid nitrogen boils at 77 K.)
d. A drill bit gets hot as it drills a hole in a metal slab.

C10T.6   The specific "heat" of water is roughly constant (within 0.2%) over a range from 5°C to 95°C, but changes significantly near its freezing and boiling points. Considering this, a change in temperature from 373 K to 373.5 K will likely be "sufficiently small" that one can use equation C10.7 to calculate accurately the thermal energy change of a certain amount of water, T or F?

C10T.7   Objects A and B are made of the same substance, but object A is twice as massive as B. Originally, object A has a temperature of 100°C, and B has a temperature of 0°C. If these objects are placed in contact, they will eventually come to a common final temperature T_f. Assuming that these objects are isolated from everything else, what is the value of T_f?
A. $T_f = 100°\text{C}$
B. $T_f > 50°\text{C}$
C. $T_f = 50°\text{C}$
D. $T_f < 50°\text{C}$
E. $T_f = 0°\text{C}$

C10T.8   Which describes the relationship between the energy E_A required to increase a 1000-kg car's speed from 0 to 23 m/s (about 50 mi/h) and the energy E_B required to increase the temperature of 1 gal (≈ 3.8 kg) of lemonade from refrigerator temperature ($\approx 5°\text{C}$) to room temperature?
A. $E_A \gg E_B$
B. $E_B \gg E_A$
C. $E_A \approx E_B$

HOMEWORK PROBLEMS

Basic Skills

C10B.1 You can convert temperatures from degrees Fahrenheit to kelvins by adding $460°$F and then multiplying by $(5\ K)/(9°F)$. Human body temperature is about $98°$F. What is this in kelvins?

C10B.2 You can convert temperatures from kelvins to degrees Fahrenheit by multiplying by $(9°F)/(5\ K)$ and then subtracting $460°$F. Using this, show that freezing water (whose temperature is 273.15 K) has a temperature of $32°$F. Also verify that the boiling point of water is $212°$F.

C10B.3 You can convert temperatures from degrees Fahrenheit to degrees Celsius by subtracting $32°$F and multiplying by $(5°C)/(9°F)$. To convert from degrees Celsius to degrees Fahrenheit, you can multiply by $(9°F)/(5°C)$ and add $32°$F. If the temperature during a Wisconsin winter night is $-40°$F, what is this in degrees Celsius? The temperature during an extremely hot day in the desert might be about $55°$C. What is this in degrees Fahrenheit?

C10B.4 The Space Shuttle enters the atmosphere traveling at a speed of roughly 8 km/s, but by the time it lands, its speed has decreased to about 100 m/s. The gravitational potential energy of the earth-shuttle system has also decreased. Where does all this energy go? Explain.

C10B.5 Estimate how much energy it would take to increase the temperature of a 500-g horseshoe from room temperature to about $1000°$C. What assumption(s) do you have to make to calculate this?

C10B.6 Compare the thermal energy that a cup (250 g) of tea loses in going from $95°$C (nearly boiling) to room temperature ($22°$C) to the kinetic energy that your body would lose if you ran into a brick wall at 5 m/s (11 mi/h).

C10B.7 A hot bath can require 40 gal of water whose temperature has been increased from about $55°$F ($13°$C) to $140°$F ($60°$C). Estimate the energy that this requires. If electric energy costs about \$1 per 25 megajoules (MJ), how much does this bath cost if you have an electric water heater?

C10B.8 An average residential swimming pool might contain 15,000 gal. About how much energy would it take to heat such a pool from $63°$F (about $17°$C) to a comfortable swimming temperature of $75°$F (about $24°$C)? If electric energy costs about \$1 per 25 MJ, what does this cost if you use electric energy to do this?

How much does this cost to heat?

Synthetic

The starred problems are especially well suited to practicing the use of the problem-solving framework and conceptual model diagrams.

*C10S.1 Imagine that in the Joule experiment shown in figure C10.1 the weights each have a mass of 10 kg and there is 8 kg ($\approx$ 2 gal) of water in the insulated container. About how far would the weights have to drop to increase the water's temperature by $0.5°$C?

*C10S.2 A 22-kg block of iron drops out of the back of a pickup truck traveling at 55 mi/h. The block slides on the road for 150 m before coming to rest. By roughly how much has the temperature of the iron increased? (Assume that it gets about one-half of the thermal energy produced by its interaction with the road.)

*C10S.3 A 65-kg stunt person climbs to the top of a tower 65 m tall and dives into a tank of water shaped like a cube 3.0 m on a side. The initial temperature of the water is about the same as body temperature. After the splash and wave energy gets converted to thermal energy, by about how much has the temperature of the water increased in this process? (Assume the water gets 90% of the thermal energy produced.)

*C10S.4 A 180-g granite stone is given an initial temperature of 100°C and then is placed in an insulated tub holding 850 g of water at 0°C. What is the final common temperature of the stone and water?

*C10S.5 Imagine that we slowly pour 1 gal of water ($\approx$ 3.8 kg) from a pitcher into an insulated bucket 75 cm below the lip of the pitcher. If the temperature of the water is exactly 22°C before it is poured, what is the temperature of water in the bucket after everything settles down?

*C10S.6 Starting from rest, a railroad car rolls down a hill 20 m high and hits another identical car at rest. The cars lock together after the collision. What fraction of the first car's change in potential energy is converted to thermal energy in the collision? (*Hint:* This collision conserves *momentum* as well as energy.)

*C10S.7 Assume that the brake shoes in your car have a mass of about 3.0 kg per wheel. Let's also assume that your car has a mass of 1500 kg. Very roughly estimate the final temperature of your brake shoes if you go down a 300-m hill while braking to maintain a constant speed. (*Hint:* Treat the car body, its wheels, and the earth as separate objects in your interaction diagram. The part of the brake shoe connected to the wheel rubs against the part connected to the car body when the brakes are applied. Make a reasonable guess for the specific "heat" of whatever is used to make brake shoes.)

Rich-Context

C10R.1 The rate $Q/\Delta t$ at which heat flows from inside a house to the environment outside depends on the house's surface area A, the temperature difference ΔT between the inside and the outside, and the quality of the house's insulation. Under normal conditions, the relationship looks like this:

$$\frac{Q}{\Delta t} \approx \frac{A \Delta T}{R} \tag{C10.12}$$

where R is the thermal resistance of the house's insulation. In the U.S. construction industry, thermal energy is measured in British thermal units (Btu) (1 Btu = 1055 J), areas in square feet, and temperature differences in degrees Fahrenheit (a temperature difference of $1°F = \frac{5}{9}°C$), so R-values are expressed in square feet times degrees Fahrenheit

times hours, divided by British thermal units ($ft^2 \cdot °F \cdot h/Btu$).

(a) For the sake of simplicity, consider a small, one-story cottage 30 ft wide, 20 ft deep, and 12 ft tall, whose floor, walls, and ceiling are all insulated to an R-value of 18 (in these units). At what rate (in Btu/hr) will heat flow out of this house if the temperature is 68°F inside and 20°F outside?

(b) When designing a solar-heated house, you would like to ensure that a house is able to store thermal energy that it collects from the sun during the day long enough to at *least* keep the house comfortable during the night. Imagine that the house has collected enough energy so that at nightfall, the interior temperature of the house is 73°F. Imagine also that the house's interior surfaces (the part of the house inside the insulation) are constructed of standard gypsum wallboard that is $\frac{3}{4}$ inch (in.) thick. Gypsum can store 20.2 Btu of thermal energy per cubic foot per degree Fahrenheit of temperature increase. Assume that the cottage has one 20-ft by 12-ft interior wall that essentially divides the house in two. (This wall will have two gypsum wallboard faces about 6 in. apart.) If the house is unheated, about how long will it take for the house's interior temperature to decrease to an uncomfortable 63°F? (*Hint:* You can use the rate of energy loss you calculated for part a as a pretty good approximation to the rate of loss during this entire period, because it was calculated for the temperature halfway between these extremes.)

(c) I'll bet you forgot to take account of the amount of thermal energy that the air enclosed by the house can store. Redo your calculation to include the contribution from the air. Does it matter much? (*Hint:* There is enough information in table C10.1 and the inside front cover to do this calculation.)

A house heated by solar energy.

(d) Instead of gypsum wallboard, imagine that we build the house's interior and exterior walls, ceiling, and floor using 8-in.-thick solid concrete slabs inside the insulating layer. Concrete can store 31.7 Btu per cubic foot per degree Fahrenheit of temperature increase. Now how long would it take the temperature of the house to fall to 63°F? Roughly how far would the temperature fall in the 14 h between sunset and sunrise?

(e) If you were designing such a house, which type of construction (wallboard or concrete) would you recommend for a solar-heated house? Why?

(f) If you haven't done so already, describe some of the simplifying assumptions you have made in your calculations.

*C10R.2 Imagine that in 2021, a practical teleportation device is invented. The only problem is that it converts any difference in gravitational potential energy between an object's starting position and its final position to thermal energy in the teleported object. Roughly how great an elevation change could you experience during teleportation and still survive? (Make appropriate estimates.)

ANSWERS TO EXERCISES

C10X.1 The gravitational potential change in this case is

$$\Delta V = -mgh = -(4.0\,\text{kg})\left(9.8\,\frac{\text{N}}{\text{kg}}\right)(0.5\,\text{m})$$

$$= 19.6\,\text{J}\left(\frac{1\,\text{cal}}{4\,186\,\text{J}}\right) = 4.7\,\text{cal} \qquad\text{(C10.13)}$$

This would be enough energy to increase the temperature of 1 g of water by 4.7°C, so it should raise the temperature of 4000 g of water by 4.7°C/4000 = 0.0012°C. (Joule probably used larger weights and cycled them a number of times to get a measurable ΔT.)

C10X.2 Equation C10.4 does apply to helium, so

$$U = \frac{3}{2}Nk_BT = \frac{3}{2}(7.5\times10^{23})\left(1.38\times10^{-23}\,\frac{\text{J}}{\text{K}}\right)(295\,\text{K})$$

$$= 4600\,\text{J} \qquad\text{(C10.14)}$$

If you have a mass $m = 55$ kg, then the speed v at which you would have to move to have this energy is given by

$$\frac{1}{2}mv^2 = U$$

$$\Rightarrow\quad v = \sqrt{\frac{2U}{m}} = \sqrt{\frac{2(4600\,\text{kg}\cdot\text{m}^2/\text{s}^2)}{55\,\text{kg}}} = 13\,\frac{\text{m}}{\text{s}}$$
$$\text{(C10.15)}$$

(about 28 mi/h) to have this much kinetic energy.

C10X.3 Let's assume that the force is constant in magnitude and direction during this process, and assume that the book slides in a straight line. Under these circumstances, the book's total displacement $d\vec{r}$ is small enough that $[dK] = \vec{F}\cdot d\vec{r}$ applies. Since the force acts in a direction opposite to the book's displacement,

$$[dK] = -F\,dr = -(20\,\text{N})(2\,\text{m}) = -40\,\text{N}\cdot\text{m} = -40\,\text{J}$$
$$\text{(C10.16)}$$

This is how much kinetic energy the book loses, so this must be how much thermal energy it gets.

C10X.4 Heat, work, work, work, heat. (The whole point of a microwave oven is that it uses microwaves, not a temperature difference, to increase an object's U.)

C10X.5 Assume that the glass of milk contains 1 cup, implying that the milk has mass $m = 0.25$ kg, and that the specific "heat" of milk is about 4200 J/kg (the same as water). The milk's temperature change is $\Delta T = -15°C = -15$ K in this case. So its change in thermal energy is

$$\Delta U^{\text{th}} \approx mc\,\Delta T = (0.25\,\text{kg})(4200\,\text{J}\cdot\text{kg}^{-1}\cdot\text{K}^{-1})(-15\,\text{K})$$
$$= -15{,}700\,\text{J} \qquad\text{(C10.17)}$$

C11 Energy in Bonds

▷ **Introduction**

▷ **Conservation of Momentum**

▽ **Conservation of Energy**

  Introduction to Energy

  Some Potential Energy Functions

  Force and Energy

  Rotational Energy

  Thermal Energy

  Energy in Bonds

  Power, Collisions, and Impacts

▷ **Conservation of Angular Momentum**

Chapter Overview

Introduction

In this chapter, we explore even more deeply hidden forms of energy, further broadening the range of interactions and processes to which we can apply the law of conservation of energy. Along the way, we will discuss *potential energy diagrams*, a powerful tool for analyzing the motion of objects that we will find useful in units N, T, and especially Q.

Section C11.1: Potential Energy Diagrams

A **potential energy diagram** for a two-object system is simply a graph of its total interaction potential energy $V(r)$ versus the objects' separation r. Such diagrams are easiest to interpret if the objects move only in one dimension and if one of the objects is much more massive than the other: we can then consider the massive object to be essentially at rest at the origin and r to be equal to the other object's position along an x axis.

We represent the system's fixed total energy E as a horizontal line on a potential energy diagram. The light object's kinetic energy K at any given x is $K = E - V(x)$. Since K cannot be negative, regions of the x axis where $V(x) > E$ are **forbidden regions,** while regions where $E > V(x)$ are **allowed regions.** The points where $E = V(x)$ are **turning points:** the light object's velocity reverses direction at such points to keep it from entering a forbidden region.

The force that the total interaction exerts on the light object has an x component given by $F_x = -dV/dx$, so it is easy to read F_x from the graph's slope. Points along the x axis where the slope of $V(x)$ is zero (implying $F_x = 0$) are **equilibrium positions** where the light object could in principle remain at rest. If such a point corresponds to the bottom of a valley in the potential energy function, it is a **stable equilibrium position;** otherwise it is an **unstable equilibrium position.**

The point is that we can learn quite a bit about how a system will behave by simply looking at its potential energy diagram.

Section C11.2: Bonds

A typical potential energy curve for a two-object system that can form a **bond** has a valley flanked by an infinite barrier at smaller values of x and a hill of finite height at larger values of x, as shown to the left. This curve at least qualitatively describes the total interaction potential energy between two molecules in a liquid or solid, between two atoms in a molecule, and between nucleons (protons or neutrons) in an atomic nucleus. The system will form a bond if, while the objects happen to have a separation within the range corresponding to the valley, some process removes enough energy that the system's total energy falls below that of the top of the hill. This makes the hill a forbidden region that prevents the objects' separation from becoming very large.

Note that the system must lose energy to form a bond. Similarly, we can break the bond by increasing the system's total energy above the top of the hill, which removes the forbidden region preventing the objects from coming apart.

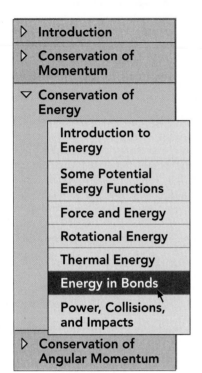

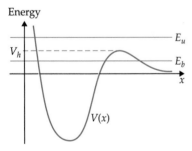

The system is bound if its total energy is $E_b < V_h$ and unbound if its total energy is $E_u > V_h$.

Section C11.3: Latent "Heat"

Molecules in a gas condense to form a **liquid** by forming loose intermolecular bonds. Molecules in a liquid freeze to form a **solid** by making new, more restrictive bonds. Forming such bonds releases energy, and breaking them requires energy. We call the internal energy a substance stores when its intermolecular bonds are broken its **latent energy** U^{la}. When a substance condenses or freezes, this latent energy is converted to thermal energy; when it melts or vaporizes, thermal energy is converted to latent energy:

$$\Delta U^{th} = +mL \qquad \Delta U^{la} = -mL \qquad \text{for condensation or freezing}$$
$$\Delta U^{th} = -mL \qquad \Delta U^{la} = +mL \qquad \text{for vaporization or melting} \qquad \text{(C11.4)}$$

Purpose: These equations describe the energy flows in phase transformation processes.

Symbols: ΔU^{th} and ΔU^{la} are the changes in an object's thermal and latent energies, respectively; m is the object's mass; and L is the **latent "heat" of transformation** (latent energy change per unit mass) for the substance the object is made of.

Limitations: These equations assume that latent energy is converted directly to thermal energy and vice versa (typically a pretty good assumption).

(The quotation marks remind us we should *really* say latent "internal energy" instead of latent "heat.") Latent energy changes during phase changes are on the order of 1000 kJ/kg and are thus much larger than thermal energy changes for typical temperature changes.

During a phase change, energy that flows into a substance goes to breaking bonds, not to increasing its temperature. For example, heat flowing into boiling water simply increases the rate of boiling without increasing the water's temperature above 100°C.

Section C11.4:   Chemical and Nuclear Energy

Chemical reactions rearrange bonds between atoms. Since such bonds are stronger than those between molecules, chemical reactions can release energies on the order of 50 MJ/kg. Nuclear reactions, which rearrange the still stronger bonds between nucleons in a nucleus, can release on the order of 100 to 200 terajoules per kilogram (TJ/kg).

An object's thermal energy U^{th}, **latent energy** U^{la}, **chemical energy** U^{ch}, and **nuclear energy** U^{nu} are all subcategories of its internal energy U.

Section C11.5:   Other Forms of Hidden Energy

We can represent the hidden energies carried by electric currents, **electromagnetic waves** (such as light and radio waves) and **mechanical waves** (such as sound waves and seismic waves) by assigning them internal energies U^{el}, U^{em}, and U^{snd}, respectively.

C11.1   Potential Energy Diagrams

What is a potential energy diagram?

A **potential energy diagram** is simply a graph of the potential energy $V(r)$ of the interaction of two isolated objects as a function of their separation. Such a diagram provides a powerful tool for illustrating the implications of conservation of energy in a given situation. We can often make a variety of qualitative statements about how objects will move in a given context simply by looking at their potential energy diagram.

First simplification: motion in one dimension

While one can construct a potential energy diagram for *any* system of two objects, it helps at first to restrict our attention to pairs of objects that move directly toward or away from each other along a line, which we will define to be the *x* axis. Figure C11.1 shows potential energy diagrams for three different kinds of systems fitting this description. The vertical scale in each diagram is not marked and is not really important: we'll see that the *shape* of the potential energy curve is what contains the important information.

Second simplification: one object is very massive

We will also limit ourselves at present to cases where we have a light object interacting with a very massive object that is initially essentially at rest in our reference frame. Then, for the same reasons that we can ignore the earth's motion and kinetic energy, we can ignore the massive object's motion and kinetic energy, even though it does respond *slightly* to the interaction. The objects' separation is then essentially determined by the lighter object's *x*-position.

Representing a system's total energy on a potential energy diagram

If an isolated system is set up initially so that it has total energy E, then conservation of energy implies that the system (once it is isolated) *always* has that total energy E, no matter what the separation between its objects might be. Since the system's total E is independent of separation, we represent it on a potential energy (PE) diagram by a *horizontal line* at a vertical position determined using the same energy scale used to plot $V(x)$, as illustrated in figure C11.1.

Note that how we initially set up a system fixes its total energy E. For example, if we hold the light object at *rest* at some *x*-position, then the system's total energy E is *equal* to the interaction's potential energy $V(x)$ when the object is at that position. When we release the object, the system becomes isolated, and during its subsequent evolution, E remains equal to the value $V(x)$ had when the object was released. For example, the system shown in

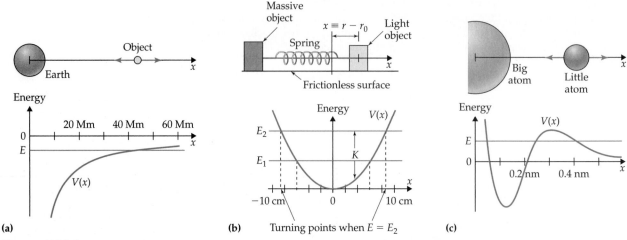

Figure C11.1
Examples of potential energy diagrams.

figure C11.1b will have total energy E_1 if the light object is released from rest at $x = \pm 6$ cm and total energy E_2 if it is released at $x = \pm 8.5$ cm.

As long as the energy in a system is only transferred between kinetic and potential forms, then $E = K + V(x)$, where K is the light object's kinetic energy (the massive object's kinetic energy ≈ 0). Therefore

Reading the light object's kinetic energy from the diagram

$$K \text{ (at } x) = E - V(x) \tag{C11.1}$$

We can thus read the light object's kinetic energy at a given position x directly from the diagram: it is equal to the difference between the total energy E and the system's potential energy $V(x)$ at that position, as shown in figure C11.1b.

We can also read from the diagram the x component F_x (the x-force) that the interaction exerts on the light object at any position. If that object moves only along the x axis, then $dy = dz = 0$, and the k-work for this interaction during a small displacement is simply

Reading the x-force F_x acting on the light object from the slope of $V(x)$

$$[dK] = \vec{F} \cdot d\vec{r} = F_x\,dx + F_y\,dy + F_z\,dz = F_x\,dx \tag{C11.2}$$

Any contribution the interaction makes to the light object's kinetic energy comes at the expense of the interaction's potential energy, so

$$-dV = [dK] = F_x\,dx \quad \Rightarrow \quad F_x = -\frac{dV}{dx} \tag{C11.3}$$

As shown in figure C11.2a, dV/dx evaluated at a given position corresponds to the *slope* of the potential energy function at that position. So the x-force on the light object at any given point is -1 times the slope of $V(x)$ at that point.

In figure C11.1b, there are two positions where the potential energy curve crosses a given energy line (these positions are at $x = \pm 6.0$ cm when $E = E_1$). As the light object approaches either of these critical positions from closer to the origin, it will slow down (since $K = E - V$ becomes smaller) until it comes to *rest* exactly at the critical point (since $K = E - V = 0$ there). The object cannot *remain* at rest there, though: the slope of $V(x)$ is nonzero, so $F_x \neq 0$, meaning that the interaction is still transferring momentum to the object. In fact, you can see from the graph that F_x is *negative* at $x = +6.0$ cm (because dV/dx is positive there) and *positive* at $x = -6.0$ cm; so in both cases the interaction will turn the object around and push the object back toward the origin. These critical positions where $E = V(x)$ are thus called **turning points**. If the system in figure C11.1b has energy E_1, the light object will then move back and forth between the turning points at $x = \pm 6.0$ cm.

Turning points

The light object can never be found where $V(x) > E$ (since it would have to have $K < 0$ there, which is absurd); we call such regions **forbidden regions**. Regions where $V(x) < E$ are **allowed regions**. For the energy E_1 in figure C11.1b, the forbidden regions are $x > +6.0$ cm and $x < -6.0$ cm.

Forbidden and allowed regions

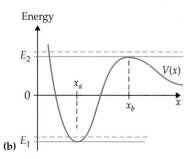

Figure C11.2
(a) Evaluated near a point x, dV/dx is the slope of the graph of $V(x)$ at that point. (b) At x_a and x_b, $F_x = 0$ (since $dV/dx = 0$). If we place the light object at rest at one of these points (which means it will have energy E_1 or E_2, respectively), it will remain at rest. If we increase the energy a bit (dotted lines), it will oscillate back and forth near x_a but fly away from x_b.

Stable and unstable
equilibrium positions

Equation C11.3 implies that the x-force on the light object will be zero at any position where $dV/dx = 0$ [that is, where the graph of $V(x)$ is horizontal]: such a position is called an **equilibrium position.** The slope of $V(x)$ will always be zero at the exact bottom of a "valley" (local minimum) and the exact top of a "hill" (local maximum) in the graph of $V(x)$. In principle, an object placed at rest at one of these positions *could* remain at rest when we release it. Imagine that we place the object at rest at a position corresponding to the bottom of a valley. If some external influence jostles the object (increasing the system's energy slightly), then the object will oscillate back and forth between turning points close to the equilibrium position (see figure C11.2b). On the other hand, if we set it at rest at the top of a potential energy *hill*, increasing its energy slightly enables it to move away from that point with increasing speed, possibly never to return. We thus call an equilibrium position where $V(x)$ has a local minimum a **stable equilibrium position;** all other equilibrium positions are **unstable.**

Example C11.1

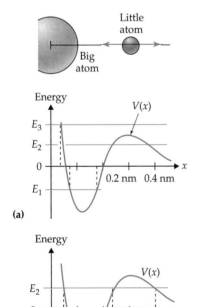

(a)

(b)   Forbidden regions

Figure C11.3

(a) Graph of a possible potential energy function for a system of two interacting atoms. (b) The system's forbidden regions when $E = E_2$.

Problem   Consider the hypothetical potential energy graph for an isolated system of two atoms (one much more massive than the other) shown in figure C11.3a. What are the possible motions for this system if it has energy E_1? If it has energy E_2? If it has energy E_3?

Solution   If the system has energy E_1, the only allowed region for the little atom's position x is the region between the turning points at roughly 0.07 nm and 0.17 nm. This means that the lighter atom will oscillate back and forth within this range of separations from the big atom. As long as the system has this energy, the little atom cannot escape from the big atom: the two are bound together as a molecule.

If the system has energy E_3, there is only one turning point at roughly $x = 0.03$ nm. If the little atom is initially approaching the big atom, it will slow down as it approaches the bump in the potential energy function at $x = 0.30$ nm, speed up as it passes the valley centered at about $x = 0.12$ nm, and finally bounce off the big atom, getting no closer than $x = 0.03$ nm. The little atom will then return to large separations without forming a molecule.

If the system has energy E_2, two qualitatively different kinds of motion are possible. If the little atom is initially within the allowed region between about $x = 0.04$ nm and $x = 0.22$ nm, it will oscillate between these two turning points. In this case, the system is a molecule (although it oscillates a bit more wildly than it would if its energy were E_1). If the little atom is initially in the allowed region where $x > 0.40$ nm and is approaching the big atom, it will be turned back when it reaches the turning point at $x = 0.40$ nm: the atom will thus bounce off the big atom without forming a molecule.

The only way for a little atom to come in from very large x and then form a molecule with the big atom is for the system's energy to be reduced (say, from E_3 to E_2) while the little atom is in the neighborhood of $x \approx 0.15$ nm. In a real chemical reaction, there must be some mechanism for doing this: the system might emit the extra energy in the form of a photon of light or somehow transfer it to a third atom. A molecule cannot be formed unless some energy is removed from the system.

The main point to understand here is that we can extract a lot of information about how the light object in a system will move simply by studying a graph of the system's potential energy.

Exercise C11X.1

Where are the stable equilibrium positions (if any) for the potential energy graphs shown in figure C11.1a and b?

Exercise C11X.2

Where are the turning points and forbidden regions for the system shown in figure C11.1b when $E = E_2$?

Exercise C11X.3

"As the system's total energy in figure C11.1b increases, the amplitude of oscillation increases." Is this true? Explain.

Exercise C11X.4

For separations greater than 0.30 nm, is the interaction between the atoms in figure C11.3a attractive or repulsive? Explain.

C11.2   Bonds

Figure C11.3 illustrates a typical potential energy curve for a **bond.** The qualitative reasons behind the potential energy curve for the interaction between two atoms (which is due to imperfectly canceled electromagnetic interactions between their charged parts) are as follows. Imagine the atoms start at a large separation and move inward. When their separation is very large, the atoms are like uncharged particles to each other, so that the force that the interaction exerts, and thus the *slope* of $V(r)$, is initially almost zero. As the atoms get closer, their negative electron clouds eventually begin to overlap, causing the cloud electrons to repel each other more strongly than they are attracted to the approaching nuclei. Repulsion means that dV/dr is negative, so $V(r)$ increases as r gets smaller. As the atoms get still closer, their electron clouds often find new configurations with a lower potential energy, leading to a valley in the $V(r)$ function. As the atoms get closer still, the very strong electrostatic repulsion between the nuclei and other repulsive effects again turns dV/dr negative, implying that $V(r)$ again increases sharply as r becomes still smaller.

Real potential energy functions for interactions between atoms look pretty much like the graph shown in figure C11.3, except that the hill is *commonly* much lower (its height is often 10 or more times smaller than the valley is deep). This varies, though. For certain pairs of atoms, there may be essentially no hill; for others, there may be no valley.

The potential energy for the interaction between two protons is qualitatively similar. The electrostatic repulsion between the protons at large separations provides the outer slope of the hill in $V(r)$, while the attractive strong nuclear interaction (which kicks in only at small separations) provides the valley's outer wall, and various strongly repulsive effects that kick in at very small separations create the valley's rising inner wall. For protons or neutrons interacting with neutrons, there is no electrostatic repulsion, so the potential energy function has essentially only a valley.

The characteristic potential energy curve for a bond

Making bonds releases energy

All these potential energy functions have this much in common: the force between the objects goes to zero as r becomes large, meaning that the slope of $V(r)$ goes to zero, meaning that $V(r)$ flattens out toward an asymptotic value as r becomes large. The reference separation for such an interaction is invariably chosen to be at $r = \infty$ so that this asymptotic value is *zero* [$V(r) \to 0$ as $r \to \infty$].

Consider now a pair of objects whose interaction potential energy curve has the shape shown in figure C11.3. If the objects initially have a very large separation and nonzero kinetic energy, then their total energy $E > 0$. An isolated system under these circumstances is *not* bonded: there will be a turning point either on the hill's outer side (if $E < V_{hill}$, where V_{hill} is the potential energy at the hill's top) or at very small r (if $E > V_{hill}$), and if the objects approach each other, they simply bounce off this turning point and go back out to infinity. To get the objects close enough to bond, the system's initial energy must be greater than V_{hill}. To then actually form the bond, we have to reduce the system's energy from its initial energy to some $E < V_{hill}$ (such as energy E_1 in figure C11.3) while the separation between the objects is smaller than r_{hill}. The objects' separation will then be constrained to values between the turning points on the inner and outer valley walls: the objects are now bound together.

So two atoms initially separated by a large distance can only form a bond if there is some mechanism (e.g., an interaction with a third object or emission of a photon) that enables them to release energy while they are close together. Thus *when bonds form, energy is released*, which often goes (at least at first) to increasing the thermal energy of the surroundings.

Breaking bonds absorbs energy

On the other hand, consider a system that is already bonded and thus whose initial energy $E < V_{hill}$. To *break* this bond (i.e., to cause the objects to split apart to large separations), we have to *add* energy to make $E > V_{hill}$. Therefore, *when bonds break, energy is absorbed*, again often from the thermal energy in the system's surroundings (at least at first).

Example C11.2

Problem   A mixture of hydrogen and oxygen gas will not burn at room temperature. Assuming that the potential energy of interaction between a hydrogen molecule and an oxygen molecule looks like that shown in figure C11.3, estimate the minimum height of the hill in the potential energy function.

Solution   The average kinetic energy of a hydrogen molecule at room temperature will be *very* roughly $k_B T \approx (1.4 \times 10^{-23} \text{ J/K})(300 \text{ K}) = 4 \times 10^{-21}$ J. Since the atoms are presumably not bonding because they do not get past the hill in the potential energy function, the hill must have at least this height.

C11.3   Latent "Heat"

Definition of latent "heat"

One of the macroscopic consequences of the issues discussed in section C11.2 is that when a substance undergoes a phase change (e.g., from solid to liquid or liquid to solid), it usually either absorbs or releases energy. The energy a given substance absorbs or releases per kilogram during a given change of phase is called the **latent "heat"** for that substance undergoing phase change. In this section, we will see that this energy flow is a consequence of making or breaking microscopic bonds between molecules. (The quotation marks again remind us that we should be thinking "internal energy" when we see the word *heat*.)

The molecules of almost every kind of substance attract each other weakly, making it possible to form weak bonds between molecules. At high temperatures, the molecules have so much kinetic energy that the total energy of any two-molecule system is typically much greater than zero, implying that the molecules are unbound. A substance whose molecules are unbound is a **gas:** gas molecules thus bounce freely and randomly back and forth between the walls of whatever container holds the gas, completely filling its volume.

As the temperature of a gas decreases, though, the collisions between molecules become less and less violent, allowing them eventually to form weak bonds with each other. As such bonds form, the substance condenses to form a **liquid.** In a liquid, the bonds are not so much between two individual molecules but between each molecule and the rest of the liquid. This means that molecules are reasonably free to move around *within* the liquid but cannot easily escape it.

As the substance's temperature decreases further, each molecule's kinetic energy becomes so small that it can begin to form tight bonds with specific neighboring molecules. As these specific bonds form, molecules become essentially locked into specific locations relative to their neighbors in a more or less rigid lattice: the substance is now a **solid.** The molecules will still vibrate about these positions, but are no longer free to roam around.

So as a substance condenses from a gas to a liquid, intermolecular bonds form: this releases energy. Conversely, to convert a liquid to a gas, we must supply the same amount of energy in order to break those bonds. For example, the energy required to vaporize 1 kg of water is 2256 kJ. This is a *lot* of energy: if adding this much energy to a kilogram of water didn't vaporize it, it would increase its temperature by 539 K! The energy involved in making and breaking the intermolecular bonds associated with phase changes is much greater than that associated with moderate changes in a substance's temperature.

Exercise C11X.5

Verify that supplying 2256 kJ of thermal energy to 1 kg of water would increase its temperature by 539 K if it didn't vaporize.

Similarly, when a liquid freezes to become a solid, the formation of new, tighter intermolecular bonds releases energy. Melting the solid requires supplying the same amount of energy in order to break the bonds. The energy required to melt 1 kg of water is 333 kJ.

So when we boil water in a pan on a stove, the thermal energy the stove supplies goes to breaking the bonds that hold water molecules in the liquid. It turns out that breaking these bonds soaks up all the energy that you supply during the phase change. If you attempt to raise the temperature of a substance undergoing a phase change by supplying more energy, this energy simply gets channeled to breaking bonds instead, making the phase change more rapid but not increasing the substance's temperature. So the boiling water in a pan maintains a constant temperature of 373 K (that is, 100°C) until all the water is boiled away. Similarly, a glass of ice water has a constant temperature of 273 K (0°C) until the ice completely melts.

We constantly take advantage of these characteristics of phase changes in our daily lives. Humans keep cool by sweating: as the sweat evaporates, it absorbs thermal energy from the skin and carries it away. Placing an ice cube in a cold drink cools it better than putting in an equal amount of water at 0°C would: as the ice melts, it absorbs a *lot* of thermal energy from the drink. Refrigerators work by forcing a liquid to boil in cooling coils inside the refrigerator (thus making the liquid absorb thermal energy from the refrigerator's contents) and then forcing the liquid to condense in coils on the refrigerator's exterior (thus releasing this energy into the environment). Fruit growers spray water on fruit trees to protect the fruit from a cold snap because the fruit's internal temperature will not drop below freezing until all the water on the fruit's outside has frozen (and this may take longer than the cold snap lasts). The fixed temperature of boiling water also makes predictable cooking possible. Cooking food by boiling water in a pan (at sea level) exposes the food to a constant temperature of 373 K whether the pan is on an electric stove, on a gas stove, or over a fire, no matter how hot the stove or fire itself might be.

Latent energy

We call the internal energy a substance has in the form of broken intermolecular bonds its **latent energy** U^{la} (*latent* because absorbing or releasing this energy does not manifest itself in a change in temperature, so the energy transfer is thus even more hidden than usual). When a substance condenses or freezes, this latent energy is converted to thermal energy; when it melts or vaporizes, thermal energy is converted to latent energy:

Table C11.1 Latent "heats" of various substances

Substance and Phase Change	Latent "Heat" (kJ/kg)
Melting O_2	13.8
Melting H_2	58.6
Melting Al	105
Melting Cu	205
Melting H_2O	333
Boiling O_2	213
Boiling H_2	452
Boiling H_2O	2,256
Boiling Cu	4,730
Boiling Al	11,400

$$\Delta U^{th} = +mL \quad \Delta U^{la} = -mL \quad \text{for condensation or freezing}$$
$$\Delta U^{th} = -mL \quad \Delta U^{la} = +mL \quad \text{for vaporization or melting}$$
(C11.4)

Purpose: These equations describe the energy flows in phase transformation processes.

Symbols: ΔU^{th} and ΔU^{la} are the changes in an object's thermal and latent energies, respectively; m is the object's mass; and L is the **latent "heat" of transformation** (latent energy change per unit mass) for the substance the object is made of.

Limitations: These equations assume that latent energy is converted directly into thermal energy and vice versa (typically a pretty good assumption).

Latent "heats" for various substances are listed in table C11.1.

Example C11.3

Problem   If thermal energy from burning natural gas costs about 2¢ per megajoule, how much does it cost to completely boil 1 gal of water already at 100°C?

Solution   One gallon = 4 quarts (qt) ≈ 4 liters (L) ≈ 4 kg of water. Vaporizing this much water, even if it is already at the boiling point, involves increasing its latent energy by $\Delta U^{la} = +mL = (4 \text{ kg})(2.256 \text{ MJ/kg}) = 9.0$ MJ. If this comes at the expense of thermal energy at a cost of 2¢ per megajoule (and no energy is wasted), then it will cost 18¢.

Example C11.4

Problem   Imagine that you put a 60-g ice cube (at 0°C) into a glass holding 250 g [roughly 8 ounces (oz)] of water at 15°C. What is the water's final temperature?

Model and Translation   The system is composed of the ice cube and the water. We will assume that this process goes so quickly that the system is momentarily isolated from external energy flows (probably a bad assumption, but what else can we do?). Let's consider this process in two steps: first let's see what the temperature of the water is after the ice has completely melted to water at 0°C, and then let's allow the two batches of water to transfer thermal energy until they come into equilibrium. During the first phase, conservation of energy implies that

[handwritten annotations: → how much energy in the ice]

$$0 = \Delta U_{\text{water}}^{\text{th}} + \Delta U_{\text{ice}}^{\text{la}} \quad \Rightarrow \quad \Delta U_{\text{ice}}^{\text{la}} = -\Delta U_{\text{water}}^{\text{th}}$$

[handwritten annotations: L₁ how much energy needed to thaw ; mL = -Mc\,\Delta T]

$$mL = -Mc\,\Delta T \qquad (C11.5)$$

where m is the mass of the ice, L is the latent "heat" of ice, M is the mass of the water, c is the specific "heat" of water, and ΔT is the water's temperature change. We know everything except ΔT, so we can solve for ΔT.

Solution

$$\Delta T = -\frac{mL}{Mc} = -\frac{(0.060\ \text{kg})(333\ \text{kJ·kg}^{-1})}{(0.250\ \text{kg})(4.2\ \text{kJ·kg}^{-1}\text{·K}^{-1})} = -19\ \text{K} \qquad (C11.6)$$

Evaluation   Since the water's initial temperature is 15°C and 1°C of temperature change is the same as 1 K, the water's final temperature is −4°C according to this calculation. This is absurd: the final temperature of the water cannot be below that of the ice! What must really happen is that enough ice melts to cool the water to 0°C. The water and ice will then be at the same temperature, and (assuming no energy flows from outside) no further change occurs. Under this scenario, we know that $\Delta T = -15°\text{C} = -15\ \text{K}$, so we can solve equation C11.6 for the mass of the ice that melts:

$$m = -\frac{Mc\,\Delta T}{L} = -\frac{(0.250\ \text{kg})(4.2\ \text{kJ·kg}^{-1}\text{·K}^{-1})(-15\ \text{K})}{333\ \text{kJ·kg}^{-1}} = 0.047\ \text{kg} \qquad (C11.7)$$

So what we have at the end is 13 g of ice floating in the water, all at a temperature of 0°C.

Exercise C11X.6

How much ice would you need to cool a 500-g drink of water from room temperature (about 22°C) to 0°C?

C11.4   Chemical and Nuclear Energy

The bonds between molecules of a substance are generally much weaker than the bonds between the atoms in a given molecule. Chemical reactions, which make and break atomic bonds, can therefore absorb or release much more energy per kilogram of substance than is involved in a phase change. For example, burning 1 kg of gasoline releases roughly 46 MJ of thermal energy, roughly 20 times the thermal energy released by 1 kg of condensing water. Burning 1 kg of natural gas releases about 55 MJ.

Typical energies released by a chemical reaction

Nuclear energy

In turn, the protons and neutrons in an atomic nucleus form bonds much stronger than the bonds between atoms, mostly because the strong nuclear interactions involved are *much* stronger than the electromagnetic interactions between atoms. Nuclear reactions can rearrange these bonds to form more tightly bound nuclei, releasing enormous amounts of energy.

For example, a **deuterium** (^{2}H) nucleus contains a proton bound to a neutron. A **tritium** (^{3}H) nucleus consists of a proton bound to two neutrons. If we force these nuclei together, we can create a helium (^{4}He) nucleus (two protons and two neutrons) and a free neutron. This type of nuclear reaction, which creates a more massive nucleus from lighter nuclei, is called a **fusion** reaction. The formation of new bonds in this process releases 340 TJ (340×10^{12} J) of energy per kilogram of ^{2}H-^{3}H mixture. This is roughly 7×10^6 times the energy released by burning 1 kg of gasoline, and it represents enough energy to supply the electrical needs of about 10,000 average U.S. households for a year. Nuclear **fission** reactions (which involve breaking apart large nuclei into smaller but more tightly bound fragments) can produce roughly 70 TJ per kilogram of fuel.

The enormous amounts of energy produced by nuclear reactions make nuclear reactions an attractive source of energy, but it is not easy to produce this energy safely. All currently operating nuclear reactors are fission reactors, which produce large amounts of intensely radioactive waste. No one knows how to store this waste safely for the millennia required to render it harmless, and so people do not want it stored in their backyards. Fission plants also produce nuclear fuel that can be used to make atomic bombs. Finally, the most common designs for fission plants can (under unusual circumstances) fail catastrophically, releasing large amounts of radioactive substances into the environment, and addressing all these problems is very costly. For these reasons and others, utilities in the United States are no longer building nuclear power plants.

Fusion reactors would produce far more energy per kilogram of fuel, would use fuel that is much more readily obtainable, would produce much less (but not zero) radioactive waste, would not produce materials that

(a)

(b)

Figure C11.4

(a) A fission power plant. (b) A fusion power plant.

can be used to make bombs, and cannot "melt down" the way that fission reactors can. However, commercially viable fusion reactors are still decades away (although progress is made every year). Even so, there is one excellent and highly reliable fusion reactor in operation today, which has been de-signed to require no maintenance for an enormous span of time, which has its own built-in radioactive waste disposal system, and which has been thoughtfully located at an appropriately safe distance from all living things. I refer, of course, to the sun (see figure C11.4).

Thermal, latent, chemical, and *nuclear* energy are all subcategories of the general category of internal energy, since in each case energy is stored in the microscopic motions and/or interactions inside the substance. An object's **chemical energy** U^{ch} changes if and only if its chemical composition changes as a result of internal chemical reactions. Similarly, an object's **nuclear energy** U^{nu} changes as the result of internal nuclear reactions. An object's latent energy U^{la} changes during phase changes. An object's **thermal energy** U^{th} changes if its temperature changes. Thermal energy often is the common cur-rency for internal energy changes. For example, a decrease in an object's chemical energy usually shows up first as an increase in its thermal energy; likewise if an object's chemical energy increases, this almost always comes at the expense of its thermal energy (at least at first).

The following is an example of a conservation of energy problem involv-ing internal energies of various forms. Note how I have represented the vari-ous interactions and internal energy flows in the interaction diagram: use this as a model when you do similar problems. (This is the kind of problem where a conceptual model diagram can really help you organize your thoughts!)

Symbols for chemical and nuclear energy

Example C11.5

Problem   Beth, whose mass is 52 kg, climbs up a hill 400 m high. She evap-orates 0.5 kg (about a pint) of water from her skin and lungs during the process. What is the minimum amount of food energy she "burns" in this process? Express your answer in food calories. [One **food calorie,** abbrevi-ated 1 Cal (with a capital C), is defined to be 1000 physics calories = 1000×4.186 J = 4186 J.]

Translation

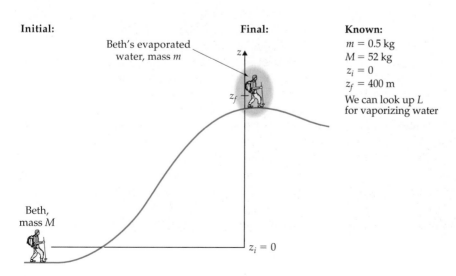

Initial:

Beth's evaporated water, mass m

z_f

Final:

z

Known:
$m = 0.5$ kg
$M = 52$ kg
$z_i = 0$
$z_f = 400$ m
We can look up L
for vaporizing water

Beth, mass M

$z_i = 0$

Conceptual Model Diagram

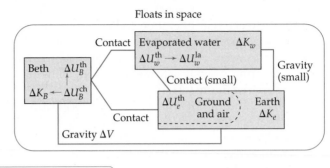

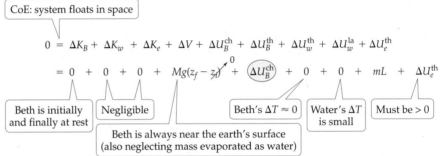

Prose Model   The system here is Beth, the earth (including the environment), and the water which evaporates. The system is isolated because it floats in space. Beth interacts gravitationally with the earth, and she participates in contact interactions with the earth and the water. Conservation of energy therefore implies that $0 = \Delta K_B + \Delta K_w + \Delta K_e + \Delta V + \Delta U_B^{\mathrm{th}} + \Delta U_w^{\mathrm{th}} + \Delta U_e^{\mathrm{th}} + \Delta U_w^{\mathrm{la}} + \Delta U_B^{\mathrm{ch}}$, where the first two terms refer to Beth's and the earth's kinetic energies, respectively; the next to the gravitational interaction between Beth and the earth; the next three terms to changes in Beth's, the water's and the earth's thermal energies (reflecting the contact interactions between Beth, the water, and the ground and air), respectively; and the last two to the water's change in latent energy and Beth's change in chemical energy, which represent internal changes in Beth and the water. Because Beth is essentially at rest at the beginning and end of the trip (her kinetic energy is going to be totally negligible anyway) $\Delta K_B \approx 0$. Because the earth is so massive, $\Delta K_e \approx 0$ and the water's change in kinetic energy will also be negligible. Because Beth always remains near the earth's surface, we can use $\Delta V = Mgz_f - Mgz_i$ (note that $z_i = 0$). Because Beth's body strives to maintain a constant temperature (this is the point of evaporating the water) $\Delta U_B^{\mathrm{th}} \approx 0$, and the water's change in temperature is also small. If L is the latent "heat" of vaporization for water, then $\Delta U_w^{\mathrm{la}} = +mL$. Air friction will probably be negligible, but Beth's feet hitting the ground will give the earth an unknown amount of thermal energy: the most that we can say is that $\Delta U_e^{\mathrm{th}} > 0$. But since we know everything else, even knowing this much allows us to put a lower limit on ΔU_B^{ch}. Let's treat Beth's mass M as constant, even though it changes slightly as the water evaporates.

Solution   So our conservation of energy equation becomes

$$0 = 0 + 0 + 0 + [Mgz_f - 0] + 0 + 0 + \Delta U_e^{\mathrm{th}} + mL + \Delta U_B^{\mathrm{ch}}$$
$$\Rightarrow \quad \Delta U_B^{\mathrm{ch}} < \Delta U_B^{\mathrm{ch}} + \Delta U_e^{\mathrm{th}} = -Mgz_f - mL$$

$$\Rightarrow \quad \Delta U_B^{ch} < -(52\ kg)\left(9.8\ \frac{N}{kg}\right)(400\ m)\left(\frac{1\ kJ}{1000\ N\cdot m}\right) - (0.5\ kg)\left(\frac{2256\ kJ}{kg}\right)$$

$$= -(200\ kJ + 1130\ kJ)\left(\frac{1\ Cal}{4.2\ kJ}\right) = -320\ Cal \qquad (C11.8)$$

Evaluation Because Beth's chemical energy is being converted to other forms of energy, ΔU_B^{ch} should be negative. To say that ΔU_B^{ch} is more negative than -320 Cal means that $|\Delta U_B^{ch}| > 320$ Cal, meaning that Beth has used up *at least* 320 Cal of food energy. This seems reasonable. (Note how all the units are consistent.)

C11.5 Other Forms of Hidden Energy

There are other forms of "hidden" energy besides thermal, latent, chemical, and nuclear energy. As we will see in unit E, **electric energy** is a form of electrostatic potential energy carried by electric currents flowing in wires. Since the electrostatically interacting electrons are microscopic, it is easiest from a macroscopic viewpoint to treat this as a form of internal energy U^{el}. We will also see that light and other **electromagnetic waves** (including radio waves, microwaves, infrared rays, X-rays, and gamma rays) can carry energy, which we can usefully express by assigning an internal energy U^{em} to such waves. **Mechanical waves** involving oscillation of some medium, such as sound waves, seismic waves, ocean waves, and so on, also can carry energy, which we can likewise express by assigning them an internal energy U^{snd}. There are many other hidden forms of energy that we will learn about in this course, but these are the most important to know about at present.

TWO-MINUTE PROBLEMS

C11T.1 An object is free to move along the x axis. It is connected through two identical springs to two points $\pm y_0$ on the y axis. When the object is at $x = 0$, both springs are equally compressed. What kind of position is $x = 0$?
A. Unstable equilibrium.
B. Stable equilibrium.
C. Not an equilibrium position.

C11T.2 If your stove burner provides thermal energy at a rate of 4500 J/s, about how much water can you boil in a minute?
A. 2 kg
B. 120 kg
C. 0.002 kg
D. 0.12 kg
E. Other (specify)

C11T.3 A 300-g hunk of ice at 0°C is placed in a thermos bottle containing 1 kg of water at 20°C. If the thermos perfectly insulates the ice-water system from the outside world, what will be the final temperature of the system?
A. Below 0°C.
B. Almost exactly 0°C.
C. Somewhat above 0°C.
D. Very roughly 10°C.
E. Somewhat below 20°C.
F. Almost exactly 20°C.

C11T.4 The thermal energy of a block of ice at 0°C melting to a puddle of water at 0°C
A. Increases
B. Decreases
C. Doesn't change

C11T.5 An egg will not cook any faster in furiously boiling water than it will in gently simmering water, true (T) or false (F)?

C11T.6 A 100-g sample of a certain substance undergoes a transformation of some kind that releases about

20,000 J of energy. What kind of transformation is this likely to be?

A. A temperature change.
B. A phase change.
C. A chemical reaction.
D. A nuclear reaction.
E. It is impossible to guess.

C11T.7 If you were to climb about 10 stories worth of stairs, roughly what is the *minimum* number of food calories that you would have to burn? (Select the closest.)

A. 70,000 Cal
B. 4000 Cal
C. 70 Cal
D. 4 Cal
E. Less than 1 Cal

Problems C11T.8 through C11T.11 all refer to the situation in which two atoms interacting with each other have the potential energy shown in figure C11.5. You may assume that the massive atom's mass is much larger than the light atom's mass, the light atom can only move along the x axis, and $V(x) \to 0$ smoothly as $x \to \infty$.

C11T.8 Imagine that the little atom approaches the big atom from infinity with an initial kinetic energy $K = 5 \times 10^{-21}$ J. How close to the big atom does it get?

A. $x = 0$
B. $x = 0.04$ nm
C. $x = 0.11$ nm
D. $x = 0.2$ nm
E. $x = 0.3$ nm
F. Other (specify)

C11T.9 Imagine that at a certain instant of time, the little atom is at position $x = 0.11$ nm and has a kinetic energy of 5×10^{-21} J. About how much energy would we have to add to break the bond?

A. 1×10^{-21} J
B. 6×10^{-21} J
C. 12×10^{-21} J
D. None: bond is already broken

C11T.10 Imagine that at a certain instant of time, the little atom is at rest at $x = 0.20$ nm. What is the closest that it will ever get to the big atom subsequently (in the absence of external effects)?

A. 0.03 nm
B. 0.05 nm
C. 0.20 nm
D. Other (specify)

C11T.11 If this system has a total energy of $+3 \times 10^{-21}$ J and the little atom is at $x = 0.11$ nm at a certain instant of time, the atoms are

A. Bound.
B. Unbound.
C. It depends on the little atom's initial direction of motion.
D. It depends on the little atom's initial speed.

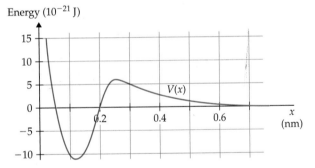

Energy (10^{-21} J)

Figure C11.5
Potential energy diagram for problems C11T.8 through C11T.11.

HOMEWORK PROBLEMS

Basic Skills

C11B.1 Assume that the two-atom system shown in figure C11.5 has a total energy of -5×10^{-21} J. Where are the turning points and what are the allowed and forbidden regions in this case?

C11B.2 Assume that the two-atom system shown in figure C11.5 has a total energy of $+5 \times 10^{-21}$ J. Where are the turning points and what are the allowed and forbidden regions in this case?

C11B.3 Assume that the two-atom system shown in figure C11.5 has a total energy of zero. Where are the turning points and what are the allowed and forbidden regions in this case?

C11B.4 Imagine that at a certain instant of time the little atom shown in figure C11.5 is at $x = 0.11$ nm, has a kinetic energy of about 7×10^{-21} J, and is moving away from the big atom. Describe its subsequent motion as completely as you can.

C11B.5 Imagine that at a certain instant of time the little atom shown in figure C11.5 is at very large x, has a kinetic energy of about 2×10^{-21} J, and is moving toward the big atom. Describe its subsequent motion in as completely as you can.

C11B.6 Imagine that at a certain instant of time the little atom shown in figure C11.5 is at rest at $x = 0.20$ nm. Describe its subsequent motion in as completely as you can.

C11B.7 Imagine that at a certain instant of time the little atom shown in figure C11.5 is at very large x, has a kinetic energy of about 10×10^{-21} J, and is moving toward the big atom. About how much energy must be removed from the system (at the appropriate time) for the atoms to become bound?

C11B.8 Imagine that at a certain instant of time the little atom shown in figure C11.5 is at $x = 0.11$ nm and has a kinetic energy of about 10×10^{-21} J. About how much energy must be added to the system for the atoms to become unbound?

C11B.9 Imagine that a stove burner provides thermal energy at a rate of 4500 J/s. What is the minimum time that it would take to melt 1 qt (about 800 g) of ice in a pan placed on that burner?

C11B.10 A natural gas furnace produces 20,000 J of thermal energy per second. How much gas does it use per hour?

C11B.11 The current *total* energy consumption of the United States is on the order of magnitude of 10^{20} J/yr. If we could produce all this energy by nuclear fusion, how many kilograms of deuterium-tritium mix would we need per year?

Synthetic

The starred problems are particularly well suited to practicing the use of the problem-solving framework and conceptual model diagrams.

C11S.1 A light object that is free to move along the x axis interacts with a massive object at $x = 0$. The graph shows the potential energy function for their interaction. Draw a quantitatively accurate graph of the

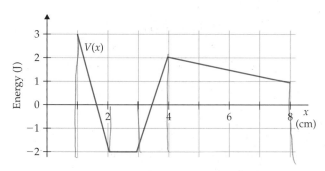

x component of the force acting on the light object as a function of x.

C11S.2 Imagine a plastic bead with a charge of +1 nano-coulomb (nC) sliding along a wire that defines the x axis. Two fixed beads with a charge of +1 nC are placed at $x = 0, y = \pm 5$ cm.
   (a) Draw a quantitatively accurate graph of the potential energy of this system as a function of the position of the sliding bead.
   (b) Is there an equilibrium position for this bead? Is it stable? Explain your answer.

C11S.3 People whose feet are wet can walk on hot coals for a short while. (*Do not try this at home!*) Why is it important that the feet be wet? Why does this offer protection only for a limited time?

C11S.4 A standard hair dryer produces about 2500 J of thermal energy per second. What is the maximum amount of ice that you could melt in 1 min?

*C11S.5 A 120-g block of ice at $0°$C is placed in an insulated thermos containing 420 g of water at $22°$C. What is the final temperature of the water? Is there any ice left? If so, how much?

*C11S.6 A 12-g block of ice at $0°$C is placed in an insulated thermos containing 450 g of water at $22°$C. What is the final temperature of the water? Is there any ice left? If so, how much?

*C11S.7 What is the minimum amount of ice that would cool a 15-kg container of lemonade from $27°$C to $0°$C?

*C11S.8 Imagine that a person whose mass is 60 kg burns 1600 Cal while climbing a mountain 1300 m high.

What fraction of the food energy is converted to thermal energy and/or latent energy in the environment?

*C11S.9   A certain solid-propellant model rocket engine releases a total of 6000 J of energy as it burns. If this engine carries a model rocket having a mass of 320 g to an altitude of 270 m, what fraction of the chemical energy released by the engine is wasted in the form of thermal energy in the air?

How much of this energy is wasted?

*C11S.10   Imagine that you were to eat 1 kg of snow. Your body will burn whatever food energy resources it has to maintain your internal temperature at 37°C. How many food calories will your body have to burn as a consequence of your meal of snow? (*Note:* This is *not* recommended as a diet plan.)

C11S.11   Icebergs present real hazards to shipping, so many ways have been considered to destroy them. Why

not just melt them? Estimate the energy required to melt a small iceberg with a volume of 1 km^3 (the density of ice is about 0.91 g/cm^3). Compare to the energy released by an atom bomb ($\approx 4 \times 10^{14}$ J).

C11S.12   If your car gets 25 mi/gal when driven on the highway at 55 mi/h, about how many joules of chemical energy does the engine convert to other forms per second? Please show all your work and estimates.

Rich-Context

*C11R.1   You are preparing for a 5-day backpacking trip where you plan to use a gasoline cook stove for about 30 min each morning and night. The description of your cook stove brags that the stove can warm 1 L of water to boiling in about 12 min.
(a) Estimate the *minimum* amount of gasoline you should take on your trip.
(b) Explain why the assumptions you made in your calculation for part a mean that the amount of gas you actually need will probably be somewhat larger.

*C11R.2   Imagine that your car can travel 25 mi on 1 gal of gas when traveling on a level road at 55 mi/h. Estimate your gas mileage while traveling at 55 mi/h up an incline that gains 3 m in elevation for every 100 m one goes forward along the incline (such an incline is called a 3% incline). Assume that your car (including passengers) has a mass of 1500 kg.

C11R.3   (This problem requires some simple differential calculus in the last step.) You may know that an object floating in water sits in the water at such a level that the mass of water it displaces is equal to its mass. We can use energy arguments to prove this pretty easily for an object of constant horizontal cross-sectional area A (such as an upright cylinder or a cube).

Our system here consists of the object, the earth, and the body of water. Let the water's density be ρ_w and the object's density be $\rho < \rho_w$. Let us also define a z axis that points vertically upward, with $z = 0$ at the original water level before the object is placed in it. Let's also define the total potential energy $V(z)$ of interactions between the object and the water and the earth to be zero when the object's bottom is at $z = 0$ (just before it enters the water). Let the object's height be h.
(a) As the object sinks into a body of water, the net effect is to cause the body's water level to rise slightly, as if the water that the object displaces had been lifted and spread out as a thin layer on the body's surface. Assuming that the body of water is so huge that the change in level is negligible, argue that if the object's bottom sinks to a (negative) vertical position $z = -|z|$, the *average* distance that the water it displaces has been raised is $\frac{1}{2}|z|$.

(b) Argue that the total gravitational potential energy function for the system (the sum of the potential energies for the sinking object and the lifted water) is

$$V(z) = \rho A g z + \tfrac{1}{2} \rho_w A g z^2 \qquad \text{for } 0 \geq z \geq -h$$

(C11.9)

(c) Draw a quantitatively accurate plot of $V(z)/(\rho_w A g h^2)$ as a function of z/h (assume that $\rho/\rho_w = 0.6$ for the sake of concreteness). You should see that the graph has a minimum value at some specific z between 0 and $-h$.

(d) Explain, using energy arguments, why the object will eventually come to rest at the depth of this minimum, no matter whether it was gently lowered into the water or dropped vertically into the water. (*Hint:* If it was dropped into the water, it will bob up and down for a while. Why? Why will it eventually stop bobbing?)

(e) This minimum occurs where $dV/dz = 0$. Use this to show that at this position, the mass m_w of the water displaced is equal to the object's mass m.

Advanced

C11A.1 Imagine that two objects with masses m and M interact only with each other, and that their potential energy is given by $V(r)$, where r is their separation. Imagine that the two objects move only along the x axis. Let us also choose our reference frame so that the center of mass of this isolated system is at rest at the origin.

(a) If x is the position of the object with mass m some time later, show that the definition of the center of mass implies that the other object's position at that time is $X = -mx/M$ and that $r = bx$, where $b \equiv 1 + m/M$.

(b) Show also that the system's total kinetic energy is bK, where K is the kinetic energy of the lighter object.

(c) If I were to draw a graph of $V(x)$, how would it be related to a graph of $V(r)$? How is the difference $E - V(x)$ related to the kinetic energy of the lighter object at position x? Do you get the expected results when M becomes very large compared to m? (These results would help you interpret a potential energy diagram for a system whose interacting objects have comparable masses instead of very different masses.)

ANSWERS TO EXERCISES

C11X.1 There are no equilibrium positions at all for the potential energy curve shown in figure C11.1a. The potential energy curve shown in figure C11.1b has a single stable equilibrium point at $x = 0$.

C11X.2 The turning points are at about $x = \pm 8.5$ cm. The forbidden regions are values of x such that $|x| > 8.5$ cm.

C11X.3 This is true: as the system's total energy increases, the line corresponding to that energy on the diagram gets higher, and the turning points move outward.

C11X.4 The slope of $V(x)$ is *negative* for $x > 0.30$ nm, so the x-force F_x is *positive*, meaning that it pushes the little atom in the $+x$ direction. This is *away* from the big atom, so the interaction is repulsive.

C11X.5 If we assume that water's specific "heat" c is constant over this whole range (a crude assumption at best), then $\Delta U^{\text{th}} \approx mc\Delta T$, implying that

$$\Delta T \approx \frac{\Delta U^{\text{th}}}{mc} = \frac{2256 \text{ kJ}}{(1 \text{ kg})(4.186 \text{ kJ·kg}^{-1}\text{·K}^{-1})} = 539 \text{ K}$$

(C11.10)

C11X.6 *Translation:* Let the mass of the ice be m, the mass of the water be M, the latent "heat" of melting be L, and the specific "heat" of water be c. The water's temperature change is $\Delta T = -22°C = -22$ K.

Model and solution: Assuming that the system of the ice and the water is functionally isolated, conservation of energy implies that (since the ice and water are at rest)

$$0 = \Delta U^{\text{la}}_{\text{ice}} + \Delta U^{\text{th}}_{w} = +mL + Mc\Delta T$$

$$\Rightarrow \quad m = -\frac{Mc\Delta T}{L}$$

$$= -\frac{(0.5 \text{ kg})(4.2 \text{ kJ·kg}^{-1}\text{·K}^{-1})(-22 \text{ K})}{333 \text{ kJ/kg}}$$

$$= 0.138 \text{ kg}$$

(C11.11)

Evaluation: This seems reasonable, and the sign and units work out.

C12

Power, Collisions, and Impacts

▷ **Introduction**

▷ **Conservation of Momentum**

▽ **Conservation of Energy**

    Introduction to Energy

    Some Potential Energy Functions

    Force and Energy

    Rotational Energy

    Thermal Energy

    Energy in Bonds

    Power, Collisions, and Impacts

▷ **Conservation of Angular Momentum**

Chapter Overview

Introduction

This is the summer-movie chapter of the unit, where we explore some interesting applications of the ideas we have learned starting in chapter C5. We begin with a discussion of *power,* expresses the rate at which energy is transformed by a process. We then look at elastic and inelastic *collisions,* which give us a chance to apply both conservation of momentum and conservation of energy. This material is essential preparation for unit R, where we will look at relativistic collision processes. We close the chapter and the unit subsection on energy with an examination of asteroid *impacts,* which provides an interesting context in which to review a variety of energy and momentum concepts.

Section C12.1:   Power

Power expresses *the magnitude of the rate at which energy flows into or out of a given form* in the course of some interaction or process:

$$P \equiv \left| \frac{dK}{dt} \right| \quad \text{or} \quad \left| \frac{dV}{dt} \right| \quad \text{or} \quad \left| \frac{dU}{dt} \right| \quad \left(\begin{array}{c} \text{whichever form of} \\ \text{energy is of interest} \end{array} \right) \quad \text{(C12.1)}$$

    Purpose: This equation defines the power P involved in a process.
    Symbols: dK, dV, and dU are small changes in an object's kinetic energy, an interaction's potential energy, or an object's internal energy, respectively, during a tiny time interval dt.
    Limitations: The time interval dt should be small enough that $P \approx$ constant during dt.
    Note: The SI unit of power is the **watt,** where $1 \text{ W} \equiv 1 \text{ J/s}$.

Utilities measure electrical energy in **kilowatt-hours,** where $1 \text{ kW·h} = 3.6 \text{ MJ}$. A typical household uses about 700 kWh of electrical energy a month, which costs about 13¢/kW·h in southern California currently.

If a specific interaction exerts a force on a moving object, the rate at which energy is transformed by that particular interaction is

$$P = \left| \frac{[dK]}{dt} \right| = |\vec{F} \cdot \vec{v}| \quad \text{(C12.7)}$$

    Purpose: This equation specifies the power P involved in a specific interaction that exerts a force $\vec{F}$ on an object moving with velocity $\vec{v}$.
    Symbols: $[dK]/dt$ is the rate at which the interaction contributes k-work to the object.

> **Limitations:** The time interval dt must be very small compared to the time required for either $\vec{F}$ or $\vec{v}$ to change significantly.
>
> **Note:** The power $P = |[dK]/dt|$ involved in a specific interaction is to energy what the magnitude of the force $\vec{F} = [d\vec{p}]/dt$ exerted by a specific interaction is to momentum.

Section C12.2: Types of Collisions

An **elastic** collision is a collision in which the colliding objects' kinetic energy is conserved. Most collision processes between macroscopic objects are at least a bit **inelastic**, meaning that some of the objects' kinetic energy is converted to internal energy (although in some cases, so little that the elastic model is a good approximation). A collision in which the objects stick together is **completely inelastic:** such a collision converts as much energy as possible to internal energy. We can consider an explosion to be a **superelastic** collision that converts internal energy to kinetic energy.

Section C12.3: Elastic Collisions

The laws of conservation of momentum and kinetic energy provide enough information to completely determine the final velocities of two objects involved in a one-dimensional elastic collision from their masses and initial velocities. In a two-dimensional elastic collision of two objects, these laws and a single piece of information about the final velocities (such as the direction of one of the final velocities) allows one to solve for the remaining final velocity components.

The examples in this section illustrate the process of solving such problems. The basic approach involves using conservation of momentum to eliminate the unknowns in the conservation of kinetic energy equation. It is usually helpful in such problems to divide through all equations by one of the masses, expressing them in terms of the unitless mass ratio $b = m_A/m_B$. Because the conservation of kinetic energy equation is quadratic, it will generate two solutions, one of which is typically a trivial solution that is of no physical interest.

Section C12.4: The Slingshot Effect

A close encounter with a planet can dramatically increase a spacecraft's speed. NASA space probes often use this **slingshot effect** to reduce the fuel required for a mission. In this section, we see that we can model such an encounter as an elastic collision, and use the techniques of the previous section to calculate the boost in speed.

Section C12.5: Inelastic Collisions

In a completely inelastic collision, conservation of momentum alone provides enough information to calculate the objects' common final velocity in terms of masses and initial velocities, but to solve *partially* inelastic collisions, we must either supply more equations or reduce the number of unknown final velocity components. If the problem supplies information about how much energy the collision converts to internal energy, we can use conservation of energy as an additional equation. Alternatively, if we are given enough information to solve the problem without using conservation of energy, then we can calculate how much energy is converted to internal energy.

Section C12.6: Asteroid Impacts

In this section, we use conservation of energy and conservation of momentum to analyze some of the physical consequences of a 10-km asteroid hitting the earth at about 20 km/s, the kind of impact that killed the dinosaurs. We will see that given just a few bits of information and some basic physics, we can predict a number of important consequences.

C12.1   Power

The definition of *power*

In physics, **power** is a technical term that expresses *the magnitude of the rate at which energy flows into or out of a given form* in the course of some interaction or process:

$$P \equiv \left| \frac{dK}{dt} \right| \quad \text{or} \quad \left| \frac{dV}{dt} \right| \quad \text{or} \quad \left| \frac{dU}{dt} \right| \quad \left(\begin{array}{c} \text{whichever form of} \\ \text{energy is of interest} \end{array} \right) \quad \text{(C12.1)}$$

Purpose: Definition of the power P involved in an energy transformation.
Symbols: dK, dV, and dU are small changes in an object's kinetic energy, an interaction's potential energy, or an object's internal energy, respectively, during a tiny time interval dt.
Limitations: The time interval dt should be small enough that $P \approx$ constant during dt.
Note: The SI unit of power is the **watt**, where $1 \text{ W} \equiv 1 \text{ J/s}$.

For example, a 100-W lightbulb converts 100 J of electrical energy to light and thermal energy (mostly the latter) every second. Table C12.1 lists some benchmarks for the power involved in various physical processes.

The kilowatt-hour

Electric power, even in everyday life, is measured in the SI unit of watts: an appliance's label will often state its power consumption in watts. Electrical energy, on the other hand, is commonly measured in **kilowatt-hours** instead of joules. A kilowatt-hour is defined to be the energy you would consume in 1 h at the rate of 1 kW: it turns out that $1 \text{ kW·h} = 3.6 \text{ MJ}$. Since a typical household of four people uses about 700 kW·h of electricity a month, this is a conveniently large unit for billing purposes. According to my recent bills, the cost of residential electrical energy in southern California is about 13¢/kW·h for the first 350 kW·h or so (the price increases above that baseline to encourage conservation).

Exercise C12X.1

Prove that $1 \text{ kW·h} = 3.6 \text{ MJ}$ of energy.

Table C12.1   Power benchmarks

Active Agent	Power	Energy Transfer Involved
The sun	3.9×10^{26} W	Nuclear energy → electromagnetic waves
A large electric power plant	≈ 1000 MW	Nuclear or chemical energy → electrical energy
An SUV or large car	≈ 150 kW	Chemical energy → thermal, kinetic, and/or potential energy
A large radio station	≈ 10 kW	Electrical energy → electromagnetic waves
A typical home furnace	≈ 10 kW	Chemical energy → thermal energy
A typical toaster	≈ 1500 W	Electrical energy → thermal energy
One horsepower (1 hp)	≈ 746 W	
Resting human metabolism	≈ 60 W	Chemical energy → thermal energy (mostly)
A commonly available He-Ne laser	≈ 1 mW	Electrical energy → electromagnetic waves

If a speci
can calculate
action as follc

Purpos
interaction
Symbo
k-work to
Limitat
the time re
Note:
teraction i
erted by a

This equ
power with f
on an airplar
of 100 m/s. S
equation C1:
from the pla
(1000 N)(100
duce at least

C12.2   T

As we have
involved in
system *just*
is very shor
mentum or
   While tl
served, the s
of the collid
ergy). How
to other forr
the collisior
energy; but
kinetic ener
   We call
ergy an **ela**
perfectly ela
Examples ir
billiard ball
itationally
member th
microscopi
whenever
is often the

Exercise C12X.2

Roughly what does it cost to leave a 100-W lamp on overnight? How much does this cost per month if you do this consistently?

Example C12.1

Problem   A 1200-kg car descends a 5% incline with its brakes on, maintaining a constant speed of 11 m/s ($\approx$ 24 mi/h). (A 5% incline means that the object moves vertically a distance equal to 5% of what it moves along the incline.) At what rate is energy being transformed to thermal energy in the car's brakes? (Ignore air friction.)

Translation   Let the car's mass be m, its speed be v, and the thermal energy in its brakes be U^{th}. Let's define a reference frame whose z axis points upward.

Model   The system comprises the car and the earth, which is isolated because it floats in space. The car participates in gravitational and contact interactions with the earth. We will ignore the earth's kinetic energy and the normal part of the contact interaction. The friction part of the contact interaction primarily converts the car's kinetic energy into thermal energy in the brake pads (ignoring small thermal energy increases in the air, the tires, and the road). So conservation of energy requires that for any small time interval dt, $0 = dK + dV + dU^{th}$, where the terms refer to changes in the car's kinetic energy, the gravitational interaction's potential energy, and the brakes' thermal energy, respectively. Since the car is close to the earth's surface, we can use $V(z) = mgz$ for the potential energy. Since the car's kinetic energy is constant by hypothesis, and since we can calculate the rate at which $V(z)$ decreases, we can determine the rate at which the brakes' thermal energy increases.

Solution   Dividing the conservation of energy equation by dt yields

$$0 = \frac{dK}{dt} + \frac{dV}{dt} + \frac{dU^{th}}{dt} = 0 + mg\frac{dz}{dt} + \frac{dU^{th}}{dt} \qquad \text{(C12.2)}$$

We know that the car's forward speed is $v = 11$ m/s $= ds/dt$, where ds is the distance the car moves down the incline in time dt. But we are also told that the car moves vertically a distance equal to 5% of its displacement along the incline, so in this case

$$dz = -0.05\,ds \quad \Rightarrow \quad \frac{dz}{dt} = -0.05\frac{ds}{dt} = -0.05v \qquad \text{(C12.3)}$$

Therefore

$$\frac{dU^{th}}{dt} = -mg\frac{dz}{dt} = +0.05mgv$$

$$= 0.05\,(1200\text{ kg})\left(9.8\frac{N}{kg}\right)\left(11\frac{m}{s}\right)\left(\frac{1J}{1\,N\cdot m}\right)\left(\frac{1\text{ W}}{1J/s}\right) = 6500\text{ W} \qquad \text{(C12.4)}$$

Evaluation   While this is a credibly small fraction of the total power involved in automobile travel (see the benchmarks in table C12.1), it is still the thermal power of more than four toasters, so it is easy to see why the brake shoes get hot!

the object's center of mass, and $\vec{v}_{CM}$ is the velocity of the center of mass relative to O.

Exercise C13X.7

Verify equation C13.16.

Now, the definition of the center of mass and the fact that the object's total momentum is equal to the object's total mass M times the velocity of its center of mass state (respectively) that

$$M\vec{r}_{CM} = \sum_{i=1}^{N} m_i \vec{r}_i \quad \text{and} \quad M\vec{v}_{CM} = \sum_{i=1}^{N} m_i \vec{v}_i \quad \text{(C13.17)}$$

Using equations C13.15, C13.16, and C13.17, you can fairly easily show that

$$0 = \sum_{i=1}^{N} m_i \vec{q}_i \quad \text{and} \quad 0 = \sum_{i=1}^{N} m_i \vec{u}_i \quad \text{(C13.18)}$$

Exercise C13X.8

Verify equation C13.18.

Using the distributive property of the cross product, we see that the object's total angular momentum around the point O is given by

$$\vec{L} \equiv \sum_{i=1}^{N} \vec{r}_i \times m_i \vec{v}_i = \sum_{i=1}^{N} [(\vec{r}_{CM} + \vec{q}_i) \times m_i (\vec{v}_{CM} + \vec{u}_i)]$$

$$= \sum_{i=1}^{N} [\vec{r}_{CM} \times m_i \vec{v}_{CM} + \vec{r}_{CM} \times m_i \vec{u}_i + \vec{q}_i \times m_i \vec{v}_{CM} + \vec{q}_i \times m_i \vec{u}_i] \quad \text{(C13.19)}$$

We are perfectly free to write this sum of four terms as four separate sums. In the third term, $\vec{q}_i \times m_i \vec{v}_{CM} = m_i \vec{q}_i \times \vec{v}_{CM}$ by the linear property of the cross product, and the distributive property means that we can pull out any cross-product factor that appears in all terms of any sum. So we can write this as

$$\vec{L} = \vec{r}_{CM} \times \vec{v}_{CM} \left(\sum_{i=1}^{N} m_i \right) + \vec{r}_{CM} \times \left(\sum_{i=1}^{N} m_i \vec{u}_i \right)$$

$$+ \left(\sum_{i=1}^{N} m_i \vec{q}_i \right) \times \vec{v}_{CM} + \sum_{i=1}^{N} (\vec{q}_i \times m_i \vec{u}_i) \quad \text{(C13.20)}$$

Equations C13.18 imply that the middle two terms in this expression are zero. Since the sum over all particle masses is the object's total mass M, the first term is equivalent to $\vec{r}_{CM} \times M\vec{v}_{CM}$, which is the angular momentum of the object's center of mass about O computed as if it were a particle. The last term would be the object's angular momentum if it were only rotating about its center of mass and not moving. Therefore $\vec{L} = \vec{L}^{cm} + 0 + 0 + \vec{L}^{rot}$, as claimed.

C13.6   Twirl and Torque

An interaction between two objects can transfer angular momentum from one to the other as well as ordinary momentum. Let's call the amount of angular momentum that an interaction contributes to an object during a time

If a specific interaction exerts a certain force $\vec{F}$ on a moving object, we can calculate the rate P at which energy is transformed by that specific interaction as follows:

$$P = \left|\frac{[dK]}{dt}\right| = \left|\frac{\vec{F} \cdot d\vec{r}}{dt}\right| = \left|\vec{F} \cdot \frac{d\vec{r}}{dt}\right| = |\vec{F} \cdot \vec{v}| \qquad \text{(C12.7)}$$

Purpose: This equation specifies the power P involved in a specific interaction that exerts a force $\vec{F}$ on an object moving with velocity $\vec{v}$.

Symbols: $[dK]/dt$ is the rate at which the interaction contributes k-work to the object.

Limitations: The time interval dt must be very small compared to the time required for either $\vec{F}$ or $\vec{v}$ to change significantly.

Note: Note that the power $P = |[dK]/dt|$ involved in a specific interaction is to energy what the magnitude of the force $\vec{F} = [d\vec{p}]/dt$ exerted by a specific interaction is to momentum.

This equation is useful in circumstances when one wants to connect power with force. For example, imagine that we know that the drag force $\vec{F}_D$ on an airplane has a magnitude of 1000 N and the plane is flying at a speed of 100 m/s. Since the angle between the force and the velocity vectors is 180°, equation C12.7 implies that the rate at which kinetic energy is being removed from the plane by the drag interaction is $|\vec{F}_D \cdot \vec{v}| = F_D v|\cos 180°| = F_D v = (1000 \text{ N})(100 \text{ m/s}) = 100{,}000$ W. The airplane's engine must therefore produce at least this much power to keep the plane's speed steady.

C12.2   Types of Collisions

As we have seen, the total energy and total momentum of almost *any* system involved in a collision are very nearly conserved (as long as we examine the system *just before* and *just after* the collision), because if the collision process is very short, external interactions have too little time to transfer much momentum or energy into or out of the system.

Why we can treat a system involved in a collision as if it were isolated

While the *total* energy of a system involved in a collision might be conserved, the strong internal collision interactions usually transfer at least *some* of the colliding objects' kinetic energy to internal energy (usually thermal energy). However, some kinds of collisions transform very little kinetic energy to other forms. For example, colliding rubber balls deform each other during the collision, converting kinetic energy to microscopic forms of potential energy; but this deformation energy is almost entirely converted back into kinetic energy as the balls rebound.

We call a collision that conserves the colliding objects' total *kinetic* energy an **elastic** collision. Collisions involving macroscopic objects are never *perfectly* elastic, but some are close enough to make it useful as a model. Examples include fairly gentle collisions between rubber balls, steel balls, or billiard balls, as well as collisions between objects that interact strongly gravitationally or electromagnetically as they pass closely without touching (remember that objects do not have to touch to "collide"). Collisions between microscopic systems such as atoms or molecules can be *perfectly* elastic whenever quantum mechanics forbids energy transfers to internal energy (as is often the case).

Categories for collisions

An **inelastic** collision converts some kinetic energy to internal energy (and thus does not conserve kinetic energy). A collision in which the objects remain stuck together is **completely inelastic:** such collisions convert as much kinetic energy to internal energy as conservation of momentum allows. We can consider an explosion to be a collision that converts internal energy to kinetic energy: we might call this a **superelastic** collision. But a normal collision (that does not somehow trigger a release of chemical or nuclear energy) will be at best elastic and usually inelastic, never superelastic.

C12.3   Elastic Collisions

The following examples show how we can usefully apply both conservation of energy and conservation of momentum to problems involving elastic collisions.

Example C12.3

Problem   (A One-Dimensional Collision) Imagine that a cart with mass m_A moving horizontally at a speed v_0 in a direction we define to be the $+x$ direction collides elastically with another cart of mass m_B at rest. After this head-on collision, both carts move along the $\pm x$ axis. What are their x-velocities just after the collision?

Translation

Prose Model   The system of the two carts is momentarily isolated here. Conservation of momentum tells us that the system's initial total momentum must be equal to its final total momentum, which in this case means that

$$\begin{bmatrix} +m_A v_0 \\ 0 \\ 0 \end{bmatrix} + \begin{bmatrix} 0 \\ 0 \\ 0 \end{bmatrix} = \begin{bmatrix} m_A v_{Ax} \\ 0 \\ 0 \end{bmatrix} + \begin{bmatrix} m_B v_{Bx} \\ 0 \\ 0 \end{bmatrix} \qquad \text{(C12.8)}$$

Since the problem describes the collision as "elastic," the system's total *kinetic* energy is also conserved. In collision problems, it is usually easiest to express this law in this form: initial total K = final total K. In this situation this becomes

$$\tfrac{1}{2} m_A v_0^2 + 0 = \tfrac{1}{2} m_A v_A^2 + \tfrac{1}{2} m_B v_B^2$$

$$\Rightarrow \quad \tfrac{1}{2} m_A v_0^2 = \tfrac{1}{2} m_A v_{Ax}^2 + \tfrac{1}{2} m_B v_{Bx}^2 \qquad \text{(C12.9)}$$

since $v_{Ay} = v_{Az} = v_{By} = v_{Bz} = 0$. Equation C12.9 and the first row of equation C12.8 give us two useful equations, and since the problem statement "gives" us m_A, m_B, and v_0, we have two unknowns v_{Ax} and v_{Bx}, so we can solve the problem.

Solution   In elastic collision problems it is almost *always* useful to divide all equations by one of the masses (say, m_B), because the answer always depends *only* on the mass ratio $b \equiv m_A/m_B$, and writing the equations in terms of the mass ratio usually makes them easier to solve. So if we divide the momentum equation by m_B and the energy equation by $\frac{1}{2}m_B$, we get the stripped-down equations

$$bv_0 = bv_{Ax} + v_{Bx} \qquad \text{and} \qquad bv_0^2 = bv_{Ax}^2 + v_{Bx}^2 \qquad \text{(C12.10)}$$

where $b \equiv m_A/m_B$. We can solve this by solving the first equation for v_{Bx} and using this to eliminate v_{Bx} in the second equation, as follows.

$$v_{Bx} = b(v_0 - v_{Ax}) \qquad\qquad\qquad\qquad\qquad\qquad \text{(C12.11a)}$$
$$\Rightarrow \quad bv_0^2 = bv_{Ax}^2 + b^2(v_0 - v_{Ax})^2 = bv_{Ax}^2 + b^2v_0^2 - 2b^2v_0v_{Ax} + b^2v_{Ax}^2$$
$$\Rightarrow \quad 0 = (b + b^2)v_{Ax}^2 - 2b^2v_0v_{Ax} + (-b + b^2)v_0^2$$
$$\Rightarrow \quad 0 = (1 + b)v_{Ax}^2 - 2bv_0v_{Ax} - (1 - b)v_0^2 \qquad\qquad \text{(C12.11b)}$$

In the last step, I simply divided both sides by b. This is a simple quadratic equation, so we can use the quadratic formula to solve for v_{Ax}:

$$v_{Ax} = \frac{+2bv_0 \pm \sqrt{4b^2v_0^2 + 4(1 + b)(1 - b)v_0^2}}{2(1 + b)} = \frac{2bv_0 \pm 2v_0\sqrt{b^2 + 1 - b^2}}{2(1 + b)}$$

$$= \frac{bv_0 \pm v_0}{1 + b} = v_0, \ \frac{b - 1}{b + 1}v_0 \qquad\qquad\qquad \text{(C12.12)}$$

Note that one of the two solutions is simply $v_{Ax} = v_0$: this amounts to the first cart going right through the other cart, without interacting with it at all! While this solution certainly conserves momentum and energy (which is all the *equations* care about), it is not realistic: the second solution is the one of interest. Plugging this solution into equation C12.11a yields

$$v_{Bx} = b\left(v_0 - \frac{b - 1}{b + 1}v_0\right) = bv_0\left(\frac{b + 1 - b + 1}{b + 1}\right) = \frac{2bv_0}{b + 1} \qquad \text{(C12.13)}$$

Evaluation   How do we check the validity of a *formulas* like equations C12.12 and C12.13? First note that the units are correct in each equation: since b is unitless, the right side of each equation has the same velocity units as v_0, which are appropriate units for v_{Ax} and v_{Bx}. Second, we can check some limiting cases where we can guess the answer intuitively. Note that if $v_0 = 0$, we have no collision, so it makes sense that the formulas predict that v_{Ax} and v_{Bx} are zero as well. If the mass of the second cart becomes extremely massive relative to the first, so that $b \equiv m_A/m_B \to 0$, then we see that equation C12.13 predicts that the second cart will essentially remain at rest, while equation C12.12 predicts that $v_{Ax} = -v_0$, meaning that the first cart simply bounces off the essentially immovable second cart. This is plausible. Note also that we can easily check these results for v_{Ax} and v_{Bx} by plugging them back into the original equations C12.8 and C12.9 and checking that those equations are indeed satisfied.

Exercise C12X.3

Do this.

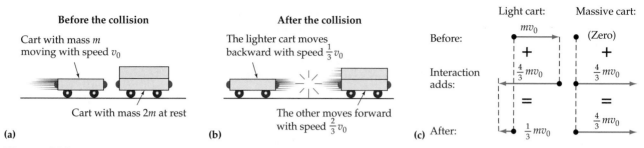

Figure C12.1

The cart collision shown in figure C3.5. Part c shows that this collision transfers a forward momentum of $\frac{4}{3}mv_0$ to the front cart.

The collisions discussed in chapter C3 were elastic

We can apply these formulas to the collision between carts shown in figure C12.1, which is a duplicate of figure C3.5. In this case, $m_A = m$ and $m_B = 2m$, so $b \equiv m_A/m_B = \frac{1}{2}$. Equations C12.12 and C12.13 then predict that

$$v_{Ax} = \frac{\frac{1}{2}-1}{\frac{1}{2}+1}v_0 = \frac{-\frac{1}{2}}{\frac{3}{2}}v_0 = -\frac{1}{3}v_0 \qquad v_{Bx} = \frac{2(\frac{1}{2})}{\frac{3}{2}}v_0 = +\frac{2}{3}v_0 \qquad \text{(C12.14)}$$

as shown in figure C12.1b. In chapter C3, we argued that these would be the results if the carts' bumpers were "sufficiently springy." We can now state more formally that these results apply if the collision is *elastic*.

Exercise C12X.4

Argue that the collisions described in figures C3.3 and C3.4 are also elastic.

In chapter C3, you may have wondered what determines how much momentum is transferred in the collision. We can now see that this is determined by the mass ratio and the degree to which the collision is elastic. An inelastic collision transfers *less* momentum than an elastic one, as exercise C12X.5 illustrates.

Exercise C12X.5

If the two carts in figure C12.1 were to stick together instead of elastically rebounding, then $v_{Ax} = v_{Bx}$. Show that this statement and the law of conservation of momentum provide enough information to solve the problem, that $v_{Ax} = +\frac{1}{3}v_0$, that the momentum transferred is only $\frac{2}{3}mv_0$ instead of the $\frac{4}{3}mv_0$ transferred in the elastic collision, and that kinetic energy is *not* conserved in this collision.

Example C12.4

Problem (A Two-Dimensional Collision) A pool ball moving at speed v_0 strikes an identical ball at rest a glancing blow. The collision deflects the first ball by an angle θ. If the collision is elastic, what are the balls' speeds immediately afterward? In what direction is the second ball traveling?

Translation

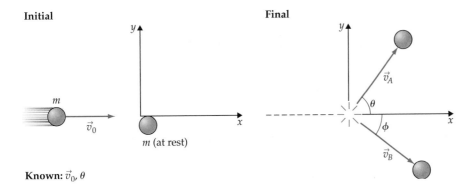

Initial   **Final**

Known: $\vec{v}_0, \theta$

Prose Model   The system consisting of the two balls is momentarily isolated. Conservation of momentum implies in this case that

$$\begin{bmatrix} mv_0 \\ 0 \\ 0 \end{bmatrix} + \begin{bmatrix} 0 \\ 0 \\ 0 \end{bmatrix} = \begin{bmatrix} mv_A\cos\theta \\ mv_A\sin\theta \\ 0 \end{bmatrix} + \begin{bmatrix} mv_{Bx} \\ mv_{By} \\ 0 \end{bmatrix} \qquad \text{(C12.15)}$$

I could have written the components of $\vec{v}_B$ as $v_B\cos\phi$ and $v_B\sin\phi$, but it turns out that when a vector's magnitude and direction are *both* unknown, it is almost always easier to use the vector's components. Since the collision is elastic, kinetic energy is conserved:

$$\tfrac{1}{2}mv_0^2 + 0 = \tfrac{1}{2}mv_A^2 + \tfrac{1}{2}mv_B^2$$

$$\Rightarrow \tfrac{1}{2}mv_0^2 = \tfrac{1}{2}mv_A^2 + \tfrac{1}{2}mv_{Bx}^2 + \tfrac{1}{2}mv_{By}^2 \qquad \text{(C12.16)}$$

The m's will cancel out. Equation C12.16 and the top two lines of equation C12.15 provide three meaningful equations, so we should be able to solve for the three unknowns v_A, v_{Bx}, and v_{By}.

Solution   After we divide out the m's and other common factors and solve the momentum equations for v_{Bx} and v_{By}, our equations become

$$v_{Bx} = v_0 - v_A\cos\theta \qquad \text{(C12.17a)}$$
$$v_{By} = -v_A\sin\theta \qquad \text{(C12.17b)}$$
$$v_0^2 = v_A^2 + v_{Bx}^2 + v_{By}^2 \qquad \text{(C12.17c)}$$

We can solve for v_A by using equations C12.17a and C12.17b to eliminate v_{Bx} and v_{By} in equation C12.17c:

$$\begin{aligned} v_0^2 &= v_A^2 + (v_0 - v_A\cos\theta)^2 + v_A^2\sin^2\theta \\ &= v_A^2 + v_0^2 - 2v_0v_A\cos\theta + v_A^2\cos^2\theta + v_A^2\sin^2\theta \\ &= 2v_A^2 + v_0^2 - 2v_0v_A\cos\theta \qquad \text{(C12.18)} \end{aligned}$$

since $\cos^2\theta + \sin^2\theta = 1$. Canceling the v_0^2 term from both sides, we get

$$0 = 2v_A^2 - 2v_Av_0\cos\theta \quad \Rightarrow \quad 0 = v_A^2 - v_Av_0\cos\theta \qquad \text{(C12.19)}$$

Here we have another quadratic equation, which we *could* solve for v_A using the quadratic formula. However, in this case it is clear that $v_A = 0$ is one solution, but not the one that the problem writer had in mind, since the problem describes ball A as being "deflected," not brought to rest. If $v_A \neq 0$, we can cancel it from both sides of equation C12.19 to get

$$v_A = v_0 \cos \theta \tag{C12.20}$$

Plugging this into equations C12.17a and C12.17b, we get

$$v_{Bx} = v_0 - v_0 \cos^2 \theta = v_0 \sin^2 \theta \tag{C12.21a}$$
$$v_{By} = -v_0 \cos \theta \sin \theta \tag{C12.21b}$$

where in the first equation, I have used $\cos^2 \theta + \sin^2 \theta = 1 \Rightarrow 1 - \cos^2 \theta = \sin^2 \theta$. We can now find the magnitude and direction of $\vec{v}_B$ in the usual way:

$$\text{mag}(\vec{v}_B) = \sqrt{v_{Bx}^2 + v_{By}^2} = \sqrt{v_0^2 \sin^4 \theta + v_0^2 \sin^2 \theta \cos^2 \theta}$$

$$= v_0 \sin \theta \sqrt{\sin^2 \theta + \cos^2 \theta} = v_0 \sin \theta \tag{C12.22a}$$

$$\phi = \tan^{-1}\left|\frac{v_{By}}{v_{Bx}}\right| = \tan^{-1}\left|\frac{v_0 \cos \theta \sin \theta}{v_0 \sin^2 \theta}\right| = \tan^{-1}\left|\frac{\cos \theta}{\sin \theta}\right| \tag{C12.22b}$$

Evaluation Note that the *units* work out correctly in equations C12.20, C12.21, and C12.22a (we have units of velocity on both sides) and we are taking the inverse tangent of a unitless number in equation C12.22b. The formula also makes sense when we set the "given" quantities to values where we can intuit the result. In this case, if we take $v_0 \to 0$, there is essentially no collision, so we would *expect* both balls to simply sit there afterward, and equations C12.20 and C12.22a agree. Also, taking the deflection angle $\theta \to 0$ means that the incoming ball just barely brushes the other, so we would expect that $v_B \to 0$ in this limit, and this is indeed what equation C12.22a says. So our solution seems plausible.

Comments on solving elastic collision problems

These are both pretty simple problems, the first because it is one-dimensional, and the second because it involves objects of equal mass. Two-dimensional collisions between objects of unequal mass are not more difficult to solve *in principle* (if the masses are given, one still has three equations in three unknowns), but *in practice* such problems can be very difficult algebraically. Because the kinetic energy equation is quadratic, one almost always ends up with a quadratic equation to solve, which can get very ugly very fast. However, *one* of the two solutions to the quadratic equation will often *obviously* satisfy conservation of energy and momentum, such as the no-collision solution to the first example and the $v_A = 0$ solution in the second case, so getting such a trivial solution is a good sign.

An interesting thing to notice is that in a one-dimensional elastic collision, we can determine the object's final velocities given *only* their initial velocities: the momentum and kinetic energy equations provide two equations in the two unknown final x-velocities v_{Ax} and v_{Bx}. But in a two-dimensional problem, the two nontrivial momentum equations and kinetic energy equation only provide three equations in the four unknown final velocity components v_{Ax}, v_{Ay}, v_{Bx}, and v_{By}. Therefore, to successfully solve a two-dimensional elastic collision problem, we need to know *something* about the final velocities. This could be one of the components, one velocity magnitude, or (as in the last example) a direction for one of the velocities.

We will not do any three-dimensional collision problems in this course (cue the celebratory music).

C12.4   The Slingshot Effect

A close encounter with a planet can dramatically increase a spacecraft's speed. NASA space probes often use this **slingshot effect** to boost their speeds so that they can visit more distant planets (this saves money by reducing the fuel they have to carry). How does this work?

Let's consider a specific case where (in the reference frame of the solar system) the initial velocities of the probe and planet are perpendicular, with speeds v_0 and v_{P0}, respectively, in a reference frame attached to the sun. Imagine that we have aimed the probe so that the gravitational pull of the planet sweeps the probe's direction around by about 90° as it passes the planet, so that it ends up traveling in the same direction as the planet, as shown in figure C12.2. What is the probe's final speed v?

Let the probe and planet have masses m_A and m_B, respectively. Note that in the solar system frame, we cannot ignore the gravitational effects of the sun; but let's assume that the encounter is sufficiently brief that the energy and momentum the probe-planet system gets from this external interaction is small. Let's also assume that both initially and finally the probe is so far from the planet that their gravitational interaction's potential energy is $V = -Gm_A m_B/r \approx 0$, implying that $\Delta V \approx 0$. This is the only significant interaction between the probe and planet (if the probe does not enter the atmosphere), so conservation of energy tells us that the system's total *kinetic* energy will be conserved. We can model this encounter, therefore, as an elastic collision.

Expressed in the reference frame shown in figure C12.2, the law of conservation of momentum implies that

$$\begin{bmatrix} 0 \\ +m_A v_0 \\ 0 \end{bmatrix} + \begin{bmatrix} +m_B v_{P0} \\ 0 \\ 0 \end{bmatrix} = \begin{bmatrix} m_A v \\ 0 \\ 0 \end{bmatrix} + \begin{bmatrix} m_B v_{Px} \\ m_B v_{Py} \\ 0 \end{bmatrix} \qquad \text{(C12.23)}$$

where the two vectors on each side describe the momenta of the probe and planet, respectively (v_{Px} and v_{Py} are the components of the planet's final velocity). Conservation of kinetic energy implies that

$$\tfrac{1}{2}m_A v_0^2 + \tfrac{1}{2}m_A v_{P0}^2 = \tfrac{1}{2}m_A v^2 + \tfrac{1}{2}m_B v_P^2 \qquad \text{(C12.24)}$$

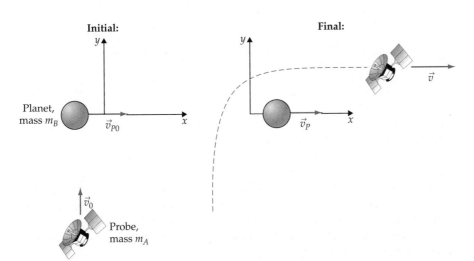

Figure C12.2

Initial and final situations for an encounter between a space probe and a planet that will result in the probe's gaining speed through the *slingshot effect*.

Again, let's divide the equations through by m_B and use $b \equiv m_A/m_B$. If we do this, divide the kinetic energy equation by $\frac{1}{2}$, and use the fact that $v_P^2 = v_{Px}^2 + v_{Py}^2$, we can write the top two lines of equation C12.23 and equation C12.24 in the stripped-down forms

$$v_{P0} = bv + v_{Px} \quad \Rightarrow \quad v_{Px} = v_{P0} - bv \tag{C12.25a}$$

$$bv_0 = v_{Py} \tag{C12.25b}$$

$$bv_0^2 + v_{P0}^2 = bv^2 + v_{Px}^2 + v_{Py}^2 \tag{C12.25c}$$

Plugging the first two into the third to eliminate v_{Px} and v_{Py}, we can show that v_{P0}^2 terms on both sides of the equation cancel, leaving (after a bit of work)

$$0 = (1+b)v^2 - 2v_{P0}v - (1-b)v_0^2 \tag{C12.26}$$

Exercise C12X.6

Verify equation C12.26.

Applying the quadratic formula to equation C12.26, we find that

$$v = \frac{2v_{P0} \pm \sqrt{4v_{P0}^2 + 4(1+b)(1-b)v_0^2}}{2(1+b)} = \frac{v_{P0} \pm \sqrt{v_{P0}^2 + (1-b^2)v_0^2}}{1+b} \tag{C12.27}$$

Now, the planet's mass m_B is typically huge compared to the probe's mass m_A, so $b \equiv m_A/m_B \ll 1$ and equation C12.27 becomes

$$v \approx v_{P0} \pm \sqrt{v_{P0}^2 + v_0^2} \qquad \text{if } b \ll 1 \tag{C12.28}$$

One of these solutions is negative, which is impossible for a vector magnitude (this solution actually corresponds to what happens if the probe loops to the left instead of the right). But the other solution shows that no matter how small v_0 might be, the probe's speed after the encounter exceeds twice the planet's initial speed. Since the orbital speed of Venus, for example, is about 41 km/s, this can give a probe a tremendous boost.

The probe's extra kinetic energy must, of course, come from the planet's orbital motion, so the planet's speed after the encounter is a *bit* smaller than it was before. Because of the huge difference in masses, though, the effect is so small as to be immeasurable.

Encounters involving more complicated angles can be *much* more difficult to calculate, but the basic idea is the same. As long as the probe spends most of its encounter time close to the trailing edge of the planet, the planet's gravitational field will pull it along with the planet and boost its speed.

C12.5   Inelastic Collisions

General comments about inelastic collisions

In problems involving *completely inelastic collisions* between two objects (where the objects stick together afterward), conservation of momentum *alone* always provides enough information to determine the objects' common final velocity from their initial velocities and masses. Knowing the final velocity, we can determine the objects' initial and final kinetic energies and thus also calculate how much energy has been converted to other forms in the collision.

Exercise C12X.7

By counting equations and unknowns, argue that the first sentence in the previous paragraph is true for an arbitrary three-dimensional collision. (If it is true for *arbitrary* three-dimensional collisions, it will be true for one and two-dimensional collisions as well.)

When the two objects collide but *don't* stick together, we need more equations and/or fewer unknowns to determine the two final velocities (one more equation or one fewer unknown for one-dimensional collisions and two for two-dimensional collisions). In elastic collisions, conservation of kinetic energy provided an extra equation. In partially inelastic collisions, we can still use conservation of energy as an equation if we know how much energy the collision converts to *internal* energy. Otherwise, we need to reduce the number of unknowns by specifying one or more of the final velocity components, magnitudes, or directions.

Example C12.5 illustrates a two-dimensional problem in which we are given the final directions of *both* objects' velocities. This allows us to use conservation of momentum alone to solve for the final velocities and then use conservation of energy separately to estimate the energy converted to internal energy during the collision.

Example C12.5

Problem (A Nice Day for Croquet) A 0.45-kg wooden ball moving at a speed of 1.0 m/s in the $+x$ direction collides with a wooden ball with the same mass at rest. Just after the collision, the velocities of *both* balls make a 30° angle with the $+x$ direction. What *fraction* of the system's original kinetic energy has been converted to internal energy in this collision?

Translation Let's orient our reference frame so the first ball's final velocity lies in the xy plane. We will shortly see that the second ball's final velocity must then lie in the xy plane as well. Figure C12.3 shows the initial and final states of the system in this situation, given this.

Model We can consider the system of the two wooden balls to be momentarily isolated. Conservation of momentum then tells us that

$$\begin{bmatrix} +mv_0 \\ 0 \\ 0 \end{bmatrix} + \begin{bmatrix} 0 \\ 0 \\ 0 \end{bmatrix} = \begin{bmatrix} mv_1 \cos\theta \\ mv_1 \sin\theta \\ 0 \end{bmatrix} + \begin{bmatrix} mv_{2x} \\ mv_{2y} \\ mv_{2z} \end{bmatrix} \qquad \text{(C12.29)}$$

We can see immediately from the third line of this equation that v_{2z} must be zero. Therefore, $\vec{v}_2$ *does* lie in the xy plane, and since it makes an angle of $\theta = 30°$ with the $+x$ axis, we must have components $v_{2x} = v_2 \cos\theta$ and $v_{2y} = \pm v_2 \sin\theta$. The second line of equation C12.29 only makes sense if v_{2y} is negative (so it can cancel the first term on the right), so $v_{2y} = -v_2 \sin\theta$ (this is consistent with what I have drawn in figure C12.3b). Then the second line of equation C12.29 reads

$$0 = mv_1 \sin\theta - mv_2 \sin\theta \qquad \Rightarrow \qquad v_1 = v_2 \qquad \text{(C12.30)}$$

Just before:

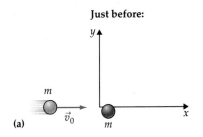

(a)

Just after:

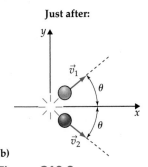

(b)

Figure C12.3
The situation considered in example C12.5.

Plugging this into the first line, we get

$$mv_0 = 2mv_1\cos\theta \quad\Rightarrow\quad v_1 = \frac{v_0}{2\cos\theta} \quad \left(= \frac{1.0\text{ m/s}}{2\cos 30°} = 0.58\text{ m/s}\right)$$
(C12.31)

Conservation of energy implies that $0 = \Delta K + \Delta V + \Delta U$, where ΔK, ΔV, and ΔU are the changes in the system's total kinetic energy, internal potential energy, and internal energy, respectively. The gravitational interaction between these balls is insignificant, and "just before" and "just after" the collision, they are not participating in any *other* long-range internal interactions, so $\Delta V = 0$. So conservation of energy in this case implies that $0 = \Delta K + \Delta U$, which means that

$$\Delta U = -\Delta K = -\left(\tfrac{1}{2}mv_1^2 + \tfrac{1}{2}mv_2^2 - \tfrac{1}{2}mv_0^2\right) = m\left(\tfrac{1}{2}v_0^2 - v_1^2\right)$$

$$= m\left(\frac{v_0^2}{2} - \frac{v_0^2}{4\cos^2\theta}\right) = \tfrac{1}{2}mv_0^2\left(1 - \frac{1}{2\cos^2\theta}\right) \tag{C12.32}$$

The fraction of the system's original kinetic energy $\tfrac{1}{2}mv_0^2$ that ΔU represents is

$$\frac{\Delta U}{\tfrac{1}{2}mv_0^2} = \frac{\tfrac{1}{2}mv_0^2}{\tfrac{1}{2}mv_0^2}\left(1 - \frac{1}{2\cos^2\theta}\right) = 1 - \frac{1}{2\cos^2 30°} = 0.33 \tag{C12.33}$$

This is unitless (as a ratio of energies should be). It is also *positive*, which is very important (normal collisions do not *decrease* a system's internal energy). It is also less than 1, which makes sense (we would not expect this collision to convert more energy than was originally available!).

C12.6   Asteroid Impacts

The impact that killed the dinosaurs

Many scientists currently believe that the dinosaurs became extinct due to consequences of an asteroid hitting the earth 65 million years ago. This asteroid, which dug a crater about 175 km across in the Caribbean, probably had a diameter of 10 km, had a mass of about $m \approx 10^{15}$ kg, and was likely moving with a speed of $v_0 \approx 20$ km/s relative to the earth when it hit. Analyzing the effects of such an impact is a good way to review and apply some of the ideas we have developed in the last six chapters. For maximum effect, I strongly recommend doing the exercises: perhaps you will be astonished at what you can calculate given only a few things about energy, momentum, and power.

The total energy released

It might be hard to *comprehend* the enormous amounts of energy released in such an impact, but it is not hard to calculate it. In a floating frame where the earth is initially at rest, the asteroid's kinetic energy is simply

$$\tfrac{1}{2}mv_0^2 \approx \tfrac{1}{2}(10^{15}\text{ kg})(20{,}000\text{ m/s})^2\left(\frac{1\text{ J}}{1\text{ kg·m}^2/\text{s}^2}\right) \approx 2\times 10^{23}\text{ J} \quad\text{(C12.34)}$$

To put this energy into perspective, the energy released by a typical atomic bomb in the U.S. arsenal is about 4×10^{14} J, so this impact will release an energy equivalent to about 500 million atomic bombs. Since the kinetic energy of the earth-asteroid system after the impact is still a negligible fraction of this energy, essentially all this energy will go to various consequences, which are listed in table C12.2.

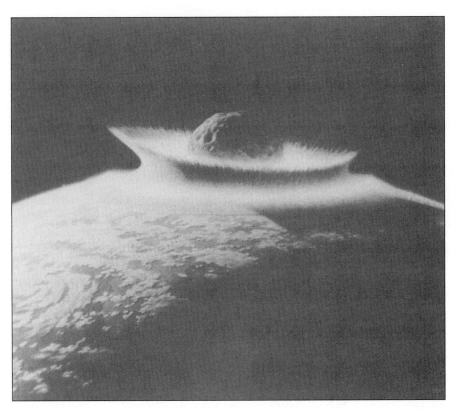

Figure C12.4
An artist's conception of an asteroid impact in the ocean.

Table C12.2   Consequences of major asteroid impact in the ocean

Agent	Consequence	Duration	Scale
Shock wave	Pressure, winds	Very brief	$r < 1000$ km
Splash	Incredibly large tsunamis	Very brief	$r < 3000$ km
Fires	Burning	Months	Global
	Cooling from soot	Months	Global
	Toxins and acid rain	Months	Global
Lofted dust	Cooling	Years	Global
	No photosynthesis	Months	Global
	Too dark to see	Months	Global
	Heavy metal pollution	Years	Global
Nitrogen oxides	Ozone loss	Years	Global
	Cooling due to smog	Years	Global
Sulfur dioxide	Cooling due to smog	Years	Global
	Acid rain	Years	Global
Water and CO_2	Warming	Decades	Global

(Adapted from Toon et al., "Environmental Perturbations of Asteroid Impacts," in *Hazards due to Comets and Asteroids*, ed. T. Gehrels, Tucson: University of Arizona Press, 1994. Most of the information in this section comes from that book.)

Exercise C12X.8

Use conservation of momentum to argue that the kinetic energy of the earth-asteroid system after the impact is less than 10^{-11} of the asteroid's initial kinetic energy.

Immediate effects

    An asteroid of such a size is not even noticeably slowed by the earth's atmosphere, and at 20 km/s, it will only take about 5 to 10 s to pass through the atmosphere to the earth. The magnitude 11.5 earthquake that results is the least of one's worries. After the impact, rock and water that have been vaporized by the impact are lofted into the atmosphere, much of it following the relatively rarefied channel left by the asteroid's passage through the atmosphere. This causes the channel to become incandescent, with most of the light energy that reaches the ground coming from altitudes above 25 km. Enough energy is radiated to cause anything within a direct line of sight of this channel (i.e., within a radius of about 1000 km) to burst into flame within seconds. (The tsunamis may help put out some of these fires along the coast when they arrive some minutes to hours later.)

The effects of vaporized rock

    Of much more serious consequence is the vaporized rock lofted into the atmosphere. Estimates from computer models are that an amount of rock equal to about twice the mass of the asteroid is converted into vapor, and roughly 100 times the mass of the asteroid is not vaporized but is lofted as pulverized rock into the upper atmosphere. If we estimate that the latent "heat" of rock is about 8000 kJ/kg, then the energy that goes to vaporizing rock is very roughly

$$\Delta U^{la} \approx (2 \times 10^{15} \text{ kg})(8 \times 10^6 \text{ J/kg}) = 1.6 \times 10^{22} \text{ J} \qquad \text{(C12.35)}$$

which is about 10% of the impact energy. If we estimate that the average energy of the pulverized rock is such that it would be lofted to a height of 30 km or so if launched vertically, then the energy that goes to lifting pulverized rock is very roughly 15% of the impact energy.

Exercise C12X.9

Check this number. (The published results of computer simulations seem to give a fairly consistent result for the amount of rock lofted, but it is harder to estimate the height number from the data: the estimate I have given is probably only good to within a factor of 2.)

    The vaporized rock is a huge problem, because about one-half is moving fast enough to leave the atmosphere with orbital speeds of 8 km/s or greater. In addition to its latent energy, this rock carries a total kinetic energy about equal to 15% of the impact energy:

$$K \approx \tfrac{1}{2}(10^{15} \text{ kg})(8000 \text{ m/s})^2 = 3.2 \times 10^{22} \text{ J} \qquad \text{(C12.36)}$$

(Its gravitational potential energy is small compared to this kinetic energy.) So this rock can essentially orbit the earth before it drops back within some tens of minutes and deposits its energy into the middle atmosphere. If we assume that this energy is released evenly over a period of 3000 s (the better part of an hour) and that the ground gets about one-quarter of this energy (the rest being radiated to space or remaining in the atmosphere), the average power per square meter that the earth receives over its entire surface is very roughly 5000 W/m^2 during this time.

Exercise C12X.10

Check this number.

For comparison, the average intensity of sunlight is 1000 W/m². This will be enough to light fires essentially anywhere on the planet. Indeed, the evidence of soot left in the rocks formed at the time of the dinosaur impact suggests that a significant fraction of the world's biomass burned.

Cooling by dust

This is just the first hour of consequences! It turns out that of the pulverized rock lofted, an amount about equal to 10% of the asteroid's mass is lofted in the form of submicron dust particles, which can remain in the upper atmosphere for years. This is enough dust to reduce the intensity of sunlight around the globe to about 10^{-10} of its normal intensity. This is so dark that human beings cannot see anything, and needless to say, photosynthesis is not going to occur either. Also, earth's surface does not receive any sunlight, and it soon becomes quite cold, well below freezing in the middles of continents according to the models. This dust shroud is mostly gone after 6 months, but global cooling persists for years, because it takes a very long time for the oceans to recover their normal temperature.

For yet more consequences, see the problems. It is easy to see how all this might lead to global extinction, though! (Fortunately for us, impacts of this magnitude are extremely rare, roughly one event per 100 million years. Worry first about getting hit by lightning.)

TWO-MINUTE PROBLEMS

C12T.1 A trained bicyclist in excellent shape might be able to convert food energy to mechanical energy at a rate of 0.25 hp for a reasonable length of time. Imagine such a person pedaling a stationary bike connected to a perfectly efficient electrical generator. Could such a person generate enough electrical power to run a toaster (T = yes, F = no)? How about a single ordinary lightbulb (T = yes, F = no)?

C12T.2 An object moving with a speed of 5 m/s in the $-x$ direction is acted on by a force with a magnitude of 5 N acting in the $+x$ direction. At what rate does the interaction exerting this force transform this object's kinetic energy to some other form of energy (or vice versa)?
A. +25 W
B. −25 W
C. 5 W
D. −1 W
E. 0
F. Other (specify)

C12T.3 An object moving with a velocity whose components are [4 m/s, −1 m/s, 3 m/s] is acted on by a force whose components are [−5 N, 0, +5 N]. What is the power of the energy transfer involved in this interaction?
A. −35 W
B. −5 W

C. 0
D. +5 W
E. +35 W
F. Other (specify)

C12T.4 Momentum is not conserved in an inelastic collision, true (T) or false (F)? Energy is not conserved in such a collision, T or F?

C12T.5 An object with mass m moving in the $+x$ direction collides head-on with an object of mass $3m$ at rest. After this elastic collision, the first object
A. Moves in the $+x$ direction.
B. Is at rest.
C. Moves in the $-x$ direction.
D. The answer depends on moving object's initial speed.

C12T.6 An object moving with speed v_0 collides head-on with an object at rest that is very much more massive. If the collision is elastic, how does the lighter object's speed v *after* the collision compare with its original speed v_0?
A. v is about equal to v_0.
B. v is noticeably less than v_0.
C. v is one-half of v_0.
D. v is very small.

(more)

E. v is exactly zero.

F. $v \approx -v_0$.

C12T.7 If two moving objects collide, we can *always* orient our reference frame so that the collision takes place entirely in the *xy* plane, T or F?

C12T.8 A object of mass m (object *A*) moving in the $+x$ direction collides with another object at rest (object *B*) whose mass is unknown. After the collision, object *B* is observed moving in the $+y$ direction. This collision *cannot* be elastic, T or F?

HOMEWORK PROBLEMS

Basic Skills

C12B.1 Imagine that Leslie, whose mass is 55 kg, climbs a rope at a speed of about 0.5 m/s. How is energy being transformed in this process? What is the power associated with this energy transformation?

C12B.2 A bicyclist produces energy at the rate of 0.30 hp with her legs, which keeps her bike traveling at a constant speed of 12 m/s on a level road against a headwind. What is the approximate magnitude of the air friction force on the bike? Assume that friction in the wheels is negligible.

C12B.3 An electric motor uses 300 W of electrical power. If this motor is attached to a winch, what is the maximum rate at which it could lift a person whose mass is 60 kg?

C12B.4 A typical refrigerator uses about 350 W of power. If the refrigerator actually runs for an average of 8 h every day, about how much does the electricity used by the refrigerator cost per month?

C12B.5 Does it cost more to leave a 100-W lightbulb on all the time or run a 4000-W electric clothes dryer an average of about 45 min/day? Explain your response.

C12B.6 A rubber ball with mass m moving at a speed of 1.0 m/s in the $+x$ direction hits another rubber ball of mass $2m$ at rest. If the collision is elastic, what are the speeds and directions of motion of the two balls afterward?

C12B.7 A 6-kg bowling ball moving at 2.0 m/s elastically collides with a bowling pin of mass 1.5 kg head-on. What is the speed of the bowling pin after the collision?

Synthetic

C12S.1 In chapter C11, I claimed that the 340 TJ of energy released in the nuclear fusion of 1 kg of deuterium-tritium mixture was enough to supply the energy needs of roughly 10,000 households for 1 year. Using the information provided in section C12.1, verify this claim.

C12S.2 Imagine that you drive a 2000-kg truck up a 3% slope at a roughly constant speed of 16 m/s. If your truck engine is converting chemical energy to other forms of energy at a rate of 100 kW, roughly what fraction of the engine's energy ultimately goes to increasing the system's gravitational potential energy?

C12S.3 Jenny knows that she can produce no more than about 0.12 hp of mechanical power indefinitely while riding a mountain bike. If her mass plus the mass of the bike is 63 kg, what is the *minimum* time that she should allow for a trip to the top of a 6500-ft mountain if the bike trail starts at an elevation of 1200 ft?

C12S.4 Imagine that you plan to generate electrical power for your 60-W study lamp by raising an object of mass 32 kg (70 lb) a vertical distance of 2.5 m (about 8 ft) with a rope, wrapping the rope around the axle of an electrical generator, and then allowing the object to sink slowly back to the floor (unwrapping the rope and thus turning the generator). About how long will it take the mass to sink to the floor if the generator is to produce electrical power at a roughly constant rate of 60 W? (Assume that the generator is roughly 100% efficient.)

C12S.5 Approximately 3.3×10^5 m^3 of water every minute drops roughly 50 m as it flows over Niagara Falls. If

Niagara Falls

you could use a hydroelectric power plant to convert 80% of the change in gravitational potential energy involved into electrical energy by (without incurring the well-founded wrath of people for destroying this beautiful natural treasure), how much power could you produce? If you sold this power at $0.06 per kilowatt-hour, what would be your annual gross income?

C12S.6 A 1.0-kg cart with frictionless wheels moving along the $+x$ axis at an initial speed of 1.5 m/s collides elastically with another cart of mass 0.75 kg moving in the $-x$ direction with a speed of 2.0 m/s. If the carts continue to move along the x axis after the collision, what are their x-velocities afterward?

C12S.7 A 7.2-kg bowling ball traveling at a speed of 3.5 m/s collides with a 1.2-kg bowling pin at rest. After the collision, the pin moves with a speed of 3.0 m/s at an angle of 60° with respect to the original direction of motion of the bowling ball. What is the final velocity of the ball (magnitude and direction)? Is the collision approximately elastic?

C12S.8 A 7.2-kg bowling ball traveling at a speed of 3.5 m/s collides elastically with a 1.2-kg bowling pin at rest. After the collision, the pin moves an angle of 30° with respect to the original direction of motion of the bowling ball. What are the final speeds of both the ball and the pin after the collision?

C12S.9 A 230-g hockey puck originally sliding on ice in the $+x$ direction with a speed of 0.50 m/s collides with another puck of equal mass at rest. After the collision, the first puck is seen to move with a speed of 0.20 m/s in a line that makes an angle of 37° with the x axis ($\cos 37° \approx \frac{4}{5}$, $\sin 37° \approx \frac{3}{5}$). What is the velocity of the other puck? Is this collision approximately elastic?

C12S.10 In a certain physics experiment, a helium atom traveling at a speed of 240 km/s hits an oxygen atom at rest. If the helium atom rebounds elastically from the oxygen atom at an angle of 90° with respect to its original direction of motion, what are the final velocities of both atoms (magnitude and direction)? (*Hint:* The mass of the oxygen atom ≈ 4 times that of the helium atom.)

C12S.11 Prove that after a two-dimensional elastic collision between a moving object and an identical object at rest, the objects' final velocities are *always* perpendicular. (*Hint:* Use the results of example C12.4 and remember the dot product.)

C12S.12 One of the consequences of an asteroid impact not discussed in section C12.6 was the water that would be vaporized and/or lofted into the atmosphere as a result of the impact. Consider the impact described in that section.

(a) Computer simulations suggest that for large-energy impacts like this one, water having about 3 times the mass of the asteroid is essentially instantly vaporized in an ocean impact. What fraction of the asteroid's energy does the energy required to do this represent?

(b) An amount of water equal to about 30 times the mass of the asteroid will simply be splashed into the stratosphere above about 15 km. Roughly what fraction of the impact energy does this represent?

(c) The stratosphere is currently very dry, holding only something like 3×10^{12} kg of water total, and it is estimated that the stratosphere simply cannot hold more than about 250 times this mass (the water will simply precipitate out). Does the amount of water vaporized and splashed into the stratosphere by the impact exceed this limit? Explain.

(d) If the ocean where the asteroid hits is shallow, the crater rim might be high enough to exclude the ocean. If it is not, or if cracks form quickly that let water in, then the ocean will boil over the hot spot at the center of the crater for months. If this boiled water ends up carrying away 10% of the impact's energy, how much water is boiled? How does this amount compare to the total amount of water currently in all parts of the atmosphere (about 10^{16} kg)?

Closing comments: It is not completely clear what the effect of adding all this water to the atmosphere would be. Adding huge amounts of water to the lower atmosphere will clearly cause unbelievable precipitation, leading to floods, tremendous storms, and so on. Water is also a very potent greenhouse gas, so the water injected into the stratosphere may cause significant greenhouse warming once the dust dissipates. On the other hand, the formation of ice crystals in the upper atmosphere might reflect sunlight to space, leading to cooling. Either way, significant effects on the earth's climate are projected to last for decades after the impact.

Rich-Context

C12R.1 On an icy road one day, a car with mass m (car A) traveling due east hits another car of mass $2m$ (car B) in the center of an intersection. After the accident, marks in the ice show that car A skidded at an angle of 60° south of east, while car B skidded at an angle of 60° north of east. The driver of car A claims in court to have been traveling the speed limit of 40 mi/h, but car B ran the stoplight and was moving northward at 20 mi/h at the time of the accident. The driver of car B does not dispute that car A was traveling at 40 mi/h but claims that car B was stalled in the center of the intersection at the time of the accident, so car A should have had plenty of time to stop. You are the judge. Which story is more consistent with the physical facts?

(*Hints:* Can this collision be superelastic? It also may help you to know that $\cos 60° = \frac{1}{2}$, $\sin 60° = \frac{\sqrt{3}}{2}$. Plug these into the equations as *fractions*, not their decimal equivalents!)

C12R.2 Everyone knows that bullets bounce off Superman's chest. If bad guys shoot 180 rounds per minute of 3-g bullets with a speed of 620 m/s, will the average force exerted by this stream of bullets require superstrength to resist, or could an ordinary person (with a similarly impervious chest) resist being bowled over? (*Hint:* Remember

that $\vec{F} = [d\vec{p}]/dt$.)(Adapted from D. Halliday, and R. Resnick, *Fundamentals of Physics*, 3/e, New York: Wiley, 1988.)

Advanced

C12A.1 In the situation described in problem C12R.1, find the *range* of northward speeds that car *B* might have had before the collision that would be consistent with the physical evidence and the idea that the collision should be inelastic.

ANSWERS TO EXERCISES

C12X.1 This problem simply involves a unit conversion:

$$1\,\text{kW·h} = 1\,\text{kW·h}\left(\frac{1000\,\text{W}}{1\,\text{kW}}\right)\left(\frac{60\,\text{min}}{1\,\text{h}}\right)\left(\frac{60\,\text{s}}{1\,\text{min}}\right)$$
$$\times\left(\frac{1\,\text{J/s}}{1\,\text{W}}\right)\left(\frac{1\,\text{MJ}}{10^6\,\text{J}}\right)$$
$$= 3.6\,\text{MJ} \qquad\qquad (\text{C12.37})$$

C12X.2 Leaving a 100-W lamp on overnight ($\approx$ 8 h) consumes about (0.1 kW)(8 h) = 0.8 kWh, which costs about 10¢ in southern California. If you do this for 30 days, though, the cost is about $3.00.

C12X.3 Plugging $v_{Ax} = (b-1)v_0/(b+1)$ and $v_{Bx} = 2bv_0/(1+b)$ into the right side of the top line of equation C12.8 and using the fact that $m_B = m_A/b$ yield

$$m_A\left(\frac{b-1}{b+1}\right)v_0 + \frac{m_A}{b}\left(\frac{2b}{b+1}\right)v_0$$
$$= m_A v_0\left(\frac{b-1+2}{b+1}\right) = m_A v_0 \qquad (\text{C12.38})$$

in agreement with the left side of that equation. Plugging these results into the right side of equation C12.9 yields

$$\frac{1}{2}m_A\left(\frac{b-1}{b+1}v_0\right)^2 + \frac{1}{2}\frac{m_A}{b}\left(\frac{2b}{b+1}\right)^2$$
$$= \frac{1}{2}m_A v_0^2\left[\frac{(b-1)^2 + 4b}{(b+1)^2}\right]$$
$$= \frac{1}{2}m_A v_0^2\left(\frac{b^2 - 2b + 1 + 4b}{b^2 + 2b + 1}\right)$$
$$= \frac{1}{2}m_A v_0^2\left(\frac{b^2 + 2b + 1}{b^2 + 2b + 1}\right) = \frac{1}{2}m_A v_0^2 \qquad (\text{C12.39})$$

which is again consistent with the right side. So both equations are indeed satisfied.

C12X.4 In figure C3.3, the carts have equal mass, so $b = 1$. Therefore equations C12.12 and C12.13 predict that the final x-velocities in an elastic collision would be

$$v_{Ax} = \frac{b-1}{b+1}v_0 = \frac{1-1}{1+1}v_0 = 0$$
$$v_{Bx} = \frac{2bv_0}{b+1} = \frac{2(1)}{1+1}v_0 = +v_0 \qquad (\text{C12.40})$$

consistent with what is shown in figure C3.3b. In figure C3.4, $m_A = 2m$, and $m_B = m$, so $b = 2$. Equations C12.12 and C12.13 then predict that

$$v_{Ax} = \frac{2-1}{2+1}v_0 = +\frac{1}{3}v_0 \qquad v_{Bx} = \frac{2(2)}{2+1}v_0 = +\frac{4}{3}v_0 \qquad (\text{C12.41})$$

C12X.5 If we plug $v_{Ax} = v_{Bx}$, $m_A = m$, and $m_B = 2m$ into equation C12.8, we get

$$mv_0 = mv_{Ax} + 2mv_{Ax} = 3mv_{Ax}$$
$$\Rightarrow \quad v_0 = 3v_{Ax} \quad \Rightarrow \quad v_{Ax} = +\tfrac{1}{3}v_0 \qquad (\text{C12.42})$$

Since $v_{Ax} = v_{Bx}$, $v_{Bx} = \frac{1}{3}v_0$ also. Since the massive cart has been accelerated from rest to a speed of $\frac{1}{3}v_0$, its change in momentum (and thus the momentum that has been transferred in the collision) is indeed $(2m)\frac{1}{3}v_0 = \frac{2}{3}mv_0$. The system's final total kinetic energy is

$$\tfrac{1}{2}mv_{Ax}^2 + \tfrac{1}{2}(2m)v_{Bx}^2$$
$$= \tfrac{3}{2}mv_{Ax}^2 = \tfrac{3}{2}m\left(\tfrac{1}{3}v_0\right)^2$$
$$= \tfrac{3}{2}\tfrac{1}{9}mv_0^2 = \tfrac{1}{3}\left(\tfrac{1}{2}mv_0^2\right) \qquad (\text{C12.43})$$

Since the system's initial kinetic energy was $\frac{1}{2}mv_0^2$, we see that the system lost two-thirds of its kinetic energy in this collision.

C12X.6 If we plug equations C12.25a and C12.25b into equation C12.25c, we get

$$bv_0^2 + v_{P0}^2 = bv^2 + (v_{P0} - bv)^2 + b^2 v_0^2$$
$$= bv^2 + v_{P0}^2 - 2bv_{P0}v + b^2 v^2 + b^2 v_0^2 \tag{C12.44}$$

Canceling the v_{P0}^2 term and moving the bv_0^2 term to the right side, we get

$$0 = (b + b^2)v^2 - 2bv_{P0}v + (b^2 - b)v_0^2 \tag{C12.45}$$

Dividing both sides by b and pulling the minus sign out in front of the last term yield equation C12.26.

C12X.7 In an arbitrary three-dimensional collision, if we know the objects' initial velocities and masses, we only have three unknowns: the three components of the objects' common final velocity. The three components of the conservation of momentum equation provide three equations for these three unknowns, so we can always solve.

C12X.8 Let the mass of the asteroid be m, its initial speed be v_0, the final speed of the asteroid-earth combination be v_f, and the combination's total mass ($\approx$ the mass of the earth) be M. Assuming that the earth is initially at rest in our frame, conservation of momentum implies that

$$mv_0 = Mv_f \quad \Rightarrow \quad v_f = \frac{m}{M}v_0 \tag{C12.46}$$

Therefore, the ratio of the final kinetic energy to the asteroid's initial kinetic energy is

$$\frac{\frac{1}{2}Mv_f^2}{\frac{1}{2}mv_0^2} = \frac{M(mv_0/M)^2}{mv_0^2} = \frac{Mm^2v_0^2}{mM^2v_0^2} = \frac{m}{M}$$
$$\approx \frac{10^{15} \text{ kg}}{6 \times 10^{26} \text{ kg}} = 1.7 \times 10^{-12} \tag{C12.47}$$

C12X.9 Since $g \approx 10$ N/kg, the change in the gravitational potential energy associated with the interaction between this rock and the earth at the peak of the rock's trajectory (where its kinetic energy would be zero if it were lofted vertically) is about

$$\Delta V = mg(z_f - z_i)$$
$$= (10^{17} \text{ kg})(10 \text{ N/kg})(30{,}000 \text{ m} - 0)$$
$$= 3 \times 10^{22} \text{ J} \tag{C12.48}$$

This is indeed about 15% of the impact energy.

C12X.10 The surface area of the earth is $4\pi R_e^2$, where R_e is the earth's radius = 6380 km. If one-quarter of the energy in equation C12.36 is evenly distributed over this area during a period of 3000 s, the average power received per square meter is

$$\frac{P}{A} = \frac{0.8 \times 10^{22} \text{ J}}{(3000 \text{ s})4\pi(6{,}380{,}000 \text{ m})^2}\left(\frac{1 \text{ W}}{1 \text{ J/s}}\right)$$
$$= 5200 \frac{\text{W}}{\text{m}^2} \tag{C12.49}$$

C13 Angular Momentum

▷ **Introduction**

▷ **Conservation of Momentum**

▷ **Conservation of Energy**

▽ **Conservation of Angular Momentum**

　　Introduction to Angular Momentum

　　Conservation of Angular Momentum

Chapter Overview

Introduction

This chapter launches a two-chapter subsection about conservation of angular momentum by discussing how we can calculate the angular momenta of particles and extended objects, and by defining the *twirl* and *torque* exerted by an interaction. (The latter idea will be important in chapter N5 as well.)

Section C13.1: The Case of the Rotating Person

An empirical examination of the rotation rate of a person on a frictionless rotating stool implies that a quantity that is different than rotational kinetic energy is conserved: we call the new conserved quantity *angular momentum*.

Section C13.2: The Cross Product

We will find it easiest to describe a particle's angular momentum in terms of a new kind of vector product. We define the **cross product** $\vec{u} \times \vec{w}$ of two arbitrary vectors $\vec{u}$ and $\vec{w}$ to be a *vector* quantity whose *magnitude* is

$$\mathrm{mag}(\vec{u} \times \vec{w}) = uw \sin\theta = w_\perp u = u_\perp w \tag{C13.1}$$

where $u \equiv \mathrm{mag}(\vec{u})$, $w \equiv \mathrm{mag}(\vec{w})$, θ is the angle between the directions of $\vec{u}$ and $\vec{w}$, $u_\perp$ is the magnitude of the component vector of $\vec{u}$ that is perpendicular to $\vec{w}$, and $w_\perp$ is the magnitude of the component vector of $\vec{w}$ perpendicular to $\vec{u}$. The direction of $\vec{u} \times \vec{w}$ is perpendicular to both $\vec{u}$ and $\vec{w}$ in the direction of one's right thumb when one's right finger and long finger point in the directions of $\vec{u}$ and $\vec{w}$. See table C13.1 for a list of properties of the cross product.

Section C13.3: The Angular Momentum of a Particle

We define a particle's **angular momentum** as follows:

$$\vec{L} \equiv \vec{r} \times \vec{p} = \vec{r} \times m\vec{v} \tag{C13.6}$$

Purpose: This equation defines a particle's angular momentum $\vec{L}$ around some point O.

Symbols: $\vec{r}$ is the particle's position relative to O, m is its mass, $\vec{v}$ is its velocity, and $\vec{p}$ is its (linear) momentum.

Limitations: Technically, this equation only applies to particles (but see section C13.5).

Note: This quantity has SI units of kilograms times meters squared, divided by seconds ($\mathrm{kg \cdot m^2/s}$).

The angular momentum of a particle moving at a constant velocity is conserved around *any* reference point O. The magnitude and direction of a system's angular momentum depends on one's choice of O, but the conservation of $\vec{L}$ does not.

Section C13.4: The Angular Momentum of a Rigid Object

This section argues that the total angular momentum of a symmetric rigid object rotating around its center of mass is

$$\vec{L} = I\vec{\omega} \qquad \text{(C13.13)}$$

Purpose: This equation describes how an extended object's angular momentum $\vec{L}$ around its center of mass is related to its angular velocity $\vec{\omega}$ of rotation around an axis through its center of mass.

Symbols: I is the object's moment of inertia for rotations around the axis specified by $\vec{\omega}$.

Limitations: The object must be **symmetric** for rotations around that axis: for every particle on one side of the axis, there must be another of the same mass the same distance directly across the axis.

Note: This equation is directly analogous to $\vec{p} = m\vec{v}$.

Section C13.5: The Angular Momentum of a Moving Object

This section proves that if an extended object is both moving and rotating around its center of mass, then its total angular momentum around a given point O is simply

$$\vec{L} = \vec{L}^{\text{cm}} + \vec{L}^{\text{rot}} \qquad \text{(C13.14)}$$

where $\vec{L}^{\text{rot}}$ is the object's **rotational angular momentum** around its own center of mass (computed as if it were at rest) and $\vec{L}^{\text{cm}}$ is its **translational angular momentum** around O due to the motion of its center of mass around the point O (computed as if the object were a particle located at its center of mass).

Section C13.6: Twirl and Torque

We will call an interaction's contribution to an object's total angular momentum during a short time interval dt the **twirl** $[d\vec{L}]$ that the interaction delivers. The total change in an object's angular momentum during dt is the sum of all the twirls it gets from various interactions. **Torque** is the *rate* at which an interaction delivers twirl:

$$\vec{\tau} \equiv \frac{[d\vec{L}]}{dt} \qquad \text{(C13.22)}$$

$$\frac{d\vec{L}}{dt} = \frac{[d\vec{L}]_A}{dt} + \frac{[d\vec{L}]_B}{dt} + \cdots = \vec{\tau}_A + \vec{\tau}_B + \cdots \qquad \text{(C13.23)}$$

Purpose: This equation defines the torque $\vec{\tau}$ that an interaction exerts and how the torques exerted by all interactions affect an object's angular momentum.

Symbols: $[d\vec{L}]_A, [d\vec{L}]_B, \ldots$ are the tiny twirls that interactions $A, B, \ldots$ deliver to an object during a very short time interval dt; $\vec{\tau}_A, \vec{\tau}_B, \ldots$ are the torques exerted by those interactions; and $d\vec{L}$ is the object's change in angular momentum during that interval.

Limitations: The time interval dt must be so brief that $\vec{\tau}$ is approximately constant during the interval.

Note that twirl and torque are to angular momentum what impulse and force are to linear momentum and k-work and power are to energy.

If an interaction exerts a force $\vec{F}$ on an object at a well-defined position $\vec{r}$ relative to the reference point O, then the interaction exerts a torque

$$\vec{\tau} = \vec{r} \times \vec{F} \qquad \text{(C13.28)}$$

on that object.

C13.1   The Case of the Rotating Person

The experiment

Consider the following experiment. A person sits on a stool that is free to rotate about a vertical axis. The person holds a weight in each hand with arms outstretched, as shown in figure C13.1a. If we set the person rotating (and the stool's bearings are almost frictionless), the person will rotate essentially indefinitely with the same angular velocity $\vec{\omega}$. The system consisting of the person, the weights, and the stool is therefore functionally isolated for rotational motion in the same way that a system of gliders on a level air track is functionally isolated for linear motion.

Imagine now that the person draws in the weights to his or her lap, as shown in figure C13.1b. If you have ever seen this situation demonstrated, you know that the person's rate of rotation increases dramatically. If the person then holds the weights again at arm's length, the person's original rotation rate is restored.

It is plausible that *something* is being conserved here: the person's angular velocity $\vec{\omega}$ does not change with time if the person does not change the position of the weights, and though moving the weights does change $\vec{\omega}$, the person can restore the original $\vec{\omega}$ simply by restoring the weights to their initial position. But what quantity is being conserved?

Could the conserved quantity be rotational kinetic energy?

It is *possible* that the quantity conserved in this experiment is the system's rotational kinetic energy $K^{\text{rot}} = \frac{1}{2} I \omega^2$, where I is the system's moment of inertia. Note that $I \equiv \sum m_i r_i^2$, where m_i is the mass of the ith particle in the system, r_i is its distance from the axis of rotation, and the sum is taken over all particles in the system. Therefore, drawing in the weights makes their particles closer to the axis of rotation, making I smaller. Restoring the weights to their former position restores I to its original value. So if K^{rot} were conserved, making I smaller would require ω to become larger, as we observe in this experiment.

We can in fact make a quantitative prediction about how ω varies with I if rotational kinetic energy is conserved. Let the system's initial and final moments of inertia (with the weights extended and pulled in, respectively) be I_0 and I, respectively. Let the system's corresponding angular speeds be ω_0 and ω, respectively. Conservation of rotational kinetic energy then

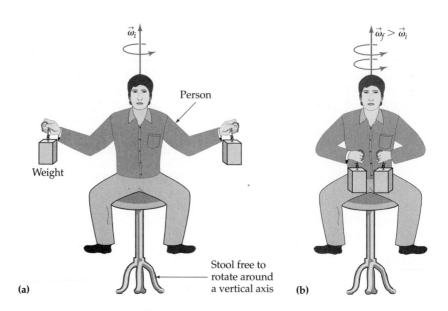

Figure C13.1

(a) A person on a stool that is free to rotate about a vertical axis rotates slowly about an axis while holding two weights with extended arms. (b) If the person now draws the weights in closer to the axis of rotation, the person's angular velocity increases dramatically in magnitude.

requires that

$$K^{\text{rot}} = \frac{1}{2}I_0\omega_0^2 = \frac{1}{2}I\omega^2 \quad \Rightarrow \quad \frac{I}{I_0} = \frac{\omega_0^2}{\omega^2} \quad \Rightarrow \quad \frac{\omega}{\omega_0} = \sqrt{\frac{I_0}{I}} \quad \text{(C13.1)}$$

To put this another way, the system's angular speed ω should be proportional to the inverse square root of its moment of inertia I.

However, if we actually *measure* moments of inertia and angular speeds in this situation, we find that the angular speed increases more rapidly than this equation would predict, more as I^{-1} instead of $I^{-1/2}$. Therefore, *the system's rotational kinetic energy is not conserved in this experiment!*

This model fails!

This is not a disaster, because the system's *total* energy of the system can still be conserved. In fact, it turns out that the person converts chemical energy to rotational kinetic energy when hauling in the weights, and letting the weights out again converts this rotational kinetic energy to thermal energy. What this experiment makes clear, though, is that if something is conserved in this experiment, it is *not* rotational kinetic energy.

The conserved quantity here is called *angular momentum*. At the deepest level, conservation of angular momentum is a consequence of the symmetry principle stating that the laws of physics are independent of one's orientation in space. We will be exploring this important conservation law in this chapter and in chapter C14. This chapter will focus on the definitions of angular momentum and associated quantities, while chapter C14 focuses on applications of conservation of angular momentum.

C13.2   The Cross Product

When we set out to define momentum in chapter C3 and energy in chapter C6, we found it easiest to start by defining these quantities for simple particles before trying to work with extended objects. I will follow the same approach here. Moreover, just as we found it convenient to express k-work in terms of the dot product of vectors, we can most conveniently express a particle's angular momentum in terms using a mathematical tool called the *cross product* of two vectors.

The **cross product** $\vec{u} \times \vec{w}$ of two arbitrary vectors $\vec{u}$ and $\vec{w}$ is defined to be a *vector* whose magnitude is

$$\text{mag}(\vec{u} \times \vec{w}) = uw \sin\theta \quad \text{(C13.1a)}$$

where $u \equiv \text{mag}(\vec{u})$, $w \equiv \text{mag}(\vec{w})$, and θ is the angle measured from the direction of $\vec{u}$ to the direction of $\vec{w}$. (Note that $\vec{w}$ is just an arbitrary vector here. Please don't confuse it with an object's angular velocity $\vec{\omega}$: note that ω is the Greek letter *omega*, not the Latin letter w.)

As figure C13.2 shows, we can consider $\vec{u}$ to be a sum of two component vectors $\vec{u}_\parallel$ and $\vec{u}_\perp$ parallel and perpendicular to $\vec{w}$, respectively. Similarly, we

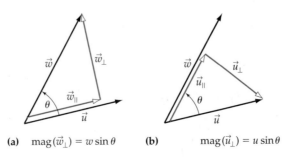

(a) $\text{mag}(\vec{w}_\perp) = w \sin\theta$ **(b)** $\text{mag}(\vec{u}_\perp) = u \sin\theta$

Figure C13.2
We can think of the magnitude of $\vec{u} \times \vec{w}$ as being either $uw_\perp$ or $u_\perp w$, where $w_\perp = \text{mag}(\vec{w}_\perp)$ and $u_\perp = \text{mag}(\vec{u}_\perp)$.

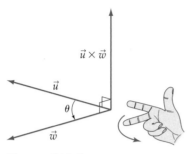

Figure C13.3
The right-hand rule that defines the direction of $\vec{u} \times \vec{w}$.

Mathematical properties of the cross product

can consider $\vec{w}$ to be a sum of component vectors $\vec{w}_\parallel$ and $\vec{w}_\perp$ parallel and perpendicular to $\vec{u}$. The figure shows that we can interpret the magnitude of the cross product as being either the magnitude of $\vec{u}$ times the magnitude of $\vec{w}_\perp$, or vice versa:

$$\text{mag}(\vec{u} \times \vec{w}) = u_\perp w = w_\perp u \qquad \text{(C13.1b)}$$

where $u_\perp \equiv \text{mag}(\vec{u}_\perp)$ and $w_\perp \equiv \text{mag}(\vec{w}_\perp)$.

Unlike the dot product (which is a *scalar*), the cross product of two vectors is a *vector*. The direction of $\vec{u} \times \vec{w}$ is defined to be perpendicular to both $\vec{u}$ and $\vec{w}$ in the sense defined by the following right-hand rule: if you point your right index finger in the direction of $\vec{u}$ and your second finger in the direction of $\vec{w}$, your thumb points in the direction of the cross product, as illustrated in figure C13.3.

Note that the definition of the direction of the cross product implies that

$$\vec{u} \times \vec{w} = -\vec{w} \times \vec{u} \qquad \text{(C13.2)}$$

Try it! If you point your right index finger in the direction of $\vec{w}$ and your second finger in the direction of $\vec{u}$, your thumb points the opposite direction from what it does if you do it the other way round. Because the cross product of two vectors changes sign when you reverse the order of the vectors, we say that the cross product is **anticommutative.**

One can also see from the definition of the cross product that

$$(b\vec{u}) \times \vec{w} = \vec{u} \times (b\vec{w}) = b(\vec{u} \times \vec{w}) \qquad \text{(C13.3)}$$

Why? Multiplication by a *positive* scalar b changes only the *magnitude* of a vector, not its direction; so the directions of all three products will remain the same, and their magnitudes will all be $buw \sin\theta$, with b being the same in each case. Multiplication by a *negative* scalar is equivalent to multiplying by a positive scalar and then reversing the direction of the vector multiplied. You can check with your right hand that flipping either $\vec{u}$ or $\vec{w}$ flips the direction of the cross product as a whole. Thus the directions of the three products are the same even when b is negative, and the magnitudes are all equal to $|b|uw \sin\theta$.

In what follows, we will find the cross product's *distributive* property

$$\vec{u} \times (\vec{w} + \vec{q}) = \vec{u} \times \vec{w} + \vec{u} \times \vec{q} \qquad \text{(C13.4)}$$

very useful. This property also follows directly from the definition, although its proof is more difficult than the others. (The proof from equation C13.5 below is not so bad; see problem C13A.1).

Exercise C13X.1

The hour and minute hands on a clock are 8 cm and 10 cm long, respectively. Let $\vec{u}$ be the displacement vector from base to tip of the hour hand, and let $\vec{w}$ be the displacement vector from base to tip of the minute hand. At exactly 10 o'clock, what are the magnitude and direction of $\vec{u} \times \vec{w}$?

The cross product in terms of vector components

The cross product in component form is as follows:

$$\text{If} \qquad \vec{q} = \vec{u} \times \vec{w} \qquad \text{then} \qquad \begin{bmatrix} q_x \\ q_y \\ q_z \end{bmatrix} = \begin{bmatrix} u_y w_z - u_z w_y \\ u_z w_x - u_x w_z \\ u_x w_y - u_y w_x \end{bmatrix} \qquad \text{(C13.5)}$$

By breaking up $\vec{u}$ and $\vec{w}$ into component vectors, one can show that this follows directly from the definition of the cross product and its distributive and linear properties.

How to remember this formula

This formula looks horribly complicated, but there is a very simple way to remember it. First, note that all three rows of equation C13.5 have the same basic form: a component of the cross product is equal to a product of a component of $\vec{u}$ times a component of $\vec{w}$ minus another such product. Consider the circle in figure C13.4, which has the subscripts x, y, z arranged in alphabetical order clockwise around the circle. Note that in each line, the subscripts of q and the components of $\vec{u}$ and $\vec{w}$ in the *first* product follow the order in which they appear as you go *clockwise* around the circle; and the subscripts of q and the components of $\vec{u}$ and $\vec{w}$ in the *second* product follow the order in which the subscripts appear as you go *counterclockwise* around the circle. For example, in the second line of equation C13.5, the subscript on the q is y. We thus find the subscripts for the first product of $\vec{u}$ and $\vec{w}$ components by going clockwise around the circle from y: the subscripts are z and x, and so the first product is $u_z w_x$. We find the subscripts for the second product by going counterclockwise from y: the subscripts are x and z, so the second product is $u_x w_z$. You can check for yourself that this mnemonic trick works for the other two lines as well.

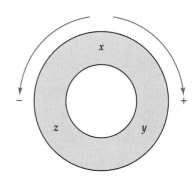

Figure C13.4
A memory aid for equation C13.5.

Exercise C13X.2

Two displacement vectors $\vec{u}$ and $\vec{w}$ have components given by $\vec{u} = [3\text{ m},\ -2\text{ m},\ 0\text{ m}]$ and $\vec{w} = [-2\text{ m},\ 5\text{ m},\ 0\text{ m}]$. What are the components of $\vec{u} \times \vec{w}$? Does the direction of your result make sense, considering that both $\vec{u}$ and $\vec{w}$ happen to lie in the xy plane in this case?

Table C13.1 summarizes the definition and properties of the cross product (and compares them with those of the dot product).

Table C13.1   A comparison of the properties of the dot and cross products

	Dot Product	Cross Product
Symbolic representation	$\vec{u} \cdot \vec{w}$	$\vec{u} \times \vec{w}$
Type of quantity produced	Scalar	Vector
Definition	$\vec{u} \cdot \vec{w} = uw \cos\theta$	$\text{mag}(\vec{u} \times \vec{w}) = uw \sin\theta$ Direction: $\perp$ to $\vec{u}$ and $\vec{w}$, use the right-hand rule
Product of a vector with itself	$\vec{u} \cdot \vec{u} = u^2$	$\vec{u} \times \vec{u} = 0$
Product is zero when:	Vectors are perpendicular	Vectors are parallel
Commutative or anticommutative?	$\vec{u} \cdot \vec{w} = +\vec{w} \cdot \vec{u}$	$\vec{u} \times \vec{w} = -\vec{w} \times \vec{u}$
Linear property	$(q\vec{u}) \cdot \vec{w} = \vec{u} \cdot (q\vec{w}) = q(\vec{u} \cdot \vec{w})$	$(q\vec{u}) \times \vec{w} = \vec{u} \times (q\vec{w}) = q(\vec{u} \times \vec{w})$
Distributive property	$\vec{q} \cdot (\vec{u} + \vec{w}) = \vec{q} \cdot \vec{u} + \vec{q} \cdot \vec{w}$	$\vec{q} \times (\vec{u} + \vec{w}) = \vec{q} \times \vec{u} + \vec{q} \times \vec{w}$
Component form	$\vec{u} \cdot \vec{w} = u_x w_x + u_y w_y + u_z w_z$	$\vec{u} \times \vec{w} = \begin{bmatrix} u_y w_z - u_z w_y \\ u_z w_x - u_x w_z \\ u_x w_y - u_y w_x \end{bmatrix}$

C13.3   The Angular Momentum of a Particle

We define particle's **angular momentum** around a given point O as follows:

$$\vec{L} \equiv \vec{r} \times \vec{p} = \vec{r} \times m\vec{v} \qquad (C13.6)$$

Purpose: This equation defines a particle's angular momentum $\vec{L}$ around some point O.
Symbols: $\vec{r}$ is the particle's position relative to O, m is its mass, $\vec{v}$ is its velocity, and $\vec{p}$ is its (linear) momentum.
Limitations: Technically, this equation only applies to particles (but see section C13.5).
Note: This quantity has SI units of kilograms times meters squared, divided by seconds (kg·m²/s).

Definition of a particle's angular momentum

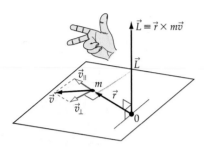

Figure C13.5
The definition of a particle's angular momentum about a point O. Note that $\text{mag}(\vec{L}) = mrv_\perp$.

Note, as shown in figure C13.5, that we can consider a particle's velocity $\vec{v}$ to be a sum of two component vectors $\vec{v}_\parallel$ and $\vec{v}_\perp$ parallel to and perpendicular to $\vec{r}$, respectively. According to equation C13.1b, the magnitude of $\vec{L}$ is

$$L \equiv \text{mag}(\vec{L}) = mrv_\perp \qquad (C13.7)$$

where $v_\perp \equiv \text{mag}(\vec{v}_\perp)$. Thus the magnitude of $\vec{L}$ depends on the particle's mass, the distance it is from point O, and the component of its velocity that causes it to go "around" O (as opposed to directly toward or away from O).

The angular momentum of a particle moving in a circle

Indeed, if the particle happens to be moving in a *circle* of radius r around O, the distance between the particle and O does not change, so the particle's velocity component vector $\vec{v}_\parallel$ parallel to $\vec{r}$ is zero and $v_\perp$ is equal to the particle's speed. According to equation C9.4, the particle's speed under these circumstances is $v = r\omega$, where ω is its angular speed. Therefore, equation C13.7 thus tells us that the magnitude of the particle's angular momentum is $L = mr(r\omega) = mr^2\omega$. Moreover, you can see from figure C13.5 that the particle's angular momentum $\vec{L}$ around O points along the axis of the particle's rotation around O in the direction indicated by your right thumb if you curl your fingers in the direction of the rotation, which is the *same* way that we defined the direction of the particle's angular velocity $\vec{\omega}$ in chapter C9. Therefore, in the case of circular motion around O, we can write a particle's angular momentum as follows:

$$\vec{L} = mr^2\vec{\omega} \qquad \text{for a particle in circular motion} \qquad (C13.8)$$

The angular momentum of an isolated particle is conserved

We will find this result helpful in section C13.4.

Consider now an isolated particle moving through space. If the particle is truly isolated from all interactions, it will move at a constant velocity $\vec{v}$ in a straight line. Consider an arbitrary point O that is a distance $r_{\min}$ from the closest point on this line, as shown in figure C13.6. What is the particle's angular momentum as a function of time?

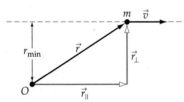

Figure C13.6
A particle moving at a constant velocity in a straight line that passes a distance $r_{\min}$ from point O has a constant angular momentum of magnitude $L = mr_{\min}v$ about that point.

In this case, it is helpful to consider the particle's position $\vec{r}$ relative to O to be the sum of two component vectors $\vec{r}_\parallel$ and $\vec{r}_\perp$ parallel to and perpendicular to its velocity $\vec{v}$, respectively. According to equation C13.1b, the magnitude of the particle's angular momentum is

$$L \equiv \text{mag}(\vec{L}) = mr_\perp v \qquad (C13.9)$$

But as the diagram shows, $r_\perp \equiv \text{mag}(\vec{r}_\perp)$ is the same as $r_{\min}$, which is a fixed number. Moreover, $\vec{L}$ has a fixed direction (perpendicular to the plane containing $\vec{r}$ and $\vec{v}$, directly away from the viewer in figure C13.6). We see, therefore, that the angular momentum $\vec{L}$ of an isolated particle around *any* point O

is a conserved quantity, just as the particle's momentum and kinetic energy are conserved. This is an encouraging sign that our definition of $\vec{L}$ is correct.

It is important to note that a particle's angular momentum depends not only on the particle's mass and velocity, but also on its position vector $\vec{r}$ relative to some origin O. The magnitude and direction of the particle's angular momentum therefore *depend on the choice of O*. (You may have noticed how I keep saying "the particle's angular momentum *about O*" as a way of emphasizing this.) As a consequence, we must be sure to specify the location of O whenever we work with angular momentum.

However, the argument regarding the isolated particle indicates while the *value* of $\vec{L}$ is different for different choices of O, the fact that it is *conserved* for an isolated particle does *not* depend on our choice of O. We will see that this extends to systems of particles as well. Therefore, while it is crucial when you are doing an angular momentum problem to specify what O you are using (and then use that O *consistently* throughout the problem), you have a great deal of freedom at the beginning of a problem to choose a location for O that makes solving the problem easier.

The *value* of a particle's $\vec{L}$ depends on one's choice of O, but conservation of angular momentum does not

---

Exercise C13X.3

A 0.5-kg particle is moving once every 2.0 s around a circle with radius 2.0 m. What is the magnitude of its angular momentum?

Exercise C13X.4

At a given instant of time, a 2.0-kg particle is 3.0 m away from a point O in the $+y$ direction and is moving with a velocity whose x, y, and z components are [0, 3 m/s, 4 m/s]. What are the magnitude and direction of the particle's angular momentum around O at that instant?

C13.4   The Angular Momentum of a Rigid Object

Consider now a rigid object whose center of mass is at rest and which is rotating about a certain fixed axis with angular velocity $\vec{\omega}$. We'd like to be able to calculate this object's total angular momentum around its center of mass (which, for a variety of reasons, ends up being a good choice for O).

Let's focus on a single particle of mass m at an arbitrary position $\vec{r}$ relative to O. As shown in figure C13.7a, we can consider $\vec{r}$ to be the sum of component vectors $\vec{r}_\parallel$ and $\vec{r}_\perp$ parallel and perpendicular to $\vec{\omega}$, respectively. (Please note that we are defining these component vectors relative to the

The angular momentum of a particle in a rotating object

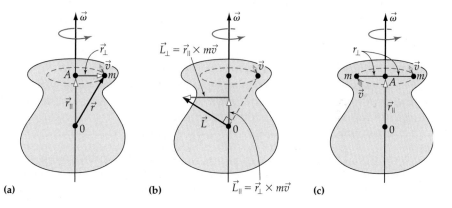

(a)   (b)   (c)

Figure C13.7
Vectors associated with a symmetric rotating object.

direction of $\vec{\omega}$, not $\vec{v}$, as we did in section C13.3.) According to the associative rule of the cross product, the particle's angular momentum around the center of mass is

$$\vec{L} \equiv \vec{r} \times m\vec{v} = (\vec{r}_\parallel + \vec{r}_\perp) \times m\vec{v} = \vec{r}_\parallel \times m\vec{v} + \vec{r}_\perp \times m\vec{v}$$

$$\Rightarrow \quad \vec{L} = \vec{L}_\perp + \vec{L}_\parallel \quad \text{where} \quad \vec{L}_\perp \equiv \vec{r}_\parallel \times m\vec{v} \quad \text{and} \quad \vec{L}_\parallel \equiv \vec{r}_\perp \times m\vec{v} \tag{C13.10}$$

It looks as if I have the subscripts backward on $\vec{L}_\perp$ and $\vec{L}_\parallel$, but if you apply the right-hand rule for the cross product, you will see that $\vec{L}_\perp \equiv \vec{r}_\parallel \times m\vec{v}$ is indeed a vector *perpendicular* to the angular velocity $\vec{\omega}$, while $\vec{L}_\parallel \equiv \vec{r}_\perp \times m\vec{v}$ points in the *same direction* as $\vec{\omega}$ (see figure C13.7b). Indeed, since $\vec{r}_\perp$ is the particle's position relative to the closest point on the axis of rotation (point A in figure C13.7a), and since the particle travels in a circular path of radius $r_\perp = \text{mag}(\vec{r}_\perp)$ around this point as the object rotates, equation C13.8 implies that

$$\vec{L}_\parallel = mr_\perp^2 \vec{\omega} \tag{C13.11}$$

Because $mr_\perp^2 \geq 0$ always, this can never be opposite to $\vec{\omega}$.

The total angular momentum of a symmetric object

The object's *total* angular momentum is simply the sum of the angular momenta of its particles. We can see that *in general*, the object's total angular momentum about its center of mass will have components both perpendicular and parallel to $\vec{\omega}$. However, let's additionally assume that the object is **symmetric** about the axis of rotation in the sense that for every particle in the object, there is a corresponding particle with the same mass that is the same distance $r_\perp$ directly across the rotation axis, as shown in figure C13.7c. Since $\vec{r}_\parallel$ is the same for both particles but their velocities $\vec{v}$ are equal in magnitude but opposite in direction, their angular momentum component vectors $\vec{L}_\perp \equiv \vec{r}_\parallel \times m\vec{v}$ will *also* be equal in magnitude but opposite in direction, implying that they will cancel when added. So if the object is *symmetric* around the axis of rotation, the perpendicular components of the particles' angular momenta cancel in pairs, and the object's total angular momentum ends up being parallel to its angular velocity:

$$\vec{L} = \sum_{i=1}^{N} \vec{L}_{\perp,i} + \sum_{i=1}^{N} \vec{L}_{\parallel,i} = 0 + \sum_{i=1}^{N} m_i r_{\perp,i}^2 \vec{\omega} = \left(\sum_{i=1}^{N} m_i r_{\perp,i}^2 \right) \vec{\omega} \tag{C13.12}$$

where the i subscripts label values calculated for the ith particle, and N is the total number of particles. Now, the quantity in parentheses is the mass of each particle times its squared distance from the axis of rotation, summed over all particles. As we saw in chapter C9, this is the definition of the object's moment of inertia I. Therefore, the angular momentum of a symmetric object is simply

$$\vec{L} = I\vec{\omega} \tag{C13.13}$$

Purpose: This equation describes how an extended object's angular momentum $\vec{L}$ is related to its angular velocity $\vec{\omega}$.

Symbols: I is the object's moment of inertia for rotations about the axis specified by $\vec{\omega}$.

Limitations: The object must be symmetric for rotations around that axis: for every particle on one side of the axis, there must be another of the same mass directly across the axis.

Note that if the object is *not* symmetric, the off-axis components of the angular momenta of its particles will *not* generally cancel, and the object's total $\vec{L}$ is *not* generally parallel to the object's angular velocity $\vec{\omega}$! This case has some very interesting consequences that are often explored in a sophomore- or junior-level course in classical mechanics. In such courses, one learns how to redefine I as a *matrix* to make equation C13.13 work in all cases. However, we will deal with only symmetric objects in this course, for which I is a simple scalar.

We saw in chapter C9 when comparing the rotational kinetic energy formula $K^{rot} = \frac{1}{2}I\omega^2$ to the translational kinetic energy formula $K = \frac{1}{2}mv^2$ that I and $\vec{\omega}$ are to rotational motion what m and $\vec{v}$ are to translational motion. We see the same pattern at work when we compare the angular momentum formula $\vec{L} = I\vec{\omega}$ to the (linear) momentum formula $\vec{p} = m\vec{v}$. An easy way to remember these formulas for rotational motion therefore is to simply remember that "I and $\vec{\omega}$ are to rotational motion what m and $\vec{v}$ are for translational motion."

Exercise C13X.5

Is a rectangular book (approximately) symmetric around an axis perpendicular to its face and going through its center of mass? Is it symmetric around an axis going diagonally from one corner to the other?

Exercise C13X.6

What is the magnitude of the angular momentum of a 5.0-kg bowling ball with a radius of 12 cm that is spinning at a rate of 5 turns per second?

C13.5   The Angular Momentum of a Moving Object

What if an object is rotating about its axis and also is moving as a whole about some reference point O? As was the case with kinetic energy, it turns out that we can divide the angular momentum of an object rotating *and* moving about any point O into the sum of two parts

$$\vec{L} = \vec{L}^{cm} + \vec{L}^{rot} \qquad (C13.14)$$

where $\vec{L}^{rot}$ is the object's **rotational angular momentum** about its own center of mass and $\vec{L}^{cm}$ is its **translational angular momentum** about O due to the motion of its center of mass around the point O (computed as if the object were a particle located at its center of mass). This means that if an object is *not* rotating about its own center of mass but is moving relative to the reference point O, we can model it as *a simple point particle*. If it *is* rotating, then we only have to add in the object's rotational momentum *computed as if it were at rest* (e.g., using equation C13.13) to find the object's total angular momentum about O. This theorem makes calculating angular momenta for extended objects in realistic situations relatively straightforward.

We can prove this fairly easily using the nice properties of the cross product. Let $\vec{r}_i$ be the position of the object's ith particle relative to O, $\vec{r}_{CM}$ be the position of the object's center of mass relative to O, and $\vec{q}_i$ be the position of the ith particle relative to the object's center of mass, all evaluated at a certain instant of time. As figure C13.8 shows, these quantities are related as follows:

$$\vec{r}_i = \vec{r}_{CM} + \vec{q}_i \qquad (C13.15)$$

If you subtract this equation from the same equation evaluated a short time dt later, and then divide by dt, you can show that equation C13.15 implies

$$\vec{v}_i = \vec{v}_{CM} + \vec{u}_i \qquad (C13.16)$$

where $\vec{v}_i$ is the ith particle's velocity relative to O, $\vec{u}_i$ is its velocity relative to

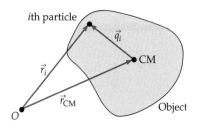

Figure C13.8
The relationship between $\vec{r}_i$, $\vec{r}_{CM}$, and $\vec{q}_i$.

A proof of this theorem

the object's center of mass, and $\vec{v}_{CM}$ is the velocity of the center of mass relative to O.

Exercise C13X.7

Verify equation C13.16.

Now, the definition of the center of mass and the fact that the object's total momentum is equal to the object's total mass M times the velocity of its center of mass state (respectively) that

$$M\vec{r}_{CM} = \sum_{i=1}^{N} m_i \vec{r}_i \quad \text{and} \quad M\vec{v}_{CM} = \sum_{i=1}^{N} m_i \vec{v}_i \qquad \text{(C13.17)}$$

Using equations C13.15, C13.16, and C13.17, you can fairly easily show that

$$0 = \sum_{i=1}^{N} m_i \vec{q}_i \quad \text{and} \quad 0 = \sum_{i=1}^{N} m_i \vec{u}_i \qquad \text{(C13.18)}$$

Exercise C13X.8

Verify equation C13.18.

Using the distributive property of the cross product, we see that the object's total angular momentum around the point O is given by

$$\vec{L} \equiv \sum_{i=1}^{N} \vec{r}_i \times m_i \vec{v}_i = \sum_{i=1}^{N} [(\vec{r}_{CM} + \vec{q}_i) \times m_i(\vec{v}_{CM} + \vec{u}_i)]$$

$$= \sum_{i=1}^{N} [\vec{r}_{CM} \times m_i \vec{v}_{CM} + \vec{r}_{CM} \times m_i \vec{u}_i + \vec{q}_i \times m_i \vec{v}_{CM} + \vec{q}_i \times m_i \vec{u}_i] \qquad \text{(C13.19)}$$

We are perfectly free to write this sum of four terms as four separate sums. In the third term, $\vec{q}_i \times m_i \vec{v}_{CM} = m_i \vec{q}_i \times \vec{v}_{CM}$ by the linear property of the cross product, and the distributive property means that we can pull out any cross-product factor that appears in all terms of any sum. So we can write this as

$$\vec{L} = \vec{r}_{CM} \times \vec{v}_{CM} \left(\sum_{i=1}^{N} m_i \right) + \vec{r}_{CM} \times \left(\sum_{i=1}^{N} m_i \vec{u}_i \right)$$

$$+ \left(\sum_{i=1}^{N} m_i \vec{q}_i \right) \times \vec{v}_{CM} + \sum_{i=1}^{N} (\vec{q}_i \times m_i \vec{u}_i) \qquad \text{(C13.20)}$$

Equations C13.18 imply that the middle two terms in this expression are zero. Since the sum over all particle masses is the object's total mass M, the first term is equivalent to $\vec{r}_{CM} \times M\vec{v}_{CM}$, which is the angular momentum of the object's center of mass about O computed as if it were a particle. The last term would be the object's angular momentum if it were only rotating about its center of mass and not moving. Therefore $\vec{L} = \vec{L}^{cm} + 0 + 0 + \vec{L}^{rot}$, as claimed.

C13.6   Twirl and Torque

Definition of twirl

An interaction between two objects can transfer angular momentum from one to the other as well as ordinary momentum. Let's call the amount of angular momentum that an interaction contributes to an object during a time interval dt the **twirl** $[d\vec{L}]$ that interaction delivers. The brackets around the dL reminds us that a twirl is just a specific interaction's *contribution* to the object's angular momentum: the actual change $d\vec{L}$ in the object's angular momentum during dt is the vector sum of the twirls $[d\vec{L}]_A, [d\vec{L}]_B, [d\vec{L}]_C, \ldots$ it receives from interactions $A, B, C, \ldots$ during that interval:

$$d\vec{L} = [d\vec{L}]_A + [d\vec{L}]_B + [d\vec{L}]_C + \cdots \qquad (C13.21)$$

Twirl $[d\vec{L}]$ is thus to angular momentum what *impulse* $[d\vec{p}]$ is to ordinary momentum and what *k-work* $[dK]$ is to kinetic energy. (There actually is no widely accepted name for this quantity, although there certainly *should* be. The name *twirl* is my invention for the purposes of this course.)

Just as *force* expresses the rate at which an interaction delivers impulse to an object and *power* expresses the rate at which it transforms energy, so **torque** $\vec{\tau}$ expresses the rate at which an interaction contributes twirl to an object:

$$\vec{\tau} \equiv \frac{[d\vec{L}]}{dt} \qquad (C13.22)$$

The definition of torque

$$\frac{d\vec{L}}{dt} = \frac{[d\vec{L}]_A}{dt} + \frac{[d\vec{L}]_B}{dt} + \cdots = \vec{\tau}_A + \vec{\tau}_B + \cdots \qquad (C13.23)$$

Purpose: This equation defines the torque $\vec{\tau}$ an interaction exerts on an object and how the torques exerted by all interactions affect the object's angular momentum.
Symbols: $[d\vec{L}]_A, [d\vec{L}]_B, \ldots$ are the tiny twirls that interactions $A, B, \ldots$ deliver to an object during a very short time interval dt; $\vec{\tau}_A, \vec{\tau}_B, \ldots$ are the torques exerted by those interactions; and $d\vec{L}$ is the object's change in angular momentum during that interval.
Limitations: The time interval dt must be so brief that $\vec{\tau}$ is approximately constant during the interval.
Note: τ is the Greek letter tau.

We can use the cross-product definition of $\vec{L}$ to express the torque on a point particle in a form that will help us develop a more intuitive understanding of the concept. Imagine that during a short interval of time dt a particle's momentum changes by $d\vec{p}$ while its position relative to our chosen reference point O changes by $d\vec{r}$. The change in the particle's angular momentum is

The torque expressed in terms of force

$$\begin{aligned} d\vec{L} &= (\vec{r} + d\vec{r}) \times (\vec{p} + d\vec{p}) - \vec{r} \times \vec{p} \\ &= (\vec{r} \times \vec{p} + \vec{r} \times d\vec{p} + d\vec{r} \times \vec{p} + d\vec{r} \times d\vec{p}) - \vec{r} \times \vec{p} \\ &= \vec{r} \times d\vec{p} + d\vec{r} \times \vec{p} + d\vec{r} \times d\vec{p} \end{aligned} \qquad (C13.24)$$

where I have used the distributive property of the cross product in the middle step. Now note that $\vec{p} = m\vec{v}$ and (as long as dt is sufficiently small) $d\vec{r} = \vec{v}\, dt$, so

$$d\vec{r} \times \vec{p} = m\, dt(\vec{v} \times \vec{v}) = 0 \qquad (C13.25)$$

since the cross product of any vector with itself is zero. Moreover, if dt is very small, then $d\vec{r} \times d\vec{p}$ will be very small compared to $\vec{r} \times d\vec{p}$. So in the small-dt limit, the change $d\vec{L}$ in the particle's angular momentum is

$$\begin{aligned} d\vec{L} &= \vec{r} \times d\vec{p} = \vec{r} \times ([d\vec{p}]_A + [d\vec{p}]_B + [d\vec{p}]_C + \cdots) \\ &= \vec{r} \times [d\vec{p}]_A + \vec{r} \times [d\vec{p}]_B + \vec{r} \times [d\vec{p}]_C + \cdots \end{aligned} \qquad (C13.26)$$

where $[d\vec{p}]_A, [d\vec{p}]_B, [d\vec{p}]_C, \ldots$ are the impulses contributed to the particle by interactions $A, B, C, \ldots$, respectively, during dt. If we compare this with equation C13.21, we see that the twirl a given interaction contributes to the particle must be $[d\vec{L}] = \vec{r} \times [d\vec{p}]$, and the torque it exerts must be

$$\vec{\tau} \equiv \frac{[d\vec{L}]}{dt} = \vec{r} \times \frac{[d\vec{p}]}{dt} = \vec{r} \times \vec{F} \qquad (C13.27)$$

This formula provides an easy way to calculate torques in a variety of contexts, and it will be a great help to us in chapter N5.

The meaning of torque

We can see what this formula means by considering a door that is initially at rest but free to rotate about the axis defined by its hinges. Imagine that you push on the door with your hand, exerting a force $\vec{F}$ that is fairly localized at a point whose position relative to the nearest point O on the door's hinge axis is $\vec{r}$ (see figure C13.9). When you push on a particular part of the door, the interaction between your hand and the door contributes twirl at a rate of $\vec{\tau} = \vec{r} \times \vec{F}$ to the door particles that your hand touches. If the door is rigid, these particles will transfer this angular momentum to the rest of the door via internal interactions, causing the door's rotation rate about its hinges to change. As we will see in chapter C14, *internal* interactions do not change the door's total angular momentum about O, so any change in the door's *total* angular momentum about O ultimately comes from the twirl contributed by this interaction.

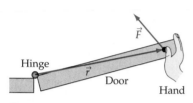

Figure C13.9
Pushing on a door with one's hand.

Is this model consistent with your years of experience with doors? You *know* that the most effective way to open a door is to exert a force $\vec{F}$ perpendicular to the plane of the door, and that pulling or pushing on the door directly toward or away from its hinges (parallel to the plane of the door) does nothing to help turn the door on its hinges. This is consistent with the formula $\text{mag}(\vec{\tau}) = \text{mag}(\vec{r} \times \vec{F}) = rF\sin\theta$, where θ is the angle between $\vec{F}$ and $\vec{r}$, which says that a force exerted perpendicular to the door (and thus to $\vec{r}$) should be more effective than one exerted directly toward or away from its hinges. Similarly, you know that it is easier to open the door by pushing on it at a point far from the hinges than by pushing on it at a point close to the hinges. This is again consistent with $\tau = rF\sin\theta$: to transfer angular momentum to the door at a given desired rate, the strength of the force that you have to exert is inversely proportional to the distance from the hinges of the point on which you push. My point is that equation C13.27 seems to describe correctly how an interaction exerting a force does in fact change the door's angular momentum.

Torque exerted by a force on an extended object

This is a specific illustration of a general principle. *An interaction that supplies a force $\vec{F}$ to an extended object at a specific point whose position is $\vec{r}$ relative to some point O contributes twirl about O to that object at the rate*

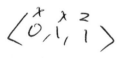

$$\vec{\tau} = \frac{[d\vec{L}]}{dt} = \vec{r} \times \vec{F} \qquad (C13.28)$$

This equation has the same form but not quite the same meaning as equation C13.27. In equation C13.27, we were talking about the torque exerted on a *point particle*; here we are talking about the force exerted on an *extended object*. In equation C13.27, $\vec{r}$ referred to the *position of the particle* relative to the reference point O; here it refers to a well-defined *position* (relative to O) *where the force is applied* to the object.

Example C13.1

Problem   A disk with a mass of 3.0 kg and a radius of 12 cm is freely spinning at a speed of 15 turns per second. Imagine that you grab the rim of the disk with your hand. What is the magnitude of the friction force you would have to apply to bring the disk to rest within 2.0 s?

Translation See figure C13.10. Note that we are taking the reference point O to be the disk's center of mass.

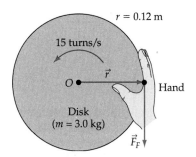

Figure C13.10
Slowing down a rotating disk.

Model The friction force is tangent to the rim and thus perpendicular to the position vector $\vec{r}$ between O and the point where the force is applied, so torque associated with the friction interaction thus has a magnitude of

$$\tau = r F_F \sin 90° = r F_F \qquad \text{(C13.29)}$$

and a direction that (according to the right-hand rule for the cross product) is perpendicular to the plane of the drawing and *away* from the viewer.
  The disk's initial angular momentum has a magnitude of

$$\vec{L}_i = I\vec{\omega}_i = \tfrac{1}{2}mr^2\vec{\omega}_i \qquad \text{(C13.30)}$$

where $\vec{\omega}_i$ is its initial angular velocity and I is the moment of inertia for a disk (which I have looked up in chapter C9). The direction of $\vec{L}_i$ is perpendicular to the plane of the drawing and toward the viewer. If the friction interaction is the *only* interaction that exerts torque on the disk, then this interaction's twirl $[d\vec{L}]$ is equal to the disk's change in angular momentum $d\vec{L}$. If we also assume that the torque is constant during the time interval $dt = 2.0$ s, the torque needed to bring the disk to rest is

$$\vec{\tau} = \frac{[d\vec{L}]}{dt} = \frac{d\vec{L}}{dt} = \frac{\vec{L}_f - \vec{L}_i}{dt} = \frac{0 - \vec{L}_i}{dt} = \frac{-\tfrac{1}{2}mr^2\vec{\omega}_i}{dt} \qquad \text{(C13.31)}$$

This states that the direction of the torque that we *need* to slow down the disk is opposite to $\vec{\omega}_i$ and thus perpendicular to the plane of the drawing and *away* from the viewer. This is consistent with the direction of the torque that the friction interaction actually *supplies*, as discussed below equation C13.29 (it is good to check this!). So if we set the magnitude of equation C13.31 equal to equation C13.29, we know everything except $F_F = \text{mag}(\vec{F}_F)$, so we can solve for that force magnitude.

Solution

$$r F_F = \tau = \frac{\tfrac{1}{2}mr^2\omega_i}{dt} \qquad \Rightarrow \qquad F_F = \frac{mr\omega_i}{2\,dt} \qquad \text{(C13.32)}$$

$$F_F = \frac{(3.0\text{ kg})(0.12\text{ m})(15\text{ rev/s})}{2(2.0\text{ s})}\left(\frac{2\pi\text{ rad}}{\text{rev}}\right)\left(\frac{1}{1\text{ rad}}\right)\left(\frac{1\text{ N}}{1\text{ kg·m/s}^2}\right) = 8.5\text{ N}$$

$$\text{(C13.33)}$$

Evaluation The units are correct, and the force seems reasonable (about 2 lb).

TWO-MINUTE PROBLEMS

C13T.1 A child swings a 0.1-kg ball on a string in a horizontal circle of radius 2.0 m once every 0.63 s. The ball's angular momentum about the child has a magnitude of
A. 0.63 kg·m²/s
B. 2.0 kg·m²/s
C. 4.0 kg·m²/s
D. 10 kg·m²/s
E. 20 kg·m²/s
F. Other (specify)

C13T.2 If you are standing 30 m due east of a car traveling at 25 m/s southwest, what is the direction of the car's angular momentum relative to you?
A. Southwest
B. Northeast
C. East
D. West
E. Up
F. Down

C13T.3 You are standing 30 m due east of a 50-kg person who is running at a speed of 2.0 m/s due west. What is the magnitude of that person's angular momentum about you?
A. 3000 kg·m^2/s
B. 1000 kg·m^2/s
C. 300 kg·m^2/s
D. 100 kg·m^2/s
E. 0
F. Other (specify)

C13T.4 The lengths of the hour and minute hands of a clock are 4 cm and 6 cm, respectively. If the vectors $\vec{u}$ and $\vec{w}$ represent the hour and minute hands, respectively, then $\vec{u} \times \vec{w}$ at 5 o'clock is
A. 24 cm^2 up
B. 24 cm^2 down
C. 21 cm^2 up
D. 21 cm^2 down
E. 12 cm^2 up
F. 12 cm^2 down

C13T.5 The letter N is symmetric (in the sense discussed in section C13.4) for rotations about an axis pointing in which of the directions listed below?
A. →
B. ↑
C. Perpendicular to the plane of the letter
D. A and B
E. A and C
F. A, B, and C

C13T.6 A disk with a mass of 10 kg and a radius of 0.1 m rotates at a rate of 10 turns per second. The magnitude of the disk's total angular momentum is
A. 63 kg·m^2/s
B. 31 kg·m^2/s
C. 10 kg·m^2/s
D. 6.3 kg·m^2/s
E. 3.1 kg·m^2/s
F. 1.0 kg·m^2/s
T. Other (specify)

C13T.7 Imagine that you are the pitcher in a baseball game. The batter hits a foul ball vertically in the air. If the ball has a weight of 2 N and an initial upward velocity of about 30 m/s, and you are 40 m from where the ball is hit, what is the gravitational torque

(magnitude and direction) on the ball about you just after it is hit?
A. 2400 N·m upward
B. 2400 N·m to your left
C. 2400 N·m to your right
D. 80 N·m upward
E. 80 N·m to your left
F. 80 N·m to your right
T. Other (specify)

C13T.8 As the ball described in problem C13T.7 continues to rise, the magnitude of the torque on the ball about you due to the ball's weight
A. Increases.
B. Essentially remains the same.
C. Decreases.

C13T.9 A cylinder rolls without slipping down an incline directly toward you. The contact interaction between the cylinder and the incline exerts a friction torque on the cylinder about the cylinder's center of mass. What is the direction of this torque?
A. Toward you.
B. Away from you.
C. To your right.
D. To your left.
E. Upward.
F. Downward.

C13T.10 Imagine that you are looking down on a turntable that is spinning counterclockwise. If an upward torque is applied to the turntable, its angular speed
A. Increases.
B. Decreases.
C. Remains the same.

C13T.11 A wheel of radius 50 cm rotates freely on an axle of radius 0.5 cm. If you want to slow the wheel to rest with your hand, you can either exert a friction force with your hand on the wheel's rim (call the magnitude of this force F_{rim}) or exert a friction force on the wheel's axle (call the magnitude of this force F_{axle}). If you had to bring the wheel to rest in 2.0 s either way, how would the force that you'd have to exert on the rim compare to the force that you'd have to exert on the axle?
A. $F_{rim} = 100 F_{axle}$
B. $F_{rim} = 10 F_{axle}$
C. $F_{rim} = F_{axle}$
D. $10 F_{rim} = F_{axle}$
E. $100 F_{rim} = F_{axle}$
F. Other (specify)
T. Depends (specify on what)

HOMEWORK PROBLEMS

Basic Skills

C13B.1 A 1200-kg car turns left around a curve with a radius of 130 m at a speed of 22 m/s. What is the car's angular momentum around the center of the curve (magnitude and direction)?

C13B.2 At a certain time, a 55-kg person is 25 m due north of you and is walking at a speed of 1.2 m/s exactly southwest. What are the magnitude and direction of this person's angular momentum about you?

C13B.3 A simplistic model of the hydrogen atom imagines the electron to be in a circular orbit around the proton. The electron's orbital radius in this model is 0.053 nm, and its speed is about $c/137$, where c is the speed of light. What is the magnitude of this electron's orbital angular momentum? Compare your answer to $h/2\pi$, where h is Planck's constant $= 6.63 \times 10^{-34}$ kg·m²/s.

C13B.4 Displacement vector $\vec{u} = [3 \text{ m}, 0, -2 \text{ m}]$ and displacement vector $\vec{w} = [-1 \text{ m}, 5 \text{ m}, 2 \text{ m}]$. Find the components of the cross product of these vectors.

C13B.5 A 7-kg bowling ball whose radius is 0.13 m is rolling directly toward you, turning 3 times per second. What are the magnitude and direction of its rotational angular momentum about you? What is its translational angular momentum about you?

C13B.6 A diver whose mass is 42 kg jumps vertically off the high diving board into the water while you watch from the side of the pool. When the diver enters the water, you are 12 m away. What is the torque around you that gravity exerts on the diver just before he or she enters the water? The diving board is 3.0 m above the water. What is the torque around you that gravity exerts on the diver just after he or she leaves the board?

C13B.7 Using the concept of torque, explain why using a long wrench makes it easier to loosen a stubborn nut or bolt than using a short wrench would.

C13B.8 A wheel 60 cm in radius is connected to an axle that is 1.5 cm in radius. Someone pulls with a force of 50 N on a thin cord wrapped around the axle. How much force do you have to exert on the wheel's rim to hold it still? Please explain your response.

C13B.9 A 6-kg bowling ball with a radius of 14 cm is spinning about a vertical axis (with its center of mass motionless) at an initial rate of 3 turns per second. Friction with the floor, however, causes the bowling ball to rotate more and more slowly until it stops after about 22 s. What was the average torque

that the friction interaction applied to the bowling ball?

Synthetic

C13S.1 Prove that the magnitude of $\vec{u} \times \vec{w}$ is the same as the area of the parallelogram whose sides are $\vec{u}$ and $\vec{w}$.

C13S.2 A 0.15-kg baseball is hit at a speed of 52 m/s in a horizontal line 1.4 m above the ground. When the baseball is 12 m from home plate, what is its angular momentum about home plate? Explain your response carefully.

C13S.3 Many subatomic particles (including the electron) behave as if they were spinning around their axis. Measurements indicate that the electron has a spin angular momentum of $h/4\pi$, where h is Planck's constant. A simplistic model imagines the electron to be a spinning spherical ball of uniform density. Other measurements indicate that if the electron really is a spherical ball, its radius must be less than 10^{-18} m. Show that if the simplistic model were true, the speed of the surface of the electron would be much faster than the speed of light. (A more sophisticated quantum-mechanical model of electron spin avoids this paradox.)

C13S.4 A Frisbee has a mass of about 165 g and a radius of about 13 or 14 cm. *Estimate* the magnitude of its rotational angular momentum when it is thrown normally, and describe the reasoning behind your estimate. (*Hint:* A Frisbee is somewhere between a hoop and a disk; a significant part of its mass is on its rim. Performing some experiments might help improve your estimate of the spin rate, but an estimate good to within a factor of 3 or so is fine.)

C13S.5 A 280-kg cylindrical piece of concrete pipe 1.0 m in diameter, 1.3 m long, and 3 cm thick is rolling toward you at a speed of 5 m/s. What is its approximate rotational angular momentum (magnitude and direction)?

C13S.6 A 6-kg bowling ball with a radius of 12 cm rolls in a straight line past you at a speed of 3 m/s. At its point of closest approach, it is 3 m away from you. Say that we define our coordinate system centered on you so that the ball rolls parallel to the $+y$ direction and the z direction is vertically upward. What are the components of the ball's total angular momentum about your position?

C13S.7 Imagine that you wrap a string around a 5.0-kg spool whose radius is 5.0 cm and that is free to rotate about its axis of symmetry. If you then pull on this string with a constant force whose magnitude is 2 N, how long will it take to spin the spool up from rest to a rotation rate of 10 turns per second?

C13S.8 A basketball with a mass of 0.15 kg and a radius of 0.15 m is thrown to you rotating 5 times per second. What is the magnitude of the frictional force that you have to exert on it with your hands to stop it rotating within 0.1 s when you catch it? (*Hint:* The moment of inertia of a spherical shell is $\frac{2}{3}MR^2$, where M and R are the shell's mass and radius, respectively.)

C13S.9 A 3.0-kg sphere with a radius of 5.0 cm rolls from rest without slipping 3.0 m down an incline, reaching a speed of 3.0 m/s after rolling for 2.0 s. What is the average torque that the friction interaction between the sphere and the incline exerts on the sphere?

Rich-Context

C13R.1 One possible way to create a long-term space habitat is to take a roughly cylindrical asteroid, hollow it out, fill it with air, and then set it spinning on its long axis so that people walking on the inner curved surface feel an effective gravitational force away from the axis of rotation (for reasons we will understand in chapter N9). Consider iron asteroid (density ≈ 7900 kg/m³) shaped like a cylinder 5.0 km long and 3.0 km in diameter. Imagine that we hollow it out so that what remains is a canlike shell 100 m thick. The spin rate required to give an effective gravitational force of at least one-half of what one experiences on earth turns out to be about 1 revolution (r) per 100 s for an asteroid of this size. We are going to spin up the asteroid using two rocket engines attached on opposite sides of the asteroid's "equator" (considering the asteroid's flat ends to be its "poles"). These advanced nuclear rocket engines deliver an impulse per unit fuel mass of 20,000 m/s.
   (a) How much fuel is required to spin up the asteroid?
   (b) How large is the mass of this fuel compared to the mass of the hollowed-out asteroid?

C13R.2 Jetliner tires take a terrible beating during landing. A plane might be traveling at 60 m/s (≈ 130 m/h) when they hit the ground. The length of the skid marks on a runway suggests that the wheels spin up to that speed in maybe 0.2 s. Assume for the sake of a crude approximation that the force that the friction interaction between the tire and runway exerts

on the tire is constant during that time interval, and that the jet is so massive that it does not change speed much during that interval.
   (a) What fraction of the k-work contributed by this friction force goes to thermal energy? (*Hint:* The calculation will involve thinking about the torque required to increase the tire's angular momentum!)
   (b) What is the approximate rate at which thermal energy is being created in watts per kilogram of tire during the spin-up interval, given the information above? (*Hint:* Make some reasonable assumptions about the tires' moment of inertia.)

Advanced

C13A.1 In mathematically proving the properties of the cross product, it is actually somewhat easier to take the component definition in equation C13.5 as the fundamental definition of the cross product, and then prove that both the geometric definition given by equation C13.1 and the distributive property of the cross product follow from it.
   (a) Prove that equation C13.5 implies that $\vec{u} \times \vec{w}$ is perpendicular to both $\vec{u}$ and $\vec{w}$. [*Hint:* Use the component definition of the dot product to show that $\vec{u} \cdot (\vec{u} \times \vec{w}) = 0 = \vec{w} \cdot (\vec{u} \times \vec{w})$.]
   (b) Prove that equation C13.5 implies that $\text{mag}(\vec{u} \times \vec{w}) = uw \sin\theta$. [*Hint:* Use the pythagorean theorem and the component definition of the dot product to show that $\{\text{mag}(\vec{u} \times \vec{w})\}^2 = u^2w^2 - (\vec{u} \cdot \vec{w})^2$ and then use the geometric definition of the dot product.]
   (c) Prove that equation C13.5 implies that the dot product is distributive. (*Hint:* This is simply a matter of grouping terms creatively.)

C13A.2 Here is a way to derive the component equation for the cross product (equation C13.5) from its definition in equation C13.1. Imagine that $\vec{e}_x, \vec{e}_y$, and $\vec{e}_z$ are three vectors that point in the x, y, and z directions, respectively, and have magnitude 1. Argue that $\vec{u}_x = u_x\vec{e}_x$ for both signs of u_x: analogous equations follow for the other component vectors of $\vec{u}$ and $\vec{w}$. Write $\vec{u}$ and $\vec{w}$ in terms of component vectors in this way, and compute the cross product, using the properties of the cross product listed in table C13.1. (*Hint:* Use the definition of the cross product to argue that $\vec{e}_x \times \vec{e}_x = 0, \vec{e}_x \times \vec{e}_y = +\vec{e}_z$, and so on. Find these products for all pairs of e vectors before doing anything else.)

ANSWERS TO EXERCISES

C13X.1 At 10 o'clock, the angle between the hands is 60°, so

$$\text{mag}(\vec{u} \times \vec{w}) = (8\text{ cm})(10\text{ cm})\sin 60°$$
$$= 69\text{ cm}^2 \qquad\qquad (C13.34)$$

Since the vectors lie on the clock's face, the cross product must be perpendicular to that face. If I point my right index finger in the direction of the hour hand and my long finger in the direction of the minute hand, my thumb points directly into the clock.

C13X.2 According to equation C13.5, we have

$$\vec{u} \times \vec{w} = \begin{bmatrix} u_y w_z - u_z w_y \\ u_z w_x - u_x w_z \\ u_x w_y - u_y w_x \end{bmatrix}$$

$$= \begin{bmatrix} (-2\,\text{m})(0\,\text{m}) - (0\,\text{m})(5\,\text{m}) \\ (0\,\text{m})(-2\,\text{m}) - (3\,\text{m})(0\,\text{m}) \\ (3\,\text{m})(5\,\text{m}) - (-2\,\text{m})(-2\,\text{m}) \end{bmatrix}$$

$$= \begin{bmatrix} 0\,\text{m}^2 \\ 0\,\text{m}^2 \\ 11\,\text{m}^2 \end{bmatrix} \tag{C13.35}$$

Since both vectors lie in the xy plane, it makes sense that $\vec{u} \times \vec{w}$ points in the z direction, since it is perpendicular to both vectors by definition.

C13X.3 *Translation:* Let m be the particle's mass, ω be its angular speed, and r be the radius of its circular path. *Model and solution:* The angular momentum of a particle in circular motion is

$$\text{mag}(\vec{L}) = mr^2\omega$$

$$= (0.5\,\text{kg})(2.0\,\text{m})^2 \left(\frac{1\,\text{rev}}{2.0\,\text{s}}\right)\left(\frac{2\pi\,\text{rad}}{1\,\text{rev}}\right)$$

$$\times \left(\frac{1}{1\,\text{rad}}\right) = 6.3\,\text{kg·m}^2/\text{s} \tag{C13.36}$$

C13X.4 The particle's position relative to O is $\vec{r} = [0\,\text{m}, 3\,\text{m}, 0\,\text{m}]$, and its velocity is $\vec{v} = [0\,\text{m}, 3\,\text{m}, 4\,\text{m}]$. One can find the angular momentum using equation C13.5, but one can also note that the magnitude of the component of $\vec{v}$ perpendicular to $\vec{r}$ is $|v_z|$, so

$$\text{mag}(\vec{r} \times m\vec{v}) = mrv_\perp$$

$$= (2.0\,\text{kg})(3.0\,\text{m})(4.0\,\text{m/s})$$

$$= 24\,\text{kg·m}^2/\text{s} \tag{C13.37}$$

Since both vectors lie in the yz plane, the product must be in the $\pm x$ direction, and a bit of work with one's right hand shows that the correct direction in the $+x$ direction.

C13X.5 (a) Yes (or at least nearly so): for every particle on one side of the axis, there is a particle on the other side.

(b) No: in this case, the book sticks out farther from the axis in the upper right than on the upper left (or vice versa), so not every particle on one side of the axis has a counterpart on the other side.

C13X.6 According to chapter C9, the moment of inertia of a sphere of mass M and radius R is $I = \frac{2}{5}MR^2$, so the magnitude of the sphere's angular momentum when it spins at an angular speed of ω is

$$\text{mag}(\vec{L}) = I\omega = \tfrac{2}{5}MR^2\omega$$

$$= \frac{2}{5}(5.0\,\text{kg})(0.12\,\text{m})^2\left(\frac{5\,\text{rev}}{\text{s}}\right)$$

$$\times \left(\frac{2\pi\,\text{rad}}{1\,\text{rev}}\right)\left(\frac{1}{1\,\text{rad}}\right) = 0.90\,\frac{\text{kg·m}^2}{\text{s}^2} \tag{C13.38}$$

C13X.7 Let $\vec{r}_i = \vec{r}_{\text{CM}i} + \vec{q}_i$ be the ith particle's position relative to O at a certain instant of time and $\vec{r}_{if} = \vec{r}_{\text{CM}f} + \vec{q}_{if}$ be its position a very short time dt later. Subtracting the first of these equations from the second, we get

$$\vec{r}_{if} - \vec{r}_i = \vec{r}_{\text{CM}f} - \vec{r}_{\text{CM}i} + \vec{q}_{if} - \vec{q}_i$$

$$\Rightarrow \quad d\vec{r}_i = d\vec{r}_{\text{CM}} + d\vec{q}_i \tag{C13.39}$$

where $d\vec{r}_i$ is the displacement of the particle, $d\vec{r}_{\text{CM}}$ is the displacement of the center of mass, and $d\vec{q}_i$ is the particle's rotational displacement during the time interval dt. If we divide both sides by dt, assume that dt is short enough so that the particle's velocity does not change much during dt, and use the definition of velocity, we get

$$\frac{d\vec{r}_i}{dt} = \frac{d\vec{r}_{\text{CM}}}{dt} + \frac{d\vec{q}_i}{dt} \quad \Rightarrow \quad \vec{v}_i = \vec{v}_{\text{CM}} + \vec{u}_i \tag{C13.40}$$

which is equation C13.16.

C13X.8 If we plug equation C13.15 into the first of equations C13.17, we get

$$M\vec{r}_{\text{CM}} = \sum_{i=1}^{N} m_i\vec{r}_i = \sum_{i=1}^{N} m_i(\vec{r}_{\text{CM}} + \vec{q}_i)$$

$$= \sum_{i=1}^{N} m_i\vec{r}_{\text{CM}} + \sum_{i=1}^{N} m_i q_i \tag{C13.41}$$

Since $\vec{r}_{\text{CM}}$ is common to all the terms in the first sum, we can pull it out in front of the sum. Then note that the sum over m_i over all particles is simply the object's total mass M, so

$$M\vec{r}_{\text{CM}} = \vec{r}_{\text{CM}}\sum_{i=1}^{N} m_i + \sum_{i=1}^{N} m_i q_i = \vec{r}_{\text{CM}}M + \sum_{i=1}^{N} m_i q_i$$

$$\Rightarrow \quad \sum_{i=1}^{N} m_i q_i = M\vec{r}_{\text{CM}} - M\vec{r}_{\text{CM}} = 0 \tag{C13.42}$$

as claimed in the first of equations C13.18. The proof of the second of equations C13.17 is essentially identical with $\vec{r} \rightarrow \vec{v}$ and $\vec{q} \rightarrow \vec{u}$.

C14

Conservation of Angular Momentum

▷ **Introduction**

▷ **Conservation of Momentum**

▷ **Conservation of Energy**

▽ **Conservation of Angular Momentum**

    Introduction to Angular Momentum

    Conservation of Angular Momentum

Chapter Overview

Introduction

The first two sections of this chapter build on chapter C13's discussion of torque by considering cases in which an interaction exerts on an object a torque that is *not* parallel to the object's initial angular momentum. The remaining sections focus on the law of conservation of angular momentum and its implications. This completes our discussion of the three great conservation laws.

Section C14.1: Precession of a Top

The gravitational interaction between a leaning top and the earth exerts a horizontal torque on the top that is always perpendicular to the top's angular momentum. If the top were not rotating, this torque would simply cause the top to fall over. When the top is rotating, this torque instead causes the tip of the top's angular momentum to **precess**, that is, move in a circle about a vertical axis, maintaining a constant angle with that vertical axis. A calculation shows that the **period** of the top's precession (the time it takes the top to precess once around the vertical axis) is

$$T = \frac{2\pi(I/M)\omega}{r_{CM}g} \qquad \text{(C14.6)}$$

where ω is the top's angular speed, r_{CM} is the distance that its center of mass is from its bottom, g is the earth's gravitational field strength, and I/M is the top's moment of inertia per unit mass (since $I \propto M$, this ratio depends only on the top's shape). Note that T does *not* depend on the lean angle.

Section C14.2: Applications

Because the earth bulges a bit at its equator and is tilted relative to the plane of the moon's orbit, the moon exerts a gravitational torque on the earth that causes the earth's axis of rotation to precess with a period of about 26,000 years. This means that the North Star will not always coincide with the earth's rotational axis: in fact, the axis will be close to the star Vega in about 14,000 years.

Knowing how a spinning object responds to a perpendicular applied torque also explains how one can skip a Frisbee off a hard surface. If the right edge of a thrown Frisbee rotating clockwise hits the ground first, the contact interaction with the ground exerts a forward torque on the Frisbee about its center of mass (as you can check, using the right-hand rule for the cross product). The net twirl contributed by the impact will thus cause the Frisbee's downward-pointing spin axis to shift somewhat forward, causing the Frisbee to lift back into the air.

Section C14.3: Conservation of Angular Momentum

In this section, we see that if an interaction between two particles exerts forces on the particles that (1) are equal in magnitude and opposite in direction (as required by conservation of momentum) and (2) also act parallel to the line connecting the particles, then one can show that the twirls (around *any* reference point O) the interaction delivers to the particles add to zero, meaning that the interaction transfers angular momentum from one particle to the other without changing the pair's total angular momentum. Since *all* known fundamental interactions satisfy the second criterion in the newtonian limit, this means that the total angular momentum of any isolated system will be conserved.

Section C14.4: Some Worked Examples

A system is isolated if it *floats in space,* if it is *functionally isolated* (i.e., subject to external interactions that contribute no net twirl to any of its parts), or if it is involved in a *collision.* The translation step for a conservation of angular momentum problem should include

1.   Pictures showing the system in its initial and final states.
2.   Reference frame axes.
3.   A clearly indicated reference point O.
4.   Labels defining symbols, particularly *masses, velocities, moments of inertia,* and/or *angular velocities* of system objects.
5.   The usual list of known quantities.

Conceptual model diagrams should include an interaction diagram (emphasizing *external* interactions) and an equation expressing the law of conservation of angular momentum (abbreviation: CAM). This equation should be written in column vector form unless the system is a single object whose moment of inertia changes.

The examples illustrate the use of this framework. Example C14.1 provides a final analysis of the experiment we considered back in section C13.1, and example C14.3 illustrates a problem that involves all three conservation laws.

Section C14.5: Application: Neutron Stars

This section illustrates an astrophysical application of conservation of angular momentum. At the end of its life, a massive star's core can undergo a catastrophic collapse that initiates a supernova explosion. The core survives the process as a **neutron star,** a ball of neutrons about 12 km in radius. Taking the sun's rotation rate as typical, one can use conservation of angular momentum to estimate that the newly formed neutron star should have a rotational **period** of about 1 ms. If a neutron star is aligned correctly relative to the earth, we can receive radio pulses linked to the star's rotational period (we call the neutron star a **pulsar** in such a case). Consistent with the calculation, no pulsars have been observed with periods much less than 1 ms, and those that on other grounds appear to be most recently formed seem to have the shortest periods.

C14.1 Precession of a Top

At the end of chapter C13, we saw that an interaction can exert a torque $\vec{\tau}$ on an object that, if it acts steadily for a short time dt, contributes a twirl $[d\vec{L}] = \vec{\tau}\, dt$ toward changing the object's angular momentum $\vec{L}$. In chapter C13, we considered only cases in which the direction of $\vec{\tau}$ was either the same as or opposite to that of $\vec{L}$. In such cases, the twirl only contributes to increasing or decreasing the magnitude of $\vec{L}$, respectively.

If $\vec{\tau}$ and $\vec{L}$ are *not* parallel, things become more complicated. The equation $[d\vec{L}] = \vec{\tau}\, dt$ implies that a torque's direction specifies the direction in which it seeks to *change* the object's angular momentum. Therefore if the total torque acting on an object is not aligned with its initial angular momentum, the object's angular momentum will change *in the direction of the total applied torque*. This can have some strange consequences, as the examples below illustrate.

For example, you know that a spinning top will not fall over, whereas the same top will simply topple over if it is *not* spinning. Why is this? Imagine that you set a top on a table so that its bottom touches the table and its axis of symmetry makes an angle θ with the vertical. Then you release the top. What happens if the top is not spinning? What happens if the top is spinning?

Figure C14.1 shows a picture of the situation. Let us take the point where the top touches the tabletop to be our reference point O, and let $\vec{r}_{CM}$ be the position of the top's center of mass relative to that point. After you release the top, there are two interactions acting on it: a gravitational interaction which exerts a downward force $\vec{F}_g$ on the top's center of mass and a contact interaction with the table that exerts an upward force on the top at point O. The latter interaction exerts zero torque around point O (since the distance between O and the point where its force is applied is zero). The gravitational force, on the other hand, exerts a torque $\vec{\tau} = \vec{r}_{CM} \times \vec{F}_g$ on the top about point O whose direction points directly *into* the plane of the drawing in figure C14.1. If we ignore friction, this is the only interaction that exerts a significant torque on the top, so the change $d\vec{L}$ in the top's angular momentum during a short time dt will be essentially equal to the twirl $[d\vec{L}] = \vec{\tau}\, dt = (\vec{r}_{CM} \times \vec{F}_g)\, dt$ that the gravitational interaction contributes during that time.

If the top is *not* initially spinning, this twirl will simply give the top an angular momentum in the same direction as the twirl, which (by the right-hand rule) will cause it to rotate clockwise about point O with increasing angular speed, meaning that it topples over. On the other hand, if the top is spinning, it already has a large angular momentum $\vec{L}$ parallel to its axis of symmetry. In a tiny time interval dt, the twirl contributed by the gravitational interaction will thus *change* the top's angular momentum by $d\vec{L} \approx (\vec{r}_{CM} \times \vec{F}_g)\, dt$, causing the top's angular momentum $\vec{L}$ (and thus its axis of rotation) to shift slightly *into the plane of the drawing* in figure C14.1.

By definition, though, $\vec{r}_{CM} \times \vec{F}_g$ is always strictly perpendicular to both $\vec{r}_{CM}$ (which is parallel to $\vec{L}$) and the vertical force of gravity $\vec{F}_g$. So as $\vec{L}$ changes direction in response to the gravitational torque $\vec{\tau} = \vec{r}_{CM} \times \vec{F}_g$, the direction of the torque shifts as well, always remaining both horizontal and perpendicular to $\vec{L}$. Since the change $d\vec{L} \approx \vec{\tau}\, dt$ in the top's angular momentum never has a component parallel to $\vec{L}$, it can only change the *direction* of $\vec{L}$, not its magnitude, and since it never has a vertical component, it cannot change the angle θ either. The net effect of this changing gravitational torque, therefore, will be to move the tip of the top's angular momentum vector $\vec{L}$ in a horizontal circle about the vertical direction as time passes, with $\vec{L}$ maintaining a constant angle θ with respect to that direction. This means that

A torque can change the orientation of an object's axis of rotation

Spinning top example

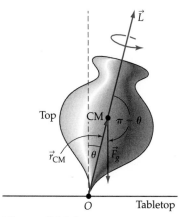

Figure C14.1
A leaning top. The torque around O exerted by the gravitational interaction points directly into the plane of the picture.

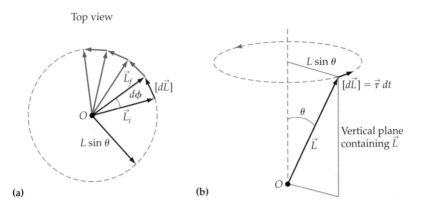

Top view

(a)   (b)

Figure C14.2
(a) A top view of the precessing top's angular momentum. Since the gravitational twirl contributed during a short time interval dt is always perpendicular to $\vec{L}$, it drags $\vec{L}$ around the circle as shown. (b) A side view shows that the radius of this circle is $L\sin\theta$.

instead of falling over, the top's axis of rotation will "wobble" about the vertical direction, as shown in figure C14.2. This kind of orderly wobbling is called **precession** around the vertical direction.

We can actually calculate the rate of precession as follows. Imagine that the top shown in figure C14.1 has a moment of inertia I, a mass M, and a spin angular speed ω about its axis of symmetry, and let the position of the top's center of mass relative to its bottom be $\vec{r}_{CM}$. Now, by definition, an angle in radians is proportional to the arclength along a circle subtended by the angle divided by the circle's radius. In this case, the tip of the top's angular momentum vector $\vec{L}$ moves in a circle whose "radius" is effectively $L\sin\theta$, where $L \equiv \text{mag}(\vec{L})$, as shown in figure C14.2. During a very short time interval dt, this tip moves through an arclength approximately equal to $\text{mag}(d\vec{L})$. Therefore, during dt the tip moves through a horizontal angle of

The rate of precession

$$d\phi = \frac{\text{mag}(d\vec{L})}{L\sin\theta} \tag{C14.1}$$

as long as dt is so short that $\text{mag}(d\vec{L}) \ll L$. Now, according to figure C14.1, the angle between the vectors $\vec{r}_{CM}$ and $\vec{F}_g$ is $\pi - \theta$, so

$$\text{mag}(d\vec{L}) = \text{mag}(\vec{r}_{CM} \times \vec{F}_g)\,dt = r_{CM}F_g\sin(\pi-\theta)\,dt \tag{C14.2}$$

where $r_{CM} \equiv \text{mag}(\vec{r}_{CM})$ and $F_g \equiv \text{mag}(\vec{F}_g)$. However, $F_g = Mg$, and there is a trigonometric identity that says that $\sin(\pi - \theta) = \sin\theta$, so this simplifies to

$$\text{mag}(d\vec{L}) = r_{CM}Mg\sin\theta\,dt \tag{C14.3}$$

Note also that since the top is symmetric by hypothesis,

$$L = I\omega \tag{C14.4}$$

Plugging equations C14.3 and C14.4 into equation C14.1, we find that

$$d\phi = \frac{r_{CM}Mg\sin\theta\,dt}{I\omega\sin\theta} \quad\Rightarrow\quad \frac{d\phi}{dt} = \frac{r_{CM}Mg}{I\omega} \tag{C14.5}$$

Note that this precession rate does not depend on θ, which is interesting. Moreover, since $I \propto M$, the precession rate is independent of M as well. Note that the precession rate is inversely proportional to the spin rate ω, so a rapidly spinning top will precess only very slowly.

Let T be the time required for the top to precess once around the circle (a quantity we call the **period** of the top's precession). "Going once around the circle" means that ϕ changes by 2π. Since equation C14.5 predicts $d\phi/dt$ is constant during the process, the ratio of 2π to T will be the same as that of $d\phi$ to dt:

$$\frac{2\pi}{T} = \frac{d\phi}{dt} = \frac{r_{CM}Mg}{I\omega} \quad\Rightarrow\quad T = \frac{2\pi(I/M)\omega}{r_{CM}g} \tag{C14.6}$$

Exercise C14X.1

Do all tops necessarily precess counterclockwise, as shown in figure C14.2? Explain your response.

C14.2   Applications

The concept of precession has a number of interesting applications in realistic physical situations. For example, people have known for many centuries that the earth's rotation axis moves very slowly relative to the distant stars. Isaac Newton was able to offer the first explanation of this phenomenon in *Principia*, as part of his general effort to illustrate how his laws of physics explained celestial as well as terrestrial phenomena. (If this explanation had been his *only* contribution to physics, his name would be recalled and honored by students of physics and astronomy today, but this important theoretical discovery has been all but overshadowed by his even greater contributions to physics.)

Newton's explanation of the earth's precession

Newton's explanation goes like this. The earth is not *quite* spherical: it bulges slightly at the equator. Since the plane of the moon's orbit is inclined at an angle relative to the earth's equator, the moon's gravitational attraction actually exerts a small torque on the earth around the earth's center of mass (because it pulls on the closer front bulge somewhat harder and at a more nearly perpendicular angle than on the back bulge, the gravitational torques around the center of mass do not quite cancel out). This is illustrated (and greatly exaggerated) in figure C14.3. The gravitational pull of the sun exerts another torque on the earth for the same reason.

Because the earth is rotating, these torques (which act perpendicular to the earth's axis) causes the earth to process as a top does. Because the torque is weak and the earth is very massive, this precession is rather slow: the combined effects of the moon's and sun's gravitational torque cause the earth to precess once every 26,000 years.

This precession makes the axis around which the stars appear to rotate when viewed from the earth shift with time. In the northern hemisphere, the stars *currently* seem to rotate about the star we call Polaris (the North Star): this star currently marks the direction of the north celestial pole. But the North Star has only been a good approximation to the location of this pole for a handful of centuries: the precession of the earth causes the location of the pole to shift around the sky as time passes. About 3000 years ago, a star named Thuban was very close to the north celestial pole. In about 14,000 years the bright star Vega in the constellation Lyra will be very close to the north celestial pole. Of course, about 26,000 years from now, Polaris will again be the North Star.

This effect is also called the *precession of the equinoxes* because as the axis of the earth shifts, the two places in the sky where the earth's equatorial plane intersects the plane of its orbit (which are called the *equinoxes*) also shift.

Figure C14.3
The gravitational interaction between the moon and the earth's equatorial bulges exerts a torque on the earth that points directly out of the plane of the drawing. This torque causes the earth's rotation axis to precess relative to the distant stars.

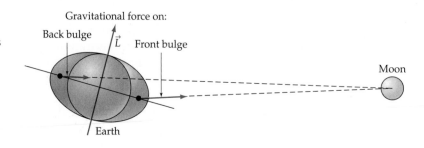

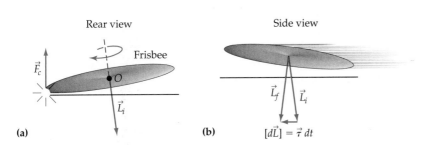

Rear view   Side view

(a)   (b) $[d\vec{L}] = \vec{\tau}\, dt$

Figure C14.4
(a) When the Frisbee hits the
ground on its left edge, the force
of impact exerts a torque around
O that points forward into the
plane of the diagram. (b) This
causes the Frisbee's angular
momentum to shift forward, which
causes it to climb into the air.

Skipping a Frisbee

Knowing how a spinning object responds to a perpendicular applied torque also helps explain how one can skip a Frisbee off a hard surface. Experienced Frisbee players know that if a right-handed player throws a Frisbee at a slight angle so that its *left* edge (as seen by the player) hits the ground first, then the Frisbee will angle upward back into the air after it hits. Why? What would happen if the right edge were to hit first?

Figure C14.4a shows the situation just as the Frisbee hits the ground. The normal part contact interaction between the ground and the Frisbee exerts a brief torque about the Frisbee's center of mass whose direction (by the right-hand rule) is directly *into* the plane of the picture, that is, parallel to the direction of flight. When a Frisbee is thrown in the normal (backhanded) manner by a right-handed player, it spins clockwise, so its angular momentum is downward, as shown in the drawing. The forward twirl $[d\vec{L}]$ contributed by the impact causes the Frisbee's angular momentum to shift forward, as shown in figure C14.4b. This lifts the Frisbee's leading edge, allowing it to climb back into the air. The torque applied to the Frisbee must point in the *forward* direction to do this, so the Frisbee *must* strike the ground on its left edge. (For example, if the Frisbee's right edge hits the ground first, the torque will point opposite to its motion, *out* of the plane of figure C14.4a, which causes the Frisbee to dig into the ground.)

Exercise C14X.2

Predict what will happen if you throw the Frisbee so that its trailing edge hits the ground first.

C14.3   Conservation of Angular Momentum

Consider two interacting particles A and B located at positions $\vec{r}_A$ and $\vec{r}_B$, respectively, relative to some arbitrary reference point O, as shown in figure C14.5. Since any interaction between these particles can only *transfer*

Interactions *transfer* angular momentum

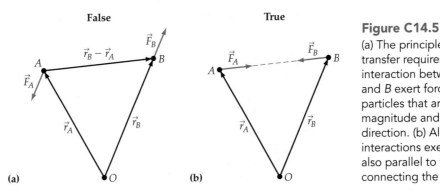

False   True

(a)   (b)

Figure C14.5
(a) The principle of momentum
transfer requires that any
interaction between particles A
and B exert forces on those
particles that are equal in
magnitude and opposite in
direction. (b) All *fundamental*
interactions exert forces that are
also parallel to the line
connecting the particles.

momentum from one to the other, the impulse $[d\vec{p}]_A$ that particle A receives from the interaction during a given tiny time interval dt must be the vector inverse of the impulse $[d\vec{p}]_B$ that particle B receives during that same time interval. Since $\vec{F} \equiv [d\vec{p}]/dt$, this means that the forces the interaction exerts on these particles must be vector inverses:

$$\vec{F}_A \equiv \frac{[d\vec{p}]_A}{dt} = -\frac{[d\vec{p}]_B}{dt} \equiv -\vec{F}_B \tag{C14.7}$$

(We called this *Newton's third law* in section C3.3.) Now, in principle, these forces could point in any direction (see figure C14.5a): they will still be consistent with the concept of momentum transfer as long as they are equal in magnitude and opposite in direction. But let's also *assume* that the forces act parallel to the line connecting the particles, as shown in figure C14.5b. (The diagram shows each force vector pointing *toward* the other particle, reflecting an attractive interaction, but each vector could instead point *away* from the other particle, as would be the case in a repulsive interaction.)

The torques about O exerted by the interaction on particles A and B are $\vec{\tau}_A = \vec{r}_A \times \vec{F}_A$ and $\vec{\tau}_B = \vec{r}_B \times \vec{F}_B$, respectively. Now note that

$$\vec{\tau}_A + \vec{\tau}_B = \vec{r}_A \times \vec{F}_A + \vec{r}_B \times \vec{F}_B = \vec{r}_A \times (-\vec{F}_B) + \vec{r}_B \times \vec{F}_B$$
$$= (\vec{r}_B - \vec{r}_A) \times \vec{F}_B = 0 \tag{C14.8}$$

The final cross product is zero because $\vec{r}_B - \vec{r}_A$ is the displacement from A to B, which is a vector parallel to $\vec{F}_B$, and the cross product of parallel vectors is zero. Now $\vec{\tau}_A + \vec{\tau}_B = 0$ implies that

$$0 = \vec{\tau}_A\, dt + \vec{\tau}_B\, dt = [d\vec{L}]_A + [d\vec{L}]_B \tag{C14.9}$$

meaning that this interaction contributes *zero* net twirl about O to this pair of particles, and thus contributes nothing to the total angular momentum of any system involving these particles. This means that any angular momentum gained by one particle is lost by the other, which in turn implies that just as an interaction transfers linear momentum from one particle to the other, so an interaction transfers angular momentum from one to the other, leaving the pair's total angular momentum unchanged. Note also that this derivation works *independent of our choice of reference point O*.

What conservation of angular momentum requires

The forces an interaction exerts on the interacting particles *must* act parallel to the line connecting the particles for this to work. In the context of newtonian mechanics, saying that angular momentum is conserved is equivalent to asserting that all fundamental interactions between particles must behave in this way, and experiments show that this is indeed true for all known interactions in the newtonian limit. (Superficially, this idea seems unrelated to the symmetry principle that the laws of physics are independent of orientation, which I had earlier stated as being connected with this conservation law; but the two ideas are in fact connected.)

If all fundamental interactions do behave in this way, then interactions between particles in a system only move angular momentum around within the system without affecting its total amount. In the absence of external interactions, angular momentum cannot either enter or leave a system. Therefore, *an isolated system's total angular momentum about any reference point O is conserved.*

The argument above applies only in the newtonian limit. In the theories of relativity and quantum mechanics, things become more complicated, partly because the interactions themselves can store both linear and angular momentum in those theories. However, because these theories still assert that the laws of physics are independent of one's orientation in space, angular momentum is still exactly conserved in these theories.

C14.4   Some Worked Examples

As we have asserted before, no system is ever completely isolated. However, a system floating in space behaves as if it *were* isolated with regard to angular momentum transfers just as it seems isolated with regard to transfers of linear momentum and energy. We can consider a person rotating on a nearly frictionless stool to be *functionally isolated,* because although the person participates in significant interactions with the earth, these interactions do not supply any net external twirl to the system. We can also apply conservation of angular momentum to a system that is not isolated at all if it is undergoing a short-duration collision and if we look at the system's angular momentum just before and just after the collision.

Isolation in conservation of angular momentum problems

The following examples illustrate the kinds of problems we can solve using conservation of angular momentum. Your conceptual model diagram for a conservation of angular momentum problem solution should start with an interaction diagram. As in conservation of linear momentum problems, the main purpose of an interaction diagram is to help you define the system and its *external* interactions so as to focus your thinking about how the system is isolated. Internal interactions are less crucial: we know that whatever they are, they will conserve angular momentum. (In contrast to conservation of energy problems, there is also no need to label boxes or interactions with symbols for kinetic or potential energies.)

The conceptual model step in conservation of angular momentum problems

Your model diagram should also include a master equation expressing the law of conservation of angular momentum, which states that a suitably isolated system's total momentum before some process of interest is equal to its total angular momentum *after* that process:

$$\vec{L}_{1i} + \vec{L}_{2i} + \vec{L}_{3i} + \cdots = \vec{L}_{1f} + \vec{L}_{2f} + \vec{L}_{3f} + \cdots \qquad \text{(C14.10)}$$

where the subscripts 1, 2, 3, ... refer to the objects in the system and the *i* and *f* subscripts mean initial and final, respectively. Adapt this equation for the number of objects in the system in question, and use the equation $\vec{L} = \vec{r} \times m\vec{v}$ or $\vec{L} = I\vec{\omega}$ to rewrite the angular momenta in terms of either masses and velocities or moments of inertia and angular velocities. In general, you should write out this equation in column-vector form unless the system consists of only a single object whose moment of inertia changes. Your explanation for the equals sign in this equation should include this principle's abbreviation CAM followed by some statement of how this system is isolated.

The *translation* step for any conservation of angular momentum problem should include all the items on the following checklist:

The translation step in a conservation of angular momentum problem

1. Pictures showing the system in its initial and final states.
2. Reference frame axes on *each* picture to define coordinate directions.
3. A clearly indicated reference point O for computing all angular momenta.
4. Labels defining symbols for *masses* and *velocities* (or *moments of inertia* and *angular velocities*) of all system objects (as well as any other useful quantities).
5. The usual list of known quantities.

Including these items will prepare you well for the conceptual model step.

Example C14.1

Problem   Consider the experiment discussed in section C13.1 where a person sits on a nearly frictionless rotating stool while holding weights either at arm's length or in his or her lap. Assume that the person's moment of inertia while sitting (*excluding* the person's arms but including the stool top) is about 2.9 kg·m^2, that the person's arms have a combined mass of about 8 kg, and that the person holds a 5-kg weight in each hand. (a) If, when the person's arms are extended, the person rotates at a rate of 0.25 rev/s, what is the person's rotation rate while holding the weights in his or her lap? (b) By roughly what factor does the system's rotational kinetic energy increase when the person draws in the weights?

Translation

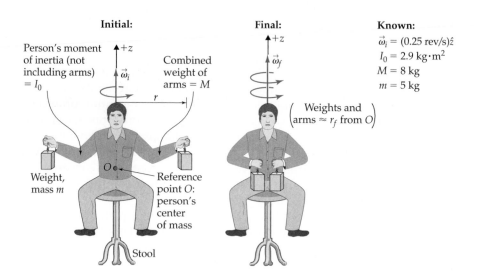

Initial: **Final:**   **Known:**

$\vec{\omega}_i = (0.25 \text{ rev/s})\hat{z}$
$I_0 = 2.9 \text{ kg·m}^2$
$M = 8 \text{ kg}$
$m = 5 \text{ kg}$

Person's moment of inertia (not including arms) $= I_0$

Combined weight of arms = M

$\left(\begin{array}{c}\text{Weights and}\\ \text{arms} \approx r_f \text{ from } O\end{array}\right)$

Weight, mass m Reference point O: person's center of mass

Stool

Conceptual Model Diagram

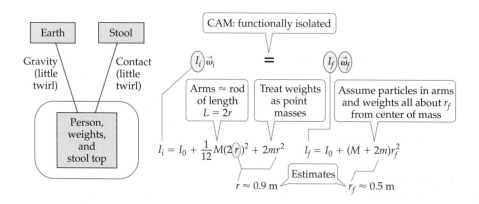

Earth   Stool

Gravity (little twirl)   Contact (little twirl)

CAM: functionally isolated

$I_i \vec{\omega}_i = I_f \vec{\omega}_f$

Person, weights, and stool top

Arms ≈ rod of length $L = 2r$ Treat weights as point masses   Assume particles in arms and weights all about r_f from center of mass

$I_i = I_0 + \frac{1}{12}M(2r)^2 + 2mr^2$ $I_f = I_0 + (M + 2m)r_f^2$

Estimates

$r \approx 0.9 \text{ m}$ $r_f \approx 0.5 \text{ m}$

Prose Model   The system of the person, the weights, and the rotating stool top is functionally isolated. If we assume that the system is at least approximately symmetric when the weights are extended and when they are retracted, and if we choose the origin O to be the system's center of mass, then its angular momentum is given by $I\vec{\omega}$ and conservation of momentum implies that

$$I_i \vec{\omega}_i = I_f \vec{\omega}_f \qquad \text{(C14.11)}$$

Since we know $\vec{\omega}_i$, we need to find I_i and I_f to calculate $\vec{\omega}_f$. Let's model the weights as point masses whose centers of mass are $r = 0.9$ m from the axis of rotation and the person's outstretched arms as being a rod with a mass $M = 8$ kg and a length $L = 2r = 1.8$ m. According to table C9.1, the moment of inertia of a rod rotating about its center is $\frac{1}{12}ML^2$, and the moment of inertia of each weight will be mr^2, so the system's total initial moment of inertia is

$$I_i = I_0 + \tfrac{1}{12}ML^2 + 2mr^2 = I_0 + \tfrac{1}{12}M(2r)^2 + 2mr^2 \qquad \text{(C14.12)}$$

When I hold my arms with my hands in my lap, it seems that the particles in my arms and in the weights are all roughly $r_f = 15$ cm (plus or minus a few centimeters) from my axis of rotation, so

$$I_f = I_0 + (M + 2m)r_f^2 \qquad \text{(C14.13)}$$

We know all the quantities on the right sides of equations C14.12 and C14.13, so we can solve for the person's final angular speed $\omega_f \equiv \text{mag}(\vec{\omega}_f)$. Once we know ω_f, we can compute the change in the system's rotational kinetic energy, using $\Delta K^{\text{rot}} = \tfrac{1}{2}I_f\omega_f^2 - \tfrac{1}{2}I_i\omega_i^2$.

Solution   It will help us in both parts to know the numerical values of I_i and I_f, so plugging numbers into equations C14.12 and C14.13, we get

$$I_i = 2.9\,\text{kg·m}^2 + \tfrac{1}{12}(8\,\text{kg})(1.8\,\text{m})^2 + 2(5\,\text{kg})(0.9\,\text{m})^2 = 9.1\,\text{kg·m}^2 \quad \text{(C14.14a)}$$

$$I_f = 2.9\,\text{kg·m}^2 + (18\,\text{kg})(0.15\,\text{m})^2 = 3.3\,\text{kg·m}^2 \qquad \text{(C14.14b)}$$

(a) Solving equation C14.11 for $\vec{\omega}_f$ and taking the magnitude of both sides, we get

$$\omega_f = \frac{I_i}{I_f}\omega_i = \frac{9.1\,\text{kg·m}^2}{3.3\,\text{kg·m}^2}\left(0.25\,\frac{\text{rev}}{\text{s}}\right) = 0.69\,\frac{\text{rev}}{\text{s}} \qquad \text{(C14.15)}$$

which corresponds to one turn every 1.5 s instead of the initial rate of one turn every 4.0 s.
(b) The ratio of the final to the initial kinetic energy is

$$\frac{K_f^{\text{rot}}}{K_i^{\text{rot}}} = \frac{\tfrac{1}{2}I_f\omega_f^2}{\tfrac{1}{2}I_i\omega_i^2} = \frac{I_f}{I_i\omega_i^2}\left(\frac{I_i}{I_f}\omega_i\right)^2 = \frac{I_i}{I_f} \qquad \text{(C14.16a)}$$

$$= \frac{9.1\,\text{kg·m}^2}{3.3\,\text{kg·m}^2} = 2.76 \qquad \text{(C14.16b)}$$

Evaluation   The units and signs all look correct. Note that $\omega_f \propto I_f^{-1}$, as claimed in section C13.1. Note also that the system's rotational kinetic energy almost triples in this process! This energy comes from chemical energy being converted to mechanical energy in the person's body. This is not a good weight-loss exercise, though, because the rotational energy increase is only about 0.005 food calories.

Exercise C14X.3

Verify this claim.

Example C14.2

Problem   A student with a moment of inertia of 2.9 kg·m^2 about a vertical axis is sitting (initially at rest) on a stool free to rotate about the vertical axis. The student is holding a bicycle wheel with a mass of 1.0 kg and a moment of inertia of 0.35 kg·m^2 that is rotating counterclockwise around a vertical axis at a rate of 3 rev/s. The wheel's axle is about 0.40 m from the student's axis. If the student turns the wheel over, what happens? Be as descriptive as you can!

Translation

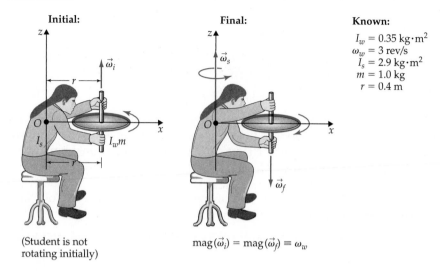

Initial:

(Student is not
rotating initially)

Final:

$\text{mag}(\vec{\omega}_i) = \text{mag}(\vec{\omega}_f) \equiv \omega_w$

Known:

$I_w = 0.35 \text{ kg·m}^2$
$\omega_w = 3 \text{ rev/s}$
$I_s = 2.9 \text{ kg·m}^2$
$m = 1.0 \text{ kg}$
$r = 0.4 \text{ m}$

Conceptual Model Diagram

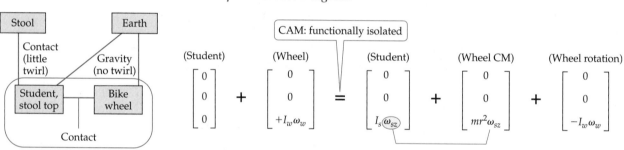

CAM: functionally isolated

$$
\underset{\text{(Student)}}{\begin{bmatrix} 0 \\ 0 \\ 0 \end{bmatrix}} + \underset{\text{(Wheel)}}{\begin{bmatrix} 0 \\ 0 \\ +I_w\omega_w \end{bmatrix}} = \underset{\text{(Student)}}{\begin{bmatrix} 0 \\ 0 \\ I_s\omega_{sz} \end{bmatrix}} + \underset{\text{(Wheel CM)}}{\begin{bmatrix} 0 \\ 0 \\ mr^2\omega_{sz} \end{bmatrix}} + \underset{\text{(Wheel rotation)}}{\begin{bmatrix} 0 \\ 0 \\ -I_w\omega_w \end{bmatrix}}
$$

Stool — Earth
Contact (little twirl) — Gravity (no twirl)
Student, stool top — Bike wheel
Contact

Prose Model   The system here is the student, the stool, and the bicycle wheel, which is functionally isolated. We will assume that the student is symmetric (although this is clearly only an approximation!) and take our reference point O to be the student's center of mass so that the student's final angular momentum is given by $I_s\vec{\omega}_s$. (Because the wheel's mass is so small compared to the student's, we will neglect the difference between the student's and system's centers of mass.) The wheel *is* symmetric about its center of mass, so its angular momentum about its center of mass is $I_w\vec{\omega}_i$ initially and $I_w\vec{\omega}_f$ finally. However, if the student rotates in the final situation, then the wheel's center of mass will also rotate around O with the same angular velocity as the student. According to equation C13.14, this means that the wheel's *total* angular momentum about O will be $\vec{L}^{\text{cm}} + \vec{L}^{\text{rot}} = mr^2\vec{\omega}_s + I_w\vec{\omega}_f$. Note that the wheel's initial and final angular velocities $\vec{\omega}_{wi}$ and $\vec{\omega}_{wf}$ are upward and downward, respectively, and if we assume the bearings are frictionless, then they cannot exert any torque on the wheel that would change its rotational speed, implying that $\text{mag}(\vec{\omega}_i) = \text{mag}(\vec{\omega}_f) \equiv \omega_w$. Also note that the student is not rotating originally, and since the student is constrained to rotate about the vertical axis, the student's final angular momentum must be vertical. Conservation of angular momentum therefore implies in this case that

$$
\begin{bmatrix} 0 \\ 0 \\ 0 \end{bmatrix} + \begin{bmatrix} 0 \\ 0 \\ +I_w\omega_w \end{bmatrix} = \begin{bmatrix} 0 \\ 0 \\ I_s\omega_{sz} \end{bmatrix} + \begin{bmatrix} 0 \\ 0 \\ mr^2\omega_{sz} - I_w\omega_w \end{bmatrix} \tag{C14.17}
$$

Only the bottom line of this equation tells us anything meaningful, but we know all quantities except the z component ω_{sz} of the student's final angular velocity, so we can solve.

Solution   Extracting the bottom line of equation C14.18 and solving for ω_{sz} yield

$$I_w\omega_w = (I_s + mr^2)\omega_{sz} - I_w\omega_w \quad \Rightarrow \quad (I_s + mr^2)\omega_{sz} = 2I_w\omega_z$$

$$\Rightarrow \quad \omega_{sz} = \frac{2I_w}{I_s + mr^2}\omega_w = \frac{2(0.35 \text{ kg·m}^2)}{2.9 \text{ kg·m}^2 + (1.0 \text{ kg})(0.4 \text{ m})^2}\left(\frac{3 \text{ rev}}{\text{s}}\right)$$

$$= 0.69 \text{ rev/s} (\approx 1 \text{ rev per } 1.5 \text{ s}) \qquad\qquad \text{(C14.18)}$$

Evaluation   The units clearly work out. The fact that ω_{sz} is positive means that $\vec{\omega}_s$ is vertically upward, which makes intuitive sense: if the wheel's angular momentum was originally upward and finally downward, the student must gain some upward angular momentum to conserve angular momentum. The student's rotation rate also seems plausible.

Exercise C14X.4

Two children of mass m riding on a disk-shaped playground merry-go-round of mass $2m$ are initially both standing on opposite sides of the merry-go-round rim a distance R from the merry-go-round's center while it rotates with angular speed ω. The children both move in toward the center until each is a distance $\frac{1}{2}R$ from the center. (a) By what factor will the merry-go-round's rotational speed increase? (b) By what factor does the children's rotational speed $v = r\omega$ increase?

Example C14.3 illustrates a situation where all three conservation laws come into play! (For the sake of brevity, I have not included a prose version of the conceptual model.)

Example C14.3

Problem   A 65-kg astronaut working in the International Space Station asks a partner for a wrench. The partner, in a playful mood, cries "Catch!" and tosses the 2-kg wrench at a speed of 3 m/s. The first astronaut, who was floating at rest, catches the wrench just as it passes 35 cm to the left of the astronaut's center of mass. (a) Estimate the astronaut's rotation rate after the catch. (b) How does the astronaut's center of mass move after the catch? (c) What percentage of the wrench's kinetic energy ends up as thermal energy in this process?

Translation

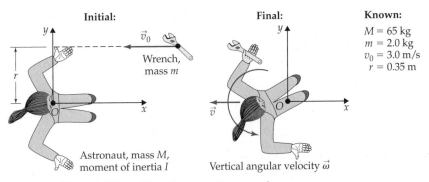

Initial:
$\vec{v}_0$
Wrench, mass m
y
x
r
Astronaut, mass M, moment of inertia I

Final:
y
$\vec{v}$
x
O
Vertical angular velocity $\vec{\omega}$

Known:
$M = 65$ kg
$m = 2.0$ kg
$v_0 = 3.0$ m/s
$r = 0.35$ m

O is the initial position of astronaut's center of mass

Conceptual Model Diagrams   We will model the astronaut as being a roughly cylinder of radius $R \approx 15$ cm and ignore the fact that the astronaut will not *quite* be rotating around his or her personal center of mass while holding the wrench.

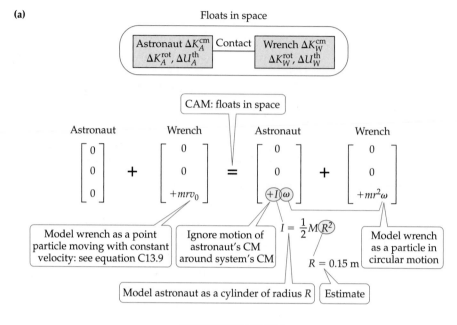

(a)

(b)

(c)   In this particular problem it is easiest to calculate the changes in the *total system's* translational, rotational, and thermal energies.

Solution   (a) The z component of the conservation of angular momentum equation reads

$$mrv_0 \approx (I + mr^2)\omega \quad \Rightarrow \quad \omega \approx \frac{mrv_0}{I + mr^2} = \frac{mrv_0}{\frac{1}{2}MR^2 + mr^2}$$

$$\Rightarrow \quad \omega \approx \frac{(2\text{ kg})(0.35\text{ m})(3\text{ m/s})}{\frac{1}{2}(65\text{ kg})(0.15\text{ m})^2 + (4\text{ kg})(0.35\text{ m})^2}\left(\frac{1\text{ rad}}{1}\right)$$

$$= 1.23\frac{\text{rad}}{\text{s}}\left(\frac{1\text{ rev}}{2\pi\text{ rad}}\right) = 0.20\frac{\text{rev}}{\text{s}} = \frac{1\text{ rev}}{5.0\text{ s}} \tag{C14.19}$$

(b) The x component of the conservation of momentum equation implies that

$$-mv_0 = (M + m)v_x$$

$$\Rightarrow \quad v_x = -\frac{m}{M + m}v_0$$

$$\Rightarrow \quad v_x = -\frac{2\,\text{kg}}{67\,\text{kg}}\left(3\,\frac{\text{m}}{\text{s}}\right) = -0.09\,\frac{\text{m}}{\text{s}} \qquad \text{(C14.20)}$$

(c) Solving the conservation of energy equation for ΔU^{th} yields

$$\Delta U^{\text{th}} = \tfrac{1}{2}mv_0^2 - \tfrac{1}{2}(m + M)v^2 - \tfrac{1}{2}(I + mr^2)\omega^2$$

$$= \frac{1}{2}mv_0^2 - \frac{1}{2}(m + M)\left(\frac{mv_0}{m + M}\right)^2 - \frac{1}{2}(I + mr^2)\left(\frac{mrv_0}{I + mr^2}\right)^2$$

$$\Rightarrow \quad \frac{\Delta U^{\text{th}}}{\tfrac{1}{2}mv_0^2} = 1 - \frac{m}{m + M} - \frac{mr^2}{\tfrac{1}{2}MR^2 + mr^2}$$

$$= 1 - \frac{m}{m + M} - \frac{1}{\tfrac{1}{2}MR^2/mr^2 + 1}$$

$$= 1 - \frac{2\,\text{kg}}{67\,\text{kg}} - \left[\frac{\tfrac{1}{2}(65\,\text{kg})(0.15\,\text{m})^2}{(2\,\text{kg})(0.35\,\text{m})^2} + 1\right]^{-1}$$

$$= 1 - 0.03 - 0.25 = 0.72 \qquad \text{(C14.21)}$$

Evaluation   All the units come out correctly, and the sign of v_x makes sense. Note that the fraction of the wrench's kinetic energy converted to thermal energy comes out less than 1, which is a good sign. The last calculation in fact tells us that 3% of the wrench's energy goes to kinetic energy of the system's center of mass and 25% to rotational kinetic energy.

C14.5   Application: Neutron Stars

A normal star supports itself against its own gravitational field because thermonuclear interactions keep its core hot, and a hot gas has a high pressure that resists compression. As the star ages, "ashes" from the thermonuclear reactions begin to build up in the core. Since these ashes cannot produce thermal energy to keep pressure in the core high, the core begins to contract. If the star is fairly massive, the core will eventually accumulate about 1.4 solar masses of ashes within a radius of about 10,000 km (with a density > 10^9 g/cm³!).

Up to this point, the pressure of electrons rattling around the core keeps it from shrinking too quickly. But at this density, electrons mingle so closely with atomic nuclei that electrons start to react with protons to form neutrons and neutrinos ($p + e^- \rightarrow n + v$). This nuclear reaction eats up the very electrons that support the core against collapse. The core thus begins to shrink. This squeezes electrons into yet closer proximity to protons, which encourages the reaction, which increases the rate of contraction, and so on.

This positive feedback effect rapidly converts the contraction into a catastrophic collapse. Once the reaction begins, the core's radius goes from about 10,000 km to about 12 km within about 0.3 s. At this radius, the star is entirely comprised of neutrons, and the density is so high ($\approx 10^{14}$ g/cm³) that the

Why stars go supernova

Pictures of a region of the Large Magellanic Cloud before and after Supernova 1987A.

Neutron stars and pulsars

Estimating the rotation speed of a neutron star

neutrons touch, making the core strongly resistant to further collapse. As material outside the core crashes down on the suddenly solid core, a shock wave is formed that blows much of that material away in a gigantic explosion. This is a supernova.

After the explosion is over, what is left behind is a tiny, rapidly rotating **neutron star.** Such objects usually have an intense magnetic field that is swept around with the star as it rotates. This radiates radio waves that pulse in step with the neutron star's rotation. A neutron star emitting detectable pulses of radio waves in this manner is called a **pulsar.**

How fast should a pulsar spin? The sun (whose radius is 700,000 km) rotates about once every month (≈ 2.6 Ms). Assume that when a typical stellar core (which contains 1.4 solar masses) has this radius, it also rotates once every 2.6 Ms. Since the star is an isolated object, conservation of angular momentum implies that the core's angular momentum *after* collapse should be the same as its angular momentum originally.

Assuming that the core is essentially a uniform sphere at all sizes, the magnitude of its angular momentum will be $L = I\omega = \frac{2}{5}MR^2\omega$. During the contraction and collapse of the core, M remains the same, but R decreases by a factor of about 60,000. Therefore, ω must increase by a factor of $(60{,}000)^2 = 3.6 \times 10^9$ to keep L the same. Since $\omega = 2\pi \text{ rad}/T$, where T is the **period** of the star's rotation (the time required for the star to rotate once), increasing ω by a factor of 3.6×10^9 means that T must decrease by the same factor, from 2.6×10^6 s to about 0.7 ms (0.7×10^{-3} s).

Astronomers have indeed observed a handful of pulsars with periods on the order of 1 ms. Most have rotational periods 10 to 1000 times longer. This is probably because the pulsar sweeps an intense magnetic field around thousands of times a second. Interactions between this magnetic field and gas surrounding the pulsar slowly drain energy from the pulsar, which comes at the expense of its rotational kinetic energy. Over hundreds of millions of years, this gradually slows the neutron star's spin rate: pulsars with long rotational periods are thus ones that have been around for quite a while. But consistent with this model, no pulsars have been observed with periods much *less* than 1 ms.

In 1987, a supernova was detected in the Large Magellanic Cloud: this was the nearest supernova to the earth in several centuries. Consistent with the supernova model described above, a burst of neutrinos was detected just before the explosion became visible. After the debris from the explosion clears, we should see a neutron star remnant rotating with a period of about 1 ms.

Incidentally, the huge moment of inertia of a neutron star and its excellent isolation mean that its rotation rate is *very* constant. This makes pulsars excellent clocks, better by orders of magnitude than anything available on earth (even if we take account of the slowing effect discussed above).

Pulsars as clocks

Exercise C14X.5

No star is a uniform sphere, but rather becomes more dense as one gets closer to its center. This means that the star's moment of inertia is not $\frac{2}{5}MR^2$ but rather αMR^2, where α is a number less than $\frac{2}{5}$ whose exact value depends on the star's density profile. Argue that no matter what α is, if it remains roughly constant as the star collapses, the star's final period is still 0.7 ms.

TWO-MINUTE PROBLEMS

C14T.1 When I was a teenager, I saw a "Candid Camera" sequence in which they filmed a person struggling with a suitcase that (unknown to that person) contained a large and rapidly spinning gyroscope. Imagine that you are carrying a suitcase containing a gyroscope whose angular velocity is horizontal and points directly away from your legs as you carry it with your right hand. Imagine that you make a 90° turn to the left as you walk. What does the suitcase do?
   A. It turns to the left along with you.
   B. It turns to the right as you try to turn left.
   C. Its bottom edge flips up away from your legs as you make the turn.
   D. Its bottom edge flips in to tangle with your legs.
   E. Its front end dips toward the ground.
   F. Its back end dips toward the ground.
   T. It attempts to maintain its original orientation.

C14T.2 Experienced players can throw a Frisbee using forehand motion that causes the Frisbee to rotate counterclockwise (when thrown by a right-handed person). If a Frisbee thrown in this way is to skip off the ground, which edge has to hit the ground first?
   A. The back edge.
   B. The front edge.
   C. The left edge.

(more)

D. The right edge.

E. One can't make the Frisbee thrown in this way skip.

C14T.3 Which of the following changes in a top's design will cause the largest decrease in the top's precession rate?

A. Increasing its mass by 10%.

B. Decreasing its height by 10%.

C. Increasing its radius by 10%.

D. Increasing its angular speed by 10%.

E. Changes B, C, and D have the same effect.

F. None of these design changes modify the precession rate.

C14T.4 A person is sitting at rest on a stool that is free to rotate about a vertical axis while holding in one hand a bicycle wheel that is rapidly spinning counterclockwise when viewed from above. The person then stops the wheel with the other hand. What happens to the person as a result?

A. The person must rotate counterclockwise.

B. The person must rotate clockwise.

C. The person will rotate in a direction that depends on which hand does the stopping.

D. Nothing; the wheel's angular momentum is carried away by external interactions.

E. Nothing; the wheel's angular momentum is simply dissipated by the friction interaction.

C14T.5 An astronaut floating at rest in space throws a ball to another astronaut, using a side-arm motion that ends up releasing the ball well to the astronaut's right as he or she faces the direction of the ball's forward motion. After throwing the ball, the astronaut (when viewed from above)

A. Remains completely at rest.

B. Rotates clockwise, but his or her center of mass remains at rest.

C. Rotates counterclockwise, but her or his center of mass remains at rest.

D. Rotates clockwise and his or her center of mass moves opposite to the ball's motion.

E. Rotates counterclockwise and her or his center of mass moves opposite to the ball's motion.

F. Other (specify).

C14T.6 If global warming proceeds during the next century as anticipated, it is possible that the polar ice caps will melt, substantially raising sea levels around the world (and flooding coastal cities such as New York). Would this shorten, lengthen, or have strictly no effect on the duration of the day?

A. Lengthen the day slightly.

B. Shorten it slightly.

C. Have strictly *no* effect on the length of the day.

HOMEWORK PROBLEMS

Basic Skills

C14B.1 Imagine that you are carrying a suitcase that contains a gyroscope whose large angular velocity is directed horizontally forward. As you attempt to turn the suitcase to the left, describe what happens to the suitcase and why.

C14B.2 Imagine that you are carrying a suitcase that contains a gyroscope whose large angular velocity is directed horizontally forward. As you attempt to go up a staircase, describe what happens to the suitcase and why.

C14B.3 Consider a simple top consisting of a disk 10 cm in diameter pierced through the center by a very light-weight rod 4 cm long, as shown in figure C14.6.

(a) If the top is rotating at a rate of 30 rev/s, what is its precession rate $d\phi/dt$?

(b) What is the period of the precession?

C14B.4 A person is sitting at rest on a stool that is free to rotate about a vertical axis while holding at one's knees an electric drill connected to a large flywheel at rest. The person then turns on the drill, which

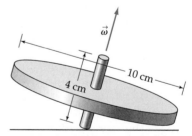

Figure C14.6
A top consisting of a disk pierced by a rod.

causes the flywheel to spin counterclockwise (when viewed from above) about a vertical axis. Does the person rotate? If so, in which direction? Explain your reasoning.

C14B.5 When our sun runs out of fuel, it will eventually become a white dwarf star with about the same radius as the earth. Estimate the sun's rotational period when it is that size. (The sun's current radius is about 700,000 km, and its current period of rotation is roughly 2.6 Ms.)

Synthetic

C14S.1 Imagine that you throw a boomerang vertically so that its axis of rotation is horizontal and the boomerang rotates counterclockwise when viewed by someone to your left (see figure C14.7). Because each blade moves faster with respect to the air when it is on top than it does when it is on the bottom, whichever blade is on top will exert more lift than the blade on the bottom. This exerts a torque on the boomerang around its center of mass. What will this do to the boomerang's axis of rotation? (*Hint:* Due to this effect, the boomerang travels in a horizontal circle back to the thrower. See "The Aerodynamics of Boomerangs" in the November 1968 issue of *Scientific American* for more details.)

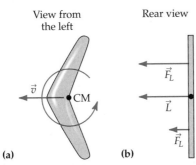

View from the left   Rear view

Figure C14.7
(a) A boomerang just as it is released, as viewed by a person standing to the thrower's left.
(b) The same boomerang as seen by the thrower (showing the different lift forces on the two wings).

C14S.2 A certain playground merry-go-round is essentially an 80-kg iron disk 2.0 m in radius. Two children, each with a mass of 44 kg, are originally standing on opposite sides of the disk near its outer edge. The merry-go-round is turning essentially without friction about a vertical axis once every 5 s. The children then clamber toward each other so that they are only 1.0 m from the center. How long does it take the merry-go-round to complete a revolution now?

C14S.3 Two astronauts of roughly equal mass are floating in space. They both hold onto a light rod 20 m long, and the whole system is rotating about the center of the rod about once every 30 s.
(a) What is the ordinary speed of each astronaut?
(b) Now imagine that the astronauts pull themselves along the rod until they are 10 m apart. What is their ordinary speed now?
(c) Where do you think that their increased kinetic energy came from?

C14S.4 A dining table has a 3.0-kg turntable in the middle for serving food. The turntable is a wooden disk 0.8 m in diameter. It is rotating at a rate of 1 rev per 5 s when someone puts a 0.25-kg coffee cup on it near its edge. What is its rotation rate now?

C14S.5 A cat is sitting on the rim of a wooden turntable that is free to turn about a vertical axis. The turntable's mass is 3 times the cat's mass, and it is initially at rest. The cat then starts walking around the rim at a speed of 0.6 m/s relative to the ground. How fast does the turntable's rim move relative to the ground?

C14S.6 A person holds a 5-kg weight in each hand with arms outstretched while standing at rest on a light-weight platform that is free to turn about a vertical axis. Other people then set the person turning at a rate of one turn per 7.2 s. The person then lowers the weights until they are alongside the person's legs. At this point, the person is spinning once every 1.2 s. Estimate the person's moment of inertia.

C14S.7 The current generation of electric cars performs poorly because currently available batteries store *much* less energy per kilogram than a tank of gas. An alternative way to create an emission-free car is to use flywheels to store energy in the form of rotational kinetic energy. A well-designed electric motor can also be used as an electric generator. If we were to attach a motor/generator to an appropriately designed flywheel, we could use it as a motor to *store* electrical energy in the flywheel (by increasing its rotational speed) and as a generator to extract electrical energy from the flywheel's rotational energy.

Engineers have recently built a working carbon-fiber flywheel whose mass is 23 kg, whose radius is 15 cm, and which rotates safely at 1700 rev/s without flying apart. At these kinds of rotation speeds, the flywheel has to rotate in a vacuum on magnetic bearings that actually suspend the flywheel in space. Magnets on the flywheel axle interact electromagnetically with coils in the case to convert the flywheel's rotational kinetic energy to electrical energy, or vice versa. The complete package has a mass of about 41 kg.
(a) Show that such a flywheel can store about 15 MJ of energy.
(b) A lead-acid battery stores about 90 kJ/kg. Gasoline stores about 46 MJ/kg, but an internal combustion engine can only convert about 20% of this energy to mechanical energy, whereas 80% to 90% of stored electrical energy can be converted to mechanical energy. Also the figure for gasoline does not include the mass of the tank and engine, which is about 300 kg for a smallish car that can hold 45 kg of gasoline: an electric motor with comparable power is much less massive (let's estimate about 50 kg).

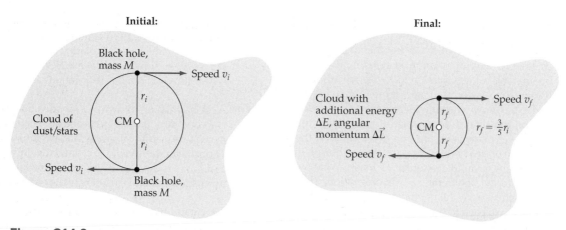

Figure C14.8

A pair of black holes loses orbital energy and angular momentum to a dust cloud as the holes move around their common center of mass (problem C14S.8).

Considering these factors, compare flywheel energy storage with energy storage in batteries and gasoline.

(c) Sixteen such flywheel packages could give an efficient car an effective range of about 300 mi. Such packages would have to be arranged in pairs that rotate in opposite directions. Why? What would happen if they were all lined up in the same way?

(d) Imagine that one of the flywheels fails, shredding into fibers that eventually come to rest through friction interactions with the case. Assume that the 18-kg case is made mostly of aluminum and, even though it successfully contains the fibers, gets about one-half the thermal energy created by the failure. What is its approximate increase in temperature?

(e) Assume that the failed flywheel's original angular velocity was directed horizontally forward. If an 800-kg car were completely free to rotate about a horizontal forward axis, very roughly how fast would it rotate after the failure? (This result will give us an idea about how violently the car would respond to such a failure.)

Closing comments: In addition to possible problems associated with flywheel failures, the main problem with flywheel energy storage is expense: even when mass-produced, a 16-flywheel package would cost an estimated $13,000 (this does not include the car!). For more information about flywheel energy storage, see W. Hively, "Reinventing the Wheel," *Discover*, **17**(8), August 1996; and R. Post et al., *Scientific American*, **229**(6), 1973.

C14S.8 Astronomers currently believe that every galaxy has a supermassive black hole at its center and that a typical galaxy has collided with other galaxies several times since the beginning of the universe.

Imagine that the central black holes of two colliding galaxies end up after the collision in an essentially circular orbit about their common center of mass, orbiting each other in the middle of a cloud of dust and stars. In this situation, the black holes' friction-like interactions with the cloud will cause them to lose energy and slowly spiral in toward each other as time passes. Assume that the black holes have the same mass M (which may be several million times the sun's mass!). If their orbits remain approximately circular as they slowly spiral in, the speed of each in its circular orbit will be $v = \frac{1}{2}(GM/r)^{1/2}$, where G is the universal gravitational constant and r is the distance between each black hole and their common center of mass. (We will be able to prove this result in unit N: for right now, just accept it as true.) Assume that the initial value of r is r_i and that after some given amount of time, the black holes have spiraled in enough that r becomes $r_f = \frac{3}{5}r_i$, as shown in figure C14.8. During this time, what is the change ΔE in the cloud's energy? What is the magnitude ΔL of the change in its angular momentum? Express both answers in terms of G, M, and r_i (and make sure that the units of your expressions are correct).

Rich-Context

C14R.1 You are working on digital effects for the next *Star Wars* episode. You are responsible for a scene where a small, fast-moving fighter crashes and embeds itself in a long, skinny Empire battle cruiser initially at rest. You want to make sure that the physics is right so that your rendering looks realistic. Let's model the fighter as a point particle and the cruiser as a skinny rod. You estimate the cruiser's mass to be $20m$, where m is the fighter's mass, and the cruiser's length to be 100 m. You also estimate that the fighter is traveling at 500 m/s when it hits.

Assume also that the fighter hits close to one end of the cruiser and is traveling perpendicular to the cruiser when it hits.

(a) What is the cruiser's final rate of rotation after the collision (in revolutions per second)?

(b) At what speed does the cruiser's center of mass move after the collision?

(c) Assume that the fighter is made of aluminum and gets one-half of the thermal energy created in the collision. What will its final temperature be? Will it melt or vaporize?

C14R.2 When jumping from a platform, a high diver initially holds his or her body essentially extended and straight and rotates slowly while falling. The diver then tucks into a compact shape and tumbles rapidly. As the diver nears the water, she or he straightens out again and again rotates only slowly while entering the water. Roughly estimate how much faster you would tumble when compacted in a ball than you would when your body was extended and straight. (*Hints:* Think of simple shapes that you can use as models for your body in both

configurations, and make some measurements or estimates about radii or lengths.)

Advanced

C14A.1 Consider Newton's explanation of the earth's precession. Let's crudely model the bulges at the earth's equator as two point particles on the earth's surface on opposite sides of the equator, each with mass m, sitting on top of an otherwise perfectly spherical earth. Assume that the earth's equator is tipped at an angle of 23° relative to the plane of the moon's orbit. Remember that the gravitational force exerted on each of these particles is directly toward the moon with magnitude $F_g = GMm/r^2$, where M is the mass of the moon and r is the distance between the particle and the moon's center. Using data from the inside front cover, estimate the value of m required to give the observed precession rate, and compare to the earth's mass. (For our model to make sense, m had better be pretty small compared to the earth's mass.)

ANSWERS TO EXERCISES

C14X.1 If the top is initially rotating clockwise instead of counterclockwise, then it will also precess clockwise. To see this, consider figure C14.2. In this top view, $\vec{L}$ now points mostly away from the viewer, and so points to the *left* of O if the top leans to the right. A twirl $[d\vec{L}]$ toward the top of this diagram causes $\vec{L}$ (and thus the axis of rotation) to change in the clockwise direction.

C14X.2 If the Frisbee's trailing edge hits first, the right-hand rule for the cross product implies that the normal part of the contact interaction exerts a leftward torque on the Frisbee. If the Frisbee is spinning clockwise, so that its angular momentum points downward, then shifting the tip of this angular momentum vector to the left causes the Frisbee to tip toward the right. So the Frisbee will veer off to the right if its trailing edge hits first.

C14X.3 The system's initial rotational kinetic energy is

$$\frac{1}{2}I_i\omega_i^2 = \frac{1}{2}(9.1 \text{ kg·m}^2)\left(0.25 \frac{\text{rev}}{s}\right)^2\left(\frac{2\pi \text{ rad}}{1 \text{ rev}}\right)^2$$

$$\times \left(\frac{1}{1 \text{ rad}}\right)^2\left(\frac{1 \text{ J}}{1 \text{ kg·m}^2/s^2}\right)$$

$$= 11.2 \text{ J} \qquad \text{(C14.22)}$$

The system's change in kinetic energy (which we are presuming comes at the expense of chemical

energy) is

$$K_f^{\text{rot}} - K_i^{\text{rot}} = 2.76(11.2 \text{ J}) - 11.2 \text{ J} = 19.8 \text{ J}$$

$$= 19.8\text{J}\left(\frac{1 \text{ Cal}}{4186\text{J}}\right)$$

$$= 0.0047 \text{ Cal} \qquad \text{(C14.23)}$$

C14X.4 Treat the children as point particles. Since the total moment of inertia of the merry-go-round plus children is the sum of the moments of inertia of its parts, initially the system's total moment of inertia is

$$I_i = \frac{1}{2}(2m)R^2 + mR^2 + mR^2 = 3mR^2 \qquad \text{(C14.24)}$$

remembering that the moment of inertia of a disk of mass M and radius R is given by $\frac{1}{2}MR^2$. When the children move in to radius $\frac{1}{2}R$, the system's moment of inertia becomes

$$I_f = \frac{1}{2}(2m)R^2 + \frac{1}{4}mR^2 + \frac{1}{4}mR^2 = \frac{3}{2}mR^2 \qquad \text{(C14.25)}$$

(a) Since the system's moment of inertia has gone down by a factor of 2, if its total angular momentum $\vec{L} = I\vec{\omega}$ is to be conserved, then the system's angular velocity $\vec{\omega}$ must increase by a factor of 2.

(b) Each child's rotational speed $v = r\omega$ remains the same in this case, because although ω increases by a factor of 2, their distance r from the center of rotation has decreased by a factor of 2.

C14X.5 Conservation of angular momentum in this case
implies that

$$I_i \omega_i = I_f \omega_f \quad \Rightarrow \quad \frac{I_f}{I_i} = \frac{\omega_i}{\omega_f} = \frac{2\pi/T_i}{2\pi/T_f} = \frac{T_f}{T_i}$$

$$\Rightarrow \quad \frac{T_f}{T_i} = \frac{\alpha M R_f^2}{\alpha M R_i^2}$$

$$= \left(\frac{R_f}{R_i}\right)^2 \qquad \text{(C14.26)}$$

This equation clearly shows that the ratio of the initial to final rotational periods is equal to the square of the ratio of the initial to final radii, irrespective of the value of α (as long as it is constant). So the final rotation time we found assuming that $\alpha = \frac{2}{5}$ will be the same as we would get for any other value of α.

Glossary

absolute zero: the temperature at which all random molecular motion ceases. (Section C10.3.)

allowed region: any continuous range of light object positions where the system's potential energy is less than its total energy. Such a position is *allowed* because the kinetic energy of the light object is positive there. (Section C11.1.)

angular momentum $\vec{L}$ (around a given point O): For a particle, by definition, $\vec{L} = \vec{r} \times \vec{p}$, where $\vec{r}$ is the particle's position relative to O and $\vec{p}$ is its ordinary momentum. If the particle is moving in a circle around O, then $\vec{L} = mr^2\vec{\omega}$, where $\vec{\omega}$ is the particle's angular velocity in its circular trajectory. For a symmetric extended object rotating about any O lying along its axis of rotation, $\vec{L} = I\vec{\omega}$, where $\vec{\omega}$ is the object's angular velocity. The total angular momentum of an isolated system about any arbitrary origin O will be conserved. (Section C13.3.)

angular speed ω: the rate $|d\theta/dt|$ at which a particle's angular position changes with time. *Angular position* here means the angle (in some specified plane) between the particle's position vector and some specified direction. The angular speed of a rigid extended object rotating about some axis is the angular speed of any particle in the object around that axis. The SI units for angular speed are radians per second (rad/s), and most equations involving ω will not come out correctly if ω is not expressed in radians per second. (Section C9.3.)

angular velocity $\vec{\omega}$: a vector describing an object's rotational motion whose magnitude is the object's angular speed and whose direction is along the axis of rotation in the direction indicated by your right thumb when your fingers curl in the direction of rotation. (Section C9.3.)

anticommutative (operation): a product (such as the cross product) for which changing the order of its factors changes its sign: $\vec{u} \times \vec{w} = -\vec{w} \times \vec{u}$. (Section C13.2.)

antiparticle: a particle having the same mass and (most) other properties as a given elementary particle but having the opposite charge. (Section C1.5.)

average force: the impulse delivered during a time interval dt divided by dt. We use this term when we suspect $\vec{F}$ is *not* constant during dt, as required by equation C3.6. (Section C3.3.)

(coordinate) axis: one of the three mutually perpendicular lines in space defined by a reference frame. These lines are called the x, y, and z axes, respectively. (Section C2.8.)

basic SI units: the SI units considered by the SI committee to be fundamental. In addition to the *second*, the *meter*, and the *kilogram*, we will use the following basic units: the *kelvin* (for temperature), the *ampere* (for electrical current), and the *mole* (for the number of molecules). The seventh unit is the *candela* (for luminous intensity): we will not use the candela in this course. (Section C1.8.)

Boltzmann's constant k_B: a constant equal in value to 1.38×10^{-23} J/K. The average molecular translational kinetic energy in a substance (if T is expressed in kelvins) is about $\frac{3}{2}k_B T$. Total thermal energies per molecule at a given temperature T typically range between $k_B T$ and $10k_B T$. (Section C10.3.)

bond: an interaction between two objects such that they remain bound together, maintaining a roughly constant separation. Making a bond releases energy; breaking the bond consumes energy. (Section C11.2.)

caloric: a hypothetical, self-repelling fluid that fills hot objects (according to the caloric model, which was accepted between the 1770s and the 1840s). (Section C10.2.)

calorie: the amount of caloric required to raise the temperature of 1 g of water by $1°C$ (1 cal $= 4.186$ J). Note that a *food calorie* is 1000 times larger. (Section C10.2.)

center of mass (of a system): a mathematical point representing the weighted average of the positions of all the particles in the system. Mathematically,

$$\vec{r}_{CM} \equiv \frac{1}{M}(m_1\vec{r}_1 + m_2\vec{r}_2 + \cdots + m_N\vec{r}_N) \qquad \text{(C4.2)}$$

where $M = m_1 + m_2 + \cdots + m_N =$ total mass of the system. (Section C4.3.)

charge: a property possessed by a particle or object that enables it to participate in an electromagnetic interaction. (Sections C1.5, C7.1.)

chemical energy U^{ch}: the part of an object's internal energy that changes if the object undergoes an internal chemical reaction. (Section C11.4.)

collision: a relatively brief but powerful internal interaction between objects in a system. (Note that objects do not have to actually touch to collide according to this definition.) If we look at the system's total momentum *just before* and *just after* such a collision, we will find it to be approximately conserved because external interactions just don't have enough *time* to transfer much momentum. (Section C5.2.)

column vector: a method of representing a vector that involves a vertical list of its components enclosed in square brackets. (Section C2.3.)

column vector rule: the rule stating that in any equation, you should be able to substitute a column vector for any symbol with an arrow over it *without* changing the meaning of that equation. This rule helps distinguish legal from illegal equations involving vector symbols. (Section C3.6.)

commutative (operation): a mathematical operation for which reversing the order of operands yields the same result. Addition and multiplication of scalars, addition of vectors, and the dot product of vectors are all commutative operations. (Section C2.2.)

completely inelastic (collision): a collision in which the colliding objects stick together afterward. Such a collision converts the maximum possible amount of a system's original kinetic energy to internal energy. (Section C12.2.)

component vectors (of a vector): the set of three unique vectors whose directions are parallel to the coordinate axes defined by the reference frame and whose vector sum is equal the vector of interest. The component vectors for a vector $\vec{u}$ are written $\vec{u}_x$, $\vec{u}_y$, and $\vec{u}_z$. (Section C2.6.)

components: a set of three signed numbers that provide an alternative and completely numerical representation of any vector. If a vector's symbol is $\vec{u}$, its components are written u_x, u_y, and u_z, and the vector itself is described by the ordered triplet $[u_x, u_y, u_z]$. (Section C2.3.)

compression interaction: a macroscopic interaction that opposes the merging of two macroscopic objects. (Section C1.6.)

conceptual model: (1) A simplified mental image of a phenomenon that helps us understand it and think about it. (Section C1.1.) (2) The part of the problem-solving framework in which you think about the physical equations and principles that link quantities of interest in a problem, select approximations and assumptions that make the problem solvable, and develop a plan for solving the problem. (Section C5.3.)

conceptual model diagram: a tool for compactly and visually representing the conceptual model step of a problem solution. Such diagrams are usually less work and more helpful than writing out the equivalent material in prose. (Section C5.4.)

conservation law: a law asserting that for an isolated set of interacting objects, the total value of some quantity does not change with time. The most important such quantities are **energy, momentum,** and **angular momentum,** which are conserved because the laws of physics do not depend on what time it is, where you are located, and how you are oriented (respectively). Note that the quantity called *momentum* is sometimes called *linear momentum* to distinguish it from

angular momentum; but in cases where there is no ambiguity, the qualifier is usually dropped. (Section C1.2.)

contact (interaction): an interaction between two macroscopic objects that arises only from direct physical contact. Such interactions include *friction* interactions that oppose the relative motion of the interacting objects, *compression* interactions that resist intermingling of the objects' atoms, and *tension* interactions that oppose the separation of joined objects. *All* known contact interactions can be placed into one of these three categories. (Section C1.6.)

coordinate directions: a general term for the mutually perpendicular $+x$, $+y$, and $+z$ directions defined by a reference frame. (Sections C2.3, C2.6.)

coordinate system: see **reference frame.**

coordinates: an ordered set of numbers x, y, z that specify an object's position in a given reference frame by specifying the distance and direction (positive or negative) that one would have to travel along each axis direction to get from the frame's origin to the object. (Section C2.8.)

coulomb: the SI unit of charge, approximately equivalent to the charge of 6.242×10^{18} protons. (Section C7.1.)

Coulomb constant k: a fundamental physical constant that expresses the potential energy involved in the electrostatic interaction between two particles with unit charge separated by unit distance. If charge is measured in coulombs and distance in meters, then $k = 8.99 \times 10^9$ J·m/C^2. (Section C7.1.)

cross product $\vec{u} \times \vec{w}$ (of two vectors $\vec{u}$ and $\vec{w}$): a vector whose *magnitude* is $uw \sin \theta$ (where θ is the angle from the direction of $\vec{u}$ to that of $\vec{w}$) and whose *direction* is perpendicular to both $\vec{u}$ and $\vec{w}$ in the sense indicated by your right thumb when your right fingers curl from $\vec{u}$ to $\vec{w}$. (Section C13.2.)

degree: a unit of angular measure equal to $\pi/180$ radians.

derived units: SI units that are defined in terms of combinations of basic units. These include the *newton, joule, watt, pascal, coulomb, volt,* and *ohm.* (Section C1.8.)

deuterium: a hydrogen atom whose nucleus contains a proton and a neutron (instead of just a proton, as is usually the case). (Section C11.4.)

direction (of a vector): the aspect of the vector that specifies its orientation in space. (Section C2.1.)

directionals ($\hat{x}$, $\hat{y}$, $\hat{z}$): symbols that provide a shorthand notation for the phrases "in the $+x$ direction," "in the $+y$ direction," and "in the $+z$ direction," respectively. (These are sometimes called unit vectors, but this is an unnecessary complication at this stage.) (Section C2.3.)

displacement: a vector indicating a shift in position. Its components specify the distance and direction that one would have to travel in the x, y, and z directions to get from the initial position to the final position. (Equivalently, each component is simply the difference between the corresponding initial and final coordinates of the points.) The magnitude of a displacement indicates the straight-line distance between the positions. (Section C2.2.)

dot product (of two vectors): a product of two vectors that yields a *scalar* value, defined as follows:

$$\vec{u} \cdot \vec{w} = uw \cos\theta = u_x w_x + u_y w_y + u_z w_z$$

The dot product behaves algebraically pretty much as the ordinary product of two numbers. (Section C8.2.)

drag: the part of a contact interaction between an object moving through a fluid (such as water or air) that exerts a force on the wing opposite to the object's velocity relative to the fluid. (Section C8.7.)

elastic (collision): a collision in which the kinetic energy of the colliding objects is conserved: no energy is converted to internal energy. (Section C12.2.)

electrical energy: the term for energy delivered to a system in the form of electrons flowing through a circuit. We can treat this as a form of internal energy U^{el}. (Section C11.5.)

electromagnetic field theory: a theory of the electromagnetic interaction that represents a good approximation to relativistic quantum field theory when applied to objects and distances much larger than single atoms in fairly weak electromagnetic fields. (Section C1.2.)

electromagnetic interaction: one of the four fundamental interactions. The electromagnetic interaction acts between all particles with electrical charge, and is only weaker than the strong nuclear interaction. (Section C1.5.)

electromagnetic wave: a wave associated with the electromagnetic interaction that can carry energy. Radio waves, microwaves, infrared rays, light, ultraviolet rays, X-rays, and gamma rays are all examples of electromagnetic waves. We can treat the energy carried by such waves as a form of internal energy U^{em}. (Section C11.5.)

electrostatic: pertaining to the part of the electromagnetic interaction that would operate between two charged particles if they were at rest (i.e., the velocity-*independent* part of the electromagnetic interaction). (Section C7.1.)

electrostatic interaction: one of the possible long-range interactions between macroscopic objects. To participate in an electrostatic interaction, at least one of the objects must be electrically charged. (Section C1.6.)

elementary (particle): a subatomic particle that has no known substructure. Each has an **antiparticle** with almost identical properties except opposite electric charge. (Section C1.5.)

energy: (see **total energy.**)

equilibrium position: any position of a light object where it would experience zero force due to interaction with the massive object. The slope of the potential energy curve is zero at such a position. (Section C11.1.)

escape speed: the speed an object would have to have at a given point to be able to escape entirely the gravitational field of another object. (Section C7.5.)

evaluation: the part of the problem-solving framework in which you check your result's (1) units, (2) sign, and (3) magnitude, to see that they make sense. (Section C5.3.)

extended object: a set of particles having a well-defined *surface* that defines its boundary and encloses a nonzero volume. The object need not be rigid as long as its boundary is clear. Examples of extended bodies range from atoms to baseballs to planets to galaxies. (Section C4.1.)

external interaction: an interaction between two particles, one inside a system of interest and the other outside that system. The momentum transfers mediated by such interactions can affect the system's total momentum. (Section C4.1.)

fission: a type of nuclear reaction in which very large nuclei are split to create more tightly-bound smaller nuclei. (Section C11.4.)

(a frame that) **floats in space:** a nonrotating frame attached to the center of mass of a system whose only external interactions are gravitational interactions with objects far away compared to the size of the system. Objects in such a frame behave as if they were in an *inertial* reference frame as long as we *ignore* the external gravitational interactions(!). (Sections C4.5, C5.2.)

food calorie (Cal): 1 Cal = 1000 cal = 4186 J. This unit is typically used to express the energy content of foods. (Section C11.4.)

forbidden region: any continuous range of light object positions where the system's potential energy would exceed its total energy. Such a position is *forbidden* because the kinetic energy of a light object would have to be negative there, but $K = \frac{1}{2}mv^2$ cannot possibly be negative. (Section C11.1.)

force $\vec{F}$ (exerted by an interaction on a particle): the rate $[d\vec{p}]/dt$ at which the interaction causes momentum to flow to that particle (the impulse delivered per unit time). (Section C3.3.)

force law: an equation that specifies how the force exerted on an object by an interaction with another object depends on the two objects' separation. (Section C8.6.)

friction (interaction): one of the possible types of contact interaction between macroscopic objects. When two *solid* objects are involved, a friction interaction is the part of the contact interaction that exerts a force on each object that is parallel to the contacting surfaces. When a solid object is moving through a fluid such as water or air, a friction interaction opposes the object's motion. (Section C1.6.)

functionally isolated (system): a system whose significant external interactions cancel for each object in the system, so that its total momentum is conserved anyway. (Section C5.2.)

fundamental interaction: one of the ways in which elementary particles can interact. The four known fundamental interactions are the *gravitational, electromagnetic, strong nuclear*, and *weak nuclear* interactions. See table C1.2. (Section C1.5.)

fusion: a type of nuclear reaction in which very small atomic nuclei are combined to make larger nuclei that are more tightly bound. (Section C11.4.)

gas: a possible phase for a substance. The molecules of a gas are not bound to each other and thus move freely within whatever encloses the gas. (Section C11.3.)

general relativity (GR): the currently accepted comprehensive theory of gravitation. (Section C1.2.)

Global Positioning System (GPS): a contemporary example of an actual reference frame. The system consists of a number of satellites orbiting the earth that constantly radiate signals detailing their position and the time when the signal was sent. By detecting signals from several satellites, a receiver on earth can calculate its own three-dimensional position to within several meters. (Section C2.8.)

gravitational field vector $\vec{g}$: a vector quantity that expresses the constant of proportionality between an object's weight and its mass at a given point in space. Near the surface of the earth the **gravitational field strength** $g = \text{mag}(\vec{g}) = 9.8$ N/kg. (Section C3.4.)

gravitational interaction: one of the four fundamental interactions. The gravitational interaction acts between all particles (including mediators), but is the weakest (by far) of all the fundamental interactions. At the macroscopic level, we categorize the gravitational interaction as a *long-range* interaction. (Section C1.5.)

heat: hidden energy that flows across the boundary between two objects, driven by a temperature difference alone. (Section C10.5.)

ideal spring: an idealized massless spring whose potential energy is exactly proportional to the square of the distance by which it is compressed or expanded. This is a good approximation to the behavior of realistic springs. (Section C7.4.)

impulse $[d\vec{p}]$: the amount of momentum that a specific interaction contributes to a particle's momentum during a short time interval. (Section C3.3.)

inelastic (collision): a collision in which some of the kinetic energy of the colliding objects is converted to internal energy (usually thermal energy). (Section C12.2.)

inertial reference frame: a reference frame in which Newton's first law is observed to be valid (i.e., a frame in which an isolated object is observed to move at a constant velocity). (Section C4.5.)

interaction: some physical relationship between two objects that (in the absence of other interactions) *changes* the motion of each. (Section C1.4.)

interaction diagram: a diagram that displays a system and its important interactions. In an interaction diagram, objects both inside and outside the system are represented by labeled rectangular boxes and interactions by labeled lines connecting those boxes. A circle around the boxes representing objects inside the system defines the system. (Section C5.4.)

internal energy U: the energy that an object contains within its boundaries in various hidden (microscopic) forms. We consider various types of internal energy in chapters C10 and C11. (Section C10.5.)

internal interaction: an interaction between two particles that are both *inside* the system of interest. The momentum transfers mediated by such interactions remain in the system and therefore do not change the system's total momentum. (Section C4.1.)

inverse sine, inverse cosine, and **inverse tangent** (functions): trigonometric functions that convert the value of a sine, cosine, or tangent, respectively, of an angle to the angle. (Section C2.5.)

isolated system: a system that does not participate in any external interactions. (Section C4.2.)

joule: the standard SI unit of energy: $1 \text{ J} \equiv 1 \text{ kg·m}^2/\text{s}^2$. (Section C6.1.)

k-work $[dK]$: the amount of energy that a particular interaction contributes toward changing an object's kinetic energy. The tiny amount of k-work that an interaction contributes during a very short time interval dt is $[dK] = \vec{F} \cdot d\vec{r} = \vec{v} \cdot [d\vec{p}]$, where $\vec{F}$ is the force the interaction exerts, $d\vec{r}$ is the displacement of the object's center of mass during dt, $\vec{v}$ is its velocity, and $[d\vec{p}]$ is the impulse the interaction delivers during time dt. The k-work is a scalar quantity that is negative if the interaction is reducing the object's kinetic energy instead of increasing it. (Section C8.3.)

kelvin: the SI unit of temperature, defined so that a temperature *change* of 1 K is equal to a change of 1°C. The zero of the Kelvin scale is defined to be absolute zero, which is −273.15°C. (Therefore to convert a temperature in degrees Celsius to one in kelvins, we simply need to add 273.15 K.) (Section C10.3.)

kilogram (kg): the SI unit of mass, equivalent to the mass of a specific platinum-iridium metal cylinder kept under carefully controlled conditions near Paris, France. (Section C1.9.)

kilowatt-hour: a unit of energy commonly used by power companies, equal to the total amount of energy used in 1 h if it is used at the rate of 1 kW· 1 kW·h = 3.6 MJ. (Section C12.1.)

kinetic energy K: the energy an object has by virtue of its motion. The kinetic energy of an object with mass m moving at a speed v is defined to be $K \equiv \frac{1}{2}mv^2$. (Section C6.1.)

latent energy U^{la}: the part of an object's internal energy that changes when its phase changes. (Section C11.3.)

latent "heat" (of transformation): the energy per unit mass released or absorbed by a substance undergoing a phase transformation. The latent "heat" involved in a phase transformation from a solid to liquid or vice versa is called the **latent "heat" of fusion,** while that involved in a transformation from liquid to gas or vice versa is called the **latent "heat" of vaporization.** The quotation marks indicate again that "heat" is not quite the correct term here: we are really talking about internal energy, not heat. (Section C11.3.)

law of cosines: the mathematical law that asserts that if the legs of a triangle have lengths a, b, and c, then

$$a^2 = b^2 + 2ab\cos\theta + c^2$$

where θ is the *outside* angle between legs b and c, as shown in figure C8.1. (If you want θ to be the angle between b and c *inside* the triangle, then make the cosine term negative.) (Section C8.1.)

leptons: a set of six fairly lightweight elementary particles, called the *electron, electron-neutrino, muon, muon-neutrino, tau,* and *tau-neutrino*. See table C1.1. (Section C1.5.)

lift: the part of a contact interaction between a wing and the passing air that exerts a force on the wing perpendicular to the wing's motion. (Section C8.7.)

liquid: a possible phase for a substance. The molecules of a liquid are bound to each other, but in a way that still permits considerable freedom of movement. (Section C11.3.)

long-range (interaction): an interaction between two objects that affects their motion even when they are not in direct contact. The *only* types of long-range interactions relevant for macroscopic objects are *gravitational* interactions (which act between all objects), *electrostatic* interactions (which involve at least one electrically charged object), and *magnetic* interactions (which involve at least one magnet). (Section C1.6.)

macroscopic (object): an object consisting of more than a handful of atoms. Categories, quantities, or concepts apply "at the macroscopic level" if they are useful in situations involving macroscopic objects. (Section C1.6.)

magnetic interaction: one of the possible long-range interactions between macroscopic objects. To participate in a magnetic interaction, at least one of the objects must be a magnet. (Section C1.6.)

magnitude: the numerical value associated with a vector. This quantity can be calculated from a vector's components in a given reference frame by squaring the components, adding them, and taking the square root (in a manner analogous to the pythagorean theorem). The magnitude of a vector $\vec{u}$ is written either mag($\vec{u}$) or simply u. (Section C2.1.)

mass: a quantity equivalent to the ratio of the magnitudes of the impulse delivered to an object and its resulting change in velocity. Qualitatively, mass expresses an object's resistance to changes in its motion. (Section C3.4.)

mechanical waves: waves that involve the physical displacement of particles in a medium. Examples are sound waves, seismic waves, and water waves. Such waves can store and transport energy: we can represent the energy stored in such a wave as an internal energy U^{snd}. (Section C11.5.)

mechanics: the area of physics dealing with how the physical interactions between objects affect their motion. (Section C1.4.)

mediator (particle): a particle that represents a fundamental interaction in quantum-mechanical calculations and that (under the right circumstances) can appear as free particles. The mediators for the strong nuclear, weak nuclear, electromagnetic, and gravitational interactions are *gluons, vector bosons,* the *photon,* and the *graviton,* respectively. (Section C1.5.)

meter: the SI unit of length, defined to be the distance that light travels in 1/299,792,458 of a standard second. (Section C1.9.)

moment of inertia I (around a given axis): the quantity mr^2 summed over every particle in a rigid extended object, where m is the particle's mass and r is its distance from the axis of rotation. (Section C9.4.)

momentarily isolated: another way to say that the total momentum of a system involved in a collision does not have *time* to change much during the brief collision process, even if the system participates in fairly significant external interactions. (Section C5.2.)

momentum $\vec{p}$ **of a particle** at a given instant of time: a vector whose *magnitude* is the particle's mass times its speed at the given instant and whose *direction* is the particle's direction of motion at that instant. Mathematically, $\vec{p} \equiv m\vec{v}$, with components $[p_x, p_y, p_z] = [mv_x, mv_y, mv_z]$. (Section C3.2.)

momentum-transfer principle: the assertion that any interaction between two objects *transfers momentum* from one to the other. (Section C3.2.)

multitap model: a model for predicting a particle's trajectory by treating all its interactions as if they exerted small "taps" on the particle. (Section C3.5.)

multiplication by a scalar: multiplication of a vector and a scalar produces a vector whose components are simply the scalar value times the corresponding components of the original vector. This is equivalent to multiplying the vector's magnitude by the absolute value of the scalar, and flipping the vector's direction if the scalar is negative (otherwise, the direction is unchanged). (Section C2.6.)

neutron star: the compact "cinder" left behind after a star goes supernova. Such objects have a typical mass of 1.4 solar masses and a radius of 12 km, are composed essentially entirely of neutrons, and rotate from once to 1000 times per second. (Section C14.5.)

newton (N): the SI unit of force, defined to be the amount of force that delivers to an object 1 kg·m/s of impulse per second. $1 \text{ N} \equiv (1 \text{ kg·m/s})/\text{s} = 1 \text{ kg·m/s}^2$. (Section C3.3.)

Newton's first law: the law that states that any object that does not interact with something else moves with a *constant speed* in a *fixed direction*. (Section C1.4.)

Newton's law of universal gravitation: the force law stating that the force which a gravitational interaction between two objects A and B exerts on either object is $\vec{F}_g = -(Gm_A m_B/r^2)\hat{r}$, where m_A and m_B are the objects' masses, r is the separation of their centers of mass, and $\hat{r}$ is a directional meaning "away from the other object." (Section C8.6.)

Newton's third law: the law that states that a given interaction between particles A and B must exert on B a force that is equal in magnitude and opposite in direction to the force that it exerts on A: $\vec{F}_{\text{on } B} = -\vec{F}_{\text{on } A}$. Note that the forces linked by this law must be forces that are the two ends of the *same* interaction. (Section C3.3.)

newtonian mechanics: a theory of physics that accurately predicts physical phenomena involving objects much larger than single atoms that move much more slowly than light in fairly weak gravitational fields. (Section C1.2.)

noninertial reference frame: a reference frame in which Newton's first law is observed to *fail*. The model of motion we have been developing assumes that we are using an *inertial* reference frame to make measurements: trying to analyze a situation in a noninertial frame using our models yields paradoxical results. (Section C4.5.)

normal (part of a contact interaction involving a surface): the part of the contact interaction that exerts a force perpendicular to the interacting surfaces. (*Normal* here is being used in the sense of "perpendicular.") (Section C8.7.)

nuclear energy U^{nu}: the part of an object's internal energy that changes if the object undergoes a nuclear reaction. (Section C11.4.)

ohm: a derived SI unit for electrical resistance defined to be 1 volt per ampere. (Section C1.9.)

operational definition: a procedure that defines a physical quantity by describing how to measure it. An operational definition of *mass* is given in section C3.4. (Section C3.4.)

origin: an arbitrarily chosen point in a reference frame that we use as the reference position against which all other positions are compared. (Section C2.8.)

particle: an idealized object having mass but zero volume, so that its position always corresponds to a well-defined mathematical point in space. (Section C3.1.)

particle model: model stating that a system's center of mass responds to external interactions exactly as a point particle would respond to the same interactions. (Section C4.4.)

pascal (Pa): a derived SI unit of pressure equal to 1 newton per square meter (1 N/m^2). (Section C1.9.)

period (of precession or rotation): the time required to precess or rotate exactly once. (Sections C14.1, C14.5.)

phase (of a substance): any one of a number of qualitatively different ways that a substance's molecules can be organized: solid, liquid, and gas are different possible *phases* for a typical substance. (Section C10.6.)

position $\vec{r}$ (of a point in a given reference frame): a vector equal to the displacement between the frame's origin and the point in question. The components of $\vec{r}$ are the point's coordinates $[x, y, z]$ in that frame; $r \equiv \text{mag}(\vec{r})$ is the *distance* between the origin and the point. A displacement $\Delta\vec{r}$ *between* two points is the vector *difference* of the points' position vectors: $\Delta\vec{r} = \vec{r}_{\text{final}} - \vec{r}_{\text{initial}}$. (Section C2.8.)

potential energy V: the energy involved in an interaction between two objects. All fundamental interactions have well-defined potential energy functions that depend *only* on the separation between the two interacting particles. At the macroscopic level, all long-range interactions between macroscopic objects have well-defined potential energy functions, but contact interactions (which involve complex microscopic processes) may not. (Section C6.1.)

potential energy diagram: a graph of the potential energy curve for a given interaction between two objects as a function of their separation, with a horizontal line indicating the system's total energy. Such a diagram is simplest to interpret if the system involves a very massive object interacting with a light object that moves in only one dimension (which we can take to be the x axis). Subsequent definitions will assume this situation. (Section C11.1.)

pound (lb): an English system unit of force that is equal to 4.45 N. A 1-kg object near the earth's surface has a weight of $9.8 \text{ N} = 2.2 \text{ lb}$. (Section C3.3.)

power: the rate at which energy is transformed from one form to another in a process (i.e., the amount of energy transformed per unit time). (Section C12.1.)

precess: a verb describing what an spinning top does in response to an applied horizontal torque that is always perpendicular to the object's angular momentum. In such a case, the tip of an object's angular momentum moves in a circular path around the vertical direction while maintaining a constant angle with respect to that direction. (Section C14.1.)

prose model: the conceptual model step of a problem written out in prose instead of using a conceptual model diagram. (Section C5.4.)

pulsar: a rotating neutron star whose intense rotating magnetic field interacts with nearby gas to create detectable radio signals that pulse at the same rate as the star rotates. (Section C14.5.)

(relativistic) quantum field theory: the theory of physics that in principle describes physical phenomena at all distance scales as long as very strong gravitational fields are not involved. This theory and the theory of general relativity are the most fundamental currently accepted theories in physics. (Section C1.2.)

quantum mechanics: an approximate version of relativistic quantum field theory that accurately predicts physical phenomena involving objects of all sizes moving much more slowly than light in fairly weak gravitational fields. (Section C1.2.)

quarks: a set of six fairly massive elementary particles, called the *up, down, strange, charmed, top,* and *bottom* quarks. Protons and neutrons are constructed of combinations of the up and down quarks. See table C1.1. (Section C1.5.)

radian, degree, revolution: different possible units for expressing angles: $1 \text{ rev} = 2\pi \text{ rad} = 360°$. The radian is the preferred SI unit. All these "units" are unusual since an angle as defined by the equation $\theta = s/r$ is really unitless. We can treat these as unitless as long as we recognize that the radian (and only the radian) can be removed from or added to a quantity's units at will. (Section C9.2.)

reference frame: an imaginary cubical lattice (or its functional equivalent) that we superimpose on space in order to quantify an object's position. Reference frames are also called **coordinate systems.** (Section C2.8.)

reference separation: the separation between two objects participating in a long-range interaction where the potential energy of that interaction is *defined* to be zero. (Section C6.3.)

reproducible experiment: a clearly designed context for making meaningful measurements that other scientists can reproduce. An experiment may or may not actively manipulate the conditions under which the measurements are made (e.g., this is difficult in astronomy) but should be designed to test the consequences of some hypothetical model in a logically convincing way. (Section C1.1.)

revolution (rev): a unit of angular measure equal to 2π radians. The angle subtended by a complete circle corresponds to 1 revolution. (Section C9.2.)

right-handed (reference frame): a frame whose x, y, and z directions correspond to the directions indicated by a person's right index finger, middle finger, and thumb, respectively, when these fingers are held so that they are mutually perpendicular. Reference frames are conventionally constructed to be right-handed. (Section C2.8.)

rigid (object): an extended object whose shape and dimensions do not change with time. (Section C4.4.)

rotational angular momentum $\vec{L}^{\text{rot}}$: the part of an object's angular momentum about an arbitrary reference point O that is due to the object's rotation about its center of mass. (Section C13.5.)

rotational kinetic energy K^{rot}: the part of an extended object's total kinetic energy associated with its rotation about some axis. $K^{\text{rot}} = \frac{1}{2}I\omega^2$. (Section C9.4.)

rotational speed v: the ordinary speed (in meters per second) that a particle in a rotating object has by virtue of the object's rotation. Note that this speed is $v = ds/dt = \omega r$, where ds is the arclength the particle covers in time dt, r is its distance from the axis of rotation, and ω is the object's angular speed. (Section C9.3.)

scalar: a quantity that (in contrast to a vector) has a numerical value but *no* associated direction, meaning that it can be adequately represented by a *single* number. The standard symbol for a scalar is a simple italic letter (for example, m, t, E). (Section C2.1.)

scalar multiple (of a vector): a vector whose components are the product of the scalar and the components of the original vector. Multiplying a vector by a scalar stretches the vector's length by the absolute value of the scalar and reverses its direction if the scalar is negative. (Section C2.6.)

science: a *process* that has proved to be a prolific producer of powerfully predictive conceptual models, involving a community of scholars committed to some fundamental theory and to developing models that are logically self-consistent and consistent with reproducible experiments. (Section C1.1.)

second: the SI unit of time, defined to be 9,192,631,770 oscillations of the radio waves emitted by a cesium-133 atom under specified circumstances. (Section C1.9.)

SI units: the internationally accepted system of units for scientific measurements. (Section C1.8.)

significant digits: the number of digits in an uncertain and/or measured quantity counted from the leftmost non-zero digit through the first digit whose value is uncertain. A calculated result will not contain any more significant digits than the quantity used in the calculation that has the *least* number of significant digits. In writing a number, zeros are considered significant if they appear to the right of a decimal point, but not if they are at the right end of a large integer. (Section C7.6.)

slingshot effect: an effect that allows a spacecraft to extract some of a planet's kinetic energy during a close encounter. (Section C12.4.)

solid: a phase of matter in which the atoms of a substance are essentially locked into fixed positions. (Section C11.3.)

solution: the part of the problem-solving framework in which equations identified in the conceptual model step are manipulated to arrive at a symbolic solution for a quantity or quantities of interest. (Section C5.3.)

special relativity: a theory of physics that accurately predicts physical phenomena involving objects and distance scales much larger than single atoms in fairly weak gravitational fields. (Section C1.2.)

specific "heat" c: the ratio $(dU^{\mathrm{th}}/dT)/m$, which has a fairly constant value for a substance in a given phase (c only weakly depends on temperature). Since *specific "heat"* doesn't really talk about *heat*, the quotation marks are meant to indicate that this actually refers to the *"specific thermal energy change per unit temperature change."* (Section C10.6.)

specific impulse: a measure of rocket engine performance, defined to be the momentum transfer delivered to the rocket per unit weight of propellant. Its numerical value (in its standard units of seconds) is equal to about 0.1 times the exhaust speed, expressed in meters per second. (Problem C5S.1.)

speed v: a numerical quantity that specifies how fast an object is moving at an instant in terms of how far it will move if it continues at that rate for a given time interval. (Section C1.7.)

spring constant k_s: a constant that expresses the potential energy involved in a spring interaction when the spring is extended or compressed by a unit length. This constant essentially expresses how *stiff* the spring is. (Section C7.4.)

stable equilibrium position: the equilibrium position at the lowest point of a valley (local minimum) in the system's potential energy function. If the light object is placed at rest at such a position, it will remain at rest. If it is then jostled slightly, its position will undergo small oscillations around the equilibrium position. (Section C11.1.)

standard model (SM) of particle physics: a combination of several relativistic quantum field theories that represents the currently accepted theory of particle physics. (Section C1.2.)

standard orientation: a frame on the surface of the earth if its x, y, and z directions point *east, north,* and *up,* respectively. (Section C2.8.)

statistical mechanics: a theory of physics that describes the behavior of complex objects consisting of *many* interacting particles. This theory is fundamentally based on quantum field theory. (Section C1.2.)

strong nuclear interaction: one of the four fundamental interactions. This interaction only acts between quarks and/or gluons (the strong nuclear interaction's mediator). It is the strongest of all the interactions, but has an effective range of roughly 10^{-15} m, making it irrelevant for any object larger than an atomic nucleus. (Section C1.5.)

subtend: to bracket, as when the two lines that define an angle bracket a portion of the circumference of a circle centered on the intersection of those lines. (Section C9.2.)

superelastic (collision): a collision in which internal energy is converted to kinetic energy. This *doesn't happen* with ordinary passive collisions: the collision must trigger an explosion that releases chemical or nuclear energy. (Section C12.2.)

symmetric object (around an axis of rotation): an object whose particles are paired so that each particle on one side of the axis of rotation has a partner with the same mass directly across the axis that is the same distance from that axis. The angular momentum of such an object is $\vec{L} = I\vec{\omega}$, where $\vec{\omega}$ is the object's angular velocity and I is the object's moment of inertia around the axis in question. (Section C13.4.)

symmetry: a property of some given set of physical laws that states they do not change even when the situation to which they are applied changes in a specified way. (Section C1.2.)

system: any set of interacting objects and/or particles having a well-defined "boundary" that determines whether any given particle is inside or outside the system. (Section C4.1.)

system of units: a coherent set of standards for measuring physical quantities. Originally, such a system would involve a set of standardized artifacts to which other objects could be compared. Now most units are described more abstractly, but the principle is the same. (Section C1.9.)

temperature T: a quantity that reflects the average kinetic energy associated with the random motion of the molecules in a substance. (Section C10.3.)

tension interaction: a macroscopic interaction that opposes the separation of two macroscopic objects. (Section C1.6.)

theory: an especially comprehensive conceptual model that embraces a whole range of phenomena. (Section C1.1.)

thermal contact interaction: a contact interaction between two objects that allows heat to flow from one to the other. (Section C10.7.)

thermal energy U^{th}: the part of an object's internal energy that depends on its *temperature* (as opposed to changes in its chemical or nuclear composition). It includes the kinetic and potential energies of random translational, rotational, and vibrational molecular motions. (Sections C10.3, C10.5.)

thermal insulator: a substance that does not allow much heat to flow through it, even if driven by a fairly large temperature difference. (Section C10.7.)

thermal physics: the study of phenomena having to do with heat and temperature. (Section C10.2.)

three-reservoir model: a model for predicting a particle's trajectory that involves imagining its momentum components to be like reservoirs containing certain levels of fluid. Interactions can either fill or drain a reservoir. (Section C3.5.)

torque $\vec{\tau}$: the rate at which a particular interaction contributes twirl to an object. (Section C13.6.)

total energy E: the numerical sum of the kinetic energies of all particles in the system plus the potential energies of all their internal interactions. (Section C6.1.)

total momentum $\vec{p}_{tot}$ (of a system): the vector sum of the momenta of the system's constituent particles. (Section C4.2.)

translation: the part of the problem-solving framework in which you assign mathematical symbols to various quantities involved in a problem, almost always with the help of a picture of the situation being described. (Section C5.3.)

translational angular momentum $\vec{L}^{cm}$: the part of an object's angular momentum around an arbitrary reference point O that is due to the motion of the object's center of mass relative to that point. (Section C13.5.)

translational kinetic energy K^{cm}: the part of an extended object's total kinetic energy K associated with the motion of its center of mass. Previously, we have assumed that $K^{cm} = K$, which is true if the object is not rotating. (Section C9.6.)

tritium: a hydrogen atom whose nucleus contains a proton and two neutrons (instead of just a proton, as is usually the case). (Section C11.4.)

turning point: any position x for a light object where the system's potential energy is equal to the system's total energy: $V(x) = E$. As the light object approaches a turning point, it slows down, comes instantaneously to rest exactly at the turning point, and then turns around and starts moving in the opposite direction. (Section C11.1.)

twirl $[d\vec{L}]$: the contribution that a particular interaction makes to an object's angular momentum during a certain time interval. (Section C13.6.)

unit operator: a ratio (equal to 1) of equivalent quantities expressed in different units. Unit operators are used to perform unit conversions. (Section C1.9.)

universal gravitational constant G: a fundamental physical constant that expresses the potential energy involved in the gravitational interaction between two particles with unit mass separated by unit distance. If mass is measured in kilograms and distance in meters, then $G = 6.67 \times 10^{-11}$ J·m/kg^2. (Section C7.2.)

unstable equilibrium position: any equilibrium position that is not at the bottom of a valley in the system's potential energy function. If the light object is placed at rest at such a position, it will remain at rest; but if it is then jostled slightly, it will move a large distance away from the equilibrium position and may never return. (Section C11.1.)

vector: any mathematical quantity having both a numerical magnitude and an associated direction. Any vector can be represented graphically by an *arrow* whose direction indicates the vector's direction and whose length is proportional to the vector's magnitude. The standard symbol for a vector in this text is any italic letter with a small arrow placed over it (for example, $\vec{v}$, $\vec{F}$, and $\vec{p}$). (Section C2.1.)

vector difference: a vector operation performed by inverting the vector to be subtracted and then adding. The resulting vector difference can also be constructed geometrically by placing the two vectors tail to tail, and then drawing an arrow from the head of the vector to be subtracted to the head of the other vector. (Section C2.2.)

vector inverse: a vector whose magnitude is the same as the original vector but whose direction is opposite. The components of the inverse are found by negating the components of the original vector. (Section C2.2.)

vector sum: a vector whose components are the sum of the corresponding components of the vectors being summed. This is equivalent to placing those vectors so the head of one coincides with the tail of the other, and then drawing an arrow from the remaining tail to the remaining head. The sum vector is then the arrow that starts at the tails of the original vectors and goes along the diagonal of the parallelogram. (Section C2.2.)

velocity $\vec{v}$ (of a particle at a given instant of time): a vector whose *magnitude* is the particle's speed and whose *direction* indicates the particle's direction of motion at the given instant. Mathematically, $\vec{v} \equiv d\vec{r}/dt$, where dt is a time interval around the given instant short enough that the velocity is essentially constant during dt, and $d\vec{r}$ is the particle's displacement during dt. The components of this vector are $[v_x, v_y, v_z] = [dx/dt, dy/dt, dz/dt]$, where dx is the change in the particle's x coordinate during dt, etc. (Sections C1.7, C3.1.)

volt: a derived SI unit for electrical energy per unit charge defined to be 1 joule per columb. (Section C1.9.)

watt: the SI unit of power. 1 W = 1 J/s. (Section C12.1.)

weak nuclear interaction: one of the four fundamental interactions. This interaction acts between quarks and leptons, but not mediator particles. Its effective strength is somewhat less than that of the electromagnetic interaction, but is still much stronger than the gravitational interaction. This interaction has an effective range of only 10^{-18} m, making it irrelevant for any object larger than an atomic nucleus. (Section C1.5.)

weight $\vec{F}_g$**:** the gravitational force exerted on an object. Note that weight and mass are *completely distinct* concepts (e.g., *weight* is a vector but *mass* is a scalar). (Section C3.4.)

work: any hidden energy that flows across the boundary between two objects that is *not* being driven by a temperature difference (i.e., that is not *heat*). (Section C10.5.)

x axis, y axis, z axis: names for the three mutually perpen-dicular lines that go through the origin of a reference frame. We define one side of each of these lines (starting at the origin) to be the positive side and the other to be the negative side. (Section C2.8.)

+x direction: the direction we point in if we stand at the origin and point along the x axis toward the side of the axis we have defined to be its positive side. The **−x direction** is the opposite direction. The **±y direction** and **±z direction** are defined analogously. (Section C2.3.)

zero vector: a vector having zero magnitude and no well-defined direction. The components of the zero vector are all zero. (Section C2.2.)

Index

Entries followed by *t* and *f* refer to tables and figures respectively

absolute zero, 179

airplanes. *See* **wings**

algebraic solution step, in problem solving, 85

allowed regions, in potential energy diagrams, 195

ampere (unit), 17

angle(s), measurement of
in degrees, 156–157
in radians, 157–158, 157*f*
units for, 17

angle of attack, of wing, 92, 92*f*

angular momentum
conservation of. *See* **conservation of angular momentum**
and cross products, 235–237, 235*f*
of moving object, 241–242, 241*f*
of particle, 238–239, 238*f*
of rigid object, 239–241, 239*f*
translational, 241
twirl and torque in, 242–245

angular speed
vs. center of mass speed, 166
definition of, 158, 158*f*

angular velocity, 158–160
vs. angular momentum, in extended object, 240
definition of, 159
right-hand rule for, 159, 160*f*

anticommutative property, of cross products, 236, 237*t*

antimatter/matter engines, 93, 94*f*

antiparticles, 11

Aristotelian mechanics, 9–10

asteroid impact, 224–227, 225*f*, 225*t*

atom(s)
interactions between
electromagnetic, 119–120
potential energy functions for, 197
in structure of matter, 10, 10*f*

Black, Joseph, 176

boldfaced terms, significance of, 16

Boltzmann's constant, 178

bond(s)
chemical, 119–120
energy release and absorption in, 198
potential energy diagrams for, 196*f*, 197–198

caloric, 176

caloric model of thermal energy, 176–178

calorie(s)
definition of, 176–177
food (Cal), 203

candela (unit), 17

Celsius degrees (unit), 179

center of mass (CM)
speed of, *vs.* angular speed, 166
of system, 66–69
calculation of, 66–69
definition of, 66
motion in, 69–72
particle model of, 71

charge, electrical
SI units of, 17, 118
sign of, 118–119

chemical bonds, 119–120

chemical energy, 201–205
symbol for, 203

CM. *See* **center of mass**

CoE. *See* **conservation of energy**

collision interactions
completely inelastic, 216
definition of, 83–84
elastic, 215–220
slingshot effect in, 221–222, 221*f*
inelastic, 216, 222–224
asteroid impact as, 224–227, 225*f*, 225*t*
superelastic, 216
thermal energy transfer in, 180
types of, 215–216

column vector(s), 30

column vector rule, 58

CoM. *See* **conservation of momentum**

commutative property
of dot products, 139, 237*t*
of vector addition, 28

completely inelastic collisions, 216

component form
addition in, 34–35, 34*f*
of cross product, 236–237, 237*t*
of dot product, 140, 237*t*
subtraction in, 35

component vectors, 29–30
definition of, 29
notation for, 37–38

compression interactions, 13, 13*f*
in contact interaction, 82–83, 83*f*

conceptual model diagrams, 4, 85–88
in conservation of angular momentum problems, 257
in conservation of energy problems, 110
in conservation of momentum problems, 88

construction of, 86–88
prose form of, 88

conservation of angular momentum, 255–256, 255*f*
model of, 234–235
in neutron star formation, 263–265
in particles, 238–239
problem-solving framework in, 257
symmetries underlying, 8
worked examples, 257–263

conservation of energy (CoE)
abbreviation for, 110
friction and, 146–147, 146*f*
in interactions, 100–101, 100*f*
contact, 108–109
with Earth, 143–144
law of, 100, 108–109
problem-solving framework in, 109–112, 147
subtlety of concept, 100, 176
symmetries underlying, 8

conservation of momentum (CoM)
abbreviation for, 87
in airflow around wing, 92, 92*f*
in conceptual structure of physics, 7–8, 7*f*
friction and, 82–83, 83*f*
in interactions with Earth, 143–144
in isolated systems, 64–66
law of conservation of momentum, 66
and Newton's third law, 53
problem-solving in, 88–92
in rocket propulsion, 93, 93*f*
symmetries underlying, 8
without isolation, 82–83, 82*f*–83*f*

contact interactions, 12–13, 13*f*
conservation of energy in, 108–109
conservation of momentum in, 82–83, 83*f*
frictional part of, 146, 167
k-work in, 146–149, 146*f*
normal part of, 146
with thermal energy changes, problem-solving framework for, 184–188

coordinate(s), of reference frame, 37–38

coordinate directions, 29

coulomb (unit), 17, 118

coulomb constant, 118

cross product, 235–237, 235*f*
component form of, 236–237, 237*t*
definition of, 235
properties of, 236, 237*t*
right-hand rule for, 236, 236*f*

Deep Space 1 probe, 93, 94*f*
degree (unit), 157
deuterium, 202
direction, of vector, 26
directionals
  definition of, 29
  notation for, 29–30
displacement
  definition of, 27, 27*f*
  vector as, 27, 27*f*
distributive property
  of cross products, 236, 237*t*
  of dot products, 139, 237*t*
dot product
  component form of, 140, 237*t*
  definition of, 139
  interpretation of, 139, 139*f*
  properties of, 139–140, 237*t*
drag. *See* **wings**

Earth. *See also* **gravitational interactions**
  asteroid impact on, 224–227, 225*f*, 225*t*
  interactions with, frames of reference in, 74–76
  kinetic energy of, ignoring, 102–103, 143–144
  precession of, 254, 254*f*
Einstein, Albert, on nature of physics, 9
elastic collisions, 216–220
  definition of, 215
  slingshot effect in, 221–222, 221*f*
electric energy, as hidden energy, 205
electric power, measurement of, 212
electrical charge
  SI units of, 17, 118
  sign of, 118–119
electromagnetic field theory
  in conceptual structure of physics, 7, 7*f*
  history of, 5, 6*f*
electromagnetic interactions, 11, 12*t*
  in atoms, 119–120
  electrostatic potential energy, 118–120, 119*f*
electromagnetic waves, as hidden energy, 205
electron(s)
  properties of, 11*t*
  in structure of matter, 10, 10*f*
electron-neutrino, properties of, 11*t*
electrostatic interactions, 12–13, 13*f*
electrostatic potential energy, 118–120, 119*f*
electroweak theory
  in conceptual structure of physics, 7*f*
  history of, 6*f*
elementary particles, 11
energy. *See also* **total energy**
  conservation of. *See* **conservation of energy**
  hidden forms of
    in contact interactions, 108–109
    types of, 176, 205
  latent, 200
  nuclear and chemical, 201–205
  potential. *See* **potential energy**

equilibrium position, in potential energy diagrams, 196
equinoxes, precession of, 254, 254*f*
escape speed, 126–128
evaluation step, in problem solving, 85–86
experiments, reproducible, as hallmark of science, 4–5
extended object(s). *See also* **systems**
  angular velocity *vs.* angular momentum in, 240
  definition of, 64
  examples of, 65*f*
  Newton's first law for, 70
  potential energy between, 121
external interactions
  definition of, 64
  and momentum of system, 66, 70

fission reactions, 202
floating in space
  and isolation, 73, 83–84
  notation for, 88
food calorie (unit), 203
forbidden regions, in potential energy diagrams, 195
force
  average, 53
  definition of, 52
  of gravitational interaction
    on astronomical scale, 144–145
    near Earth's surface, 144
  vs. power, 215
  units of, 17, 52
force laws, 144–145
frames of reference. *See* **reference frames**
freely falling frames, 73
friction interactions, 13, 13*f*
  in conservation of energy problems, 146–147, 146*f*
  in conservation of momentum problems, 82–83, 83*f*
  in Newtonian mechanics, 9–10
  thermal energy in, 179–180, 180*f*
  problem-solving framework for, 184–188
frisbees, angular momentum and, 255, 255*f*
functional isolation
  in conservation of angular momentum problems, 257
  definition of, 83
  testing for, 83
  in thermal energy problems, 185
fusion reactions, 126–127, 202

Galilei, Galileo, 5
gas(es), phase change and, 199
general relativity
  in conceptual structure of physics, 7, 7*f*
  history of, 5–7, 6*f*
Global Positioning System (GPS), 38
gluons, in mediation, 12*t*
GPS (Global Positioning System), 38

gravitational field strength, 54
gravitational field vector, 54
gravitational interactions, 11–13, 12*t*, 13*f*
  and Earth's precession, 254, 254*f*
  force of
    on astronomical scale, 144–145
    near Earth's surface, 144
  Newton's law of universal gravitation, 145
  potential energy formula, 120–121
    graph of, 120, 120*f*, 122–123, 123*f*
    for objects near Earth, 103–107, 104*f*, 106, 121–123, 123*f*
  slingshot effect in, 221–222, 221*f*
gravitons, as mediators, 12*t*
Greek philosophical tradition, 4

heat. *See also* **latent "heat"; specific "heat(s)"**
  definition of, 181, 181*f*
  vs. specific "heat," 183
  vs. thermal energy, 181
helping diagrams
  in conservation of energy problems, 110
  in conservation of momentum problems, 88
  in problem-solving process, 86
hidden forms of energy
  in contact interactions, 108–109
  types of, 176, 205

impulse(s)
  addition of, 51
  definition of, 50–51
  vs. K-work, 142–143
  vs. momentum, 51
  multiple, modeling of, 51–52, 55–56, 55*f*
  per unit mass, 93
inelastic collisions, 222–224
  asteroid impact as, 224–227, 225*f*, 225*t*
  definition of, 216
inertial reference frames, 72–74
  definition of, 72
  distinguishing from noninertial, 73
  examples of, 73–74
  and interactions with Earth, 74–76
interaction diagrams
  in conservation of angular momentum problems, 257
  in conservation of energy problems, 110
  in conservation of momentum problems, 88
  in thermal energy problems, 184
interactions. *See also specific types of interactions*
  conservation of energy in, 100–101, 100*f*, 108–109, 143–144
  definition of, 9
  in describing motion, 14–15
  external
    definition of, 64
    and momentum of system, 66, 70

fundamental, 10–12, 12*t*
internal, definition of, 64
macroscopic, 12–14, 13*f*
momentum transfer in, 48–50, 48*f*–49*f*
internal energy, types of, 203
internal interaction, definition of, 64
ion engines, 93, 94*f*
isolated systems
conservation of angular momentum
in, 257
conservation of energy in, 100–101
conservation of momentum in, 64–66
definition of, 66
degrees of isolation, 83–84
in thermal energy problems, 184–185

Joule, James Prescott, 102, 177–178, 177*f*
joule (unit), 17, 102

kelvin (unit), 17, 178–179
Kelvin temperature scale, 179
kilogram (unit), 17, 54
kinetic energy, 101–103
alternative expression for, 102
definition of, 101
of Earth, ignoring, 102–103, 143–144
in interactions, 100, 100*f*
in momentum change, 138–140, 138*f*
in multiple interactions, 140–142
rotational. *See* **rotational kinetic
energy**
SI units of, 102
translational, 164–165
k-work
in contact interactions, 146–149, 146*f*
definition of, 141–142
and Earth's kinetic energy, 143–144
and force laws, 144–145
vs. impulse, 142–143
meaning of, 142–143
vs. work, 142

Large Magellanic Cloud, 264*f*, 265
latent energy, 200
latent "heat," 198–201
definition of, 198
in phase changes, 198–200
of transformation, 200
of various substances, 200*t*
**law of conservation of
energy,** 100, 108–109
law of conservation of momentum, 66
law of cosines, 138
lepton(s)
mediators for, 12*t*
properties of, 11*t*
in structure of matter, 10, 10*f*
lift. *See* **wings**
linear property of dot products, 139, 237*t*
liquid(s), phase change and, 199
long-range interactions, 12–13, 13*f*

macroscopic interactions, 12–14, 13*f*
macroscopic objects, definition of, 12
magnetic interactions, 12–13, 13*f*
and kinetic energy, 120
magnitude, of vector, 26, 57
definition of, 31
notation for, 31
mass
center of. *See* **center of mass**
definition of, operational, 53–54
vs. weight, 54
master equation
in conservation of angular momentum
problems, 257
in conservation of energy problems, 110
in problem-solving process, 86–87
matter, fundamental structure
of, 10–12, 10*f*
matter/antimatter engines, 93, 94*f*
mechanical waves, as hidden energy, 205
mechanics
commonsense models of, 8–9
in conceptual structure of physics, 7, 7*f*
definition of, 8
history of, 5, 6*f*, 8–10
mediators, in fundamental interactions, 11
meter (unit), 17
models. *See also* **conceptual model
diagrams; standard model**
common-sense, 8–9
conceptual, 4
good, characteristics of, 4
limitations of, 4
of momentum, 49–50, 49*f*, 55–57,
56*f*–57*f*
particle model of center of mass, 71
of phase change, 199–200
of thermal energy, 176–178
of thermal physics, 178–179
mole (unit), 17
moment of inertia, 160–161
calculating, 161–164
definition of, 161
for various objects, 164, 164*t*
momentary isolation
in conservation of angular momentum
problems, 257
definition of, 84
in thermal energy problems, 185
momentum
conservation of. *See* **conservation of
momentum**
and kinetic energy, 138–140, 138*f*
in multiple interactions, 140–142
of particle
definition of, 49
vs. impulse and momentum in
general, 51
of system, 66, 70
total, definition of, 64
transfer of, 48–50, 48*f*–49*f*
in modeling motion, 55–57, 56*f*–57*f*
momentum-transfer
principle, 50, 66
symmetry in, 50
vector model of, 49–50, 49*f*

motion
modeling of
momentum flow in, 55–57, 56*f*–57*f*
speed *vs.* velocity in, 14–16
of system center of mass, 69–72
multitap model of motion, 55–56, 55*f*
muon, properties of, 11*t*
muon-neutrino, properties of, 11*t*

neutron(s), in structure of
matter, 10–11, 10*f*
neutron stars, 263–265, 264*f*
Newton, Isaac
and conservation of energy, 100, 176
on Earth's precession, 254
in history of physics, 5
and motion of extended objects, 66
newton (unit), 17
Newtonian mechanics
in conceptual structure of physics, 7, 7*f*
history of, 5, 6*f*
motion in, 9–10
Newton's first law, 9
for extended objects, 70
reference frames and, 72–73
**Newton's law of universal
gravitation,** 145
Newton's third law, 53, 256
Noether, Emmy, 7
Noether's theorem, 7–8
noninertial reference frames
definition of, 72–73
distinguishing from inertial, 73
normal part, of contact interactions, 146
North Star, 254
nuclear energy, 201–205
symbol for, 203
nuclear reactors, 202–203, 202*f*

ohm (unit), 17
operational definition, definition of, 53
origin, of reference frame, 37

particle(s)
angular momentum of, 238–239, 238*f*
definition of, 46
elementary, 11
momentum of
definition of, 49
vs. impulse and momentum in
general, 51
velocity of, 46–47, 47*f*
definition of, 46
intuitive definition of, 15–16
particle model, of system center
of mass, 71
pascal (unit), 17
period, in precession, 253
phase changes
latent heat in, 198–200
microscopic model for, 199–200
photon(s), as mediators, 11–12, 12*t*

physics, history of,   5–7, 6f
position, of reference frame,   37
potential energy
absolute, inability to
determine,   105–106
in electromagnetic
interaction,   118–120, 119f
between extended objects,   121
gravitational,   120–121
graph of,   120, 120f, 122–123, 123f
for objects near Earth,   103–107,
104f, 106, 121–123, 123f
in interactions,   100, 100f
measurement of,   103–107, 104f
negative, meaning of,   107–108
problem-solving framework
for,   126–130
reference separation in,   105–106,
121–122
between spherical objects,   121
of spring,   123–125, 125f
potential energy diagrams,   194–197
for bonds,   196f, 197–198
definition of,   194
examples of,   194f
reading of,   195–196
total system energy in,   194–195
pound (unit),   54
power
benchmarks for,   212, 212t
definition of,   212–215
vs. force,   215
precession,   252–254, 252f–253f
applications,   254–255, 254f–255f
precession of the equinoxes,   254, 254f
Principia (Newton),   254
problem solving
sign errors, avoiding,   86–87
significant digits,   130–131
vector algebra, common errors,   57–58
problem-solving framework,   84–86
in conservation of angular momentum
problems,   257
in conservation of energy
problems,   109–112, 126–130
in conservation of momentum
problems,   88–92
constructing model diagrams in,   86–88
for thermal energy problems,   184–188
proton(s)
interactions between, potential energy
functions for,   197
in structure of matter,   10–11, 10f
pulsars,   264–265

quantum chromodynamics, history of,   6f
quantum electrodynamics, history
of,   5, 6f
quantum mechanics
in conceptual structure of physics,   7, 7f
history of,   5, 6f
quark(s)
mediators for,   12t
properties of,   11t
in structure of matter,   10–11

radian(s),   157–158, 157f
radioactive waste,   202–203
reference frames
conventions for,   39
floating in space,   73, 83–84
notation for,   88
inertial,   72–74
definition of,   72
distinguishing from noninertial,   73
examples of,   73–74
and interactions with Earth,   74–76
Newton's first law and,   72–73
noninertial
definition of,   72–73
distinguishing from inertial,   73
right-handed,   39
selection of,   74–76
standard orientation of,   39
for vectors,   37–39
reference separation, in potential energy
calculation,   105–106, 121–122
relativistic quantum field theory,   5, 6f
relativity. *See* **general relativity; special
relativity**
reproducible experiments, as hallmark of
science,   4–5
right-hand rule
for angular velocity,   159, 160f
for cross product,   236, 236f
right-handed reference frames,   39
rigid object
angular momentum of,   239–241, 239f
definition of,   71
motion of,   71–72
rocket propulsion, and conservation of
momentum,   93, 93f
rotational angular momentum,   241
rotational kinetic energy
angle measurement in,   156–158
angular velocity in,   158–160
right-hand rule for,   159, 160f
definition of,   160
formula for,   161
moment of inertia in,   160–161
calculating,   161–164
for various objects,   164, 164t
total kinetic energy
and,   156, 164–168, 168f
rotational speed, definition of,   158–159
Rumford, Count,   177

scalar(s)
definition of,   26, 26f
notation for,   26
scalar components, of vector,   30
scalar division, of vector,   36
scalar multiplication
of cross products,   236
of vector,   35, 35f, 37
science, nature and history of,   4–5
second (unit),   17
SI units,   17
of charge,   118
conversion of,   18–19
derived units,   17

of force,   52
intuitive understanding of,   17–18, 18f
of kinetic energy,   102
standard prefixes for,   17, 17f
of temperature,   178–179
sign errors, avoiding,   86–87
significant digits, conventions
for,   130–131
slingshot effect,   221–222, 221f
solid(s), phase change and,   199
Space Shuttle, inertial frames
of reference in,   73
special relativity
in conceptual structure of physics,   7, 7f
history of,   5, 6f
specific "heat(s)",   182–184
definition of,   182–183
for various substances,   183, 183t
speed
angular
vs. center of mass speed,   166
definition of,   158, 158f
in describing motion,   14–16
escape,   126–128
rotational,   158–159
spherical objects, potential energy
between,   121
spring, ideal
force exerted by,   145
potential energy formula,   123–125
graph of,   124–125, 125f
uses of,   124–125
spring constant,   124–125, 125f
stable equilibrium position, in potential
energy diagrams,   196
standard model
fundamental interactions in,   11
history of,   5–7, 6f
quarks in,   11
standard orientation, of reference
frames,   39
statistical mechanics
in conceptual structure of physics,   7, 7f
history of,   6f
strong nuclear interaction,   11, 12t
summation notation,   160
Sun, as fusion reactor,   202f, 203
superelastic collisions,   216
supernovas,   264–265, 264f
swinging object, k-work and,   147
symmetric object, angular momentum
in,   239f, 240–241
symmetry principles
in conceptual structure of
physics,   7–8, 7f
in momentum transfer,   50, 53
three basic,   8
systems. *See also* **isolated systems**
center of mass of,   66–69
calculation of,   66–69
definition of,   66
motion in,   69–72
particle model of,   71
definition of,   64
momentum of,   66, 70
total energy of,   101

tau, properties of, 11*t*
tau-neutrino, properties of, 11*t*
technical terms, learning correct
    use of, 16
temperature
    absolute zero, 179
    definition of, 178
    Kelvin scale, 179
    SI units of, 178–179
    vs. thermal energy, 178–179,
        182–183, 182*f*
tension interactions, 13, 13*f*
theories, in science, 4–5
thermal contact interactions, problem-
    solving framework for, 184–188
thermal energy
    caloric model of, 176–178
    in collisions, 180
    definition of, 181
    and friction, 179–180, 180*f*
    vs. heat, 180–182, 181*f*
    problem-solving framework
        for, 184–188
    vs. temperature, 178–179, 182–183, 182*f*
    work in, 180–182, 181*f*
thermal insulators, in thermal energy
    problems, 185
thermal physics
    contemporary model of, 178–179
    history of, 176–178
Thompson, Benjamin, 177
three-reservoir model of
    motion, 55–57, 56*f*–57*f*
tops, precession in, 252–254, 252*f*–253*f*
torque
    definition of, 243
    nonparallel to angular
        momentum, 252–254, 252*f*–253*f*
    parallel to angular
        momentum, 242–245
total energy
    absolute, inability to determine, 108
    in interactions, 100–101, 100*f*
    of multiparticle system,
        definition of, 101
    negative, meaning of, 108
    in potential energy diagrams, 194–195
total momentum, definition of, 64
translation step
    in conservation of angular momentum
        problems, 257
    in conservation of energy
        problems, 109–110
    in conservation of momentum
        problems, 88–89
    in problem solving, 84–85
translational angular momentum, 241
translational kinetic energy, 164–165
tritium, 202

turning points, in potential energy
    diagrams, 195
twirl
    angular momentum and, 242–245
    definition of, 242–243

unit(s). *See also* **SI units**
    for angles, 17
    consistency in use of, 19, 85–86
    purpose of, 16
    of vectors, 37
unit operators, 18–19
unit vectors, 29–30
universal gravitational constant, 120–121
unstable equilibrium position, in potential
    energy diagrams, 196

vector(s)
    addition of, 27–28, 27*f*
        common errors in, 57–58
        commutative property in, 28
        in component form, 34–35, 34*f*
        in one dimension, 31–32, 32*f*
    algebra with, common errors, 57–58
    column, 30
    column vector rule, 58
    components of, 29–30
        notation for, 37–38
        scalar, 30
    cross product of, 235–237, 235*f*
    definition of, 16
    as displacement, 27, 27*f*
    dividing by scalar, 36
    dividing by vector, 36, 57
    dot product of
        in component form, 140, 237*t*
        definition of, 139
        interpretation of, 139, 139*f*
        properties of, 139–140, 237*t*
    magnitude of, 26, 57
        definition of, 31
        notation for, 31
    notation for, 26
    in one dimension, 31–32, 32*f*
    reference frames for, 37–39
    scalar components of, 30
    scalar multiplication of, 35, 35*f*, 37
    vs. scalars, 26, 26*f*
    subtraction of, 27–28, 28*f*
        in component form, 35
    in two dimensions
        computing components
            from magnitude and
            direction, 32–33, 33*f*
        computing magnitude and direction
            from components, 33

    unit, 29–30
    units of, 37
    zero, definition of, 28
vector bosons, as mediators, 12*t*
vector difference, definition of, 28
vector inverse
    calculation of, 35
    definition of, 28
vector model of momentum, 49–50, 49*f*
vector sum, definition of, 27–28
velocity
    angular. *See* **angular velocity**
    of particle, 46–47, 47*f*
        definition of, 46
        intuitive definition of, 15–16
volt (unit), 17

watt (unit), 17, 212
weak nuclear interaction, 11, 12*t*
weight
    definition of, 54
    vs. mass, 54
wings
    angle of attack in, 92, 92*f*
    drag of
        as contact interaction, 146, 146*f*
        power used in, 215
    lift of
        and conservation of
            momentum, 92, 92*f*
        as contact interaction, 146, 146*f*
work
    definition of, 181, 181*f*
    vs. k-work, 142
    types of, 142

***x* axis,** of reference frame, 37
***x* component,** of vector, definition
    of, 30
***x* direction,** definition of, 29
***x*-force,** in potential energy
    diagrams, 195

***y* axis,** of reference frame, 37
***y* component,** of vector,
    definition of, 30
***y* direction,** definition of, 29

***z* axis,** of reference frame, 37
***z* component,** of vector,
    definition of, 30
***z* direction,** definition of, 29
zero vector, definition of, 28

Periodic Table of the Elements

1 1A																		18 8A
1 **H** 1.008	2 2A												13 3A	14 4A	15 5A	16 6A	17 7A	2 **He** 4.003
3 **Li** 6.941	4 **Be** 9.012												5 **B** 10.81	6 **C** 12.01	7 **N** 14.01	8 **O** 16.00	9 **F** 19.00	10 **Ne** 20.18
11 **Na** 22.99	12 **Mg** 24.31	3 3B	4 4B	5 5B	6 6B	7 7B	8	9 8B	10	11 1B	12 2B		13 **Al** 26.98	14 **Si** 28.09	15 **P** 30.97	16 **S** 32.07	17 **Cl** 35.45	18 **Ar** 39.95
19 **K** 39.10	20 **Ca** 40.08	21 **Sc** 44.96	22 **Ti** 47.88	23 **V** 50.94	24 **Cr** 52.00	25 **Mn** 54.94	26 **Fe** 55.85	27 **Co** 58.93	28 **Ni** 58.69	29 **Cu** 63.55	30 **Zn** 65.39	31 **Ga** 69.72	32 **Ge** 72.59	33 **As** 74.92	34 **Se** 78.96	35 **Br** 79.90	36 **Kr** 83.80
37 **Rb** 85.47	38 **Sr** 87.62	39 **Y** 88.91	40 **Zr** 91.22	41 **Nb** 92.91	42 **Mo** 95.94	43 **Tc** (98)	44 **Ru** 101.1	45 **Rh** 102.9	46 **Pd** 106.4	47 **Ag** 107.9	48 **Cd** 112.4	49 **In** 114.8	50 **Sn** 118.7	51 **Sb** 121.8	52 **Te** 127.6	53 **I** 126.9	54 **Xe** 131.3
55 **Cs** 132.9	56 **Ba** 137.3	57 **La** 138.9	72 **Hf** 178.5	73 **Ta** 180.9	74 **W** 183.9	75 **Re** 186.2	76 **Os** 190.2	77 **Ir** 192.2	78 **Pt** 195.1	79 **Au** 197.0	80 **Hg** 200.6	81 **Tl** 204.4	82 **Pb** 207.2	83 **Bi** 209.0	84 **Po** (210)	85 **At** (210)	86 **Rn** (222)
87 **Fr** (223)	88 **Ra** (226)	89 **Ac** (227)	104 **Rf** (257)	105 **Db** (260)	106 **Sg** (263)	107 **Bh** (262)	108 **Hs** (265)	109 **Mt** (266)	110	111	112	(113)	114	(115)	116	(117)	

Key:
1 **H** 1.008 — Atomic number, Symbol, Atomic mass

58 **Ce** 140.1	59 **Pr** 140.9	60 **Nd** 144.2	61 **Pm** (147)	62 **Sm** 150.4	63 **Eu** 152.0	64 **Gd** 157.3	65 **Tb** 158.9	66 **Dy** 162.5	67 **Ho** 164.9	68 **Er** 167.3	69 **Tm** 168.9	70 **Yb** 173.0	71 **Lu** 175.0
90 **Th** 232.0	91 **Pa** (231)	92 **U** 238.0	93 **Np** (237)	94 **Pu** (242)	95 **Am** (243)	96 **Cm** (247)	97 **Bk** (247)	98 **Cf** (249)	99 **Es** (254)	100 **Fm** (253)	101 **Md** (256)	102 **No** (254)	103 **Lr** (257)